_____

Beyond Boundaries

_____

To Althea

From Selwa

With every best

wish

July 25, 2008

Beyond Boundaries

THE INTELLECTUAL TRADITION
OF TRINIDAD AND TOBAGO IN
THE NINETEENTH CENTURY

Selwyn R. Cudjoe

Calaloux Publications

Wellesley, Massachusetts

DISTRIBUTED BY
UNIVERSITY OF MASSACHUSETTS PRESS
Amherst & Boston

Distributed by the University of Massachusetts Press
P.O. Box 429, Amherst, MA 01004
www.umass.edu/umpress

First published 2003 by Calaloux Publications

Printed in the United States of America.

Library of Congress Cataloging-in-Publication Data

Cudjoe, Selwyn Reginald.
   Beyond boundaries : the intellectual tradition of Trinidad and Tobago
in the nineteenth century / Selwyn R. Cudjoe.
      p. cm.
Includes bibliographical references and index.
   ISBN 1-55849-318-2 (lib. cloth ed. : alk. paper) -- ISBN 1-55849-391-3
(pbk. : alk. paper)
1. Trinidad and Tobago literature (English)--History and criticism.
2. Trinidad and Tobago--Intellectual life--19th century.   3. Trinidad
and Tobago literature--History and criticism.   I. Title.
   PR9272 .C83 2002

Paperback printing
1   3   5   7   9   10   8   6   4   2

Cloth printing
1   3   5   7   9   10   8   6   4   2

For
Yashica

Also for
BJ, Joel, Bridget,
Merle, and Everton

Contents

Acknowledgments

When I began this literary journey ten years ago, I never thought it would take so long to complete. Along the way, many people and institutions have offered their assistance, without which it would have been impossible to complete my task. Therefore, I would like to thank those who stayed with me throughout and those who provided aid along the way. First of all, I want to thank Yashica Olden who was there at the beginning as she helped to decipher and transcribe some nearly undecipherable scripts at the British Library and who has stuck with me to the end. Biodun Jeyifo of Cornell University and Joel Krieger of Wellesley College have also been with me from the beginning and have always offered spiritual and intellectual sustenance. Bridget Brereton, former Vice Principal of the University of the West Indies, read some of the early chapters and offered instructive suggestions. She remains a scholar's scholar and a friend. Merle Hodge of the same institution has always been inspirational, and each day, I learn from her courage and magnanimity. I wish to thank Doreen Sealy who opened up her home and her library to me and provided me with her insights into such literary personalities as C. S. Assee and E. Bernard Acham. I also owe much thanks to Fr. Anthony de Verteuil for exposing me to the contributions the French Creoles made to Trinbagonian society's literature and for his pioneering work in this early phase of Trinidad and Tobago literature. I also wish to thank Jagessar Ganesh, president of the Dow Village Ramleela Cultural Organization, Trinidad, and Lakhan Balroop of the First Felicity Ramleela Group, also of Trinidad, who shared their information about the ramleela festival in Trinidad with me.

Many persons assisted in the translation of various texts (mostly from Spanish, French, and Latin into English). In this regard, I am grateful to Jacqueline Morin of the Lycee Saint-Louis, Paris; Benedicte Alliot, University of Paris; Michele Lemettais, formerly of Wellesley College; Barry Lydgate (French Department), Carlos Vega (Spanish Department), and Carol Doughtery (Classics Department) of Wellesley College. I also thank Professor Doughtery who assisted me in evaluating Assee's *Laus Reginae.*

I owe a great deal to the late Peter Khan, professor emeritus at Cornell University, who helped me interpret Jean Cazabon's paintings, and the late Trudy Calvert, also of Cornell University, who edited early drafts of this manuscript. John Campbell and Franka Phillip, presently and formerly of the University of the West

Indies, respectively, were worthy research assistants during the early stages of this project. Pauline Walters also assisted in copying many articles at the Trinidad and Tobago Archives. I also wish to thank William Cain, Wellesley College, and Lauren Zygorie, a student at the University of Texas School of Law, with whom I generated two publications while this larger project was being undertaken, and John Raphael, former Mayor of Port of Spain, who launched my edited work on Michel Maxwell Philip in 1999. Additional thanks go to Gregson Davis, Duke University, who supported me during my time of domestic travail; Carl Jacob and Maxie Cuffie, former editors of the *Trinidad Guardian* and the *Trinidad Express,* respectively, each of whom gave me the opportunity to write a weekly column for their newspapers. I am indebted to Cuffie for reining in my verbosity.

I also wish to thank the librarians at the Commonwealth Collection at Cambridge University; Regeant's Park College at Oxford University; the British Library (both the Main Library and the Newspaper Library at Colingdale); the Royal Botanic Gardens at Kew, London; the Methodist Collection at SOAS Library, University of London; the West Indiana Collection and the National Herbarium of Trinidad and Tobago at the University of the West Indies; the National Archives of Trinidad and Tobago; the Comparative Zoology and Widener Libraries at Harvard University; Boston Public Library; Olin Library at Cornell University; and Knox College, Toronto, for providing access to the *Scrapbooks of John and Sarah Morton.* I also wish to thank Shelley Wong, Associate Professor of English and Director of the Asian American Studies Program at Cornell University, who allowed me to participate in her course, "Geography, Literature and Critical Social Theory," at the Society for the Humanities during the fall of 1996. She will never know how much it opened up to me a field of study of which I knew little nor how much it shaped the texture of this work. I also owe a great deal of thanks to the library and staff at Clapp Library, Wellesley College, particularly Karen Jensen and her staff at Interlibrary Loans. I am sorry I bugged you guys so much.

I am thankful for two fellowships and a summer stipend from the National Endowment for the Humanities and annual faculty awards from Wellesley College that made possible my frequent traveling to various collections to gather data. Without Wellesley's financial generosity this project would have taken much longer to complete. I also wish to thank Louis Lee Sing, Linus Rogers and Patricia Majias, chairmen respectively of the National Lotteries Board; Airports Authority; and Tunapuna-Piarco Regional Corporation (of Trinidad and Tobago) for generous grants that assisted in the publication of this study. Lively discussions while I was a Senior Fellow at the Society for the Humanities, Cornell University, and a Visiting Scholar at the W. E. B. Du Bois Institute for Afro-American Research, Harvard University allowed me to work out many of my ideas about this study. I am also grateful to Henry Louis Gates, Jr., Chairman of the Afro-American Studies Department, for inviting me to be a Visiting Scholar of the Afro-American Studies Department, Harvard University, for the past ten years. I also wish to thank Arnold

Rampersad, now at Stanford University, for allowing me to present some of the ideas developed in this book at his colloquium at Princeton University and am grateful for the encouragement Toni Morrison rendered on that occasion. My participation in many of the colloquia at the Du Bois Institute also allowed me to clarify my ideas. So, too, did my discussions with Anthony Appiah, Princeton University; Wellington Nyangoni, chairman of the Afro-American Studies Department at Brandeis University; and Paget Henry and Lewis Gordon of the Afro-American Studies Department, Brown University.

I also wish to thank Bruce Wilcox, director of the University of Massachusetts Press, and George Whipple of Cornell University Press for their assistance over the past fifteen years. They have acted as family and, as such, have been luminous companions amidst the tumult and bruising demands of having one's work published.

Although Everton Smith came into my life very late, he exemplifies the kind of self-made and self-taught scholars who constituted the backbone of Trinidad and Tobago's intellectual culture during the nineteenth and early twentieth centuries. I also want to honor him for the support he has given to the work we do in the National Association for the Empowerment of African People. Little does he know how much he has been a quiet inspiration to me. He reminds me of the efforts of my father and those of his generation who strove toward excellence and the acquisition of an intellectual culture. They are the backbone of all we have achieved intellectually. This is one reason why Smith is one of the persons to whom I have dedicated this book.

Lastly, my debt of gratitude would not be complete if I did not thank my sister Margaret and my cousins Marva, Rhonda, Anthony, Don, Junior, Ronnie and Judith for all the assistance and comfort they have provided—and continue to provide. They remain the bedrock from which all good things flow.

SELWYN R. CUDJOE

Wellesley, Massachusetts

Beyond Boundaries

Stickfighting or the Calinda in Tacarigua, Trinidad, the spiritual and cultural womb out of which the author came. The two figures in the hats (from left to right) are Archie Cudjoe, a relative, and Hamilton Cudjoe, an uncle.

Introduction

What is past is past. I suppose that was the general attitude [of people in Trinidad and Tobago]. And we Indians, immigrants from India, had that attitude to the island. We lived for the most part ritualized lives, and were not yet capable of self-assessment, which is where learning begins…

As a child I knew almost nothing, nothing beyond what I had picked up in my grandmother's house. All children, I suppose, come into the world like that, not knowing who they are. But for the French child, say, that knowledge is waiting. That knowledge will be all around them. It will come indirectly from the conversation of the elders. It will be in the newspapers and on the radio. And at school the work of generations of scholars, scaled down for school texts, will provide some idea of France and the French.

—V. S. Naipaul, "Nobel Lecture," 2001

When V. S. Naipaul of Trinidad and Tobago won the 2001 Nobel Prize in Literature, his accomplishment signaled a culmination of a literary and intellectual process that had its origins in the narrative[s] of Louisa Calderon in 1803. In his Nobel lecture, Naipaul bemoaned that, when he began to write, there were no local models for him to follow. He argued that, unlike the French child, Trinidad and Tobago possessed no tradition of literature into which he could delve, no tradition of scholarship into which he could have immersed himself.

In a sense, Naipaul is correct. Although there is an existent tradition of writing, cultural practices, customs, uses of language, etc., which have helped to produce and influence a host of significant Trinbagonian writers, up to and including Naipaul, it has not been mapped, historicized, or examined in detail. This tradition exists in tracts, novels, newspapers, travel writings, dramatic performances, open-air theatre, sermons, and poetry. It can be found in all of those practices—within the recesses of history, as it were—that scholars seldom examine. The challenge lies in rescuing this tradition from the oblivion into which it has fallen, much of which it suffered from its inception.

Beyond Boundaries attempts to save this intellectual tradition from obscurity and to impose a way of reading and understanding it so that no Trinbagonian can ever say, "As a child I knew almost nothing, nothing beyond what I had picked up at my grandmother's house." Instead, like the French, English, or Spanish child, s/he can be proud of a tradition of literature and scholarship. We can hope that in the future transmission of this important, but too long neglected, tradition of Trinbagonian letters and scholarship shall be through school texts.

This study also puts to rest the notion that Caribbean literature in English started at the beginning of the twentieth century. West Indians have been writing and speaking about their experiences since they arrived in these islands, whether it took the form of open-air theatre as in the case of Carnival, hosay, or ramleelas; the telling of *kheesas* (Indian folk tales) or anancy stories; or the rendering of proverbs and riddles for the benefit of children's education. While the more fortunate members of the society were putting their pens to paper to tell their stories, others told their tales to those who recorded them for posterity. Some writers and storytellers described the fauna of the islands, while others offered portraits of their society.

In the search to rescue Trinidad and Tobago literary and intellectual history, it is clear that the savants of the nineteenth century took a broader view of what constituted the literary or the imaginative. For them, the humanities, agriculture, geography, and history were creative and imaginative enterprises. In a way, they saw these as humanistic endeavors of self development. The only criterion was that these productions contribute to the edification and cultivation of citizens. As Terry Eagleton asks in another context, "Under what social conditions does creativity become confined to music and poetry, while science, technology, politics, work and domesticity become drearily prosaic?"[1] This is why so much of the educational process was carried in and through newspapers. The idea of intellectual cultivation was not intended to confine itself to a tiny group of men and women who were satisfied to call themselves literary or cultured.

In this current study, I have used this broader concept of literary and intellectual thought to describe what these early writers had in mind when they spoke about what they did. In their own age, these authors would not have been averse to my calling their discourses literary since that word would have encapsulating the broad interests shared by such writers in human letters. Thus, within this context, my study's subtitle, "the Intellectual Tradition of Trinidad and Tobago in the Nineteenth Century," represents a concession to contemporary taste and nomenclature.

I have also made little distinction between those who were born on the islands and those who were not. Although narratives such as *Warner Arundell* and *The Slave Son* were written by English (Creole) writers, I textualize them as part of the local literature since they inculcate and/or embody aspects of local language and culture. They give a vision of how others saw the islands and, thereby, extend our knowledge about the truth of Caribbean experiences. I have tried to capture the underlying symmetry of ideas that characterized these writings and have sought to

1. Terry Eagleton, *The Idea of Culture* (Oxford: Blackwell, 2000), p. 21.

demonstrate how all the writers are associated with and contributed toward a collective enterprise called Trinidad and Tobago literary and intellectual thought. I have also made the point that the notion of Trinidadianness and Tobagonianness (Trinbagonianism, for short) was/is an evolving concept that the society is still trying to stabilize within itself. Postmodernists would say that our national identity is a sentiment that is constructed over time or, better yet, within time.

Most of all, I have tried to demonstrate that these writers and thinkers did not work in isolation, untroubled by the events that were taking place around them. In its broadest sense, the literature of Trinidad and Tobago was influenced by (and at times influencing) all the major currents of the age, even as the writers explicated what was particular to the land in which they lived and worked. In other words, they were constantly affected by what was taking place beyond their boundaries, in very much the same way that C. L. R. James suggested that, in the islands, much of what was significant about the game of cricket took place beyond the boundary. Many of our writers and thinkers studied abroad and made frequent trips to the metropolitan centers (particularly London and Paris), as well as throughout the Caribbean. Meanwhile, the newspapers, of which there were many, kept the general society informed about the ideas that traversed the world. So, although the people of the islands lived in a small, confined world, their ideas were influenced by the classical thinkers of the ancient world, Enlightenment concepts, English literature, African philosophy, Hindu theology, Islamic passion plays, and the culture of Carnival. Just as it is impossible "to understand intellectual formation in Britain in the nineteenth century outside the context of the relationship between Britain and the rest of the world,"[2] so too, it is difficult to understand intellectual currents in Trinidad and Tobago without understanding its relationship to Britain and other parts of the world.

This study, therefore, traces the development of the literature of Trinidad and Tobago and how various practices led toward its construction. The first three chapters deal with the literature up until the end of apprenticeship in 1838. The first chapter, "The Menace of Color," recounts the story of Louisa Calderon through many of the documents that were published about her torture at the hands of Governor Thomas Picton. In the process, this chapter offers a good representation of a "nascent" Trinidadian in the first decade of the nineteenth century. The second chapter, "*Free Mulatto* and Early Expressions of Trinidad's Literature," examines *Free Mulatto* (1824), Jean-Baptiste Philippe's seminal work, along with the various letters and poems that were written during that early period. It also demonstrates how much *Free Mulatto* was influenced by Enlightenment ideas. "Children of the Dark," the third chapter, looks at Pierre M'Callum, *Travel in Trinidad* (1805), M. Dauxion-Lavaysse's *A Statistical, Commercial, and Political Description of Venezuela, Trinidad, Margarita, and Tobago* (1812), and "The Narrative of John

2. Faith Lois Smith, "John Jacob Thomas and Caribbean Intellectual Life in the Nineteenth Century," Ph.D., dissertation, Duke University, 1995, p. 99.

M'Donald" (1837), as well as the poems and petitions of this period. In this chapter, I am concerned primarily with how Africans are treated in the literature.

Chapters four through six focus on the literature from apprenticeship to 1859. Chapter four, "The Textuality of Colonialism," is devoted primarily to E. L. Joseph's *Warner Arundell* (1838), a trilogy, whereas chapter five, "Jamettization of the Culture (1838–1851)," examines the literary development from 1838–1851. This chapter concerns itself with works such as "Jim the Boatman" (1846); *Ca qui pas bon pour z'oies pas; Pas bon pour canards* (1847), a play; *The Interesting Narrative of Maria Jones*, one of the earliest slave narratives; and the religious proselytizing of John Law through the establishment of the Baptist Press. Chapter six, "The Emergence of a National Voice (1852–1858)," looks at three of the more exciting literary pieces of the period: *Adolphus: A Tale* (1853); Maxwell Philip's *Emmanuel Appadocca* (1854), the first indigenous novel of the tradition; and Mary Fanny Wilkins's *The Slave Son* (1854). It ends with a discussion of Captain and Mrs. Swinton's "Journal of a Voyage with Coolie Emigrants from Calcutta to Trinidad" (1859).

Chapters seven through nine examine the literature of the 1860s. Chapter seven, "Naming the Land," argues that naming the space (or the land) was a necessary precondition in order to experience the national territory. It critiques the paintings of Jean Michel Cazabon (1813–1880); L. A. A. de Verteuil's *Trinidad* (1858), a work on geography; and Antoine Leotaud's *Oiseaux de l'île de la Trinidad* (1866), a study of the birds of the island. Chapter eight, "Cultural Resistance: The Emergence of the Carnivalesque," examines William Gamble's *Trinidad: Historical and Descriptive* (1867), the Keenan *Report* (1869) and J. J. Thomas's *The Theory and Practice of Creole Grammar* (1869): three texts that opened a discourse on varied ideological practices that shaped the society. Chapter nine, "Signs Taken in Wonder: Race and Race-Consciousness," is devoted exclusively to Charles Kingsley's *At Last* (1869), a response to Charles Darwin's magisterial work *On the Origin of Species* (1859).

Chapters ten and eleven make the case for the emergence of a self-conscious literary tradition and the unleashing of powerful indigenous forms that reveal different dimensions of the society. Chapter ten, "Bodies *in* the West…," examines *The Diaries of Abbé Masse, 1876–1883*, written by a Roman Catholic curate, and Pierre-Gustave Borde's *Histoire de l'île de la Trinidad sous le gouvernement espagnol 1498 á 1797* (1876, 1882). It also describes what I call the "hosay" and "carnival continua," forms of open-air theatre that have been ignored shamelessly by our literary theorists. Chapter eleven, "Cultural Self-Assertion: Savagery versus Civilization," examines notions of savagery and civilization that are utilized by the dominant class to undercut the growing self-awareness of the colonized. It also examines "the Calypso," and its African provenance, the *ramleelas*, a retelling of the *Ramayana* in the wilderness as I have described it, and "Joseph Annajee" (1879), a conversion narrative.

In the 1880s, the Amerindian functioned as an important trope, which expressed nationalistic sentiments and rewrote these original inhabitants back into the region's history. This is the subject of chapter twelve, "The Romanticization of the Amerindian," in which I examine L. B. Tronchin's *Inez: Or the Last of the Aroucas* (1885); Jean-Charles de St. Avit's *Les Deux Premiers Martyrs de la Trinidad* (1885), a dramatic piece; and Horatio Nelson Huggins's *Hiroona: An Historical Romance in Poetic Form* (written in the 1880s but not published until 1930), "the Caribbean's fist epic poem," as Paula Burnett labeled it. Chapter thirteen, "The Negro's Grievance: Literature in the Service of a Cause," discusses *Froudacity* (1889), J. J. Thomas's stinging rebuttal to James Anthony Froude's *The English in the West Indies* (1888), and the French verse of the Creoles, especially the poetry of Sly Devenish (1819–1903), which was so prominent in the second half of the nineteenth century.

Chapters fourteen and fifteen round out the account by examining the rise in nationalist sentiments amidst attempts to be faithful to elements of colonial ideology. Chapter fourteen, "Knights of the Mask," looks at James Collens's *Who Did It?* (1891), a detective novel that opens with a game of cricket; several works by Lewis O. Inniss (*The Adventures of Reginald Osborn* [1895], *Centennial Tourists' Companion to Trinidad* [1897], and *Carmelita: The Belle of San Jose* [1897]); Henry Martiol Rodrigues's *The Siren Goddess of South America* (1897), a romantic text set in South America; Ivry Hart's *Centenary Reminiscences* (1897) and *Some Sketches and Songs* (1898); Eugene Francis Chalamelle's *Some Reflections on the Carnival of Trinidad* (1897), a pamphlet that details the transgressive sexual practices of Carnival; and Anthony Richard Delamere's *The Old Bar and the New Bar*, a work that traces the development of the legal profession during the nineteenth century.

Chapter fifteen, "The Revindication of the Races," focuses on two works with contradictory views: C. S. Assee's *Laus Reginae* (1902) and Stephen Nathaniel Cobham's *Rupert Gray: A Tale of Black and White* (1907). While Assee celebrates the greatness of Queen Victoria and imperialist practices, Cobham examines the emerging racial pride of Afro-Trinbagonians even as he discusses the forbidden nature of their relationships with white women. Such an examination is to be seen against the background of the great poetry row of 1902, the growing importance of Pan-Africanism in the society, and the significant place Sylvester Williams, Canon Philip Douglin, and Cobham play in disseminating such ideas.

I have tried to let the work speak for itself by employing a strategy that organizes the various texts into a logical pattern, the overlapping discursiveness of which, as Edward Said says, reveals their transgressive tendencies. It is this crossing over, this "moving from one domain to another, the testing and challenging of limits, the mixing and intermingling of heterogeneities, cutting across expectations, providing unforeseen pleasures, discoveries, experiences,"[3] that allow for the most fruitful examination of this complex period of Trinidad and Tobago's intellectual development. More importantly, I have tried to demonstrate that, before one can construct

---

3. Edward Said, *Musical Elaborations* (London: Vintage, 1992), p. 55.

a theory of the postcolonial, one first has to chronicle and understand the development of national literatures of societies such as Trinidad and Tobago.

I hope that this study, a product of ten years of intellectual labor, allows for the self-assessment that Naipaul suggests is so necessary for learning and provides a history of ideas that he believes is so easily available to the French and English child. Since the ideas in these narratives, apart from emanating from the experiences of the local environment, were shaped and influenced by intellectual currents circulating in and around the Atlantic, it is not merely a Trinidad and Tobago story, but a New World story in that it takes and reshapes ideas from home and abroad to reveal a New World, Atlantic sensibility. Three days before this study went to press, I obtained a copy of Kris Rampersad, *Finding a Place: IndoTrinidadian Literature* (Kingston: Ian Randle, 2002) that makes the case for the development of an Indian literary sensibility (consciousness) in Trinidad between 1850 and 1950. However, the major part of the study (chapters three through 7) examines the written literature of the twentieth century. An important study, it demonstrates the impact of Indian oral literatures in the making of Trinidad's literary culture.

Finally, I trust that this study contributes to a better understanding of the archeology of knowledge that has been fashioned in nineteenth century Trinidad and Tobago. Like *Beyond a Boundary*, James's classic study of the game of cricket in a colonial society, *Beyond Boundaries* hopes to demonstrate that the discussions of race, politics, literature, art, theology, science, and culture that were taking place in Trinidad and Tobago were part of similar discussions taking place beyond the islands' boundaries. In this sense, I see this study as a tribute to James's intellectual brilliance as well as to what he tried to accomplish in his *ouvre*. Although he did not write a study on Maxwell Philip as he promised in 1931, I hope that this examination of a tradition that produced such important writers and thinkers as Jean Baptiste Philippe, J. J. Thomas, Eric Williams, Oliver Cromwell Cox, Sylvester Williams, George Padmore, the Naipauls (Seepersad and Shiva), Earl Lovelace, Arnold Rampersad, Merle Hodge, and James fulfills that deep intellectual chasm he hoped to fill. It is also my hope that this study offers an alter-native prism through which we may view Trinbagonian society and deepens our appreciation of the work that our foreparents produced when it was very difficult to pursue literary and intellectual endeavors, a fact to which so many of them testified. This book represents an act of solidarity with what they did, pays tribute to what they accomplished, and expresses a profound respect for the faith they showed in their society. May it lead to a better understanding of our society and ourselves.

CHAPTER 1

The Menace of Color

The culture that the intellectual leans towards is often no more than a stock of particularisms. He wishes to attach himself to the people; but instead he only catches hold of their outer garments. And these outer garments are merely the reflection of a hidden life, teeming and perpetually in motion. That extremely obvious objectivity which seems to characterize a people is only the inert, already forsaken result of frequent, and not always very coherent, adaptations of a much more fundamental substance which itself is continually being renewed.

—FRANTZ FANON, The Wretched of the Earth

Conde does not dissociate culture and collective consciousness from the socioeconomic context. She examines the formation of Caribbean identity in terms of chains of relations rooted in the slave/(neo)colonial system and the interplay of strategies of assimilation and subversion, submission and revolt. Analyzing the oral literary tradition, Conde attempts to recapture the memory of the past and its echoes in the present.

—MARIE-DENISE SHELTON, "Conde: The Politics of Gender and Identity"

The pride of Englishmen and the Glory of the Nation—the TRIAL by JURY—which has ever been considered the Palladium of British liberty! Long may it continue, and its Innovators become the Objects of universal Detestation. Let him who tramples on Humanity and Justice be for ever annihilated from Society—let him tremble at the horrid Cruelty to injured Innocence—a helpless Female—whom *Nature* made him her *Protector* and not her *Prosecutor*.

—J. LEE, The Trial of Governor Picton

The Evolution of Society

The modern social history of Trinidad and Tobago coincided with the transfer of the governance of the island from the Spanish to the English and what James Millette calls "the genesis of Crown Colony Government," a form of governance that transformed the British Caribbean between 1860 and 1962 when formal independence occurred.[1] Trinidad was part of the Spanish Captaincy-general of Venezuela when Sir Ralph Abercromby captured it from the Spanish in 1797. It finally became a British territory when the Treaty of Amiens was signed in 1802.

Because Spanish colonial society was extremely concerned about maintaining legality, there developed "an unadulterated bureaucracy"[2] that made the administration of Spanish law cumbersome, expensive, and fraught with difficulties and delays. In *The Spanish Empire in America*, C. H. Haring writes that the Spaniards "like the Romans…were preeminently creators of laws and builders of institutions. Of all the colonizing peoples of modern times, the Spaniards were the most legal-minded. In the new empire they speedily developed a meticulously organized administrative system such as the world had rarely seen."[3] Yet, as Millette explains, these difficulties were not the fault of the code but resulted from "Spanish attempts to resolve the ever present conflict between law and justice [that] were painstaking and detailed."[4]

The excessive concern with law and legality meant that slavery in the Spanish islands was milder than it was in the other West Indian islands, an imbalance that had tremendous effects on the people of color in Trinidad before the arrival of the British. Bridget Brereton writes that the people of color "held minor posts in the administration in many Spanish colonies by the 1780s, and they were commissioned as officers in the local militias. More significantly, Chacon (governor of Trinidad, 1784–1797) was a man of liberal intent, and he chose to ignore the laws that existed in the Spanish colonies against the free coloureds."[5]

Slave laws also played an important part in shaping the tone and character of Caribbean society. According to E. V. Goveia, "both in their content and in their enforcement, the West Indian slave laws follow a remarkably consistent pattern, imposed by the function of the law in maintaining the stability of those forms of social organisation on which rested the whole life of the West Indian colonies in the 18th century." She also notes that, because Spanish societies in the West Indies were less "generally dependent" on Negro slavery (as were those in the French-, Dutch-, and English-speaking Caribbean), "the proportion of whites and free people in their population was higher than was usual in any of the colonies where plantation slavery was dominant." Although this observation suggests that the free people of color were more integrated into Spanish society and enjoyed more rights than their black counterparts in the non-Spanish territories, they were still subject to severe restrictions. Indeed, "they were supposed to live under the supervision of a patron,

---

1. See James Millette, *Society and Politics in Colonial Trinidad* (Curepe & London: Omega Bookshops & Zed Books, 1985), on which I draw heavily in sketching this early period of Trinidad's history.

2. The term is Lewis Bobb's and is taken from his foreword to Millette's *Society and Politics,* p. xxiv.

3. J. C. Haring, *The Spanish Empire in America* (New York: Harcourt, Brace, and World, 1963), p. 25.

4. Millette, *Society and Politics,* p. 47.

5. Bridget Brereton, *A History of Modern Trinidad, 1783–1962* (Kingston: Heinemann, 1981), p. 24.

even though they were free, and by a special law, they were forbidden to wear gold, silk, cloaks or other kinds of clothing considered unsuitable to their station in society." Yet, the relatively humane treatment the free people of color received stemmed directly from the nature of the *Siete Partidas,* "the earliest legal view of the slave and slavery in the history of the West Indies," in which "the slave is considered as part of the 'familia,'" resulting in a fuzzy distinction between slaves and serfs. Goveia remarks that "throughout the 18th century, Puerto Rico followed the practice of giving asylum to fugitive slaves from non-Spanish islands, with very little variation from the principle that, once they had embraced the Roman Catholic religion, they were not to be returned."[6] Such benign treatment changed once the British began their rule in Trinidad, and this change led to ill feelings between the British authorities and the people of color.

In a way, it was unfortunate that Great Britain captured Trinidad at a time when the constitutional theories by which Britain governed its overseas territories were being transformed. Until the nineteenth century, the English government "had never displayed so careful and sustained an interest in slave regulations as had the government of Spain from the earliest times."[7] The laissez-faire ideas of the early period of British capitalism, however, were giving way to a greater authoritarianism. Millette believes that "this transformation from tolerance to authority was prompted by many factors but, perhaps in the long run, particularly by two: the need to blunt the savage edge of the entrenched white minorities in the colonies, and the necessity to cope with the rising 'menace of colour' and particularly with the threat of black or coloured people in government."[8] During the early period, Abercromby's desire to follow Spanish law as closely as possible did nothing to clarify the new social and political situation, nor did it make the position of the free people of color and the free blacks any more secure. More importantly, the ambiguous constitutional status during this early period led to many atrocities, none of which were more disastrous than the manner in which Thomas Picton handled the case of Louisa Calderon.

In its early period, Trinidad was also exposed to revolutionary ideas. Residents of the Spanish-speaking colonies of Trinidad and Venezuela were affected by ideas emanating from the British colonies in North America and from the French Revolution. These ideas found fertile ground in "a world tired of colonial rule, and where there was already a current of feeling for self-government. The Creole felt capable of ruling himself, and struggled for full mastership of the State to complement his mastership of the land and the slaves."[9] Indeed, for New World Africans, the Haitian revolution was decisive, for it established how they saw their position

6. E. V. Goveia, *The West Indian Slave Laws of the 18th Century* (Bucks: Caribbean Universities Press & Ginn and Company, 1987), pp. 53, 11, 18, 13–14.

7. Ibid., p. 19.

8. Millette, *Society and Politics,* p. xi.

9. Guillermo Moron, *A History of Venezuela,* trans. John Street (London: George Allen & Unwin, 1964), p. 96.

in that part of the world, and it set in motion ideas about their own liberation. As Millette writes:

> In the West Indies, following on the outbreak of revolution in St Domingue and on the triumph of the Jacobins in France, the struggle became quite as bitter as it was in Europe. Indeed, because the obsession of both the principal belligerents with a West Indian strategy, the whole West Indian area was in the greatest turmoil. In addition, liberty, equality and fraternity, the radical objectives of the French Revolution, were sentiments that appealed powerfully to the subject slave and free coloured populations scattered throughout the West Indies....
>
> In Trinidad, as elsewhere in the West Indies, it was the fate of the Revolution to introduce a new element of instability into a fundamentally unstable society. The ideas of freedom and democracy, no longer the monopoly of abstract philosophers constituted in the West Indies as in Europe the severest attack on established positions and institutions. As ideologues of progress and liberation they gave rise to new theories of social organization based on the exciting premise that liberty equality and fraternity were the rights of all men. Spokesmen like Oge, Sothonax, Polverell, and Victor Hugues brought the messages to the West Indies. Toussaint, Dessalines, Christophe, the masses of oppressed slaves, and even planters like the coloured man Fedon, repudiated slavery and all its works. However imperfectly the new ideas were appreciated, the examples of resistance and revolt were powerful precepts for action everywhere in the West Indies.[10]

In Trinidad, where free blacks and people of color outnumbered the white population, these ideas took on enormous importance and had important consequences for social and political development. They even affected the constitutional arrangements for the future development of the society.

The People of Color

Because the people of color and free blacks greatly outnumbered the whites, they became important elements in Trinidadian society. Coming in large numbers from the other islands because of the Royal Cedula of Population (a scheme proposed by Roume St. Laurent and accepted by the King of Spain, that brought French immigrants to Trinidad), and the Haitian War of Independence, the people of color brought their families, their slaves, and everything they possessed. According to Millette, "as legal immigrants encouraged to come to the Island by the cedula of 1783, they had rights and they meant to assert them... They had a legally defined status that made their social position better by comparison than that of any other coloured community in the West Indies. And it was from this eminence that they were to take their stand on the constitutional question in future years."[11]

As the British began to administer the island, the rights the Creoles enjoyed

10. Millette, *Society and Politics*, pp. 22–24.
11. Ibid. p. 33.

under the Spanish were eliminated gradually. Colonel Thomas Picton who managed the country after the departure of Abercromby adopted a policy of silent (we
would now call it benign) neglect toward the people of color that resulted in new
tensions between these two groups. From an initial stance of neglect and concilia-
tion, Picton moved to a policy of terror and brutality that led Pierre M'Callum to
assert that Picton "was invested with the supreme authority of a commercial colony,
before he obtained the knowledge of governing himself." [12]

Picton saw Spanish laws that protected the people of color as unnecessary
encumbrances to the enforcement of his will and designs. Further, before a new constitution could be put into place, Picton had to destroy the legal status of the free
people of color. During his short reign (1797–1803), he did everything in his power
to compromise and ultimately violate the rights of the people of color. Under his
administration, torture of and brutality toward them grew by alarming proportions.

Additionally, Picton, it seemed, feared that the revolt that took place in St.
Domingo would occur ultimately on Trinidad and wanted to avoid such an occurrence at any cost. He believed that all of the island's free people of color had come
to Trinidad "hotfoot from the revolutionary orgies of the neighboring islands"[13] and
so were natural troublemakers. Cruelly disregarding the feelings of these citizens,
Picton set about to subject them to public humiliation by placing severe restrictions
on their social lives.[14] This vendetta set the stage for two of the earliest narratives in
Trinidad and Tobago's literature.

Inhuman Torture: The Story of Louisa Calderon

"The Narrative of Louisa Calderon"[15] and Jean-Baptiste Philippe's *Free Mulatto*,
two of the first narratives of Trinidad and Tobago's literary tradition, must be examined in the context of the increasing tyranny imposed upon the people of color.
Although approximately twenty years separate these documents—one, subjective,
the other objective—each examined the conditions under which the free coloreds
lived and the cruelties to which they were subjected. Their contents thereby give us
a glimpse of a society in formation, and the response of a people under pressure.

"The Narrative of Louisa Calderon," the first document of our literature, tells of
the fate of a young woman under the tyranny of Picton. Through her direct testimony during the one-day trial of Governor Thomas Picton in London on February
24, 1806, and through the various accounts of this incident that are given in
Trinidad and in London, one can begin to discern the subject[16] and reconstruct her

12. Pierre M'Callum, *Travels in Trinidad* (Liverpool: W. Jones, 1805), p. 141.
13. Ibid., 109–110.
14. See ibid. pp. 111–12 for an outline of the restrictions placed on the people of color.
15. "The Narrative of Louisa Calderon" refers to the extracts from various trial testimonies in which
she speaks for herself and describes her suffering.
16. In attempting to *dis-cern Louisa Calderon*, I conflate two related definitions of the old English
word "to cern," which means to accept an inheritance or a patrimony, and "to cerne," which means to
encircle or enclose. Each meaning alerts the reader to how I intend to treat this subject: to encircle

narrative voice.[17] Indeed, the narrative discloses a policy of abuse that is important for an understanding of Trinbagonian literary tradition.

Yet, for purposes of this analysis, the accuracy of the various transcriptions is not the salient concern—(the records were all taken down in shorthand),even though the various chroniclers could be construed as performing either the function of *enscribano* as the latter acted under Spanish law[18] or of the familiar *amanuensis* that we observe in the production of some Caribbean slave narratives.[19] Rather, in this analysis, I interrogate the performative aspects of Calderon's narrative, being more concerned with the epistemological dimension of the text (what and how we know) than with its praxeological aspect (what was done to the young woman). Although one may be inclined to view Calderon's account of her torture as a transparent or a self-serving gesture, I am more concerned with the circumstances of her utterances and what they tell us about her subjectivity. Using the language of the classical rhetoricians, I argue that the questions raised in this narrative refer "less to a knowledge of the truth than to a knowledge of verisimilitude." Tzventan Todorov contends that, even though an author (amanuensis/enscribano) may be "mistaken, or lying, his text is no less significant than when he is speaking the truth; the important thing is that the text be 'receivable' by contemporaries" or be so regarded by its producer. From this point of view, the notion of 'false' is here irrelevant."[20] Speaking specifically about the Caribbean, Frantz Fanon observes that, when a story flourishes in the heart of a folklore, it is because in one way or another it expresses an

---

Calderon in such a way as to retrieve her inheritance and her patrimony for the society. See Paul Smith's *Discerning the Subject* (Minneapolis: University of Minnesota Press, 1988), to which I am indebted.

17. One can reconstruct Calderon's text by examining her direct testimony, the supplementary evidence of other witnesses, and the descriptions of several commentaries that were written about this very famous trial. Eric Sundquist makes a similar case for the narrative voice of Nat Turner as it is revealed in Thomas Gray's account of Turner's "confessions." He notes "that Nat Turner's voice—and hence his thought, his vision, and his leadership—remains strongly present in the historic 'text' that may be reconstructed from the accounts of his revolt and his published document" (Eric Sundquist, *To Wake the Nations* [Cambridge: Harvard University Press, 1993], p. 21). In *I, Tituba, The Black Witch of Salem*, Maryse Conde uses Tituba's confession to construct a narrative of her life. As Conde remarks in an interview with Ann Armstrong Carrboro, "I really invented Tituba." I wrote "her story out of my dreams" (*I, Tituba* [New York: Ballantine Books, 1992], pp. 201, 199). See also Elaine Breslaw, *Tituba, Reluctant Witch* (New York: New York University Press, 1996), a biography that traces Tituba's Amerindian past in South America, to her stay in Barbados, on to the infamous Salem witch trial in 1692. Incidentally, Tituba and Calderon have a few things in common. Each was questioned intensely for several days; each was placed in prison for a considerable time; and each was represented by the authorities as a threat to her community.

18. An *enscribano* always attended the *alcalde* (the Spanish judge) and was responsible for taking notes of all the proceedings of the court. He is described as a "Scrivener, or notary, and also an officer who draws up the charges against a criminal, with all the circumstances, according to legal form" (*The Trial of Governor T. Picton for Inflicting the Torture on Louisa Calderon* [London: Dewick & Clark, 1806], p. 15).

19. See, for example, Mary Prince, *The History of Mary Prince, A West Indian Slave* (1831; rpt. London: Pandara Press, 1987).

20. Tzventan Todorov, *Conquest of America* (New York: Harper, 1984), p. 54.

aspect of 'the spirit of the group.'"[21] In the Trinidad and Tobago context, the narrative of Louisa Calderon expresses the grievances of a member of this emerging society.

Louisa Calderon, a nascent Trinidadian, was shaped by the confluence of forces that emerged in early nineteenth-century Trinidad. Born in Port of Spain, Trinidad, on August 25, 1786,[22] Calderon was the daughter of Maria del Rosario Calderon, who was born in Cariaco in the province of Cumana in Venezuela. Drawing on a representation of the torture she underwent at the hands of Vallot, Picton's gaoler, one is made privy to an eyewitness account of her life and how her fate was imbricated within the laws of the society.

The facts of the case are simple. On December 7, 1801, Louisa Calderon, a young colored woman of Port of Spain, lived in a state of concubinage with a white Spaniard, Pedro Ruiz. With the aid of Carlos Gonzalez, she robbed Ruiz of $2,000. Discovering his loss, Ruiz made a report to Lieutenant Governor Picton who immediately committed Calderon to prison with the warning that, "if she did not confess who had taken the money, he would order the hangman to put his hand upon her."[23] Two days later, Picton instructed St. Hilaire Beggorat, an *alcalde*, to investigate the claim, which Beggorat did until December 21.[24]

On December 22, dissatisfied with Calderon's replies to his interrogation, Beggorat applied to Picton for permission to torture her. One day later, permission was given and Calderon was tortured for fifty-four minutes. On December 24, she was tortured again for twenty-three minutes. Finally, she was "immediately put in irons, rather in an erect position, in a garret in the goal, where she could not stand upright, and continued in this horrid place for eight months."[25] While she was being tortured, Beggorat wrote, "the said Luisa [*sic*] cried *Ay, ay,* repeating the same several times, calling on God and the Holy Virgin."[26]

After Calderon was released, Colonel William Fullarton, one of three English commissioners sent to the island during this crisis, took her to London to testify against Picton, who was tried subsequently, in London for her torture.[27] Don Chandos, in whose arms Calderon fainted, supported her testimony and added that

21. Frantz Fanon, *Black Skin; White Masks* (New York: Grove Press, 1967), p. 64.

22. E. L. Joseph offers much evidence to support Calderon's birth in 1786 rather than 1788 (*History of Trinidad* [1838: rpt. London: F. Cass, 1970], chap. 16).

23. Pierre McCallum, *The Trial of Thomas Picton* (London: W. Lewis, 1806), p. 17.

24. Don de Castro, an *escrivano*, or notary; Vallot, the goaler and hangman; and Raphael Chandos, the *alguazil* or constable, attended Beggorat in his examination and subsequent torture of Calderon.

25. McCallum, *The Trial of Thomas Picton*, p. 15.

26. Quoted in V. S. Naipaul's *The Loss of El Dorado: A History* (London: Andre Deutsch, 1969), p. 176. In this book (pp. 172–79), Naipaul offers a good dramatic recreation of Calderon's torture.

27. The actual practice was called picketing, picquetting, and in this particular case, "picton-ing, "in which the defendant's left hand "was tied up to the ceiling, by a rope, with a pulley; her right hand was tied behind, so that her right foot and hand came in contact, while the extremity of her left foot rested on the wooden spike....She swooned each time before she was taken down, and was then put into irons called Grillo; this was a long piece of iron, with two rings for the feet, fastened to the wall; and in this situation she remained for eight months. The effect from this picketting was excruciating pain; her

FIGURE 1. A depiction of Louisa Calderon as she is tortured by Vallot, Picton's goaler, who is holding the keys. St. Hillarie Begorrat is one of the persons in the drawing.

"the room in which she was in irons for eight months by the legs, was so low that it would not admit of her fitting erect, but she was obliged to crouch down."[28] Although Picton was found guilty after a one-day trial and a five-minute jury deliberation, he was eventually freed. This case became a cause célèbre in London because it pitted some of the most powerful pro- and antislavery advocates against each other. Even Vallot admired Louisa's courage under torture. He remarked that "I was surprised at her being resolute."[29]

Although enslaved Africans in Trinidad underwent much more severe punishments in their everyday existence, McCallum seemed to be particularly aggrieved because Vallot, the gaoler, apparently "shewed her [Calderon] the treatment which certain Negroes, accused of sorcery, divination, etc., had undergone from a similar punishment."[30] Significantly, picquetting was introduced into the island in 1797 by Picton "to torture four or five negroes" who, he was convinced, had "held converse with the devil."[31] During Picton's trial, the prosecutor noted:

> In order to operate on her imagination, two or three negresses were brought before her in the apartment where torture was usually applied, and these unhappy wretches were to suffer the horrid ceremony under a charge of witchcraft, as a means of extorting confession.[32]

In 1803, in letters sent back to England (reprinted as *Travels in Trinidad*), McCallum first brought Picton's cruelty to the attention of the British public even though he encountered some difficulty in having his book published. One com-

---

wrists and ankles were much swollen, and the former bore the marks to the present day" (*The Trial of Governor Picton* [London: J. Lee and W. Mantz, 1806]) This text is not paginated, so in future citations of this text, I differentiate between it and the previously cited, *The Trial of Governor T. Picton* by using the name of the publisher.

28. McCallum, *The Trial of Thomas Picton*, p. 20.

29. Quoted in *The Loss of El Dorado*, p. 177.

30. Ibid, p. 15.

31. Ibid., pp. 20–21.

32. *The Trial of Governor Picton*, p. 8.

mentator remarked that it "would shock the human mind, to read the black cata-logue of crimes which our traveler exhibits against Picton."[33] McCallum also doc-umented Picton's treatment of Negroes. In 1812, in his *Appeal*, John Sanderson noted even more horrendous tyrannies against the slaves: "Tortures to exhort con-fession of sorcery, witchcraft, and obeism [Obeahism], public mutilations in the marketplace for such chimerical crimes; and even the burning of the living and dead together in the streets of Trinidad have stained the character of that unfortunate colony with the blood and ashes of the devoted victims of superstitious cruelty, practised under the authority of ignorant judges."[34]

The case of Calderon and the subsequent trial of Picton are important for sev-eral reasons. First, they introduce us to the language of colonialism that posits a clear and unequivocal distinction between *them* (white and European) and *us* (black and African) that is captured clearly and vividly when Mr. Garrow, the prosecutor in Picton's trial, outlined his case against Picton:

> Louisa Calderon, on whose treatment the present prosecution is founded, was of the age of ten or eleven years, when she was induced to live with a person of the name of Pedro Ruiz in the character of his mistress. With our habits it appears very extraordinary that she should be in such a situation at this tender period of life, but in that hot country the puberty of females is much accelerated, and they become mothers frequently when they are only twelve years old.[35]

Another account argued:

> Louisa Calderon, then of the age of about TEN or ELEVEN years, had been seduced by a person of the name Pedro Rouis [*sic*], with whom she had lived as his mistress; that to us in England, appeared most horrible, but in that country, young women became mothers at the age of TWELVE, and those who had not the good fortune to form an honourable connection, got into a state of concubinage at an early age.[36]

Pitting *their* habits against *ours* posits that the physiological development of young women in hot countries differed from that of their counterparts in cold countries. Moreover, the condition of Calderon is rendered as typically licentious, an attribute that has characterized black women from the time of slavery. Even as late as 1889, when an ordinance was proposed to lower the age of consent from six-teen years to thirteen years, the non-official members of the Trinidad Legislative Council who represented the plantocracy argued that "girls developed more rapid-ly in tropical climates and sooner attained the age of puberty."[37]

33. Quoted in McCallum's *The Trial of Thomas Picton*, p. 36.
34. Quoted in Millette, *Society and Politics*, pp. 54–55.
35 . *The Trial of Governor T. Picton*, pp. 6–7.
36. *The Trial of Governor Picton* (J. Lee, 1806).
37. Quoted in David Trotman, *Crime in Trinidad: Conflict and Control in a Plantation Society, 1838–1900* (Knoxville: University of Tennessee Press, 1986), p. 180.

Calderon's narrative and Picton's subsequent trial also alert us to the important question of language that remained at the heart of the colonial experience, a subject that J. J. Thomas addressed in the middle of the century. When the English conquered the island, Spanish, French, and Creole were the predominant languages spoken. The conquest introduced yet another language: English. Thus, from its inception, the experiment and interpretation of language were closely related to defining the colonial subject. The possession or nonpossession of a particular language almost stood as a mark against the colonized person.[38]

Calderon was taken to England to testify about the torture Picton had inflicted upon her. One version of the trial began with the observation that Calderon "was attended by two interpreters, the one for the Spanish language, the other for the Creole corruptions, or variations from that language."[39] Another account stated that Calderon spoke English "but very indifferently."[40] Yet to speak of Creole as a corruption loses sight of the tremendous linguistic mix (*mestizaje*) that was taking place in Trinbagonian society at the time, a process that was on display at the trial. Extracts of Spanish law had to be translated into English for the benefit of the court. The Attorney General, whose function was to interpret the law, neither spoke nor understood Spanish; Calderon testified in Spanish; and some interpreters had to be replaced because they could not translate between Spanish and English.

By defining Creole as a corruption of another language, rather than "a metalanguage through which the Caribbean people transcend paralyzing historical antimonies,"[41] colonialist culture displayed its tendency to deny colonial people their subjectivity and their agency, thereby making them think of themselves as inferior. In the process, little attention was paid to the fact that both Calderon and the discourse she inhabited possessed their own history and memory, which suggests that, when Thomas published *Theory and Practice of Creole Grammar*, he was responding to a problem of language, as well as to the identity that lay at the heart of the Trinbagonian and Caribbean condition.[42] As though coming full cycle in 1997, in her manual for Caribbean speakers, Merle Hodge argued that the majority of the people from the English-speaking Caribbean are not "English-speaking. We are a

38. I am not here concerned with how language shapes identity but with how language is used to differentiate between *them* and *us*, the latter being branded as inferior because they cannot attain to the "higher" language of the other.

39. *The Trial of Governor Picton*, p. 13.

40. *The Trial of Governor Picton* (W. Lee).

41. Marie-Denise Shelton, "Conde: The Politics of Gender and Identity," *World Literature Today*, (Autumn 1993), p. 717.

42. Drawing on Jacques Lacan and Louis Althusser, John Mowitt makes the following observation about the relationship between language and identity: "First, because human reality is irreducibly mediated by language and because language is the differential system described by Saussure, the subject that arises in language is structured by the differential logic of the linguistic signifying chain...Second, the linguistic constitution of the subject predisposes it toward its others: the unconscious and the social domain of other subjects.... Third, the subject's desire (structured by its linguistically mediated intersubjective constitution) not only destabilizes the subject, but also attaches the impossible structure of the subject to the lived inadequacy of social reality (*Discerning the Subject*, pp. xiv–xv).

Creole-speaking people. We have a language of our own, and English is another language that we have to learn."[43]

The "Narrative of Louisa Calderon" also opens up the question of what it meant to be a person in a slave society even when one was dubbed "a free person of color" and how the legitimacy of these early inhabitants was established or determined through legal texts. In this specific case, the enmity between Fullarton and Picton brought the issues to the fore. Nonetheless, to the degree that this incident spoke to the powerlessness of colonial people, it alerts us to the difficulty these citizens had in establishing their claims to fairness, legitimacy, equality, and justice. Roberto Gonzalez Echevarria notes that "[l]egal rhetoric always implies a textual exchange or dialogue, a petition or appeal or an answer to some sort of accusation. Like the pillory, which served to let the individual expiate his deviance in a public display of shame, writing, coming clean, is an act through which pardon, reunification with the body politic is pursued."[44] Thus Picton's trial and the several written versions of it preview the emergent Trinidadian subject and, in the process, expose the difficulty of establishing one's identity in a repressive, colonial society. Moreover, this trial made the public aware of the deteriorating position of colored persons in the society.

Essentially, Calderon's narratives and Philippe's address give us a sense of how colored people were represented and the conditions under which they lived. They also give us an insight into the feelings of these early inhabitants and how they used language to express and to deny feelings and sensibilities. Through these works, we see how the creative use of language and the imagination—that is, the fictional— begin to construct a Trinbagonian sensibility. In this context, Echevarria's concept of notarial rhetoric can be viewed as a point of departure from which to investigate the early literature of Trinidad and Tobago, or what I call the literary topography of Trinidad and Tobago.

The Trial

Although Picton's trial raised many points in British jurisprudence, it was played out among those who thought him guilty and felt he had sullied British law and those who believed that he was being tried unjustly for doing his duty.[45] Each side tried to convince the public of Picton's guilt or innocence and of why he needed to be punished or exonerated. The very titles of the accounts of the trial suggest how

43. Merle Hodge, *Knots in English: A Manual for Caribbean Users* (Wellesley, Mass.: Calaloux Publications, 1997). p. xi.

44. Roberto Gonzalez Echevarria, *Myth and Archive* (New York: Cambridge University Press, 1990), p. 70.

45. Sebastian Ventour, a jurist, argues that as famous as this trail was, it offers no precedent for law in contemporary Trinidad. Mr. Dallas, Picton's counsel, argued in similar terms. His defense was that Picton's "offense was committed in a foreign country" and that "no two systems of jurisprudence more materially differed than those of this country [England] and our colonies [that is, Trinidad]" (McCallum, *The Trial of Thomas Picton*, p. 23).

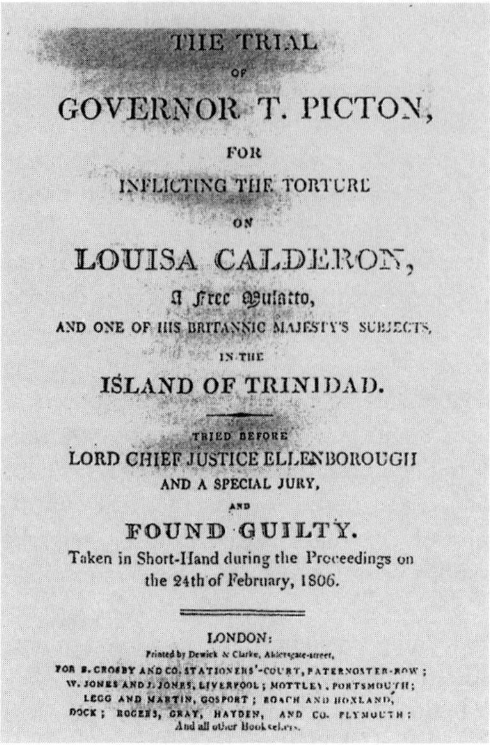

THE TRIAL
OF
GOVERNOR T. PICTON,
FOR
INFLICTING THE TORTURE
ON
LOUISA CALDERON,
A Free Mulatto,
AND ONE OF HIS BRITANNIC MAJESTY'S SUBJECTS,
IN THE
ISLAND OF TRINIDAD.

TRIED BEFORE
LORD CHIEF JUSTICE ELLENBOROUGH
AND A SPECIAL JURY,
AND
FOUND GUILTY.
Taken in Short-Hand during the Proceedings on
the 24th of February, 1806.

LONDON:
Printed by Dewick & Clarke, Aldersgate-street,
FOR B. CROSBY AND CO. STATIONERS'-COURT, PATERNOSTER-ROW;
W. JONES AND J. JONES, LIVERPOOL; MOTTLEY, PORTSMOUTH;
LEGG AND MARTIN, GOSPORT; ROACH AND HOXLAND,
DOCK; ROGERS, GRAY, HAYDEN, AND CO. PLYMOUTH:
And all other Booksellers.

FIGURE 2. Cover of *The Trial of Governor T. Picton for Inflicting the Torture on Louisa Calderon.*

inflamed sentiments were. Indeed, the broadsides had to be as graphic as possible to convince their readers. One summary of the trial is titled *The Trial of Governor Picton, for having Maliciously and with a view to Oppress Louisa Calderon, one of His Majesty's Subjects in the Island of Trinidad, By Inflicting The Torture on Her, by Suspending her by the Wrist, by a rope from the Ceiling, without any Resting Place for her Foot, But A Spike of Wood, in the Month of December, 1801.* Nothing could be more graphic. Another account, taken in shorthand during the trial, is *The Trial of Governor T. Picton, for Inflicting the Torture on Louisa Calderon, a Free Mulatto, and One of His Britannic Majesty's Subjects, in the Island of Trinidad.* Although this broadside does not mention how Calderon was tortured, it reproduces a drawing in watercolor that was presented to the court by the prosecutor of the case and that showed Calderon being suspended by her wrist from a rope without any resting place for her foot.[46] One account of the trial states that "[t]he pride of Englishmen

46. This drawing played an important part in the trial. After it was shown to Calderon during the trial, "this exhibition occasioned her to shudder in a way which nothing but the terrific recollection of her sufferings could have excited." Seeing this response, Mr. Garrow suggested to Lord Ellenborough, "I wish the position of your Lordship, could have enabled you to have seen this involuntary expression of the sensations of the witness, on the inspection of the drawing." In his address to the jury Mr. Dallas, the defense lawyer, described this drawing as a "florid representation" and "a most scenic display" that was designed "to influence the judgement, and to inform the passions of the public" (*The Trial of Governor Picton,* pp. 16, 50, 51). See page 14 for a reproduction of this drawing.

and the Glory of the Nation—the *TRIAL* by *JURY*—which has ever been considered the Palladium of British Liberty! long may it continue, and its Innovators become the Objects of universal Detestation. Let him who tramples on Humanity and Justice be for ever annihilated from Society—let him tremble at the horrid Cruelty to injured Innocence—a helpless Female—whom *Nature* made him her *Protector* and not her *Prosecutor*."

In McCallum's version, taken in shorthand, the author boasts proudly on the title page that he "was a Prisoner in the same Cell where the unfortunate Young Lady was TORTURED, and who was the Means of Bringing Picton's Horrid Crimes to Light."[47] Needless to say, because of McCallum's encounter with Picton, his depiction of the trial is vituperative and biased. He charges that, while he was imprisoned with Calderon, "the jailor Vallot gave me poison, and, when that did not take the desired effect, he [Picton] banished me to America in a vessel that had the yellow fever on board. For what? Why, to prevent me from enquiring further than I did into his crimes."[48]

McCallum claims that his work played an important part in bringing Picton to justice. He prefaces his version of the trial with an address to William Garrow in which he makes "no apology for conveying to you, through the medium of the press, my grateful tribute of approbation for your extraordinary exertions on behalf of an oppressed fellow-creature." He calls Picton an "unworthy and despotic governor," accuses him of "curs[ing]" the island "by ordering the erection of this barbarous engine for torture," and describes him as "a man who had too long considered Trinidad a forest, and his inhabitants his game."[49] This description reminds one of Bartolome de Las Casas's depiction of the Spanish treatment of the Indians.[50] Further, McCallum also outlines the circumstances under which torture was permissible under Spanish law. He concludes that Picton was acting outside the law when he tortured Calderon and therefore unjust.

Picton, for his part, had no respect for Calderon. Six days after the trial, in a letter to Sir Samuel Hood, his friend and colleague, he describes Calderon as "a common mulatto girl, of the vilest class, and most corrupt morals," and represents his position in the following manner:

47. McCallum, *The Trial of Thomas Picton*.
48. Ibid.,, pp. 3–4.
49. Ibid., pp. 3, 16, 17.
50. In *The Devastation of the Indies: A Brief Account*, Bartolome de Las Casas speaks of the Spaniard's behavior toward the Amerindians: "Yet into this sheepfold, into this land of meek outcasts there came some Spaniards who immediately behaved like ravening wild beasts, wolves, tigers, or lions that had been starved for many days. And Spaniards have behaved in no other way during the past forty years, down to the present time, for they are still acting like ravening beasts, killing, terrorizing, afflicting, torturing, and destroying the native peoples, doing all this with the strangest and most varied new methods of cruelty, never seen or heard before, and to such a degree that this Island of Hispaniola, once so populous...has now a population of barely to hundred persons" (trans. Herman Briffaulty [Baltimore: Johns Hopkins Press, 1992], p. 29).

I was placed, without any solicitation…in a most extraordinary situation, at the head of a new conquest, without any legal adviser to guide me in the administration of an intricate system of foreign laws, written in a foreign language; without any Magistrate legally constituted or acquainted with the jurisprudence of the country to execute them; without any law except such as I could causally pick up upon the spot; without any council with whom I could share the responsibility, and without any detailed instructions to supply the deficiency; and that, so situated, I was left, for nearly six years, solely to my own judgment and discretion, to carry on the business of the Colony in the best manner I could….

I was ordered to administer an intricate system of laws of which I was totally ignorant, and then I am made accountable for the errors I involuntary committed, and criminally prosecuted for what I could not possibly avoid.[51]

Hood, an erstwhile defender of Picton, said that Calderon was fifteen rather than fourteen years when the torture occurred and therefore Picton was not guilty of an illegal act. However, rather than Calderon's age, the case turned on whether Spanish law allowed torture and whether it was practiced in the island before Picton's governorship.

The evidence suggests that Picton took it upon himself to torture Calderon to exact a confession from her. In her testimony, Calderon stated that her "wrist was tied up to a pulley at the ceiling, and the toe of one foot was on a spike of wood. The other hand and foot was tied together." The torture, she said, "occasioned a great deal of pain." After she was taken down from the piquet, iron fetters were placed around her legs. On the second day she was tied up by both arms and "drawn up by the rope and pulley" so that the end of her toes could just touch the spike of wood beneath her.[52] After being tortured on the second day, she fainted, was taken into prison, placed in iron fetters and remained in that condition for eight months until Colonel Fullarton arrived in the country. It was Fullarton's intervention that led to Picton's trial in England.

The charges against Picton turned on whether he transcended his jurisdiction when he inflicted a penalty upon Calderon that was not in force in the island when Spain ruled the country. Through the authority of various legal texts, the defense had to prove that the law of Old Spain (which authorized the administering of torture) prevailed while Picton governed the island.[53] According to Lord Chief Justice Ellenborough, who presided over the trial, the central question in the trial revolved around whether any "syllable" in *The Royal Schedula of His Majesty the King of Spain* (which contained the laws that governed the people of Trinidad) or the *Recopilacion de Leyes De Indias* (*The Royal Letters and Orders*), the law of Indies, "justifie[d] the infliction of torture [on Louisa Calderon.]"[54]

51. Joseph, *History of Trinidad*, pp. 253–55.
52. *The Trial of Governor Picton*, pp. 15, 17, 19.
53. In the words of the Chief Justice, the defense had to prove whether "by the authority of a text writer they [the defense] can establish that the law of Spain prevailed" during Picton's governorship (ibid., p. 69).
54. Ibid., p. 87.

In his defense, Picton argued that he acted lawfully and without malice in accordance with the laws of Spain that he claimed he had sworn to uphold. The jury's verdict proved otherwise, and he was found guilty of torture. In a subsequent trial on June 11, 1808, Picton could only obtain a special verdict that "no malice existed in the mind of the defendant against Luisa [*sic*] Calderon independent of the illegality of the act," even though there was a strong predisposition to find Picton guilty of the act. The opinion of Lord Chief Justice De Grey, who presided at the final trial on February 10, 1810, of the special verdict of 1808, supported Lord Ellenborough's judgment. He ruled that "[t]he torture, as well as banishment was the old law of Minorca, which fell of course when it came into our possession. Every English governor knew he could not inflict torture; the Constitution of this country put an end to the idea."[55]

"The Narrative of Louisa Calderon" is a valuable literary and generalized representation of how the newly emerging Trinidadian subject was viewed in this slave society. Embedded in a transcultural setting (she was a mulatto of Spanish origins and her grandmother was a slave) and a trilingual condition (she spoke Spanish, English, and Creole), Calderon heralds the cosmopolitan nature of the society and the differences that personify modern Trinidad and Tobago.[56] (Later, Trinidad would be influenced also by the presence of Indian languages.) Calderon's narrative offers the first glimpse of a modern Trinbagonian subject. It alerts us to the fact that, at the inception of Trinbagonian society, the narrative itself was embedded within a several contexts (legal, cultural, linguistic) that marked the emergence of the subject. As one collapses the identity of the Trinbagonian subject into a larger Caribbean identity, one reemphasizes that Caribbean identity is embedded in a social system that involves "the interplay of strategies of assimilation and subversion, submission and revolt."[57] It is to those contradictory impulses that the narrative of Louisa Calderon speaks.

55. Joseph, *History of Trinidad,* pp. 259–60.

56. This argument needs to be refined somewhat. Hodge argues that two types of Creole are spoken in the Caribbean: Trinidadian and Jamaican. She argues that, "although the basic structure of Creole is the same across the Caribbean, the region can be sub-divided into two groups of Creole speakers with differences in certain details of their grammar. The speech of different Caribbean populations shows features of the one or the other. The language of Tobago, for example, is of the Jamaican type, not the Trinidadian, although Trinidad and Tobago are one country." Given the close affinity between language and identity, it becomes clear (as most Tobagonians know) that Trinidadians and Tobagonians do not, in any simple sense, possess a common identity. That we will not be able to examine this phenomenon is a shortcoming, but unfortunately, such an examination is beyond the scope of this study, nor is this author equipped to make such an examination.

57. "Conde: The Politics of Gender and Identity," pp. 717–18.

CHAPTER 2

Free Mulatto and the Early Expressions of Trinidad's Literature

> Whether it be the fault and glimpse of newness,
>   Or whether that the body public be
>   A horse whereon the governor doth ride,
>   Who, newly in the seat, that it may know
>   He can command, lets it straight feel the spur;
>   Whether the tyranny be in his place,
>   Or in his eminence that fills it up,
>   I stagger in.
> —WILLIAM SHAKESPEARE, *Measure for Measure*

My Lord, it is to be feared, that, in Trinidad, every species of criminality is lost in the blaze and glare of whiteness, and that nothing appertaining to that qualification can suffer the taint of guilt....

Man can brook every variety of misfortune, but cannot meekly endure sarcasm or affront. To these the coloured are constantly exposed from the white inhabitants; and, from the principles laid down by His Excellency, their every complaint is construed into mutiny. He had learnt enough of politics to know, that amongst despotic rulers it is a maxim, that to govern with arbitrary power it is requisite to divide the population.

—JEAN-BAPTISTE PHILIPPE, *Free Mulatto*

The key to the literary situation in early Trinidad was the fact that most of the French creoles—as many of them who could afford it—sent their children back to France for their education. For the girls, and the boys as well, part of their education was something called *ecriture*. When they returned to the island they all lived on the estates. Having received a very cultured education in Latin, Greek and French and training in penmanship and so on, when they came home they would write to one another and some of them, like this Le Cadre fellow, just wrote to suit himself.

—ANTHONY DE VERTEUIL, "An Interview with Selwyn R. Cudjoe"

The Deteriorating Condition of the Colored People

If the "Narrative of Louisa Calderon" alerts us to the problems colored people underwent and the treacherous business of affirming one's identity in a new society, then Jean-Baptiste Philippe's *Free Mulatto*[1] confirms how widespread the problem had become by 1824. To be sure, during that early period, most of the inhabitants were newcomers to the island, although their different subject-positions made all the difference in the world. If Governor Picton was boorishly racist, Governor Ralph Woodford (1813–1827), the first civilian governor of the island, was just as determined to create "an ordered society in which every race and class would know its place"[2] and which in effect would deny colored citizens their legal and human rights.[3] So that while the torture of Louisa Calderon signaled *the* moment when the conditions of the colored population began to deteriorate, Philippe's sterling account depicts the nadir to which conditions descended. It also announces to the world that, as a collective entity, colored people would not accept such second-class treatment. Indeed, it could be argued that *Free Mulatto* adumbrates the other level of resistance to which the colored people had taken their struggle for dignity.

In making his case against Governor Woodford, Philippe locates the legal basis for the troubles of the colored people in an act that was committed by one of Picton's advisers. Speaking of the "harsh treatment that he [Colonel Picton] exercised on that inoffensive, and, till then, happy people," Jean-Baptiste Philippe notes that it was St. Hilaire Beggorat, "the confessed adviser of the torture of Louisa Calderon," who drew up the code of instructions that reduced the freedoms of the colored inhabitants. He continues:

> There it was, for the first time, the persons of colour saw the statue of their liberty, raised by the liberality of the former government, dashed to the ground and trampled on; and their charter, the twelfth article of capitulation, violated, and in effect annulled, whilst they themselves were held up as objects of contemptuous distinction.[4]

In a paradoxical way, it was Beggorat who was instrumental in drawing up the laws that resulted in the first sustained written act of resistance: Philippe's address to the Right Honorable Earl of Bathurst, Britain's principal secretary of state for the colonies. This address argues for "the claims which the coloured population of Trinidad have to the same civil and political privileges with their white follow-sub-

---

1. Although this work has come to be known as *Free Mulatto*, its original title is *An Address to the Right Hon. Earl Bathurst, Relative to the Claims which the Coloured Population of Trinidad have to the Same Civil and Political Privileges with their White Fellow Subjects by a Free Mulatto of the Island* (London: S. Gosnell, 1824).

2. Carl Campbell, *Colony and Nation* (Kingston: Ian Randle, 1992), p. 8.

3. Perhaps, just as significantly, the contemporary national anthem of Trinidad and Tobago proclaims: "Here every creed and race finds an equal place."

4. *An Address to the Right Hon. Earl Bathurst* (London: S. Gosnell, 1824), p. 30. All further references to this work will be noted in the text as *FM*.

jects."[5] Therefore, when Philippe begins to make his case against the British administration's denial of the rights of colored people in Trinidad in 1823 (and the treatment of the Amerindians, the Spanish peons, and the liberated African-Americans), it is Beggorat's "Code Noir" that he dissects (deconstructs) to advance the cause of the colored people.[6] Strangely enough, Philippe does not blame Picton for the humiliating conditions the colored people endured ("[h]e was a severe disciplinarian, an inexorable judge; but by no means prejudiced against the class of colored persons"). Rather, he attributes these misdeeds to the "evil advisers in whom he placed unbounded confidence" (*FM.*, p. 34). Although diplomacy may have prevented Philippe from condemning Picton, the objective conditions of the society had produced a Picton and a Woodford. Another way of saying this is that the social conditions caused Picton and Woodford to behave in an identical manner.

Even before Philippe launched his formal attack against Beggorat's "Code Noir" in 1819, M. Dauxion-Lavaysse, a French outsider upon whose objectivity we can rely and a liberal of de Tocquevillian dimensions, made a similar case against the ill treatment of the colored people in Trinidad. Having resided in the island from about 1800 to 1815 and having traveled extensively throughout the area, Dauxion-Lavaysse had an excellent opportunity to view the conditions under which black and colored peoples in the West Indies and South America lived. In *A Statistical, Commercial, and Political Description of Venezuela, Trinidad, Margarita, and Tobago* (1820), Dauxion-Lavaysse notes the "the fate of those unfortunate [coloured] people is at least as much to be pitied as that of the negroes.... There are none, even to the negroes, who do not arrogate to themselves the privilege of despising them; and the hatred which is continually fermented between these two classes, is one of the great pivots of colonial policy."Although the hatred between the Africans and the coloreds seemed great, the disdain with which the whites held the coloreds was of far greater intensity. Dauxion-Lavaysse tells the story of "a rich and immoral magistrate" of Martinique who, in 1798, fathered a child with a colored woman: "In 1802, this child, of whom it was positively asserted that the said magistrate was the father, ran after him crying 'papa, papa!' whilst he was riding in Lamentin. The wretch made his horse trample on the poor child, and struck it with his horsewhip; saying to the unhappy mother, 'this will teach you how to make that little serpent call me father again.'" Speaking of the unfortunate condition in which the mulattoes found themselves, Dauxion-Lavaysse writes:

> Whatever education a man or woman of colour may have received, whatever may be their virtues, however considerable their fortunes, nothing can raise them to a

5. The subtitle of Philippe's address.

6. It is not stressed sufficiently that *Free Mulatto* also protests against the treatment of the Amerindians, the Spanish peons, and the liberated African-American refugees (who were promised liberty and protection when they deserted their plantations and fought on the side of the British in the 1812 War) under the British, especially under the hands of Robert Mitchell, Commandant of North Naparima and Savanna Grande. *Free Mulatto* is also a powerful defense of the colored women of Trinidad.

level with the meanest white, who is authorized by the prejudices of the country to treat them with insolence. And yet those men and women of colour are daily seen to practise the kindest hospitality towards unfortunate whites abandoned by everyone else. I could fill a volume with instances of generosity and humanity in the negroes and people of colour.[7]

It is against the background of this growing divide between the two segments of the population—the mulattoes and the whites—and the increasing hostility toward the latter that the indigenous Creole elite sought to assert itself. In 1810, under the leadership of John Welsh Hobson, the coloreds formed their own organization to fight the growing infringement on their rights. Observing how the English colonists systematically deprived them "of all their charters of liberty merely that they themselves might usurp the entire authority," the colored citizens wrote to His Excellency, Thomas Hislop, governor of Trinidad, to inform him of their grievances and to seek permission "to prepare and transmit to their gracious Sovereign, a dutiful, loyal, and affectionate Address, humbly and fervently imploring him to take into his royal consideration, the present state of existence of his faithful subjects of colour in the island of Trinidad, and to extend unto them (under whatever system of jurisprudence his royal wisdom may deem expedient for the future government of this colony) such a participation in its operation as may secure to them (on a permanent and inviolable footing) their personal security and social happiness" (*FM.*, p. 229). When, therefore, in 1824, Philippe and Dr. Cognet, another leader of the coloured citizens, submitted their address to Lord Bathurst, their pamphlet grew naturally out of a tradition of letters and memorials that were used to address those in authority; it was a form of communication used routinely during that period.

Perhaps, the most significant thing about the letter written to Governor Hislop is its elevated and respectful tone and the deference it paid to his authority. Rich in symbolic language and determined not to offend, the letter nonetheless states its sentiments in an unambiguous way. The writers open their letter by subscribing themselves as "His Majesty's dutiful, loyal, and affectionate subjects," humbly approaching His Excellency "with sentiments of high and unalterable respect and consideration, not only appertaining to your Excellency, as the representatives of their august and benevolent Sovereign, but flowing voluntarily from their hearts" (*FM.*, pp. 227–28). After affirming their continued loyalty and respect to their Sovereign, the petitioners go on to state:

Conscious of the rectitude of their intentions, and of the faithful discharge of their duties as members of society, they are inevitably led to a serious contemplation of the situation in which it is their fate to be placed in that society; and, with every tender and delicate consideration towards all the circumstances connected with that situation, they cannot avoid perceiving that at a moment when the feelings and

---

7. M.Dauxion-Lavaysse, *A Statistical, Commercial, and Political Description of Venezuela, Trinidad, Margarita, and Tobago.* trans. and ed. E. B. (London: G. and W. B. Whittaker, 1820), pp. 395–96.

pursuits of their fellow-colonists are ardently and actively exercised, projecting and soliciting new systems of government, and political regulation, from the parent state (in which not only the comfort and happiness of His Majesty's subject of colour are entirely overlooked, but the very existence of such a class appears to be forgotten), it becomes their duty to employ such means as appear to them necessary (and, at the same time, consistent with the principles of order, respect, and obedience towards their government, which they profess to act upon, and from which they will never be found deviating), to awaken the reflection, that there exists in this colony a numerous, opulent, and useful class of free subjects, who are entitled to *something* (*FM.*, pp. 228-29).

This letter, characterized by its pedantry, embodies a circumlocutory mode of expression, and possessed a spirit of equivocation. It does not possess the concreteness and particularity that one encounters in *Free Mulatto*. Philippe notes that "the petition was not sufficiently explicit, and the words 'entitled to *something,*'" looked equivocal" and was "penned with the very essence of humility" (*FM.*, pp. 44–45). Indeed, the timidity and tentativeness of the letter can be ascribed to the fact that during that period the colored population was accused of contemplating acts of conspiracy merely by complaining about their condition and thus had to be careful.[8] However, despite its shortcomings, this and other letters were a preparation for the philosophical/political essay that Philippe submitted to Lord Bathurst.

After Sir Ralph Woodford became the governor of the island in 1813, conditions for the colored population deteriorated rapidly. In typical fashion, on June 19, the coloreds wrote a very solicitous letter of welcome to Woodford in which they congratulated him on his appointment and rejoiced in his safe arrival in the island:

The paternal solicitude of the sovereign authority, for the welfare and prosperity of the inhabitants of this colony, has been unequivocally manifested in its anxiety to extend to them such a system of regulations, as might best conduce to the happiness of all. And in the choice of your Excellency to carry into execution this benevolent intention, we are persuaded, that our gracious Prince has wisely selected a representative, of talents, zeal, and integrity, commensurate to the arduous duties of his station, and eminently calculated to realize the flattering expectation of colonial improvement, prosperity, and happiness. Fully confiding in your Excellency's authority, as well as capacity, to correct the errors, and reform the habits, which have long obstructed the prosperity of a colony, wherein our interest and happiness are deeply implanted, we fondly contemplate, in the result of your exalted labours, such a favorable change in its character, and genuine advantages, as accords with the enlightened and dignified view, in which the subjects appears to have been contemplated by the government of our Sovereign (*FM.*, pp. 233–34)

This eloquent plea of cooperation and fealty to the Crown occasioned a terse ver-

8. Philippe notes that "serious propositions were agitated among the public to banish the ringleaders from the colony" and an eighty-year-old man was publicly horsewhipped for signing the letter to the governor (*FM.*, p. 45).

bal response from Woodford: "I thank you for the very flattering address with which you have this day presented me; and I have to inform you, that whilst you continue to pay proper obedience to the laws, you shall receive my protection" (*FM.*, p. 66). Such a reply set the tone for his relations with the coloreds. Philippe observes that, since his arrival in the colony, "[h]is Excellency has apparently shown a rooted antipathy to everything having the semblance of, or appertaining to the class of colored persons; and by the *effect* of his conduct, both public and private, it would appear that no opportunity has been lost, by which that class could be insulted or degraded. I do not fear contradiction when I aver, that they have suffered more affronts and more injuries during his government, than they have experienced since the commencement of the annals of the country" (*FM.*, p. 69).

In 1823, the leadership of the colored group passed on to Jean-Baptiste Philippe. His superior education made him the logical choice to articulate their sentiments to an authority higher than the governor.[9] Undoubtedly, Philippe's personal condition must have contributed to his disdain for Woodford and the way the governor treated the free colored population.[10] More importantly, the Orders in Council of September 16, 1822 that called for the corporal punishment of the coloreds for the most trivial offense brought their anger to a fever pitch and precipitated them into action.[11] An ad-hoc committee of the free colored group, consisting of "the most respectable coloured inhabitants and proprietors in the Island" determined to vindicate their position, decided to make representation to Lord Earl Bathurst on behalf of their group.[12] *Free Mulatto*, a pamphlet submitted to Lord Bathurst by Philippe and Dr. Cognet on behalf of the committee, articulated their claims. Intended to be treated as a private document (they requested that the pamphlet "not be shown to any third person"), it was not published officially until 1882 by Allers and Blondel when J. J. Thomas wrote an introduction to the text. All evidence, however, seems to suggest that Philippe was the principal author of the text.

9. See Selwyn R. Cudjoe's introduction to *Free Mulatto* (Wellesley, Mass.: Calaloux, 1996) for a discussion of Philippe's early life and education.

10. In his address to Lord Bathurst, Philippe made his personal grievance known. He notes that, despite his being a graduate of a university, the son of a wealthy planter, and the only trained physician practicing medicine in the southern part of the island, he was compelled to enter "the line as a private in the militia; whereas all the other *pretenders* to physics officiated as surgeons or lieutenants" (*FM.*, p. 101). After his petition to Lord Bathurst, he was allowed to practice in the latter capacity.

11. According to this ordinance, colored persons could be punished by cart whip or placed in chains if they were found "landing a vessel without permission, amusing one's-self with dancing after nine o'clock at night without permission, taking a walk in the streets after ten o'clock in the evening, together with a variety of other deprivations from municipal orders, many of them of comparatively trifling importance, and the greatest part of them directed exclusively against the coloured inhabitant" (*FM.*, p. 123). As it noted, "if the power of inflicting the punishment of flagellation and chains rest upon the vague and undefined principle on which it is placed by the new criminal modifications, the legislative authority of the Sovereign would be rendered nugatory for the protection and security of his coloured subjects" (*FM.*, p. 126).

12. Daniel Hart, *Trinidad and the Other West India Colonies* (Port of Spain: The Chronicle Publishing Office, 1866), p. 168. The committee consisted of persons such as Dr. Cognet, Desire Fabien, J. W. Hobson, C. Rousseau, J. C. Forget, and J. Edwards.

Philippe was uniquely qualified to undertake this assignment. One of the first Trinidadians to study literature abroad formally, he impressed his literature master, one Mr. Wanostrocht, so much with his love of the subject that the latter prophesied that Philippe would be "a great man one day."[13] After Phillipe returned to Trinidad, he continued his study of literature. His complaint that a "small literary society of youths was broken up, and the owner of the house condemned to pay a fine for hiring the room in which they met" (*FM.*, p. 198) indicates that there was a serious concern for literary matters among his peers and some interest in the society at large for that pursuit. Philippe, it would seem, was also fond of reciting poems. His eulogist noted that he possessed "a soul of fire in his bosom. If, in, these poetical intercommunications, we were not alone, he grew impatient at being understood by no one but me. He wrote down the verses which he declaimed, and I with the lucky or unlucky facility of which I have never lost the habit, translated them with a pen as rapid as his own."[14] Undoubtedly, poetry and rhetoric moved Philippe. As Campbell notes, literature was Philippe's "second love," and it came in handy when he decided to write to Lord Bathurst.

In 1812, Phillipe entered the University of Edinburgh where he eventually became a medical doctor three years later at about the age of 19.[15] His thesis for this degree, "Hysterical Moods," seems to have concerned itself with psychology. Nonetheless, after he received his medical degree at Edinburgh, he traveled throughout Europe, attending "several lectures of the celebrated professors, especially at the University of Leyden and at Montpellier."[16] In Europe, Philippe was exposed to the most advanced ideas of his time, French having replaced Latin as the international language. It must have been with feelings of elation, satisfaction, and hope that he proceeded to his homeland to serve his people and to enjoy the prestige to which his highly won honors had entitled him.

Philippe was not accepted enthusiastically on his return to Trinidad. Apart from the mulattoes, his return did not generate much excitement or adulation. Under Woodford's governorship, the colored people were the objects of contempt, as Woodford transmitted to them by how he spoke to them. Woodford's policy resulted more from his personal agenda than the demands of the socio-economic or political situation in the colony. As Campbell notes, more than any previous governor, Woodford placed himself "at the head of the white people's preoccupation to control, discipline and humiliate the coloureds; and he was attempting to build the prejudice deeper into the structure of the social institutions of the colony."[17] Disgusted completely with such a posture and policy, after many epistolary com-

---

13. "A Oration," In *FM,* Part II (1987), p. 6.

14. Ibid. p. 8. I am not too sure exactly what Philippe's eulogist had in mind when he made the observations above. Did he mean that Philippe wrote down the verses he declaimed in French/Creole which he (the eulogist) translated into English or that Philippe did indeed compose his own poems?

15. I am indebted to Campbell's "Man from Naparima" (in *FM* [1987]) for most of the biographical information on Jean-Baptiste Philippe.

16. *FM.* (1987). pp. 7-8.

17. *FM.*, p. xx.

munications with local administrators, Philippe and his colleagues decided that they would be humiliated no longer by Woodford. The time had arrived to take their complaints to the highest official level.

Free Mulatto

Free Mulatto, the product of a first-class literary mind, is the culmination of what Campbell calls "the politics of private discussion" and "the quiet collection of signatures" and a chronicle of the "sunk and mortifying conditions to which they [the coloreds] have been degraded by the illiberal prejudices of the whites, publicly countenanced as they have been by the illegal proceedings of some of their successive governors."[18] Although *Free Mulatto* embodies the collective response of the colored community to the pressures brought against them by the English, it also displays Philippe's acquaintance with Enlightenment ideals and an intimate knowledge of the works of the French essayists and pamphleteers of the previous century.[19] Like Abbé Raynal's A *Philosophical and Political History of the Settlements and Trade of the Europeans in the East and West Indies,* upon which Philippe structured his work, *Free Mulatto* was the result of conversations and debates of which Philippe was the most prominent figure. Undoubtedly, Philippe must have been struck by Raynal's conviction that "Natural liberty is the right which nature has given to every one to dispose of himself according to his will."[20] As Dorinda Outram suggests, Raynal's *Philosophical and Political History* was the *"locus classicus* for Enlightenment discussions of colonialism."[21] Philippe's critique of British policy in Trinidad, an application of Enlightenment thought to a slave society, demonstrates how these ideas, outside their European provenance, took on a new life.[22] Many of the ideas in *Free Mulatto* can be located within the genre of the philo-

18. Ibid., p. 2.

19. In compiling his address, Phillipe drew on the work of many of the eminent scholars of his and previous times. In addition to Raynal, these scholars include William Shakespeare *(Measure for Measure),* Bernardin de Saint-Pierre *(Études de la nature),* John Gay *(Gay's Fables),* Jean Racine *(Andromaque),* William Paley *(The Principles of Moral and Political Philosophy),* Guy Fables, Henry Kames *(Sketches of the History of Man)* Virgil *(Aneid),* Bryan Edwards *(History of the West Indies,* of which he was critical), William Robertson *(History of Scotland),* and Benjamin Franklin *(The Works of Benjamin Franklin).* Phillipe also drew on other popular writings, such as William Wilberforce's speeches on the abolition of the slave trade, the Holy Bible, George Pinckard's *Notes on the West Indies,* and such legal writings as *Recopilation de Castile* and William Blackstone's *Commentaries on the Laws of England.* Many Latin American authors drew on similar sources to construct their narratives. In this regards, see Antonio Benitez-Rojo, "The Nineteenth century Spanish American novel," in Roberto Gonzalez Echevarria and Enrique Pupo-Walker, eds. *The Cambridge History of Latin American Literature, Vol. 1* (Cambridge: Cambridge University Press, 1996), pp. 417–89.

20. Quoted in C. L. R. James, *Black Jacobins* (New York: Vintage, 1989), p. 25.

21. Dorinda Outram, *The Enlightenment* (Cambridge: Cambridge University Press, 1995), p. 73. Outram notes that Diderot, a leading philosophe, assisted Raynal with his work.

22. Franco Ventriri notes that it was on the fringes of Europe—meaning Italy, Greece, the Balkans, Poland, Hungary, and Russia—that the stresses and strains "within Enlightenment ideas could be best analysed." It also might be that, in societies such as Trinidad where scholars had taken back those ideas, one could also see these strengths and weaknesses. See Outram, *The Enlightenment,* p. 6; and A. Owen Aldridge, ed., *The Ibero-American Enlightenment* (Urbana: University of Illinois Press, 1971).

sophical/political essay, a form that was "not so much a technical discipline as a stance toward the world, a critical freedom."[23] A disquisition by and about colored people of Trinidad during the slave era, it explores "the nature of man and of his response to his environment and his own conscience." Marked by a tradition of inquiry into causes, the text involves the work of a "progressive-minded intellectual" who throws much light on the colored subject "as a social being" and "points to a theoretical solution of the problems of the age [that] could be comprehended within it."[24] To have studied in France at that time meant that Philippe was educated in this tradition. Unconsciously, he accepted aspects of Enlightenment discourse that conflicted with notions of slavery. Dorinda Outram notes that, while some aspects of the Enlightenment thought were "powerful in allowing certain groups to think of change,... they could not overcome the limits to change which they envisaged as possible for the social order. This contradiction between support for supposedly universal rights and the actual exclusion of large numbers of human beings from the enjoyment of those rights is central to, and characteristic of, Enlightenment thought."[25] As we will see, even this contradiction was present in Philippe's life.

Philippe used the pamphlet, the preferred form of the philosophes, to air his accusations against the English. A popular literary form in Trinidad when he wrote, many of his fellow colored rebels used the pamphlet to express their dissatisfaction with the conditions under which their people lived.[26] Carl Campbell notes that in the 1820s, because of the popularity of French culture and "the fundamental lack of freedom of expression in the newspaper, Trinidad was an island given to pamphleteering."[27] Moreover, if we see literature as one aspect of "the general history of ideas" and accept the notion that within the philosophe "the writer and the specialist often merge to take on the appearance of a superior kind of journalism," then it can be asserted that this stunningly eloquent piece of philosophical cum investigative prose stands at the entrance of Trinidad and Tobago's literature and constitutes the first literary essay of the tradition.

23. Peter Gay, *The Enlightenment: An Introduction* (New York: Norton, 1966), p. 159.

24. Geoffrey Brereton, *A Short History of French Literature,* 2nd edition (Harmondsworth: Penguin, 1976), pp. 51, 92. A *philosophe* also referred to a Frenchman of a particular type. Peter Gay argues that philosophe is a "French word for an international type" and so used the term in his work of the Enlightenment. According to Gay, France "fostered the type that has ever since been taken as *the* philosophe: the facile, articulate, doctrinaire, sociable, secular man of letters. The French philosophe, being the most belligerent, was the purest specimen" (*The Enlightenment: An Introduction,* p. 10).

25. Outram, *The Enlightenment,* p. 122.

26. Francis De Ridder, another coloured priest who was rebelling "against the social and political attitudes of the Church hierarchy towards the coloureds" in Trinidad, also seized upon the pamphlet as a weapon of attack against the Roman Catholic authorities. As he notes in his January 1830 polemic aimed at Dr. Daniel Macdonnell, the Roman Catholic Bishop of London, "publicity is the strong weapon that supports the bulwark of liberty of a British subject; and in this country it is the only one I have, and with which I can, with safety and all confidence, meet your Lordship in defending my character" (Carl Campbell, "The Rebel Priest: Francis De Ridder and the Fight for Free Coloureds' Rights in Trinidad," *Journal of Caribbean History,* 15, pp. 38, 35).

27. Ibid. p. 36.

Thomas understood this dimension of Philippe's work. In 1882, he described *Free Mulatto* as "a work of high literary ability. [I]t was singularly well suited for its purpose, and lofty withal, not only in its general tone, but as regards mere style, in many of its remarkable paragraphs. The cardinal merit of the work, however, is not in either of these particulars. That merit is shown in the double aspect of its conception and execution." Philippe argues that his aim is "not literary reputation—my motive is an earnest desire, by a true portraiture of facts, to dispel the clouds of misrepresentation in which prejudice has long enveloped every circumstance relative to the coloured population of Trinidad." Still, Campbell insists that *Free Mulatto* is "one of the earliest pieces of indigenous polemical literature by a nonwhite in the British Caribbean."[28] In 1890, Jose Bodu praised Philippe's audacity and fearlessness and noted that "to publish [such] a work at a moment when slavery was still in existence, and colour prejudice at its height, must have required courage of no mean order."[29]

Both an unknown eulogists at Philippe's death and Thomas's introduction to the 1882 edition underscored the importance of *Free Mulatto*. Each acknowledged the work's moral seriousness and Philippe's insight into the conditions of nonwhites, even though his emphasis is on the mulatto. Further, each used a mode of discourse to match the eloquence and intelligence of Philippe's masterpiece. Such an approach was especially important when one recognizes that the "critical freedom" of enquiry (philosophical) that Philippe pursued clashed with the established orthodoxy of the age (the correctness and inflexibility of slavery and the superiority of white people). He also used a specific literary medium to make a case for the equal rights of members of his group (political). Using clear, simple concepts of justice and a biting wit, Philippe pointed out why the criminal behavior of the whites (read colonists) had to cease. As such, he provided a counterdiscourse to the oppressive discourses and political practices of the dominant social group that were intent on negating the hard-won freedoms of his group.

Although Philippe did not wish to establish a "literary reputation," *Free Mulatto* had all the markings of the French literary essayists and pamphleteers. Framed by a multiple of literary, political, and philosophical references, Philippe offered a work of considerable literary merit. Although he wanted to present "a true portraiture of facts," he had no problems using rich, evocative language to describe the Arcadian landscape St. Laurent beheld when he visited Trinidad:

> On his landing in Trinidad, he beheld an island gifted with every blessing which nature in her greatest prodigality of favour could possible lavish: a soil the most exuberant, diversified with every variety of ground; extensive plains, hill and dale, rivers, capable of navigation far into the interior, offering at every season a plentiful supply of water; mountains traversing the island in four groups; and withal, separated from the north-east point of Terra Firma by a beautiful basin, offering a safe

---

28. *FM.*, pp. xxv–xxvi.
29. Jose M. Bodu, *Trinidadiana* (Port of Spain: A. C. Bondel, 1890), p. 7.

anchorage throughout, at the most tempestuous seasons. The whole island, too, was covered with forests containing every species of durable wood, and holding forth every advantage to a government that knew in what way to avail itself of such resources (*FM.*, pp. 3–4).

The convention of the form, it would seem, demanded that Phillipe use elaborate, perhaps romantic, language to describe the bucolic possibilities of the island even as he sought to convince Lord Bathurst about the wrongs that were committed against him and his people. This, of course, is not meant to suggest that Lord Bathurst was entirely convinced by Philippe's arguments, as his instructions to Lieutenant Colonel Young, protector of the slaves in Guyana, make clear.[30] It suggests, however, that Philippe used all his persuasive powers to make his case.

Philippe's Enlightenment

The philosophical implications of *Free Mulatto* are articulated in its final section, its summary as it were. In this section, Philippe takes issue with Woodford and others who denied colored citizens their ability to develop intellectually and morally, who prevented them from participating in free and open discourse, and who discouraged them from aspiring to higher and nobler causes. Drawing on the work of William Paley, an important figure for Philippe, and other philosophical writings, Philippe makes the ultimate moral case against the slave system. More than likely a deist, Philippe deduces that, because men and women are born of the same Heavenly Father, reason, the cardinal virtue of Enlightenment, ought to prevail over superstition and illogical prejudice:

> My Lord, we live in an enlightened age. The human mind has, it is supposed, expanded in the sphere of reason, and still we see such despicable prejudices continuing to exist in these lamentable climes. Surely, surely, we possess an atom of the emanation of the Deity equally with the whites, feelings as strong, minds as capable of improvement, hearts as susceptible of generous emotions, as keenly alive to the sense of obligation, as readily fired by the infliction of injustice. We are endued, too, with souls exposed as much to the bountiful providence of the Almighty Father; alike objects of his mercy and care: from the throne of grace he contemplates with equal complacency the actions of the white and coloured; and at the final day of retribution, when all our dooms will be fixed for ever, surely, the Divine Creator of mankind will make no difference in his judgements, but what will be commensurate with the relative proportions of individual sin and virtue (*FM.*, pp. 206–207).

30. Writing to Lieutenant Colonel Young around the same time that Philippe offered his petition, Lord Bathurst offers the following observations about the relationship that should exist between master and slave: "You must exercise a constant discretion in impressing upon the minds of the slaves in the most forcible manner, that the measures which have been provided for their protection are in no degree to interfere with the unremitting practise of industry and obedience, to which under prescribed regulations, their owners are by law entitled; but on the contrary, that these duties are the more strictly to be observed by them in proportion as the law and regulation interpose, to prevent any improper exercise of the authority of the master" (*Port of Spain Gazette,* June 28, 1826).

Phillipe willingly concedes that "in the *aggregate* [they] coloured people could [not] pretend to an equality with the whites of Europe, in points of morality and mental endowment" (*FM.*, p. 214) and viewed slaves, "that ignorant class of men," as being similarly disadvantaged. However, he asserts this position not because of their color—he takes pride in and acknowledges that African blood flowed through his veins—but because they lack formal education, good breeding, and virtue, the "essentials" of good character. For Philippe, good character is the paramount virtue. One ought to be accepted and rewarded for what one achieves, not for the color of one's skins or one's social position. Superiority, he says, is not "*inherent* in the difference of complexion, but only…arises from the possession of *superior understanding* and virtue" (*FM.*, p. 214). Prejudice, he continues, "cannot long maintain its power; it may for a while stop the ebb of civilization (nay it has done so for two hundred years back); but the mind will not be involved in perpetual darkness. It will finally break the bonds which have so long shackled it, and, springing from the gloom of obscurity, will expiate freely in the regions of science, of sentiment, and of liberty" (*FM.*, p. 216). The social order, he suggests, can only be based on equality and fairness.

Undoubtedly, Philippe's judgment on slavery was affected by his being a slave owner. It led to his taking an inconsistent position on the question of social equality. In 1826, when one of his slaves ran away, Philippe quickly placed the following notice in the *Port of Spain Gazette* of September 20: "Last Saturday, the 23rd instant, a young negro slave well known in the town and formerly belonging to Mr. Mackworth escaped at the undersigned. The reward mentioned will be paid to all persons who take him to the Royal Jail. He has recently been seen at St. Joseph." In April 1827, Philippe "bought Aurore estate in Laventille at a judicial sale for £2,422. It was a small estate of only three and a quarter carreaux, but it had nine slaves, also building and livestock." Campbell suggests that Philippe bought the estate "in order to acquire the slaves, who were possibly removed to the family estate in the Naparimas."[31] Although Philippe was very critical of Bernardin de St. Pierre, who was an "unenlightened discipline of Jean Jacques Rousseau"[32] and who justified slavery and cited *Genesis* ("[c]ursed be Canaan; may he be, with regard to his brothers, the slave of slaves") to support his proslavery stance, he seems to sympathize with the latter's sentiments:

> It is not difficult to guess whence Bernadin de St. Pierre drew his creed concerning the sons of Africa. He had a brother, a slaveholder in the Isle of France, and wished to smother any qualms of conscience, by quoting Scripture in support of the most horrible traffic that ever disgraced human nature. But the flimsy argument is equally atrocious and absurd; elucidating wonderfully how easy it is for cunning, or fanaticism, to cite the Holy Writings in vindication of every selfish passion, or as a cloak for covering the basest malignity (*FM.*, p. 53).

31. Carl Campbell, *Cedulants and Capitualants,* (Port of Spain: Paria, 1992), p. 245.
32. Private Notes, February 1996. Lemettais describes de St. Pierre as being pre-Romantic in style and a gifted observer of nature.

Philippe was a walking, talking contradiction. Although he protested the treatment of his colored brethren, he had no problems with owning African slaves. Many of his colored brethren were the same. When slavery was abolished in 1834, free coloreds rather than whites owned the majority of slaves. Anthony de Verteuil concludes that there was "probably little difference between the treatment meted out to slaves by coloured and white owners taken as a whole...[T]reatment varied immensely between individual owners."[33] On the other hand, Bridget Brereton observes that "free coloureds were less significant slave-owners than land-owners: land was cheaper, and easier to obtain, than slaves."[34] But, as Lemettais notes, because *Free Mulatto* was written in 1824, some thirty years after the French Revolution, "it might have reflected Voltaire's fear of giving power to an ignorant and illiterate people. The masses were to be feared. In Trinidad, the masses were the slaves. Like the French masses, they, also were to be feared. Even Voltaire, the great defender of freedom, had commercial interests in the slave trade."[35] Thus, possessing slaves and fighting for the rights of coloreds were not seen as inconsistent. They were merely signs of a contradictory age.

It is quite possible that Phillipe treated his slaves in a benevolent manner because of his liberal posture. Carl Campbell describes him as a "moderate reformer," who had no "desire to effect radical social changes. He expected education and virtue regardless of colour or race to be rewarded with social recognition...He envisaged that persons like himself, wealthy, well-educated, well-bred, would be among the social and political leaders." Yet, Philippe's attitude toward slavery was "enigmatic," for as Campbell reiterates, he never called for the abolition of slavery.[36] He never connected the greater liberties of coloreds with the slaves' freedom. To him, reason and good character were the supreme virtues.

Thus, as a child of the Enlightenment, Philippe's ambivalent behavior was not entirely out of character.[37] Like the philosophes on whom he fashioned himself, Philippe sought to explain his world in a rational manner and to reject the racial prejudice of his time. Yet, in a paradoxical way, he remained a prisoner of his age, subservient to the ideology of distinction and the hierarchical ordering that characterized his world. Gay notes that "[s]eeking to distinguish themselves, the *philosophes* had little desire to level all distinctions; seeking to be respected, they had no intention of destroying respectability. Their gingerly treatment of the masses,

33. Anthony de Verteuil, *Seven Slaves and Slavery, Trinidad: 1777–1838* (Port of Spain: Script-J Printers, 1992), pp. 38, 40.

34. Bridget Brereton, *A History of Modern Trinidad, 1783–1962* (Port of Spain: Heinemann, 1981), p. 64.

35. Private notes, February 1996.

36. Campbell, *Cedulants and Capitulants*, p. 244.

37. Philippe's behavior parallels that of the Abbé Raynal, a leading thinker of the Enlightenment, whom the former quoted profusely. Raynal, whose radical *Historie* was immediately proscribed after its first publication in 1770, never ceased to represent the colonists as tyrants. Yet, according to M. Dauxion-Lavaysse, it was "well known that Raynal held shares in the slave ship of the houses of D....of Nantes, and in those of the firm of Sollier, or Marseilles" (*A Statistical, Commercial, and Political Description of Venezuela, Trinidad, Margarita, and Tobago*, p. 393).

which became less patronizing as the century went on, reveals their attachment to the old order and their fear of too drastic upheaval."[38] The philosophes' desire to privilege knowledge and to promote a cultural elite who would lead the peasant (in this case, the slave) masses out of their ignorance cohered with Philippe's notion that the key to social advancement consisted in the possession of formal education, good breeding, superior understanding and virtue.

Philippe's major concern, then, was for himself to be treated as equal to Europeans. Further than that he was not prepared to go. He was not prepared to effectuate or struggle for a radical overthrow of the social order as Daaga[39] or the slaves of 1805 were prepared to do.[40] Even though he castigated slavery, like Abbé Raynal, he did not argue for its abolition. As so many other theorists of the Enlightenment, Philippe "stopped short at the point where prescription would have to turn into practice."[41] His was a liberal ideology that called for moderate reform rather than a radical restructuring of society. Because there was congruence between his ideas and those of the dominant class, Philippe believed that social change was possible within the system. The slaves who planned their revolt in 1805, Daaga and the Mandingo ex-slaves, who defined themselves as "African Subjects" and who pleaded to return to their country of origin, saw no redemptive capacity in the slave society in which they lived. The first wanted to tear the system apart, while the latter opted to leave.[42] Philippe was committed to reforming the system even if it entailed (as it did) the continued enslavement of Africans whose behavior did not

38. *The Enlightenment: An Introduction,* p. 26.

39. Daaga, who led a mutiny of 280 recruits in June 1837, sought to overthrow the system and return to Guinea. Of much more importance to this study, however, is the distinction between the those who saw redemptive possibilities for the social order (as in the case of Philippe) and those who saw no redeeming values in the slave system (as in the case of Daaga). This dichotomy is also discernible in African-American intellectual thought. In his very thoughtful critique, Cornel West makes very much the same criticism of W. E. B. Du Bois's attitude to America as opposed to that of the Black nationalists. He argues that "[e]ven when Du Bois left for Africa in 1961 ... his attitude toward America was not that of an Elijah Muhammad or a Malcolm X. He was still, in a significant sense, disappointed with America, and there is no disappointment without some dream deferred. Elijah Muhammad and Malcolm X were not disappointed with America. As bona fide black nationalists, they had no expectations of a white supremacist civilization; they adhered neither to American optimism nor to exceptionalism." Henry Louis Gates, Jr., and Cornel West, *The Future of the Race* (New York: Alfred A. Knopf, 1997), pp. 72–73.

40. In 1805, the slaves in Carenage planned a well-organized revolt against their masters. It was nipped in the bud and many slaves executed. See the *Barbados Mercury and Bridgetown Gazette,* February 1, 1806.

41. Outram, *The Enlightenment,* p. 74.

42. On January 12, 1838, several Mandingos petitioned Lord Baron Glenelg to assist them to return to their original home in Africa. It was also the case that Africans who had arrived recently in the island were more committed to the violent overthrow of the society. As one observer noted, "[I]t is an indispensable fact, that a new negro is more prone to insurrection than the creole slave [a slave born in the islands]: the latter, subdued by habit and education, is more reconciled to his hard lot than the former, whose spirit is not enough broken by example to bear with patience the cutting lash of the whip. The negro troops already trained, are ready when an opportunity offers, to plunge their bayonets into the bowels of the whites, and will aid the endeavours of their colour in the work of emancipation" (Pierre M'Callum, *Travels in Trinidad* [Liverpool: W. Jones, 1805]).

measure up to the ideals he considered desirable. In contrast, the slaves condemned the system en masse. Indeed, Philippe's desire for respectability overcame a desire for genuine equality and this, more than anything, limited the intellectual reach of his appeal.

Sixty years after Philippe wrote *Free Mulatto*, Thomas recognized the intellectual importance and moral guidance that such a work offered to future generations. Thomas seemed to have endorsed Philippe's appeal for a "talented tenth" or the establishment of a cultural elite that undergirds Philippe's work:

> Despite the alarming inroad of the purely materialistic views of life, which, at the present day, rule the heart and conduct of many who, for the want of better men, are seen in the higher places of our society, there is hope in the consciousness of a few that an education deeper, wider, and more humanizing, is yet to do its work of elevating Creoles above the sordid interests of the passing hour. It is when this work shall have truly begun, that the memory of the great Patriot of our Country will be the object of that general veneration which will be at once the justification of those who praise, and the inspiration of those who shall emulate him.[43]

Still, in 1925, when Arthur Schomburg celebrated the achievement of the race internationally and cited the "significant pioneering initiative in social service and reform, in efforts toward race emancipation, colonization and race betterment," he drew upon the example of Philippe's work. He notes "the dramatic and history-making expose of John Baptist Phillips [*sic*], African graduate of Edinburgh, who compelled through Lord Bathurst in 1824 the enforcement of the articles of capitulation guaranteeing freedom to the blacks in Trinidad."[44] It did not matter that Schomburg did not reflect seriously on the complexity of Philippe's position within the context of Trinidad society. It mattered that Philippe's work affected the international conscience and became an important part of the scorecard of African achievement in the world.

Free Mulatto, the work of a liberal philosopher, is inundated with Enlightenment values. Written at the commencement of modern Trinidad, it posed an important intellectual challenge to the dominant manner of speaking about slavery and freedom. It also forced the English to take another look at how they treated their coloured inhabitants. Although Phillipe's interpretation of the human condition is colored by contradictory sentiments, his *Free Mulatto* signals the beginning of an indigenous literary/intellectual tradition that, bearing many diverse and stimulating fruits, reached beyond the boundaries of Trinidad and Tobago.

Orations, Letters, Poems, and Diaries

Apart from Philippe's address, the first third of the nineteenth century offered other forms of literary endeavors, the most conspicuous of which were orations, let-

---

43. "Publishers' Preface," In *FM*. (1987). This essay is not paginated.
44. Arthur Schomburg, "The Negro Digs Up His Past," in Alain Locke, ed., *The New Negro* (New York: A and C Boni, 1925), p. 234.

ter writing, diaries, memorials, autobiographies, and poems. Orations, it would seem, were one of the more popular forms of addresses. Sometimes they were published as pamphlets and distributed. For example, whenever a governor arrived or left the country, a principal was installed or left a school, or someone of importance died, an oration constituted the appropriate form of welcome, remembrance, or sorrow.

The eulogy of Philippe, given by an unknown eulogist demonstrates how members of the society used this formalized mode of persuasive rhetoric that was prominent in the French education of the day. Significantly, it is entitled an oration rather than a eulogy. In this eulogy, one notices not so much by the elaborate praises—that is what a eulogy is supposed to contain—but by the florid manner and elevated language of the prose:

> The public gratitude evinced by the inhabitants of Trinidad in attending his funeral obsequies, their dark habiliments, hallowed emblems of internal sorrow, the faltering accents with which his name is mentioned in the interchange of mutual sympathies and regrets, the signs which heave their bosoms, and the tears which gush from every eye, eloquently proclaim the intensity of their grief, and exhibit the noblest testimonies of his worth. It is just that he should be honoured by the emotions of others, who by his own deeds had established his claims to virtue.[45]

In speaking about Philippe's love of country and the sacrifices he made to serve his fellowmen, the eulogist rhapsodizes about one of Philippe's amatory encounter:

> Above the age of eighteen, a period when, for the West Indian, every cord of the soul is bent on the charms of love, and when beauty, combined with true merit and diverting accomplishments, has that powerful influence on the mind of man in general, that his faculties are at once captivated when seized by amatory flames as by the endearment of an enchanting spirit, our young traveler met at Aken one, whose loveliness, whose advantageous situation in life, whose amiable features and accomplished manners, promised every comfort a happy and prosperous matrimony was likely to ensure. The darling moments of their intercourse, the mellifluous suavity of their conversations, the sparkling fire of their eyes betrayed their hearts, unfolded the reciprocity of their feelings, and both pleased and flattered the doting expectation of the young lady's parents. Gratitude, politeness, amiability, future prospects, impelled him to love, but his country, his brethren of the same soil, called upon him to redress their wrongs, and to immolate his love on the altar of his native home. Great indeed was the struggle! Bitter the sacrifice! But our hero needed not the stern resolves of an aged Mentor to force him from the coast of pleasure, and to fling him with violence into an ocean of trouble. No: the warning voice of a friend was enough. "You have no alternative—you must either abandon this object of your tenderest attachment, or relinquish all the noble plans which you have formed for the welfare and happiness of your country." His decision was as rapid as it was firm

---

45. "An Oration," in *FM.* (1987), p. 3.

and unalterable; for the very following day he left Aken, began preparations to return to his country, and, in fact, arrived in Trinidad at the age of nineteen.[46]

Although this euloguim is about Philippe's life, it also allows the eulogist to offer an imaginative rendering of what Philippe must have felt when he made his decision to return to Trinidad. Indeed, the speaker could not have met the young traveler whom Philippe met at Aken or have seen the sparkling fire of her eyes. Such a writing strategy called for a leap of the eulogist's imagination and the exercise of enormous creative ability. As a result, this eulogy stands out as a literary performance in its own right.

Letter writing was another prominent literary form of the period. As indicated earlier, most of the French families who possessed the means sent their children to France to learn how to live "in a cultured way, to be able to provide for their own entertainment at home, to become a lady or gentleman, so that they could lead a full, happy life."[47] In France, the children's education consisted of *ecriture;* the study of Latin, Greek, French; and penmanship. Central to this education was the emphasis on the formal properties of penmanship and writing that acceded to the well-established rules of composition. Rhetoric was also a part of the curriculum.

Having received such an elaborate education, the following problem arose: what was one to do when one returned to the remoteness and literary thinness of early nineteenth-century Trinidad? Given the difficulty of travel at the time, as well as having a lot of time on one's hands, most of the members of this class corresponded with one another to pass the time. Indeed, letter writing became the primary way these people communicated with one another. Father Anthony de Verteuil notes that "the letter became a literary exercise in which one found bits of poetry in the letter that the letter writer composed."[48] Additionally, these letters contained quantities of sentimentality, and flowery language. Such writing also served as a means of embracing and domesticating the landscape, as one discovers in Sly Devenish's poems of the latter half of the century.

The poem also enjoyed an honored place in this culture during the early nineteenth century. De Verteuil called Trinidad a festival culture in which poems were composed for baptisms, weddings, and similar celebratory occasions, with baptismal poetry being the most popular. These poetic exercises were mainly private efforts, recited to and circulated primarily within families, such as the de Gannes, the La Cadres, and the de Lapeyrouse. For example, when George Le Cadre sought the hand of his deceased brother's widow, he wrote a mock epic to her:

> In this harsh climate, do not doubt
> The burning sun one cannot flout.
> I have good reason thus to speak,

---

46. Ibid, pp. 9-10.
47. Anthony de Verteuil, *And Then There Were None* (Port of Spain: Litho Press, 1992), p. 76.
48. Personal interview with Anthony de Verteuil, March 28, 1995. I am indebted to Fr. de Verteuil for information on this aspect of the literature.

> O hear me, and I'll be content,
> That to my plea an ear you've lent,
> With attention meek.
> For, of the strong and burning sphere
> With your complexion do beware,
> It is so beautiful and fresh,
> Framed by the bonnet's veil and mesh.
> Tis only at dawn of day,
> When Phoebus yet holds full sway,
> I love to see you then appear
> So clothed in tasteful, simple style
> As to enhance your beauty, while
> You also are addition clear
> To nature's beauty in the morning,
> And in the purest moment's dawning.[49]

Although Le Cadre's verse is not the most imaginative use of language, it is representative of the kind of poetry that was written at the private level.

During this same period, poets also published their poems, written in French and English, in the various newspapers. Much of this poetry was similar to those that were circulated privately. For example, the *Port of Spain Gazette* published several poems on November 23, 1825. Three were by an anonymous author; D. F. B signed another written in French. A fourth poem, "To My Daughter Adelaide Felicity," traces the development of the poet daughter's from an infant to woman. The first, second, fourth and fifth stanzas of this poem reveal the sentimental poetic language of the time:

> Before the infant lips could frame,
> With lisping tone a parent's name,
> When first a smile of playful grace
> Was seen upon thy Cherub face;
> While dandled on thy mother's knee-
> Think'st thou that smile was dear to me?
> Twas, Adelaide-Felicity.
>
> When thou, at last could run alone,
> And lisp over names with dulcet tone;
> And like the lamb, in frolic play,
> Didst while the laughing hours away:
> Thy father's bosom throbb'd with glee,
> While love maternal guarded thee,
> 'Twas, Adelaide-Felicity.

---

49. Quoted in Anthony de Verteuil, *And The There Were None*, p. 67.

....

And when with cultivated mind,
By knowledge stored, by art refined,
Thy faithful heart, thy hand, thy will,
Were pledged to one who holds them still,
One who is worthy even thee,
What, think you, owed the youth to me?
Twas, Adelaide Felicity.

And when thy lengthened absence o'er,
I'll hold they in my hands once more,
And kiss thy pearls of joy away,
And see the smiles of rapture play,
About thy lips from sorrow free
What thinkest thou, calls this tear from me,
Tis Adelaide.

Another of these original poems, "The Firefly," compares the life of human beings to that of a firefly. It ends as follows:

Then let us not whist journeying here
Forget there is another sphere
Where joys eternal reign;
But strive that all our actions may
Shine forth as lights upon our way.
And our admittance gained.

The last poem, a sonnet to love is written to one Eliza and is entitled, "Is it a Crime to Love!":

If it be crime to love the eye
That speaks so bright divinity;
If it be crime to love the smile
That can my gloomiest thoughts beguile;
It be crime to love the tone
That seraphs love- so much their own;

If it be crime to love the mind
With love and elegance refined;
If it, in fact, be crime to love,
Think thou no more of bliss above;
For who they loveliness can view
Nor only love—but worship too?
Alas for thee! Since tempters share
The punishment their victims bear.

There were other poetic endeavors. Some are metaphysically problematic (such as "A Lady's Choice")[50], while others are bland (such as "The Reading Room").[51]In spite of their claims to originality, many of these poems reflect the sentimentality and deep-seated religious feelings of their authors. Straining after poetic effects, they show a concern for home and the sanctity of family, sentiments that are at the center of *Free Mulatto*. Whatever these poem's aesthetic shortcomings, they give the reader a sense of the verse written at the time and of the sentiments that mattered most to that segment of the population.

Another popular form of literary activity was the autobiography. Ferdinand Le Cadre wrote one of the more important autobiographies under the guise of a hermit telling the tragedy of his life. Written in French in an exercise book, Le Cadre finished his piece in 1828 a year before he died of yellow fever on October 7, 1829, at the age of twenty-one. As de Verteuil tells the story, Le Cadre was educated in Paris, returned to Trinidad, and subsequently married Josephine de Gannes de La Chancellerie in 1827. After a year of marriage, the union produced a son, Charles Leon St. Hilaire. When his uncle Stanilas died, Le Cadre had to take charge of his uncle's estate and the slaves attached to it. Although opposed to slavery, Le Cadre was forced by the exigencies of his circumstances to continue a practice he hated, for if he did not, he would have gone bankrupt. Retreating from the Diego Martin Valley, he settled on Colombia Estate, owned by his mother-in-law and located in Cedros in the south of the island. Overcome by sorrow and depression, he wrote the story of his life, which ends with the following words: "O, my son, my cup of sorrow is overflowing. I left all to come and see in these vales of my childhood, a day's refuge to await my death." According to de Verteuil, Le Cadre was buried "with scant ceremony in the shade of the trees near the estate house."[52]

During the early 1800s, several planters, overseers, and merchants' clerks kept diaries. Two of the more important ones were written by Edouard Le Cadre and by

---

50. "A Lady's Choice," *Port of Spain Gazette*, April 4, 1827. This poem, a reflection of a kind of spiritual torment, springs from a woman's attachment to a system of values that she detests. It reads as follows:

> I do not like a man that's tall,
> A man that's little's worst than all;
> I much abhor the man that's fat,
> A man that's lean is worse than that;
> A young man is a constant pest.
> An old man would my room infest.
> Nor do I like the man that's fair,
> A man that's black I cannot bear,
> A man of sense I could not rule,
> And from my heart I hate fool;
> A sober man I will not take,
> A drunken man my heart would break—
> All these I do sincerely hate.
> And yet—I LOVE THE MARRIAGE STATE.

51. "Original Poetry," *Port of Spain Gazette*, January 20, 1827.

52. *And Then There Were None*, pp. 64–65. This book tells the story of the Le Cadre Family of the West Indies. The first two chapters are based on Le Cadre's diary, while the third chapter is based on Ferdinand's autobiography.

Friedrich Gottfried Wilhelm Urich.[53] While the former deals with Martinique as well as Trinidad, the latter, in German, tells of Urich's experiences in Trinidad from September 1830 to October 1832. Urich, who came out to Trinidad at the age of twenty-one, spent his time as a merchant's clerk in Port of Spain and then some months as a manager of a sugar estate in Naparima.[54] Although he lived in Venezuela for two years (1832–1834) and returned to Germany to be married in 1841, Urich spent most of his adult life in Trinidad, where he set up his own business, fathered three sons, and died in 1883.

One important event recorded in Urich's diary is the reaction to the January 6, 1832, Order in Council that was meant to improve the conditions of the slaves on Trinidad. Unsurprisingly, the island's planters fiercely opposed the measure. According to Urich, "[t]he whole of the white population is protesting and are to send a petition to the King as well as to both Houses of Parliament." In Contrast, the Africans welcomed the new law and became "sulky and unwilling to do their daily tasks, which they could do easily between the hours of 6 a.m. and 6 p.m."[55]

Slavery ended six years later, four years having been given over to apprenticeship. Abolitionism would usher in a new type of narrative that spoke of liberation and that articulated a new consciousness. Such narratives would begin to compete with those of the colored and white segments of the community.

53. See for example, Friedrich Urich, *The Urich Diary: Trinidad 1830–1832*, trans. Irene Urich and ed. Anthony de Verteuil (Port of Spain: Litho Press, 1995).

54. Merchants' clerks, it seems, were not too well respected in the community. Writing in the *Port of Spain Gazette* on January 20, 1835, one poet notes in "The Merchant's Clerk":

Ere wide awake and breakfast o'er,
To business I must run,
Thro' town I go in sun or rain,
A sort of living din.
Without success, the rulers frown,
While debtor's call you shark,
Thus smiles and sunshine seldom beam
To greet a merchant's clerk....

I am not awkward in the dance,
And sing I think I can—
I'm told I'm not by any means
An ugly looking man;
But mothers all are wrapt in frowns,
And cast their glances dark,
On daughters who too kindly smile
Upon a merchant's clerk.

They tell me in some forty years,
They'll take me in the firm,
When I'm a full grown meat, forsooth,
For some long greedy worm.
What's riches when we can't enjoy
No frolics, fun, nor lark,—
Oh! Little boys and unborn babes,
Now don't be merchant's clerks.

55. Urich Diary, pp. 108, 113.

CHAPTER 3

Children of the Dark

Political subordination, however hateful to a liberal mind, is as bright as day when compared to the dark and hopeless bondage of the negro; a bondage that combines pangs of intellectual misery, with the sufferings of a brute; and under that impression Toussaint's brave colleagues were averse to submit to the subordination of the European freebooters.

—PIERRE M'CALLUM, *Travels in Trinidad*

> The son of Afric's savage coast regard,
> His tatoo'd body, his high cheeks deep scar'd,
> His lengthy jaw, his bilious eye of lead,
> His acts of awkwardness, his heavy tread;
> His gait ungraceful, melancholy air,
> His grotesque gesture, and incessant stare;
> His tongue unwieldy; halting voice, whose sound
> Mocks ev'ry language, does each word confound.

—UNKNOWN POET, *Port of Spain Gazette* (1825)

I was born free…and I wish to die free. I ask no remuneration for my servitude of fifty years: the church to which I belong will support me for the few days I have yet to live.

—SLAMANK, a Mandingo priest

Travels in Trinidad (1805)

While the whites and mulattoes were telling their stories, the African population was constructing another narrative. Needless to say, the story of the children of slavery, refugees from America, and free blacks from other West Indian territories offered another portrait of Trinidad, Tobago, and Caribbean realities. Although their story remained essentially an oral one (slave and colonial authorities gave precedence to scribal over oral cultures), their activities were subjected to enormous exaggeration and biases, glimpses of which can be gleaned through a narrowly written record.[1] Of course, theirs was a story written in blood, as they tried to locate themselves within the society.

When the British arrived in 1797, the majority of the population were enslaved Africans and people of color (approximately 15,000 of the 18,627 inhabitants of the island); the slave population quickly grew to 21,000 by 1803. Most of the slaves came from St. Domingo and the other British colonies. Those actually from Africa came between 1797 and 1805. Although the Ibos constituted the largest African ethnos that came to Trinidad, the Congo, Moco, Mandingo, Kormantyn, and Fanti also came to the island during that period. The Africans who came to Trinidad "were generally all young, well formed and healthy, as their importation took place subsequent to the Act of Parliament which regulated their treatment in the Middle Passage."[2]

Pierre M'Callum, a Scottish gentleman who visited Trinidad from February to April 1803, offers one of the earliest observations of Africans living in Trinidad. In an extremely revealing account, he offers two conceptions of the Africans in the Caribbean. In the first section of the text, the period in which he resided in Trinidad, he seems to have a particular conception of the African. In the second section of the text, after he was deported from Trinidad, he presents another conception of the African. In the first section, where he indicts Picton for the horrible crimes he committed against blacks and his fellow whites, M'Callum supports the stereotype of black inferiority. In the second, however where he speaks of the French behavior toward Toussaint L'Ouverture and the atrocities committed by some whites in the other British West Indian colonies, he tends to be sympathetic to African aspirations and sees these people as fellow human beings. In the latter instance, he contrasts their humanity with the inhumanity of his fellow Europeans. M'Callum's sympathy arises from his support of resistance activities of Caribbean people because such activities are directed against Britain's enemies.

The first section opens with a disruption of its idyllic setting. Lying under the "fragrant shade of the hospitable linden-tree, thinking of the many hours that glided during my delightful solitude in the woods near Perth-Amboy," his reverie is

1. The well-known Anansi tales of the West Indies, a part of the prose genres of African oral literature, were taken from Ashanti (Akan) legends. Creolized to fit the Caribbean condition, the hero of these stories is usually represented as a sly, cunning person who usually wins out in the end. There is every reason to believe that the "smart man," one of Trinidad and Tobago's legendary characters, takes its resonance from the Anansi character. The proverbs, another aspect of oral African prose literature was taken from the Hausa traders from northern Nigeria, the Congo, and the Akan ethnoi. The Fulani who were not as extensive as the other ethnic groups (approximately 171 came in the early period) were the chief repository of the riddle, another aspect of oral African prose literature. Fr. Anthony de Verteuil believes that several of "the traditional Trinidadian proverbs" originate in Martinique. See, Anthony de Verteuil, *Seven Slaves and Slavery, Trinidad: 1777–1838* (Port of Spain: Scrip-J Printers, 1992), p. 13. See, also, Ruth Finnegan, *Oral Literature in Africa* (Oxford; Oxford University Press, 1976), for a discussion of these literary forms.

2. See de Verteuil, *Seven Slaves and Slavery*, pp. 8–9, 22. According to the 1813 slave census, there were 13,984 African slaves of which the Ibo consisted of 2,863; Congo, 2,450; Moco 2,240; Mandingo, 1,421 and Fanti, Ashanti, 1,068.

broken by a thing most brutish: a couple of females slaves "with large heavy iron chains, which hung all round them, riveted to an iron collar round the neck, and again to their ankles." According to M'Callum, "these chains were so weighty that the poor unfortunate creatures were almost sinking under the grievous load, fastened on by the wicked followers of Christianity." Observing this fiendish scene, M'Callum exclaims, "Good God! I thank thee forever for having given my body a white colour—What misery have I escaped."[3]

He also describes his visit to the prison, the Bastille. He notes that in an area of about twenty square feet "were lodged no less than one hundred negroes, with large ugly heavy chains riveted about their necks, waists, &c. and, to my great astonishment, several British seamen confined in the *same* filthy hole of an apartment along with them" (*TT.*, p. 130, my italics). In other scenes, he observes a slave whose ears were cut off and a free man who was imprisoned because he asked his employer to repay him part of the money the latter had borrowed from him. When certain slaves were accused of planning a revolt in Carenage in 1805, three of them (Sampson, Baptiste, and Carlos) "were sentenced to be hanged and their heads severed from their bodies; the latter had to hanged in chains, and their heads stuck up." Other slaves associated with the plot had their ears cut off and flogged; still others were flogged and had ten-pounds iron rings affixed to their legs, while some were flogged and banished from the colony.[4]

It is against this tableau of brutality that the initial encounter between black and white (African and European) takes place and out of which the nascent discourse of the society is inscribed: on the one hand, the inestimable brutality against female slaves; on the other, the exultation of security and privilege that the possession of a white skin offers.[5] While it seemed natural to imprison an African, the violation of

---

3. Pierre M'Callum, *Travels in Trinidad* (Liverpool: W. Jones, 1805), pp. 35–36. All other references to this text will be noted as *TT.*

4. In early December 1805, Governor Thomas Hislop discovered a well-organized plan "of the most sanguinary nature" to take over the island and to annihilate the whites. According to his report, the slaves intended to adopt the behavior of the Africans of Haiti: "The huckster negro women and slaves proved incontestable evidence alluding to the approaching annihilation of the whites in the words: 'Bread is white meat, wine is white blood. We are going to eat white bread; we are going to drink white blood,' and their companions responded with the refrain: St. Dominique." "Threatened Revolt of the Slaves," *Barbados Mercury and Bridgetown Gazette,* February 1, 1806.

5. M'Callum also takes objection to slavery of blacks in the Caribbean. In an appendix to his book, "Horrors of West Indian Slavery," he recounts the story of the unprovoked killing of a black woman who was pregnant and noted that "[t]wo gentlemen were witness of this horrid action. One of them, Mr. Harding, the manager of the Codrington College estate, went up to Halls and spoke harshly to him, and said he ought to be hanged, for he never saw a more unprovoked murder, and that he would certainly carry him before a magistrate. Hall's [the offending party] reply is very remarkable. 'For what?' said he (with the utmost indifference as to the crime) "for what? *FOR KILLING A NEGRO!!!*" This is a short but a significant sentence, strongly confirming an important truth which has frequently been asserted, viz. that the Negroes are regarded by their white skinned oppressors as an inferior order of beings, and, under the influence of this sentiment, are naturally enough denied the common rights of humanity, and excluded from the pale of that sympathy, which a sense of common nature and a common extraction is calculated to inspire" (*TT.*, p. 341).

the rights of "a British subject" seemed a travesty, a threat to the foundation of "English freedom." Thus, M'Callum asks loudly that "[w]here is the justice of the country? Where are those rights which Britons have vainly called their own?" (*TT.*, p. 169)[6]

It is within the articulation of these oppositional categories that the identities of whites and blacks are constructed. The African is depicted as being primitive, inhuman, unknown, and unknowable, whereas the Englishman is depicted as the embodiment of rationality and order, the quintessence of civilized behavior. M'Callum describes Africans in the following manner:

> There are two Negro Regiments stationed here, composed of negroes taken from the French colonies, and commanded by French officers. The arming and training so many hirelings, after the mournful scenes and horrid barbarities of their committing we have witnessed in St. Domingo, is surely not the prudent dictates of wisdom....Pray, what tie is there to bind a black hireling to be faithful to his duty? Has he that vernacular attachment, animated with the sacred flame of *amour patria*, that distinguish the soldiers of other free nations? No, my friend, all his actions spring from lust and brutality, without which his bosom would be an empty void. The late ferocity of one of the Negro Corps in Dominica [an account he reproduced in his book], where they murdered their officers (mostly British, I believe), is a striking presage of their future conduct....
>
> Many of them were, you know what, in St. Domingo, &c.—Hence, devoid of every principle which distinguishes the human species from the brute creation, a ferocious excitement stimulates them to crimes, as much as crocodiles of the Nile when they seize and devour young children (*TT.*, pp. 26–27).

This excerpt articulates a nascent colonialist discourse that intensifies as imperialism (and colonialism) became more intense.[7] Africans are depicted as being no better than animals. They are a degenerate species, who are incapable of loyalty and lack the softening influences of humanity. They act as they do because of constitutive reasons. As a colonialist writer, M'Callum is intent on depicting Africans as the ultimate savage, and thus paves the way for the degenerate, lazy characters that Anthony Trollope, James Anthony Froude, Thomas Carlyle, and other negrophobes would develop later in the century. M'Callum concludes:

> I am also convinced they do not know the meaning of loyalty. To find a Negro that does, would be as singular a phenomenon as a preposterous birth—fishes feeding

6. This notion that the English upheld a free and fair legal system in spite of its practice of slavery and the denial of the rights of African people is one that the English carried about in their heads even when they were saying and doing the most savage things to others. Such a notion would find its fullest embodiment in the works of Rudyard Kipling and G. A. Henty.

7. Elleke Boehmer defines colonialist literature (and hence a colonialist discourse) as one that reflects a colonial ethos and is concerned specifically with colonial expansion. She notes that colonialist literature was written "by and for colonizing Europeans about non-Europeans colonized by them...[and] was informed by theories concerning the superiority of European culture and the rightness of empire" (*Colonial and Postcolonial Literature* [Oxford: Oxford University Press, 1995], pp. 2–3.)

on dry land—or a pregnant mule, which Naturalists, with much truth, maintain to be incapable of breeding—or even a shower of pebbles from the clouds! (*TT.*, p. 28)

M'Callum is not intent on depicting Africans only as savage and degenerate. He is also concerned with Empire and empire building, which explains his enthusiasm for the immigration of Scottish Highlanders to the island and his hysterical attack on Africans. Because colonialism, as Elleke Boehmer notes, involved "a complicated web of economic exchange and flow of goods and money" wealth making and the ideology of work were promoted as supreme virtues.[8] M'Callum alludes to these virtues when he writes:

I do not mean to deny the negro has his share of sufferings also; it is, however, a negative share. He is not only exonerated from the care of providing for the present, but for the future. The only thing he can complain of, is, the hardships necessarily attached to his condition. When he eats his banana, he goes contentedly to sleep; the world or its cares have no effect on his mind,—though a hurricane or a fire destroy the sanguine anticipation of his tyrant; though volcanos [*sic*] ingulf [*sic*] towns and cities; though war and pestilence succeed with all their horrors; all that is nothing to the negro,—he sits in the posture of contentment, smoaking [*sic*] his pipe, and views, with a tranquil mind, the siderated prospects of a whole generation,—therefore, the unhappiness of the negro is local and negative; that of the Highlander labourer universal and positive(*TT.*, p. 84).

In this passage, M'Callum outlines a major "negro" stereotype that will become popular in colonialist literature as he contrasts the degenerate, lazy, malingering, good-for-nothing negro with the white man, "the archetypal worker and provident profit-maker," the builder of cities and harbingers of a new civilization.[9] It is this conception—the inevitable colonialist strategy—that leads M'Callum to characterize the African's interests and his joys as negative and local, and those of the white person as universal and positive. As a result—and this is one variation of a theme that lasts well into the twentieth century—white people write about universal subjects; black people write about local concerns.

After saying many terrible things about African people in Trinidad, M'Callum offers a sympathetic depiction of African activity in Haiti. Following M'Callum feeling the sting of Picton's tyranny and being deported from Trinidad by the latter, he changed his mind about the Negroes' capacities and abilities.[10] It may have helped that he was describing the French, rather than "free born" Britons, whose "pestilential contagion of…principles has sapped the foundation of humanity, reli-

---

8. Boehmer, *Colonial and Postcolonial Literature*, p. 37.

9. Ibid., p. 39.

10. In a revealing statement, M'Callum notes that, with all Napoleon's "sagacity and military knowledge, he, fortunately for the Western Hemisphere, mistook the character of the negroes; they were no longer a horde of runaway slaves. No, they were united together in the bonds of an indissoluble freedom, and had been a considerable time in the actual enjoyment of it, therefore they were not to be hoodwinked by the shallow maneuvers of the upstart Ruler" (*TT.*, p. 323).

gion, and morality...[and] completely changed the national character" of Holland"
(*TT.*, p. 320).[11] Writing from New York, M'Callum is supportive of the black
struggle in Haiti in general and Toussaint in particular. Of the Haitian blacks, he
says:

> If the cold cruelty of despotism have no bounds, what can we expect from the
> paroxysm of despair? Surely ample allowance ought to be made, if, in this instance
> enormities were committed; for they were taught the example from their oppres-
> sors, of which I beg leave to notice a sample that will freeze your very soul with
> horror. Here a white, (yes, a beautiful French lady,) lately plunged a negro into a
> burning oven—another white dashed out the brains of a child in the presence of its
> father—a third fed a slave with his own proper flesh. These are the monsters who
> have to account for the barbarity of the revolted negroes. Millions of Africans have
> perished on this soil of blood. You break at every step, the bones of the inhabitants
> to whom nature had given these islands, and you shudder at the retaliation of their
> vengeance. In this dreadful struggle, the crimes of the whites are yet the most hor-
> rible; they are the offspring of despotism, whilst those of the negroes, originate in
> the hatred of slavery, the thirst for vengeance (*TT.*, pp. 316–17)

Although M'Callum argues that there was some justification for black retaliation in Haiti (he sees vengeance as an important element of their struggle), he is
not able to let go of the feeling that mulattoes were far "more cruel than the whites."
This, he argues, is one reason why Toussaint "thought it advisable, with the con-
current voice of his fellow-soldiers, to contest every inch of ground with them [the
mulattoes]" (*TT.*, p. 318). M'Callum presents Toussaint in a very just and favorable
light. He argues that "[t]owards his bitterest enemies he never swerved from the
rules of justice; and if he used all the means that were in his power to conquer, he
sought as much as he could, to allay the horrors of war, and spare human
blood....By the oblivion of errors and faults, he wished to cause the lawful and
sacred cause of liberty to be revered, even by his vilest enemies" (*TT.*, p. 318).

M'Callum also uses Toussaint as an example of how a public servant ought to
behave and how public service ought to be conducted. Implicitly, Toussaint's conduct is used to criticize Picton's behavior and the manner in which the latter abused
public office to gratify his private ends:

> He constantly made his brethren in arms, both generals and officers, remember
> that the distinction they were raised to, ought to be considered but the reward of
> honor, courage, and unblemished conduct in private life; having been raised above
> their countrymen, the more prudent and circumspect all their actions ought to
> be—that the misconduct of public men brought on society more fatal consequences
> than that of other citizens—that the honors and offices they were invested with,
> were given to them, not to promote their fortunes, or serve their ambition, but had

---

11. Of the French republican system of government, M'Callum says, "[i]t is an irrational, unprinci-
pled, proscribing, confiscating, plundering, ferocious, bloody, and tyrannical democracy!" (*TT.*, p. 321).

for their motive and object the public welfare; that they imposed on them public duties to be fulfilled, before they should think of themselves, that impartiality and justice ought to dictate all their decisions—that they ought to repress all vices, continually stimulating their activity, watchfulness and zeal (*TT.*, pp. 318–19).[12]

In spite of these brave statements, M'Callum feels that the newly freed slaves of St Domingo would be a threat to British interests and argues that it is necessary to settle Trinidad and the other islands with white people. In other words, in spite of their bravery, black people cannot be trusted. To justify his position, M'Callum says, "we [the British] shall always be able to make conquests highly important to the British empire, or to yield succors to [white] Jamaica, in case it should be attacked" (*TT.*, p. 115) by the newly liberated blacks from St. Domingo.

In spite of M'Callum's sympathetic stance toward Toussaint and the Haitians, his interest in the Empire mattered most. As a colonialist text, *the* primary function of *Travels in Trinidad* was to secure the interest of the mother country, contribute to and reinforce the perception that Britain was the dominant power in the world, and to secure the interest of whites. Such an ideology translated to a modern version of "white first." Any action or notion that spoke in a contrary voice, no matter how noteworthy and honorably, had to be negated. All conquests, all actions, as M'Callum notes, should always be "highly important to the British empire." This was the criteria by which all actions should be measured.

Dauxion-Lavaysse's Travels (1812)

M. Dauxion-Lavaysse, a landed proprietor in Trinidad during the first fifteen years of its existence as a British territory, also offers his observations of Africans in the Trinidad in *A Statistical, Commercial, and Political Description of Venezuela, Trinidad, Margarita, and Tobago* (1812).[13] Defending African people against ideas expressed in M'Callum's *Travels in Trinidad* (he describes the latter book as "a severe philippic against General Picton,") Dauxion-Lavaysse presents the earliest systematic refutation of M'Callum's invective against African people in the Caribbean,[14] as well as the first spirited defense of the African population in

12. In this context, it is instructive to compare M'Callum's treatment of Toussaint with that of C. L. R. James's treatment of Toussaint in *The Black Jacobins.* For purposes of this study, however, it's important to note how central an examination of Toussaint's behavior was in framing the character and nature of blacks from the inception of the literary experience in 1803 to the James analysis in 1938.

13. M. Dauxion-Lavaysse, a Frenchman who spent fifteen years in the West Indies (circa 1795–1810), used Trinidad as his base as he traveled extensively in the Caribbean and Latin America. Commenting on his work, his English editor and translator notes that a "strong bias of national jealousy, aggravated by a sense of injustices, whether real or imaginary, has evidently stimulated our traveler's pen in some parts of his book, and hence it was no easy portion of the editorial task to qualify the author's expressions, by divesting them of that acrimonious turn, which is never essential to the support of truth" (*A Statistical, Commercial, and Political Description of Venezuela, Trinidad, Margarita, and Tobago* [London: G. and W. B. Whittaker, 1820], p. x; hereafter noted in the text as *Statistical Description*).

14. Dauxion-Lavaysse translated M'Callum's *Travels in Trinidad* as *Voyages.* Both in his account of Picton's trial and in *Travels in Trinidad,* M'Callum wages a vindictive verbal war against Thomas Picton.

Trinidad and the Caribbean.[15] Considered a *nigrophilus*[16] by some, Dauxion-Lavaysse argues that "the colonial system in the American islands is a monstrous anomaly. The slave trade makes every European shudder, who has human feelings, when he sees herds of negroes landed, who are sold like beasts of burden."[17] Speaking of how Africans were perceived, he observes:

> A great deal has been written on the negroes, and very learned men have published many falsehoods and absurdities on the subject. As if it were not enough that the institutions of their country and those of Europeans condemn them to slavery, it is also necessary to represent them as monsters in the physical and moral world! The celebrated Camper quotes the opinion of different writers who have discussed this point from the times of Herodotus, Strabo and Pliny, down to our own days. Will it be believed that there have been amongst those, men, who were so ignorant of the first principles of zoology, as to suppose negroes to be a race produced between man and the ourang outang?…One opinion rather generally entertained is, that the negroes are a race of men very inferior in their intellectual faculties to Europeans, the savages of America, and even other Africans with straight hair, known by the name of Moors. I would ask of those who are so little informed on the noblest part of natural history, comparative anatomy, as to suppose organization to have no relation with intelligence, if it be astonishing that men, such as the negroes, born in countries destitute of every institution for intellectual culture, should not have made any progress in the liberal arts and sciences?
>
> It has been proved by numerous examples, that whenever negroes had the means of receiving education, they have profited by it, like the rest of mankind. And even while this sheet goes to the press has not the Institute of France received astronomical observations on the comet of 1811, made in the Mauritius, by M. Lilet, a negro born in Madagascar, and who has arrived at a knowledge of the superior sciences, without education, and by the mere force of genius (*Statistical Description*, pp. 366–68)

Refuting the use of skulls to prove black inferiority (another practice that would perfect itself in the latter part of the century), Dauxion-Lavaysse observes that "[w]hat, in fact would be said of an African or Asiatic philosopher, if such there are, as they have been, in those countries, who, seeing some ill-shapen sculls [*sic*] of Europeans, would decide that the Europeans are necessarily a stupid race of men?"

In *Travels,* he describes Picton as "a mighty praetor, whose knife was set in oil that it might cut the deeper, and never hesitated to engulf the reeking blade into the warm bowels of a fellow-creature, nor to pour *aqua-fortis* into the bleeding wound, in order to provoke the innocent object to a state of madness" (*TT.*, p. 20).

15. Dauxion-Lavaysse is responding to all the negrophobes of the period.

16. A nigrophilus, a term of reproach, is ascribed to someone who is considered a lover of negroes, or in its more derogatory dimension, a lover of niggers. It is usually intended as a gross insult as in "he is a *nigrophilus.*"

17. *Statistical Description*, p. 387.

(*Statistical Description*, p. 369)[18] As he reflects in one of his footnotes, "It is not the history of negroes that I pretend to write; I merely wish to dispel the prejudices that are unfavourable to them" (*Statistical Description*, p. 370). Like M'Callum, Dauxion-Lavaysse uses the achievements of Africans in the Haitian revolution to prove their bravery and courage and quotes Baron de Vastey, a former slave, to support his point:

> Five and twenty years ago… we were plunged in the deepest ignorance, we had no notion of society, no distinct ideas of happiness, no powerful feelings; our faculties, both physical and moral, were so overwhelmed under the load of slavery, that I myself who am writing this, thought the world finished at the horizon which bounded my sight; my ideas were so limited that things the most simple were incomprehensible to me; and all my countrymen were as ignorant, and, if possible, even more so than myself! I have known many of them, who learned to read and write themselves without the help of a master; I have seen them walking with their books in their hands, inquiring of the passengers, and begging them to explain the signification of such a character or such a word, and in this way, have many, already advanced in years, become able to read and write without the benefit of education. Such men have become notaries, attornies [*sic*], advocates, and judges, astonishing the world by the sagacity of their judgment; others have become painters and sculptors from their own exertions, and have also surprized strangers by their reproductions" (*Statistical Description*, pp. 372–73)

Dauxion-Lavaysse attributes most African vices to the condition of slavery. The "cruelties and ferocities which they exercised on the whites in Surinam, St. Domingo, and the British colonies, where they have revolted" could be explained and justified by the revolutionary situation that was taking place in the society. He says, "[r]ead the dismal history of revolutions, in all times and amongst all nations, and you will every where see that whenever slave have succeeded in breaking their chains, they have forged arms from them to exterminate their masters" (*Statistical Description*, p. 374). Quoting Bryan Williams's *History of the British Colonies in the West Indies* and I. G. Stedman's *Narrative of a Five Year Expedition Against Revolted Negroes of Surinam*, Dauxion-Lavaysse notes the extraordinary bravery of Africans under the worst possible conditions. He also offers other slave accounts of mistreatment and acts of enormous bravery. C. L. R. James would adopt a similar method when he wrote *The Black Jacobins* (1938).

Speaking about the unproductive nature of slavery (free labor, the author con-

---

18. The ideas discussed in this work have important ramifications for the entire black Atlantic. The experiments that were carried on by Louis Agassi, the chairman of Harvard's Comparative Zoology Department in the middle of the century arise directly out of the concerns expressed by Dauxion-Lavaysse. In other words, so much that was taking place in terms of intellectual ideas in the Trinidadian or in the Haitian world of the late eighteenth and early nineteenth century was of great significance to the Atlantic world.

FIGURE 3. Rose Hill was the residence of Edward Jackson. Richard Bridgens describes this elegant home as "the residence of a Gentleman well known in the colony for his classic and enlightened appreciation of everything connected with the arts and literature." Emily Goodwood, a Cambridge scholar, observes that through "his cultivation of the arts, the master/owner of the plantation transforms the site of literal cultivation (the plantation on which the sugar cane is grown) into a scene in which cultivation is an aesthetic process. This process is made the subject of (commissioned) sketches, or the subject matter of poetry. It brings to mind the idea of OEpastoral, a term which connotes both rusticity and poetry simultaneously, and a literary genre which craftily makes poetry (a leisured activity which has traditionally been the preserve of a privileged elite) out of other people's labour." From Richard Bridgens, *West India Scenery with Illustrations of Negro Character* (1837).

tends, is less costly), Dauxion-Lavaysse argues that it is the mortality rate among the negroes that has ruined many a planter. He describes that the wonted killing of Africans: "of a thousand [Africans] transported from Africa, grief or ill-usage destroys one third, in the first three months after their arrival; and at the end of six or seven years, seven or eight tenths of the others are dead!" In Trinidad, Tobago, and Grenada, it was "considered very fortunate when of thirty young negroes bought in the course of a year, there may be six in good health five years afterwards" (*Statistical Description*, p. 389). Drawing on the benign treatment the slaves on Sir William Young's plantation in St. Vincent enjoyed and their resultant prosperity, Dauxion-Lavaysse concludes that "[t]he negro population increases on all the plantations that are administered with humanity" (*Statistical Description*, p. 392).

Although Dauxion-Lavaysse believed in the gradual liberation of slaves, his is one of the earliest descriptions of slaves behaving as intelligent beings who possess qualities that are worthy of emulation. Animals they are not. Given an opportunity, they can raise themselves to "higher heights," as the Rastafarians says. Their failure to do so may lead to the retrogression of all, hence Dauxion-Lavaysse's important, final observation:

> When negroes succeed in obtaining their liberty, they are generally found to form new plantations, and some of them, by dint of labour and economy, become greater proprietors in the end. Others act as extensive traders, and such are seen in all the colonies, especially at Trinidad, where they often become considerable merchants. I have thought it necessary to make this remark, in order to point out a marked difference between the character and dispositions of the Negroes and savages. Such a form of government, and law, as may be good for the one, is not fit for the others: this then is what those who undertake to superintend their civilization ought to be convinced of; for if they do violence to nature, they will cause her to retrograde instead of advancing (*Statistical Description*, pp. 394–95).

The African in Verse

In spite of Dauxion-Lavaysse's staunch defense of Africans and the bravery they showed during the Haitian War of Independence, there were those in the society (including the coloreds) who saw them only in a negative light and who were inclined to project all of their fears and suspicions upon the Negro. When the slaves attempted their revolt in 1805, the colored members of the population sent the following letter to Governor Hislop supporting his actions against the slaves and pledging their fealty to the Crown:

> "We, His Majesty's most dutiful and loyal subjects, the People of Colour of the island of Trinidad, beg leave, most humbly to approach your Excellency with our sincere congratulations on the timely discovery of the detestable conspiracy which now occupies the investigation of your Excellency and His Majesty's honourable Council: a conspiracy in which the over-ruling hand of Providence has miraculously interposed to shield us from relentless fury and horrid dislocation, and which the firm and energetic measures of your Excellency's administration affords us the consolatory hope of arresting in its earliest stages.[19]

A revealing poem published in *Port of Spain Gazette* in June 1825—perhaps by a white poet—differentiates between Africans born on the continent and those creolized Africans who were born on the island. For our purposes, the more important aspect of the poem deals with how the poet represents the former, whom he makes feel inferior by comparing him unfavorably with the latter in an attempt to demonstrate the positive benefits of slavery.

The first section of this poem represents the African as primitive, savage, and inhuman:

19. "Threatened Revolt of the Slaves," *Barbados Mercury and Bridgetown Gazette*, February 1, 1806.

FIELD NEGRO.

FIGURE 4. An enslaved African is seen with the implements employed in the cultivation of the sugar cane: the hoe, the cutlass, and the sandal. On his arm "is a too-too in a coarse netting of lien, termed by the Negroes tie-tie." From *West India Scenery with Illustrations of Negro Character*.

The son of Afric's savage coast regard,
His tatoo'd body, his high cheeks deep scar'd,
His lengthy jaw, his bilious eye of lead,
His acts of awkwardness, his heavy tread;
His gait ungraceful, melancholy air,
His grotesque gesture, and incessant stare;
His tongue unwieldy; halting voice, whose sound
Mocks ev'ry language, does each word confound.

The adjectives the poet employs to describe the African reveal the bestiality and savagery in which he has envisioned the latter. Adjectives such as "savage," "tatoo'd," and "grotesque," as well as the characteristics attributed to him ("his lengthy jaw" and "his bilious eye of lead"), depict the African as less than human and puts in place a process of othering in which the colonized person, in reference to the European, is represented as being "less human, less civilized, as child or savage, wild man, animal, or headless mass." Boehmer astutely observes that it is this "symbolic complex of the Other" that becomes "the keystone of colonialist ideology."[20] The entire strategy is intended to depict the African as a lesser being.

The second part of the poem employs all the historic ethnic stereotypes that were used to imprison the African:

20. Boehmer, *Colonial and Postcolonial Literature*, p. 79.

> Next view, when dancing, his distorted mien,
> View (if thy nerves admit it void of pain)
> His features, body muscles, limbs, that try
> With vile contortion to distress the eye;
> Mark, how when o'er him passion holds her sway,
> His lineaments the Cannibal betray.
> Whether he be of Moco's savage race,
> Or Eboe's saddened looks o'ercloud his face,
> Or sulky Beby, or Aranda wild,
> Or Coromantin's sanguinary child,
> Or less fierce Widah, or Angola tall,
> The traits enumerated suit them all.

The poet suggests that it hurts one's eye to view this cannibal, a pain that supposedly increases whenever he is caught in mindless sexual passion, a traditional stereotype of the Negro. Indeed, the African is most like a beast when "passions hold sway," a sentiment that precedes Fanon's thesis of the Negro. In this section, the poet uses all of the ethnic stereotypes ("traits that suit them all") to nail the African in his place.[21] Yet, the desire to insert the African into a prescribed social position also speaks to a general unease on the colonizer's part: the ever-present fear of disorder and a libidinous temptation that the latter can never quite keep under control.

The creolized African, on the other hand, embodies elements of civilization: at least, those aspects of European civilization that makes him more acceptable. He seems closer to the European in that he is depicted as having the "tender" sentiments associated with the latter. Importantly, he is presented as being once removed from the "savage" African. In the islands, away from the motherland, he has been "refined" or "re-fined"—as in the verb re-found—within this new geographical context.[22] Observing the creolized African, the poet writes:

> His creole offspring to inspect begin,
> His form of symmetry and glossy skin,
> A form whose mould full oft might not disgrace,
> Thy master hand, Conova great, to trace.

---

21. According to James Walvin, the planters and their propagandist "searched for evidence which both justified their involvement with slavery and placed the African beyond the pale of English comprehension. The writings of Edward Long and Bryan Edwards exemplified this kind of literature…The major themes, occurring time and again in their caricatures of the Negro were the African's blackness and 'animal' features, his alleged indolence and untrustworthiness and his unusual sexual powers. Long, for instance, referred to the features of the Negro to prove the African's relationship to the orang-outan." Both Long and Edwards emphasize "the lust and brutality which, they claimed marked black sexuality." The Negro, they allege, "had an appetite for unnatural and excessive sexual experiences and…no capacity for the refined and tender feelings of the white man" (*The Black Presence* [New York: Schocken Books, 1972], pp. 22–23).

22. See the previous footnote.

Note his bold laugh, rapidity of talk,
Oft I regret this stooping gait of mine,
And envy Creole! the firm step of thine.

"Symmetry" is the one word that captures the behavior of the creolized African, as opposed to the contorted frame of the African from the continent. But even as the poet places the Creole on a higher level than the African and demonstrate the former's transformed condition within the context of slavery, the author still depicts him as a mindless, acculturated being:

That education ne'er refined each sense,
A happier gift is his—contended ignorance.
What tho' proud learning n'er illumed his mind,
Yet, to him, Nature has been far more kind,
For she with cunning hath his judgement lit,
And given him humour and a ready wit.

Finally, the poet contrasts "the form of Guinea's offspring wild" with the "less fierce, and more happy, Creole child." Then, he compares "the debasing bondage of these isles" with the "savage freedom of his native coast." He concludes that the system of slavery can only serve to make the creolized African view his African ancestors with contempt and loathing:

Black as the stigma is, that brands the fame,
And weds th' oppressors with the Planter's name—
E'en at whose sounds, Hypocrisy her eyes
Upturns with pious horror to the skies,
Yet Planters rear a race which will aspire
With pity and contempt to view its African sire.

It is obvious that the poet is articulating a developing colonialist stereotype: the notion that the Creole is better formed and more cultivated than his African counterpart. In 1850, this stereotype reached its apogee when Lafcadio Hearn quoted Dr. E. Rufz who argues that:

The Creole Negro is gracefully shaped, finely proportioned: his limbs are lithe, his neck long,—his features are more delicate, his lips less thick, his nose less flattened, than those of the African. Rarely can you discover in him, the sombre fury of the African, rarely a surly or savage mien; his is brave, chatty, boastful. His skin has not the same tint as his fathers—it has become more satiny; his hair remains wooly but it is finer wool. All his outlines are more rounded—one may perceive that the cellular tissue predominates, as in cultivated plants, of which the ligneous and savage fibre has been transformed.

Such descriptions verge on scientific racism, a point that Dauxion-Lavaysse alludes to in his description of the experiments that were being carried on earlier in the century. While it is true that intermarriage may have resulted in more Caucasian features in the creolized African, it does not follow that these newly achieved features are more aesthetically pleasing, nor do they make one "more handsome." Indeed, all that is transmitted is a colonialist notion that ennobles all things European and that, in the process, ascribes beauty and superiority to those things. The intent of our unnamed poet and Dr. Ruifz, then, is to argue for the evolution of a superior being rather than to make a case for phenotypical variations within the African family. This point is made obvious when writers who make this distinction emphasize "the strength and beauty of form" of the Creole, as opposed to "the savagery and ugliness" of the African.

The Narrative of John M'Donald

"The Curious History of a Black Man" (1833), or "The Narrative of John M'Donald,"[23] one of the first Trinidadian slave narrative, refutes the earlier McCallum depictions and those found in the unnamed poet above. In his own way, M'Donald (the subject of this narrative) releases himself from the narrowly constricting and constricted definition of what constitutes an African's humanity and speaks in his own voice. Because he is allowed to speak for himself, he can begin to reconstruct the outlines of an identity and counter the notions of savagery and bestiality that have been ascribed to his person.

"The Narrative of John M'Donald" chronicles the life of John M'Donald, a slave born in Grenada. Orphaned at an early age, he received his freedom during the French Revolution and became a domestic servant of Colonel M'Donald, from whom he evidently took his name and whom he accompanied to St. Lucia, Puerto Rico, Jamaica, Honduras, the Bahamas, Holland, Prussia, and India. John M'Donald also accompanied Sir Ralph Abercromby to Egypt and served under the Duke of Wellington and Sir John Moore, "a thirty-shillings-a-day military governor in the West Indies," as V. S. Naipaul calls him. [24] After his travels in the Caribbean, Europe, and Asia, M'Donald decided to return to Grenada to see if any members of his family were still alive. In doing so, he sought to prove that he possessed the human feelings that many of his adversaries claimed that he lacked:

> [A]lthough it has always been the aim of the slavers to try and convince the British people that we are vile and ungrateful, and more like brutes than any thing else, in order that they may work us as they do like beasts of burden, and rob us of our daily labour; yet a black possesses as correct a feeling of God, and is blessed with a heart as alive to acts of charity, as the unlettered white man of his class; and I challenge any slaver, atheist, or whatever he may be, to disprove this fact.[25]

---

23. For the purposes of this study and in keeping with generally accepted appellation, I call this work "The Narrative of John M'Donald."

24. V. S. Naipaul, *The Loss of El Dorado: A History* (London: Andre Deutsch, 1969), p. 131.

25. Studholme Hodgson, *Truths from the West Indies* (London: William Ball, 1838), p. 175. Hereafter, reference to this work will be noted as *Truths*.

Such sentiments, differ little from those of Mary Prince who, two years earlier, expressed similar thoughts, as she too sought to illustrate her humanity and to criticize the negative propaganda of the proslavery parties in Britain.[26]

Grenada was not as hospitable to M'Donald on his arrival as he had hoped. After remaining in the island for three months, he was apprehended as a runaway and thrown in jail for three months until his owner was found. Since he had no owner—he was a free man—he languished in prison, was sold to recover his "jail expenses," and purchased by Francis Robinson, a trader in goods from Grenada to Trinidad. Robinson eventually took M'Donald to Trinidad

In Trinidad, things did not work out well for M'Donald. When Robinson died, M'Donald was sold to John Dawson Parke, who being second in a fatal duel, had his property confiscated. The consequences were dire for M'Donald:

> His brother Benjamin Parke, took me to his house, but always told me I was as free as he was. He died two years afterwards, and I then was free by having no master; and remained so for three years. One Mr. Perry, who is now here, then sent a policeman for me, and put me into jail; and I was sold by Mr. Jones, the Escribano, for a debt due to Captain Percy (about 250 dollars) by Mr. Dawson Parke, contracted in America. A Guinea negress, called Zabet, bought me. And here am I, free by rights so many times, who have often conversed with, and waited on, the lamented Mr. Wilberforce, at Greenwich, the servant of Colonel M'Donald. I, the English soldier, and wounded in the service of England. Here am I, the slave of a French African! (*Truths,* p. 178)

Having previously tasted the sweetness of liberty and after having seen so much of the world, M'Donald had much to lament. Although he tried to claim his liberty in Trinidad, he was told he "had no proofs" (*Truths,* p. 178) of it. When he and other slaves complained to the authorities about the cruelty of their masters, they were "sent back with a pass, which we think is an order for our oppressor to give an account of his conduct, but as soon as we arrive we are put into the iron stocks, and then flogged on the following day by order of the commandant. If we again complain, we are told that the commandant did perfectly right, as we had no business to come away without a pass, when it is notorious the slavers always refuse us passes" (*Truths,* pp. 179–80). In the end, M'Donald won his freedom after he petitioned and was assisted by the colonial secretary of the island.

M'Donald is aware of the intricacy of the system. He knows that the planter class controls the society and that little can be done about their power. This realization does not prevent him and others from challenging the evil perpetrated against them, but as a consequence, they are placed on the treadmill, flogged, and beaten at will. "The masters," he says, "gratify their rage with impunity, and there are many of us who have carried bruises and cuts upon our bodies, which have been

26. Mary Prince, *The History of Mary Prince, a West Indian Slave* (London: F. Westley and A. H. Davis, 1831).

refused as evidence" (*Truths*, p. 181). Despite the fact that some of the whites protest the cruelty against the slaves—even free men who were arbitrarily cast back into slavery—the barbarity against them continued. According to M'Donald, the slaves' condition was compounded by the impending freedom of the Negro: "Since our oppressors know that we are to be half-free in August next, their rage, which always falls on our bodies, knows no bounds. Oh, if I could describe all the miseries I have seen and endured in Trinidad!—but it would take up too much time" (*Truths*, p. 182). The narrative ends with M'Donald pleading with Studholme Hodgson to help him escape "this accursed restraint, by which I am robbed of my labour as if I were a felon in jail! Do help a poor creature, suffering the ignominious and cruel yoke of slavery, and God will reward you in the other world, and I will pray for you in this" (*Truths*, p. 182).

There is little reason to deny the truth of this narrative since a similar narrative told by James Williams of Jamaica a year after emancipation (1835) was corroborated fully by an English commission that visited that island.[27] The one element that remains worthy of discussion is *how* Hodgson, acting as amanuensis, captured the truth of M'Donald's story. In recording the latter's story, Hodgson tried to be as accurate as possible. He notes that "[a]lmost the very words of the poor fellow are here given" (*Truths*, p. 173). As if to give greater emphasis to his role as amanuensis, at the end of the text, Hodgson writes that "[s]uch is the plain, unvarnished tale of John M'Donald, a black; the observations and reasonings are altogether his own. I might have rendered them more interesting by placing the incidents in a connected form, and by translating them into the negro idiom, but I did not wish to have recourse to what might seem an artifice to gain attention" (*Truths*, p. 180). Continuing, Hodgson says that he "repeatedly conversed with, and cross-examined [M'Donald] in the strictest manner, without the power of detecting any discrepancies in his statements" (*Truths*, p. 173).

In recording/transcribing M'Donald's narrative, Hodgson acted in a manner consistent with that of Susana Strickland who transcribed both *The History of Mary Prince* and *The Narrative of Ashton Warner*, two early Caribbean slave narratives.[28] Like Hodgson, Strickland assures us that she tried to be faithful to the subject's language and sentiments. In Warner's case, she notes that she "adhered strictly to the simple facts, adopting, wherever it could conveniently be done, his own language, which, for a person in his condition, is remarkably expressive and appropri-

27. James Williams, *A Narrative of Events since the 1st of August, 1834, by James Williams together with the Evidence taken under a Commission appointed by the Colonial Office.* (London: Central Emancipation Committee [sold by G. Wightoman], 1838.) As the commissioners, Messrs. George Gordon and J. Daughtrey, wrote on October 21, 1837, in their letter to Sir Lionel Smith, "[i]n reporting the general results of this extended inquiry, it has become the duty of the commissioners to state, that the allegations of James Williams's Narrative have received few inconsiderable contradictions, whilst every material fact has been supported and corroborated by an almost unbroken chain of convincing testimony" (p. 14).
28. See Selwyn R. Cudjoe's *Caribbean Slave Narrative* for a discussion of these works.

ate."[29] Although Hodgson did not feel it necessary to adhere to M'Donald's "negro idiom," the evidence suggests that he remained faithful to M'Donald's sentiments.

In following the patterns established by other Caribbean slave narratives, most of which were transcribed during the same period, "The Narrative of John M'Donald" demonstrates a link with the emerging patterns of literary expressions among Africans in the Caribbean. Although M'Donald's account is not as extensive or as detailed as the other narratives in the tradition, it suggests that many Africans told their stories, even though few of these tales remain for the eyes of their descendants. Like *Free Mulatto*, "The Narrative of John M'Donald" opens up the horizons of our literary landscape and suggests an alternative way of viewing the world.

Petitions

The many petitions that Africans submitted to those in authority also augment the written tradition of Trinidad and Tobago literature. Analogous to the memorials, addresses, and orations of the mulattoes and the diary and letter writing of the whites, the petitions marked another dimension of literary activity among the Africans.[30] If as Boehmer notes, "[e]mpire was itself, at least in part a textual exercise,"[31] the response of the colonial/slave involved a form of textuality. Individually and collectively, Africans used the petition as an instrument to appeal to the officials about their condition. As a result, between 1800 and 1838, Africans submitted innumerable petitions to the governors and, in extreme circumstances, to the secretary of state for the colonies, to plead for their freedom.

Significantly, an extremely large number of petitions were written on behalf of women of whom their masters took especial advantage after the law prohibiting the whipping of female slaves was passed prior to abolition. One of the most riveting examples of this type of petition was that of Veronique, a cripple. Written by Veronique's mother, Marie Jeanne, to Lieutenant-Governor Sir George Hill, the petition reads as follows:

> Four years ago, Veronique was abandoned by her master, Toussaint Leroux, because he thought her worthless as a slave and past work, owing to general debility and an ulcerous habit of body, occasioned by the hardships she had suffered. She sought an asylum with a discharged African soldier, named Hunt, by whose care she partially recovered, with the loss, however, of the greater part of one of her feet. Toussaint

29. Aston Warner, *Negro Slavery described by a Negro, being the Narrative of Ashton Warner, a Native of St. Vincent's* (London: Samuel Maunder, 1831), p. 13.

30. *Free Mulatto* resulted from the many petitions made to the colonial authorities. Carl Campbell writes that "[t]here is a sense in which *Free Mulatto* stands outside the mainstream of development; the free coloureds' case was based essentially on petitions; the November 1823 petition which came before the book [*Free Mulatto*], and the subsequent petitions which came after it. The investigation of the free coloureds' case by James Stephen Jr. was based on these petitions" (*Cedulants and Capitulants* [Port of Spain: Paria, 1992], p. 242).

31. Boehmer, *Colonial and Postcolonial Literature*, p. 12.

Leroux, hearing of this, arrested her. Being again badly treated, she ran away; and again arrested, was ordered to jail with one month's hard labour on the treadmill, on which I saw my poor child last Wednesday. I implore you not to let her, a cripple, a woman, be longer kept at it (*Truths*, pp. 353–54).

Although it is entirely possible that Marie Jeanne got someone to write this petition for her, the same was not the case for the Mandingo slaves who petitioned the secretary of state for the colonies for assistance to return to Africa. A proud people, the Mandingos always considered themselves spiritually free in spite of their physical enslavement.[32] They always had among them one or two priests who could read and write in Arabic, sought to maintain their African heritage, and kept themselves together through religious solidarity. Forming themselves into "a kind of self-help association,"[33] they also assisted one another to secure freedom. Therefore, it comes as no surprise that, after slavery was abolished and apprenticeship ended, these ex-slaves petitioned Her Majesty's government for their freedom.

The first significant thing about their petition is that the Mandingos themselves composed it. Second, they never refer to themselves as slaves. They always call themselves "natives of Africa and of the Nation or Tribe called Mandingo." Third, they reiterate the evil consequences of slavery by noting that, during the slave trade, they "were torn from their beloved Country, their friends and relations, delivered into the hands of Slave Merchants, who imported Your Memorialists into the West Indies and sold them as Slaves." Fourth, before slavery ended, the Mandingos "had long before unfettered themselves, their tribe and their families, by the fruits of their joint and industrious efforts."[34] All this group requested of the British government was transportation to Africa. From that point on, the Mandingos would *be* on their own and would *find* their people. Predictably, the British government never granted their wish. Instead, they were left in a foreign land (Trinidad) to flounder.

Another member of the Mandingo nation who also petitioned the governor for his freedom was Slamank, an eighty-five year old Mahomedan priest. His story is as touching as that of Veronique:

That he was thirty-five years of age when he was sold into slavery; and notwith-standing his sacred profession, has been forced to labour in the fields, and undergo the sufferings and degradation of slavery for fifty years.

That all his family has been separated from him in his old age, his children from time to time have been sold; and that he now remains alone on the Marli estate without family or friend.

That on the 1st August, 1834, the petitioner, then eighty four years old, was told

32. Apart from the two examples noted in this text, the example of Sayeb, a "Mahomedan" Mandingo, cited in volume one of Edward Joseph's *Warner Arundell*, speaks to the intelligence, dexterity, and principles of this group of people. See appendix 1, pp. 78–82.

33. Brereton, Bridget, *A History of Modern Trinidad, 1783–1962*. (Port of Spain: Heinemann, 1962), p. 68.

34. This petition is contained in Gertrude Carmichael, *The History of the West Indian Islands of Trinidad and Tobago, 1498–1900* (London: Alvin Redman, 1961), pp. 414–16.

that the King had made him free, but that he must still be an apprentice to learn the same trade of digging cane which he had been practising for fifty years.

The petitioner, whose blood had warmed at the prospect of enjoying freedom, even for the last few days of his wretched existence, must now abandon hope of living to see the day of his redemption.

He implores your Excellency to allow him *to go free*. He was born free, and he wishes to die free. He renounces all claims to remuneration for fifty years' servitude. The Mandingo church in Port of Spain will support him (*Truths*, p. 358).

Hodgson, who heard Slamank recite the above was troubled by what he heard. Turning to the sympathy of his English readers, he dared anyone who "had read over the petition taken from the lips of the broken-hearted old man,…to find epithets, if there be any in our language strong enough, to do justice to that master who rendered that prayer necessary, or to that governor who, so far from deigning a reply to the appeal, suffered its author to drop into the grave a despairing slave!" (*Truths*, p. 152).

Slaves who had suffered much were finding outlets to express their feelings and to agitate for their liberty. These petitions also provided them with a vehicle to articulate an identity. In most instances, the predominant sentiment behind these petitions was the enormous pain these men and women felt on being separated from their families and their societies. Thus, M'Donald returned to the West Indies to seek his family, while the Mandingos wished to return to Africa to reintegrate themselves into their ethnic group and, where possible, into their individual families. At the end his earthly life, all Slamank wished was once more to feel the solidarity of and to bind himself into his holy church which, he was sure, "will support me for the few days I have yet to live" (*Truths*, p. 152). It is these words and letters of our ancestors that allow us one hundred and sixty four years after the end of slavery to enter into a lost world of courage and bravery.

The Role of the Press

As we study the literary space in which our ancestors acted during this early period of Trinbagonian development, it is instructive to examine, however briefly, the role the press played in the burgeoning desire of these natives to express themselves. At one level, the press provided the dominant class a means to engage in amateur literary activities by publishing a number of poems. Certain elements of the press also did its best to keep the infamous institution of slavery alive. Not only did this segment reveal a proslavery attitude, it blackmailed and ostracized anyone who spoke out against this monstrous system. Rather than expose the horrible and cruel aspects of slavery, the press tried its best to camouflage many of the institution's horrors. Those journalists who questioned the value of slavery were, as Hodgson points out, were in serious trouble:

Not very long since, the life of the editor of the *Jamaica Courant* was sought after with demoniac rage; the monstrous crime of which he had been guilty consisted in advocating emancipation; it was the same with Loving of Antigua, with Anderson of Trinidad, and many others of different islands. No journal advocating the cause of humanity can continue long. All advertisements are withheld from it—the merchants, or storekeepers, will not, at any price, supply paper—they will combine together on hearing that a vessel has arrived with some, and purchase up the whole, by which the editor is repeatedly forced either to put off his publication altogether, or to send it forth on the coarsest description of material (*Truths*, pp. 196–97)

The *Port of Spain Gazette*, which Hodgson calls "the vilest [journal] that ever disgraced the press of any country" (*Truths*, p. 198), acted on behalf of the planters and generally spat its venom on anyone who spoke of the virtues of emancipation. Throughout 1832–1833, as the planters' bitterness mounted against provisions that were designed to allow the slaves more freedoms, "the columns of the *Port of Spain Gazette* were filled with hysterical articles and letters."[35] Daphne Gloria Cuffie observes that, for many years the editor and proprietor of the *Port of Spain Gazette* was the government printery. Established in 1825, this newspaper served as the official organ of the government until 1833 when the *Trinidad Royal Gazette*, a four-page publication, began to appear twice weekly.[36] To circumvent the influence of the *Port of Spain Gazette*, Young Anderson, at great expense to himself, began an alternative journal. Hodgson writes that it was

[the] best conducted journal which for many years had appeared in the West Indies; and while he mildly but firmly exposed the wrongs of the negroes, he, at the same time, in treatises breathing the spirit of the purest benevolence, pointed out to the planters the line of proceeding, which, in the actual state of public feeling, it behooved them to adopt, whether as good men, or as *wise* men. As uselessly might he have spoken to the winds! Every form of abuse was lavished upon him, but he swerved not. Orators were brought into the lists against him—they quailed before the eloquence of truth. Disgusting pamphlets were circulated, the writers of which, whether the bloated dandy of Port of Spain, or the itinerant mountebank from Glasgow, alike groveled in the mire under his literary lash (*Truths*, pp. 202–203).

Such then was the literary landscape of the society as it faced a world without slavery and as a people reached beyond the narrow confines of their once-fettered lives. There was no instant outpouring of literary activity, but as Africans accustomed themselves to freedom and began to acquire the rudiments of "'riting and 'rithmetic," they began to express their feelings about varied aspects of their world. They examined different aspects of their culture to domesticate and control their world and to make it more meaningful to them. Because colonialism presumed an imaginative dimension, the colonized person relied on a semiotics of language that utilized the conative, the cognitive, and the representational, as well as the rhetori-

35. Brereton, *A History of Modern Trinidad*, p. 62.
36. See Daphne Gloria Cuffe, "Problems in the Teaching of English in the Island of Trinidad from 1797 to the Present Day" (MA Thesis, Institute of Education, University of London, 1963, p. 93).

cal, to respond to the colonizer's onslaught and to define his/her position, that is, his/her identity, vis-à-vis the colonizers' within the colonial space. In this endeavor, functional texts such as law reports, journalistic articles, and ethnographic and anthropological writings played as important a part as poems, novels, and dramas in clearing a space to express and chart the imaginative landscape of the society.

CHAPTER 4

The Textuality of Colonialism

The fact is, our bondsman, unless it is for himself, works like a slave—
that is to say, most indolently: when he diverts himself, he feels, for the
moment, that he is free. By looking at the very slave's walk, one
acquainted with them knows if they are walking on their own master's
business, or their own.

—E. L. JOSEPH, *Warner Arundell*

To name a foreign land, to make of that land and its ways a textual arti-
fact, was to exercise mastery.

—ELLEKE BOEHMER, *Colonial and Post Colonial Literature*

Much remains to be learned about the extent to which Creoles, from
the Americas, Africa, or Asia, participated in the dialogues that gave
rise to both colonialist and anti-colonialist doctrines, not just in the
eighteenth century, but from the beginnings of the European colo-
nialisms that produced them.

—MARY LOUISE PRATT, *Imperial Eyes*

Emancipation and its Aftermath

The physical emancipation of Africans in 1838 (when apprenticeship terminat-
ed) did not end racial prejudice or, for that matter, diminish the negative stereotyping of the Negro by most Europeans. For many of the latter, it presaged a return
to barbarism.[1] William Wilberforce seemed prophetic when, in 1823, he remarked

---

1. Leaving Trinidad on the eve of emancipation, A. C. Carmichael, the wife of an English planter
observed that "[w]e had now determined upon returning to Europe, there seemed to be no longer any
rational prospect for doing good, in any sense of the word; the toil became insupportable, where the best
intended efforts all failed, either for improvement of the people, or the benefit of the estate. We felt that
the really important influence of the proprietor was gone; that even personal security was in danger; and
in fine, that there was no longer any incentive to remain. There were some good and faithful
negroes,...but in the event of any rising, their numbers could have been of no avail...the certainty that
we were no longer safe, and were no longer able to effect any good, determined us to leave" (*Domestic
Manners and Social Condition of White, Coloured, and Negro Population of the West Indies, Vol. 2* [London:
Whittaker, Treacher, 1834], pp. 334–35).

that, although "the old prejudice, that the Negroes are creatures of inferior nature, is no longer maintained in terms, there is yet too much reason to fear that all latent impression arising from it still continues practically to operate in the colonies."[2] Despite the process of emancipation generating considerable discussion about the advantages of free over slave labor, the colonial authorities sought to maintain the notion of white supremacy through the educational system, particularly through the deployment of literary images.[3] Even though colonialism is primarily an economic and military affair, it still did much to promote racial stereotypes and ideas of white dominance via the literature of the period. Elleke Boehmer, a literary theorist, has noted that colonialism, a textual and symbolic enterprise, "also involved an act of the imagination" and relied on "energizing ideas and propaganda" to promote the imperial ideal.[4] Literary texts, therefore, were an integral part of the colonial enterprise.

Significantly, the social development of Trinidad and Tobago coincided very nearly with the opening up of Spanish America to European colonization, the rise of the British colonial empire (1837–1901), a transition from slave to wage labor, and a period in which the tenets of England's civilizing mission were codified. In 1884, an ardent defender of the colonial system argued that "the very existence of these colonies, as civilized communities, is dependent on the continuation of the sugar cultivation, for which they are particularly fitted...with the ruin of the sugar industry the European element will promptly disappear, and the great progress made of late by the emancipated classes will not only be stopped, but without the civilizing influence of European thought and European intelligence they will promptly retrograde."[5]

Although Trinidad consisted of many isolated communities, it was during this period (1838–1901) that the society formed itself into a distinct entity as it absorbed the various ethnic groups that came into the islands.[6] In this context, literary texts played an important part in shaping the consciousness of the society. Just as "literary texts helped sustain the colonial vision, giving reinforcement to an

2. Quoted in Walvin, *The Black Presence: A Documentary history of the Negro in England* (New York: Schocken, 1972), p. 30.

3. David Trotman sees 1838–1900 as a period in which the English struggled to maintain cultural hegemony over society and maintains that the latter struggle was linked to the labor demands of a plantation economy. See "The Struggle for Cultural Hegemony" in Trotman's *Crime in Trinidad* (Knoxville: University of Tennessee Press), 1986.

4. Boehmer, *Colonial and Postcolonial Literature*, p. 31. Boehmer writes that, in its heyday, the British Empire "was conceived and maintained in an array of writings—political treatise, diaries, acts and edits, administrative records and gazetteers, missionaries' reports, notebooks, memoirs, popular verse, government briefs, letters 'home' and letters back to settlers. The triple-decker novel and the best-selling adventure tale, both definitive Victorian genres, were infused with imperial ideas of race pride and national prowess" (p. 13).

5. Quoted in Trotman, *Crime in Trinidad*, p. 41.

6. Prior to the development of a proper road system, the implementation of a telegraph service, and the establishment of a railway system in the 1870s, Trinidad consisted of a number of isolated, self-contained communities. See William Burnley, *Observations on the Present Condition of the Island of Trinidad* (London: Longman, Brown, Green and Longmans, 1842) for a sense of the isolated nature of the society during the 1840s.

already insular colonial vision," the texts produced in the colonized world by colonized people served to articulate a concept of an evolving national self.[7] Thus, the various narratives (fictional, creative, and particularly journalistic)[8] produced in Trinidad and Tobago during the last sixty years of the nineteenth century exemplified how Trinidadians and Tobagonians imagined themselves as a people during that critical period of nation-making.[9] The functional, as well as creative, texts that arose in this period articulated an evolving national sensibility, asserted a people's humanity, combated negative racial stereotypes, and insisted on the humanity of colonized people.[10] To the degree that other immigrant groups became involved in the national story—as victims of negative stereotypes that served to portray them as inferior—they, too, had to come to terms with and rise above limiting and limited notions of self-definition. Such limits, among other things, suggested that colonialism involved "a transaction between cultures."[11] In other words, the views of each group—the colonizer and the colonized—were conditioned by the nature of their encounter, which too, was tempered by the internal dynamics of the society.

7. Although writers such as Boehmer and Griffiths, Tiffin, and others (see *The Empire Writes Back*) consider the early writings of the colonized that contested the imposed images of the colonizer as manifestations of postcolonial literature, I am more inclined to use the term colonial or national writings and will do so in this study.

8. One does not always appreciate the importance of newspapers in the formation of national consciousness (particularly in nineteenth-century Trinidad), the essentially fictive aspect of that process, and the role imagination plays in the creation of a national community. A Laventille resident who has never visited Barackpore (or vise versa) can only possess a sense of that community through an act of imagination. In this sense, reading a newspaper involves the employment of the fictive (a creative act) and the unconscious arrangement of ideas. As Benedict Anderson reasons, "[r]eading a newspaper is like reading a novel whose author has abandoned any thought of a coherent plot" (*Imagined Communities: Reflections on the Origin and Spread of Nationalism* [London: Verso, 1991], p. 33.) My grandfather who was born around 1870 and lived in Tacarigua, a village in Trinidad, visited Port of Spain, the capital of the island, once in his lifetime. He certainly relied on gossip and the newspaper to experience Trinidad in the most expansive sense of that team.

9. Benedict Anderson's thesis that nation-making always involves an imaginary leap is very useful in thinking of a society's development. Such a notion dramatizes the idea that a nation is more a symbolic formation than a natural essence. Thus, a nation exists in so far as its citizens experience that state via its varied print narratives. Needless, to say, as Anderson also adds, "radio made it possible to bypass print and summon into being an aural representation of the imagined community where the printed page scarcely penetrated." In terms of visual representation, television acted in a similar manner. Ibid., p. 57.

10. Anderson sees the novel and the newspaper as "the basic structure of two forms of imagining which first flowered in Europe in the eighteenth century" (Ibid. pp. 24–25). In Trinidad and Tobago, the newspaper played the primary role in the construction of national consciousness. The literature of Africans played an important part in countering negative stereotyping that were planted in the minds and emotions of Europeans. According to Walvin, not only did Olaudah Equiano's autobiography play a powerful role in counteracting negative stereotypes of Africans at the end of the eighteen century, but the works of Ignatius Sanchez and Ottobah Cugoano "contributed significantly towards the upsurge of abolitionist sentiment in the 1780s" (*The Black Presence*, p. 81).

11. Boehmer, *Colonial and Postcolonial Literatures*, p. 22. Between 1838 and 1867, 10,000 Africans, 2,500 Chinese, and 1,298 Portuguese settled on Trinidad. Between 1838 and 1917, 141,000 East Indians settled on the island.

Warner Arundell: A Creole at Home

In 1817, Edward Lanza Joseph (1792–1838), an Englishman, came to Trinidad on his way to join Simon Bolivar's forces that were fighting for independence in South America. In the end, Joseph did not fight with Bolivar, but instead, he remained in Trinidad for the rest of his life becoming one of the more prominent journalists and authors of his time. He edited the *Port of Spain Gazette* for a short while (about eight months); wrote and acted in various plays; authored *Warner Arundell: The Adventures of a Creole* (1838), a three-volume novel; and composed the *History of Trinidad* (1838), the first history of the island. Scholars Bridget Brereton, Rhonda Cobham, Mary Rimmer, and Lise Winer, who introduced *Warner Arundell* recently, observed that "Joseph frequently contributed articles to the local newspapers, usually 'sketches of West Indian society and manners'...[and] the British *Monthly Magazine*."[12] When he died, Joseph had spent an equal amount of time in England and Trinidad, but identified the latter as his "adopted country."[13]

A historical romance written in the form of a travel narrative, *Warner Arundell* is one of the earliest texts to appear at the beginning of the colonial era in the Anglophone Caribbean[14] and is one of the first textual acts in England's renewed strategy of dominance. Despite this intent, one can perceive the outlines of a national community within its formulations. The novel also reveals how the British felt toward the French advocacy of liberation in the Caribbean. Although the book's primary function was to promote white solidarity and to maintain European privilege within the reconfigured space of colonialism, it is also true that within its pages one begins to see the emergence of a distinctly Trinidadian society. *Warner Arundell* centers around the life of its title character—(one reviewer remarked that the novel was written in the form of an autobiography[15]).—Warner is descended from "one of the most ancient English families known in the West Indies" and the son of a mother who died while giving birth to him in Grenada in 1795 during

12. E.L. Joseph, *Warner Arundell: The Adventures of a Creole*, edited by Lise Winer (Barbados: University of the West Indies Press, 2001), p. xx. This work possesses a fine introduction to Joseph and his work.

13. Ibid., p. xxv.

14. *Warner Arundell* can be placed in the same genre of travel writings that includes such works as Francois Le Vaillant's *Voyages de F. Le Vailliant dans l'interieure de l'Afrique 1781–85* and John Stedman's *Narrative of a Five Years' Expedition Against Revolted Negroes of Surinam in Guiana* [1772–1777] that arose in the later eighteenth and early nineteenth centuries. However, Tobais Smollett's *The Adventures of Penegrine Pickle* (1751), a picaresque novel to which Joseph alludes, is the more important literary progenitor of *Warner Arundell*. Each novel uses a similar literary archetype (a young man launching out in life) and follows a similar ternary rhythm: loss of innocence, going through many ordeals, and the achievement of final happiness. The scholars who introduced the recent edition of *Warner Arundell* also argue that "The title of this original manuscript—*The Life, Adventures and Opinions of Warner Arundell, Esquire*—echoes that of Laurence Sterne's rambling novel, *The Life and Opinions of Tristram Shandy, Gentleman* (1759–67)" (*Warner Arundell* (2001), p. xxix).

15. "A Review of *Warner Arundell: The Adventures of a Creole*" *Trinidad Standard*, March 23, 1838. This review was republished from *The Metropolitan*, an English newspaper.

Fedon's Rebellion.[16]   Warner's adventures, one reviewer writes, actually "began before he was born, for his mother was carried up in the mountains by the insurgents of Grenada and died in giving birth to him in the midst of negroes, mulattoes and poor creoles who had adopted all the doctrines of the Jacobins and Sans Culottes at Paris."[17]   The romance ends in Trinidad when Warner marries Maria Josefa, a descendant of a noble Spanish Castilian family.

In this picaresque *tour d'horizon*, Africans, pirates, planters, West Indian doctors, magistrates, lawyers, merchants, Spanish dons, freedom fighters, South American Indians, monks, and missionaries inhabit a world shaped by incessant conflicts, especially the wars of liberation that took place in the Caribbean and in South America between 1795 and 1824. Seen through the eyes of an English Creole and written primarily for an English audience (the narrator frequently interrupts his text to explain the unfamiliar for these readers), the romance seeks to bring to the attention of the secretary of states for the colonies, "the many abuses in our West Indian Colonial System, which call loudly for correction."[18]   As an enlightened Creole,[19] Arundell thought it his duty "to mitigate the evils of slavery by punishing its abuses, without regard to what might be said or thought elsewhere" (*WA.*, I, p. 227). Although he presents himself as a benevolent slave master who condemns the system, Warner does not see fit to emancipate his slaves, for he feels they enjoy a better position under slavery than they would under free conditions:

It was a glorious day on both my plantations when I took charge of them [that is, the slaves]. Oxen were roasted, and the poor slaves wept with joy. Under the direction of Keen and Leech, they were overworked and ill-treated: under my father they were well off. I promised to follow up my parent's system, and I hope I have kept my word. I believe my people are as happy and contented as any labourers on earth. To have emancipated them before the glorious measure of general freedom was taken by the English nation, would not have served them so well as treating them humanely as bondsmen. I believe, had I offered freedom to any of my people prior to the general emancipation, the boon would not have been considered a favour (*WA.*, III, pp. 251–52).

16. *Warner Arundell: The Adventures of a Creole, Vol. 1* (London: Saunders and Otley, 1838), p. 1. Further references to this work will be as *WA.*, accompanied by the volume number. As his birth year implies, Warner Arundell was born in Grenada two years before Sir Ralph Abercromby captured Trinidad for the British. As it turned out, Abercromby also crushed Fedon's Rebellion in Grenada in June 1796 and set a reward for the capture of Julien Fedon who led the rebellion against the English on that island.

17. *Trinidad Standard*, March 23, 1838.

18. WA., I, Dedication page.

19. As a group, the Creoles emerge as problematic figures in the national liberation struggle in the Caribbean and South America. Although they sought independence from the colonial powers—France, England, Spain—they had little interest in freeing the African slave or the Amerindian peasant. As Anderson notes, "[e]ven if he was born within one week of this father's migration, the accident of birth in the Americas consigned him to subordination—even though in terms of language, religion, ancestry, or manners he was largely indistinguishable from the Spain-born Spaniard. There was nothing to be

In this romance, Joseph mixes various genres into a Caribbean literary calaloux. Writing within what Mary Louise Pratt calls the "contact zone," *Warner Arundell* explores the implications of the meeting of two disparate cultures as they grapple with different signifying practices.[20] Thus could the fictional editor of *Warner Arundell* argue that his narrative "is taken from a very voluminous manuscript, which partakes of the mixed nature of memoirs, a journal, an autobiography, and a collection of letters and essays" (*WA.*, I, p. vii). Travelling extensively in the Caribbean and South America, Warner sees that it is "necessary for him who would undertake to become the historian of this important revolution, to visit all the principal cities on the great South American continent; in order to inspect such few scattered records as were preserved during this most sanguinary civil war, and to consult with all the surviving chiefs who figured in the contest, whether living in the New World or in Europe" (*WA.*, I, p. viii).[21]

Although the objective of this text is to inform the secretary of state (and through him, the British public) of the conditions in the colonies, at its epistemological core it seeks to acquaint Europe with an exotic, non-European landscape, to compare the life of the freeborn European with that of the enslaved Caribbean person, and to reiterate the superiority of European civilization. Moreover, the romance is designed to soften the terrifying impact of slavery through the idealized love of Warner and Maria, through Arundell's embrace of his colored siblings—the result of his father's concubinage—and through the kindness he shows his slaves.

Warner is intent on maligning the motives and activities of anyone—for example, Julien Fedon, a colored person, or Victor Hughes, a colored official of the French Revolutionary Government, who proclaims the abolition of slavery in Guadeloupe—who challenges British rule in the Caribbean.[22] Staunchly British and anti-French in his attitude, Joseph promoted the English cause while he lived in Trinidad. Louis La Grenade, a mulatto who "threw the weight of his power into the scale of the British," is described as being "more sagacious" [*WA.*, p. 14] than

done about it: he was *irremediably* a Spaniard [or English] " (Anderson, *Imagined Communities,* pp. 57–58). Such ambivalence led to contradictory behaviors as we see in the case of Warner Arundell.

20. Mary Louise Pratt, *Imperial Eyes* (London: Routledge, 1992), p. 4. Pratt describes "contact zones" as "social spaces where disparate cultures meet, clash, and grapple with each other, often in highly asymmetrical relations of domination and subordination—like colonialism, slavery, or the aftermaths as they are lived out across the globe today" (p. 4).

21. At the time in which this romance is set, Trinidad was connected more centrally with the affairs of South America principally because it was still tied to the Spanish legal system and retained links with Venezuela. One critic points out that Venezuela was "the crucible of the creole independent movement in South America" (*Imperial Eyes,* p. 113). As most of these early accounts (including V. S. Naipaul's *The Loss of El Dorado*) assert, much of Trinidad's early political activity is connected with that of South America.

22. Victor Hugues, a mulatto, was public prosecutor at Rochefort during the Reign of Terror. According to J. W. Fortescue, "[h]e possessed...audacity and vigour as well as brutality, and as a leader of an excitable race such as the negroes was most formidable" (*A History of the British Army, Vol. 4* [London: Macmillan, 1915], p. 370.)

Fedon. A present day scholar who examined Fedon's Rebellion has written in con-siderable variance with Joseph. He describes La Grenade as an "assimilationist" who "had generally ingratiated himself with the [British] authorities."[23] Joseph also reflects a pro-British attitude in his *History of Trinidad*.[24]

There is another twist to Warner Arundell's story. As an English Creole born in the Caribbean, his mission was twofold: at the very moment he seeks to make the colonized world available to his European peers, he also reveals the heteroglos-sic nature of his undertaking. In order to heighten the "nationalist" aspect of his tale, it is interspersed with "creolisms" that he picks up while living in Trinidad and that he knows "will scarcely be understood on the other side of the Atlantic" (*WA.*, I, pp. xvii–xviii). Significantly, the author inscribes himself "E. L. Joseph of Trinidad" and represents himself as speaking a "'Creole French,' a lingo principally made up of corrupt French, but mixed with African, Spanish, and English words. However, this *patois* is the mother-tongue of about a million and a half people in this part of the world." This patois was also spoken by Europeans (certainly the buccaneers) "who had been long enough amongst the island" (*WA.*, I, p. 76). In pointing out to his readers the distinct language spoken by these people, Joseph is alerting them to the emergence of a national society that is forming during this period.

Opening up such a linguistic space allows Joseph to inundate his text with Creole expressions. In so doing, he deploys a repertoire of images that would come to signify Trinidadian society. Further, he also granted his readers "an insight into the mental habits and capabilities of the people who invented them."[25] As a creative text, *Warner Arundell* shows the evolution of a Creole language and culture—as its subtitle suggests—not so much "in terms of separateness or apartheid, but in terms of co-presence, interaction, interlocking understanding and practices…within rad-ically asymmetrical relations of power."[26] In other words, we can begin to see *Warner Arundell* as a colonialist text that takes account of the specificity of the island's emerging self.

In the first and third volumes of the novel, there are various descriptions of the island and of Trinidadians (and Caribbean peoples), detailing characteristics of the latter with which they would be associated as the society developed further. Moreover, Joseph's examination of the society grants us a unique vision of what it means to live in a contact zone and allows us to see the evolution of a society. The author's description of the sacredness with which the African male holds his moth-

23. Cox, *Free Coloreds in the Slave Societies of St. Kitts and Grenada*, p. 84.

24. Given the imaginative liberties he takes, Joseph's description of Daaga whom he interviewed after the latter's revolt in Trinidad in 1837 resides more in the realm of fiction than history. It is also interesting to compare Joseph's descriptions of Daaga and Fedon. See *History of Trinidad* (1838, London: F. Cass, 1970), pp. 259–72.

25. John Jacob Thomas, *The Theory and Practice of Creole Grammar* (London: New Beacon, 1989), p. 120.

26. Pratt, *Imperial Eyes*, p. 7.

er and how easily he is offended when his mother is insulted is emblematic of a kind of Trinidadian we have come to know over the years. Speaking of an encounter in Grenada between Cojo, a Coromantee, and Yoyo, another African character, the narrator notes that "[t]hirst of vengeance, and not treachery, caused the African thus prematurely to level his piece. 'Damn Yoyo,' muttered the negro, lowering his arm: 'me want for pay him, because he curse my mamma in Guinea, and call me black nigger-dog; Goromighty make black man first, white man after; but devil put it in a buckra man and nigger woman head to make (beget) mulatta bastard'" (*WA.*, I, pp. 19–20). After killing Yoyo in combat, Cojo exclaims with his last dying breath, "'Ah, ah! Yoyo, no go curse me mother again; me go." Here a slight tremor shook his frame, and he expired.'" (*WA.*, I, p. 21). This episode also demonstrates how the African saw himself in relation to the European and his colored brethren, a problem raised earlier in *Free Mulatto*.

In *Warner Arundell*, other aspects of Creole life and culture are also made available to an English audience. The West Indian's love of butting (celebrated in Ralph Ellison's *Invisible Man*),[27] a description of the calinda dance (stickfighting), the presence of African spirits ("the *jumby*), the wisdom of African proverbs ("I sell the story for the same price I bought it") are present in the text. Africans are described as becoming "blue vex," while local descriptions of flora, such as the sappotilla, calabashes, and cocoa-nut shells, give the book a Caribbean feel. There is also the familiar ring of a Bajan (a citizen of Barbados) who has no place "to cock up" his legs, the sarcastic remark of a mulatto servant who is taken to England ("This country cold for true; and everybody heart cold like the country" [*WA.*, II, p. 42]), and the sight of mate and crew "join[ing] in these 'skylarkings'" (*WA.*, II, p. 87) while they are on the sea.

Some of the descriptions in this romance are strongly visual and specific. For example, the narrator describes the local birds as he approached Trinidad's coast:

> As the sun arose I saw a flight of more than ten thousand flamingoes winging their way from Trinidad to the Spanish main, having the appearance of a triangular body of fire, as they majestically flew over our vessel.
>
> To this succeeded flights of millions of the parrot tribe, varying in size, from the seven-coloured parroquet, about the dimensions of a lark, to the large and gaudy macaw (*WA.*, I, p. 143).

As Warner comes closer to the shore, he describes a sight that would be explicitly related Trinidad and that would define the island for much of its modern history:

> By means of a telescope, I was enabled to see thousands of brilliant hummingbirds, the appearance of whose waving, ruby, topaz, and golden plumage, and grace-

---

27. After a fight aboard the Saucy Jack, a whaler that was taking Arundell and others to the Caribbean, Warner says that he butted a shipmate "until his 'human face divine' was, as the Barbadians say, 'mashed up like a sour sop.'" (*WA.*, II, p. 87).

ful forms, delighted my youthful eye. Here, the humming-birds are so numerous, and so beautiful, as to justify the original name which the aborigines gave to this island; and by which it is still known, by their few descendants, who yet inhabit the isle of their fathers: I mean 'Iere,' that is to say, island of the humming-bird (*WA.*, I, pp. 143–44)

When Arundell lands in Port of Spain, he offers a description of the interior of the island:

We now approached town; and the apertures between the mountains, which form the beautiful valleys of Cuesa, and Diego Martin, relieved the sameness of the hills, which bounded the view from the gulf. The sombreness of the virgin forest was here and there contrasted by the cultivation of man; and the dense woods themselves assumed a smiling aspect; for, amid the waving expanse of dark foliage, here and there blossomed the ponij [could this be the poui], a tree as tall as any which Europe produces, and the flowers of which are of most brilliant golden hue; while below, rows of majestic 'bois-immortelles,' with their deep rose-coloured foliage, glowed like fire, as the sun shone on them: these gave a grateful shade to the peasant alleys of cocoa. The scene was diversified with a hundred different kinds of palm, including the palmiste, or palmetto, which here rises at least fifty feet higher than do any I had seen in the other islands. Here and there I observed cane plantations, but these appeared to lack that neatness which the sugar estates have in Antigua; yet the canes of the latter place bear as great a resemblance, in point of size, to those of Trinidad, as a porpoise bears to a whale. Altogether, the prospect of the coast, sailing from the Bocas to Port of Spain, is the finest I ever beheld, or ever hope to view (*WA.*, I, p. 145).

These passages are among the earliest written descriptions that we have of the flora and fauna of the island. For the first time, the island is fictionalized and made available to the reader as the author names the sounds and sights that are associated specifically with the islands of Trinidad and Tobago.

Joseph also presents the rich texture of life in Port of Spain, as his narrator compares the latter with the drabness of London: "The bustle of this place astonished me; as did also the mixed hue and costume of the population, and the Babylonish varied of tongues" (*WA.*, I, p. 146). Because Warner possesses a "great facility in acquiring languages" (*WA.*, I, p. 152), he appreciates the languages spoken by the people in Port of Spain. According to him, their "dialects...were as mixed as their complexions and dresses. Chinese, corrupt Arabic, spoken by the Mandingo negroes; a hundred different vernaculars from Guinea; English, with its proper accent, and then with its creole drawl; Spanish, with its true Castilian pronunciation, as well as with the slight corruption with which the South American speak it; Creole French, European French, Corsican, various kinds of *patois*, German, and Italian, were all spoken in this town" (*WA.*, I, pp. 147–48).

In an interesting exchange between the captain of the Pickled Timber and Arundell, Joseph captures the cadence and syntax of black speech, even though he wishes to make fun of what then was called broken English, but what now is recognized as the emergence of another form of English:

> "Could I see the captain?" said I, as I got on board.
>
> "I *is* the captain," said a very good-looking, middle-aged black man. "I *is* the captain, at service."
>
> "Do you go to St. Kitt's and St. Thomas's?"
>
> "I *does*, please the Lard. Do you want a passage, sir?"
>
> "No, my friend: but I wish to know if you are acquainted with a man of colour in St. Christopher's called Rodney Arundell?"
>
> "To be sure I *does*, and all his fam'ly, brothers and sisters, and all: good people they *is*, too. I knowed the father from whom they *is* degenerated (he meant descended). They *is* as well to do as any brown people in the West Indies."
>
> "Thank God! thank God!," said I.
>
> "Why, Lard bless me, sir, sit down on the hen-coop, until the boy brings a chair. *Is* you relations to the Arundells?"
>
> "I am their brother."
>
> "You their brother! Are you the young gentleman that went away against their consent for to learn to be a doctor, but of who they could never find out what had become? For the Lard's sake, Mr. Arundell. Come with me to St. Kitt's; they'll all be *too* glad to see you. Your poor sister Jane is my oldest boy's godmother. Many a day has she come to my house, and cried until her heart was ready to break, because she did not know what had become of you. Why did you not write to them?"
>
> "I did, my good fellow; I wrote twenty times, but never got an answer" (*WA.*, III, pp. 94–96).

This is one of the earliest and more sustained examples of black speech in the development of a Creole language and literature.

Warner Arundell does more than make a non-European landscape available to Europeans, it also produces non-European subjects for a colonial audience. In so doing, it attempts to neutralize the behavior of colonized people by placing them in a timeless past and denying them any self-knowledge or historical consciousness. Such a strategy prevents Europeans from confronting the enormous crimes they had committed against colonized people, particularly at a time when Caribbean folks were stoutly resisting their advance.[28] Hence, the Maroon War in Jamaica in 1795 when Africans forced the English to sign a treaty with them is projected as arising merely from the "flogging of two maroons," while the "naked Indians" are presented as being "two thousand years in civilization behind the modern English"

---

28. For an example of Caribbean resistance around this period see Richard Price, *First Time: The Historical Vision of Afro-American People* (Baltimore: Johns Hopkins Press, 1983), on the Surinam maroons; C. L. R. James, *Black Jacobins* (New York: Vintage, 1963), for the Haitian maroons; and Mavis Campbell, *The Maroons of Jamaica, 1655–1796* (Granby, Mass.: Bergin & Garvey, 1988) for the Jamaican maroons; Cox for Fedon and others.

(WA., II, p. 220).[29] In like manner, Fedon's rebellion occurs because "the basest of white men...spit on me and called me a mulatto dog" (WA., I, p. 38).[30] Quashy, an African, joins the rebellion because Victor Hugues "take me from massa plantation, and tell me to fight for liberty and 'quality" (WA., I, p. 30).[31] Needless to say, the actions and abilities of characters such as Fedon who opposed slavery are presented as outlandish and despicable. Not only is he "destitute of courage and ordinary abilities," he is also seen as "the tool of the monster Victor Hugues" (WA., I, pp. 14, 27).[32] Africans, it seems, can have no volition of their own. They can only fight when Europeans tell them to do so or when they are violated personally by white persons.

Obviously such absurd motivations do not explain the massive insurrections that were taking place simultaneously throughout the Windward Islands (Guadeloupe, Martinique, St. Vincent, St. Lucia, Grenada, and Dominica), Jamaica, and Haiti between 1794 and 1796 nor the gallantry of African freedom fighters in these battles. Between 1794 and 1796, over 36,000 British soldiers were killed in the West Indies. More than personal slights were at stake in this massive conflict.

In St. Lucia, Africans displayed "a coolness and intrepidity" in the face of British assaults.[33] In St. Vincent, "[British] soldiers, who a few months earlier had shown the greatest gallantry, now refused to face the enemy."[34] To put it another way, the

29. Of course, Joseph puts it more felicitously in his text. He writes that "[t]he last Maroon war in Jamaica, in 1795–6, which kept, for eighteen months, that island in a state of alarm, and cost one million in sterling, arose from flogging two Maroons. Had they been shot, their comrades would not have noticed it." Contrasted with the British and their finer sensibility, he continues: "We all know that in the British army flogging is absolutely necessary for the maintenance of its morality and discipline...but savages conceive that flogging is fit only for dogs and slaves" (*WA.*, I, p. 220) The "we" he addresses is, of course, his English compatriots who, in this context, are the civilized, while the Africans are the savages and slaves.

30. See Cox, *The Free Coloreds in the Slave Societies of St. Kitts and Grenada,* pp. 80–88 for an explication of the cause of Fedon's Rebellion.

31. Because Victor Hugues was mulatto, Joseph distorted Hugues's motives and maligned him considerably. See J. W. Fortesque, *A History of the British Army, Vol. 4* [London: Macmillian, 1915], pp. 424–56, for a discussion of Hugues's activity in the British Caribbean.

32. Fedon's response to this despicable charge is important. Noting that he fought neither for revenge nor ambition, he acknowledged that he became the leader of the rebellion against the English because "I fought for liberty and equality; not as these words are, I find, understood by the hollow-hearted French, but I aimed at emancipating the slaves, although I myself possessed a valuable gang. I wished to make the negro respected despite his inky skin, to induce the mulatto to consider himself a man, although his brown complexion told him he was the son of the tyrannical white man. Yes, Arundell, when I reflect on the myriads brought from Africa, and sacrificed in these islands to European greediness, I sigh when I recollect that I have not in my veins the pure blood of the naked and savage African. Look on these lovely islands: did the Supreme Creator bid them raise their verdant heads from the Atlantic that they should be made altars whereon that insatiate devil, European avarice, should sacrifice millions of the dark children of Guinea, after having immolated the whole race of Indians" (*WA.*, I, p. 39)? Noble as these sentiments are, we hear nothing more from Fedon than his maniac ravings in the last volume of the *Warner Arundell.* Needless to say, the implications of Fedon's sentiments are not worked out in the text. Maxwell Philip also alludes to these notions in *Emmanuel Appadocca.*

33. Fortescue, *A History of the British Army,* p. 435.

34. Ibid., p. 446.

Africans had the English busy during that period. Enslaved men fighting for their freedom are always a more formidable force than soldiers who battle solely for "prize-money." Eventually, in order to secure their position, the British were forced to raise African troops, such as the Second West India Regiment, which fought its first battle in 1796. In Dominica, the British "owed its salvation simply to the loyalty of the slaves."[35] It was only the arrival reinforcements led by Sir Ralph Abercromby in 1796 that saved British control of the Windward Islands.

Similarly, in *Warner Arundell,* South Americans peasants are presented as beings bereft of civilization and without any sense of historical consciousness. In spite of the fact that the Incas, Aztecs, and Mayas achieved civilizations unparalleled in Europe and in spite of the kindness of South American inhabitants and their ability to create a tolerable existence for themselves, *Warner Arundell* offers a picture of a land unfit for human habitation. Thus, in speaking of a South American *hato,* a breeding farm, he writes:

> What a beautiful place is a South American hato! With its flocks of wild dark-bay horses, each squadron led by its captain; its immense droves of horned cattle; its general appearance of plenty, content, and, I had almost said, happiness: but happiness is not merely the absence of misery; it is a positive, not a negative enjoyment. Man was not made to live in the wild seclusion of a South American hato; the inhabitants of which, having little to think of, seemed to think of nothing [in anticipation of Naipaul]. The poor woman who owned the place appeared scarcely able to command sufficient words, in her native language, to express limited ideas (*WA.,* II, p. 268).

South America's sin is that it is not England. To Arundell, it is inconceivable to accept a way of life in which people are sparse in their speech and, perhaps, more reflective in their thinking. Although he does not (cannot) fully understand the language of a woman he encounters, he knows, that is, speaks authoritatively, that she is unable to possess a sufficiently large vocabulary and that she lacks the capacity to think as expansively as a European. Hence, the limited nature of her ideas. (These notions will be later expanded upon by the Froudes and the Naipauls.) Although this South American woman's only saving grace is her kindness ("She, however, was most kind to us" [*WA.,* II, p. 268])—a trifle to be tolerated and perhaps awarded a few points on the scale of human achievement—it cannot be considered a serious accomplishment in the scheme of civilized development. No wonder, Warner is so surprised when she declines his offer of money in exchange for the kindness she has rendered him. He remarks that she was "most thankful for five or six charges of powder, which we gave her. She thought herself overpaid." Arundell suggests that a culture that cherishes equal exchanges is a thing of the past, and in time, such a society, he argues, must be conquered by colonial-capitalism:

---

35. Ibid., p. 450.

The time has arrived when battles are to be decided on the Exchange. Believe me, the small bunch of keys in the hands of Rothschild is more potent than the legions of the despot. While Napoleon warred against the bigoted sovereigns of continental Europe, his military genius prevailed; but when, maddened by revenge against England, he attempted to war on commerce, civilisation rose against him, and he fell. His ruin was more owing to his frantic Berlin decree than the swords of Russia, his reverses at Leipzig, or his defeat at Waterloo (*WA.*, III, p. 3)

A Creole Abroad

Warner Arundell is also concerned with what can be called the backward glance. In addition to telling the English about Trinidad, Warner wishes to describe London to his fellow-colonists who have never had the opportunity to visit the mother country. He warns his readers that his narrative (at least, this part of it) will not be like *Domestic Manners and Social Condition of the White, Coloured, and Negro Population of the West Indies,* an apology of slavery that A. C. Carmichael, the wife of an English planter who lived in the West Indies for five years, published about the negroes of St. Vincent and Trinidad in 1833.[36] Rather, Arundell says, his narrative will be "A Creole's Notion of 'Home.'" The final word of this title is italicized to suggest a Creole's sojourn abroad, but not really in a foreign land, but in a country in which he feels at home and that has provided him all his virtues and the means by which to value his achievements. Indeed, Warner's every sentiment is filled with what he considers the proper/appropriate manner for an Englishman to behave under every circumstance.

To Arundell, then, London is a place to be adored and admired. His first act consists in contrasting the city with the tropical Caribbean he left behind:

I found myself, during my journey, in a new world: the climate, the lofty houses, with glass windows, and chimneys; the immense population; the total absence of black, coloured, and Indian people; the rosy looks of the women, so different from the languid and lily complexions of my fair countrywomen; the ruddy appearance of the children; the masculine, and often corpulent, figures of the gentlemen; the clownish aspects of the country people, with their smockfrocks, worsted stockings, and ponderous laceboots; the immense size and fatness of the horned cattle; the noble figures of the horses; the sheep, clad in thick wooly coats, so different from the light hairy jackets in which Nature has arrayed the sheep of the Caribbean Islands; the endless variety of the costume of all the people I met, so different from the eternal white jackets and trousers of the Antilles; the dissimilarity of the feathered tribe; the absence of palms of a tropical climate, and the total difference of all vegetable nature—for not a tree, shrub, fruit, legume, leaf, flower, nor even blade of grass, was exactly like aught I ever beheld,—all, all I saw made me feel as though I was transported into another planet (*WA.*, II, pp. 1–2).

36. In the third volume of his work, Arundell also comments on Dauxion-Lavaysse's book "firstly, because it was a well-written work; secondly, because I had lately passed through the countries described; and, lastly, because in the course of my travels, I had met with the author" (*WA.*, III, pp. 7–8).

Even the English landscape suggests differences between the two cultures:

> Towns, villages, farms, and cottages, sprang up before my eyes in endless variety.
> True it is, that, in England, I looked in vain for the noble mountains and deep val-
> leys of the West Indies, or the more stupendous scenery of South America; but,
> instead, I viewed a country *rendered pre-eminently beautiful by cultivation,* where
> every hut and rustic gate seemed to me to be placed to increase the picturesque
> effect of the landscape (*WA.*, II, p. 3).

London is cultivated in a way that the Caribbean and South America are not.
The former has been made virtuous by the hands of men and women, whereas the
latter remains virgin territory to be explored.   England is "a land of freedom."
Arundell is further impressed by "the civility of the hostess, the activity and intelligence of the servants" and rejoices at the superiority of free over slave labor.

Disputing the effect of climate on behavior, offered often as the reason for the
laziness of the slave, Arundell argues that the slave's behavior can be explained by
the repugnance with which he holds forced labor:

> At a negro ball, the sable dancers use thrice as much exertion, and continue thrice
> as long, as any set of dancers in England? Notwithstanding the oppressive heat of
> the climate, a negro sportsman, when engaged in a pedestrian hunt in Trinidad,
> uses violent efforts from which an English fox-hunter would shrink. The fact is,
> our bondsmen, unless it is for himself, works like a slave—that is to say, most indo-
> lently: when he diverts himself, he feels, for the moment, that he is free. By look-
> ing at the very slave's walk, one acquainted with them knows that if they are walk-
> ing on their master's business, or their own (*WA.* II., p. 5).

The so-called laziness of the slave masks his capacity to resist his enslavement.
To Warner's credit, he recognizes the slaves' possession of agency and common
sense.

Elaborating on this notion of agency and his capacity for humanity, Arundell
describes the charitable practices of West Indians as he compares their activities
with what he calls the "apparent want of charity in the people of England":

> Often I have witnessed acts of benevolence from persons in the colonies, who have
> a multiple of sins for their charity to cover. Many a wretched white man, when
> attacked at one and the same time by poverty and the yellow fever, has been suc-
> coured by poor mulatto women of the most unfortunate and degenerate descrip-
> tion; many a houseless white has been nursed into health by those women, or
> decently buried them, although the names even of the parties in whose behalf their
> has been exerted were unknown to them. It is remarkable that this has been the
> common practice of poor mulatto women since the earliest days of colonialisation
> in this part of the world, as we learn from the oldest Spanish historians of these
> islands. In the Antilles, even the poor slaves allows no child of want to solicit in
> vain, while he has the power of relieving him. Often had I seen sailors who had lost

their way up a West Indian colony, or who had been turned adrift for misconduct—often have I seen such feeding out of a calabash of the poor negroes (*WA.*, II, pp. 17–18).

Needless to say, such acts of benevolence demonstrate further that in spite of the condition of slavery, enslaved persons fashioned a culture that consisted of both sharing and giving.

While in Columbia, acting as a volunteer and surgeon in the South American Liberation Army, Arundell falls in love with Senorita Maria Josefa Ximenes, a seventeen-year old Spanish Creole. He, "a tall and handsome Englishman," is attracted to "her queenly form and noble features, in which seemed to be united the Castilian traits of romance with the indications of creole benevolence" (*WA.*, II, p. 237). Termed "the angel of mercy," she is also smitten by him. After a four-year separation, they are reunited in Port of Spain during the Carnival season when he returns the lost treasure of her grandfather. A few weeks later, on St. Joseph's Day, they are married. "Since that day, the current of my life has been too smooth, and my happiness has been too uniform, for a description of it to be interesting. Hence the creole, Warner Arundell, has no more adventure to recount" (*WA.*, III, p. 282). The romance ends of that note: the achievement of final happiness for our hero.

White Prestige and Colonial Resistance

Positioned as it is, at the beginning of the colonial phase of social development in the Caribbean, *Warner Arundell* serves to buttress many colonial claims about colonized societies. Although Joseph is careful to speak of the humane aspects of the slaves' behavior, his novel is intent on depicting Africans and Amerindians as lacking civilization, constantly in need of European guidance, and always solicitous of European concerns. At the very moment that black troops kill several black women who are paying their final respects to Arundell's mother, these same men, indifferent to their cold-blooded murder, "shed tears at seeing my father recognise the body of his wife" (*WA.*, I, p. 26). The suggestion seems to be that, while Africans can be sympathetic to the suffering of this noble English gentleman, they can find no tears for the African women they have just killed.

The novel also seeks to portray some of the masters as benevolent and kind. Although Bearwell Arundell has "absolute authority" over his slaves, he and Warner "were most affectionately attached" (*WA.*, I, p. 46) to the slaves who enjoyed an idyllic existence. Bearwell Arundell's plantation, it seems, is the quintessence of ease and kindness. The slaves of Warner's father "either hired themselves…[and] gave my father what they pleased out of their earnings; he scarcely took account of what his slaves paid him….Their time was chiefly spent in eating *wangoo* (boiled Indian corn-flour), fish, land-crabs, and yams; sleeping; beating the African drum,…dancing, quarrelling, and making love after their own peculiar mode, the notion of tender passion being very similar to that of Tom Pipes in 'Peregrine Pickle'" (*WA.*, I, p.

45).[37] Given such a paternal relationship with his slaves, there is no reason why Bearwell's Africans should ever want to be free. Indeed, three slaves whom he emancipates become even more attached to him.

However, it is in the idealized union between Warner and Maria that we see the invidious way in which Joseph attempts to negate the harsh realities of slavery and to obscure the sharp divisions in the emerging society. Without any ceremony, we are introduced to Bearwell's first family:

> We were half over [between Basseterre and Antigua] before I recollected that I had not read the letter. I broke the seal, and found it to be from one of my brothers; for it appears [as casual as that] I had five, and two sisters, of whose existence, up to that moment, I never heard. The fact was, that previous to my father's marriage he had a large family of coloured children: these, although neglected and looked down upon in consequence of having committed the sin of bearing a brown complexion, were, in every sense of the word, respectable (WA., I, p. 233).

In this amazing scene, we learn nothing of the black mother of these "brown" children, nor for that matter, is she even identified. She does not have a name, nor do we know what kind of relationship she enjoyed with Warner's father. Her common-law husband, it seems, was entirely indifferent to her needs since the family was "looked down upon" and did not enjoy the protection of his enormous power. After all, Bearwell went over to England and became a Member of Parliament to protect the interest of the dominant group—the sugar cane planters. However, this unknown woman, the mother of his seven children, is absolutely erased from history, whereas Warner's mother, the second wife of his old age, is portrayed as an angelic being. The former is recovered only to demonstrate Warner's kindness and generosity of spirit, hence his maudlin affectations:

> While reading this affecting and affectionate letter, I was obliged to pause repeatedly, in order to wipe away the first warm tears I had shed for many years. My kind brothers and sisters were offering to act as my parents, and yet addressing me in the humble style of slaves, fearing to give offence while they were inspiring me with gratitude (WA., I, pp. 234-35)

In other words, *the novel* asks us to sympathize with Arundell, to compliment him on his generosity, to recognize his large-heartedness, and to share in his abhorrence for "the abominable prejudice of the West Indies" that support "the accursed distinction…between members of the same family, whose complexion is different" (WA., I, p. 235). The English reviewer, who probably saw nothing unusual in Bearwell's behavior or Warner's conduct, utters not a word of remorse for or condemnation against Bearwell. We are asked only to look at what the reviewer calls Warner's "unusual condescension" towards his brothers and sisters:

---

37. See chapter five of volume one for a description of life on the Arundell plantation.

At St. Christopher, the hero met a host of full grown sisters and brothers, the children of his father before his marriage by a black housekeeper. Although Master Warner had been kept in ignorance of their existence, he received them on the footing of relations; and this *unusual condescension* awakens the liveliest affections and gratitude in the breasts of the poor brownies who lay all that they possessed in the world (and they are well to do in it) at the feet of their half brother. The whole of this passage may be particularly noticed as a happy blending of humour and pathos. It produces those smiles which are the sweeter from being mixed with a few natural tears. Warner though poor at times refuses to profit from these generous offers, and he sails to England.[38]

As far as the reviewer is concerned, "the poor brownies" should feel honored at having Warner acknowledge their relationship.

Such a textual strategy only seeks to neutralize Bearwell's concubinage and his complete indifference to his colored, common-law wife. Joseph is trying to blur the boundaries between the races (even though he must reconstruct them later on) so as to reinforce the color hierarchies upon which the slave system was based and through which colonialism maintained its hegemony. Whereas such promiscuity and exploitation of black women as Bearwell's was deemed acceptable during the eighteenth century, in the nineteenth century it was looked down upon and condemned by colonial officials. Governor Woodford noted that concubinage was "one of the moral failings...[that] lower the moral tone of the society."[39] In 1873, Sir Joseph Needham, chief justice of the island (1870–1885), thought it his "duty to reprobate in the strongest terms the practice on the part of managers and overseers [and owners] of cohabiting with female coolies [East Indian women], and to point out that amongst a jealous and susceptible people it sometimes led directly to the murder of the woman."[40] By glossing over Bearwell's "failing" and opting for the sanctity of holy matrimony, Joseph reaffirms the rightness of white superiority and thereby names this behavior as the proper conduct for a white gentleman in the age of colonialism. But, as Ann Stoler reminds us:

No description of European colonial communities fails to note the obsession with white prestige as a basic feature of colonial mentality. White prestige and its protection loom as the primary cause of a long list of otherwise inexplicable colonial postures, prejudice, fears, and violence. As we have seen, what upheld that prestige was not a constant; concubinage was socially lauded at one time and seen as a political menace at another. White prestige was a gloss for different intensities of racist practice, gender-specific and culturally coded. Although many accounts contend that white women brought an end to concubinage, its decline came with a much

38. *Trinidad Standard,* March 23, 1838 (my italics).

39. Quoted in Carl Campbell, "The Rebel Priest: Francis DeRidder and the Fight for Free Coloureds' Rights in Trinidad, 1825–32," *Journal of Caribbean History,* 15, p. 22.

40. Quoted in Trotman, *Crime in Trinidad,* p. 172. This conflict between the female East Indian indenture and the overseers becomes the central conflict in A. R. F. Webber's *Those that Be In Bondage* (1917, Wellesley: Calaloux, 1988).

wider shift in colonial relations along more radically segregated lines—in which the definitions of prestige shifted and in which Asian, creole, and European-born women were to play new roles.[41]

While Bearwell Arundell refused to acknowledge his concubine, Warner accepts and receives his colored brothers and sisters as equals. Just when the colonial order is threatened, it is saved with the union of the descendants of two distinguished Creole families as if to suggest that they are the legitimate heirs of the New World heritage. Through the nobility of their actions (the accomplished English gentleman and the estheticized and altruistic member of the Castilian race who served the wounded during the South American war of liberation), we are presented with what is supposedly the desirable conduct of Europeans who live in the colonial world. Necessarily then, the actions and abilities of such characters as Fedon who opposed slavery are presented as outlandish and despicable, whereas the behavior of colonized women is seen as loose and threatening, corrupters of the morals of Europeans.

In *Warner Arundell,* Joseph tries to soften the impact of the slave system, particularly on women, by exempting Bearwell Arundell from the condemnation of his colored offsprings for whom he took no responsibility. In *Emmanuel Appadocca,* Maxwell Philip takes an opposite position as he condemns his white father for abandoning his colored mother and mulatto son. The lineage of the idealized Maria Josefa contrasts with the bastard origins of the non-English women of African descent, and Maria's union with Warner is meant to discourage transracial relationships.

While it is true that slavery ended primarily because of economic reasons, the colonial authorities tried to justify their behavior on the grounds that they conducted their system in a benevolent manner. This is the dilemma in which the planters found themselves. As editor of the *Port of Spain Gazette,* the planters' journal and a supporter of slavery, Joseph had to justify the English enslavement of nonwhites by speaking of the relative kindness of a system of which he was a part. Needless to say, *Warner Arundell* can be read as a product of those conflicting and conflicted emotions.

This crucial period in English colonial history also demanded reinterpretation. It needed a narrative that could speak to English hegemony and control in ways that were neither threatening nor politically obvious. Casting the political as erotic and resolving such political uncertainties within the sphere of the family seemed an easy "non-political" way to address these concerns. Stoler notes that formulations to secure European rule during this period pushed in two directions: "on the one hand, away from ambiguous racial genres and open domestic arrangements, and on the other hand, toward an upgrading, homogenization, and a clearer delineation of

41. Ann Laura Stoler, "Carnal Knowledge and Imperial Power: Gender, Race, and Morality in Colonial Asia," In Micaela di Leonardo, ed., *Gender at the Crossroads of Knowledge: Feminist Anthropology in the Postmodern Era* (Berkeley: University of California Press, 1991), p. 63.

European standards; away from miscegenation towards white endogamy; away from concubinage toward family formation and legal marriage."[42] The seventeenth- and eighteenth-century Caribbean could have accepted concubinage and its consequence; nineteenth century Trinidad could not afford to do so. It is these pragmatic political concerns that *Warner Arundell* addresses in its romance.

As a journalist and amateur historian, Joseph found himself in an apt position to conduct this ideological work for his class. Because he was accustomed as a journalist to piling fact upon fact, it became even easier to pile adventure upon adventure as he navigated his way through the tortuous history of the Caribbean and South America. Yet, he never lost sight of the implicit moral reach of his endeavor and this is the most outstanding aspect of his novel.[43] And even though he was forced to inculcate—and perhaps show a new respect for—indigenous forms, Joseph's primary concern was the securing of English hegemony in the region in the age of colonialism via literary creativity. At a time when Europe was experimenting with new ways to control the subjects within her empires, literature proved to be an important ideological tool in the cultural and intellectual array of those armaments.

Indigenous Voices

As was typical of colonialism, both the colonizer and the colonized were trapped by the limits of his/her cultural framework. It stood to reason, therefore, that Joseph envisaged the unfolding colonial drama quite differently from that of a former slave who had to make his way in a new and different world. Each party had to establish an identity in a world in which assumptions were changing rapidly and in fundamental ways. Concomitant with such rapid transformation was the quest for voice and language that was reflected in the emanation of different literary expressions within the public (informal) and private (formal) spheres. Symbolically, Joseph ends his romance on the day Trinidad celebrates its annual Carnival, a gigantic masquerade ball of African and French origins:

> The day after this, our old friend, Moses Fernandez, arrived, and was overjoyed at my good fortune. He solicited, and obtained, a private interview with Senoritta Ximenes. The evening of this day, the town of Port of Spain seemed possessed with the demon of mirth. It was carnival, and in no part of the New World is the mummery of carnival kept up with such spirit and buffoonery as in Trinidad. Every one appeared in some kind of masquerade, from the man of wealth, who rode through the town richly clad in the dress of a Turk or grandee, to the ragged negro-boy, who covered his black face with a sheet of brown paper. I turned from the harmless but noisy mirth, and made for the quiet residence of Maria Josefa (*WA.*, III, p. 280).

42. Stoler, "Carnal Knowledge and Imperial Power," p. 74.

43. In speaking of Smollett's work, Paul-Gabriel Bouce notes that "the moral significance of the adventures lived through by Smollett's heroes does not lie at the end of the story; it runs through it, sustains it and underpins it all the time" (*The Novels of Tobais Smollett* [New York: Longman, 1976], p. 103). The same can be said of *Warner Arundell*.

Significantly, the last we see of Maria is her masquerading in the identical costume (or dress) she wore at the Casa del Rey of Alt Gracia where she met Warner for the first time and where they fell in love. Says Warner:

> I attempted to embrace her. She retreated into the back apartment, set down the lamp, and then placed herself at my side.
> "Sweet love," said I, "do you not wish to ride or walk about the town with me to see the maskers?"
> "No, dearest heart; I wish to remain here, and see and listen to you alone (*WA.*, III, p. 281.)

The carnival celebration was a major aspect of the nation's dramatic expression. At the formal level, the theatre seems to have taken hold in Port of Spain just as the slave era was coming to an end. Martin Banham, Errol Hill, and George Woodyard note that, between 1826 and 1831, five theatres existed in the city: three amateur theatre companies (two English and one French), one professional English touring company, and one professional French lyric company: "The amateurs played once a month, the professionals twice and three times a week."[44] Even at this early date, the theatre was associated with the Carnival celebrations. John Crowley writes that "[t]heatrical performances, under the Governor's license and patronage, also became popular. Pre-Shrovetide dramas were staged, such as 'The Tragedy of the Orphans' followed by the French Farce of 'George Daudin' advertised for performance at the Amateur Theatre, St. James Street on 21 February 1827."[45] Jose Bodu observes that the first dramatic performance in the island took place in 1828.[46] He memorialized this event by recalling a rather humorous incident associated with this play:

> During this year the first Amateur Dramatic Performance took place at the old Theatre in Pierre's house, later Police Station, which was highly successful, notwithstanding the fact that Mr L.____, one of the leading performers, had to rely on the prompter for his knowledge of his lines. These were simple and consisted in repeating "oh! ciel," with a look at the flies, "oh! terre," with a glance at the stage, "quelle

44. Martin Banham, Errol Hill, and George Woodyard, ed. *The Cambridge Guide to African and Caribbean Theatre* (Cambridge: Cambridge University Press, 1994), p. 225.

45. John Crowley, *Carnival, Camboulay and Calypso: Tradition in the Making* (Cambridge: Cambridge University Press, 1996), p. 42.

46. Loften Mitchell remarks that "[t]heatre in America was virtually nonexistent until the middle of the eighteenth century." The other Anglo-Caribbean countries seemed to be in better shape. Jamaica had a formal theatre in 1682; Barbados had an organized theatre by 1728; Antigua opened its first theatre in 1788; Guyana had its earliest performance in 1810; Grenada in 1828; and St. Lucia in 1832. The African Grove Theatre, spearheaded by James Hewlett, an Afro-Caribbean, was the first African American theatre company. It offered its first performance in 1821. Significantly, William Henry Brown's *The Drama of King Shotaway*, recognized as "the first black drama of the American theatre, has as its subject the 1795 Carib uprising against the British government on the island of St. Vincent." See Jonathan Dewberry, "The African Grove Theatre Company," *Black American Literature Forum*, 16, No. 2 (Winter 1982), pp. 128–31; Loften Mitchell, *Black Drama* (New York: Hawthorn Books, 1967), p. 14; Banham, Hill, and Woodyard, *The Cambridge Guide to African and Caribbean Theatre*, pp. 141–51.

immensité." The words were remembered with exactness, but the stage directions were reversed to the great delight of the audience. The prompter, enraged, exclaimed "L____, qu'est-ce que vous faites?" which were solemnly repeated, as was a supplementary "Tonnerre, L____, que vous étés bête." The prompter caused the unfortunate tragedian to be removed from the stage amid frantic applause.[47]

In his diary, Freidrich Urich recorded eleven plays performed in English and French that he saw in Port of Spain (St Ann's) and the Naparimas between 1830 and 1832. In fact, so entrenched was this activity among the upper echelon of the society that two performances were offered in August and September 1831 for the benefit of the victims of a Barbados hurricane. The first performance, put on by the whites, consisted of two comedies: "The Green-Eyed Monster" and "All the World's a Stage." The second performance was put on by the "creoles," by which I think Urich meant the mulattoes. The title of other plays put on during this early period were *No Song, No Supper, Postmortem Will, William Tell, Thresa*, and *Tom and Jerry*.

Some of the plays were warmly received, while others were thought to be frivolous. Yet, importantly enough, from as early as 1828, there was much formal drama in the society. Urich's descriptions of some of these plays are instructive. They are also the earliest known example of literary criticism in the society (even though a private exercise) and offer a valuable analysis (commentary) of these early works:

20th Jan., [1831]. Pollonais persuaded me to go to the theatre. There was a vaudeville show "Frontin Mari" and the opera "La Fête du village voisin." Music by Beaujeldieu was played. The music is pretty and the songs pleasant. The singers acted quite well but they are somewhat lacking in voices. This is also true of the ladies of the cast, but Madame Meyret is an exception, for she has a nice, well trained and fairly powerful voice. It is a pity though that she is not good looking, and that she does not act better and sing with more expression....

1st March, 1831. Christian takes us to the theatre. The play is: Werther on "Les égarements d'un coeur sensible" (The Mistakes of a Tender Heart)—a travesty. The piece is quite amusing but the jokes disgusting. Real French nastiness. It was followed by "Paroles de Sedaine", music by Gretry. It would be a nice piece if properly played for the music is pretty, but these singers massacre it. Christian is very restrained, and won't give any sign that might show that he regrets the money spent for the tickets....

30th July [1831]. Christian and Muller went to Naparima. I went to the theatre in the evening. "Amateurs et Acteurs" and "Lover's Vows" were presented. Miss Virginai for whose benefit both pieces were performed, received bouquets from Mademoiselle Shine. "Lovers Vows" is really a translation of Kotzbue's "Child of Love" and it does not amount to very much. The morals and most of the characters are bad. Some of the best and finest speeches are entirely spoilt by stupid and

---

47. Jose M. Bodu, *Trinidadiana* (Port of Spain: A. C. Blondel, 1890), p. 7.

ridiculous jokes by which the whole effect is lost. For example, the scene between Agatha and the country folk is wrecked by the inane remarks of the countryman's wife.[48]

During this same period, Joseph also wrote and produced several local plays that were performed by the Brunswick Amateurs. Messrs. Banham, Hill, and Woodyard add that he also translated German plays for local production.[49] His two outstanding musical farces were *Martial Law in Trinidad* (1832) and *Past and Present* (183?). Although the former was performed on December 15, 1832, presumably to a great reception, little is known about the production of the latter.[50] In *Martial Law in Trinidad*, Joseph "attempts to delineate Men and Manners which he daily beholds," playing on the absurd recourse to duels (the inherent manifestation of one's honor) that was so prevalent in the society of the time.[51]

At the informal or public level, another kind of popular theatre was taking place. In this period, we saw the rise of Carnival as a national dramatic expression within the society. In fact, it might have been the only public activity that transcended narrow village lines and involved the entire African (Creole) population in a common "national" activity. In his diary, Urich notes the performance of Carnival as early as 1831. He writes that "[w]e follow various masked bands. The dances are usually African dances, and the enthusiasm of the negroes and negresses amuse us very much, for these dances are stupendous."[52] Thus, by 1831, African people in Trinidad were involved in the Carnival celebration. By 1838, they seemed to have taken it over completely. Insulted by this African presence, a defender of the plantocracy observed:

> We will not dwell on all the disgusting and indecent scenes that were enacted in our Streets—we will not say how many we saw in a state so nearly approaching to nudity, as to outrage decency and shock modesty—we will not particularly describe the African custom of carrying a stuffed figure of a woman on a pole, which was followed by hundreds of negroes yelling out a savage Guinea song (we regret to say nine tenths of these people were Creoles)—we will not describe the ferocious fight between the 'Damas' and 'Wartloos' which resulted from this mummering—but we will say at once that the custom of keeping Carnival, by allowing the lower order of

48. Friedrich Urich, *The Urich Diary: Trinidad, 1830–1832, t*rans. Irene Urich and ed. Anthony de Verteuil (Port of Spain: Litho Press, 1995), pp. 39, 48, 77.

49. Banham, Hill, and Woodyard, *Cambridge Guide to African and Caribbean Theatre*, p. 225.

50. Performed on December 15, 1832, *Martial Law in Trinidad* was published on May 21, 1833.

51. *Martial Law in Trinidad: A Musical Farce in Two Acts* (1833). *This play* is not so much "a musical satire on the militia" (*Cambridge Guide to African and Caribbean Theatre*, p. 225), as Messrs Banham, Hill and Woodyard contend. It is more a satire that speaks to the folly of men who used the cover of martial law to practice the deathly game of dueling, which under normal circumstances, was prohibited. It is also reflective of the proclamation of martial law over the Christmas and New Years holidays to forestall slave insurrections, many of which were known to occur during this period.

52. Urich, *The Urich Diary,* p. 46.

society to run about the Streets in wretched masquerade, belongs to other days and ought to be abolished in our own.[53]

However the white population was prepared to interpret Carnival or the nature of the social order, the end of Apprenticeship on August 1, 1838, marked the beginning of another form of social relationship among the populace that was reflected in the literary accounts that manifested themselves in the next generation of writers, artists, and thinkers.

53. Quoted in Crowley, *Carnival, Camboulay and Calypso,* pp. 30–31.

CHAPTER 5

Jamettization of the Culture, 1838–1851[1]

I thus conceive the immediate thrust and counterhegemonic discourse on Black drama—the Afrocentric and the post-Afrocentric—as a refusal of subjection, of subjectivity imposed by the hegemonic Eurocentric discourse, a refusal to be Europe's civilization and silent Other.

Irrespective of the appropriateness or otherwise, or even the success or failure, of its specific strategies, the Afrocentric's quest for "authentically black" drama is a renunciation in part of what is perceived as an imposed identity, a crippling intellectual dependence on, or, in [Y.] Mudimbe's description, an undue "epistemological filiations" to, the West.

—Tejumola Olaniyan, *Scars of Conquest/Marks of Resistance*

I am the King of Dahomey, but I also rule over many countries that I have conquered. Do you now visit my dominions to offer your subjugation, or do you come as an enemy to dispute my rule.

—The chant of a Pierrot, a Carnival figure

Oju to wo gelede ti dopin iran (The eyes which have beheld gelede have seen the ultimate in drama.)

—Yoruba proverb.

The years 1838 through 1851 witnessed the emergence and subsequent articulation of the African presence in Trinidad. In 1838, according to Errol Hill,

1. Jamettization (from the French *diamètre*, the "other half") refers to a very lively underworld of Carnival characters that exploded in the 1870s. Energized by "the lower class" (which we now understand to be the substance of the society), these characters consisted of stickmen, singers, drummers, dancers, prostitutes (another meaning of *jamette*) bad johns, matadors (madames), *dunois* (*jamette* rowdies), *makos* (panders), obeahmen (practitioners of magic), and corner boys. This underground eruption of the culture represented a moment when the masses of people began to assume their original selves and asserted the integrity of their being. For women specifically, it meant the expression of female independence that was threatened by official society. Camboulay, or cane burning, the opening feature of the Carnival celebrations after slavery, became symbolic of the liberating possibilities of the people. The use of the flambeaux signaled the burning away of old slave ways, a purification of a corrupted past, and the illuminating light of the future. The title, "The Jamettization of the Culture," refers to that newly energized and enfranchised phase of the society, a process of adaptation and creolization of the culture.

"Suddenly, a new class of over 22,000 free men was created, allied to the free coloureds by racial ancestry, [yet] separated from them by the stigma of recent serf-dom."[2] With the emergence of this new class of people, the Carnival celebration, previously of French-Creole origins, took on a new dimension as Africans began to make their presence felt in the public arena. In a period in which the masked balls of the upper class, a holdover from the preslavery days, remained an important fea-ture of the Carnival celebrations, the immersion of Africans in this festival allowed them to release an energy and to display a sense of self that had not been possible previously. Even the use of masks (and masking), which they practiced/adopted after they took over Carnival, signified a commitment by the African to continue "the traditions of his predecessors" and to maintain "the reputation of his lineage."[3] Hill observes that it was the artillery masquerade band of 1834 mimicking "the best Militia Band that has ever been embodied in the West"[4] that represents the secular starting point for the postemancipation Carnival and reflected the determined efforts of a people to give its own signature to the Carnival celebration.

Carnival was also a time when the talents of native artists, poets, musicians, actors, dancers, and craftsmen were on display. For Africans, Carnival represented a time of reconnecting with their old societies and an opportunity to find their rhythm in a new social environment. Tejumola Olaniyan has observed that "the for-mer slaves, appropriating Carnival with their own forms, insisted on connectedness of histories by their cultural eclecticism, [while] the whites violently clung to dif-ference and purism, even at the cost of giving up and labeling inferior a form they had evidently enjoyed so much."[5]   R. P. M. Bertrand Cothonay, a French Dominican father who visited a Carenage parish in 1883, wrote in his journal:

I told you that the Trinidad blacks, particularly those in Carenage, are ex-slaves or sons of slaves. Following emancipation, which took place on August 1, 1833, they resolved annually to celebrate this day by a solemn festival for perpetual memory.

2. Errol Hill, *The Trinidad Carnival: Mandate for a National Theatre* (Austin: University of Texas Press, 1972), p. 9.

3. Onuora Enekwe, *Igbo Masks* (Lagos: Department of Culture, Federal Ministry of Information and Culture, 1987), p. 59. Masks, the heart of African culture, "represent the revelation of divinities and spirits to the world of men which at the same time is animated by a supernatural and metaphysical breath.....The aesthetic truth of the African mask puts art at the service of the sacred. The work of art is a tool, a system of drives to idealize the world. It allows men to make their imagination communicate while addressing the gods and things." Yacouba Konate, *Côte d'Ivorie Contrastes* (Abidjan: Edipresse, n.d.) Among the Yorubas, there are two types of masking traditions: the *Egungun* masks that honor the ancestors and the *Oro* masks that serve as an instrument of social control. Enekwe writes that "[t]he Egungun are associated with visual displays, including dancing and drama. They are therefore similar to Igbo masks" (Ibid, p. 59). Even as Africans in Trinidad donned their masks—from the ole mass of Jour Ouvert morning to the fancy sailors of Carnival Tuesday afternoon—they revealed an important aspect of their emotional lives, a specific connection to their African ancestry and hinted at a deeper spiritual level of their being.

4. Ibid., p. 23.

5. Tejumola Olaniyan, *Scars of Conquest/Masks of Resistance* (New York: Oxford University Press, 1995), p. 16.

FIGURE 5. Negro dancing and drumming. From Richard Bridgens, *West India Scenery with Illustrations of Negro Character* (1837).

The festival began at daybreak with a high mass, loud music, consecrated bread, a procession, etc. and it continued for three days during which, in the course of festivities, there were indescribable dances and orgies, reminiscent of African life."[6]

Essentially, Carnival tried to recreate, reassemble and resurrect an African way of life that the colonial authorities attempted to stifle during slavery.

Trinidad Carnival, however, was not merely a caricature of white society or the mere transformation of the French mardi gras. In the hands of Africans, Carnival turned out to be a festival in which the culture of the people gestated, became a stage where many talents were fused together, and turned into a springboard for exploring cultural heritage. Hill remarks:

The Ananase storyteller, for instance, sings, drums, and moves when reciting his folk tale; the calypsonian is actor and mime as well as singer and composer, often accompanying himself on his guitar and sometimes dancing in performance; the dead-wake observances include singing, competitive dancing, and rhetorical speechmaking. Accordingly, Carnival theatre exists not merely in recorded dialogue which is, however, to be found, but also in the presentation of characters in dramatic situations and confrontations, in conflict, in parody, in dumb show, in dance forms, and in songs.[7]

Elements of African oral literary tradition are inherent also in Carnival. Even

6. R. P. M. Bertrand Cothonay, *Trinidad: Journal d'un missionaire dominicain des antilles anglaises*, (Paris: Retaux et fils, 1893).p. 62.

7. Ibid., p. 4.

elements of the colonial culture are domesticated to suit local needs. In Jamaica, the slaves inculcated many foreign elements into the Christmas celebration. An English officer's son living in the West Indies during the 1820s quotes a Mr. Barclay about Christmas 1823:

> [In Jamaica I experienced] a novelty I had never before witnessed, in a rude representation of some passages of Richard III which they made sufficiently farcical. The Joncanoe men, disrobed of part of their paraphernalia, were the two heroes and fought, not for a kingdom but a queen, whom the victor carried off in triumph. Richard calling out 'a horse! a horse!' etc. was laughable enough....How the Negroes had acquired even the very imperfect knowledge they seemed to have of the play, we could form no idea.[8]

In Trinidad, stickfighting (or the calinda) provided ample opportunity for the mixing of song, dance, literature, and performance. Point out that stickfighting was both a dance and a performance, Hill emphasizes that the legend and lore that grew up around calinda were part of an oral tradition that was brought from West Africa by the slaves. He adds that the stickfighting chants, some of which memorialized great heroes of the art form, were sung by stickfighters with a supporting chorus. Adopted later by the calypso singer, its older forms reflected an important rhetorical dimension that possessed important ramifications for Trinidad's literary culture. Hill writes:

> "The stickfighting argot—the challenges and rebuttals—[utilizes] a picturesque, metaphorical language, the stuff of which dramatic dialogue is made. Apart from calinda chants, only fragmentary expressions of this colourful speech survive today. "I come to measure your grave," spoken as a solemn greeting while the challenger shows the length of his pouistick to a prospective adversary, is a sample of this language.[9]

The rhetorical range of this genre was displayed in all of its beauty and possibilities when Lord Executor, a calypsonian who began singing in 1899, went blind in 1950. He composed the following epic-tragic verse (calypso) in recognition of his blindness:

> I follow the star of the unconquered will,
> Which makes me inexorable and unbeaten still,
> As a burning diadem upon my breast,
> Invulnerable and calm and self-possessed.
> But today I cannot see at all
> Much more to fight and charge my cannon-ball,
> So come and hear the story of my fatal misfortune
> In this colony.

8. Hill, *The Trinidad Carnival*, p. 12.
9. Ibid., p. 27.

How often I have told pretenders in war
That I am a terror, four by four,
With heavy-weight cannon, power, and gun,
To make every contender tremble and run,
But now all that happen to pass,
Lord Executor is running out at last,
So come and hear the story of my fatal misfortune
In this colony.

The technical beauty of my elaborate praise
Will be mentioned by generations for many days,
I, Executor, Calypso King,
Now at this very moment I was called to sing.
What I've done for all mankind
Must be remembered as I'm getting blind.
So come and hear the story of my fatal misfortune
In this colony.[10]

The literary efforts of the stickfighters were extended and refined by the Pierrot, another Carnival figure, who Hill claims, "can trace his lineage back to ex-slave rituals."[11]   Where the stickfighter was content with his war chants and short verbal challenges, the Pierrot recited "grandiose speeches dwelling on his own prowess, his invincibility, his impressive lineal descent, and the dire things in store for all his enemies. His speeches were based on historical writings of the careers of great kings and military campaigners, or they were adaptations from the classics of English literature, including orations from Shakespeare's plays."[12]   As with similar Carnival activities, these characters attempted to domesticate Shakespeare and other writers to fit their local needs.

Carnival, then, emerged as an important platform through which a critical aspect of the society's literary heritage manifested itself. It was also a repository of the society's oral tradition.[13] Magico-religious practices, such as Shango, also possessed—and became a vehicle for— a wealth of oral literature. Super Blue's ability to merge Shango chants and rhythms into his calypso performances not only proved a fruitful and exciting combination during the nineteen eighties and nineties,[14] it also demonstrated the continuing link between oral poetry and traditional folk forms. Through the dexterous use and manipulation of language, a form of "languaging" as Lawrence Carrington has called it, the Carnival celebrations provided a

10. Quoted in Hill, *The Trinidad Carnival*, pp. 27–28.

11. Ibid., p. 28.

12. Ibid., p. 27.

13. Although more work needs to be done, the belair, Shango worship, and calypso contain a substantial store of oral literature. In this context, Funso Aiyejina, "Orisa Tradition in Trinidad" (unpublished) offers an important insight into this phenomenon.

14. Super Blue, one of Trinidad and Tobago's leading calypsonians, became very popular when he introduced the Shango beat to the calypso. After doing so, he won the Carnival monarch competition three times and was road march king for three years consecutively.

space in which the local populace expressed itself and defined its uniqueness. Unknowingly, the artists were manipulating received forms to express the new content of their circumstances. In the process, one sees the emergence of a vigorous literary tradition, as well as the skilled and vigorous use of language to express one's identity and existentially to understand one's life. Thus, from this Carnival tradition, one strand of the society's literary culture emanated.

Jim the Boatman: A Backward Glance (1846)

Slavery also left its mark on other aspects of the literary culture. "Jim the Boatman," a tale fashioned as an autobiography, appeared in the *Trinidad Spectator* on January 24, 1846.[15] A colored person wrote this tale, set in Port of Spain around 1810. It tells the story of Jim, a six-year-old boy stolen by a Bermudan slave captain who dealt in contraband goods. Made a slave, Jim works aboard his captor's ship at a time when "the slave trade was then illegal although slavery enjoyed the countenance and protection of the British Government." After keeping Jim enslaved for eight years and thinking that he has forgotten the land of his birth, the slave captain feels safe in having the young man accompany him to Trinidad on one of his illegal trading missions. Although Jim has forgotten many things about the island, his mother and friends have not forgotten him, and his mother has never stopped believing that she would see her son again.

One night, one of the illegal Trinidadian traffickers recognizes Jim. After questioning him and making sure he is the missing boy, the former returns to shore and tells Rosette, Jim's mother, the good news. Heartened, she proceeds immediately to the smugglers' ship, where she confirms Jim's identity and tries to negotiate his release. Although she appeals to some of the leading businessmen in the town to assist her, she is refused aid, for although they pity her, promise to be fair, and even make some feeble efforts to restore her son to liberty, the truth is that they are afraid to touch a single stone in the already tottering fabric of slavery, lest they should hasten its demise. They either live by the cruel practice or have invested in it. It is, therefore, not surprising that they do not exert themselves on behalf of the oppressed.

Realizing that his treachery has been discovered and that there is a possibility that he may lose his ill-gotten property, the slave captain tries to escape from the

15. The newspapers of this period were the major outlet of literary activity and political commentary. According to Daphne Cuffie, the government kept an anxious eye on the press. Lord Harris, governor of the island, kept the secretary of state for the colonies informed about the activities of the press, particularly its stand on political matters. Lord Harris claimed that the style of the *Port of Spain Gazette,* the *Trinidad Standard and West Indian Journal,* and the *Trinidad Spectator* "was generally bad, their moral tone low, their political stand vacillating and their reports of the proceedings of the Legislative Council inaccurate." More specifically, he felt that the *Trinidad Spectator* was hostile to the government and that its content was "bitter, vituperative, and scurrilous." See Cuffie, "Problems in the Teaching of English in the island of Trinidad from 1797 to the Present Day."

island as soon as he can. Frantic that she may lose her last opportunity to recover her son, Rosette asks for and receives an audience with the governor of the island. The author writes that this meeting leads to a most improbable sequence of events:

> The Governor listened with deep attention and moved, both by justice and compassion, instantly ordered his carriage, took Rosette with him, and drove with all speed to the King's wharf [and] commanded the Harbour Master without delay to man his boat, row after and arrest the vessel which was now more than two miles on her way, but making little progress, owing to the lightness of the breeze. It was done as the Governor commanded. An investigation took place, conducted by His Excellency. It was clearly proved that the young man called *Prince* was the son of Rosette, and formerly designated *Jim*. But who stole him could not at the time be proved. The Captain gave a bungling and a manifestly false account of the manner in which he became possessed of him. Jim was declared free and restored to his affectionate mother. The Governor threatened the Captain with a further investigation, but permitted him to depart. He did depart without delay, but, though he still lived and sails his own vessel, engaged in his former roving trade, he never since visited Trinidad.

As in all romances, the heart triumphs over the cold, calculating head and its horrendous deeds. Expectedly, then, at the end of the tale, Jim was reconciled to his mother. As the years pass, he proves to be "a son worthy of his mother" and labors to make her as happy and comfortable as possible "in the evening of her years." Thus, a sad story about slavery and its practices concludes on a happy note.

In "Jim the Boatman," written so closely after the abolition of slavery, three important things stand out. First, those who had suffered under slavery are still trying to come to grips with the harshness and arbitrariness of the institution. Reflecting on Jim's plight, the narrator observes that "[l]ast night he was free, but he is now a slave." Second, there is the recognition that, although some of the early English governors may have been protective of the rights of the colored and black elements of the society, those who came after (perhaps beginning with Woodford) were "neither fitted nor inclined, promptly and fearlessly, to unveil villainy."

Third, increasingly, Africans were asserting their presence in the society. For the first time in the literature, we hear the voice of a distinctive African (black) person when an assistant of the illegal traders, suspecting that the young boy may be Jim. engages in the following conversation:

> He asked at once if his name was Jim.
> The reply was, "De once called me Jim when little child, but de not call me so again. My name *Prince*."
> "Where you born?"
> "I do not know, fo de go take me to Bermudas when I young too much to member."
> "When de go take you mudder living?"
> "Yes."

"What de call her?"

"Rosette."

"You member any sister or brodder?"

"Yes, me member one sister one brodder."

"What de call them?"

"One Louise and todder Fred."

"Jim the Boatman" represents a form of advocacy literature in which the author reflects on the experiences of his group as a means of expression. The author wished to bring the plight of the free colored and the blacks to the attention of the colonial administration in the hope that means would be found to alleviate their condition. Moreover, the appearance of the tale at its particular historical moment suggests the emergence of a nascent self-confidence or self-assurance among the non-white element of the population. There is a feeling that the rights of this group have to be considered, especially as the group's members were supposed to be enjoying the rights of free men and women.

Ca Qui Pas Bon pour Z'Oies, Pas Bon pour Canards
(What's Good for the Goose is Good for the Gander) (1847)

While "Jim the Boatman" brought the plight of the coloureds and the former slaves to the fore, the carnival masqueraders, the camboulay celebrants, the chantuelles singers, the tambu bamboo performers and the calypsonians continued to fight for cultural space and social efficacy through the Carnival celebrations. As a result, Carnival and the metaphor of Carnival became important aspects in the life of the society which led Rasta to argue that "Carnival, and to a lesser extent, Christmas, became sacred to Africans."[16] Although the exact origins of the celebration of Carnival as a two-day fête on the Monday and Tuesday prior to Ash Wednesday are not known, historians agree that, by 1844, Carnival was a two-day affair. During the period 1838–1852, the African elements of the society took over Carnival and made it their national festival. In response, the colonial authority did everything in its power to label the fête as the African's return to savagery and barbarity. One observer remarked that what was good and glorious under the French elite (when even the governor took part in the masquerade balls) suddenly became a bestial degradation when Africans took Carnival to the street and made it their own.[17] *What's Good for the Goose is Good for the Gander* (hereafter *What's Good for the*

16. Conversation with Rasta, May 7, 2002.

17. As the festival of the French Creoles, Carnival "consisted of masquerade balls and visiting parties of the elite from estate to estate. Wealthy citizens, in particular Sir Ralph Woodford, governor from 1813 to 1828, gave elaborate masked balls, and in the evening during Carnival the leading members of society would don masks and drive through the streets of Port of Spain, visiting houses thrown open for the occasion." Donald R. Hill, *Calypso Calaloo: Early Carnival Music in Trinidad* (Gainesville: University Press of Florida, 1993), p. 20. See also John Crowley, *Carnival, Camboulay and Calypso* (Cambridge: Cambridge University Press, 1996), pp. 33–43 for a good description of Carnival during this period.

Goose), the only extant play we have of the period, examines the morality of the Creole Carnival—or the black appropriation of Carnival.

Written in French, this short play is set in the home of Cafarman, a merchant presumably of Port of Spain, who is described in the text as "a misanthrope." A reflective man who is given to philosophizing, Cafarman takes enormous pleasure in offering learned disquisitions about the state of the world and presumably the burning issues of his society. Probably a member of one of the governing bodies, he certainly reflects the sentiments of his class. Almost as if to prepare us for his opinions on Carnival, at the beginning of the play, Firnardeau, his business associate, announces, "You are a misanthrope, my dear Cafarman. And your ascetic lectures sometimes do you an injustice."[18]

The play opens with this conversation between Cafarman and Firnardeau, who are speculating on the quality of the French wines they are imbibing. Mrs. Cafarman uses this occasion to bring up her husband's disapproval at her attending a Carnival ball and thus provides Cafarman the opportunity to lecture on the waste and extravagance of Carnival. The Carnival ball, he says, "is a foolish waste of time. [It] is a school of immorality where one goes to have fun, to lose one's money, one's health, and sometimes other things too!" Firnardeau responds to Cafarman's cynicism by calling the latter "crazy" and claims that the ball is "a school of manners! The key to domestic happiness." Furthermore, he asks rhetorically, "Where does one make friends? At the ball. Where does one find a mistress who later can embellish our happy days? At the ball." To which Cafarman retorts, "Where does one catch cold, get into a fight, and a thousand other unpleasant things? At the ball!!!" Unable to persuade her husband about the liberating aspects of the ball, Mrs. Cafarman engages her husband in the following exchange:

> Mrs. Cafarman: To each his own....If only you would read your books, sip your favourite wine, and leave others to amuse themselves in their own way. (Drum and cries [of Carnival] are heard in the street).
>
> Mr. Cafarman: Yes! Hear the type of entertainment that goes on, for example. What's that? You tell me that those are rational beings with human faces who indulge themselves in such scandalous debauchery? Do you know of anything more absurd than these disgusting masquerades of the most backward times? More stupid than this carnival? (He serves himself some sherry and sips it.)
>
> Firnardeau: Yes, it's quite stupid, but it sells merchandise and in that respect, without the profit some of us reap....
>
> Mrs. Cafarman: Ho! Gentlemen, please let the world amuse itself as it sees fit. People don't think of doing evil when they are enjoying themselves. Beside, life isn't that gay already.
>
> Mr. Cafarman: Well, Felicity, congratulations on reasoning it out, my dear.

---

18. *Ca qui pas bon pour z'oies; Pas bon pour canards, The Trinidad Spectator,* February 24, 1847. Daaga Hill translated the play into English. All quotations are taken from this translation of the play.

In the second scene of the play, Johnny, the son of Mr. and Mrs. Cafarman, and St. Rose, Firnardeau's black valet, appear in front of the assembled company (Mr. and Mrs. Cafarman, Firnardeau, and Sarah, Mrs. Cafarman's servant) disguised as Turkish men-of-war, Mrs. Cafarman having selected her son's masquerade. Ridiculing the choice of costume and the folly of appearing before him in such an "idiotic outfit," Mr. Cafarman castigates his wife: "I'm disappointed that you haven't thought to dress him as a little nigger." At the end of the scene, however, the assembled company departs to enjoy the Carnival celebrations. Cafarman is left behind to contemplate mankind's folly and the savagery of the Africans.

It is in the third scene, seated in an armchair, drinking his sherry, and as the play-wright reminds us, "contemplat[ing] his glass lovingly," Mr. Cafarman offers his reflections on Carnival:

> One must confess that civilisation makes slow progress. Look at all these people rushing about in fury for this absurd carnival! These dances, this infamous jollifica-tion. Why don't they strive, as I do, to inculcate the principles of virtue from pious works. (He sips his drink). These books, these public papers, these are my only recreation. But how valuable are they? The are inexhaustible! (He takes the bottle to serve himself and notices that it's empty. He uncorks another and drinks) Decidedly, I am going to bring a motion against the carnival. Let's see the [news] papers…uh…*Spectator*, Coolie regulations….what does it say? But he's crazy, that man! These people are never satisfied with what's done for them. French party…tut, tut, tut. All fine gentlemen! You go to work quickly! (He drinks). Hic! If one listened to you the colonies would no longer be of any value to us. How for-tunate that my friend, Jonestown, made himself indispensable and that Milord will be compelled to leave his beautiful ideas in a briefcase! Hic! (He serves himself and drinks.)

By midnight, Cafarman has drunk himself into an alcoholic stupor. The play-wright intends that we compare his drunken ramblings with the clean, liberating fun that Carnival offers. In berating Carnival (in which all his friends and imme-diate family participate and enjoy), he is left with his maniacal ramblings which, in a confused way, reveal the distorted way in which members of his class thought about Carnival:

> Midnight! At last! Besides, my honorable friend, Burn hic! It's odd how this hic-cup tor—hic! torments me. My friend, Burnlaw, and there…and my eloquent War- hic! Warbler! (He swallows an enormous glass of sherry). Must kill this hic-cup…hic! Let's read the *Standard* and the [Port of Spain] *Gazette* to…hich…wake me up. (He opens the *Gazette* and falls asleep, saying) the morals, the good pleas-ure…stability, maintenance of existing things…sherry…hic! virtue and reli-gion….delicious wine…sherry…hic!

Mr. Cafarman remains in this drunken stupor until he is awaken about three in the morning by the returning revellers. The playwright describes him as being "in a deep sleep, a spiritual ecstasy." They all speak of the wonderful time they have had at the ball, contradicting the views of some of the members of their class that "carnival is without all virtue and morals." Finally, Mr. Cafarman comes around to the position that it is not wrong to enjoy oneself and that Carnival may not be that "atrocious" after all. Firnardeau, however, determines that Carnival may be a beneficial activity especially "when one considers the tranquility that reigns at the moment [presumably speaking about the social and political climate] and the manner in which the people behave themselves. Decidedly, there is progress among the people."

The play concludes with Firnardeau's observations: "[Carnival] is the people's only pleasure and we must let them enjoy it. They don't read, they have neither horses, nor car, nor money to procure the delicate pleasures and it is only good politics to allow people to masquerade at least once a year." As the title of the play suggest, if it's good for the rich people to go to their masked balls and enjoy themselves, then it's all right for the rest of the population to participate in carnival and enjoy themselves. Hence, "what's good for the goose is good for the gander." The festival may even possess desirable social effects, as it allows revelers to take their minds off the hardships and disappointments of their daily lives.

The Interesting Narrative of Maria Jones (1848)

Apart from the literature that was generated by the Carnival celebrations, antagonism between Protestants and Roman Catholics were also a source of considerable literary activity, the major products being the narrative of Maria Jones and the religious tracts of Rev. John Law. Although Maria Jones's name appeared in the *Missionary Herald* in 1845, her story did not come to the public's attention until 1848.[19] It may have been the first slave narrative by an African woman of the society. Born in West Africa in 1777, at the age of seven, Maria was stolen from her home and taken to St. Vincent as a slave. After residing there for a short time, she was sent to Palmiste Estate in South Trinidad, where she worked with "other negroes in the cane piece." On the plantation, she was identified as a strong-willed and determined woman. Realizing her influence on the other slaves, her Scottish master removed her from the field and put her to work in his kitchen "lest she should cultivate a similar spirit in the gang."[20] After a short stay at Palmiste Estate, Maria was transferred to Mount Pleasant, a plantation in north Trinidad, where she remained until Apprenticeship ended in 1838.

After Apprenticeship, Maria took advantage of the educational opportunities

19. Although Maria Jones's narrative was published first in the *Missionary Herald* in March 1848, it was also carried as a pamphlet, *Maria Jones: Her History in Africa and the West Indies* (1851), by the Haversfordwest Mission Press, the propaganda arm of the Baptist Missionary Society. In 1848, the story was told by Rev. George Cowen, while Rev. John Law, head of the Baptist Missionary Society signed the 1851 version as biographer. I use Cowen's 1848 text because it captures the tone, spirit, and voice of Jones's life more accurately than the Law version.

20. "Maria Jones," *Missionary Herald*, March 1848, p. 39.

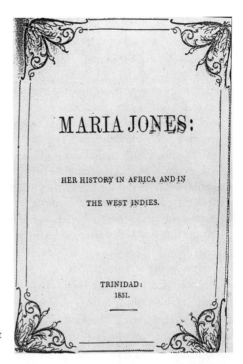

MARIA JONES:

HER HISTORY IN AFRICA AND IN

THE WEST INDIES.

TRINIDAD:
1851.

FIGURE 6. Cover illustration for *Maria Jones,*
put out by Haversfordwest Mission Press, Port
of Spain (1851).

offered by the Mico Charity Institute that opened a school at Mount Pleasant
Estate.[21] Immediately, Maria's dedication to her education became paradigmatic of
those ex-slaves who longed to be educated and who gave themselves totally to the
liberating possibilities of the word, albeit through the auspices of religion.[22] When
the school opened, like so many other former slaves, Maria rushed to take advantage of the opportunities offered and began to attend evening classes.[23] It is possi-

21. Between 1835 and 1845, Mico Charity promoted Negro education in the British West Indies.
Rev. Cowen, a schoolmaster employed by Mico Charity, became the first English Baptist to work in
Trinidad. He was accepted as a missionary by the Baptist Missionary Society and was stationed in Port
of Spain. See John Hackshaw, *The Baptist in Trinidad* (Port of Spain: Ampy and Bashana Jackson
Memorial Society, n.d.), and Brian Stanley, *The History of the Baptist Missionary Society, 1792–1992*
(Edinburgh: T&T Clark, 1992), for discussions of Cowen, the Baptist Missionary Society, and the Mico
Charity.
    22. The missionary societies provided much of the early education for the children of the island. Rev.
William Moister, pastor of the Port of Spain Wesleyan Church, stated that "[o]n New Year's Day [1840]
we opened our school, and up to the present it has succeeded beyond our most sanguine expectations.
We have 130 names on our books and the daily attendance is from 90 to 100. Our school has gained
the confidence of the public. The children of several Roman Catholic parents attend, and I do not hes-
itate for a moment to say that it is one of the best schools in Trinidad" *Wesleyan Methodist Missionary
Society Correspondences,* Box 140, no. 17.
    23. In a letter to the editor of the *Port of Spain Gazette,* Thomas Belby, secretary of the Mico Institute
in Trinidad, wrote that "the apprentices themselves not only felt a great desire to receive instruction but,
I believe, have fulfilled their daily tasks in the neighborhood of our school with cheerfulness and satisfaction to their employers; and it is not an uncommon thing to see them, after school, chanting their
hymns of joy and praise sitting with pleasure and delight listening to the voice of instruction" (April 6,

ble that her enthusiasm to gain a formal education might have been a direct reaction to the slave master's desire to keep slaves in ignorance.[24] Cowen, head of the Baptist Mission and amanuensis of Maria's story, observes:

> Curiosity brought many to witness the operations of a school for "niggers," as well as to see the "buckra gentleman who came so far for teach 'em." But Maria was a person of sounder and more sober understanding than many of her degraded class, and her noble mind sympathizing with the efforts being made in their behalf, at once resolved with all the energy of her character, let others do as they would, that she would, though aged, improve herself all she could. While many of those who accompanied her to the school simply looked and laughed at what they considered "buckra's" foolish attempt "to make nigger know book," Maria manifested determination enough to present herself to the teacher, at the age of sixty years, with her head white and her eye dim, to learn the alphabet (*Maria Jones.*, p. 39)

Maria brought an intensity of purpose to her studies. Her acquisition of the word acted as a life-giving force. Possessing what Rev. Cowen calls "a strong, masculine, craving mind, a deep desire to know" (*MJ.*, p. 39), Maria could not get enough of the word: "The more she acquired, the more she desired; the eagerness with which she sought instruction, not only from the school teacher, but on every hand, from any one she could press into her service, it is impossible to describe" (*MJ.*, p. 39). When she exhausted evening school, she demanded that she be transferred into day school, even though she had to pay for the privilege. She wished to achieve sufficient education to read and to understand the *New Testament*. According to Rev. Cowen, "Never did she rest, nor allow others to whom she had access, to rest, till she had the happiness with her own aged and dim eyes to read the book of life" (*MJ.*, p. 40).

In this context, it may not be irrelevant to observe that religious education meant different things to the master (in this case, Rev. Cowen) and the slaves. Such an education had the effect of making slaves and ex-slaves "more content, more hardworking, more obedient, and more submissive than they would be without such instruction."[25] To Maria, however, schooling was a way of liberating herself from

---

1838). In 1849, Rev. Cowen reported on the responses to his religious school: "Last sabbath I visited this place [at Sherring Ville], met twenty of them at the sabbath school, some of them, eight or ten, reading the scriptures, and all reading something; while the old people, who hitherto thought education of little use, sat listening and passing their remarks as the children read, sang, recited their hymns, and answered questions. Several adults have also profited by this school, by receiving occasional instruction, and in very many families have the scriptures and other good books, from time to time, have been read by the teacher, of which the people themselves have made mentioned to me with delight" (*Missionary Journal*, January 1850, pp. 9–10).

24. A parallel situation in the United States might be relevant here. Speaking before the Virginia House of Delegates after the legislature passed a bill that prohibited the "education" of blacks, one delegate declared, "We have as far as possible closed every avenue by which light may enter their minds. If we could extinguish the capacity to see the light, our work would be completed." Quoted in Thomas L. Webber, *Deep Like Rivers* (New York: W. W. Norton, 1978), p. 29.

25. Ibid., p. 44.

the stultifying degradation of slavery and all that it meant. Having acquired the skill of reading, Maria encouraged other former slaves to share in her passion for literacy. An advocate of the liberating capacity of education, Maria impressed upon the others the importance of reading and used herself as an example to encourage them to study. She stated "in the strongest light the advantages afforded them since freedom for improving their minds. To encourage them,[she] would dwell upon her own acquirements, and the gratification if offered her to be able to read the 'good book'" (*MJ.*, p. 40).

With her new conception of life, Maria wished to marry "after free fashion" someone with whom "for years she had lived as wife, according to the negro, or rather the slave custom." After receiving instructions from a Presbyterian minister, Maria, with "evident pride," married Jones. Thereafter, she informed Rev. Cowen that she wished to be called "Mrs. Jones, and not Maria, as beforetime. This she said purposely, in the hearing of several other females present, turning to them as she spoke, as though anxious to improve the occasion by provoking them to go and do likewise" (*MJ.*, p. 40). It also might be that she wished to lord her new status over them, taking pains "to move among them like a queen, as though conscious of some superiority over them in point of character" (*MJ.*, p. 40). Maria's behavior might also have been a reflection of what many slaves felt when they heard the gospel preached by white ministers under the auspices of slavery. Thomas Webber writes that in America, "many slaves had themselves remarried or rebaptized after emancipation. [Henry] Bibb, speaking of the fugitive slaves he met in the North after his escape, writes that '...if they professed religion, and have been baptized by a slaveholding minister, they repudiate it after becoming free, and are rebaptized by a man who is worthy of doing it according to the gospel rule.'"[26]

After her marriage, the narrative turns to her conversion and the importance of her being baptized by immersion in water (Protestantism) versus the sprinkling of water on her forehead (Roman Catholicism), an important distinction between the Protestants and the Roman Catholics of the island.[27] Once Jones came into a knowledge and understanding of the Baptist faith, she wanted to "'baptise same fashion as blessed Saviour.' She said, moreover, that she desired to be immersed, and asked me if I [Cowen] would do it." After much thought and prayer, Rev. Cowen baptized her in the manner she wished. That moment represented the most important occasion of her life, as she says:

26. Ibid., p. 82. This is an important example of mining the silences of these narratives.

27. In Port of Spain in 1851, Rev. Law reminded a Baptismal candidate that "[y]our appearance this day among us as a candidate for Christian Baptism, supposes that you are fully convinced that *believers* in the Lord Jesus are the only proper subjects of Baptism, and that *immersion* is the only mode.... That Baptism is more than external form, that it is an intelligent, personal, and spiritual act of obedience to the will of God, whereby the Christian baptised, declares his knowledge of, and believes in, the great truths of Christianity, will appear abundantly evident if the various Scripture statements and explanations, in reference to the nature and character of Baptism, are duly considered" (*The Design, Spiritual Nature and Doctrinal Import of Christian Baptism* [Port of Spain: Haversfordwest Mission Press, 1852]).

"I baptise *four* times now, but only one time right! Fore dem tief me in Africa, dem priests dere do somtin for baptise, when I came to buckra country, dem catholic priests"—for Maria was originally a Roman Catholic—"do wha dem call baptism; dem put oil on my head, salt in my mout, an make cross on me face; but now I read bible for my own self, I no find dis dere. When I join Cotch church, dem take me, 'gain and *prinkle* water in my face for baptise, but neder dis right, when I came for know better. No more one way, same fashion blessed Saviour he self do; he go right down in de water, an came up 'gain same I do now. O! tankee Fader for show me dis 'fore I go fra here for good" (*MJ.*, p. 42).

The triumph of this spiritual narrative resides in how Jones takes her life into her hands, finds her way, and then is baptized as she desires. It also suggests a reevaluation of what religiosity meant to the ex-slaves in the postemancipation context. Neither willing to take the word of Rev. Cowen nor her former Presbyterian minister at face value, Maria goes to the "good book," where she discovers her own references to guide her life. In real-life terms, the word becomes her guide to a better and more fulfilling life. Although her master possesses several valuable plantations, she affirms that "I more rich than he for a[ll] that; he poor blind buckra sinner, while Fader made me rich for ever" (*MJ.*, p. 39). Where she was blind, she now sees; where she was without direction, her faith gave her a new direction.[28]

Although the repetition of the classic Christian strategy ("Give me Jesus and keep the world") is present in this narrative, this slave woman, stolen from Africa and living a life that encompassed slavery and colonialism, used the word to negotiate her freedom on her own terms. Brian Stanley notes that "the Baptist missionaries in the West Indies came, not primarily as evangelists of the 'heathen,' but as pastors and teachers of an existing Christian negro community." Therefore, they "exercised a more decisive influence on the course of secular history than they did in any other part of the world."[29] Under such circumstances, it is easy to see how the Trinidad mission under Rev. Cowen did so much to influence the life of this strong Christian woman. She emerges as one of those exemplary African women who was determined to be her own person in spite of her past state of servitude.

---

28. The idea that the slave was happy once s/he possessed the Lord and could sneer at the riches of the planter, is one of the tropes of this genre of fiction. Written to demonstrate that "missionary labours are not in vain"(*MJ.*, p. 38), *Maria Jones* was produced to demonstrate to benefactors and supporters in London that the missionaries were doing important work in the Caribbean. The same is true of "Daniel," a narrative similar in composition and phrasing to *Maria Jones*. Daniel, an old African slave who lived on the same plantation as Jones and who Rev. Cowen also befriended, utters sentiments similar to those of Jones on the death of their masters: "A short time before Daniel was called home, his owner...died suddenly, and though wealthy, he left this world poor, and miserable, and wretched, and blind, and naked. Daniel remarked, when he heard of the event, 'he no rich yonder; ah, he poor, he poor!" *Missionary Herald,* August 1851, p. 126. Rev. Cowen also reported Daniel's story.

29. Stanley, *The History of the Baptist Mission Society,* p. 6.

John Law and the Baptist Press (1848–1852)

If the Baptist Press used Jones's life to demonstrate the superiority of Protestantism over Roman Catholicism, the innumerable tracts produced under the auspices of Haversfordwest Mission Press suggest that it wanted to challenge the influence Roman Catholicism had over a majority of Trinidad's population.[30] Although this battle was not a new one, between 1848 and 1852, the propaganda war intensified and thus earned an important place in Trinidad's literary experience. It also contributed to a vigorous writing life that was taking place in the island at the end of the 1840s and 1850s.[31] Just as importantly, the missionary pamphleteering that took place during this period was the necessary forerunner of William Gamble's *Trinidad: Historical and Descriptive* (1866) and the works of Lewis O. Inniss, both of whom were associated with the early Baptist Church in Trinidad.

The first reference to the Haversfordwest Mission Press was made in the February 1849 issue of the *Missionary Herald*, the journal of the Baptist Missionary Society. John Law, a young English evangelist working in Trinidad, notified the general secretary of the Wesleyan Society that "lately" he had "been fully occupied with the work of the Lord Jesus Christ. I am preacher, schoolmaster, and printer, or anything, as the case may require."[32] Law informed the general secretary that three months prior to November 21, 1848 (the day on which his letter was sent), a young man was doing their printing: "I have printed a Portuguese hymn book, and have also commenced a series of *Tracts of Trinidad*. The sixth number is just from

---

30. The confrontation between the Protestants and the Roman Catholics went back to the beginning of the nineteenth century. In 1814, Governor Woodford sought to prevent the Methodist missionaries from preaching to the slaves at nights. When Thomas Blackburn confronted Woodford on this subject, Woodford told him that "[y]ou must only preach upon moral duties: teach the people not to thieve and tell lies and if you succeed in prevailing to them [sic] to cleave from these things, you will have done more than any of your other preachers have done in any other colony. You must not speak at all about the mysteries of religion, you must not mention them: the people can learn them in the Established Church. You must only preach what is contained in the *New Testament*. You must not distribute any tracts of any kind until you have sent a copy of each to me for my approbation: if you do, you will get yourself into trouble." In 1817, Abraham Whitehouse, head of the Wesleyan Church in Trinidad, advised his superiors in London that "such is the influence of Popery, the malice of the Rector [of Port of Spain], and the enmity of the Governor to the Methodist religion [that] we cannot teach Methodist doctrines without trenching on the peculiar tenets of Roman Catholicism." In his most strident restrictions against the Protestants, Woodford demanded that the missionaries put up a bond £500 before they could preach and prevented them from marrying or buying slaves" (Quoted in Anne Claire Ince, "Protestant Missionary Activity in Five South Caribbean Islands during Slavery, 1765–1826," Ph.D., diss. Faculty of Modern History, Oxford University, 1984; G. C. Findlay and W. W. Holdworth, *The History of the Wesleyan Methodist Society, Vol. 2* [London: Epworth Press, 1921], p. 216).

31. According to the Fifty-Ninth Report of the Baptist Missionary Society, 6,000 tracts were distributed between 1848 and 1851 (*Missionary Herald*, 1851).

32. Trained at the Baptist Academy at Bradford, England, Law was ordained on September 10, 1845, and sent to Trinidad to work for the Baptist Mission. He devoted his life to contesting what he considered the blasphemies of Roman Catholicism and became, in the words of Rev. Cowen, "a man engaged in publishing...a series of tracts on the chief doctrines of the gospel, exhibiting them in contrast to the error, superstition and idolatries of Rome" (*Missionary Herald*, January 1852).

the press. They all treat on the subject of popery, the great curse of the land. I have just written and published my first letter addressed to the Roman Catholic Bishop of Trinidad, exposing the fearful errors contained in a catechism which he causes to be circulated among his people. 'Woe is me if I preach not the gospel' to all to whom I can have any access either by the living voice or the press. May the Lord add his rich and effectual blessing."[33] On December 13, 1850, Law announced that he had published "a new and enlarged edition of the Portuguese Hymn Book," from which he had made a profit of twenty dollars that he used to purchase "more printing materials."[34]

In July 1849, Rev. Cowen wrote to the general secretary of the Baptist Committee in London to complain that the "Romish priest" in Savanna Grande has "set himself in opposition to our efforts to teach and to enlighten those whom he had so long sealed up in darkness and profound ignorance." The tracts, one of the many ways to combat the "Romish priests" and their doctrines, led Rev. Cowen to affirm: "I distribute extensively in the neighborhood tracts on Popery. Tract distribution is among the best means we have of sowing the seeds of truth among the people. When the power to read becomes more universal, it will be a mighty means of sapping superstition."[35] The missionaries hoped that the pamphlets (tracts) would combat the "darkness," which they believed was aided and abetted by Roman Catholicism. Law informed his elders in London that, "for the purposes of making known by the press the glorious gospel of the blessed God, I have commenced *The Trinidad Evangelist,* the first and second numbers of which I herewith send you, as also number twelve of *The Tracts for Trinidad.* These tracts are eagerly sought after. I feel that life is short, and that whatsoever my hand findeth to do, I *must* do it with all my might. Still the work is of God; man is nothing but a mere instrument in His hands."[36]

And what did God, using Law as His instrument, say about the Roman Catholics and how was Law to accomplish His end? In approximately twenty-one

---

33. *Missionary Herald,* February 1849, p. 26.

34. *Missionary Herald,* March 1851, p. 39. The Portuguese who settled primarily in Trinidad and Guyana posed a special problem for the Protestants vis-à-vis the Roman Catholics. Revs. William Hudson and Edward Collier outlined the problems the Protestants encountered in St. Vincent: "The Portuguese emigration from Madeira is leading either to the introduction of Popery into these West India colonies where it had not heretofore obtained a footing, or to its firmer establishment where it had but a lingering existence. It is obvious that the Papacy is making everything subservient to the spread of Popery. In British Guyana, for instance, we have but few Romanists, until the large emigration commenced from Madeira. The emigrants were soon followed by Priests, and the Romanists have not a large establishment in British Guiana, a nunnery, a Bishop; and several of the Priests are supported from the colonial chest." Law stepped up his activities among the Portuguese in Trinidad to combat this additional influence of Popery. Not only did he publish two Portuguese hymnbooks, once a week, he preached in Portuguese, a language he learned in Trinidad (*Wesleyan Methodist Missionary Correspondences,* May 20, 1851). The letter from which this excerpt is taken was published in the *Wesleyan Missionary Notice,* 9, No. 155 (November 1851), p. 178.

35. *Missionary Herald,* October 1849, pp. 165–66.

36. *Missionary Herald,* October 1850, p. 152.

"Tracts from Trinidad," five issues of the *Trinidad Evangelist*, "Protesto de Roma Contra Papa E Papismo," and other occasional pamphlets, Law and his fellow Baptists unleashed a fierce attack against "Popery" and the "unscriptural nature" of the Roman Catholic religion.[37] Law lays out the groundwork for his theological arguments in "How to Know What God Teaches," in which he argues that the Roman Catholic system of religion is "at variance with the word of God and most ruinous to the soul of man." He repeats this contention in "Praying to Saints and Angels." He observes that, while Protestantism discovers God's will through the *Old* and *New Testaments*, the Roman Catholics ascertain God's will "by the testimony of the Catholic Church which God appointed to teach all nations all those things which He had revealed." Law believes that each Protestant is concerned about his or her personal relationship with God ("If any man will do his Will, he shall know the doctrine, whether it be of God, or whether I speak for myself" [John, viii]). Law also believes in the Bible that affirms "the power of God unto salvation to every one that believes." Roman Catholics, he argues, are concerned with corporate religion in which "the testimony of your Church must be given a flavour of the Bible before it can be received by man." Law believes that "[i]t is *cruel* and *merciless* in the extreme for the Roman Catholic thus to thrust herself between the Creator and his creatures—between the gracious and forgiving God and the guilty and perishing sinner: What crime can be compared to the violence and cruelty of this?"[38]

Law's arguments about the sufficiency of the Bible as *the* final testimony of God's word repeats many of the arguments that appeared in W. Niven's "The Sufficiency of the Bible as a Rule of Faith and Guide to Salvation" and "Infallibility." In "Purgatory," Law condemns the Roman Catholic notion of purgation ("No one who dies in the Lord is required to go to Purgatory to suffer for his sins, for every sin is washed away in that blood which cleanest from *all* sin, so that after death all believers enter immediately into rest and blessedness") and the Apostle's ability to forgive sins. In "Praying to Saints and Angels," he condemns

37. The extant pieces from the Haversfordwest Mission Press are *Maria Jones* (1851); Law, "Pastoral Counsels: An Address to a Christian on Being Received into the Church" (1852); Law, "The design, Spiritual nature, and Doctrinal Import of Christian Baptism" (1851); "Protesto de Roma Contra Papa E Papismo" (n.d.); "O Baptismo Dos Crentes Em Agua 'Em Nome do Pai e do Filho e do Espirito Santo," (n.d); W. Nivens, "The Sufficiency of the Bible as Rule of Faith and Guide to Salvation" (n.d.); W. Nivens, "Infallibility" (n.d.); Law "For Me to Live is Christ, to die is Gain" (1850); Law, "Repentance Towards God," (1850); "The Irreparable Loss" (n.d.); Law, "How to Know What God Teaches" (1849); "The 'One Mediator Christ Jesus' Fully Qualified to Make Intercession for us" (1849); Law, "Purgatory—Power to Forgive Sins" (n.d.); Law, "Praying to Saints and Angels" (n.d.); Law, "The Seven Sacraments" (1849); Law, "To the Roman Catholics of Trinidad: Luther's Conversion" (1850); J. Stantham, "Certain Assumptions Refuted" (n.d.); Law, "The Mode of Christian Baptism" (1851); Law, "Infant Baptist" (1851); James Smith, "A Few Plain Reasons for Baptism of Believers" (n.d.); E. B. Underhill, "The Distinctive Features of the Baptist Denomination" (1851); George Cowen, "The Temporal Supremacy of the Pope" (n.d.); Law, The Forged Headship" (1852); and W. Noel, "The Ministers of Christ and the Pope, Prelates, and Priests of Rome" (1852).

38. John Law, "How to Know What God Teaches?" (Port of Spain: Haversfordwest Mission Press, n.d.). Most of these tracts are not paginated.

the Roman Catholics' practice of praying to "deceased saints" and the distinction they make between "mortal" and "venial" sins. Overall, Law echoes the concerns of many of his colleagues who condemn the doctrines of Roman Catholicism.

It might be that Law and the other Protestant missionaries were afraid that the onslaught of Roman Catholicism in the Caribbean in the second half of the nineteenth century signaled "the commencement of a downward course" of their work, particularly in the eastern Caribbean. In "Papal Aggression in the Colonies and the Duties of Wesleyans in the Crisis," Rev. Hudson and Collier, writing from St. Vincent, pose the following question: "Are we to lower our standard—to strike our colours—because Popery, ay, Puseyism, and High-Churchism, too, are disputing our claim to the territories we have won from degradation, darkness, and Heathenism? The Wesleyans were the first to 'lift up their banners' in the name of the Lord, in many of these colonies." So strongly did they feel about the issue, the Wesleyans in the eastern Caribbean district were willing "to give up a portion of their allowances, [that] amounted to £200. They well knew that the Parent Society could not, at a time when Reformers were urging, 'Stop the supplies,' increase the grants."[39] Law's polemics was part of a larger Caribbean response to what was seen as the excesses of Roman Catholicism in the island.

Although Law's polemical texts (and those printed by his press) were aimed at what he saw as the excesses of Roman Catholicism, it performed an important function of opening up the society to new ideas and stimulating a culture of reading and discourse. Peter Brewer observes that "[t]here is nothing to suggest that Law was exceptionally gifted, but he was clearly an influence in the lives of such men as L. O. Lewis, the writer and later deacon of the Port of Spain Church, and W. H. Gamble, the missionary, who must have been one of the young men of whom Law was fond."[40] In his booklet on the Diamond Jubilee of the Baptist Mission in Trinidad, Lewis uses Rev. Cowen's life and Maria Jones's baptism as the starting point of his narrative.[41]

Whether many persons read these pamphlets is beside the point. That Law engaged in a fierce polemic with the Roman Catholic Church for almost ten years and used his printing press to assist his activities are important aspects of the society's literary life. These tracts certainly contributed reading stimuli for the society.

A Narrative on the Dispensation of Divine Providence (1846)

The activities of the Wesleyan missionaries produced a startling narrative of deliverance when, on August 17, 1846, the *Trinidad Standard* published Rev.

39. *Wesleyan Missionary Society Correspondences,* May 20, 1851.
40. Peter Brewer, "Ministry in a West Indian Town: John Law of Port of Spain, 1845–1870," *Baptist Quarterly* 33, No 6 (April 1990), p. 284.
41. See L. O. Inniss, *Diamond Jubilee of Baptist Missions in Trinidad, 1843–1903* (Port of Spain: Franklin's Electric Printery, 1904).

William Moister's "A Narrative of the Dispensation of Divine Providence."[42] Although sermons may not necessarily be included in a catalog of nor contribute to the development of a literary culture, "Divine Providence" is organized in such a way that it is a part of Trinidad's literature. In his sermon, Rev. Moister deploys "verbal symbolisation and signification" and what, in another context, has been called "the organizing dynamics of fiction" in a deft and sophisticated manner that marks his work as an excellent product of the fictional imagination.[43] His sermon was meant to instruct and to edify, thereby meeting two of the minimal conditions of African oral verse.[44] For our purposes, Rev. Moister's sermon is important because he used a local incident to dramatize Divine Providence, God's mercy, and His intervention in human affairs.

"Divine Providence" tells the story of a seaman who is struck dead by lightening and another who lays prostrate and senseless in a boat "whilst your minister was preserved as by a miracle from the fatal effects of thunderbolt and from a watery grave." In his sermon, Rev. Moister describes the placidity of the Gulf of Paria as he traveled to Couva to discharge his ministerial duties. "The morning was fine, and as we glided down the smooth and placid Gulph [sic] of Paria, the surrounding scenery seemed well calculated to draw out the mind in holy contemplation and joy." Concluding his business at Couva at about two-thirty in the afternoon, Rev. Moister is returning to Port of Spain when disaster strikes:

> The weather had become showery, but was not by any means more threatening than usual at this season of the year. A light breeze soon took us up as far as Carapichaima when we observed the thunderstorm gathering to the east was in dense black masses of clouds. The rain soon descended in torrents, the vivid lightening flashed around us, and the peals of thunder were fearfully long and loud. The breeze freshened and we scudded along, under full sail, without the slightest apprehension of danger, beyond what might arise from a thorough wetting at this sickly season of the year. I had been again endeavouring to draw out the boatmen in religious conversation, and it's very remarkable that we had been speaking expressly of instances of sudden death by lightening, and of the necessity of being always prepared to meet our God, when in a moment—in the twinkling of an eye—the light-

42. William Moister, a prolific writer on religious matters, was born in England. He went to the West Indies in 1834 when the Wesleyan Missionary Society sent out "eighteen additional Missionaries to the West Indies to prepare the way for the approaching freedom of the poor Negro slaves, the Act for their emancipation having just passed both Houses of the British Parliament" (William Moister, *The Story of My Life and Missionary Labours* [London: T. Woolmer, 1886] p. 115). "Extract of a Letter from Rev. William Moister," published in the *Wesleyan Missionary Notice*, London, No. 7 (November 1846), pp. 179–180, was also published in the *Trinidad Standard*. I quote from the latter, which carries a longer version of this sermon.

43. See G. G. Darah, "200 Years of Nigerian Letters," *ANA Review* (April–June 1996), in which he talks about the properties of literature, and Antonio Benitez-Rojo, "The Nineteenth-century Spanish American Novel," in Roberto Gonzalez Echevarria and Enrique Pupo-Walker, *The Cambridge History of Latin American Literature, Vol. 1* (Cambridge: Cambridge University Press, 1996), p. 436.

44. See Ernest Emenyonu, *The Rise of the Igbo Novel* (Ibadan: Oxford University Press, 1978), chapter 1, for a discussion of African oral literature.

ening flash struck the highest part of the vessel, which was the bamboo guard that goes across the mast-head to support the lug-sail. This was completely shattered to pieces. The electric fluid then descended the mast and struck William [Woodford, one of the boatmen] dead in an instant. He was reclining with his head against the mast his hilliard-rope in his hand, to be ready in case of a signal, at the time of the awful incident. The electric fluid completely scathed him, set his clothes on fire, and passed through the bottom of the boat at his feet. In the same instant, John (the other boatman), who was at the helm, was laid prostrate and senseless at my feet...After a few wild expressions of surprise, John recovered from the shock, came to my assistance, and began throwing out the ballast whilst I continued to bale. As to William, he remained just as he fell upon his face, with his arms and feet extended, and never so much as spoke, or groaned, or moved.

As their boat begins to sink, they attempt to keep it afloat. When those efforts prove futile, they cling to the overturned craft to prevent themselves from drowning in the fury of the storm. After being exposed to "immanent danger" for an hour and a half, Rev. Moister and Ovid are saved by the sloop *Atlanta*. At ten o'clock the following morning, Rev. Moister and Ovid reach Port of Spain, "tolerably well, except for a few bruises, and fatigued consequent on our exposure and exertion." As he assesses his close encounter with death, Rev. Moister can only "mediate upon our wonderful deliverance and to return thanks to our Heavenly Father for such a remarkable interposition of this preserving power."

From this remarkable incident, Rev. Moister draws five lessons that God in His Providence had chosen to teach him. First, the incident gives additional proof that there is a God. Second, it confirms the doctrine of Particular Providence, that is, the existence of a God who actively intervenes in "the minutest affairs of individuals." In his autobiography, Moister describes this incident as "a remarkable interposition of Divine Providence in my deliverance from a watery grave."[45] Third, the episode confirms the uncertainty and frailty of human life and the necessity of being prepared constantly to meet "our God." As Rev. Moister reminds his congregation, "[w]hen we arise in the morning we know not what may befall us before the shades of evening closes upon us. We know not what disease may seize upon our vitals, or what accident may overtake our course. When we go forth from our homes, we know not that we shall ever return." Fourth, as a former seaman himself, the minister advises that all sea-faring men to be persons "of deep piety and devotedness to God." Fifth, his miraculous deliverance suggests that Christians should always praise and thank God for His mercies. Moister concludes his sermon with the following verse from Psalm 101: "I will sing of mercy and judgment; unto thee O Lord will I sing."

In this sermon, the author offers a very detailed account of his travails, and it is his strong descriptive powers and dramatic presentation that enhance this well-constructed narrative. Further, Rev. Moister's strategy of repetition strikes an emotional chord that allows the reader to respond sympathetically to the author's tra-

45. Moister, *The Story of My Life and Missionary Labours*, p. 169.

vails. Buoyed by the stamp of personal experience, the sermon thus becomes a very effective literary presentation.[46] Although "Divine Providence" does not possess the same urgency and Old-Testament fervor of Jonathan Edwards, "Sinners in the Hands of an Angry God," its rhetorical power, powerful imagery, and measured cadence make it a major contribution to Trinbagonian literary culture.[47]

Occasional Poetry

The period 1838–1851 also saw the publication of local poetic efforts in the islands' newspapers. Occasional poems under the heading "Original Poetry" and "Poetry-Original and Select" appeared in the *Trinidad Spectator* and others. Although most of these poems imitate their French and English predecessors and reveal a lofty tone,[48] a few were noteworthy if only because they attempted to poeticize local concerns and conditions. "The Sugar Cane" that appeared in *The Trinidad Spectator* on May 15, 1846, celebrates the intrinsic qualities of the sugar cane by comparing it with other plants and flowers and pointing out its unique Caribbean features. Even the structure of the poem captures the litheness of the sugar cane plant as it sways in the tropical breeze. Just as important, the gold it yields is far in excess of anything the exotic plants and flowers with which it is compared can command:

> Let them talk of their Roses, Shamrocks and Thistles,
>   Or, prate of the Lily so smart;
> I think our emblem is better by far,
>   The Cane with its feathery dart.
>
>   The Hurrah for the Cane,
>   May it ever remain
> The pride of the isle of the West;
>   Let who will be foes,
>   Or whatever oppose,
> Flourish it still shall with the best.

46. In challenging those who do not believe in the glory of God, Rev. Moister offers a wonderfully alliterative rejoinder that builds to a remarkable climax: "The skeptic may ridicule the idea, but to me every star that sparkles in the sky, every flower that adorns the earth, every shower of rain that descends, every gleam of sunshine which beams forth, every peal of thunder, and every flash of lightening proclaim that *there is a God,* and especially is the conviction deepened by the awful manifestation of divine power which I have recently witnessed." This notion of seeing God's beauty and power in the immensity of his physical creation will be picked up by Charles Kingsley in *At Last* when he visits Trinidad in his effort to refute Charles Darwin's theory of evolution.

47. Jonathan Edwards (1703–1758), one of America's most influential theologian and philosophers, is best remembered for his sermon "Sinners in the Hands of an Angry God" (1741.) As John E. Smith, Harry S. Stout, and Kenneth P. Minkema observe, "[i]n a Puritan culture not given to secular pursuits or belles lettres, theology necessarily stood as the artistic and intellectual means through which the culture's highest ideas were expressed" (*A Jonathan Edwards Reader* [New Haven: Yale University Press, 1995], p. vii). In the Trinidad case, Rev. Moister's sermon reflects the intellectual activity that was taking place in the society at the time.

48. See, for example, "The Departed Year," *Trinidad Spectator,* January 22, 1848.

True the Rose is fragrant, the Lily is sweet,
   But far sweeter the Sugar Cane
It is useful while they are only for shew,
   So let it the preference obtain.

   Then Hurrah for the Cane, etc.…

The Thistle may boast its bright red and sharp torns,
   But the brighter the gold the Cane yields,
The Farmer with Thistle continually wars
   But who'd pluck the Cane from this fields.

   Then Hurrah for the Cane, etc.…

The Shamrock is green, and in vain is it trampled,
   It springs up again 'neath the feet;
But cut it, and soon all its beauty is gone,
   Cut the Cane and 'tis good to eat.

   Then Hurrah for the Cane, etc.…

As if in response to "The Sugar Cane," "Chant of the Labourers, Oppressed by the Truck Plan" appeared in the *Trinidad Spectator* on June 3, 1846. I have been unable to discover what the "Truck Plan" referred to, but the poem is obviously intended to challenge the assumptions of nobility and grandeur associated with sugar cane. In this poem, there is a sense that sugar cane production has baneful effects on the labourers, a process that was reinforced by the arrival of "the Coolies."[49] The poet suggests that such a conjuncture is even more painful when the price of sugar slumps and the conditions of the workers deteriorate. The poem reads as follows:

Cane have their time to grow,
To be cut down—or, burned:
A fitting time hath sugar to be struck,
But all hast thou! all seasons are thine own,
         Oh, Truck!

Mongst rotten fish, spoilt rice and yankee cheese,
Musty cornmeal and weevily black eye pease,
Rudely thou sit'st, and thus thy labourers pluck,
By hams and pork, that taint the healthful breeze!
Hard must we toil and sweat—and, all for these?
         Oh, Truck!

We know when Coolies come from far across the sea,
Then we prepare with them to buy our luck!

---

49. Incidentally, in both *What's Good for the Goose* and "Chant of the Labourers," Indo-Trinidadians are mentioned, and their presence suggests that, from their initial arrival, they made an impression upon the society.

But who alas! can e'er compete with Thee?
Our blood, our bones, and marrow are they fee.
                    Oh, Truck!

Is it? when cane heaps in your mill-yards lying,
Whilst fervent suns their costly juices suck,
That we "unfaithfulness promises relying,"
Said, "we did wrong," when from our work we struck,
And sad resumed our task, against the crying.
                    Deceitful Truck!

Although the identity of the poet is uncertain, he may himself have been a labor-
er since the poem strikes out against colonial oppression, especially the oppression
engendered by the rule of King Sugar. The workers, having struck against the conditions imposed upon them, return to work in good faith and in the hope that their
conditions of employment will change. Apparently, these hopes were not realized.
Throughout the poem, the sense of deceit and betrayal rings out with the repetition
of "Deceitful Truck!" or in a variation of that phrase at the end of each stanza.

The poet is also aware of the economic slump that the industry is going through
at the time, despite attempts to improve the sucrose content of the sugar cane
through administering better fertilizers. In the end, there is the painful realization
that it is the workers who suffer most when disaster comes. The master and manager can repair to his home and his shop respectively. It is the worker who is
"screwed" and made to "perish" because of the owners' shortsightedness or lack of
concern. It is the poem's awareness of the worker's well-being that demonstrates an
evolving sense of self-consciousness that becomes an important element in the literature.

African/Afro-American Presence

During the 1838–1851 period, the newspaper also increased its coverage of
events in Africa, the slavery debates in England, and the handling of the slave question in the United States. Although such articles were meant to confirm and reinforce the so-called barbarity of the Africans (especially his "abominable" religion)—
and by extension, his black descendants in the Caribbean—they highlight unique
features of African culture. For example, under the heading "African Superstition,"
the *Trinidadian* of December 13, 1848, carried the following story:

One of the most horrible and extraordinary superstitions is that connected with the
birth of twins; an occurrence looked upon as the greatest affliction that can happen
to an Ibu woman. The little victims are no sooner born than one or both are taken
away, placed in the neighborhood thicket in earthen pots or baskets, and left to
become the food of the hyenas or other wild beasts. The unfortunate mother is separated forever from her conjugal alliance. She is obliged to pass a long period of
repentance and purification, in a rude hut some distance from town; and if she out-
lives all these trials, mental and physical, and returns once more to society, she is

regarded as an especial object of Fetiche wrath, and no woman knowingly will sit in her company or hold communication with her. No wonder that it is so dreaded by Ibu women, to whom it is impossible to offer greater insult, or one which rouses their angry feelings more, than to say the word "Abo wadakri;" or, by holding up two fingers, signify that they have had twins. Another equally absurd, and scarcely less cruel superstition is the sacrifice of such children as unfortunate cut the teeth first in the upper jaw. They believe it is to indicate a wicked disposition, one hateful of the gods of the Fetiches, and therefore proper subject for immolation on the altars of their abominable worship. At a little distance from Obi's dwelling and rather to the right, we came unexpectedly on a large earthen ido, placed in a thicket, surrounded by high trees, this we believe to be the image to which most of their sacrifices are offered.

Another article, "Character and Conditions of the Liberated Africans," an extract from the *Anti-Slavery Reporter,* was published in the *Trinidadian* on October 15, 1851. After describing how the liberated Africans in the Caribbean gather together to bargain collectively for better wages and improved working conditions, the article reveals the planters' conception of the African's behavior. Speaking specifically of the Trinidad situation, the article quotes Dr. Mitchell, the superintendent of immigrants on the island, who made the following statement: "The Yaribahs [Yorubas] …exhibited a regard for truth, unusual among Africans. Some of the more savage class, who have run away from their masters, appear to have excited considerable dread in a part of Trinidad." The author notes that, although the Creoles are kind to the liberated Africans, "they generally prefer to associate with each other, or with native Africans who have formerly been settled in the colony, and [who] have manifested a desire to become Christians, thereby avoiding the reproach of heathenish which the Creoles sometimes apply to them."

The excerpts above suggest that, despite the negative stereotyping of Africans, the period immediately following the end of slavery saw Africa and its people made available for those in the society who wished to know about them. Whether in reproach of their "heathenism" or the "problems" that separated them, Africans were being seen as persons with separate histories and distinctive identities. The discussion that ensued around their differences and subsequent coming together provided the building blocks upon which the society's nascent literary culture was erected.

Creating a Literary Space

Consistent with the newly liberated condition of the society, there arose a need to create a space for the freer and fuller expression of a people's consciousness. Between 1838 and 1851, four parallel events, though seemingly unrelated, made the society more conscious of its literary responsibility. The first event was the publication of a letter to the editor of the *Trinidad Spectator* on June 13, 1846. This letter argues for the creation of what the writer calls a "literary institution." Although the letter was aimed at the elite of the society, it made an eloquent case for the value and importance of the literary life within the society. In the writer's view, the literary includes more than such expressive genres as poems and tales; rather, it also encompasses any written work in the humanities or the sciences that contributes to the edification of the citizens, narrow as the concept of the latter term might have been:

> Literary institutions have ever been found conducive to promote liberal and enlarged views of things, and may be looked upon as the surest support of our social edifice. The principle of self-love, inherent in the human mind, in this instance ennobles the man. A spirit of emasculation is aroused, and every faculty of the mind is exerted, conscious of the deep interest and importance attached to all questions on general literature. A calm and dispassionate study of the various branches of literature and science develops the ideas, expand the mind, and corrects many erroneous opinions originating in a dearth of information, while the intellectual mind ranges with fond delight over the vast and fertile field offered for its delightful contemplation.

Although the letter echoes Matthew Arnold's convictions about the elevating and ennobling aspects of literary pursuits, it also indicates an enlarged conception of what constitutes the literary. The author, a member of a self-titled member of the Debating Society, remarks that, whatever the literary encompasses, it must contribute to the deepening of one's intelligence and to the broadening of one's sensibility as the example of England, "our motherland," demonstrates so aptly. Hence his plea that "[m]y earnest convictions of the many benefits which would accrue to our community from possessing these means of diffusing intelligence—in cementing the bond of sympathy and union—inspiring a taste for literature—elevating the mind of man, and effecting a complete moral and intellectual regeneration of society, might tempt me to trespass at too great a length upon the columns of your newspaper."

The author believes these goals are attainable. Although some inhabitants wish to inject "the unhappy prejudice which has so long been a bane to the prosperity of this colony" into the proceedings, he believes a literary institution would contribute to the society.[50] His experience has taught him that organizations such as debating societies allow a person "to freely express opinions on various interesting and important questions." That his organization has cultivated these traits, suggests that others in the society could have achieved the same. His letter also suggests that there are several debating clubs on the island at that time.

The second event involved the coming together of several prominent men in

---

50. As we would see in the next chapter, in his preface to *Adolphus: A Tale* (1853), the anonymous author responded to this condition of induced forgetfulness in the following manner: "Many voices will no doubt be raised against us, as endeavouring to rouse feelings which are supposed dead, and to revive things which some would have entirely erased from memory's tablets; but, we reply, to create disagreeable feelings is not our aim. The pages of history, which unfold to us the barbarities of past ages, are not intended to throw us back into barbarism; on the contrary, it is by reading and meditating upon the evils of the past, that we find the most enriching lessons of wisdom" (*Trinidadian*, January 1, 1853).

October 1846 to form a society "denominated the Trinidad Literary Association."[51] At this meeting the first resolution called for "the encouragement of a Society having for its object intellectual pursuits, and the discussion of subjects connected with Literature and Science [which] is greatly to be desired." The second resolution made provision for "those individuals whose pursuit occupy their time during the day, or whose pecuniary means debar them from prosecuting literary or scientific inquires, [but who] could, by co-operating in such an institution, secure to themselves its advantages at a convenient hour, and at an inconsiderable expense."[52]

On November 21, 1846, the Association was officially established. Because its objectives were so all-embracing, it is helpful to outline some of its rules. It also demonstrates how the concept and functions a literary society changed over time:

> Rule 11: That the objects of the Trinidad Literary Association be the providing of a Reading Room, the formation of classes in different departments of knowledge and the Fine Arts, the establishment of a course of Lectures and Debates, and the furnishing of a Room appropriate for Conversation, with materials for Games of Skill. Cards and all Games of Chance to be excluded.

> Rule 13: That the Reading Room be provided with Newspapers, Magazines, Reviews, and such other Books as the Committee of Management may decide.

> Rule 17: That any member of the Association desirous of entering upon any course of study, do signify their intention in writing to the Secretary, and that the Committee of Management do exercise their discretion in enabling such individuals to effect their purpose, but constructing Classes, and engaging Teachers. The expenses appertaining thereto by defrayed by the parties who avail themselves to such advantages.

> Rule 20: That every member may be permitted to introduce a Stranger into the Rooms of the Association, his name to be inserted in a Visitor's Book, with the name of the party introducing him. No Gentleman to be considered a Stranger after sixty days residence in Trinidad.

> Rule 21: That any member may introduce a Lady on the Evening of the Lectures.

In addition to its wide reach, three important aspects of the Literary Association stand out. First, because the Association wished to cater to those "strangers" who had just arrived in the island, the proposed clientele were most likely the elite of the island and visiting expatriates. Second, since women could not be members of the Association and could attend only when they were invited to do so by the male members on the evenings when lectures were given, the Association's sexist orientation is clear. However, in this matter, it reflected the tendencies of its age. Third, because newspapers and magazines were made available to the members suggests the essential role these periodicals played in the development of what the Association considered literary.

---

51. *Trinidad Spectator*, October 24, 1846.
52. Ibid.

From all reports, the Association ended before 1852. A reader who congratulated the editors of the *Trinidad Free Press* on their successful fight to reduce the subscription fee at the public library requested that the books of "the late Trinidad Literary Association, now in the keeping of the Honorably Colonial Secretary" be presented to the Trinidad Public Library that was formed in 1851.[53] Whatever its successes or failure, the organization placed on Trinbagonian society's agenda the necessity of forming a literary association that spoke to the intellectual needs of some of the members of the society.

The third defining event of the event occurred in June 1851 when the *Trinidad Free Press* announced its intention to become a political, literary, and agricultural journal, "a portion of…[whose] columns shall always be supplied with Extracts from the numerous Literary Periodicals which are now published in England, and our efforts shall be used among our Friends to obtain contributions on Historical, Moral and Political subjects, thereby rendering the Paper at once interesting and instructive."[54] Thus, the *Trinidad Free Press* carried articles on the slave trade in Cuba, Lope de Vega and his works, a biographical sketch of George Washington, and a notice of the death of James Fennimore Cooper. More importantly, on November 1, 1851, the periodical carried verbatim "Sadiki, The Learned Slave," one of the few Caribbean slave narratives that was extant; the tale was reprinted from the *West Africa Colonizer*.[55] Although most of the early extracts published in the journal were taken from European and American publications, gradually the articles began to relate to the specific conditions of the society and revealed contemporary trends in literature.

On March 28, 1853, as if to state its objective more clearly, it changed its masthead to read *The Trinidad Free Press and Literary Journal*. In its first issue, the retitled newspaper ran the first chapter of Harriet Beecher Stowe's *Uncle Tom's Cabin* and carried the second and third chapters of this seminal novel on slavery in April and May. In that first issue, the journal began to promote local talent by publishing "The Natural and Political History of Trinidad from Its Discovery to the Present" by an author who styled himself "A Native of the Island." In its zeal to publish works by native sons, the paper carried L. A. A. de Verteuil's prize-winning "Essay on the Cultivation of the Sugar Cane in Trinidad" and other works that conduced to the intellectual and moral uplift of the inhabitants and to cultivate a better knowledge of their physical environment. The publication of these articles and extracts from other texts widened the base of a literary culture that began to speak to the needs of the population.

The fourth event of this time was the battle carried on by the *Trinidad Free Press*

---

53. *Trinidad Free Press*, March 26, 1852.
54. *Trinidadian*, June 28, 1851.
55. Written in Arabic, this slave narrative was translated by Robert Madden in 1834. According to Madden, "This man [slave] speaks English well and correctly for a Negro but does not read or write it. I caused him to read the original, and translated it word by word. From the little knowledge I have of the spoken language, I can safely present this version of it as a literal translation."

to democratize the Trinidad Public Library, founded in 1851, and thereby make its reading materials available to the public. At the end of it's the library's first year, it contained 868 volumes "of the most celebrated English and French writers, beside a few natural and scientific specimens which may form a nucleus for a museum." Yet, according to the editors of the *Trinidad Free Press,* the library "can go no further; books there are, but no readers."[56] The editors were infuriated because the library's Committee of Management did not understand its functions. The *Free Press* wrote that the library "not only possesses the means of useful instruction to the uninformed, but can only open a field of boundless knowledge to the more ambitious votaries of Literature and Science. And yet up to the present time it is scarcely visited, and not one single subscriber is to be found on its books, except... Lord Harris and the committee." The yearly subscription of two pounds was beyond the reach of most citizens, and a subscriber had to leave a deposit before he could borrow a book. Such a situation militated against the use of the library's material, a condition made worse when it was revealed that, in its first year of operation, the library had spent over one thousand dollars to no useful purpose.

Finding such a situation intolerable, as well as being committed to the cultivation of a literary culture, the *Free Press* organized a campaign to make the library more accessible to the general public and, thus, to expand its readership. On January 20, 1852, the *Trinidad Free Press* announced the circulation of a petition it intended to forward to the Council of Government requesting that the subscription rate be reduced. Its editorial of the same date states:

> Every man of business knows that the cheaper an article, the greater is the number of purchasers, and consequently, the larger the circulation. We have on hand, nearly a year's trial with the annual subscription of two pounds, and, there are only thirty two members; and, the greater number of these are personages such as the Chief Justice, the Attorney General, the Archbishop, the Archdeacon,—who are in no need of a Public Library. It is therefore, necessary, to reduce the subscription in order to make the Institution useful to the Public. By making it five dollars per Annum, payable half yearly in advance, there will be no cause of complaint on the ground of poverty; and the Library will be materially benefited by it from the large increase of Subscribers that will undoubtedly be the consequence. We hope the honorable gentlemen of the Council will perceive the propriety of amending the Ordinance in this respect.

By March of that year, the campaign achieved its two major objectives. The subscription was reduced to one pound, and the monetary deposit on books was withdrawn. Although this was a small victory, on September 23 the editors of the *Trinidad Free Press* wrote that, although the subscription rate was still too high, "we must acknowledge the change as a step towards improvement, that may lead to further improvement." Such a change resulted in the increased use of the library. In

56. *The Trinidad Free Press,* September 2, 1851.

contemporary jargon, it made the library more user-friendly. The cumulative effect of these two innovations was to make literary works more readily available to the public and to open up the society to a more diverse body of information.

To be sure these four events were small gestures. Initially, only a particular class benefited. Yet, these little victories placed a few more building blocks in the literary foundation of the society and contributed eventually to the construction of a literary culture. When one realizes how important the public library was to the development of subsequent generations of writers—such as C. L. R. James, Carlton Comma, Albert Gomes, and their peers—it becomes clear that these efforts, puny as they were, eventually bore fruits at the beginning of the twentieth century. Suffice it to say that the first sustained effort to construct a literary culture started with the first generation of thinkers who emerged after apprenticeship.

✸ ✸ ✸

A close examination suggests that, during the period of 1838 and 1851, the building blocks of the society's literary heritage were put in place. Although its base might have been narrow, its claims elitist, and its achievements unspectacular, one discerns several tendencies. First, in *What's Good for the Goose*, one sees a clear relationship between the culture (in this case, Carnival) and the politics of the society. Although Firnardeau recognizes that Carnival brings enjoyment to the populace at large, he also sees that support of the festival is "only good politics." Given the fears of the colonizers during this early period after emancipation, it is clear that they would do very little to disturb domestic tranquility, even if it meant accepting what they considered to be base and barbaric.

"Jim the Boatman" reveals a second tendency by demonstrating how writers used this period to clarify their relationship to slavery, especially during the second half of the nineteenth century. Such a clarification was necessary if the literature were to develop further. It was almost as though this psychological purgatory was necessary before a former slave society could begin to interrogate itself. Additionally, the activities of John Law and the Baptist missionaries did much to expand the base of and energize a literary culture.

The third tendency, less obvious than the others, was also instrumental in creating the base of a literary culture. As in Latin American, the literary independence of the Trinbagonian writers was tied inescapably to the struggle for political independence.[57] After 1838, many of the writers who articulated their views were intent on placing them at the service of the national liberation struggle. Although this phenomenon was confined to a very tiny group of thinkers, it suggests an important

57. See Jean Franco, *An Introduction to Spanish-America Literature* (Cambridge: Cambridge University Press, 1969), pp. 28–46. The writers of this early period seemed to identify with Latin America (particularly Venezuela) very strongly. Apart from the hero of *Warner Arundell*, the heroes of *Adolphus: A Tale* and *Emmanuel Appadocca*, in their struggle for liberation, identified quite closely with the early liberation struggles of Latin America and even set foot upon those shores. Perhaps, it is not coincidental that two Trinidadians founded the first newspaper in Venezuela.

link between writing, politics, and the opening up of society. Although most Africans were illiterate, a small group of colored persons who saw themselves as cultivated or striving toward cultivation provided an audience for those revolutionary voices that were attempting to articulate the nature of their condition. To the degree that one discerns the emergence of a national literature, one begins to hear voices lifted up in opposition to the harshness, arbitrariness of power, and the denial of basic human rights/writes that were, in themselves, political statements. One also sees the emergence of a people's culture during this period.

The coincidence of these early creative experiences (prose, drama, and verse) and the call for the creation of a "literary institution" suggest the opening up of the society in such a way as to make it less hostile to those who wished to hear and be heard; those who wished to write and be written about. When, for example, the author of *What's Good for the Goose* concludes that, because the nonwhite population neither reads nor possesses other forms of entertainment (even though they do) that they should be allowed to enjoy their Carnival, little does he realize that Carnival possessed a rich literary heritage that was only waiting to be liberated. To the degree that the people's festival was winning acceptance and demanding to be heard, it represented a "freeing up" of the culture that would create the necessary space for the evolution and cultivation of a national literature.

In his masterful work *Wretched of the Earth*, Frantz Fanon proposes that out of relative obscurity each generation rises up to make its contribution to a society's store of wisdom and knowledge and, by extension, its literary culture. The antagonistic relationship between the two parallel strains of Trinidad's literary culture—the written (essentially narrow and private) and the oral (essentially public and innovative)—during 1838 and 1851, demonstrated the yoked condition of the society's early literature. The education provided by the Baptist missionaries and their fierce polemic with the Roman Catholics led to a condition that made debate and discussion possible, as the case of Maria Jones demonstrated. That another strain had entered into the mix—that of the Indo-Trinidadians—indicates that the culture was in the process of opening itself up, yet again, to absorb the contributions of another segment of its rich and variegated population.

CHAPTER 6

The Emergence of a National Voice, 1852–1858

Take Afric's sons, your spade and hoe,
And to your fields with pleasure go.
By cultivating our own corn,
We may yet each fill up our horn,
With manioc, tania, potatoes, yams,
Earn gold enough to procure hams.
Look forward to your native hills
Your valleys with their ceaseless rills.
Courage, Creoles, and once again
We will send out cocoa to old Spain.

—BLACKBALL (1853)

Lead children, lead this old one from her house,
Lead, Trojan women. Raise to her feet
the fellow slave once your lady and queen.
Come carry me, lead me, lift me
taking my old hand.
Lend me your arms bent for a crutch.
And I—let me lean—I will hasten with slow
stiff-ankled steps…

O gods below earth, keep safe my son,
the only anchor left to my house.
Hidden in snowbound Thrace, he lives
guarded by his father's friend.

—EURIPIDES, *Hecuba*

"Farewell!" he said, waving his hand; "no spot on earth is more lovely than you [Trinidad]. God might have chosen you for Eden when first he created man; angels might have lived among your gardens. What dreams of prosperity, of glory, have I not had about you,— all spoiled, corrupted, poisoned by the white man! Farewell, then sweet island! The best I can wish you is that you may daily send forth slaves, flying, like myself, to be free."

—MARY FANNY WILKINS, *The Slave Son*

If the foundation blocks for the society's literary culture were put in place between 1838 and 1851, the 1850s saw the first flowering of a distinctive national voice. Indeed, the social and political turmoil of the period became the soil in which much of the literary activity was nurtured. For example, the freed colored "were resentful of discriminatory practices, real or imagined, which they now suffered because of skin color"; the ex-slaves "were jealous of their newly-won freedom and [were] determined to protect it from any form of restrictive impositions";[1] the condition of Africans and the coloreds became the subject of examination; the East Indians began to affect Trinbagonian society; and the society began to realize a sense of its Nationness.[2]

During this period, *Adolphus: A Tale* (1853), a metafictional tale; Michel Maxwell Philip's *Emmanuel Appadocca* (1854), the first novel of the tradition; and L. A. A. de Verteuil's magisterial *Trinidad* (1858), a work that is examined in the next chapter, were published. Marcella Fanny Wilkins, an English woman who presumably lived in Trinidad for some years, wrote *The Slave Son* (1854), a sentimental novel that examined the conditions of the colored population in Trinidad and offered a different resolution to the problem than did Philip.

Further, during the 1850s, the newspapers continued to play their midwifery roles in the evolution of this literary culture and carried information that opened up Trinidad to a more intense discussion of international ideas.[3] Apart from publishing literary works, the newspapers continued to cultivate the literary taste and scientific interests of its readers by encouraging the formation of debating clubs and literary associations, along with promoting public lectures and the expansion of literary facilities for the society's elite.[4] Continuing the efforts of the previous era, the 1850s placed a deeper local stamp on the literature and gave it a more distinctive Trinbagonian feeling.

1. John Crowley, *Carnival, Camboulay and Calypso: Tradition in the Making* (Cambridge: Cambridge University Press, 1996), p. 10.

2. Antonio Benitez-Rojo defines Nationness as a practice or concept that "concerns itself with the origins of a sociocultural group in a given territory." See Antonio Benitez-Rojo, "Nineteenth-Century Spanish American Novel," in Roberto Gonzalez Echevarria and Enrique Pupo-Walker, eds. *Cambridge History of Latin American Literature, Vol. 1* (Cambridge: Cambridge University Press, 1996), p. 421.

3. Nothing said here should blind us to the fact that, of a population of 70,000 people in 1853, two-thirds of the population could not speak English, seven-eighths were illiterate, and nine-tenths "go barefoot" as the *Trinidadian* reported on December 24, 1853. It is well to remember that, in terms of formal literature, one was talking about an activity that involved a small percentage of the population.

4. Although it was not their ostensible objective, the newspapers felt a sense of bitterness and frustration at not being supported by the those on the island who could afford to do so. In its last editorial, *The Trinidadian*, a newspaper that had done much to encourage the growth of a literary culture, complained that "[t]he intellectual life in Trinidad is at a low ebb. Sensual pleasure are the order of the day. The people here can support horserace and balls, and can spend half a million of dollars per annum for fermented and intoxicating drinks, but they are too poor, too mean, or too ignorant to support four or five printing offices and newspapers, as would be done by an equal number of inhabitants in any district of the northern part of the United States." *Trinidadian*, December 24, 1853.

Adolphus: A Tale (1853)

Adolphus: A Tale (hereafter *Adolphus*), one of the most important works to appear during this period, was written anonymously and serialized in the *Trinidadian* from January 1 through April 20, 1853.[5] Part of the romantic-realist tradition of the Americas, *Adolphus* shares similarities with Jean Francisco Manzano's *The Early Life of the Negro Poet* (1840), "one of the few freed slaves to achieve literary prominence in nineteenth century Cuban letters,"[6] and with Harriet Jacobs's *Incidents in the Life of a Slave Girl* (1861). The Trinidadian tale examines the callous and arbitrary manner in which colored people were treated during the first half of the nineteenth century. Using a form of self-reflexivity, the unknown author hoped his tale would allow society to examine the numerous social and political problems colored people experienced.[7] As he exposes the diminishing rights of the free coloreds, he poses a question. What redress does a person of color have when the women of his group have been dishonored by one of the elite (in this case, someone who passes for white)? (It also is a question that Philip and Wilkins pick up in *Emmanuel Appadocca* and *The Slave Son*.)   When Adolphus, the title character, prevents DeGurreinon, the antagonist, from raping Antonia, Adolphus's bethroded, he is forced to flee the country of his birth because of a law that forbids a colored person from raising his hands against a white person. Venezuela, the country to which Adolphus and his companion flee, is presented as the paradigmatic example of a free country, the kind of society the colored Trinidadian should aspire to achieve, the kind of democracy they would like to construct in their homeland. In making such

5. While *Adolphus* was being serialized, the *Trinidadian* carried running accounts of responses to *Uncle Tom's Cabin*, accounts of slavery that were similar in nature to those portrayed in *Uncle Tom's Cabin* (for example, characters who acted like Lagree or St. Clair), reports of the Anti-Slavery Society about the treatment of slaves, and excerpts on the cruelty of slavery taken from U. S. newspapers, such as the *Mississippi Clairon*. "Release from Slavery," the story of Solomon Northrop that appeared in the *New York Journal of Commerce*, was also carried in the *Trinidadian*.

6. Juan Francisco Manzano, *The Life and Poems of a Cuban Slave*, ed. By Edward J. Mullen (Hamden, Conn.: Archon Books, 1981), p. 3. G. R. Coulthard writes that *The Early Life of the Negro Poet* "is one of the most valuable documents of the period, written as it is from the inside as a protest against the injustices of slavery" (Ibid., p. 3). Richard Madden translated this slave narrative into English in 1840, even before the first Spanish edition appeared.

7. This tale can be read as what Fernando Alegria calls "romantic-realism," a text that "self-consciously and systematically draws attention to its status as an artefact in order to pose questions about the relationship between fiction and reality." Quoted in Benitez-Rojo, "Nineteenth-century Spanish American Novel," p. 429. See also Patricia Waugh, *Metafiction* (London: Routledge, 1988), p. 2. The unknown author of *Adolphus writes* in his preface that "[t]he past is the parent of the present, and to whom can the youth turn for instruction with more sanguine hopes of success, than to follow a father whose mind is ripened by age and experience? Therefore, it is we disclaim any desire to arouse bitter feelings; all we wish is, that the past, however, disgraceful it may appear to one party, and however painful to another, be not entirely buried in forgetfulness, because it is a source of lessons pregnant with utility. Hence it is we devote a few moments of leisure to the production of the following chapters, and, under the veil of fiction, we paint as in true colours as out abilities could admit, a picture of the past state of colonial society." See *Adolphus: A Tale, Trinidadian*, January 1, 1853. Other citations of this tale are noted in the text as *A*.

a comparison, Adolphus compares his island home with what awaits him in Venezuela:

> He had left a land where prejudice against colour had destroyed many of the social ties, where the soil was daily watered with the tears of slaves, and where none whatever of the descendants of Ham could claim the rights of a man and a citizen. Another picture was now before him—all was free, all men were equal. Joy reigned in every dwelling. Liberty had given life to all. The father, instead of mourning for a son who had fallen in the last campaign, felt proud and joyous at knowing that his child had offered himself as a sacrifice at the shrine of Patriotism. The tender spouse beheld with sacred admiration the glorious scar which their husbands had brought home from the scenes of combat, as the fruits of their devotion to their country's cause. Throughout the environs, the romantic sounds of the *bandolas* toll to the stranger the mirth of the peasantry.
>
> Adolphus could not behold the scenes without emotion. He could no longer restrain his delight and rising from one of his deep reveries, he exclaimed: "What a change! How unlike an unfortunate and degraded country, is this land! Ah Liberty, who can be so blind as not to admire thy grandeur! How sublime are thy lessons!!! Tell me, thy great goddess, shall thou ever smile on poor Trinidad?" [*Trinidadian*, April, 6 1853].

In Venezuela, Adolphus and his friends are saved from death by the intervention of Simon Bolivar, president of the country and a long-time friend of Adolphus's adopted father. Fortuitously, Adolphus remembers a ring his adopted father has given him, a present from Bolivar, who had saved the father's life. Finally, back in Trinidad, DeGurrinon is ruined, imprisoned, and revealed to be what he is: a Negro (or in more specific terms, "a mulatto"): "His birth is traced, his mother is found out to be a slave." Adolphus triumphs by retaining Antonia's love. And, as the tale ends, there is every indication that, through Bolivar's intervention, Adolphus would soon return to Trinidad, as a free man to rejoin Antonio.

This tale exposes many of the novel characteristics of Trinbagonian society. Adolphus is a direct descendant of a maroon family, a second-generation African in Trinidad. Cudjoe, one of the slaves, is offered equality with Adolphus and his friends, even though his character and fate are not worked out fully in the text. Africans are depicted as being honorable, courageous, and sensible as they, too, embrace freedom and its possibilities.

More importantly, *Adolphus* is used as a vehicle to promote individual freedom and to plead with the dominant class to treat its black and colored members as equals. That some members of the colored society were actively exploring the possibilities of settling in Venezuela suggests that the latter was really uncomfortable with their lot in Trinidad.[8] At the end of the story, the narrator observes that

---

8. In the 1850s, some coloreds, led by George Numa Des Sources, a proprietor of the *Trinidadian*, made a strong move to emigrate to Venezuela. A report in the *Trinidadian* explains that "[t]o the middling and labouring classes, Trinidad does not hold out any adequate recompense; they barely earn an existence, while the legislation is diametrically opposed to their interests. The political thralldom and

Figure 7. Michel Maxwell Philip, author
of *Emmanuel Appadocca*.

"[s]uch is the contempt with which the sanctity of the law is treated-—such are the
effects which bigoted prejudice take on the minds of those who are entrusted with
its administration, that justice to him whose misfortune it is to be the descent of
Afric's clime is unattainable." [*Trinidadian*, March 16, 1853] This is the sad note
that predominates as the tale ends. However, it reflects the Creole struggle for justice that shaped the experience of the 1850s, and it is one of the problems Philip
explores in *Emmanuel Appadocca*.

Emmanuel Appadocca (1854)

Although Michel Maxwell Philip's *Emmanuel Appadocca* was not the first novel
to examine the subject of miscegenation, it was the first Anglo-Caribbean novel to
do so from the point of view of a colonized person.[9] Written in solidarity with the

servility which exist is not likely to be removed for a long time. Lord Harris's anticipated return here as
Governor forebodes no good. The same system—the same cringing favorites—the same spies—the servility which characterizes the would-be respectables—the foisting (?) and corruption necessarily consequent thereon—what can be expected from such a state of things?... The granting of free political institutions here is incompatible with the safety of the whites, because the population of colour is too numerous. Our blood boils with indignation at the bare recollection of the insulting language of [Mr. Hawes
report on political reform for the society.] What then remains for you but to emigrate?...Ere many
months are elapsed, we hope to see the faithful band of pioneers leave these ungrateful shores for a new
home. Let every influence be used by the friends of Emigration to augment the number. Economize
your small means for a time, and you will find that the economy of a few months will be the corner-stone
of your independence and competency" (*Trinidadian*, October 11,1851).

9. E. L. Joseph's *Warner Arundell* was the first novel to examine interracial love. In an afterword to
Maxwell Philip's *Emmanuel Appadocca* (Amherst: University of Massachusetts Press, 1997), I discuss
Philip's life and times more fully. See also Selwyn R. Cudjoe, ed., *Michel Maxwell Philip* (Wellesley,
Mass.: Calaloux, 1999) for a discussion and other essays on Philip's life.

African American liberation struggle and the passage of the Fugitive Slave Law of 1850 in the United States, the novel is informed by the historical romance, the African American slave narrative, and the ideology of piracy. As a slave child, the product of a black mother and white father, Philip was disturbed by "the cruel manner in which the slaveholders of America deal with their slave-children."[10] He wished to add his voice to the chorus of abolitionists who were upset by the dehumanizing practices of slavery. More particularly, he was distressed by how slave children were treated, how slave mothers were abandoned by their white lovers (whom he called "violators"), and the cruel manner in which slavery dissolved the natural bonds of humanity.[11] Taking up the theme of revenge that he encountered in Euripides's play *Hecuba*, Philip asks what constitutes the correct response of slave children to the unnatural and unfilial acts of their nonslave fathers when he probes the implications of the *lex talionis* (law of just revenge)[12] as a means of responding to such crimes.[13]

Set primarily in the Gulf of Paria, the Caribbean Sea, St. Thomas, Venezuela, and Trinidad, the novel tells of the activities of a company of pirates, men from different nations, who find a sense of security in one another's company and take the law into their own hands. More specifically, it counterpoises the heroism of Appadocca, the protagonist, against the villainy of James Willmington, the antagonist, and explores the moral dilemma that such a contrast creates. As the motley company of pirates rejoice at the booty they have plundered from the Letitia of Bristol, an English ship, we get a good sense of their condition and their attitude to the world:

> Those [were] fierce men, who had abandoned the entire world for the narrow space of their small vessel, and the inhabitants of the vast universe for the few kindred

10. Maxwell Philip, *Emmanuel Appadocca: or, Blighted Life* (London: Charles J. Skeet, 1854), preface. All subsequent quotations are taken from this edition and are noted in the text as *EA*.

11. Bridget Brereton posits that Philip's mother was not "an ordinary slave woman" in that she was a member of the Philip family, a distinguished family in the island. This is one more reason why Philip was so hurt by how his father treated his mother. See Bridget Brereton, "Michel Maxwell Philip (1829–1888): Servant of the Centurion," in Cudjoe, ed., *Michel Maxwell Philip*, pp. 106–107.

12. As suggested by the epigram from *Hecuba* at the beginning of *Emmanuel Appadocca*, Philip was determined to examine the implications of betrayal and its just rewards. Undoubtedly, Hecuba's story had a powerful effect on Philip's imagination and the shaping of the text.

13. Although the *lex talionis* has been variously interpreted as the law of vengeance or the law of compensation and retaliation, it certainly has its origins in what constitutes the correct relationship between a master and his slave. Nahum M. Sarna writes that initially "the lex talionis strove to achieve exact justice: only one life for one life, only one eye for one eye, and so forth. In pursuit of this goal, however, the laws allowed physical retaliation and vicarious punishment and did not accept the principle of equal justice for all but, rather, adjusted penalties according to social class" (*The JPS Torah Commentary Exodus*, Commentary by Nahum M. Sarna [Philadelphia: Jewish Publication Society, 1991] p. 126). In Roman jurisprudence, the *lex talionis* came to be interpreted as the law of just retribution. L. B. Tronchin first raises the *lex talionis* as a theme in *Emmanuel Appadocca* when he discusses Philip's life. See L. B. Tronchin, "The Great West Indian Orator," *Public Opinion*, December 21, 1888. This article is reproduced in Cudjoe, ed., *Michel Maxwell Philip*.

spirits who were their associates—that had separated themselves, by their deeds, from the world, the world's sympathy, and the world's good and bad, that had actually turned their hands against all men, and had expected, as they had probably frequently experienced, that the hand of all men should be turned against them, could not restrain their feelings of welcome, and three loud and prolonged cheers resounded, far and wide over the silent ocean, as they were wafted, in undying echoes, over the crests of heavy and heaving billows. As comrade rejoined comrade, their grim and bearded faces appeared to relax from their wonted habit of ferocity, under the influence of a prevailing sense of joy: such a joy, those, alone, can experience who have seen every natural tie break asunder around them—who have felt the heavy hand of a crushing destiny, or have been hunted and driven, by the injustice and persecution of a friend or relative, to seek shelter in that desperate solitude, which is relieved, but, by the presence, and cheered, but, by the sympathy of the few, who, like themselves, have been picked out by fate, to suffer, to be miserable, and to be finally, cast forth from the society of mankind (*EA.*, pp. 57–58).

Given such solidarity, "a tradition of rough, quasi-democratic self-government," as Gordon Lewis labels it,[14] developed among the members of the Black Schooner, the ship on which these men sail. Each man is considered an equal as long as he follows the discipline of the ship. These men also maintain "a strict sense of honour," convinced "that the least breach of honesty among themselves would be the end of their individual security, and the dissolution of their society" (*EA.*, p. 98). Because their feeling of abandonment condemn them to establish their own values and to follow their own rules, they have adopted piracy as a way of life, "more like an adventure, in which men of spirit would engage with as much honour, as in fighting under banners of stranger kings, for the purpose of conquering distant and unoffending peoples" (*EA.*, p. 99). To these men, the pirating of booty is considered to be just as legitimate as the pirating of men, a reflection of the sentiments echoed by one Captain Bellamy, the leader of a buccaneering group.[15]

According to Appadocca, Wellmington's crime revolves around the fact that he has abandoned his offspring and thereby violated one of Nature's most sacred law, that is, "certain feelings which are implanted in us, and which are considered the laws of Creation" (*EA.*, p. 110). Appadocca believes that, by prostituting "the law of nature" for his "own selfish gratification" and neglecting that life for which he is supposed "to provide and care" (*EA.*, p. 117), Willmington has abandoned all the natural human feelings enshrined in the "law of the land" and in Nature's law. The abandonment of such natural feelings leads to (or creates) "the spoilt and blighted existence" among all those men (on sea and on land) who were so acted, hence the

---

14. Gordon Lewis, *Main Currents in Caribbean Thought* (Port of Spain: Heinemann Educational Books, 1983), p. 81.

15. Captain Bellamy is reported to have told his followers that "organized society robs the poor under the cover of the law while they, the pirates, plundered the rich under the protection of their own pirate's courage." Quoted in Lewis, *Main Currents in Caribbean Thought*, p. 80.

title, *Emmanuel Appadocca; or, Blighted Life*. Wilmington must pay a price for his transgression.

The novel responds to two important questions: when these laws are violated, who has the responsibility of enforcing them and what is the correct way of doing so? Resorting to an updated interpretation of the *lex talionis*, the narrator suggests that a person has an obligation to punish these violations while he lives. After asserting that law exists in all of nature, he uses the following ground to justify his actions:

> Man, as well as other beings, is subject to it [Law], and the penalty which its violation entails. If you establish false systems among yourselves, and consent to postpone to an imaginary period, this penalty, which ought to be made to follow closely upon every obligation of the law, surely Heaven is not to be blamed. Duty is poised between reward of virtue and retribution: man has the license to chose, between either meriting the former, or bringing down the latter, upon himself. The great error of your social physics is, that you remit this penalty to a period of time, which if it were even unimagined, would fail to afford the principal and best effect of retribution,—the deterring from crimes (*EA.*, p. 200).

The narrator goes further, saying, "Know that man himself, by law, is the avenger, the retributionist on himself or others." It is the principles of *lex talionis*, as he interprets them, to which Emmanuel turns to vindicate "the law of nature which has been violated in me, and in your child; and I swear, by the Great Being who gave me reason, that I shall not rest until I have taught my father, that the creature to whom he has given life possesses feelings and sensibility, and is capable of taking vengeance" (*EA.*, p. 203).

As prescient (and perhaps as dogmatic) as Appadocca is in his understanding of philosophy, the most intriguing aspect of his (and by extension, Philip's) interpretation of the *lex talionis* is his belief that this theological law is an integral part of ancient Africa's philosophical and theological system—of "those who dwelt on the banks of the Nile of old"—even though Europeans came to associate it with Hebraic Law.[16] He suggests that this African theological borrowing was applied incorrectly within the Judeo-Christian system. He says to Hamilton, his European counterpart, "You forgot, in your social system, the wisdom of the race which you affect to despise, while you cherish the theological philosophy which you were eager to borrow from them, and tie the hand of the avenger, and blunt the double-edged

16. In the 1850s, Egypt's importance in world history was a conscious part of the age. Reviewing a revised edition of J. Gardner Wilkinson's *A Popular Account of the Ancient Egyptians* in the *London Quarterly Review*, a reviewer remarked that, because archaeology "is now becoming a popular study— and what remains of ancient Egypt—have thrown great light upon the Assyrian monuments, we prognosticate a large sale for these volumes" (Vol. 2, No. 4 [June 1854], pp. 589–90). In *The Slave Son*, Mary Fanny Wilkins notes that the Egyptians "were the most civilized [people] on the globe; and elsewhere we find that during one period the fair-haired race was subject and slave to the Egyptians, and that the prejudice of caste was as strong in the Thebaid against the white people, as it is with us now against the Negroes" (*The Slave Son* [London: Chapman and Hall, 1854], pp. 120–21).

sort of retribution."[17] By insisting on this earth-based notion of retribution, a "now-orientation" of this theological concept, Appadocca is expressing what Mervyn Alleyne calls "an African religious and world-view continuity [that] underlies the strong desire to remove the inequalities and injustices of the status-quo which is commonly found in Afro-Jamaican religious movements."[18]

In advancing his thesis of how social and religious life ought to be ordered and the appropriateness of the *lex talionis* within the context of the slave system—in this case, the relationship between a master (his father) and his slave (his son)—Philip intends a broader indictment of Western civilization and colonialism, which he argues is nothing more than a "licensed system of robbing and thieving" around which "the civilized world turns" (*EA.*, p. 217). In defense of colonized peoples, he makes *the* important point, extensive as it is, that bears repetition:

The barbarous hordes, whose fathers, either [by] choice or some unlucky accident, originally drove to some cold, frozen, cheerless, and fruitless waste, increasing in numbers, wincing under the inclemency of their clime and the poverty of their land, and longing after the richer, and more fertile, and teeming soil of some other country, desert their wretched regions, and with all the machinery of war, melt down on the unprovoking nations, whose only crime is their being more fortunate and blest, and wrench from their enervated sway the prosperous fields that first provoked their famished cupidity. The people which a convenient position, either on a neck of land, or the elbow of some large river, first consolidated, developed, and enriched, after having appropriated, through the medium of commerce, the wealth of its immediate neighbours, sends forth its numerous and powerful ships to scour the seas, to penetrate into hitherto unknown regions, where discovering new and rich countries, they, in the name of civilization, first opened an intercourse with the peaceful and contented inhabitants, next contrive to provoke a quarrel, which always terminates in a war that leaves them the conquerors and possessors of the land. As for the original inhabitants themselves, they are driven after the destruction of their cities, to roam the woods, and to perish and disappear on the advance

17. Philip was aware of Africa's contribution to intellectual thought and scientific developments. *A Port of Spain Gazette* report on his introductory lecture on electricity delivered on July 7, 1855 at the Chacon Street Schoolhouse reads as follows: "After a few words on the derivation of the word, he entered upon the history of the science, showing that among the Greeks the knowledge of the force was confined to the bare observances of the effect of friction on amber; to another very ancient people, however—the Egyptians—or rather the priesthood of that people—he ascribed a much more extended acquaintance both with electric force, and with some of the ends to which it might be applied. He stated his belief that it was by its agency that the learned men of profane Egypt were able to initiate all but one of the miracles which Divinity empowered Moses to perform, and which enabled them also to give the world renowned voice to the statue at Memnon." Memnon, the mythical king of Ethiopia, was the son of Eos and Tithonus. He went to Troy to aid his uncle Priam, killed Antilochus, and was himself killed by Achilles, after which Zeus rendered him immortal. The voice of the statue of Memnon to which Philip alludes, refers to "the colossi of Memnon whose stones, before the restoration the statues, were said to sing at dawn, once stood before the temple of a king and are inscribed with the names Amenhotep III." See N. G. L. Hammond and H. H. Scullard, eds., *The Oxford Classical Dictionary* (Oxford: Clarendon Press, 1970), pp. 668–69.

18. Mervyn C. Allyene, *Roots of Jamaican Culture* (London: Pluto Press, 1989), p. 105.

of their greedy supplanters. Nations that are different only in the language with which they vent their thoughts, inhabiting the same portions of the globe, and separated but by a narrow stream, eagerly watch the slightest inclination of accident in their respective favours, and on the plea, either of religion—that fertile theme, and ready instigator—or on the still more extensive and uncertain ground of politics, use the chance that circumstances throw into their hands, make incursions and fight battles, whose fruits are only misery and wretchedness. A fashion springs up at a certain time to have others to labour for our benefit, and to bear 'the heat and burthen of the day' in our stead: straightway, the map of the world is opened, and the straggling and weakest portions of a certain race, whose power of bodily and mental endurance, renders them the likely objects to answer this end, are chosen. The coasts of the country on which nature has placed them, are immediately lined with ships of acquisitive voyagers, who kidnap and tear them away from the scenes that teem with the associations of their own and their fathers' happiness, load them with irons, throw them into the cruel ordeal of the 'middle passage,' to test whether they are sufficiently iron-constituted as to survive the starvation, stench, and pestilential contagion which decide the extent of the African's endurance, and fix his value. This, my dear friend, is an abstracted idea of the manner in which the world turns (*EA.*, pp. 217–19).

In this incisive disquisition of how Europeans treated Africans and other "weaker" races, the narrator outlines a myth of beginnings: a narrative of the colonial encounter. He explains that first Europeans rushed to discover warmer and more productive climes. Initially, the indigenous peoples welcomed them and shared their meager food supplies with them. When, however, it seemed as though the Europeans had come to stay, misunderstandings arose between the two parties that resulted in violent conflicts, perceived by the Europeans as treachery on the part of native peoples. In the ensuing conflict, native peoples were dispossessed. In 1986, Peter Hulme described this pattern of behavior with regards to the Americas:

There seems little doubt that as far as the Amerindians were concerned the turning point [in their relationship with the Europeans] was always the realization that their 'guests' had come to stay. The Europeans were blinded to this by their failure to comprehend that what confronted them was an agriculturally based society with claims over the land. Unable to understand the effect of their behavior the only narrative that they could construct to make sense of both the hospitality and the violence was a narrative of treachery in which the initial kindness was a ruse to establish trust before the natives 'natural' violence emerged from behind the mask.[19]

It is to Philip's credit that, as early as 1854, he understood that European discourses about their civilizing mission, their notions about the pacification of savage peoples, and their vain mouthings about their Christianizing endeavors were nothing less than the invention of disguises under which to rob and enslave native peo

---

19. Peter Hulme, *Colonial Encounters: Europe and the Native Caribbean, 1492–1797* (London: Methuen, 1986), p. 131.

ples whose only crime was "their being more fortunate and blest…[with] prosperous fields that first provoked their famished cupidity." Although the author offers a romantic alternative, that is a glorified, pristine innocence ("The mind can thrive only in the silence that courts contemplation….Commerce makes steam engines and money—it assists not the philosophical progress of the mind"), he understands that a system that depends on brutalizing others to achieve its ends and encouraging human beings to exhibit the worst aspects of human nature, vice and wickedness, cannot be construed as being civilized or Christian.

Philip grasps that the civilization from which Africans came "gave philosophy, religion, and government to the world, but who must now themselves stoop, to cut wood, and to carry water, when, by the common rules of justice, they should be permitted to enjoy the land from which they have sprung, and to participate in its dignities." That an inhabitant of Trinidad, in the middle of the nineteenth century, should demonstrate such important insights into Africa's contribution to world civilization and use it as an informing principle of his intellectual work is a remarkable achievement. That he should make a careful distinction between instinct and reason (he argues that "there is no such thing as instincts in man: he alone is distinguished from the rest of organic beings by the indefiniteness of his mind and sensibilities"), speak so perceptively about the law of revenge, and make such an resounding indictment against slavery testify to the vitality of Trinidad's intellectual culture, despite his having written the novel while he was in England. Such acute observations and perspicacity of mind demonstrate the seriousness with which these men understood their scholarly tasks and the intellectual awakening (a sense of incipient nationalism) that was taking place in the society.

Appadocca believes the most important thing in life is the courage to preserve "our honour, our consciousness of acting right," a central virtue in the buccaneer's code. Such honor, he believes, can only be achieved by dedicating one's life to avenging (justly retaliating to) the cause of one's displeasure and one's shame. It is through this process that one fulfills one's destiny, a complicated notion of what he calls "a synchronism of events and a simultaneousness of the actings of nature's general laws;…against which no man from the absence of any power to read the future can provide." Although Appadocca chooses to end his life after having completed his destined objective, he clearly proves himself a romantic. In death, his faithful followers exalt him.

Emmanuel Appadocca can be read as a nineteenth century response to the philosophies of slavery, racism, and European arrogance. Written at a time when many antislavery novels were being published, it has much in common with Blyden's "African man" and Rousseau's "natural savage," both of whom seek the solution to the problems of racism in an idealized world where men, as Emmanuel asserts, will live "happily, quietly, and far removed from the world, whose sympathy they cannot hope, and cannot care to possess." Like Blyden, Philip's thesis represents "an emotional response to the European process of denigrating Africa [and Africans] and an opposition to the exploitation that resulted from the expansionism of Europe from the fifteenth century" to when Philip wrote.[20] The passage of the Fugitive Slave Law, one of the factors impelling the writing of this novel, proved to be the final humiliation of the African in the New World. In writing *Emmanuel Appadocca*, it was Philip's intent to recuperate the African for the New World and place him at the center of his universe. When Philip died, a grieving savant made the following comment about what he meant to them:

> Yes! Trinidad's illustrious son is gone,
> Thy victory now is sure, thy work is done.
> O thou implacable and cruel death
> Revengeful for with foul Lethean's breath,
> That bringest here desolation's bitter tears
> To patriot's eyes, whose soul unknown to fears.
> In times of yore defied the tyrant's yoke,
> And liberty the blessed day evoke.
> But no! O death thy victory is vain
> And Philip's memory will still remain,
> Enthroned in love within the grateful heart
> Of those to whom the voice of faith imparts
> Sweet consolation, heavenly balm;
> O yes, his memory lives secure and calm
> Among the young who hailed his fame so fair,
> Who would not blush to weep for one so dear.
> When the eternal spark forsook its shell
> His memory lives and history will tell
> His work, the battles fought to freedom's name,
> When impious tyranny imposed its fame
> And timid liberty conceals its head;
> Assailed at last! by legitimate dread.
> O sweet breeze of the Naparima's plains,
> Repeat at times in thy melodious strains
> The name of Philip to the distant hills
> Where oft are heard the distant peals!
> And you, O friends, let not oblivion's womb
> Conceal in darkness, veil the hero's tomb.[21]

The Slave Son (1854)

Although *The Slave Son* examines many of the same issues as raised in "Jim the Boatman" (the trading of slaves when it was against official policy), *Adolphus* (the disrespect meted out to free colored women and the suppression of the coloreds), and *Emmanuel Appadocca* (the relationship between a white father and a slave son), it does so from a Christian, Eurocentric perspective. Because Wilkins sees the solu-

20. V. Y. Mudimbe, *The Invention of Africa* (Bloomington: Indiana University Press, 1988), p. 132.
21. L. B. Tronchin, "The Great West Indian Orator," *Public Opinion*, December 21, 1888.

tion to the black and color problem from a Eurocentric point of view, she reproduces many of the racist stereotypes that one finds in the work of her English counterparts. This is true even as she makes a case for the liberation of the coloreds and the blacks, without, it should be said, making too many concessions to their humanity.

In Wilkin's view, the slave world (Trinidad) out of which she writes is a hierarchical one, based on color and intelligence. The light-skinned mulattoes, nearer in color to the whites, are depicted as being much more rational and sensible than those who possess Negroid features and dark skin pigmentation. Centering her novel around the story of Belfond, the slave son of St. Hilarie Cardon, the wealthiest and most sophisticated planter on the island, and Laurine, an equally sophisticated and sensitive free colored woman, Wilkins tries to construct a Caribbean *Uncle Tom's Cabin*, in which Christian purity and religious belief ultimately triumph.[22]

Belfond who is sent to France as a valet to his white brother tastes freedom, a condition that is intensified as he becomes more educated. As Belfond becomes better educated, he begins to see things differently. In France, he attempts to run away, but is captured and taken back to Trinidad. At Tobago, on his way to Trinidad, Belfond escapes once more, swims to Trinidad, and starts a new life.

Laurine, with whom Belfond has fallen in love, goes from house to house to sell her provisions and trinkets to raise enough money to free her mother who is enslaved. After a revolt on Cardon's plantation that frees Belfond and Laurine, they leave the country to start a new life in Venezuela.[23] Filled with descriptions of the idiocy of blacks, their superstitious practices, and the evil of Obeah (Wilkins spells it Obiah and calls it "African witchcraft"), the author follows the lead of similar novels written by whites who sympathized with the plight of slaves, but who nonetheless, viewed Christianity and Europe as the sources of timeless and redeeming values for all civilizations.[24] Wilkins dismisses African theological beliefs and those of other civilizations as superstition and cant and by doing so thereby highlights the diametrically opposed ways in which the colonizers and the colonized see education. In his outstanding work on slaves' education, Thomas Webber quotes Margaret Mead in arguing that education, in its broadest sense, "is the cultural

22. Wilkins thanked Harriet Beecher Stowe for writing *Uncle Tom's Cabin*, which Wilkins says, "removed the objection" that prevented her from writing her novel. "The time has come," she observed, "thanks to Mrs. Stowe! when my subject is no longer irrelevant to the topics of the day" (*The Slave Son*, p. 14). Other quotations from *Slave Son* are noted in the text as *SS*.

23. In *Emmanuel Appadocca, Adolphus* and *The Slave Son*, Venezuela represents an important symbol of freedom.

24. Highly skilled in "bush medicine" and African lore, these practitioners of Obeah (black doctors and midwives) were valuable members of the slave community. Because of their healing powers and their knowledge of herbal medicine, they enjoyed tremendous prestige among the slaves and were feared equally by the whites since they sometimes included poisoning in their repertoire. Most importantly, they became keepers of the indigenous culture of African people. Seen in this light, it is clear that Africans in the colonies saw Obeah in quite a different manner than the Europeans.

process, the way in which each newborn infant, born with a potentiality for learn-ing greater than that of any other mammal, is transformed into a full member of a specific human culture." He concludes:

> The primary understanding of how a group views the world and operates within it must be reached, as nearly as possible, from that group's perspective. Only through the members of a given social system, through the attempt to see the world as they see it, can we hope to understand the subjective meaning with which that group and its individual members understand themselves and the world in which they live.[25]

The Slave Son is content to condemn slavery as it represents an European point of view. In the process, it repeats many of Carlyle's tirades against African people and reiterates many of the conclusions of the negrophiles of the time. Even Mr. Dorset, "a most tender-hearted, Negro-loving man, all the way from free, noble, moral England" and somewhat sympathetic to the slaves, could endorse the bene-ficial practices of slavery. He observes that "I never entirely went with the public in running down the system of slavery, for I am inclined to consider it a means per-mitted by Providence to bring the inhabitants of a vast and unknown region into more immediate and direct communication with the children of enlightened Europe, and by this means to civilize savages. It remains for me to do my part, by showing kindness, patience, and gentle teaching" (*SS.*, p. 118). Such sentiments merely reinforce the conception of the "savage" nature of blacks and their need for the guidance of whites. Similar sentiments were shared by the white author of *The Koromantyn Slave* who professed sympathy with the slaves, but who still saw Christianity and the African's proximity to whiteness as the modus operandi of their earthly and heavenly salvation.[26] Dorset (and Wilkins by extension) granted that Africans possessed elements of humanity, for as the narrator acknowledges, Dorset was "in the habit of speaking with his own Negroes every day, and he had always discovered in their conversation proofs of the same power of mind, the same reasoning faculties, the same feelings as those of white people, only not cultivated" (*SS.*, p. 119).

The complicated relationship between a white father and a black slave son is revealed when the slaves on Cardon's plantation rise up against their master, set fire to his home, and free Belfond, who was condemned to die for being insubordinate to his master. In the conflagration, Cardon refuses his son's attempt to free him from the burning house. Surprised by this refusal, Belfond reflects on the perversi-ty of his condition: "He would not let me save him, he repeated to himself; 'He would not let me save him!—I, his own son, cursed even in that!' and with his hand resting on his bosom, he bewailed his unhappy fate, and wept over the untimely

---

25. Thomas L. Webber, *Deep Like the Rivers* (New York: W. W. Norton, 1978), p. 263.

26. See *The Koromantyn Slave: or, West Indian Sketches* (London: J. Harchard, 1823.) See Barbara Lalla, *Defining Jamaican Fiction* (Tuscaloosa: University of Alabama Press, 1966) for a discussion of this text.

death of one whom he would have loved had he been permitted" (*SS.*, p. 342). Even in the face of death, his white father is unwilling to acknowledge his black son.

One sees an immediate comparison between Appadocca and Cardon with the father-son relationship portrayed in Philip's novel. However, if Appadocca is bent on seeking revenge against his father for defiling his mother, Belfond is intent on saving his father and making peace with him. The latter craves his father's love, in spite of his father's callousness and perhaps cruelty to his mother. Whereas Philip, as C. L. R. James suggests, might have been influenced by how his father treated his mother,[27] Wilkins, a white woman, used the conflict between a white father and his enslaved son to promote the saving and revivifying grace of the Christian message, the virtues of forgiveness and the triumph of God's love in this world and the one hereafter. Where *Emmanuel Appadocca* ends on a tragic note, *Slave Son* ends happily and optimistically as Belfond prepares to take his bride "beyond the sunny islands across the water,—there, where none are slaves, where Bolivar [echoes of *Adolphus*] has given to all equal rights" (*SS.*, p. 345). Thus, Christianity, in all of its vanity, triumphs.[28] Just as in *Uncle Tom's Cabin*, the *Slave* Son has Belfond confess to his wife-to-be:

> All I wanted was to feel myself something in this great beautiful world—something responsible to God. Do you see, Laurine, that fallen tree, lying prostrate on the ground? See the little twigs it sends shooting upwards—those are its endeavours to rise, but a power greater than all its forces keeps it chained to the ground: such is the poor slaves, and such are his impotent yearnings to rise. Believe me, blessed Laurine, the very spirit of rebellion I exhibited, my disgust and discontent, were but so many proofs of my worship of the Supreme (*SS.*, pp. 345–46).

As for Adolphus, de Sources, and others, Venezuela offered a sense of liberty and equality for the slave and the colored person. Bolivar, a Caribbean person in the larger sense of the term, personified a leadership that many coloreds expected to find in the land of their birth. When Belfond bids farewell to his dear land, a spot on earth that God might have chosen for his Eden, he does so reluctantly. Even as he speaks of his blasted dreams, "all spoiled, corrupted, poisoned by the white man," there is the knowledge that he wishes things were better and that, indeed, the white man recognized that all he wanted was the right to enjoy the same rights that he,

27. James writes that "[w]hile in England, he [Philip] had occasion to write his father asking for help. It seems that his father refused, or at least neglected the appeal and Maxwell Philip never forgave him. It was about this time too that he wrote and published *Emmanuel Appadocca*....It is sufficient to say here that all through it shows the powerful effect with which the misfortune of his birth weighed upon his mind" (C. L. R. James, "Maxwell Philip, 1829–1888," in Cudjoe, ed., *Michel Maxwell Philip*), p. 89.

28. The language is that of Isaiah Berlin who, in speaking of the dangers of cultural arrogance and the tendency to judge ancient societies in terms of modern values pointed out that no one had "written more pungently than Voltaire against the European habit of dismissing as inferior remote civilisations, such as that of China, which he had extolled in order to expose the ridiculous vanity, exclusiveness and fanaticism of the 'barbarous' Judaeo-Christian outlook that recognised no values besides its own" (Isaiah Berlin, *The Proper Study of Mankind* [London: Chatto & Windus, 1997], p. 362).

the white man, enjoyed. To be sure, there is, in this sentiment, many echoes of Philippe's *Free Mulatto.*

The Slave Son, as a reviewer remarked, wishes to demonstrate that slavery results in "the debasement of the mind, the deadening of every virtue, the calling into action of those weapons of defense which nature has given to the weak—cunning, deceit, treachery, and secret murder." It also sought to achieve "the restoration of a better tone of feeling between the coloured and the white man." The reviewer also saw the novel as an attempt to make the English people focus more directly on the mote within their own eyes rather than what they perceived to be the mote in the eyes of the slave holders in the United States: "If the treatment of the mulattoes in our other West Indian island be like that described in Trinidad, we have no business to exclaim against the citizens of the United States for their behavior towards men and women with black blood in their veins."[29]

From this standpoint, Wilkins achieved her goal of making her English readers compare what was happening in the Caribbean with what was taking place in the United States. Indeed, she may have seen herself as providing against Caribbean slavery the same blow that Stowe provided in the United States. Yet, in a very derogatory and sexist aside, the *Atlas* reviewer refused to take the novel seriously. He averred that "[c]ourtesy to the sex and our friendly feelings towards all novices incline us to look with indulgence upon this first effort."[30] Despite the inability of the reviewer to take *Slave Son* as seriously as Wilkins intended, the very existence of the review gives us some information of the book's impact upon its English readership. Since *Atlas,* an important English journal of arts at the time, reviewed the work, it suggests that Wilkins's work created enough of a stir to make it more than a blip upon the collective English consciousness. That Trinidad should be the setting of this novel indicates that the treatment of the coloreds deserved the enormous attention it was getting at the time.

If the English showed some interest in Wilkins' novel, the editor of the *Port of Spain Gazette,* the journal of the planter class,[31] was livid when news reached him that Wilkins had used his fair land, the spot "God might have chosen...for Eden when first He created man; [a place where] angels might have lived among your gardens" to set her novel. Intent on reading fiction as historical truth, the *Port of Spain Gazette* published the entire review and averred:

> The absurdity of representing the African Slave trade as being carried on here so late as the year 1832, even sub rosa, is so great, and the picture drawn of the complexional prejudice which once existed here, so extraordinary outré, and the extracts

29. "The Slave Son," *Atlas Supplement,* (London), January 28, 1854
30. Ibid.
31. An editorial in the *Trinidad Reporter* referred to the *Port of Spain Gazette* as a "supporter of the Government—a destroyer of the rights and liberties of the People. Principle is set aside, and rectitude of purpose is unthought of. Sordid motives seem to be the axis upon which everything connected with the paper revolves" (June 14, 1855).

elected by the *Reviewer,* which we presume may be considered as the cream of the work, possess so little interest, that we should hardly have inflicted such utter trash on the patience of our readers, but for the remarks of the Reviewer that "If the treatment of the mulattoes in other West India islands be like that here described in Trinidad, we have no reason to exclaim against the citizens of the United States for their behavior towards men and women with dark blood in their veins," thus evidently assuming that such treatment really does prevail here, and may possible prevail in the other British West India colonies.[32]

Taking evident pride that the smuggling of African slaves had long ceased to exist in Trinidad, the editors of the *Gazette,* rebuked such "a respectable paper like the *Atlas* [for] allowing such an absurd hypothesis" in its columns. Giving notice that they intended to take up the matter with the editor of *Atlas,* the article concluded:

> Many, many years have passed away, since the "free people of colour" as they were at one time invidiously termed, of the British West Indies, were placed on a full footing of legal equality with the white inhabitants. The last trace of the social inequality which once existed are fast disappearing; and it is too hard to have our follies and our vices of long gone-by days not only fished up from the gulph [*sic*] of oblivion, and grossly exaggerated, but sought to be palmed off on the world as a picture of the present state of society in these colonies.

Although the *Gazette* could have been faulted for confusing fictional creativity with historical reality, they were correct in detecting that Wilkins was indulging in a nineteenth-century convention of using a fictional work "mainly to aid the readerly concretization of the world of the book by forming a bridge between historical and fictional worlds."[33] This was another variation of romantic realism, as it were. Since Wilkins was intent on using her novel to reveal the cruelties of slavery and, through her novel, to do for the Caribbean what Stowe had done for the United States, the editor of the *Gazette* was right to forego the willing suspension of disbelief, a process that is suppose to take place when one reads fiction. He detected correctly that *The Slave Son* was intended to strip bare (to expose) the reality of their society and subject it to ridicule. As a defender of the status quo and his belief that Trinidad slavery was not as bad as United States slavery, the editor of the *Gazette* was not prepared to let such an attack go unanswered. In this sense, fiction *was* akin to reality, and no author should be allowed to substitute one for the other.

In spite of its narrow vision of the society, *Slave Son* is an important sentimental novel, which is filled with many ethnographic details. It anticipates some of the topics that de Verteuil's *Trinidad,* William Gamble's *Trinidad,* and J. J. Thomas's *Theory and Practice of Creole Grammar* would examine. Informed by the proverbs of African and Creole people, the novel captures many aspects of African wisdom and

32. *Port of Spain Gazette,* March 1, 1854.
33. Waugh, *Metafiction,* p. 32.

the richness of the Creole language. Wilkins also records the names of many local beverages and foods (such as mawbee and callaloo respectively), as well of the fruits, animals, and flowers of the people. In an enormously descriptive paragraph, she makes the following observation:

> The day was surprisingly bright and beautiful; and as he gazed on the wild and gorgeous banks of either side with delight and curiosity, he discovered that not a leaf on tree or shrub, not a blade of grass, was like anything that grew in his own England,—-vegetation so large, so varied, so rich a scale. Sometimes it was difficult to tell which was a bird and which was a flower, so brightly and confusedly were they mingled. Now his eyes followed the blue bird till it was lost in a thousand mazes, or the oriole and perroquet perched on the tree-top like some brilliant flower, then they would rest on a tuft of blooming shrubs,—the macata, the red hibiscus, the oleander, and the African rose,—through whose closely twined branches the pawpaw shot up its silvery column, with its crown of leaves and pendent racemes of odoriferous lilies, and hundreds of humming birds, all poised on their glittering wings, were spinning nectar from every cup; further on, the slim mimosa was seen hanging its delicate fringes among the thick and solid leaves of aloe and cactus, and flowering lianas twined their wreaths from bough to bough, flinging odours to the wind, and grace over the wild confusion of the woods. (*SS.*, pp. 127–28)

The white man's fear of Obeah and its strategic use as a subtext in *Slave* Son is of enormous interest. Every important aspect of the novel is driven by the fear of Obeah and its use for good and evil. To read Wilkins is to understand—though in a curiously inflated way—how difficult it is to understand the Caribbean if one does not understand how mytho-religious practices such as Obeah, myalism, vodun, and Santeria shape the lives of its inhabitants. Although she was undoubtedly English, perhaps a planter's wife, Wilkins possessed a tremendous knowledge of Trinbagonian society, its language, and its cultural practices. As a fictional work, *Slave Son* demonstrates the contradictions of the white abolitionist who genuinely wishes to repudiate slavery and its evils but who cannot free herself from an ideology that sees Africans as needing white colonial guidance and the protection of Europe and Christianity.

The East Indian Presence

After the East Indians arrived in 1845, they began to affect the general populace. Apart from the opposition to their presence from some quarters, their treatment also became a subject of lively discussion. In 1851, the *Trinidadian* carried an article entitled "Treatment of Our Indian Coolies at Trinidad," based on a report by Major Fagan, the "Coolie Stipendiary Magistrate of Trinidad," which was sent to Lord Harris.

In this article, this "Friend of India," presumably an Englishman, outlines "the wretched conditions to which the coolies have been reduced by the bad faith of the colonial authorities, and the ill-treatment of some of the Planters."[34] Calling this record of bad faith a "melancholy tale of perfidy and misery," the paper devoted considerable attention to the conditions to which the East Indians were subjected. Recounting an East Indian myth of beginning as it were, this "Friend of India" alludes to a betrayal of trust that is similar in some respects to that of the Amerindians and the Africans. He relates that "[t]he coolies, be it remembered, were engaged in Calcutta by a government agent under the guarantee of the state that they should be provided with adequate food, clothing and comfort for five years. It was solely in dependence on this pledge of the punctual payment of their wages and continuous employment, to which the honour of Government was bound, that they were led to embark for that distant colony."

Alas, such was not to be the case. When the East Indians arrived on the island, they found themselves at the complete mercy of the planter, who was able to turn them off his plantation "without paying them the wages they have earned; because," as the Stipendiary Magistrate observes, "there is no law guaranteeing their wages to them; and this infamous procedure is exhibited in a Crown Colony, with English law, English judges, English barristers and English institutions!" Such treatment had disastrous consequences for East Indians who died by the thousands.

However, the author had another objective in mind. Not only did he try to persuade the governor that the East Indian, with better treatment, had the potential to be "a more valuable labourer than the African," he also went on to draw certain sociological conclusions: "In the matter of natural intelligence, the Calcutta coolie is immeasurably superior to the African. He has all the qualities of a man, without any propensities of a brute. The African is destitute of the former, but unusually festive in the latter." It might be that this "Friend of India," like the "Apostle of the Indians" at the dawning of the New World encounter, was merely exaggerating the contrast between these two groups so as to assist the more despised party.[35] Utterances such as those by the "Apostle of the Indians" (since "the labour of one Negro was more valuable than that of four [Amer] Indians, every effort should be made to bring to Hispaniola many Negroes from Guinea")[36] and the "Friend of India" only encouraged those who believed in the African's inferiority, that he was merely another link (one of the lower links) in the chain leading from savagery to civilization.

To his credit (and that of the newspaper), the publication of the following excerpt from Major Fagan's report alerted the population that all was not well and certainly told the planters that their behavior was under scrutiny:

34. "Treatment of Our Indian Coolies at Trinidad," *The Trinidadian*, August 13–16, 1851.

35. There seems to be support for this position. Ron Ramdin notes that the Indian Mutiny of 1858 aroused bitter feelings in Britain toward the "heathen Hindoos" whom the English authorities saw as "beings of an inferior and heathen race" (Ron Ramdin, *The Other Middle Passage* [London; Hansib, 1994], pp. 36–37).

36. Quoted in Eric Williams, *From Columbus to Castro* (New York: Harper and Row, 1970), p. 37. According to Williams , once Batoleme de Las Casas had accepted this formula for solving the Amerindian problem, he put in place "the rationalisation of Negro slavery" (Ibid., p. 37).

Oh! the extent of the sufferings of this well disposed, but wretched people—wretched from neglect, injustice, and want of sympathy in their physical afflictions—-is not at present known as it ought to be, and would have been, had only a portion of that preserving industry with which the press of the West Indies has been plying the trade of slander in regard to them, been devoted to the more Christian work of exposing their sufferings and grievances, or demanding redress or transshipment to their country from which they immigrated under pledges which they complain, and complain with reason, have been violated. Their fleshless arms, their wasted frames, their haggard looks, their livid countenances, which it has been my painful lot to witness in the hospitals of the colony and on the high roads, where stretched on their bed of earth, from which I fear but few of them ever rose, looking more like skeletons than living human beings, proclaim that this is not romance, but the truth: affording but too reasonable ground for apprehending that most have perished from neglect, and not from the effects of climate.

Oh! it is an utter abomination—a crying injustice—and one that must soon or late be heard, to see in this so-called Christian and civilized land and under the eye of Heaven, a people whose sweat and toil—and that sweat and toil in many instances, unrequited—have rescued the soil from entire abandonment, made the victims of a relentless, an ungrateful and heartless neglect, to which no parallel can be found in the annals of slavery; and many of them now with the prospect before them of being doomed, when their services are no longer required, to wander through the wilderness of the land, unheeded, houseless, friendless, famishing and without covering to shield them from the night air, or night dew, so fatal to all who are exposed to their baneful influence in the tropics.

In retrospect, it seems obvious that a comparison would be made with the African condition and that of slavery. It is sufficient, though, to recognize that the Indians who came to Trinidad during the first decade suffered much and fiercely at the hands of the planters. However, the plea by the "Friend of India" that both the native and foreign press should sound the alarm about the depressing conditions of the Indians fitted in quite nicely with the role that the press played (that is, educating the population) during this period of development.

Journal of a Voyage with Coolie Emigrants from Calcutta to Trinidad (1859)

The cruelty that Major Fagan observed in his report to Lord Harris was supplemented by a chonicle of events documented in Captain and Mrs. Swinton's *Journal of a Voyage with Coolie Emigrants from Calcutta to Trinidad*, "one of only two known first-hand accounts that have survived voyages of Indian emigrant ships bound for Trinidad."[37] A remarkable narrative of a voyage of most horrid proportions (approx-

37. Ramdin, *The Other Middle Passage*, p. 22. The title of Ramdin's book reiterates the assumption made by "Friend of India" that the voyage of the Indians to the Caribbean was analogous to the trip made by Africans. Ramdim concedes that, "by comparison with the African slavers, following the abo-

imately 120 of the 340 Indians who left Calcutta aboard the *Salsette* died along the way), it illustrates the dangers that East Indians underwent as they crossed the *Kala pani* (dark water) and the horrific price they paid to supply Trinidad fields with a cheap source of labor. To be sure, the Indians themselves did not know why they were recruited (in spite of what Major Fagan says); they only knew that the trip across the Atlantic meant a better way of life. For many it did, but the attendant cruelty speaks volumes about the injustice that our forebears underwent as they traveled and adapted to a land that was not their own. As I demonstrate in the subsequent chapter, part of the process of becoming Trinidadian involved a capacity to both claim and name one's space, a process that occurred simultaneously as this brutality was taking place.

The existence of the journal itself is a remarkable phenomenon. In it, Captain Swinton kept an account of his 108-days' journey across the Atlantic, passing it on to his wife shortly before he perished off the New York coast shortly after leaving Trinidad. As James Carlile, the editor of this journal noted, Jane Swinton, "with fidelity," copied her husband's journal and made it available to posterity. Although Swinton is concerned primarily with recording the deaths of these immigrants (a not-so-inconsequential fact when one realizes that the captain was paid for the number of live bodies he delivered to his destination),[38] he also comments on the state of the Indians, the voyage, and some of the journey's attendant difficulties. In one excerpt, Swinton reflects on the tremendous mortality rate after forty-five days at sea:

> May 3rd. A woman died of dysentery. This makes seventy dead. It is dreadful mortality; still any one who had ever sailed with them would not wonder at it, as they are so badly selected at the depot, and so many diseased sent on board. Besides, their habits are so beastly, and personal cleanliness so neglected, and being such a weakly emaciated set, they require a suitable number of male and female nurses, who should be adequately remunerated, to look after and attend to them.[39]

On April 29, he wrote that he had cleared the launch boat to convert it into a hospital for the sick, "the smell below being so dreadful, though everything [was] done to prevent it" (*Journal*, p. 8.) Such unsanitary conditions, unclean water, and inadequate food contributed enormously to the deaths of the Indians. When one adds the exposure to the weather to which they were not accustomed, one realizes that Captain Swinton's observations do not really tell the entire story. Yet, there is something to be said about the general health of the persons who were recruited to

---

lition of the British slave trade and slavery, humanitarian concern and the reluctance of some officials to engage in a new system of slavery, resulted in the more spacious 'Coolie ships'" (Ibid., p. 14).

38. Captain Swinton was informed about this condition before he left as his correspondence with John Wreinholt reveals: "My dear Captain Swinton—Government will only pay you on so many Coolies landed alive" (Captain and Mrs. Swinton, *Journal Of a Voyage with Coolie Emigrants from Calcutta to Trinidad* [London: Alfred W. Bennett, 1859], p. 4).

39. Ibid., p. 8. Subsequent quotations are noted in the text under *Journal*.

travel to Trinidad. Jane Swinton's observes that "[t]he manner in which the Coolies are collected together in Calcutta is from native travellers being sent out into the country and villages, to induce them to emigrate by fine promises. These travelers bring in the scum of the villages as well as some desirable emigrants. They should be kept at least a month at the depot, to get them into a fit state to bear a three months' voyage" (*Journal*, p. 12). Two months into his journey, recognizing the tremendous human cost, Captain Swinton is forced to recognize that "[t]his mortality is dreadful, and without any means of being checked. A great reformation is required in the system of Cooley [*sic*] emigration" (*Journal*, p. 9). Without such reformation, further tragedy was inevitable.

If Captain Swinton related what happened on the voyage, it was left to Jane Swinton to analyze the meaning of what transpired. She, however, is blind to the contradictions that her very presence on that journey entails. At the heart of the journal is the pull between the promulgation of certain ideals (religiosity and Christianity) and the barbarity of the practice in which the couple is engaged. After all, Captain Swinton did not go to India (or China for that matter) because he wished to save the souls of these heathens, even though the prospect of Christianizing these Indians must have been a tantalizing prospect. His journey to India was motivated solely by profit, as his statements reveal, and it is a motivation that led to the tremendous calamity for the Indians.[40] So that while Jane Swinton can see nothing wrong in her husband's actions (removing hundreds of Indians to a land they did not know and for what purpose they were not told), she seems to be taken aback by their lack of what she calls personal morality among the Indians:

> They have no morality whatever: if they fancy each other, they become man and wife for the time being, and change again when they please. The parents of girls will sell their children for a few rupees. I may here mention that in the island, and on the plantations which I visited, I found the same immorality was carried on, and no provision for instructing them in Christianity; on the contrary, their own heathen processions were allowed to be carried on, but good care was taken of their bodies, as there was a doctor to take charge of them (*Journal*, p. 14).

Thus, while this Christian woman has no problems removing over three hundred people from their homelands to a future about which they were not aware, she is upset about their choices of mates and what she calls "their own heathen processions." Although she even pities their being "put into boats in sixes and sevens like cattle, and sent to their different destinations" (*Journal*, p. 15), she takes no responsibility for bringing these Indians to the Caribbean in the first place.

To Jane Swinton, the answer to the plight of the Indians was to instruct them in Christianity so that they might behave in a way she finds desirable. No wonder that she is gratified that some of the children are taken to the Tacarigua Coolie Home

---

40. See for example, Captain Swinton's entry of May 28.

(now the St. Mary's Children's Home) to be "instructed in Christianity" (*Journal*, p. 14). But the mandate of the Tacarigua Coolie Home, funded in part by the funds of William Burnley, was to make these children English with British values and manners, a mission that had the same effect as the famous 1857 minutes in India.

To be sure, Jane Swinton's promulgation of Christianity and her (mis)interpretation of the behavior of the East Indian women are tainted by her Eurocentric veil. Still, her sympathy for the condition of these emigrants is to be admired, as are the sensible recommendations she made to improve their lot. She seems sincere in her comments that the journal be used "towards promoting the welfare of this unfortunate race of people, and may be the means of interesting kind and philanthropic persons on their behalf." Yet, it remains true that she and her husband participated in a tremendous evil: taking a people from their home and casting them into the wilds of Trinidad. Unfortunately, they failed to appreciate the contradictions that were inherent in their actions.

* * *

Necessarily, the emerging literature of this period was a part of a wider nationalist phenomenon that was taking place in Latin America, the Caribbean, and the United States. It was a literature that identified with political and social reforms, promoted autochthonous cultural values, challenged the arbitrariness and cruelty of slavery, brought to the fore many of the injustices that the Creole population suffered, and chronicled the agonies of the Indians. As Jean Franco writes, during this period, "literature was sometimes the only form of activity left open to them [the intellectuals], so that the novel and even poetry came to be regarded as instruments for attacking injustices, and for creating a sense of patriotism and civic pride."[41]

Romanticism, the major vehicle through which the sentiments of the period were expressed, captured the contradictory impulses that informed the literature. Such a literature erected a Creole nationalism that became a driving force in the formation of the society. Ernest Gellner asserts that "nationalism is rooted in modernity." The nation, he argues, was never "an eternal entity, imperishable, transcending the ephemeral beings and generations in which it is transiently incarnated. The basic building blocks of mankind are nations, and their existence is not a contingent and morally irrelevant fact, but, on the contrary, it is central to human fulfillment. Cultural diversity is our manifest destiny and men reach fulfillment through their distinctive national cultures, not through some bloodless universality."[42]

Clearly, Trinbagonian literature of the 1850s reveals the nuances of an emerging national voice and a budding nationalism. A recapitulation of a past, as the author of *Adolphus* explained, is a necessary point of departure in understanding the present and in outlining the contours of the future. Inescapably, those past voices con-

41. Jean Franco, *An Introduction to Spanish-American Literature* (Cambridge: Cambridge University Press, 1969), p. 47.

42. Ernest Gellner, *Nationalism* (New York: New York University Press, 1997) pp. 13, 8–9.

tain the seeds of an incipient nationalism that became more insistent as the century advanced. Needless to say, the literature was a means through which the citizens of a multicultural Trinidad began to achieve a degree of human fulfillment and was also an avenue through which they began to emerge as Trinbagonians.

CHAPTER 7

Naming the Land

A cosmic painting is able to depict with a few strokes of the brush the unfathomed heavens and the microscopic organisms of the plant and animal kingdoms which we find in stagnant pools or the weathered edges of the rocks. The subject matter for the picture is every possible thing that has ever been observed during intensive study in every field up to the present day and contains the proof of its truth and faithful representation...Pleasure at the attaining of new knowledge is mingled with a wistful longing in the mind which strives ever upward and onward and is dissatisfied with the present, a longing for as yet unknown areas of knowledge which remain to be discovered.

—ALEXANDER VON HUMBOLDT, quoted in Adolph Meyer-Abich,
   Alexander von Humboldt

Place is not only a fact to be explained in the broader frame of space, but it is also a reality to be clarified and understood from the perspective of the people who have given it meaning.

   —Quoted in J. Nicholas Entrikin, *The Betweenness of Place*

Historical reality cannot be apprehended in any relation of immediacy, but can only be approached through its textual representation and inter-pretations; its absence bear the contradictory traces of the always-already-read.

   —ROBERT YOUNG, *White Mythologies*

Truly, this period in our history has been well defined as the boundary-making era. Whether we turn to Europe, Asia, Africa or America, such an endless vista of political geography arises before us, such a vast area of land and sea to be explored and developed; such a vision of great bur-dens for the white man to take up in far-off regions, dim and indefnite as yet.

   —THOMAS HOLDICH quoted in F. Driver, "Geography's Empire"

Introduction

The need to experience the national territory did not confine itself to the creative texts—novels, tales, sermons, poems, etc.—but it also resonated in the works of the visual artists, the geographers, and the natural scientists. To be sure, the newspapers also assisted in bringing these works to the fore in that painters, such as Jean Cazabon, advertised for customers in the newspapers, while L. A. A. de Verteuil made his views known by writing articles in the newspapers. The newspapers also made the works of such scientists as Alexander von Humboldt known to the public by publishing their articles and describing their travels. They reported on a geological survey of the island that was undertaken by G. P. Wall and J. G. Sawkins and that Charles Kingsley used in *At Last*.[1] On January 22, 1859, the *Port of Spain Gazette* reported that "we have often heard of the walking expeditions of Mr. Wall made matters of surprise, even amongst the hardiest of our country planters—and they are certainly not men to over-rate personal exertions. And there are few corners of the Island which have not been peeped into and made to deliver up their secrets by these investigations." Undoubtedly, the need to possess this new geographic space in all of its complexities became the object of those scientists and visual artists alike who came of age in the 1850s and 1860s, a part of the project of Nationness that possessed the writers and thinkers of the period.

This imperative to possess the land and make some meaning out of their physical environment became even more urgent as various groups of people (the Asians, the Africans, and the Europeans) came from different lands and felt isolated and (e)strange(d) in a space that was not their own, in a landscape they did not know but had to invent at least during the first and second generations. As time passed, that is, once they determined that returning to their original homes was not a viable option, they turned to making Trinidad their home.[2]

Since one can have no direct, unmediated experience of the material world, as David Turnbull observes, knowledge can only be seen "as a practical, social and linguistic accomplishment, a consequence of bringing the material world into the social world by linguistic and practical action."[3] Hence came the need of these nonfiction writers and artists felt to catalog their space, that is, to produce narratives

1. See G. P. Wall and J. G. Sawkins, *Report on the Geology of Trinidad, or, Part 1 of the West Indian Survey* (London: Longman, Green, Longman and Roberts, 1860).

2. While the colonizers who came to Trinidad possessed what cultural geographers call a "shared mental map" of the land, a collective self-conscious notion of the place they wished to colonized, it is clear that the early inhabitants (that is, those colonized by Europe) had no shared sense of the land they were to inhabit, except that they did not want to be there. One question that needs to be explored—to which I only allude in this chapter—is at what point did the many immigrants who arrived in this society during the nineteenth century begin to possess this shared sense of the space they inhabited? See Leo Marx, "The American Ideology of Space," in Stuart Wrede and William Howard Adams, eds., *Denatured Visions: Landscape and Culture in the Twentieth Century* (New York: Museum of Modern Art, 1991), pp. 62–78, for a tentative formulation of this question with regards to the United States.

3. David Turnbull, *Maps Are Territories* (Chicago: University of Chicago Press, 1993), p. 10.

about it, in order to understand its significance, to dialogue about it, and thereby to make it habitable. It was out of this need to talk about the space in which they lived—as Paul Carter notes, "[o]therwise, the landscape itself could never enter history"[4]—and to endow it with meaning that one saw a continuation of the national project that we observed among the creative writers.

It is this sense of urgency that marked the 1850s and the 1860s as a significant period in Trinidad's spatial and literary history.[5] This act of naming (the act of giving a place its form and its identity), a distinctly creative act within the context of the Christian tradition, could only take place at this moment when the inhabitants were busily engaged in trying to locate themselves in a different time and in a new space. According to Carter, "space itself was a text that had to be written before it could be interpreted."[6] As a result, the activities of the landscape painters, the geographers, and the scientists became an important self-conscious, inauguratory act, through which a people seized the initiative to locate itself in its time, "to come to grips with the Necessity its past represents for it and to imagine a creative, if only provisional, transcendence of its 'fate.'"[7] To paraphrase Antonio Benitez-Rojo, it was through these acts of naming and inscribing that citizens for the first time could have the illusion of "really experiencing the National Territory, with its rivers, mountains, valleys, flora, fauna, roads, villages, and cities—a kind of telluric matrix where collective memory preserved both the ancient toponymy and the traditions of the land."[8] Such, it seems to me, was the task that works such as L. A. A. de

4. Ibid., p. 48.

5. Drawing on the argument that Europe's encounter with the New World was presented usually as a way in which the former inaugurated "history" in these new lands, Derek Gregory points out that "geography," too, was inaugurated with conquest, "inscribed through the very instruments of navigation and survey" that made Europe's presence in the New World possible. Such a way of looking denies the original inhabitants any relationship to their own land "through a discourse which, in the course of the nineteenth century, typically 'centers landscape, separates people from place, and effaces the speaking self" (Derek Gregory, *Geographical Imaginations* [Cambridge: Blackwell, 1994], pp. 130–31). Robert Young makes very much the same point as he seeks to delineate how the colonizer and the colonized represent history alike (See *White Mythologies* [London: Routledge, 1990]). I want to argue that the works of L. A. A. de Verteuil, A. Leotaud, and J. J. Thomas are intended to recenter and reinscribe people in a new landscape.

6. Paul Carter, *The Road to Botany Bay* (London: Faber and Faber, 1987), p. 41.

7. Haden White, *The Content of the Form* (Baltimore: Johns Hopkins University Press, 1987), p. 149. The act of naming is not only of Christian origin. Speaking of how the Yolngu, the original inhabitants of Australia, linked naming and creativity together, Turnbell writes that "Yolngu knowledge is coincident with the creative activity of the Ancestral Beings. They traversed the land and in the process created the topography. What they did then provides the names of places along the path; the identity of each place is established by its connection to other places. Their actions also link groups of people. In turn, these links are given a social form and determine the social and political processes of Yolngu life. Thus the landscape, knowledge, story, song, graphic representation and social relations all mutually intersect, forming one cohesive knowledge network. In this sense, given that knowledge and landscape structure and constitute each other, the map metaphor is entirely apposite. The landscape and knowledge are one as maps, all are constituted through spatial connectivity" (Turnbull, *Maps are Territories*, p. 30).

8. Benitez-Rojo, "Nineteenth-Century Spanish American Novel," p. 420.

Verteuil's *Trinidad: Its Geography, Natural Resources, Administration, Present Condition, and Prospects* (1858), Antoine Leotaud's *Oiseaux de l'île de la Trinidad* (1866), William H. Gamble's *Trinidad: Historical and Descriptive* (1866), and J. J. Thomas's *The Theory and Practice of Creole Grammar* (1869) set themselves and what, ultimately, they represented within the discursive formation of the society's development.[9] Even the landscape sketches by Jean Cazabon that were painted during this period can be seen as being constitutive of the naming process that took place during the middle of the nineteenth century. Like John Barrell, I take it to be axiomatic that, "to describe the meaning of a picture [or painting], of the kind which relates different aspects of it into a statement about its significance, there has to be available a discourse in terms of which that meaning can be described."[10]

The need, then, to represent the world they encountered in an ordered way (a process of teaching the country to speak, as it were) and to advance a systematic knowledge of the land they encountered became major objectives of Cazabon, de Verteuil, Leotaud, Gamble, and Thomas. However, if we see place as having two major components—its location in space and a determinant of one's identity—we discover that the energies of our intellectuals and our artists, as well as the practical activities of the ordinary inhabitants, were designed to put in place discourses about their relations in space and to explore their being in a/the New World. Such discourses, one can argue, gave the members of Trinbagonian society a language through which to locate themselves in their world, to conceive themselves as existing within a rational social order, and to acquire a shared sense of community and historical consciousness.[11] Put in more graphic terms, we can say that to possess the country during this period "depended on demonstrating the efficacy of the English language there…civilizing the landscape, [and] bringing it into orderly being. More fundamentally still, the landscape had to be taught to speak."[12]

Teaching the landscape to speak (that is, charting the spatial history of the society) in order to make it available for its inhabitants assumed as much importance as the creative writers' task of describing and examining the emotional dimensions of a people's lives. Although many critics have seen the rise of the novel as being coter-

9. According to Derek Gregory, representation "draws attention to the different ways in which the world is made present, re-presented, [and] discursively constructed" (Gregory, *Geographical Imaginations,* p. 104).

10. John Barrell, "Sir Joshua Reynolds and the Englishness of English Art," in Homi Bhabha, *Nation and Narration* (London: Routledge, 1990), p. 154.

11. Colonization also revolved around and included a spatial, geographical element. With regard to the Algerians, Frantz Fanon observed that "the Algerians, the veiled women, the palm tree and the camels make up the landscape, the natural background to the human presence to the French. Hostile nature, obstinate and fundamentally rebellious, is in fact represented in the colonies by the bush, by mosquitoes, natives, and fever, and colonization is a success when all this indocile nature has finally been tamed. Railroads across the bush, the draining of swamps and a native population which is non-existent politically and economically are in fact one and the same thing" (Frantz Fanon, *The Wretched of the Earth* [New York: Grove, 1963], p. 250). For the colonized person, then, the exploration of his/her land also constituted an active engagement with colonialism through an engagement with environment.

12. Carter, *The Road to Botany Bay,* pp. 58–59.

minous with the rise of the nation-state,[13] the nonfictional narratives and painterly visions of the land also expanded our understanding/knowledge of the nation. It is to the narrative discourses of important markers of the literary and social development of the society between 1850 and 1870, Cazabon, de Verteuil, and Leotaud, that we turn as we chart the spatial history of the nation.[14]

Jean Michel Cazabon (1813–1880)

One of the earliest indigenous attempts to name the land came from the painterly vision of Jean Michel Cazabon.[15] Born eleven years after the publication of Philippe's *Free Mulatto,* Cazabon belonged to one of the wealthy families of Naparima. In fact, the Cazabons were the next-door neighbors of the Philips who lived on the adjacent Concorde estate. Like the authors of *Free Mulatto* and *Emmanuel Appadocca,* Cazabon studied in England (at St. Edmund's College), in France (at the Académie des Beaux-Arts, Paris), and in Italy.[16] In Paris, he won the Prix de Rome that allowed him "to live and work for four years in the Villa Medici, at the expense of the French government."[17] Versed in the painting techniques and philosophies of his day, Cazabon was ready to practice his craft when he returned to Trinidad in 1830.

Although Cazabon exhibited his work at the Salon du Louvre, Musée Royal, Paris (1839, 1843–1847), his most satisfying and prolific period of painting began

13. Timothy Brennan notes that "the rise of the modern nation-state in Europe in the late eighteenth and early nineteenth centuries is inseparable from the forms and subjects of imaginative literature... Flourishing alongside what Francesco de Sanctis has called 'the cult of nationality in the European nineteenth century', it was especially the novel as a composite but clearly bordered work of art that was crucial in defining the nation as an 'imagined community,'" (Tomothy Brennan, "The National Longing for Form," in Homi Bhabha, ed., *Nation and Narration* [London: Routledge, 1990], p. 48) .

14. Gregory differentiates between what he calls the *discourse* of geography rather than the *discipline* of geography. He intends the former to refer to "all the ways in which we communicate with one another, to that vast network of signs, symbols, and practices through which we make our world(s) meaningful to ourselves and to others" (Gregory, *Geographical Imaginations,* p. 11). Needless to say, in this work, I am concerned about the discourse rather than the discipline of geography.

15. Richard Bridgens, an Englishman who had gone to Trinidad some ten years earlier, captured the Negro in all of his rhythmic beauty in a sketch called "Drumming." According to Bridgens, "it may almost be said that the Negro recreation is comprised in the work of dancing. Parties to enjoy his favourite amusement are, on the largest estates, and on grand occasions, got up in a style which would surprise those who have heard of nothing but the extreme wretchedness of the Negro's lot. At such times, each displays his best attire. The ladies generally prefer white muslim, with sometimes a petticoat of gay colours, and on the head a madras handkerchief put on with considerable taste. The men appear in white jackets and trousers: but on common occasions, the appearance of the company is such as is given in the sketch here presented to the reader" (Richard Bridgens, *West Indian Scenery with Illustrations of Negro Characters* [London: Robert Jennings, 1837]). The book is not paginated.

16. According to Geoffrey MacLean, Cazabon was not officially registered at the Académie des Beaux-Arts, although he might have been a part-time student there. See Geoffrey MacClean, *Cazabon: An Illustrated Biography of Trinidad's Nineteenth Century Painter* (Port of Spain: Aquarela Galleries, 1986), p. 20.

17. Olga J. Mavrogordato, *Voices in the Street* (Port of Spain: Imprint, 1977), p. 51.

in 1848 when William Burnley and James Lamont, two of the largest ex-slave-holders of the island, commissioned him to paint several Trinidadian scenes. During this period, he also contributed to *Illustrated London News,* in which he provided sketches for *Water Riots* (1849), *Trial of the Rioters at the Court House of Port of Spain* (1849), and *The Great Fire of Port of Spain* (1850). Because of his success, Cazabon was accepted within Governor Harris's circle of friends. This allowed him to attend and to record many of the governor's social functions and excursions. For example, *Cedar Point–Mount Tamana* was executed on one of Governor Harris's picnics. He also recorded Governor and Lady Harris's wedding party as it arrived at Craig, one of the Five Islands off the northwestern tip of Trinidad.

It was in his landscape paintings that Cazabon captured and documented the emerging consciousness of the nation, especially as it was reflected in the activities of the dominant class. According to MacLean, "the oneness he felt with nature is shown in the careful and loving attention he paid to details of the natural elements: the movement of clouds; the colours and textures of earth, sea and sky; the fall and form of vegetation."[18] However, because landscape painting attempts to affirm the pastoral harmony between society and nature and because, as Richard Hartshorne has pointed out, the literal meaning of landscape is "the view of an area seen in per-spective,"[19] it can be argued that the double functions of Burnley and Lamont as colonizers and patrons of the arts were linked indubitably to their attempt to con-trol the new spatial reality and to get a better perspective of things under the changed circumstances of colonization. In this sense, Cazabon's work not only used a visual vocabulary to harmonize the spatial and social aspects of the land and to draw attention to how inhabitants accommodated themselves to their new social order, but it also brought the local landscape into the realm of social consciousness.

Although Cazabon first recorded painting of Trinidad, *Morne Jaillet in San Fernando, Naparima, Island of Trinidad,* appeared in 1845, it is in his first two com-missioned works that one finds some of his more exciting paintings. "Westview of Orange Grove" and "Orange Grove" (1849) were among the most impressive land-scapes that Cazabon rendered. The first, a watercolor of Burnley's house, represents one of the most elegant buildings in the country. De Verteuil points out that one of the residences bore "a remote comparison with English or French villas."[20] Burnley's residence in Tacarigua possessed one hundred windows, one more than the governor's residence in Port of Spain (rumor has it that Burnley had to close one window in deference to the governor's status.)

"Orange Grove" is a view of the Orange Grove Savannah, and like "Westview of Orange Grove," it offers a pastoral image of the landscape and depicts several cat-tle grazing on the Savannah. In the foreground, there is a pond for which Tacarigua

18. MacLean, *Cazabon,* p. 29.
19. Quoted in Gregory, *Geographical Imaginations,* p. 98.
20. L. A. A. de Verteuil, *Trinidad; Its Geography, Natural Resources, Administrative, Present Condition, and Prospects, Vol. 1* (London: Ward and Lock, 1858), p. 68. The other residence to which de Verteuil refers was H. Boissiere's Champ-Elysées in Maraval.

was justly famous and where many of the inhabitants of the island picnicked over the years. The picturesque Northern Range with its flamboyant blues appears in the background of the painting. Both of these paintings reveal a lushness of tropical vegetation and suggest a sense of calm and repose.

Views of Trinidad (1851), a spectacular group of eighteen drawings that shows some of the most arresting scenes of the island, was translated into itaglio sepia etchings by Eugene Circeri, a famous lithographer whom Cazabon engaged to assist him in his work. Typical of the topological veduti (views) of the time, these drawings capture the local landscape in vivid details and the activities of the inhabitants. Although each painting is intended to capture a particular aspect of the island, the inclusion of humans within most of them gives a sense of the social aspect of the work.[21] In these paintings, many of them stylized, Africans and Europeans seem at ease with one another, even though there is a striking military presence in some of them. Certain buildings (the Custom House, Trinity Cathedral, the Catholic Church, and the St. James Barracks), more English than French, reflect a late Gothic style, while the bamboo arches of St. Ann's with the light filtrating in the background is indicative of what Gordon Lewis calls "the marvelous natural architecture" of the island.[22] The late Peter Kahn, professor emeritus in the History of Art at Cornell University, observes that "these paintings do not just depict a view of the place. They also capture the action of the people as well. It is typical of Canaletto, the Venetian painter and engraver."[23] Kahn feels that the paintings are somewhat "primitive" in that they are not as "illusionary as some of the other topological painters (such as the early William Turner) who did topographical views."[24]

In 1853, Cazabon produced *Grand Trinidad Races,* and in 1857, he published "*Album in Trinidad,* another set of lithographs, in which he used the lithograph services of Levilly and the printing house of Geny-Gros. In 1860, he brought out *Album of Demerara* with A. Hartman, a photographer who was visiting from Paris. As in *Views of Trinidad,* the lithography in *Album of Demerara* was done by Circeri and the printing by Lemercier. In 1862, Cazabon relocated to St. Pierre, Martinique, from which his family had originally emigrated, and did some landscapes of that island. Returning to Trinidad in 1870, he found it difficult to pick up where he left off and from that point on, his career began to fade. The results, according to MacLean, was that "he began to drink to dull his disillusionment.... . Slowly, the quality of Cazabon's work changed, and as a man he began to lose his

---

21. MacLean writes that "Cazabon accentuated the grandeur of his landscape by diminishing their human complements, reducing his figures to colourful, faceless smudges floating like butterflies across their permanence. Often he portrays men as squat and effete and women as frivolous and simple: exaggerating and contrasting what he felt were their inner natures" (*Cazabon,* p. 30).

22. Gordon Lewis, "Distant Peace," *Times Literary Supplement,* January 24, 1986, p. 96.

23. Conversation with Peter Kahn, November 20, 1996. I am also indebted to Professor Kahn for helping me to read these paintings.

24. Ibid.

social significance. His image became that of a drunken though gentle old eccentric, hawking his paintings to anyone who would buy them, or exchange them for a drink or a meal. If all else failed he would give them away."[25] Despite this change of fortune, in 1886, Cazabon won a first prize of twenty dollars for his watercolors at the Trinidad Agricultural Exhibition. In the same year, his paintings were used to represent Trinidad at the Colonial and Indian Exhibition that was held in London with sixteen of his watercolors and twelve pen and ink drawings being exhibited. They seemed to have been well received. In 1888, he died of a heart attack.[26]

Of his post-1851 works, *Maraval Dike* (1851), *Riders in the Queen's Park* (1853), *River Scene—Evening, Thatched Huts on a Cocoa Estate* (both 1880), *Mountain Village, East Indian Group* (both 1886), *River Pool Bathers, The Blanchisseuse, Grand Trinidad Races, 5th January 1853, Bamboos and Immortelles on the Santa Cruz River* (1850), and *Creole Woman with a Parasol (nd)* are representative of his efforts. In *Grand Trinidad Races,* Cazabon reveals the social inequalities that existed on the island. MacLean calls it his "strongest social statement" and writes that, in this work, one senses "the enjoyment of the Race Meeting by all classes and ethnic shades, but also the racial and cultural divisions of the society. The hurried arrival of the 'aristocratic' British administrator in his large and well-appointed carriage contrasts with the donkey-cart of lesser citizens; the white and coloured Creoles and their different modes of dress reflect different social stations;...while the little black boys perched for better vantage in a tree, witnesses to the entire extravaganza."[27] *Bamboos and Immortelles on the Santa Cruz River,* an example of Cazabon's use of oils, shows "a sensitivity to tropical light and colour."[28] The bright orange of the immortelles, the placid, ever-present serenity of the bamboo grooves (bamboo grooves and arches are famous devices of Cazabon), and the languid, quiet-flowing stream amidst the profusion of tropical growth give one a sense of the bountiful nature of the place. Moreover, the two peasants with baskets of provision on their heads suggest that they fit quite comfortably into the environment.

Thatched Huts on a Cocoa Estate introduced another dimension of Trinidad life: cocoa cultivation and its importance in the island's economy during the nineteenth century. The presence of a tethered donkey in the foreground, a mother and child in the front of one of the huts, with clothes hanging on a clothesline to dry, indicate how thoroughly the immigrants to the island have adapted to the island and shows that these people's way of life has resonances even in how Trinidadians live

25. MacLean, *Cazabon,* p. 26.
26. In 1917, Beatrice Greig organized an exhibition of Cazabon's work at Queen's Royal College. Its failure to attract much enthusiasm led *The Port of Spain Gazette* to lament that "the Trinidad public failed lamentably to show appreciation of art-especially where as in the latter case it was the product of one of Trinidad's son whose work when in the zenith of his unsurpassed skill and fame as an artist, have been unearthed through the initiative of a comparative stranger" (July 17, 1917).
27. MacLean, *Cazabon,* pp. 28–*29.
28. Ibid., p. 106.

FIGURE 8. *East Indian Group* by Jean Michel
Cazabon.

today. The latter scene repeats itself on a grander and more organized way in
Mountain Village, which depicts a pattern of settled village life, the preferred form
of social organization for most Africans after the abolition of slavery. That such a
village is located in a mountain area suggests a desire on the part of the inhabitants
(the maroons of the country) to remove themselves from the ever-watchful eyes of
the master and to develop their own forms of social and cultural life. The painting
recalls the opening scene of *Adolphus: A Tale.*

East Indian Group and *East Indian Woman* (originally *Coolie Group* and *Coolie
Woman* respectively, but renamed by MacLean as a concession to the derogatory
implications of the word "coolie") were exhibited at the Colonial and Indian
Exhibition in London in 1886. The former captures an idealized picture of an
Indo-Trinidadian family, mother, father, and daughter, as they stand in front of
their thatched-roofed home. A rather large goblet stands at the side of the house.
Typical of the Indo-Trinidadian woman of her day is the woman's flowing sari and
the jewelry that bedecks her arms is indicative of her wealth, most of which was
converted to gold rather than put into banks that Indo-Trinidadians did not trust.
The man is dressed in traditional Hindu dhoti. As one views these watercolors, one
is inclined to offer a comment similar to that of David Lee made when he viewed
Cazabon's *Creole Woman with a Parasol* at the Commonwealth Institute, London, in
1987:

> The faint absurdity of applying a painterly practice to subjects for which they were
> not designed is emphasised in a small oil portrait of a creole woman, dressed and
> posing like Countess Howe in Gainsborough's stately picture at Kenwood. This

FIGURE 9. *Creole Woman with a Parasol* by Jean Michel Cazabon.

elegant, ebony woman, already looking uncomfortably twee, carries a parasol, which is small enough to double as a cocktail decoration, between thumb and forefinger as if it were a toothpick. The same inappositeness of sitter and style is felt in Van Dyck's portraits of the royal servants at Winsor Castle.[29]

Such an observation should not be interpreted to mean that Cazabon did not strive to lend a modicum of dignity to the lives of these Trinidadian subjects. Rather, there is an unreality to these portraits (the same is true for *The Blanchisseuse* in which one sees a Creole laundry woman and her child), although I am sure Cazabon tried to capture the natural dignity of these people.[30] Significantly, V. S. Naipaul not only purchased *East Indian Group* but used it as the cover for the 1995 edition of *The Adventures of Gurudeva,* a selection of his father's short stories. It is of some interest that Naipaul situates the geographical origins of his grandfather as Uttar Pradesh and sets his family's departure for Trinidad as "some time in the 1880s," just about the time that Cazabon would have painted *East Indian Group.*[31]

For purposes of this study, two aspects of Cazabon's art need to be emphasized. First, his work is not unique. It is representative of a period in which he "readily

29. David Lee, "Michael J. Cazabon," *Arts Review* 39 (July 1987), p. 534.

30. What is one to make of MacLean's description of *The Blanchisseuse;* "In this painting the blanchisseuse is seen leaving the river with the laundry carefully folded in her tray, balanced on her head. Hand in hand she walks with her daughter, who will have already learned the fundamentals of her mother's skills" (*Cazabon,* p. 116).

31. See Seepersad Naipaul, *The Adventures of Gurudeva* (London: Heinemann, 1995).

identified with the English landscapists whose work he had known, and the French landscape artists around him in Paris."[32] His *Views of Trinidad* shows a striking resemblance to the *Views of the English Lakes* (1868) drawn and engraved by William Banks of Edinburgh. It also has much in common with the French-Cuban painter and lithographer Frederic Mialhe (1810–1881) who worked in Cuba and "left the most complete set of views of the Cuban way of life in the mid-nineteenth century."[33] However, that Cazabon adopted a contemporary form and used it with great skill and dexterity cannot be denied.

The second relevant aspect of Cazabon's work to our study is its stylized nature and the idealized depiction of the peasants in his pieces. Although he worked in a style and technique that he learned and perfected in England and France, MacLean points out that, "as he matured, his work began to express more fluently his natural instinct."[34] Like Jean-Baptiste Philippe, Cazabon seemed trapped in the in-betweenity of his status: "a black 19th century Caribbean artist working in a European idiom."[35] Although Cazabon recognized that the peasant whom he depicted assumed a prominent place in the social landscape, his inability to break through (or away) from the formalism he had learned abroad kept these peasants tethered to an idealized conception that denied them much of their humanity and the vitality of their everyday lives (Cazabon's portraits of the high and mighty, both of their homes and their persons, seemed adequate to the style of painting he had learned). It was almost as if he was conducting a dialogue with himself rather than seeking to convey to his viewers the emotional realities of his subjects' lives. Indeed, his tragic end may have had something to do with this deep, ambiguous orientation that lay at the center of his worldview. In this context, Lee's observation seems apropos:

> Whenever I look at pictures by a painter of low life, such as George Morland, I am always left nursing the thought that the practice of painting as the artist learned and applied it was incapable of giving a convincing account of how peasants and farm workers really lived. Even if it had been, Morland's patron would undoubtedly not have tolerated it. His method supplied an idealised view which was coincident with patrician attitudes to the lot of the labouring class. As anyone who has delved even briefly into late 18th century history knows, Morland's cosy scenes of plenty are about as far from reality of country life as it was possible to get. I receive the same feeling from some of Cazabon's fascinating watercolours. Indeed, Cazabon's entire story is intriguing and fascinating.[36]

It is not coincidental, then, that Trinidad's most celebrated landscape painter of

32. MacLean, *Cazabon*, p. 20.
33. See Guilio V. Blanc, "Cuban Modernism: The Search for a National Ethos," in Martin R. Balderrana, ed. *Wilfredo Lam and His Contemporaries, 1938 -1952*, pp. 53–69. The quote is on page 53.
34. MacLean, *Cazabon*, p. 30.
35. Lee, "Michael J. Cazabon," p. 534.
36. Ibid.

the nineteenth century appeared when de Verteuil and Leotaud were writing about geography and ornithology, respectively. Pressed to know and to explain their land, they had to find as many ways as possible to represent the sites and sounds of its existence. In a world that was about to be exploited further, painting offered one means of reconciling the social with the economical, the fading grandeur of an "aristocratic class" with the rise of a newly emancipated peasant class. Indeed, the pastoral images that one sees in Cazabon's work make the landscape more human and accommodating to the latter and reveal aspects of the culture that hithertofore was not documented within the social space. In this context, we can argue that Cazabon used his visual imagination to bring the local space into the realm of discourse, rendering it distinct, concise, and conceivable. Through his mastery of the form, he transformed an imagined or illusionary landscape into a narrative presence, pregnant with meaning and possibility. Like the works of de Verteuil, Leotaud, Gamble, and Thomas, Cazabon's landscape paintings emerge as an important element in the discursive knowledge of the society, a reflection of an indigenous art that was emerging in the Caribbean. And if, as recent geographers have observed, material landscapes also "reflect power relations and dominant 'ways of seeing' the world," then it can be concluded that even Cazabon's paintings were caught up in these new relations of power engendered by the rise of colonialism in the society.

It was the impetus to extract meaning and knowledge out of his landscape—or to make his landscape more meaningful—that led Cazabon to depict his natural surroundings in ways that were assessable to those in power. When *Views of Trinidad* was reprinted in 1986, Lewis reminds us that Cazabon was doing in and for Trinidad exactly what the other Creole, European-trained painters of the Caribbean of the time (such as Campeche of Puerto Rico, Belisario of Jamaica, and Audubon of Saint Dominique) were doing for their respective societies. Lewis argues that Cazabon's paintings may be read rather profitably if read simultaneously with Charles Kingsley's *At Last: A Christmas in the West Indies* (1871), an account of an 1869–1870 visit to Trinidad, which "described in splendid prose many of the scenes drawn by Cazabon."[37] Yet the qualifications made by Guilio V. Blanc in his essays on Cuban modernism, what he calls "the search for a national ethos," are also instructive as we seek to locate Cazabon's work in its specific condition of its production:

> On the whole, the native Cuban artists of the nineteenth century were less concerned than the European visitors with the documentation of their native land and people. Founded in 1818, the Academia of San Alejandro provided solid training based on European antecedents and produced artists interested in conventional treatment of mythological, religious, and historical portraiture. Although Armando

---

37. Lewis, "Distant Peace." At the invitation of his friend, Arthur Gordon, Governor of Trinidad, Kingsley visited Trinidad in the latter part of 1869 and early 1870 and published his account of his experiences as *At Last*.

Menocal (1863–1942) and Leopeldo Romanch (1862–1951) sometimes depicted Afro-Cubans and *guajiros,* these prominent professors at San Alejandro were intent on painting images that reflected European academic standards. Their subjects are little more than props, pretexts for good compositions, and, as a result, their works convey impressions of exoticism and maudlin theatricality. In landscape painting of this period, an effort was made to record vegetation and local topography, and occasionally, Afro-Cubans, *guajiros,* and *bohios* do appear. The emphasis, however, is on the picturesque. Among the more successful nineteenth century landscapes are those of Estaban Chartrand (1840–1883), a Cuban of French descent who may have had ties to the School of Fontainebleau.[38]

As we celebrate Cazabon, we must remember that paintings of his local/African counterparts may not be available so that we can see what topics interested them. Thus, it can be argued that the emphasis of those painters, informed by a subaltern perspective as it were, would have been different from that of Cazabon, as the works of twentieth-century Trinidad painters Alfredo Codallo, LeRoy Clarke, and Marcello Hovell suggest. John Pierre notes that each of the above-named artist inculcates folk elements into his work, a reflection of the deeper and more authentic cultural filiations of a people in formation.[39] Still, in spite of, or perhaps because of, his insertion within the power circles of his day, Cazabon "left us a precious heritage in his paintings of the Trinidad which he knew and which are now among our national treasures."[40] Closer to the existential search that animated his paintings, MacLean remarks that "Cazabon's search for himself in the philosophies of Europe led him back to the simplicity of his Trinidad existence, where he was able, at least to find, the comfort that he sought in a warmer, more familiar landscape."[41] It was also a part of that imperative to name the place in which one lived, and for that alone, we need to celebrate this artist's achievements.

The Moral Implications of de Verteuil's Geography

This need to name the space in which one lives and thereby make it more meaningful and manageable found its greatest and most urgent articulation in de

---

38. Blanc, "Cuban Modernism," p. 54.
39. Speaking of the folkloric elements of Codallo's work, Pierre notes: "The common thread among many artists of Codallo's time [1913–1971] was to paint landscapes, seascapes and portraits. This was directly attributable to colonial influences [colonialism] that were depicted in the body of European works housed in colonial offices and the homes of administrative officers serving in the colonies. Codallo was not attracted to any of these painterly pursuits. All of his works expressed and abounded in folk themes employing an undisguised and undiluted idiom...His work provides us, and possibly future generations, with the lexical symbols of the mythological world of the Soucouyant, La Diablesse, Douens, etc....the only folklore we can ever know." (John Pierre, "The Social Significance of Folk Elements in the Paintings of Le Roy Clarke, Alfredo Codallo and Marcello Hovell," B.A. Thesis, University of the West Indies [Trinidad], 1988, pp. 18, 20).
40. Mavrogordato, *Voices in the Street,* p. 52.
41. MacLean, *Cazabon,* p. 30

Verteuil's *Trinidad*.[42] A member of one of the important French families of the
island, de Verteuil was the leading spokesman of the French Creoles for much of
the nineteenth century. This group which practiced "the most rigid endogamy and
extensive intermarriage," did not allow anyone with a taint of "Negro blood" to
become a part of their group. As Brereton writes, de Verteuil "was imbued with
French culture, royalist politics, devotion to the Catholic faith and, above all, family pride."[43] Such a background predisposed de Verteuil to wanting to maintain the
interest of the dominant white elite of which he was the most distinguished member. Although he dedicated his book to his fellow inhabitants in the hope that they
found it "truthful; if not as interesting or valuable as it might, under other auspices,
have been,"[44] he had another, and more important, agenda when he wrote his geography: he wanted "to make Trinidad better known to the British public in general
and to its own inhabitants in particular." Citing a trend that educators detected in
colonial education, de Verteuil observes:

> It is really surprising how uniformed even Trinidadians are regarding their own
> country. Our best school boys are able to give the names of the chief rivers, and the
> position of the principal towns in Great Britain, France, and even in Russia and
> China; but they are ignorant, perhaps, of the names of the Guataro and Oropuche
> [*sic*], or through what county the Caroni has its course. They know that San
> Fernando exists, but may not be able to say whether it is on the eastern or the west-
> ern side of the island; they can give the principal boundaries and dimensions of
> Europe, and its larger kingdoms, but are ignorant of those of their own island-
> home; they can enumerate the chief productions of England or France, but they do
> not know what are the agricultural products of their own country, or whether the
> quantity of sugar exported is 35,000 or 56,000 hogsheads.
>   Not only is such ignorance discreditable, but its effects cannot but be prejudicial
> to the best interests, and consequently to the advancement of the colony (*Trinidad*,
> pp. viii–ix).[45]

Yet, buried within this rather egalitarian ideal—that of making Trinidad better
known to his countrymen and the British public—is his desire to reveal the riches
of his land to the colonial other. As J. M. Blaut writes, "one of the primary functions of geography throughout the entire period [the nineteenth century] was to
teach European children what they needed to know about non-Europe in order to
participate in their countries' imperial and commercial activities in those regions [of

42. There is a way in which de Verteuil's work can be associated with travel writing. He certainly had
to travel around the country to observe the events/objects of which he speaks. He also had to render his
narrative, that is, use his rhetorical skills, in such a way as to make the land exciting for those who wanted to inhabit it. The same, of course, would be true for Cazabon and Leotaud.
43. Brereton, *Race Relations*, pp. 38–37. Se also Anthony de Vertueil, *Sir Louis de Verteuil: His Life
and Times* for an account of L. A. A. de Verteuil's life.
44. de Verteuil, p. iii. All other citations will be noted in the text as *Trinidad*.
45. de Verteuil spells Oropuche without the third "o".

FIGURE 10. Sir L. A. A. de Verteuil, author of
Trinidad: Its Geography, Natural Resources,
Administration, Present Condition, and Prospects.

the world]."[46] Although one may not want to implicate de Verteuil in a project in which he may not have been consciously associated or to insert his work into an enterprise that took Europeans beyond their boundaries to map the world for the glory of an imperial empire, it cannot be denied that his production had an impact on how the dominant powers saw the island and how they might have used such information to fulfill their purposes or, to retain the metaphor of imperialism, to fill in those empty spaces.[47] In fact, most writers who spoke about Trinidad after 1858 used *Trinidad* to support their arguments. However, when de Verteuil catalogued the geography and natural resources of the island, he intended to inform the British public that Trinidad was a land that was fit to be exploited.[48] Such an act, then, could not be seen as a benign activity since European geographers associated their discipline with the perceived needs of empire and saw geographical knowledge "as a

46. J. M. Blaut, *The Colonizer's Model of the World: Geographical Diffusionism and Eurocentric History* (New York: Guilford Press, 1993), p. 45. When I discuss Thomas's work, I demonstrate the ambivalent nature of colonial discourse.

47. In a charming essay "Geography and its Explorers," Joseph Conrad reveals the ambivalence with which he views the geographical experience (and which, of course, is pertinent here). While, on the one hand, he seeks to emphasize the quest for science in the geographical exercise ("the truth of geographical facts and a desire for precise knowledge"), on the other, he recognizes the political consequences of these acts ("the vilest scramble for loot that ever disfigured the history of human conscience and geographic exploration"), as he describes the rape of Africa. See Joseph Conrad, *Last Essays* (London: J. M. Dent, 1926). The quotations are on pages 19 and 25.

48. That he changed some of his major conclusions when he republished *Trinidad* (1888), at the height of the nationalist onslaught, suggests that, with hindsight, he may has seen how misguided some of his ideas were.

tool of empire, enabling both the acquisition of territory and the exploitation of resources."[49] Inescapably, one could argue that de Verteuil's geography was implicated within the project of imperial expansion and colonial discourse.[50]

Apart, then, from his desire to demonstrate the cogency of his insights, de Verteuil was determined to express the fears of his class and open up his observations for national and international discussion,[51] hence the hybridity of his text: at one level it represents an attempt by a member of the ruling class to justify the virtues of slavery, to affirm its beneficial impact on the former slaves and to assert the moral superiority of his class; at another level, it attempts to claim the space that a people inhabited and to create an awareness of the country's natural endowments.[52] In other words, de Verteuil's introduction narrativizes the relationship between the former slaves and their masters (subjective), while the body of the text catalogs the physical geography of the island (objective).[53] In the process, a slippage occurs that undermines colonial authority. Incidentally, it is only with the abolition of slavery and the gradual ability of the ex-slaves to represent themselves that the actions of the slaves (that is, the expression of their human agency) began to be taken seriously by the colonizer, a new condition that de Verteuil explores in his work. It is at this important diacritical moment of Trinidad's history (the 1850s) that one begins to see the more expansive expression of what Haden White calls "the growth and development of historical consciousness.[54]

49. F. Driver, "Geography's Empire: Histories of Geographical Knowledge." *Environment and Planning D: Society and Space*, vol. 10 (1992), p. 27.

50. Carter notes that "the true dialogue the writer conducts is not with external reality, but with language itself. What he explores is the resources of meaning implicit in the mere repetition of conventional phrases" (*The Road to Botany Bay*, pp. 142–43).

51. De Verteuil's *Trinidad* inscribes all of the Eurocentric views of the dominant Western mode of discourse. As such, it can be read as a continuation and reinforcement of the Eurocentric discourse that played itself out on the island. Rather than read *Trinidad* in this manner exclusively, I will allude only to its more glaring Eurocentric views, which are merely one aspect of this important work. See Blaut, *The Colonizer's Model of the World*, for a reading of a Eurocentric views of the world and a way in which *Trinidad* can be inscribed therein.

52. Homi Bhabha describes hybridity as "a problematic of colonial representation that reverses the effects of colonial disavowal, so that other 'denied' knowledges enter upon the dominant discourse and estrange the basis of its authority."

53. Haden White differentiates between a historical discourse that narrates, that is, simply states the facts, and a discourse that narrativizes or tells a story, that is, imposes a structure and order of meaning that these facts do not possess as mere chronology or catalog-of the events. See White, *The Content of the Form*, p. 2.

54. White notes that "interest in the social system, which is nothing other than a system of human relationships governed by law, creates the possibility of conceiving the kinds of tensions, conflicts, struggles, and their various kinds of resolutions that we are accustomed to find in any representation of reality presenting itself to us as history. This permits us to speculate that the growth and development of historical consciousness, which is attended by a concomitant growth and development of narrative capability (of the sort met with in the chronicle as against the annals form), has something to do with the extent to which the legal system functions as a subject of concern" (Ibid., p. 14). It is precisely a new form of historical consciousness, generated by the passage of the Emancipation Act and the physical liberty of the former slaves, that makes de Verteuil so concerned about their actions that he characterizes as either moral or immoral.

Superseding a desire to provide the accuracy of information about the society in which he lived (such as correcting the many "glaring errors" that occurred in previous texts), de Verteuil is also concerned with the social, economic, and cultural impact that the abolition of slavery had upon the society.[55] Thus, while, in one breath, he outlines a moral compass of his society, in another, he champions the economic possibilities of the island and opens it up for its subsequent rape. Such a model allows him the opportunity to advance his moral (and moralist) concerns about the former slaves (as he does in his introduction) and then to offer a detailed body of information (such as a description of the natural resources and the animal life of the island) in the body of his text and thereby lay the foundation for the colonial exploitation of the island. In this way, he offers a Eurocentric views of the society even as he speaks of ways to make the society better.

De Verteuil's Introduction

In his introduction to *Trinidad*, de Verteuil reflects many of his Eurocentric biases as he says many cruel and indecent things about the people of tropical climes and the ex-slaves of the island. Writing from the point of view of a colonizer, de Verteuil details the "many serious difficulties" the dominant class encountered in the transition from slavery to colonialism. In doing so, he echoes the fears of William Burnley, one of the first members of his class to examine the effects of emancipation upon the economic fortunes of the island's elite within this new colonial context. While Burnley used the information he acquired to recruit Asian immigrants, de Verteuil advances his information to increase the flow of East Indians into the island. De Verteuil's biographer informs us that "it was he who suggested the setting up of a separate agency in Calcutta for immigrants to Trinidad."[56] Although de Verteuil acknowledges that the abolition of slavery was "one of the most extraordinary social changes recorded in the history of the human race,"[57] he bemoans the fact that many Africans deserted the sugar cane plantation to make a new life for themselves:

> The amount of labour diverted into new channels was not exactly lost; but was in many cases such an exchange as tended to the great detriment of all classes-as is shown by the immense increase in the numbers of carpenters, masons, and other tradesmen, tailors, petty shopkeepers, etc. The permanent reduction for agricultural purposes was, on the contrary, a real loss to the colonies; since the cultivation of staples is the only foundation of their commerce and of their prosperity (*Trinidad*, p. 9).

55. The introduction of de Verteuil's work has less to do with geography (the location of events in place) than with history, the actions of men and women in the past, the aim of which is to represent human events "in such a way that their status as parts of meaningful wholes will be made manifest" (White, *The Content of the Form*, p. 50).

56. Anthony de Verteuil, *Sir Louis de Verteuil* (Port of Spain: Columbus, 1973), p. 119.

57. Because it is not so easy to determine what exactly de Verteuil means, one needs to explore this sentence more fully.

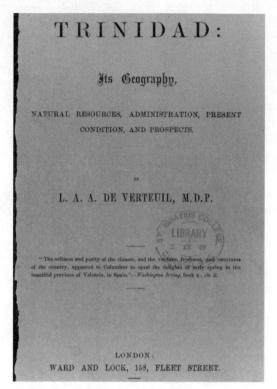

FIGURE 11. Title page of *Trinidad*, 1858 edition.

As a member of the dominant class, de Verteuil sees the abolition of slavery as having revolutionized the relationship between the social classes. Although he acknowledges that the Asian immigrants "prevented a proportionate decrease or total abandonment of sugar manufacture in these two colonies" (*Trinidad*, p. 10), he cannot help but chastise the independent path Africans have taken. Hence his claim that the latter "wantonly indulged in idleness and revelry, or squandered his time in wandering over the country, from place to place, being always certain of procuring shelter and work wherever he preferred remaining, even for a few days" (*Trinidad*, p. 12). As far as de Verteuil is concerned, the major ontological vocation of Africans was to provide a ready supply of agricultural labor for the colonizing class. The devotion of the former to the mechanical and petty trades does not coincide with de Verteuil's notion of what constituted the best interest of the society. Trinidad, he reminds all who want to hear, "is an exclusively agricultural country, and such, for an unlimited period, it must continue to be, inasmuch as its prosperity entirely depends on the cultivation of the soil, and the exportation of colonial produce" (*Trinidad*, p. 243).

Not only does de Verteuil object to the abolition of slavery because of the economic impact it has had upon his group (he also believes that Africans were not adequately prepared for emancipation), as "a Christian and philanthropist" (*Trinidad*, p. 51) and "a fervently religious man,"[58] he rues the fact that freedom has

58. *Sir Louis de Verteuil*, p. 11.

deprived the former slaves of the salvific grace of Christianity. In this view of the world, concepts such as progress and innovation are "the products of the European mind or spirit and thus ultimately products of the Christian soul."[59] Hence, de Verteuil represents Christianity as a "taming and civilising influence on the wildest and the most ignorant tribes" (*Trinidad*, p. 34). Determined to attribute all progress to the belief in a Christian God[60] and forgetting the contributions that Islamic civilization made to the world in science and philosophy from the fifth to the fifteenth centuries, he writes:

> It cannot be denied that Christianity has snatched the world from under the baneful yolk of paganism, wherever it has made its appearance; and that the worship of one holy God-Creator, Saviour, and Sanctifier-with all its rational consequences, all its beneficial emanations, all its social applications, that is to say, that sublime philosophy of the natural law, of which the grandest genius of antiquity had but a glimpse-has become, through the teaching of the Gospel, a practical science for all indistinctively, the vulgate of all nations, and diffusive as the atmosphere in which we breathe and move. It is also certain that wherever Christianity has not yet penetrated, the same frightful superstition and gross idolatry, which in former ages overspread the entire world, are still prevailing; that countries-once enlightened by the Christian doctrine, and which under its influence shone with all the brightness of intellectual greatness and practical virtues-have since, by repudiating its dictates, sunk into the abjection of degeneracy, and have remained in the darkness which ensued on the extinction of the lamp of Christianity. Asia and Africa will supply many examples of this; indeed that activity of our moral, intellectual, and social faculties; that progressive development of high conceptions, useful aims, and human fraternity, which constitute civilisation, are the result of an attractive power in Christian institutions, springing up wherever the latter are planted and fostered, disappearing or reappearing with them, retrograding or progressing, according as they are more or less respected (*Trinidad*, pp. 34–35).

This tremendous reverence for the superiority of the Christian faith leads de Verteuil to bemoan the fact that Christianity was not taught during slavery so as "to have nourished and improved the minds of the wild Africans" (*Trinidad*, p. 35). Thus, he recommends that the "local authorities and the home government to encourage, by all means, the diffusion of Christianity and aid those who have the peculiar charge of preaching evangelic morality and Scripture truth" (*Trinidad*, p. 35).[61]

   De Verteuil also regrets the impact that slavery had on the moral lives of those who were subjected to its ills. He celebrates the Eurocentric myth of the sanctity of marriage (the concept that monogamy, blessed and accepted by Christianity, was the most "rational" and "civilized" mode of organizing family life) and describes concu-

---

59. Blaut, *The Colonizer's Model of the World*, p. 19.

60. Blaut offers a insightful description of this kind of thinking. Needless to say, de Verteuil may have been blind to the influences such a history of thought had on his formulation of the world.

61. Many of these views informed Wilkins's *The Slave Son*.

binage, the preferred family arrangement of African people, as "that foul leprosy that clung to slavery" (*Trinidad*, p. 20). He also advocates the classification of African births into legitimate and illegitimate "as the means of testing the progress of a people in morals; for the proportionate number of marriages is, to a certain extent, one undoubted criterion of the morality of a population" (*Trinidad*, p. 171).[62] Shades of racism also creep into his work when he claims that the demise of the original Amerindian population resulted from their having "resisted the pressures of civilisation, and finally sunk under the ascendancy of a more intelligent race" (*Trinidad*, p. 172).[63] Determined to negate the fact that Africans, newly liberated from slavery, want to pursue new avenues of endeavors, he concludes:

> The recollections of slavery seem still to act as an *incubus* on their faculties; and they are, in general, averse to all menial occupations, and to the hired labour of the cane-fields especially. This feeling undoubtedly has its origins in human nature; but, unfortunately, they still continue to nourish a sort of repugnance to all kinds of agricultural pursuits, giving preference and precedence to any petty trade and peddling speculation, or handicraft, rather than to the adoption of the more healthy and noble occupation of agriculture. They are excessively fond of display, and of appearing to their best advantage in dress-this mistaking vanity for that rational pride which sought to govern human actions. Singularly improvident, and satisfied with the present "daily bread," they do not seem to think for a moment of the necessity of economy, in order to meet and alleviate cases of illness, accidents, or other contingencies of the future. Although thus extravagant, they use no steady exertion in

62. See Merle Hodge, "Challenges of the Struggle for Sovereignty: Changing the World versus Writing Stories," in Selwyn R. Cudjoe, *Caribbean Women Writers* (Wellesley: Calaloux, 1990), pp. 202–8 for discussion of the negative impact of the Eurocentric model on the Caribbean family life. Needless to say, Caribbean women, particularly peasant women, had a different concept of man-woman relationships. Speaking of these relationships in the Haitian context, Ira Lowenthal notes that bourgeois assumptions imposed on gendered roles in peasant societies may falsify and distort their complexities. Elaborating on this notion, Joan Dayan writes that "some fictions of female sexuality—specifically those echoing elite or Christian notions of women's place-may have little to do with how women really feel." In the specific Trinidad context, testimony to the rationality of the slave's way of ordering their domestic lives, Mrs. Carmichael, a visitor to the society in 1833, records an interesting encounter she had with a young slave woman on the Laurel Hill plantation. Discussing her plans to live with one J. P., this young slave woman say that she is going to "try live wid 'em first a little bit for trial, and den if he be one good, nigger, she [would] marry 'em." Things do not work out and they separate due in part because J. P. is "at least twenty years younger" than J. See Joan Dayan, *Haiti, History and the Gods* (Berkeley: University of California Press, 1995), p. 134, and Gertrude Carmichael, *Domestic Manners and Social Condition of the White, Coloured, and Negro Population of the West Indies, Vol. 2* (London: Whittaker, Treacher, 1833), p. 190. See also Basil Matthews, *Crisis of the West Indian Family: A Sample Study* (Mona, Jamaica: Extra Mural Department, Unviersity of the West Indies, 1953) for a discussion of the African family in Trinidad during slavery and colonialism.

63. Blaut contents that the sixteenth century discussion in Spain about the humanity of the American Indians was a crucial part of the early formation of the diffusionist theory in that it helped to explain why it was "natural for them [the American Indians] to succumb and to provide Europeans with labor, land, and products" (*The Colonizer's Model of the World*, p. 20). Also see Lewis Hanke, *The Spanish Struggle for Justice in the Conquest of America* (Philadelphia: University of Pennsylvania Press, 1949), for a discussion of the sixteenth Century Spanish debates about the humanity of the Amerindians.

earning their wages; nor, generally speaking, will they vest it advantageously in the savings banks, or otherwise, even when earned: in fact, they do not exert themselves beyond the merest necessity. As a consequence, very few individuals have sensibly progressed; on the contrary, the emancipated-as a class-may be said to have retrograded, and are now suffering severely from the general distress (*Trinidad*, pp. 175–76).[64]

Needless to say, this version of history—that is, the powerful transformative nature of Christianity and Western civilization—embodies all of the myths of Western progress and modernity. Speaking of its impact on the New World, Leo Marx points out that inherent in that myth was the idea that "civilization is chiefly associated with its presumed positive qualities: organized religion; cities; literary; knowledge of, and power over, nature, as represented by the latest advances in science and technology; social order; civility; literature; and art,"[65] the whole point of which was to justify European atrocities in the New World. Homi Bhabha has observed that such stereotyping of Africans and the native peoples of America—a problem we also find in Gamble's *Trinidad*—represents a profoundly ambivalent gesture (a "text," as he calls it) "of projection and introjection, metaphoric and metonymic strategies, displacement, overdetermination, guilt, aggressivity; the masking and splitting of 'official' and fantasmatic knowledges to construct the positionalities and oppositionalities of racist discourse."[66] It is this ambivalent nature of colonialism that allows Anthony de Verteuil, a descendant of L. A. A. de Verteuil, to characterize the latter as "the chief anti-colonialist of his time" and depict him as being antiracist as well.[67]

It can be argued that de Verteuil used his work to present the fears and prejudices of his group and to outline a new social order, and to accomplish this end, he describes the attributes of the land to excite others to share in its bounty and its possibilities. In a reciprocal gesture, he also warns that inhabitants have to pull up their socks if they wish to encourage others to participate in the development of the land, hence his plea to his fellow inhabitants that "on a careful review of our present social condition, you have no cause for despondency; but let my earnest advice prevail with you to sever all connection with the past by a steady advance in moral and industri-

64. In a letter to the *Port of Spain Gazette* regarding sugar cane cultivation in Le Reunion, de Verteuil wrote that "in Lareunion, as in Trinidad, the emancipated slaves have gradually retired, no only from cane cultivation, but also from other agricultural pursuits; a result much to be deplored, even considering only the welfare of that class, without reference to the general interest of the colony... . Immigration has saved the Mauritius, la Reunion and Trinidad from ruin, and has been the main instrument of the prosperous condition of the two former islands. This is a fact against which one may struggle, but it is a fact; and those who prefer to base their judgment on facts, may bring it forward as an unanswerable argument in favour of the principle: as to details, let them be a bone of contention" (March 30, 1859).
65. Marx, "The American Ideology of Space," p. 64
66. Bhabha, "Difference, Discrimination and the Discourse of Colonialism," p. 208.
67. *Sir Louis de Verteuil*, p. 47, 62–63. De Verteuil's obituary also described him as having played "a prominent part in the early Reform Movement" of the island ("Death of Sir Louis de Verteuil," *Port of Spain Gazette*, August 12, 1900, p. 3).

al improvement; or if the events of the past cannot be but reverted to, if its trials and struggles, its sufferings and humiliations will, of necessity, intrude-let them rather serve as beacons by which to avoid the shoals, and to steer onward in the current of the future, than as provocations to disunion, or precedents for error" (*Trinidad,* p. vi).

However, on the whole, de Verteuil sympathies cohered with those of the dominant class.[68] Although his views of the Africans changed as he grew older (Anthony de Verteuil claims that there was "a marked change" in his views of the former slaves in the revised edition of *Trinidad* [1884]),[69] it still remains true that the central theme of his book aligns itself with the colonialist ideology of its time.

Designed to open up a "fair and impartial discussion" (*Trinidad,* p. vi) of the economic and social possibilities of the society, *Trinidad* emerged as an important diacritical marker in the continuum of the island's literary and social discourse and as an important discourse on its spatial history through which the society could begin to speak about its place in the world. It asks the island's people to look at themselves with greater objectivity and recommends that they enter into a new relationship with their space and time. It also seeks to reconstruct them in such a way as to respond positively to the new social and economic conditions of colonialism. Of course, how the inhabitants read such a text was a different matter.

The Physical Impact of de Verteuil's Geography

When the English arrived in Trinidad in 1797, one of Abercromby's first act was to engage F. Mallette to make a physical inventory of the land and is properties.[70] The resulting map, *The Map of Trinidad,* was the first attempt to record the physical aspects of the island and to name its resources. By a strange coincident, Alexander von Humboldt and his partner Aime Goujaud Bonpland set sail for the West Indies in the same year but never visited Trinidad. Instead, they wound up in Venezuela and spent the next five years exploring South America and opening it up to the world. Humboldt's example certainly gave de Verteuil the necessary impetus to undertake his own task. As he sailed to the New World, Humboldt wrote to von Moll, his friend and fellow naturalist, "I shall be able to collect plants and fossils and to make calculations with these excellent astronomic instruments; I shall analyze atmosphere chemically...but all this is not the main object of my journey. My attention will always be directed to the combination of energies, to the harmony caused

---

68. By 1889, Anthony de Verteuil claims that Sir Louis was "undoubtedly the outstanding Trinidadian of his time" (*Sir Louis de Verteuil,* p. 81).

69. De Verteuil, *Sir Louis de Verteuil,* p. 81.

70. See F. Mallette, *Descriptive Account of the Island of Trinidad* (London: W. Fadden, 1802). It needs to be emphasized that maps, cultural and political practices, are meant to be understood "within the cultural specifics of the circumstances that it portrays" and to provide a particular kind of information for those who authorizes its production (Turnbell, *Maps are Territories,* p. 19). It follows then, that Mallette's map was intended for the exploitative purposes of the English rather than for the acquisition of any self-knowledge of the inhabitants of the island.

by the influences of inanimate nature and all the plants and animals of animate nature."[71] Although de Verteuil did not have as much recourse to Humboldt's work as did Kingsley, he certainly reflects Humboldt's goals in his work.

Fifty-nine years later de Verteuil offered a catalogue of what he found on Trinidad, seeking, as Humboldt did, to make a link between the animate and inanimate objects of the island. Like Humboldt, whom he quotes in his book, de Verteuil wishes to describe the geography of the island, to catalogue its natural resources, and to demonstrate how the latter can contribute to a better life for all.[72] A collective work by some of the island's more prescient members, *Trinidad* represents the most comprehensive document written about the physical geography of the island since Mallette's work. It devotes separate chapters to the geography of the island and to its natural resources and notes the richness of its animal life, the vagaries of its tropical climate, the diversity of its population (including religion and educational systems), its political governance, and its agriculture potential[73]. It also includes Antoine Leotaud's essay on "the Ornithology of Trinidad" and his catalog of fishes, as well as Herman Cruger's essay on Trinidadian flora. De Verteuil also acknowledges the assistance of Dr. Court who gave him "a pretty complete account of our most remarkable reptiles" (*Trinidad,* p. xi). A tour de force, the book represents one of the most comprehensive works written about nineteenth-century Trinidad. It also makes an important contribution to the developing science of Caribbean geography, which was just beginning to organize itself.[74]

71. Quoted in Adolf Meyer-Abich, "Alexander von Humboldt" in *Alexander von Humboldt, 1769–1969* (Bonn: Inter Nationes, 1969), p. 43.

72. Humboldt's influence is all over de Verteuil's text. Not only does the latter quote the former, but he also appropriates Humboldt's view of climate (how it fits in the geography) and remarks how the geological formation of the island (that is, the island's mountains) resemble those of the South American continent. Needless to say, Humboldt's work was also published in the *Trinidadian,* as was an allusion to his correspondence with Dr. Culton (See *The Trinidadian,* June 8 and August 13, 1853.) In the *Port of Spain Gazette* of March 8, 1854, reference was made to the work of William von Humboldt, Alexander's brother.

73. De Verteuil, it would seem, followed the general outlines of Humboldt's geographical work on Cuba, The *Island of Cuba,* which he undoubtedly read in French while he studied in Paris. Some of the same features that make Humboldt's work attractive, particularly his lifting geography out of its scientific provenance to treat of its political implications, were also present in de Verteuil's work. For example, the generous panoramas (morphologically accurate but enhanced by impressionable *apercus*), the aesthetic treatment of the landscape, the nuances of light and color that attended descriptions, and Humboldt's total involvement with his work—an essential part of the *géographie humaine*—was also present in de Verteuil's work.

74. It cannot be stressed enough how much de Verteuil's enterprise was part and parcel of what was happening in the outside world. A. H. R. Grisebach in *Flora of the British West Indian Islands* (1864) observes that "Trinidad, lying almost contiguous to the delta of the Orinoco, partakes of the flora of Venezuela and Guiana," a point de Verteuil advanced six years earlier. Moreover, Grisebach divides the British Caribbean into "five natural section, each with a distinct botanical character," of which Trinidad stands alone (p. 5). Says Guisebach, "Almost all the principal authors who have written on West Indian plants belong to the last century and consequently to the Linnaean school and a general synopsis of West Indian plants have never been attempted." Linnaeus published a paper on a small set of Jamaican plants. Dr. Cruger, a fellow countryman of Guisebach, both of them were Germans, also contributed to Grisebach's book. See A. H. R. Grisebach, *Flora of the British West Indian Islands* (London: Lovell Reeve, 1864).

Of the chapters, the most notable are those that examine animal and plant life and the topography of the island. The naming exercise in the book brings the land to life and demonstrates how the inhabitants began to possess their land, even though it may have meant different things to different members of the society. Certainly, the task of cataloguing the island's physical resources represented an indispensable task for those who wished to understand (and to exploit) the physical environment. It represented something else to those who made that environment their home. Indeed, much of the information provided by de Verteuil was gleaned from the inhabitants whom he quotes to support the assertions he made about the land. Like him, they, too, were engaged in the process of naming the land in which they lived. Although they were not acquainted with the technical nomenclature of animal and plant life, there is sufficient evidence to indicate that they made use of the plants and animals in their everyday lives since their very survival as a people depended on their knowing the value of what they found in their new environment.

De Verteuil's descriptions of the landscape also demonstrates the aesthetic pleasure he took in his word painting. Like Antoine Leotaud, de Verteuil "loved his country with the ardour of a passion. And he was over and above all things a Trinidadian."[75] Although he is concerned to show the importance of cocoa production to the development of the island (he would lead the fight to open up the land for the settlement and production of cocoa and even introduced an ordinance in the Legislative Council against the stealing of cocoa), one is impressed by the magisterial, though lovingly intimate, way in which he paints this snapshot of the cocoa plantation:

> The trees are planted at twelve or fifteen feet apart, and range from about twenty-five to thirty five feet in height; the leaves are large, and when young, of a violet-red hue: whilst from the larger branches and the stem, hang red, yellow, green, or dark crimson pods,-the "Immortel" itself forming a striking feature in the scenery. In January and February, the latter exchanges its leaves for a thick covering of bright red blossoms, the ground underneath being literally carpeted with flowers, whilst birds of various species, and of the most brilliant plumage, join in gay concert above. Several other trees become, at certain periods, like the "Immortel," a regular mass of flowers. Those of the Poui are of a brilliant yellow: of the Roble, an orange colour, and very fragrant: others, again, are white, pink, or violaceous (*Trinidad*, p. 67).[76]

De Verteuil also employs dramatic tension to enliven his description of the animal (in this sense, the insect) world which for him, is a drama worthy of the careful observing gaze of the geographer. Thus, as he describes how meticulously the

75. de Verteuil, *Sir Louis de Verteuil*, p. 55.
76. This written description of the cocoa plantation reinforces the visual representation of the land and explains further Burnley's attraction to Cazabon's art. For example, in *The Queen's Empire*, a pictorial tribute that celebrated Queen Victoria's Diamond Jubilee, readers were able to see a photograph entitled, "Drying Cocoa in Trinidad," that suggests that even this writerly description had its uses. See Driver, "Geography's Empire," p. 32.

hunter and the parasol ants organize their lives, he uses a military analogy to reveal their mode of attack:

> This ant is very active and quick in its movements, stings most severely, and may be said to be excessively fierce in its attacks. It is exclusively carnivorous, and, after killing its prey, divides its into portions, each ant carrying its share of the spoil. The hunter ants do not build nests, but choose recesses in some decayed tree, or among dry leaves, forming a sort of moss, sometimes two feet in diameter, where they congregate during the dry months; in fact, they are nomadic, being always engaged in some predatory excursion, and preferring the wet to the dry seasons for their expeditions; they carry with them their larvae close to the body. The army, or tribe, on starting, marches on a frontage of from about five to six feet, by ten feet deep; then follow three or four columns, which afterwards are formed into two, and sometimes only a single section, this rearguard being sometimes half a mile from the expeditionary corps actually engaged in spoliation. The latter beats up the ground, climbing smaller trees, groping into every hole, under every leaf, and leaving nothing unvisited. Not only insects and the smaller animals fly in every direction, but even the larger species are compelled to give way; for the hunter ants kill everything living thing in the way of their march, young birds in their nests, animals too young or too weak to escape, cock-roaches, scorpions, crickets, etc., and carry away the larvae of insects and their nymphs; they dare not penetrate, however, into the nests of the parasol-ants, which defend their townships bravely (*Trinidad*, p. 138).

De Verteuil's intimate involvement in his work and his capacity to blend the aesthetic with the scientific, the subjective and the objective, the moral with the practical allow the reader to feel the human dimension of his enterprise and to appreciate how involved de Verteuil was in charting the evolution of his society. It also demonstrates how his linguistic prowess makes the material world available for social and economic purposes. In the circumstances, one is reminded of Goethe's satisfaction when he received the first complimentary copy of Humboldt's *Essai politique sur l'île de Cuba* and realized that the author had not omitted "pointers to the incommensurable" in spite of the tremendous amount of statistics that were present in his work.[77]

Trinidad ought not to be read as a text that peripherally describes a static landmass, but "as a passage central to the spatial constitution of [Trinidad]."[78] Although the book reflects many of his Eurocentric preoccupations, it also demonstrates de Verteuil's intimate involvement with, and knowledge of, his physical environment. As one commentator wrote in 1889, de Verteuil knew "more about the colony in a

77. Goethe's comment was especially important in light of Schiller's bitter criticism of Humboldt, who Schiller complained, showed a "'poverty of understanding and perception, in spite of the great richness of the material' and especially of 'that sharp, naked reason which is impertinent enough to want to measure and fathom Nature, which must remain inscrutable and awe-inspiring in all of its aspects." Quoted in Cedric Hentscchel, "Alexander von Humboldt's Synthesis of Literature and Science" in *Alexander von Humboldt, 1769–1969*, p. 105.

78. Carter, *The Road to Botany Bay*, p. 98.

literary and practical sense than anyone else."[79] Similar to the way knowledge is produced among the Yolngu of Australia, it can be argued that the knowledge produced in this marvelous text, through its examination of landscape and geography, made the society available for its inhabitants in ways that were not previously possible and helped to recenter the speaking subject in his new world.

Antoine Leotaud (1814–1867)

The publication of Antoine Leotaud's *Oiseaux de l'île de la Trinidad* (1866) represented a parallel attempt to investigate Trinidad's physical environment. According to Frank Chapman, Leotaud's essay on the ornithology that appeared in de Verteuil's book was undoubtedly "the first paper of importance relating to the birds of Trinidad."[80] Although this remarkable essay was followed by E. Cavendish Taylor's "Five Months in the West Indies: Trinidad and Venezuela" (1864),[81] it was the publication of *Oiseaux de l'île de la Trinidad* that catapulted Leotaud into the arena of serious scientific attention, gained him the attention of ornithologists who were concerned with the tropics, and thrust Trinidad into the eyes of the ornithological world. Published at a time when papers on South American ornithology were based on personal observations, "Dr. Leotaud's many years of field experience gave him advantages which few ornithologists had possessed."[82] De Verteuil was correct when he noted that Trinidad had produced another person of science.

When Leotaud undertook his study, he had two major objectives in mind. First, he wanted to capture this aspect of the island's natural life for posterity. Second, he wished to make a case for the particularity of the island's ornithology even though zoologically and geologically, Trinidad was a part of the South American landscape:

> We lie so contiguous to the southern continent, that our ornithology must necessarily differ from that of the other West India Islands. This is a point of geographical distribution which has its importance, both as regards the science in general, as in questions of pure locality. So luxuriant and varied is our vegetation, our forests so extensive, our insects so numerous, and the disposition of the country itself so far from being uniform, that the vastness of our ornithological treasures cannot form a matter of surprise; and should I but enumerate the species, that alone would be to enregister facts which, at a remote period, may acquire an immense local interest. Our vegetation will change, our soil become impoverished, our forests will

79. *Sir Louis de Verteuil,* p. 81.

80. Frank M. Chapman, "On the Birds of the Island of Trinidad," *American Museum of Natural History,* 6, Article 1 (1894), p. 9

81. Taylor who traveled throughout Trinidad from December 22, 1862, to March 24, 1863 (he also spent a month in Venezuela during this time), catalogued 109 species of land birds and nine species of water birds. One of his most enchanting description is that of Steatornis Caripensis to which he devotes almost two pages. See "Five Months in the West Indies: Part 1: Trinidad and Venezuela," *The Ibis,* 6 (1864), pp. 73–97.

82. Chapman, "On the Birds of the Island of Trinidad," p. 10.

diminish in extent, as they yield to the axe; our marshes will disappear, and our insects cease to swarm in such numbers as at present, and, as a consequence, the ornithology of the island will then present in its aspect, a change which is even already perceptible (*Trinidad,* p. 423).

It is almost as though Leotaud was aware of the historical role he had to play: he was aware that he had to name ("enregister") the birds so that, at a future period in our history, we, too, may come to know and respect a past that has vanished. Thus, to name the island was to preserve it for posterity. But like the population itself, Leotaud seemed to realize the unique—almost god-like—position in which he found himself. He was at the beginning of a process that had to be chronicled carefully if he wished to maintain any traces of his time in the future. Thus, he observes:

On reflecting on the circumstances which thus regulate the alimentation of our birds, we are led to a first consequence, viz., that this colony being still new, and subject therefore to the changes which time may produce, our ornithology will hereafter lose its present characteristics. Not only will the number of species diminish in proportion to the reduction of alimentary resources, but new species will perhaps be naturalised, as new cultures are introduced. A species of grosbeak seems already to have become one our guests, since the cultivation of rice as been introduced (*Trinidad,* p. 431).

There arose a question that may be applied even to the human species on the island: how do we to sustain new species or even new cultures that came into the country with such amazing regularity?

The second aspect of Leotaud's intervention, and one that is more germane to our study, was his determination to identify species of birds unique to Trinidad, that is, to determine the Trinidadianness of the island's ornithology. Although he recognized that our fauna made Trinidad an integral part of South America, still he was able to identify twenty-three species of birds that were common to Trinidad and North America, a conclusion that P. L. Sclater, a reviewer of his book, responded to skeptically:

Trinidad is, in fact, nothing more or less than a bit of Venezuela, separated from the adjoining main at a very recent epoch, just as the British Islands have been divided from Europe. As Mr. Taylor has observed, there is probably no species of birds to be met with in Trinidad that is not also found in Venezuela, though many, doubtless, occur in Venezuela which do not extend their range into Trinidad. This is just as the case with England and the Continent. Dr. Leotaud seems to recognize this fact to a certain extent, though he is still hampered by the notion that Trinidad has something in common with the Antilles (which form a very distinct and isolated province of the Neotropical Region) and North America. He talks of there being twenty species common to the United States and Trinidad; but when these cases are rightly investigated it will, no doubt, be found that the greater number of these twenty species find their way to Trinidad by Venezuela, and not by direct immigration.[83]

In this context, Leotaud seems to have been more correct than Sclater. When Chapman intervened in 1893 (Chapman studied the ornithology of Trinidad from February 21, 1893, to May 7, 1893), he indicated that there were twelve species or subspecies of birds that were peculiar to Trinidad (and by now) Tobago. Chapman concludes:

> We can thus in a general way determine the relationship of Trinidad to the continent, and it is therefore of special interest to note the effects of this recent insulation of the birds of the island. Unfortunately we have not as yet sufficient exact data from the adjoining main to make a satisfactory comparison, but as before stated, the relationships of the birds of the island to those of the continent are remarkable close. As far as we at present know the following species and subspecies of birds are peculiar to Trinidad or to Trinidad and Tobago:

Merula xanthosceles	Basileuterus vermivorus olivascens
Cyclorhis flavispectus	Lanio lawerenceii
Chylorospingus leotaudi	Sporophila lineola trinitatis
Platyrhynchus mystaccus insularis	Ramphocaenus melanurus trinitatis
Myrmeciza longipes albiventris	Amazilia erythronota
Momotus swainsoni	Pipile pipile.

Most of these birds are simply insular representatives of mainland species to which they are closely allied. They serve to show that, in spite of its comparatively recent separation and proximity to the continent, Trinidad still presents a habitat sufficiently isolated to permit the differentiation of some species inhabiting it.[84]

This was certainly Leotaud's point. There was something distinctive about the society's avifauna that he had to capture both for his fellow citizens and those who were to come after him. He used a lot of French and patois words to name the birds of Trinidad, even named some after himself and the island. Also, he was especially picturesque in his description of the humming bird. However, Leotaud was responding to Taylor who claimed that Trinidad did not "possess any species [of birds] peculiar to itself."[85]

To be sure, Leotaud made several errors of classifications in this pioneering work in the literary tradition of the society. As in the case of Thomas's *The Theory and Practice of Creole Grammar*, another pioneering work, there was a paucity of sources upon which Leotaud could draw and that made his work more difficult. However,

83. P. L. Sclater, "Remarks on Dr. Leotaud's *Birds of Trinidad, The Ibis*, 3 (1867) p. 106.
84. Chapman, "On the Birds of the Island of Trinidad," p. 7.
85. Taylor, "Five Months in the West Indies," p. 77.

such circumstances only make us appreciate his effort more.[86] Still, Chapman puts Leotaud's achievement in perspective when he writes:

> At the time when Dr. Leotaud worked the correct identification of tropical birds was possible only for a few specialists. There were no general works, and a large library was a necessary adjunct to the satisfactory determination of species. With few books at his command it was to be expected that Dr. Leotaud would sometimes wrongly identify his specimens. Indeed, these errors indicated the difficulties under which he labored, and as such give evidence of the enthusiasm which enabled him to complete his work.[87]

Although Leotaud's study was a pioneering work in the field of tropical ornithology, he did not receive the recognition that he deserved. This failure of recognition might have been due, in part, to the fact that he died one year after his book was published. Yet, so glaring was/is the absence of *Oiseaux de l'île de la Trinidad* from the literature of Trinidad or tropical works on ornithology that G. C. A. Junge and G. F. Mees, authors of the authoritative *The Avifauna of Trinidad and Tobago*, were forced to make the following comments:

> We want particularly to express our admiration for the invaluable work done by Leotaud (1866). He not only prepared a charming book, but for that time also an outstanding work. In ornithological literature very little can be found about Leotaud and therefore we may add here some particulars....
>   Antoine Leotaud (1814–1867) was Trinidadian by birth. At the age of twelve he went to France, where he acquired an extensive knowledge of Anatomy, Pathology and Chemistry. He also studied Zoology. In 1839 he returned to Trinidad and started his career as a physician, and distinguished himself as such. One of his essays was awarded a gold medal by the Paris School of Practical Medicine. Another has been crowned by the Medical Association of Ghent. On the island he was highly esteemed by all. In his spare time he studied birds, purchased specimens and books required for this study, which, however, meant a heavy tax on his slender means. His book was published by national subscription in 1866. In 1867 Leotaud passed away after a painful malady of fourteen months duration.[88]

When de Verteuil used Leotaud's essay on ornithology and zoology in his appendices of *Trinidad,* he was drawing on a mutual friendship and respect for the latter's knowledge of a field that Leotaud had acquired through painstaking work, helped along by enormous enthusiasm. It was a friendship and admiration that went back to when they two men were medical students at the Sorbonne in the 1830s.[89] Speaking at Leotaud's funeral of his friend's abilities, de Verteuil said that "Dr. Leotaud was in a high degree gifted with the true medical instinct; his diagnosis was

---

86. Although he is fairly generous, Sclater points out several errors in Leotaud's work.
87. Chapman, "On the Birds of the Island of Trinidad," p. 10.
88. G. C. A. Junge and G. F. Mees, *The Avifauna of Trinidad and Tobago* (Liden: E. J. Brill, 1958), pp. 3–4.
89. Anthony de Verteuil believes that de Verteuil "seems to have shared to some extent Leotaud's extraordinary interest in zoology" while they were students at the Sorbonne (*Sir Louis de Verteuil,* p. 28).

sure and in consultation with him I always felt safe." As to the ornithologist's tremendous work in tracking down and naming numerous species of birds of the island, de Verteuil made the following observation: "To our young men I would point out Dr. Leotaud as an example which cannot be too assiduously followed. Indefatigable, preserving, devoted, his life has been a constant labour, but in return we know that the name of a Creole in Trinidad ranks high among those eminent for the promotion of Natural Science."[90] None could speak more confidently about Leotard's abilities than de Verteuil: they both engaged in a process of enregistering the island in the minds of their fellow inhabitants. Each, it seemed, named the island so as to make it known and accessible to its citizens and those who would come in contact with it.

* * *

Cazabon, de Verteuil, and Leotaud, Trinidadians in every sense of the word, were engaged in an enterprise that transcended them. Pioneers in the areas of art, geography, and ornithology, they opened up areas of discourses that were necessary for an understanding of the Trinbagonian society. Implicated in a history of ideas of which and to which they were not necessarily conscious, they were concerned only to name the place in which they lived. In a very real sense, this new colonial land had to be brought within the horizon of intelligibility (both local and foreign) through visual and written representations. As Gregory writes, "The very act of naming was a way of bringing the landscape into textual presence, of bringing it within the compass of European rationality that made it once familiar to its colonizers and alien to its inhabitants." [91] In the final analysis, however, these scholars and artist were engaged in an ambivalent project in which inhabitants were viewed as both objects and subjects in their own space. According to Paul Carter, "It was not by discovering novelties but by ordering them, rendering conceptually and culturally visible, that the great work of colonization went ahead... It was the method of giving objects great and small a place in the world, the picturesque logic of connection and contrast, that ensured they could never be lost again or overlooked."[92]

When Leotaud made the explicit observation (as would Thomas two years later) that he needed to name his spatial environment so that it would achieve greater meaning in a "remote period," I think he understood Carter's injunction in more ways than one: he had to inaugurate a discursive process whereby the physical properties of the island could literally come into being. In other words, he and the others had to name the space in which they lived and to teach it how to speak. Such, it seems to me, is the major characteristic that made the works of Cazabon, de Verteuil, and Leotaud so very important and enabling to the spatial and literary history of the island.

90. Ibid., p. 55.
91. Gregory, *Geographical Imaginations*, pp. 171–72
92. Carter, *The Road to Botany Bay*, p. 128

CHAPTER 8

Cultural Resistance:
The Emergence of the Carnivalesque

From night to night, during nearly three years, I laboured almost unceasingly at my task; sometimes threading my way with confidence, frequently having to condemn or re-write whole pages, which a chance remark of a passer-by or closer inquiry had proved erroneous: yet, though often baffled, I was never discouraged;   for I look forward to the day when, respectfully submitting to the public this imperfect Work and its object, I could claim, if not the praise of successful authorship, at least the credit of having endeavored, under great disadvantages, to supply a public want.

—J. J. THOMAS, *The Theory and Practice of Creole Grammar*

The meanings of words in a language are the community's store of established knowledge. A child learns the values and preoccupations of its culture largely by learning the language: language is the chief instrument of socialization, which is the process by which a person is, willy-nilly, molded into conformity with the established systems of beliefs of the society into which s/he happens to be born. Language gives knowledge, and allows knowledge to be transmitted from person to person. But this knowledge is traditional, not innovative, for language is a stabilizing, stereotyping, mode of communication.

—ROGER FOWLER, *Linguistic Criticism*

A nation's self-respect hinges upon its ability and willingness to defend itself, but its very existence is inconceivable without its own language.

—JOHN EDWARDS, *Language, Society and Identity*

Establishing the Terms of the Debate

The 1860s found Trinidad a society in transition. Indeed, it was a period in which the society had to absorb several different cultures and ways of life. However, apart from its heterogeneous nature in race and ethnicity (Europeans, Africans, and Asians, plus the varied ethnic groups among the Africans and the East Indians), the society was also linguistically diverse. European languages, such as Spanish, French, English, and Portuguese; African languages, such as Ibo, Hausa, and Akan; and East Indian languages, such as Tamil and Hindi, were all spoken on the island. Such an interesting mixture of languages and cultures made for an exceedingly rich, variegated, and exciting society. When, however, the English authorities chose to restructure the society through religious and secular education (that is, to conform to the values, feelings, and sentiments of the dominant group), the inhabitants resisted their oppressors by maintaining their own forms of storytelling, practicing their own religious and cultural beliefs, performing their own authentic musical forms, and following their own ideas of family organization. In short, because these people continued their own ways of life, the colonial authorities realized that they had to impose their own modes of knowledge and frames of references upon colonized people if they wished to maintain the hegemony they desired.

To achieve these ends, the colonizers forbade Shango and other religious practices, exacting tremendous penalties against violators;[1] banned the playing of African drums; and outlawed the practice of Obeah, ordering practitioners to be jailed and flogged.[2] They also deligitimized African forms of marriage and concubinage by promoting European monogamous forms of marriage[3] and demeaned the importance of African languages in the society. Thus, Africans and East Indians were treated as though they were outcasts and inferior beings, and their customs and languages denigrated, while the English language and the English way of life were advanced as the only desirable modes of behavior. Such an emphasis in official policy intensified the cultural struggle during the first three decades after emancipation, a crucial period of our development as a society.

In light of such a policy, in the 1860s, language and the language instructions assumed a major role in this larger arena of cultural struggle. While Mervyn

1. See Eudora Thomas, *A History of the Shouter Baptist of Trinidad and Tobago* (Ithaca, N.Y.: Calaloux, 1987).

2. Article 11 of the Ordinance of Governor Lt-Colonel Thomas Picton, proclaimed on June 30th 1800, read: "Any Negro who shall assume the reputation of being a spell doctor or obeah-man, and shall be found with an amulet, a fetiche, or the customary attributes and ingredients of the profession, shall be carried before the Commandant of the District, who will take cognizance of the accusation; and provided the crime be not capital, inflict proper punishment; but should it appear probable that the culprit has been the cause of death of any person by his prescriptions (as very frequently happens), the Commandant will then transmit him to the common gaol, as a criminal, to be prosecuted and dealt with according to law" (Carmichael, *History of the West Indian Island*, p. 382). As late as January 14, 1889, the following report appeared in *New Era* under the heading "The Obeah Man": "James Ramsay, the obeah man, whose case was reported in our last issues, was flogged on Tuesday at the Royal Gaol in the presence of Mr. L. M. Fraser, Inspector of Prisons, and Dr. R. H. H. Knaggs. [After] twenty out of the twenty-five lashes were administered, the man of magic [was] bellowing like the Bull of Bashan under the infliction. None can say but that the sentence was deserved and Ramsay's dupes will be interested to learn that the black art cannot take the sting out of the cat o'nine tails." One notes the pleasure the reporter takes in describing Ramsay's pain and how he mocks the latter's claims of possessing "magical" qualities. The use of the cat-o'-nine-tails to inflict punishment was a holdover from the days of slavery.

3. For example, Joseph Patrick Keenan called "the notorious prevalence of concubinage, which characterized the domestic lives of the people" the "darkest form of immorality" (See *Report Upon the State of Education in the Island of Trinidad* [Dublin: Alexander Thom, 1869] p. 29).

Alleyne has asserted that "language contact is but one instance of cultural contact,"[4] Mikhail Bakhtin has observed that culture ought to be viewed as "the symbolic exchange of language, circumscribed and permeated by a specific historical environment."[5] More importantly, as Bakhtin notes in a similar context, the novel (and literature in the larger sense) must be seen as "the site in which contesting and contested discourses of different periods, groups, or classes engage one another as sociolinguistic forces implied, rather than literature—indeed, culture in general—must be understood as a system of significations that dialogically manifests itself and its multiple meanings in all their historical specificity and social valence."[6]

As a part of this social and cultural struggle, the educational system became a principal battle site, where the struggle for the ideological control of the minds of African and Indian people took place and represented an important step in the development of identity. Although I do not wish to suggest that the major articulations of a Trinidad personality were delineated during this period, I insist that the struggle for national direction began to be played out at the social and cultural levels, and it is within that context that we begin to see the earliest formulation of what it meant to be a Trinidadian.[7] During this period, we see the promulgation of the purely formal discourses of the colonizer trying to impose his values on the population via the educational system as he sought to force English/European values upon a Creole society that represented itself largely by what can now be called the carnivalesque, that is, a culture of laughter, picong, festivity, and ole talk that regenerated itself through the dynamic of a people's experiences and defined itself paradigmatically through the first nascent outburst of the Carnival festivity in all of its polysemous and polysemantic richness.[8] In this context, the creative transformative

4. Mervyn Alleyne, *Roots of Jamaican Culture* (London: Pluto, 1989), p. 120.

5. Quoted in Robert Anchor, "Bakhtin's Truths of Laughter," *CLIO*, 14, No. 3 (Spring 1985), p. 245.

6. Ibid.

7. I do not suggest that there is an original Trinidadian—there is none—against which one can measure who or what an authentic Trinidadian is. I only wish to argue for the representation of a particular historical personality that was being articulated via a particular discursive practice. Thus, when we argue for a nascent Trinidadian, we are talking about a subject that was created, to some degree, by the images and representations of history, art, journalism, travelers' reports, and so on.

8. In *V. S. Naipaul,* I define the culture of Carnival to mean not only the pageantry of the celebrations, but also all the necessary and contingent aspects of that festival that made it so important in the lives of Trinidadians and Tobagonians. In that study, I further define the culture of Carnival as constitutive of ritual spectacle, such as pageantry, comic shows, demarche gras, dances, and other festivities before Carnival day, preparation for Carnival, the activities of the calypso tents and the steelband yards; verbal compositions (that is, the literature of Carnival), such as the calypso, the parodies of official life, the talk of the midnight robbers, the language of stickfighting, and so on; ritual dances, such as camboulay, calinda, innovative Carnival dances (e.g., the butterfly) made up for the celebrations; and ritual meaning, such as what Carnival means and what the band leaders, the calypsonians, and the ordinary Carnival revelers say that Carnival means to them. More importantly, the culture of Carnival, a distinct entity from the official culture, constantly affirms the integrity of a way of life of the oppressed masses of people. See Selwyn R. Cudjoe, *V. S. Naipaul: A Materialist Reading* (Amherst: University of Massachusetts Press, 1988) for a further discussion of this idea. "Ole talk" in the Trinidad sense represents a love of and for language and rhetoric. *Mauvais langue,* a special aspect of gossip, also fits into this pattern of language use and rhetoric.

process that was taking place in the wilderness consisted of a situation in which the Creole inhabitants (the native population) took over and transformed the Carnival from its French aristocratic origins; appropriated and transformed La Davina Pastora or the Siparia Fete from its Spanish and Roman Catholic origins and made it into their own likeness by invigorating it with their own values, desires, and feelings;[9] adapted and transformed the *Ramayana*, a Hindu epic, and the *Hosein* (or hosay), an Islamic festival, to suit their own unique desires and purposes as they all sought to impose order on disorder and symmetry and cohesion on "chaos" and thrown-togetherness. Here, of course, one saw the emergence of the subaltern, the emergence of the underground culture that was being submerged by officialdom and colonial rhetoric and practices. This is one reason why the practices of Carnival, hosein, the ramleela, and the Great Siparia Fete—the Christian, Islamic, and Hindu versions of the carnivalesque—were thought to be so destructive and lewd (that is, so subversive) by the colonial authorities. Because these practices, according to the official society, brought out the worst aspects of the Creole society, they had to be banned. Yet, apart from subverting the official culture, these practices remained the principal means through which a people kept their identity in spite of the onslaughts against their culture.

If we view the carnivalesque-and what I have called the culture of Carnival-as being polysemous, that is, meaning different things to different people, and manifesting a distinctive way of life, the production of such texts as Gamble's *Trinidad: Historical and Descriptive*, Patrick Joseph Keenan's *Report Upon the State of Education in the Island of Trinidad*, and J. J. Thomas's *The Theory and Practice of Creole Grammar* must be seen as the logical outcome of a process that reflected two separate perceptions of the society. While Keenan's *Report*, a part of a hegemonic discourse, sought to "downpress," control, and superintend the activities of the colonial subject, *Creole Grammar* seeks to unearth and celebrate the submerged dimension of a people's life that, at the time, was dismissed as being unimportant, irrelevant and valueless.[10] *Trinidad* straddles these two important impulses as it describes and comments on various linguistic and anthropological practices of the society. Unlike Keenan's *Report*, it does not seek to impose a rigid formula upon the people. It merely disparages aspects of their culture.

These texts were published between 1866 and 1869—fully one generation after the formal emancipation of the slaves—and precisely at a time when the Creole

9. See, for example, "The Great Siparia Festival," in *New Era*, May 1, 1871.

10. Roberto Gonzalez Echevarria defines hegemonic discourses as one that is "backed by a discipline, or embodying a system, that offers the most commonly accepted description of humanity and accounts for the most widely held beliefs of the intelligentsia. Within such a discourse, the individual finds stories about himself and the world that he or she finds acceptable, and in some ways obeys. Prestige and socio-political power give these forms of discourse currency. When they are abandoned, they are merely stories or myths, voided of power in the present, the way in which we read about Melquiades' scientific prowess in the early chapters of *Cien anos de soledad*" (*Myth and Archive*, p. 41). It is only necessary to point out that there was another world of ideas from which the slaves drew their values and their ways of talking about the world.

population was attempting to implant their forms of consciousness on an emerging society. Therefore, these works ought to be seen as a reflection of the symbolic order that outlined the ideological struggle that engaged the energies of the society. Because each author worked within a similar episteme, they allow us a unique glimpse into the status of Trinidad culture at a particular juncture of history. Their work ought to be seen as important modes of discourse that arose from the dialogical practices of the period, mutually reinforcing practices, sites of contested and contesting discourses that allow us to understand the nascent signs of the literary and cultural evolution of our society. Indeed, it is not coincidental that these texts appeared at the very moment when the official society was in crisis and at a time when a furious debate was taking place over the best way to anglicize the society and over the place "the children of the sun" should assume in this new dispensation.[11] Each text, it can be argued, had "a molding and modeling" effect on the other.[12]

Trinidad: Historical and Descriptive (1866)

In May 1856, after having studied at Stepney Academical Institution (now Reagent's Park College, Oxford) for two years, William Hamilton Gamble, a native of Trinidad, offered himself for missionary service in Trinidad.[13] His candidacy, sup-

11. See, for example, the discussion between the "Warnerites" and the "Gorodnites" in the *New Era*, November 22, 1869. Interestingly enough, a description of the Creole population as "children of the sun" occurs as early as *Free Mulatto*.

12. The language is that of Gonzalez Echevarria, *Myth and Archive*, p. 10.

13. Prior to Peter David Brewer's thesis, "The Baptist Churches of South Trinidad and Their Missionaries," most studies represented Gamble as an Englishman who did missionary work in Trinidad. Although it is possible that the subtitle of his work, "A Narrative of Nine Years Residence in the Island, with Special reference to Christian Missions," may have led readers to think he was a visitor to the island, all evidence points to the contrary. Gamble, a Trinidadian, went to England to study. The minutes of the Methodist General Committee of February 6, 1855, refers to Gamble as "a native of Trinidad" (p. 25) that made him especially suited for missionary work in the country of his birth. All the official records of the mission refer to Gamble as being "of European parentage, though born in Trinidad." In "The Baptist Churches of South Trinidad and their Missionaries," Brewer writes that Gamble "was the adopted son of a well-known white lady of Port of Spain, who sent him to England for an education." In 1856, when he left England to take up his duties in Trinidad, he was depicted as "entering on his work in right good earnest. He had gone back to the place where he received his first religious impressions, to labour with the missionary (Rev. Law) of Christ. Inured to the climate, knowing the manners and habits of the people, accustomed to their modes of thought, yet having advantage of two years training at Stepeny College, we may reasonable hope for a long career of devoted, useful missionary life." In Gamble's obituary, E. B. Underhill writes that: "Mr. Gamble was of European parentage, though born in Trinidad. He received his early education in London. He was about eighteen years of age when he returned to Trinidad and entered business. Ere long he married, and was baptized with his wife by the Rev. John Law. Having personal means of support, he again came to England, and attended the classes at Stepney Academical Institution, in preparation for the ministry of the Gospel. On the completion of his studies, he offered himself for mission work in his native home, and, under the auspices of the Baptist Missionary Society, he entered his labours in the month of October, 1856" (Peter David Brewer, "The Baptist Churches of South Trinidad and their Missionaries, 1815–1892," Master of Theology, University of Glasgow, 1988, pp. 128–29; E. B. Underhill, "The Late Rev. William Hamilton Gamble, of Port of Spain, Trinidad," *Missionary Herald* (October 1, 1888), p. 398. *The Baptist Handbook for 1889* (London: Alexander and Shepherd) offers the same basic information about Gamble's life.

ported by Rev. Law, with whom he had worked and under whom he had studied in Trinidad before going to London, was submitted to Dr. Angus, head of the college, who on receipt of the letter, "warmly recommended his application for Mission Service in Trinidad."[14] Accepted by the Mission in July 1856, Gamble sailed for Trinidad on September 12, arriving in Trinidad on October 17, 1856, to pick up his labors. A product of a missionary education, Gamble began his ministerial work in Trinidad under the tutelage of Rev. Law.

As a missionary, he continued the work that Rev. Cowen and Rev. Law started. Like them, he attacked the Roman Catholic Church, "the persecuting hand of pop-ery and the vile way in which the Catholics get away with all manner of sin." He believed that the Catholics exerted "a powerful religious influence throughout the country. The genius of the Catholic religion is suited to the tastes of the people. The sensuous service, the robes of the priests, the intoned liturgy, the offering up of the host, the frequent processions, the many fete days; all these things are pleasing to the greater number of people in Trinidad. The first communion has many charms for the young girls, and is certainly agreeable to parental feeling. The confession is, to the literate minds, a means of relief to a burdened conscience, while extreme ancients hold a very high place in the estimation of the people."[15] In a letter to Underhill on February 8, 1888, he writes that "today and tomorrow the people here are wild with 'Carnival,' a miserable outcome of Popery, but then no matter what defilement they contract during carnival it can be taken away by confession and absolution—so teaches the miserable system called Popery. We are progressing in primary education, and it is to be hoped that as education spreads, superstition will decrease. Such fooleries as Carnival however, die hard." He did not know how cor-rectly he spoke.

In racial matters, Gamble followed the example of L. A. A. de Verteuil, whose work the former used as a guide and to whom he confessed his "indebtedness for several facts, and a few sentences" (*T.*, p. vi). Using a rationale similar to that of de Verteuil, Gamble arrived at similar conclusions about Africans, observing that, although Africans "had enjoyed several years of the blessings of freedom, yet they were far from free from the degradation and immorality which slavery necessarily produces and entails" (*T.*, p. 1). In a letter to Mr. Baynes, secretary to the Baptist Mission in England, on July 21, 1888, two weeks after his father died, William Gamble, Jr., described his father's attitudes toward Africans: "The blacks have always been accustomed to be driven and they require the same treatment today—altho' the 1st of August 1888 is the Emancipation Jubilee—my father often said he was a nigger-driver. His experience was that the moment he ceased driving they grew indifferent if not to say careless. He said one requires to be an eternal scold

14. In *Trinidad*, Gamble describes his joining the Mission as follows: "Induced by the representations of Mr. Law, the Committee decided upon sending him help. Accordingly, in the year 1856, the writer was accepted for Trinidad, and prepared for his departure thither (p. 6).

15. William H. Gamble, *Trinidad: Historical and Descriptive* (London: Yates and Alexander, 1866), pp. 42–43), hereafter *T*.

with whip in hand always."[16] Gamble also made it clear that emancipation had not necessarily changed Africans. They possessed the same "state of morals" after slavery as they had during it: "Even now, though many years have rolled by, and the second and third generations occupy their fathers' places, still the vices of the parents are indulged in by the children. Alas! That it should be so!" (*T.*, p. 2).

"People, Languages, and Religion," the most original part of Gamble's *Trinidad*, discusses the ethnography of the island, fleshes out a draft of the island that de Verteuil began in his *Trinidad*, and prepares us for Thomas's *Creole Grammar*. Not only does it give us a sense of the diversity of the society, it lists the activities of the "motley aggregation of Africans, Asiatics, Europeans, and a few individuals of Indian or American blood" (*T.*, p. 29) who inhabited the island. Of Afro-Trinidadians, he says, they are "a tall, well-made people, rather showy in their persons, fond of dress, music, and amusements generally, especially dancing and theatricals. They have a frank manner about them, but are somewhat fickle, and lack stability of character and firmness of purpose. The liberated classes and their descendants cannot be said to have attained to any high standard of moral character. If the truth must be told, they are litigious, and somewhat lax in the principles of honesty" (*T.*, p. 30). After this brief introductory note, he describes the characteristics of the various African ethnoi: the Yorubas, the Eboes, and the Congoes.

In this work, Gamble provides a comprehensive description of the Indo-Trinidadians. Apart from their frugality, thrift, intelligence, and capacity for hard work, "the only reliable labour in the country" (*T.*, p. 31), he observes that "The Coolies are very abstemious, saving nearly all they earn, with a view to carrying back their earnings to their own country, where, with the amount of money they can save here, they will among their countrymen be considered very wealthy persons" (*T.*, p. 32). As with the Africans, Gamble differentiates between the language and customs of the Bengalis (who speak Hindustani) and the Madras who speak Tamil.

Gamble's work possesses much importance to us on the language question. He tells us of the many dialects that Africans speak and their "aptness" at learning different languages. Of the Indians, he says, their languages are so different that "English has to become the medium of communication" (*T.*, p. 33). Apart from the languages of the Portuguese and Chinese, Gamble notes that "Danes and Germans, Spaniards and Italians, Scotch and Irish, French and English, are to be found in Trinidad, with their diversified manners, different languages, and opposing creeds. The languages spoken in Trinidad are numerous and diverse" (*T.*, p. 38). Gamble records that the language of government and law was English and that a patois, "not pure French," was the language used by the Creoles of the Island. His recognition of the preeminent use of patois among the lower classes prepares us for Thomas, "one of the most intelligent and learned of the Trinidadians" (*T.*, p. 39), who was in the process of preparing a grammar on patois. Gamble also offers one of the earli-

16. Baptist Missionary Minutes, Regeant's Park College, Oxford.

est explanations of the language and concludes that, "among themselves this *patois* is the medium of thought. It is, moreover, the language which the African and the Coolie, and the stranger in general, learns first, and of course, for the simple reason that he hears it most frequently spoken. Its vituperative epithets are numerous and forcible; and I am afraid are the best known, because the most frequently in use" (*T.*, p. 39).

Gamble's chapter on the Baptist Missions in Trinidad is also instructive, even though it repeats much of what Rev. Law and Rev. Cowen said about the difficulty of propagating the faith in the island and the intransigence of Roman Catholicism. It captures the diversity of religious life in the country and reveals his frustration in gaining converts. Inniss observes that, although Gamble was a good preacher, the changing nature of his congregation made it difficult for him to enlarge it.[17] He was incorrect when he predicted that "the day is not far distant ere the many tongues and the many creeds found in Trinidad will become as one" (*T.*, p. 45).

After thirty years of missionary work, Gamble became very tired and felt he needed a rest. In a letter to Mr. Baynes on May 29, 1886, he writes that, although he had never "asked the Society for one pound for medical attention......we may yet have to beg for money for doctor's expenses but I pray not." By the end of the year, his health had taken a turn for the worse. On December 23, he wrote that he felt "run down considerable during this year, have lost weight, and suffer with increasing frequency from loss of voice and consequently an inability to discharge my ministerial duties." Within two years of this letter, Gamble died of dysentery on July 8, 1888.

In spite of all his work, Gamble was unable to dissuade his people from seeing Africans in an inferior manner, nor for that matter, were many Africans capable of seeing themselves as equals to whites. On March 16, 1889, about nine months after Gamble's death, William Gamble, Jr.,[18] complained to Mr. Baynes about how Africans were seen by the church, even though L. O. Inniss, his father's "worthy helper," as William senior called the latter, was a deacon in Gamble's church and doing a fine job:

> I understand from Mr. W[illiams, pastor of San Fernando Baptist Church], that it is the intention of the Society to transfer Mr. Wilshire of the Bahamas to Trinidad. It would be no more than right that there should be 3 missionaries in Trinidad, for there are only 2 and one is compelled to leave on account of health as in Mr. William's case or one dies, as in my father's case, the Baptist cause naturally suffers. Mr. Baynes, I may mention that laymen are not appreciated–neither is the man who

17. See L. O. Inniss, *Diamond Jubilee of Baptist Missions in Trinidad, 1843–1903* (Port of Spain: Franklin's Electric Printery, 1904), p. 11.

18. William H. Gamble, Jr., worked in the Trinidad Government Service in the Audit Office. Although his father wanted him to follow in his footsteps, the health of the former prevented him from becoming a minister in the Baptist Church. William senior expressed his disappointment at this outcome: "This grieves me much for nothing would have given me greater pleasure than to have seen him give himself to the Lord" (December 25, 1879).

is not white, even if he be a minister-there are undoubtedly prejudices; but India is not the only place in the universe wherein is to be found caste-a white face is almost a wonder, it works magic. It is not only in the Church that this is the case-I meet with it in my work. I hear the darkies express themselves very often on this point. People in England know nothing of these prejudices, these disadvantages one labours under-to them, you must live among them just in the same way would you learn their tongue. Perhaps you reply but you must teach them better. I answer nothing like trying but he who sets himself the task of overcoming caste will find that in so doing the object for which one is labouring will suffer considerable.

William junior was alluding to the diseased state of racial relations at the end of the 1880s. His father had done little to erase the false notions of African inferiority, nor for that matter, did he leave much of an impression on the society or his congregation. The *Port of Spain Gazette* reported that Gamble was gifted "with a powerful voice, a robust frame, a pleasing countenance, and most courteous manners, and was very successful in his ministrations, especially among the humbler classes of the town. His kindly voice and warm shake will be missed by members who are not members of his congregation."[19] To be sure, some of the sentiments of this obituary was contradicted by his son's testimony and the feelings Gamble expressed in *Trinidad*. Inniss, his worthy helper, believed that "he was a good preacher" and that the church was always full when he preached, but he had nothing else to say about Gamble who, nonetheless, left us an informative work that paints a vivid picture of the habits of the diverse population that inhabited the island in the mid-1860s.

The Keenan Report (1869)

The movement from a predominantly French/Creole patois to the use of English as the dominant language in Trinbagonian society was reinforced by the increased attempt to anglicize the society and rearrange the school curriculum accordingly. On January 16, 1868, after a report by a local commission consisting of Messrs. Darling and Farfan proved to be unsatisfactory,[20] Sir Arthur Hamilton Gordon, governor of Trinidad, appointed Patrick Joseph Keenan, chief inspector of schools of Ireland, "to make a diligent and full enquiry into the state of public education, whether secular or religious, in the island of Trinidad" and to recommend "the means most effective for the improvement of the public schools of that island."[21] Although Keenan's *Report* concerns itself ostensibly with education policies, it can be read as a political document intended to affect the social and cultural practices of the society.[22] Neither Keenan nor Gordon could have been unaware of Fitche's dic-

---

19. Quoted in L. O. Inniss, *Diamond Jubilee of Baptist Missions in Trinidad,* p. 11

20. See L. B. Tronchin, "The Great West Indian Orator," *New Era*, December 18, 1888, for a discussion of this issue.

21. Keenan, *Report*, p. 1. All subsequent references to this report are included in the text as *KR*.

22. See R. J. Zvobgo, *Colonialism and Education in Zimbabwe* (Harare: Sapes, 1994) for an excellent overview of how education functions in a colonial state and Carl Campbell (*Colony and Nation* [Kingston, Jamaica: IRP, 1992]), for a more specific, though not as critical, examination of early education in Trinidad.

tum that to influence the behavior of the citizen "you must do more than merely talk to him; you must fashion him, and fashion him in such a way that he simply cannot will otherwise than you wish him to will.... The education proposed by me therefore... is a reliable and deliberate art for fashioning in man a stable and infallible good will."[23]

While the *Report* may seem to bear all the signs of innocence, it was neither alien to nor independent of the discursive practices of the society. Rather, it constituted an important insertion into the ideological framework of the society. Read in this manner, it gives one a good idea of how the dominant colonial culture perceived its "subjects" and how it wished to mold them. It confirms Gonzalez Echevarria's observation that "texts never exist individually, but in relation to others ... there is no possible metatext, but always an intertext."[24] In other words, its interrelatedness with other texts and its positioning within the discursive practices of the society makes Keenan's *Report* an important formative cultural documents of the society.

In his attempt to clear away the debris before he made his recommendations to Governor Gordon, Keenan wrote that, besides the problems of race, language, and religion, "there was yet another difficulty—a social one, the existence of which could not be deliberately ignored":

> Seventeen years had passed away since the emancipation of the 20,657 slaves on the island. Many of them still survived; and many others who had been slaves in the neighbouring colonies became free settlers in Trinidad. To such people, society was only a chaos. In it they could recognise neither design, nor purpose, nor symmetry. For its duties their habits ill suited them; for its responsibilities their intuition was defective. Nevertheless, they formed a considerable proportion of the people, and it became the duty of the State to mould them into good citizens. Accordingly, in his new scheme of education, Lord Harris had to consider their conditions and necessities (*KR.*, pp. 9–10).

In Keenan's view, Africans posed three major civilizing problems. First, their values and practices were heathenistic and barbaric and thus a curriculum should be designed to turn them into good English boys and girls. This implied that English standards and values were the civilized norms to which all citizens should aspire, a restatement of the problem that Blaut identified.[25] Second, it was implied that the

---

23. Quoted in Elie Kedourie, *Nationalism* (London: Hutchinson, 1961), p. 83. It is an accepted position that apart from its purely pedagogical functions, educational programs do act as a servant to political causes. With regard to education, Kedourie argues that "the purpose of education is not to transmit knowledge, traditional wisdom, and the ways devised by a society for attending to the common concerns; its purpose rather is wholly political, to bend the will of the young to the will of the nation. Schools are instruments of state policy, like the army, the police, and the exchequer" (Ibid., pp. 83–84).

24. Gonzalez Echevarria, *Myth and Archive*, p. 9.

25. In a curious way, James would pay tribute to and accept some of these values as his own. See, for example, *Beyond a Boundary* when he talks of how he accepts the English school boy norms and how much it meant to him.

overarching philosophy that gave meaning to African lives was "chaotic" because it was non-European, which meant that Africans could recognize "neither design, nor purpose, nor symmetry" in their lives, nor could they attach any order or coherence to their world. As a result, Keenan's proposals were designed to give Africans and Indians the intellectual and religious tools that would allow them to make sense of their world, to give it coherence and order, and to bring them out of their heathenistic darkness. When Morton, another European, presented his plans to educate the East Indians he echoed many of Keenan's sentiments.[26]

Third, in this context, education was meant to oppress rather than liberate, to dehumanize rather than to humanize, to alienate rather than to reconcile the inhabitants to their society. Apart from trying to inculcate the economic skills that the colonizers required in an age of colonialism, Keenan's formulation were intended primarily "to impart the cultural, moral and behavior values of the [dominant] society, notably appropriate attitudes of respect for the rulers, their institutions and their rulers."[27] Since the colonial state could not rule by force alone, it had to adopt alternative ways to regulate and control the newly freed people. The education offered by Keenan's *Report* was not designed to make Africans more fully human. Rather, it was designed to educate people away from themselves and to spread what Alleyne calls "cultural imperialism":

> Where cultures are in contact, formal opportunities for learning may be chiefly provided through schools. Schools will then be both cultural institutions to which either all or only some have access, and institutions that dispense formal instruction in virtually the entire culture. In this way the school can serve one of two functions: it can provide people from one culture with the opportunity for formal instruction in the new culture toward which they are moving, or it can preserve and impart knowledge of the culture from which these people may be moving, that is, the "dying" culture. The school is then an instrument of both cultural change and cultural persistence or revival. The school is also an effective instrument for spreading cultural imperialism: for fostering notions about the innate or achieved superiority of one culture.[28]

According to Keenan, in 1851, when Lord Harris announced his educational plan, the major impediments to education were the questions of race, religion, language, social conduct, and the horizons of the slaves. Apart from its oppressive nature, the proposed educational reforms also constituted an attempt to stop the spread of Roman Catholicism and the further diffusion of French ideas and values. It was also designed to aid in the anglicization of the society. Ideological training was to be carried out in two major ways: the teaching of English in the schools (the only language in which children would be taught) and the nonsupport of denomi-

26. See Sarah E. Morton, *John Morton of Trinidad* (Toronto: Westminster, 1916).
27. Zuobgo, *Colonialism*, p. 2.
28. Alleyne, *Roots of Jamaican Culture*, p. 15.

national schools, which meant that Roman Catholics would suffer disproportionately because they had more schools and Protestantism would be advanced even more through the teaching of English. On the whole, most of Harris's recommendations dealt with the manner in which religious education was to be conducted.[29]

Scholars such as Carl Campbell who have analyzed the role of education in this period see the conflict as one between religions (the Anglicans versus the Catholics) rather than a struggle for cultural hegemony between English and French values. Although there is much truth in the position that the Anglicans wanted to make the system more English than French, central to the conflict was another struggle between an African- and Indo-based culture and a European-based one. There is sufficient evidence to suggest that the Africans and the Indians subscribed to an entirely different ontological system (manifested in their religious, cultural, and social practices) that gave order and coherence to their lives.[30] Committed as he was to a Eurocentric way of interpreting the world, it never occurred to Keenan that there could be any validity to African or Indian customs. It is that [mis]reading of African cultural values that Thomas challenged when he produced his theory of Creole grammar.

I do not wish to suggest that Keenan's *Report* was totally without value and that he did not perceive areas in which relatively important educational changes should be made. To his credit, he calls for the introduction of texts that reflect the needs of the society. Although he recognizes the "excellence and reputation" of the Irish National Books that were used in Trinidadian schools at the time, he expresses a wish to see "a set of books whose lessons would be racy of the colony—descriptive of its history, of its resources, of its trade, or its national phenomenon, of its trees, plants, flowers, fruits, birds, fishes, etc... .As the Irish element preponderates in the Irish books, so the Trinidad element ought to preponderate in the Trinidad books, which would then be as popular with the Trinidadians as the Irish books are with the people of Ireland" (*KR.*, p. 17).

Still, Keenan could be dismissive of the culture and its values. In pointing out the

29. The fundamental recommendations of Lord Harris's educational program were as follows: (a) that no religious instructions whatever were to be imparted in the schools; (b) that under no circumstances were schoolmasters to give religious instructions; (c) that religious instructions of the children were to be committed to their respective pastors, who upon the day set apart for the purposes in each week—the school being closed that day—were to impart such instructions in the churches and elsewhere; (d) that the instructions in the schools was to be of such a character as not to offend the religious sensibilities of any inhabitant of the colony; (e) that no school fees were to be charged; (f) that the school expenses were to be met by local rates; (g) that the entire management and control of schools, the appointment and dismissal of teachers, the determination of the course of instructions and of the books to be employed were to be vested in a Board of Education.

30. Alleyne discusses the connection between the practice of African religions and rebellion in the New World. Observing the influence the slave religions (Myalism, Convince, and Kwamina) had on Afro-Jamaicans, the English authorities resolved "to carefully investigate the means of diffusing the light of genuine Christianity, divested the dark and dangerous fanaticism of the Methodists which, grafted on the African superstitions, and working on the uninstructed minds of the negroes, has produced the most pernicious consequences to individuals, and is pregnant with imminent danger to the community." Thereafter, the Church of England began "to proselytise among and baptize the slaves" (*Roots of Jamaican Culture*, p. 27).

absence of the study of needlework among the students at the Girls' Model School, he writes that "operating upon a singular constituted community, whose wants are the results of an imperfect civilization, and whose defects are the incidents of a predominant indolence, the system of education in Trinidad ought to be, in a conspicuous degree, one of an industrial character" (*KR.*, p. 17). His view embodies a contradictory posture to the indigenous culture of the society. Whatever he meant by "an imperfect civilization" has never been really clear to this reader.

It is also to Keenan that we must turn to get a sense of the language situation in the colony, which helps us ultimately to understand why Thomas wrote *The Theory and Practice of Creole Grammar.*[31] Speaking about the "polyglot character of the people," Keenan went on to make the following observation:

The sermons in the Roman Catholic Cathedral of Port-of-Spain are nearly always delivered in French, and most of the sermons in the other Catholic churches throughout the island are preached in either French or Spanish. The Catholic children almost universally learn their prayers and their catechism in French or Spanish. There are 19 sworn interpreters of French, 9 of Spanish, 1 of German, and 1 of Hindoostanee, all officially recognised by the Government, for the purposes of law and commerce. The Coolie element in the population has increased to nearly 20,000. In point of fact, the place is quite a Babel. The operation of the Ward schools has, no doubt, extended the use of English to districts where English had been previously unknown. But this diffusion of the English language has been accomplished by the most irrational process that could possibly be conceived. French and Spanish speaking children have been set to learn English alphabets, English spelling, and English reading, without the slightest reference whatever, in the explanation of a word or the translation of a phrase, to the only language, French or Spanish, which they could speak or understand...In some of the schools the reading is a mere mechanical repetition of words, suggestive of no meaning, no idea, no sense of intelligence or pleasure. After years of schooling the mind of a child under such circumstances is still a *tabula rasa*....The desire of every lover of the colony must be to see that all the inhabitants speak English. But a language cannot be infused into the human mind by the power of a battering-ram. Rational measures must be employed. And my firm conviction is that if the French and Spanish-speaking children were first taught to read their vernacular language, and then taught English through its medium, they would acquire a facile use of English with incalculable rapidity. This is no new theory. Very eminent authorities have laid it down as the best means of introducing English into Wales, the Highlands of Scotland, and the remote parts of Ireland. At all events, the least to be attempted should be to require every teacher to know the language spoken by his pupils, and—by way of illustration and exemplification—resort to it as often as might be necessary. The padlock at present on the lips of the children of the French and Spanish-speaking districts would thus be opened, and the little creatures would no longer stand like victims to bewilderment in the presence of an examiner (pp. *KR.*, pp. 21–22).

31. Gamble also emphasizes the "polygot character" of the society and the number of languages spoken in the country at the time.

It was an attempt, then, among other things, to remove the padlock from the lips of the children and the adults that led Thomas to write his grammar of the Creole language, one of the most important texts of nineteenth-century Trinidad. It certainly represents the attempt of a people to assert their identity at the very moment when the weight of the official society was intent on snuffing it out. In a multilingual setting, though, no language operates independent of another, and as Alleyne has observed, in multilingual situations, the political dominance of the speakers involved is the important determinant in "the nature and direction of language change." He adds further:

> When two languages are mismatched, second language learning is unidirectional: speakers of the subordinate languages learn the dominant language but not vice-versa. Speakers of the subordinate languages not only learn the dominant language but surrender their own languages more or less swiftly and more or less completely, depending on the degree of unevenness in the matching of the cultures in contact. The lower languages undergo drastic change as a result of either borrowings from the dominant language or to losses in the inner form as a result of growing disuse. The dominant language, however, changes little or not at all when spoken by native speakers, though it changes drastically when acquired as a second language by speakers of the lower languages.[32]

Needless to say, the formal introduction of English at the official level (speakers of the *superstrate* language) led inevitably to the erosion of the "lower language" (the *substrate*) and losses at the "inner form" of the language. As a teacher in the educational system, Thomas could observe what he calls "the nullifying effects of the patois on English instruction among us"[33] and the disadvantages to which the French-Creole speakers were subjected as the society rapidly adopted English as the dominant language. Thomas's attempt to rescue a language and a people from oblivion drove him to devote three years of his short life to record the language of the African population.

Indian languages, particularly Hindi, did not succumb to immediate dissolution, primarily because Indo-Trinidadians steadfastly maintained their culture. They "deliberately and persistently kept their children away from the Ward Schools of the island" (*KR.*, p. 37). According to Keenan, the East Indian "is proud of his ancient lineage, is influenced by the prejudices of caste, and declines to associate intimately with, or to bring up his children in the same school, with Creoles of the African race" (*KR.*, p. 37). To the degree, however, that the English authorities imposed the English language upon Trinidadians, primarily in the areas of religion, law, and education, it ensured that social and cultural practices would result ultimately in new and different methods of expression.

---

32. Alleyne, *Roots of Jamaican Culture,* p. 121.

33. J. J. Thomas, *The Theory and Practice of Creole Grammar* (1869, London: New Beacon, 1969), preface; hereafter referred to in the text as *CG.*

In Keenan's work, we see a dichotomy between the real world of the inhabitants and the language of the "facts" in which he represents them. Africans, it seems, were guilty of an enormous sin against civilization, not only because they were born in Africa and possessed black skins, but because blackness itself was encoded as a fact of inferiority and backwardness. Keenan's depiction of Africans as "degenerate" and barbaric picks up on similar statements made by de Verteuil, Gamble, and Edward Bean Underhill in *The West Indies: Their Social and Religious Condition*. [34] Given such deep ideological beliefs, it is clear that Keenan severely distorts African culture beyond recognition and reduces their lives to a fiction. Keenan's *Report* must be viewed not so much as a representation of ontic reality, but as reflecting the views of the dominant culture, a prescription for the mental enslavement of Afro- and Indo-Trinidadians. Because of their percentage of the population and their exposure to the Ward schools, Afro-Trinidadians bore an unusually heavy burden from this ideological assault.

The Theory and Practice of Creole Grammar (1869)

The evidence suggests that Thomas was best equipped to respond to Keenan's ideological assault. Although I do not mean that Thomas's grammar was a conscious response to Keenan's *Report*—Thomas began his *Grammar* three years before Keenan arrived in the country. Proceeding intertextually, we can compare how each scholar represented the society and the value each placed on the integrity of the life and culture of the working people. Appearing as it did at the very moment that the official powers were drafting a new educational system for the society and inaugurating a specific curriculum for its teachers, *Theory and Practice of Creole Grammar* represents a counterdiscourse within the discursive space emerging at the time. Although he was concerned about the linguistic status of Creole as a language, Thomas was more concerned about what the anglicization of the society meant for those who spoke the Creole language. He writes that his study originated as a result of "considerations having a wider and more urgent importance, and bearing upon two cardinal agencies in our social system; namely Law and Religion" (*CG.*, preface). His work also seems to be in response to a Protestant minister who "expressed surprise to Thomas that there was no Creole grammar or lexicon to help learners."[35] One reviewer was pleased Thomas recorded the language of the "lower class, who cannot sufficiently appreciate their merits and applications" while a *Trinidad Chronicle* editorial observed that it took a knowledgeable and critical mind to "reduce that which has always been wild, vague, seemingly accidental, to a clear concise system."[36]

Thomas, the son of a freed slave, was born two years after slavery had officially

34. See Edward Bean Underhill, *The West Indies; Their Social and Religious Condition* (London: Jackson, Walford, and Hodder, 1862).

35. Bridget Brereton, "John Jacob Thomas: An Estimate," *Journal of Caribbean History*, 9 (May 1977), p. 23.

36. Quoted in Smith, *John Jacob Thomas*, p. 40.

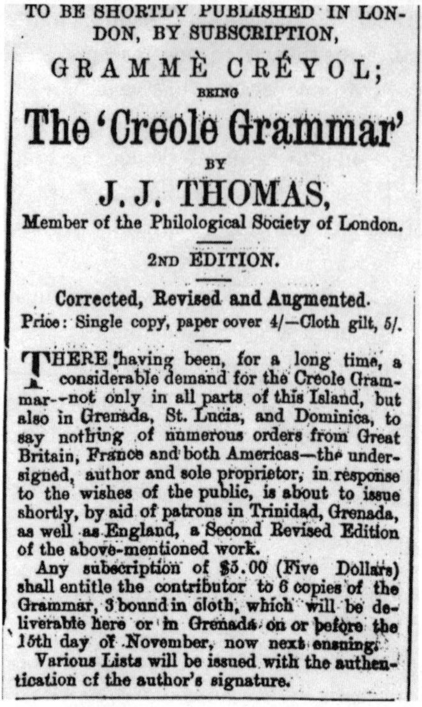

TO BE SHORTLY PUBLISHED IN LON-
DON, BY SUBSCRIPTION,

GRAMMÈ CRÉYOL;

BEING

The 'Creole Grammar'

BY

J. J. THOMAS,

Member of the Philological Society of London.

2ND EDITION.

Corrected, Revised and Augmented.

Price: Single copy, paper cover 4/—Cloth gilt, 5/.

THERE having been, for a long time, a considerable demand for the Creole Grammar—not only in all parts of this Island, but also in Grenada, St. Lucia, and Dominica, to say nothing of numerous orders from Great Britain, France and both Americas—the undersigned, author and sole proprietor, in response to the wishes of the public, is about to issue shortly, by aid of patrons in Trinidad, Grenada, as well as England, a Second Revised Edition of the above-mentioned work.

Any subscription of $5.00 (Five Dollars) shall entitle the contributor to 6 copies of the Grammar, 3 bound in cloth, which will be deliverable here or in Grenada, on or before the 15th day of November, now next ensuing.

Various Lists will be issued with the authentication of the author's signature.

FIGURE 12. An advertisement for the republication of J. J. Thomas's *The Theory and Practice of Creole Grammar* in *Public Opinion*, August 9, 1887.

ended. He was also a product of Harris's educational initiatives.[37] Gifted linguistically, by the time he reached manhood, Thomas appeared to "have been fluent not only in the Creole which was spoken round about him, but also in English and French; proficient in the classical languages, Latin and Greek; and at least acquainted with Spanish and the dialects of the neighboring islands" (*CG.*, p. v). Gerard Besson claims that, when Thomas became schoolmaster at Savonetta, "a completely Patois-speaking village," he learned the language to provide better instruction for his students.[38] As he became better acquainted with the language, Thomas grew to respect its uniqueness and took pains to point out that it was not "only mispronounced French ... but make bold to submit the illustrations in this treatise [*Theory and Practice of Creole Grammar*], as calculated to dispel an error which has often been fatal to the interests of the poor, and to supply a want to whose existence the continuance of such an error is mainly attributable" (*CG.*, p. iv).

37. A product of Lord Harris's educational initiatives, Thomas rose very quickly within the system. Selected in 1858 for special training, he became one of the first qualified teachers and, in 1859, was awarded one of the six places in the Model School to do further training. In 1860, he was appointed schoolmaster at Savonetta; in 1866, he was appointed to the office of the receiver-general; and in 1869, he was sent to Cedros as a clerk of the Peace. When Charles Kingsley visited Trinidad in 1869, Arthur Gordon, the governor of Trinidad, introduced Thomas to Kingsley. In 1870, Thomas became the secretary to the Board of Education and secretary to the Council of Queen's Royal College. See Smith, *John Jacob Thomas,* for an insightful discussion of Thomas's life.

38. Gerard Besson, *A Photographic Album of Trinidad* (Port of Spain: Paria, 1986), p. 86.

Thomas wanted his *Grammar* to assist in ameliorating the problems of the poor who were exasperated because of the change from French to English. There was also the added problem that court-appointed interpreters did not understand that Creole was a language in its own right that required as detailed a study as any other language, hence Thomas's explanation of his project:

> In the administration of Justice in this Colony, the interpreting of Creole occurs as a daily necessity. Yet it is notorious that, in spite of constant practice, our best interpreters, though generally persons of good education, commonly fail in their renderings, especially from Creole into English. No doubt this is owing in some measure to the inherent difficulty of translating off-hand, and at the same time exactly, from one language into another. But in the present case this difficulty has remained wholly undiminished, because our interpreters, like everybody else, neglect to study the idiotisms of the dialect in combination with their English equivalents (*CG.*, preface, p. iv).

Thomas's recognition of the disadvantages in which Creole speakers found themselves induced him to develop a theory and practice of the language. He recognized that the language was "a direct descendant of French as spoken by African slaves, with additions to the vocabulary drawn from African languages and speech of those other groups who have influenced Trinidad—English, Spanish and Amerindians" (*CG.*, p. vii).[39] To be taken seriously and to gain validity, Thomas had to work out a phonology (an orthography), an etymology, and a syntax of the language. He also provided a collection of idioms, proverbs and short texts to illustrate the language in its specific usage that thereby demonstrate "the divergence of the Creole from the French with regard to the import and use of individual words." For Thomas, *Theory and Practice of Creole Grammar* was intended to be a manual for those whose business it was to assist Creole speakers in their collision with the English language.

The Social and Ideological Importance of Creole Grammar

The impact of English and the attempt to anglicize the society led inevitably to many changes in spoken Creole: "though abandoned to the ignorant, and used only occasionally among instructed persons, [Creole] exhibit[ed] one of the vital characteristics of living tongues in its capability generating new terms from radicals within itself" (*CG.*, p. 73). In recognizing Creole as a new and developing language, Thomas recognized that the linguistic transformation that took place in Creole was similar to what occurred in "the development of the Romance languages from their Latin stem after the Roman empire had broken up and barbarian peoples had begun to remould Latin according to their own verbal rhythms" (*CG.*, back cover). Thomas further recognized, as contemporary linguists have, that "pidgins and

---

39. Thomas defined Creole as "a dialect framed by Africans from a European tongue" (*CG.*, p. 1).

Creoles are not wrong versions of other languages but, rather, new languages. Their words were largely taken from an older language during a period of linguistic crisis to fill an urgent need for communication... . They are new languages, shaped by many of the same linguistic forces that shaped English and other 'proper' languages."[40] Indeed, taken from its African languages, Spanish, French, and English roots, Creole arose in Trinidad to fill a need felt by an African-based society not only to communicate with one another but also to express an emerging cultural identity. It was Thomas's task to chronicle the emergence of that identity by recording the group's language.

To be sure, Thomas was not the first scholar to publish a work on the Creole languages in the New World. John Holm points out that "The first serious study of Creole languages in the Caribbean began in the 1730s when Moravian missionaries were sent to convert the slaves on St. Thomas (1732) and in Suriname (1735)." In 1829, the British and Foreign Bible Society in Britain published "the first complete edition of *Da Njoe Testament* in Sranan Creole English for the Moravians in Suriname," and in 1842, Abbé Goux, a French priest, published a fourteen-page description of the Lesser Antillian Creole, "the first systematic treatment of a French-based Creole,"[41] to which the author attached a *Catéchisme en langue Créole*. Thomas had access to the latter when he prepared his grammar on Trinidadian Creole.

These early publications were not free from criticism. In December 1829, Dr. Andrew Thomson, founder and chief contributor to *Edinburgh Christian Instructor,* attacked the translation of *Da Njoe Testament* and rebuked the Moravians for "putting the broken English of the Negroes ... into a written and permanent form" and taking pains "to embody their barbarous, mixed, imperfect phrase in the pages of schoolbooks, and to perpetuate all its disadvantages and evil consequences by shutting them up to it as the vehicle of God's word."[42] William Greenfield, a philologist, responded by discussing the history of Sranan and emphasizing that "it is obvious that it [Sranan] can no longer be denominated 'broken English' or English attempted to be spoken by the Negroes endeavouring to leave off their own tongue."[43] Anticipating the case that Thomas made for his grammar, Greenfield argues that "the process by which they [the Romance languages] have been framed

40. John A. Holm, *Pidgins and Creoles,* Vol. 1 (Cambridge: Cambridge University Press, 1988), p. 1. Pidgin and Creole studies became established as an academic discipline in the 1960s. According to Holm, pidgin can be defined as "a reduced language that results from extended contact between groups of people with no language in common; it evolves when they need some means of verbal communication." Creole, he argues, "has a pidgin in its ancestry; it is spoken natively by an entire speech community, often one whose ancestors were displaced geographically so that their ties with their original languages and sociocultural identity were partly broken. Such social conditions were often the result of slavery" (Ibid., pp. 4–9).

41. Holm, *Pidgins and Creole,* pp. 17, 21, 23.

42. John E. Reinecke, "William Greenfield, A Neglected Pioneer Creolist," in Lawrence D. Carrington, ed., *Studies in Caribbean Language* (St. Augustine: Society for Caribbean Linguistics, 1983), p. 2.

43. Ibid., p. 4

is precisely that which is presented by the Negro-English, i.e. by corruption and intermixture, and the subsequent invention of new terms, by compounding or otherwise changing those already existing."[44] Greenfield concludes his defense of the integrity of Creole by claiming that: "The human mind is the same in every clime; and accordingly we find nearly the same process adopted in the formation of language in every country. The Negroes have been proved to be in no degree inferior to other nations in solidity of judgment, or fertility of imagination.[45]

The publication of *Theory and Practice of Creole Grammar*, therefore, represents a continuation of a process that was taking place in the Caribbean: an attempt to codify and understand the emergence of a new form of social existence. As such, it signals the consolidation of a national community, a sense of self-awareness and self-consciousness that is indispensable for any national community. In this sense, the crafting of such a theory and practice signified what John Edwards calls "an emblem of groupness, as a symbol, a rallying point."[46] In this first detailed grammar of a French-based Creole, Thomas was concerned to show the uniqueness of Trinidadian Creole and to build on the achievements of Goux. Thus, he argues:

> As the Abbé does not profess to discuss systematically the peculiarities of the dialect, his observations on that point are, of course, exempt from technical criticism; but I am free to state that the *patois* of the catechism, being that of Martinique or Guadeloupe, and withal *very* strange, it would scarcely be more intelligible to a Trinidadian than real French." (*CG.*, p. V)

Thomas's attempt to preserve the integrity of the Creole language signaled an important moment in the sociocultural history of Trinidad. Apart from its communicative aspect (that is, its attempt to assist outsiders in learning the language), as an emblematic marker, the *Grammar* signifies that the majority group—primarily the African *ethnoi*—had consolidated its place in the national community. Thus the ongoing attempt of the Creole community to resist the coercion of its language (that is, the learning of English as proposed by the Keenan *Report*) emphasizes the concealment aspect of language and suggests an attempt "through language, to maintain inviolate the group's own grasp of the world."[47] When, however, one recognizes that creolization, a general cultural phenomenon, is confined not only to language, one begins to recognize the degree to which *Theory and Practice of Creole Grammar*

---

44. Ibid., p. 6.

45. Ibid., p. 7.

46. John Edwards, *Language, Society and Identity* (London: Basil Davidson, 1985), p. 17. In this work, Edwards differentiates between what he calls the *communicative* and *symbolic* functions of language. He writes that "language can be important in ethnic and nationalist sentiment because of its powerful and visible symbolism, quite apart from the revived communicative aspect which is often desired with minority groups" Ibid., p. 17. Needless to say, I am more concerned with the symbolic than I am with the communicative aspect of *The Theory and Practice of Creole Grammar*.

47. Ibid., p. 17. Edwards points out that "language can be seen as a vehicle for concealment, secrecy and fiction" (*Language*, p. 16)

constituted simultaneously a moment of resistance to and recognition of foreign/colonial impositions. It also illustrates a creolization that Faith Smith documents in *John Jacob Thomas and Caribbean Intellectual Life in the Nineteenth Century*.[48] It is in this sense that *Theory of Creole Grammar* (and Keenan's *Report*) can be read respectively as extralinguistic and extraeducational discourses.

Theory and Practice of Creole Grammar performed important foundational work within the culture. It played an important role in crystallizing and stabilizing the ideas of Trinidadian society during the culture's formation and at a moment of national crisis. Although much of the outward forms of the language disappeared gradually, the inner linguistic dimension of the language gave form and coherence to the people of the new society that was emerging. Because words and concepts allow us to express certain distinctions and relationships, Thomas's attempt to codify our social experiences helped enormously "to explore and establish the structure of our community's body of knowledge" and to preserve "a community's store of established knowledge." As an instrument of socialization, *Theory and Practice of Creole Grammar* went a long way in assisting a people to understand themselves by molding them "into conformity with the established systems of beliefs of the society into which s/he happen[ed] to be born."[49]

Even if it does not enter a society via conditions of linguistic coercion, a language never remains static. As society changes, so does the capacity of the communicative aspects of the language to express those changes and, as a consequence, the cultural content of a group's identity. Ultimately, according to Roland Barthes, "a sense of identity depends more on the continuation of group boundaries than it does upon specific elements within them."[50] The attempt, however, to record a community's store of knowledge, to signify its awareness and consciousness of itself as a distinct community, and to tell a people who they are makes *The Theory and Practice of Creole Grammar* a significant marker in the society's historical and literary unfolding. As a linguistic document, it remains one of the most important documents in our literary and linguistic history.

Trinidad, Keenan's *Report*, and *The Theory and Practice of Creole Grammar* signify important moments in Trinidad and Tobago's social, cultural, and linguistic history. Coming when they did, they tried to account for the thrown-togetherness of the society at an important moment of its transformation. Because they came out of a similar episteme and thus enjoyed a similar situation from different perspectives, they ought to be understood as important markers in the discursive formation of our society.

48. See Smith, *John Jacob Thomas*, especially chapter 2, "Thomas and His Society."
49. Roger Fowler, *Linguistic Criticism* (London: Oxford University Press, 1986), p. 97.
50. Quoted in Edwards, *Language*, p. 97.

CHAPTER 9

Signs Taken as Wonders:
Race and Race-Consciousness

> From childhood I had studied their [West Indies and the Spanish Main] Natural History, their charts, their Romances, and alas! their Tragedies; and now, at last, I was about to compare books with facts, and judge for myself of the reported wonders of the Earthly Paradise.
>
> —CHARLES KINGSLEY, *At Last*

> The negro has had all I ever possessed; for emancipation ruined me.... I am no slave-holder at heart. But I have paid my share of the great bill, in Barbados & Demerara, with a vengeance: & don't see myself called on to pay other men's!"
>
> —CHARLES KINGSLEY, quoted in Robert Bernard Martin, *The Dust of Combat*

> Racism is never a superadded element discovered by chance in the course of investigation of the cultural data of a group. The social constellation, the cultural whole, are deeply modified by the existence of racism.
>
> —FRANTZ FANON, *Towards the African Revolution*

The introduction of educational reforms fueled in part by the implementation of Keenan's *Report* and by financial incentives of 1875, provided for by Ordinance 13 of the Education Act, allowed denominational schools to educate more students at the primary level.[1] The rise of a vigorous press, "a liberal press," as it was called, among the black and coloured inhabitants opened an avenue whereby adult Africans and coloreds could comment about the goings-on in their society. These

---

1. The Education Ordinance 1890 repealed the Educational Ordinance of 1875 and granted school aid to each primary school on a uniform basis. However, providing education for the children of the lower classes did not become easier (between 1870–1901 all primary schools were fee-paying). Still, the recognition that the children of ex-slaves and indentured laborers needed to be educated became an important issue of debate during this period. See Brereton, *Race Relations in Colonial Trinidad*, chap. 4, for a discussion of the role and importance of education during the 1870–1900 period.

newspapers also offered their readers a larger diet of foreign news, which allowed them to keep in touch with international events. If the primary schools catered to the education of the children, then the liberal press not only educated the adult population, but it also provided a forum whereby the latter could express their feelings about matters that affected the society and their well-being. Added to this mélange, 1870–1900 saw the spread of the English language and the further entrenchment of the East Indians and their languages in Trinbagonian society even though patois remained the dominant language of the mass of people until the end of the century. All of these factors helped open up the society further, even as the assimilation of newcomers posed additional challenges to the prospects of national development.

Apart from opening up what can be called "the public sphere" and the expansion of civil society, the rise in education and the contingent awareness of a new self (or a new positioning within the society) created an enhanced feeling of race pride and race awareness among the black and colored masses. Indeed, this enhanced view of themselves, and a consequent rise in their solidarity, can be seen in Joseph Lewis's defense of Africans against the vilification of Charles Kingsley, the demands for political reforms, and the publication of Thomas's *Froudacity*. This spirit of defiance, it can be argued, saw its ultimate manifestation in the formation of the Pan-Africanist movement in London in 1900, under the leadership of Sylvester Williams, a Trinidadian who was raised amidst the activities of this period.[2] The black and coloured masses resented not only the racism of the dominant class, they also took exception to the latter's presumed superiority and their denial of senior positions in the civil service and other public offices to which they felt they were entitled. Thus, members of the petit bourgeois made their feelings known through the liberal press by protesting against the advantages the sugar monopoly received.[3] Later, they organized themselves around reform politics. The oppressed people (the majority of whom were the working people) made their feelings known through the camboulay and hosay riots of the 1880s and the maintenance of their cultural practices, such as indigenous dances and wakes.

With the expansion of the economy, the increased urbanization of the population, a larger pool of educated people, expanded educational opportunities (both

2. According to Brereton, the editors of the "liberal press," particularly Carter and Lewis, and writers such as J. J. Thomas "contributed to the emergence of black nationalism in Trinidad…[which] was strikingly demonstrated in 1901, with the establishment of a branch of the Pan African Association in Trinidad. H. S. Williams, the founder of the Association in London, was himself a lawyer from Trinidad, and he visited the island in 1901. He was enthusiastically received, and branches were formed in Port of Spain, San Fernando, and other towns and smaller villages" (Brereton, 38; James R. Hooker, *Henry Sylvester Williams* [London: Collings, 1975] chap. 5; and Owen Charles Mathurin, *Henry Sylvester Williams* (Westport, Conn.: Greenwood, 1976).

3. The black petit bourgeois protested the special privileges given to the sugar industry, such as state-aided immigration and a taxation system that "imposed heavy import duties on food and other articles of mass consumption while taxing property and income lightly or not at all" (Bridget Brereton, "The Liberal Press," p. 410).

formal and informal), and the greater circulation and communication of ideas, the subordinate groups of the society (the subaltern, if you wish) began to reconstitute their relationship with the dominant power as they asserted their independence and expressed their varied identities.[4] Concomitant with these concerns, were questions of race and racial consciousness that also became important issues of discussion during this period. Bracketed by Kingsley's visit to Trinidad (1869) and Sylvester Williams's return to the society in 1901, these last three decades revealed a new sense of race-consciousness and incipient nationalism. It was also a period in which the black and coloured members of the society made their feelings known at the local level and responded to criticisms offered at the international level. In this period, one also saw the extending of privileges to local culture and a deep desire on the part of the citizens to *know* and to understand their society better.

Kingsley, The Theory of Natural Selection, and Natural History

The rise of race-consciousness in the society during this period was not unconnected to events that were taking place in the "mother country." Thomas Carlyle's "Occasion Discourse on the Negro Question" (1850) and the Eyre Affair that resulted from the English brutality during the Morant Bay Rebellion in Jamaica (1865) led to a sharp rise in "anti-Negro" feeling in Britain. Such was the intensity of the debate that many intellectuals, having to take a stand, divided on the issue. For better or worse, Charles Darwin and Charles Kingsley found themselves on different sides of the issue. When Kingsley visited Trinidad in 1869, he was deeply implicated in this debate and was working through his conflicts in his own way. He was deeply disturbed also by Darwin's *On the Origin of Species* (1859), a book that turned the Victorian world upside down and inside out, aroused much discussion about the origin of human beings and heightened concerns about the nature of race and empire. *At Last*, it can be argued, was a direct response to Darwin's *On the Origin of Species* and the racial debate that was taking place in Britain at the time.

Quickly after *On the Origin of Species* was published, Kingsley, a leading naturalist of the nineteenth century, informed Darwin he was prepared to accept a conception of Deity who "created primal forms capable of self-development." In this context, Kingsley's *The Water Babies*, was "one of the first literary explorations of natural selection."[5] Yet, like so many of his colleagues, Kingsley was worried by the implications of Darwin's theory.[6] It left them with a suspicious feeling that, if

4. Robert Young views the culture of the oppressed as not simply being destroyed on impact with colonialism, but "rather layered on top of each other, giving rise to struggles that themselves only increased the imbrication of each with the other and their translation into increasingly uncertain patchwork identities." This is a useful way to describe what was taking place in Trinidadian (and perhaps Caribbean) culture at that time. See *Colonial Desire* (London: Routledge, 1995), p. 174.

5. Peter Raby, *Bright Paradise: Victorian Scientific Travellers* (London: Chatto and Windus, 1996), pp. 216–17.

6. According to Margaret Farrand Thorp, "Most of the great literary figures of the nineteenth century were rebels against or thinkers in advance of their time. Kingsley's influence was due in large part to his not being a thinker at all. He suffered all the torments endured by the average man of the period

The Botanic Gardens, Port of Spain.

FIGURE 13.   Frontispiece of *At Last,* 1887 edition.

Darwin were correct, then it was possible that creation is a random act rather than a manifestation of a grand design as the supporters of Natural History believed.[7] Kingsley, an Anglican priest and arguably the most popular writer of the period, wrote that "the scientists found themselves in a curious position, for 'they find that now they have got rid of an interfering God—a master-magician, as I call him— they have to choose between the absolute empire of accident, & a living, immanent, ever working God.'"[8]

Kingsley's *At Last* attempts to resolve the troubling ambiguity inherent in the above statement. An avid enthusiast of science, Kingsley showed a keen interest in

---

in his struggle with a changing universe; he differed from the average man in the courage with which he faced the problems of the day and the volubility with which he discussed them. He made for himself solutions which were shallow but convincing to hundreds because of their power for comfort and because of the enormous vitality and sincerity behind his presentations. His power in his time and his significance to succeeding generations lies in this, that he was not so much an artist as a fluent English gentleman" (*Charles Kingsley, 1819–1875* [Princeton: Princeton University Press 1937], pp. 1–2.

7. J.W. Burrow has observed that, in the first half of the nineteenth century, "Natural history became an approved clerical hobby. To pursue in any detail the pleasing evidences of harmony and divine purpose in the Newtonian heavens required some rather abstruse mathematics; to trace the same evidences in each leaf, stamen and antenna was well within the scope of any country clergyman with a collecting basket. To follow the workings of nature was to explore the mind of its Creator and to receive renewed assurances of his benevolence. The proudly displayed 'collection' was almost the equivalent of a Bible laid open on a table. God was sought, not in mystical exercises in one's chamber—that would have been 'enthusiasm', which was both morbid and ungentlemanly—but at the bottoms of ponds and in the midst of hedges. Natural history became something of a craze in the first half of the nineteenth century and works on it outsold popular novels" ("Introduction." in Charles Darwin, *The Origin of Species* (London: Penguin, 1985), pp. 18–19.

8. Quoted in Robert Bernard Martin, *The Dust of Combat* (New York: W. W. Norton, 1960), p. 235.

the natural world, which he used to buttress his faith in God. Thus, *At Last* can be read as a part of Kingsley's religious manifesto: an effort to demonstrate that the natural world is yet another manifestation of God's goodness and power or, as Kingsley puts it, "God's Creative Genius." In 1862, he informed F. D. Maurice of his objectives in *The Water Babies:* "I have tried, in all sorts of queer ways, to make children and grown folks understand that there is a quite miraculous and divine elements underlying all physical nature."[9] A similar intention informs *At Last*. Therefore, when Kingsley arrived in Trinidad and saw the immensity of Trinidad's forests, a manifestation of God's invincible power, he immediately contrasted it with Darwin's conception of the world and makes the following comparison:

Take your tired eyes down again; and turn them right, or left, or where you will, to see the same scene, and yet never the same. New forms, new combinations; a wealth of creative Genius—let us use the wise old word in its true sense—incomprehensible by the human intellect or the human eye, even as He is who makes it all. Whose garment, or rather Whose speech, it is. The eye is not filled with seeing, or the ear with hearing; and never would be, did you roam these forests for a hundred years. How many years would you need merely to examine and discriminate the different species? And when you had done that, how many more to learn their action and reaction on each other? How many more to learn their virtues, properties, uses? How many more to answer the perhaps ever unanswerable question—How they exist and grow at all? By what miracle they are compacted out of light, air, and water, each after its kind? How, again, those kinds began to be, and what they were like at first? Whether those crowded, struggling, competing shapes are stable or variable? Whether or not they are varying still? Whether even now, as we sit here, the great God may not be creating, slowly but surely, new forms of beauty round us? Why not? If He chose to do it, could He not do it? And even had you answered that question, which would require whole centuries of observation as patient and accurate as that which Mr. Darwin employed on Orchids and climbing plants, how much nearer would you be to the deepest question of all—Do these things exist, or only appear? Are they solid realities, or a mere phantasmagoria, orderly indeed, and law-ruled, but a phantasmagoria still; a picture-book by which God speaks to rational essences, created in His own likeness? And even had you solved that old problem, and decided for Berkeley or against him, you would still have to learn from these forests a knowledge which enters into man not through the head, but through the heart; which (let some modern philosophers say what they will) defies all analysis, and can be no more defined or explained by words than a mother's love. I mean, the cause and the effects of their beauty; that "Aesthetic of plants," of which Schleiden has spoken so well in that charming book of his, "The Plant," which all should read who wish to know somewhat of "The Open Secret."

But when they read it, let them read with open hearts.

For that same "Open Secret" is, I suspect, one of those which God may hide from the wise and prudent, and yet reveal to babes.

9. Quoted in Raby, *Bright Paradise*, p. 217.

At least, so it seemed to me, the first day that I went, awe-struck, into the High Woods; and so it seemed to me, the last day that I came, even more awe-struck, out of them.[10]

In responding to Darwin's theory of natural selection, Kingsley speaks of God's omnipotent powers and notes that God, if he desires, can have one, rather than many, sources for the evolution of human life. After viewing the beauty of another part of Trinidad's flora, Kingsley returns to the unitary source of creation:

"But what if all these forms are the descendants of one original form? Would that be one whit more wonderful, more inexplicable, than the theory that they were each and all, with their minute and often imaginary shades of difference, created separately and at once? But if it be—which I cannot allow—what can the theologian say, save that God's works are even more wonderful than we always believed them to be? As for the theory being impossible: who are we, that we should limit the power of God?"...If it be said that natural selection is too simple a cause to produce such fantastic variety: we always knew that God works by very simple, or seemingly simple, means; that the universe, as far as we could discern it, was one organization of the most simple means, it was wonderful (or ought to have been) in our eyes, that a shower of rain should make the grass grow, and that the grass should become flesh, and the flesh food for the thinking brain of man; it was (or ought to have been) yet more wonderful in our eyes, that a child should be resemble its parents, or even a butterfly resemble—if not always, still usually—its parents likewise. Ought God to appear less or more august in our eyes if we discover that His means are even simpler than we supposed. We held Him to be almighty and allwise. Are we to reverence Him less or more if we find that His might is greater, His wisdom deeper, than we had ever dreamed?...We were taught, some of us at least, by Holy Scripture, to believe that the whole history of the universe was made up of special providences: if, then, that should be true which Mr. Darwin says—"It may be metaphorically said that natural selection is daily and hourly scrutinizing, throughout the world, every variation, even the slightest; rejecting that which is bad, preserving and adding up all that is good; silently and insensibly working, whenever and wherever opportunity offers, at the improvement of each organic being in relation to its organic and inorganic conditions of life,"—if this, I say, were proved to be true, ought God's care, God's providence, to seem less or more magnificent in our eyes? (*AL.*, pp. 245–46)

In his work, Kingsley was struggling with two explanations of the origin of the human species: how to reconcile Darwin's theory of natural selection (evolution) with the Christian notion of a unitary source of beginning (creationism). As he traveled to the Caribbean, Kingsley ruminated on these questions and the centrality of God in the affairs of men. Even though he accepted Darwin's theory of natural selection, he was determined to prove that miraculous and divine elements underlay all things. Thus, he reasoned that one cannot arrive at an understanding

10. Charles Kingsley, *At Last: Christmas in the West Indies* (London: Macmillan, 1887), pp. 171–72, hereafter *AL*.

of human origins only through the use of one's head (science). One must also use one's heart and one's sensibility to contemplate nature, the seat of God's goodness and Creative Genius. "All that the scientific man can do is, to confess the presence of mystery all day long; and to live in that wholesome and calm attitude of wonder which we call awe and reverence; that so he may be delivered from the unwholesome and passionate fits of wonder which we call astonishment, the child of ignorance and fear, and the parent of rashness and superstition" (*AL.*, p. 174).

In the West Indies, Kingsley found an answer to the competing claims of religion and science, even if it descended into the realm of superstition. Reflecting on the beauty of the "resplendent Calycophyllum,"[11] or Chaconier,[12] "the jewel of these woods," Kingsley concludes that "[t]here are those who will smile at my superstition, if I state my belief that He who makes all things make themselves may have used those very processes of variation and natural selection for a final cause; and that the final cause was, that He might delight Himself in the beauty of one more strange and new creation. Be it so, I can only assume that their minds are, for the present, at least, differently constituted than mine" (*AL.*, p. 267). Given this posture, Kingsley remained one of the many persons who retained a belief in Natural History, a philosophy that was prevalent in the first half of the nineteenth century.

James Pope-Hennessy, an English novelist, described *At Last* as one of Kingsley's "less widely-known work on Natural History. This solid description of seven weeks in Trinidad is written with admirable feeling and sound knowledge. The attitude of persistent appreciation (one of the most tedious in the world?) may be cloy a little, but no one can question the book's high place in the imperialist literature of England."[13] As an imperialist drama, the book helped to promulgate the ideas of empire; as a naturalist work, it proved to be one of the important works that engaged Darwin's theory of natural selection.

Kingsley and his Imperialist Preoccupations

Kingsley's trip to the West Indies was a homecoming of sorts. His family's imperial connection with the Caribbean and Charles's fascination with this tropical region suggest that his intellectual and material fortunes were tied to colonial-capitalism in the Caribbean. These factors also prompted his Caribbean journey.[14]

11. Herman Crueger, a botanist of German descent and the director of the Trinidad Botanical Gardens (1857–1864), described the Chaconier as "the resplendent Calycophyllum" (See *At Last*, p. 267).

12. The Chaconier is the national flower of Trinidad and Tobago. Until recently, it was believed that the Chaconier, popularly known as the "chaconia," was named after Don Maria Chacon, Trinidad's last Spanish governor. Victor C. Quesnel and T. Francis Farrell reason that the name chaconier "is derived from chaconne, the dance, for which the dancers decorated themselves with little flags just as the tree seems to be decorated with little flags." See Victor C. Quesnel and T. Francis Farrell, *Native Trees of Trinidad and Tobago* (Port of Spain: Trinidad and Tobago Field Naturalists' Club, 2000), p. 128.

13. James Pope-Hennessy, *West Indian Summer: A Retrospective* (London: B. T. Batsford, 1943), p. 115.

14. See, for example, Edward Said, *Culture and Imperialism* (New York: Vintage, 1993), for a discussion of this point.

Mary Lucas, Kingsley's mother, the daughter of Nathan Lucas, a judge of Farley Hall, Barbados, was born in the West Indies. For several generations, her family were planters in Barbados and Demerara "where Judge Lucas owned estates."[15] In the parlance of the day, she came from "a family which had been 'West Indian' for generations."[16] Kingsley's father also made his fortune from his Caribbean estates. This connection was so deep-seated that when, after emancipation, Kingsley was asked for a subscription to help the freed slaves, he refused to make any such contribution. Feeling the financial loss his family suffered because of emancipation, he responded promptly: "The negro has had all I ever possessed; for emancipation ruined me.... I am no slave-holder at heart. But I have paid my share of the great bill, in Barbados & Demerara, with a vengeance: & don't see myself called on to pay other men's"[17]

Such ties to the West Indies and his attitude toward the divine rule of kings and nobility, made Kingsley an imperialist and a negrophobe at heart. In *Yeast*, his first novel, he makes it clear that "[t]he upper classes are to rule, but to rule with compassion; the lower classes must improve their moral status but accept their inferior station." Kingsley spelled out the point more clearly when he spoke about his book: "The moral of my book is that the working man who tries to get on, to desert his class and rise above it, enters into a lie, and leaves God's path for his own—with consequences."[18] He accepted the prevailing racialized cultural assumptions that described the Irish "as simian or black," saw the inhabitants of Sligo as "dreadful," "white chimpanzees,"[19] and championed the natural rights of kings and queens to rule. Absolutely and notoriously Anglophile, in 1849, when Sir James Brooke, the white Rajah of Sarawak, was charged in the House of Commons with inhumanity to the Dyaks, Kingsley was furious that his hero should be questioned. When John Malcolm Ludlow, the most radical of the Christian Socialists, complained of Brooke's bloody slaughter in Borneo, Kingsley responded indignantly that "[s]acrifice of human life? Prove that is *human* life. It's beast life."[20] Kingsley felt "a natural antipathy toward the coloured races, and in wars between white nations, his allegiance automatically was with the Teutonic side. His race pride and his patriotism, which sometimes amounted to jingoism, combined in one of his least attractive aspects.... For Kingsley the Englishman first, then the white man, was always right."[21]

15. *Dust of Combat*, p. 20.
16. Thorp, *Charles Kingsley*, p. 3.
17. Quoted in *Dust of Combat*, p. 258.
18. Ibid., p. 117. Said notes in *Culture and Imperialism* that "[t]he nineteenth century English novels stress the continuing existence (as opposed to revolutionary overturning) of England. Moreover, they *never* advocate giving up colonies, but take the long-range view that since they fall within the orbit of British dominance, *that* dominance is a sort of norm, and thus conserved along with the colonies" (p. 74).
19. Quoted in. Young, *Colonial Desire*, p. 72.
20. Ibid., p. 72.
21. Ibid., pp. 213, 215. In *Colonial Desire*, Young has demonstrated that, in the 1860s, there was a climate in Britain in which there was an obsession with race, the scientific question of hybridity, and the

It is no wonder that Kingsley enjoyed a close, personal friendship with Thomas Carlyle and James Anthony Froude, both of whom said cruel, racist things about Africans in the Caribbean. Kingsley did not only know Carlyle's books thoroughly, he acknowledge Carlyle as his literary model and as the influence in shaping his career. Carlyle also felt equally as solicitous about Kingsley and recommended *Alton Locke,* the most propagandistic of Kingsley's novels, to Chapman and Hall for publication.[22] In gratitude for all that Carlyle did for him, when Carlyle became the Rector of Edinburgh University in 1866, Kingsley acknowledged the many truths he had learned from Carlyle in his youth. He credited the older writer with having delivered him from "'phantoms & superstitions, which have made me bless the day when my dear & noble wife first made me aware of your existence. What I owe to that woman God alone knows; but among my deepest debts to her is this—that she first taught me to reverence you. Amid many failings & follies, I have been at heart ever true to your teaching."[23] Needless to say, the one concept about "Negroes" that Kingsley picked from Anthony Trollope and Carlyle, "uneasy bedfellows except in their contempt for the Negro," was the hereditary "laziness" of Africans in the Caribbean that all three took as the cornerstone of Negro behavior.[24]

Froude and Kingsley were constant companions and shared many hours in each other's company. Froude married Charlotte, the elder sister of Kingsley's wife whom he dissuaded from becoming a nun. In 1867, when Froude was doing historical research in Spain, Kingsley substituted for him as the editor of *Fraser's Magazine.* Kingsley also reviewed many of Froude's books and certainly endorsed the sentiments of *Heroes.* Eventually Kingsley became the Professor of Modern History at Cambridge, whereas Froude later became the Regis Professor of History at Oxford. For both men, "the West Indies functioned as a site of an idealized past, a past which was posited as vastly different from, and a solution to the present."[25]

As their work demonstrates, Kingsley and Froude shared similar views about the inferiority of the Africans in the Caribbean. Like Froude, Kingsley believed that Africans in the Americas were incapable of self-government and even though he called slavery an abomination, he saw Africans of whom he wrote as an inferior race:

> The negro…is quite devoid of that self-government, either personal or municipal which is the only training for political self government; & the want of which has wrecked free institutions in France & Spain-& till now, again & again in Italy. But the contact with, or rather intermingling with, free white settlers from the

---

"imaginative phantasm of racial mixing which lay behind it." Indeed, when Anthony Trollope came to the West Indies in 1859, he saw race-mixing as one of the ways to solve the race question (*Colonial Desire,* p. 142).

22. See *Dust of Combat,* p. 73.

23. Quoted in Ibid., pp. 200–201.

24. See Iva G. Jones, "Trollope, Carlyle, and Mill on the Negro: An Episode in the History of Ideas," *Journal of Negro History,* 52 (1967), p. 185; Thomas Carlyle, "The Nigger Question," *Fraser's* (1849); and Anthony Trollope, *The West Indies and the Spanish Main.*

25. Smith, *John Jacob Thomas,* p. 120.

Northern states may teach them, what the Romance nations of Europe have not taught themselves.... A system of feudalism, gradually dying out & leaving the negro quite free, would be, to judge from history, the most prudent & practical method.[26]

In one of the most dramatic yardsticks of moral outrage of the 1860s, Kingsley joined Carlyle, Ruskin, Charles Dickens, and Alfred Tennyson in publicly supporting Governor Eyre's brutal suppression of the Morant Bay Rebellion in Jamaica in 1865 during which Paul Bogle and George Gordon were killed. Kingsley and Mathew Arnold felt that the authorities should "flog the rank and file, and fling the ringleaders from the Tarpeian rock."[27] In contrast, John Stuart Mill, Huxley, Spenser, and Darwin, members of the Jamaica Committee, protested Eyre's brutality against the Jamaicans. Needless to say, there was substantial agreement between Kingsley and his intellectual friends about the need to subjugate "inferior peoples," a link, as Said remarks, we avoid at our peril.[28] In other words, Kingsley's work, a part of the imperialist enterprise, provided British imperialism with academic authority that made it such an imposing structure in the nineteenth-century Caribbean.

When Kingsley arrived in the West Indies in 1869, he brought with him "structures of attitude and reference,...[a] virtual unanimity that subject races should be ruled, that they *are* subject races, that one race deserves and has consistently earned the right to be considered the race whose main mission is to expand beyond its own domain."[29] Although he occasionally sympathized with blacks, his was a continuation of an imperial discourse that sought to maintain and assert the superiority of the white race and its culture over all other cultures. As a leading academic and popularizer of ideas, he would play a leading role in shaping the racist ideas and ideals of his age. To be sure, he included some of the scientific findings of Trinidadian scholars into his work and, thereby, encouraged what they did. Ultimately, however, Kingsley's mission embodied the claims of his class and his civilization: he would tell the natives where to get off if they wished to retain the goodwill of the master. Since imperialist discourse, as Barbara Lalla tells us, "presupposes a dialect of domination and subordination as a construct for order,"[30] Kingsley used his narrative to remind the natives about the desirability of keeping their "places" in the general scheme of things. Necessarily, Kingsley's views reflected the degree to which racism had infected European culture of the nineteenth century and how much it had become a part of the "interdisciplinary academic knowledge" of the society. As Robert Young writes:

26. Quoted in *The Dust of Combat*, p. 258.
27. Quoted in Young, *Colonial Desire*, p. 8. So enamoured was Kingsley with Arnold that he used Arnold's description of what constituted a cultivated person to characterize Indians and Amerindians. (See pages 124 and 190, respectively.)
28. Said, *Culture and Imperialism*, p. 12.
29. *Culture and Imperialism*, p. 53.
30. Lalla, Defining Jamaican Fiction, p. 32.

Racial theory cannot be separated from its own historical moment: it was developed at a particular era of British and European colonial expansion in the nineteenth century which ended in the Western occupation of nine-tenths of the surface territory of the globe. There is an obvious connection between racial theories of white superiority and the justification for that expansion, which raises questions about the complicity of science as well as culture: racism knows no division between the sciences and the arts."[31]

When, therefore, the leaders of the Trinidad working class contested Kingsley's (and later Froude's) ideas about their society, they were participating in an international struggle against racism and concepts of white superiority that were directed against colonial people everywhere. Thus, theirs was not an isolated struggle, but rather part of a larger struggle against racial prejudice that would engulf the world during the latter nineteenth century, as well as much of the twentieth, a point that Said makes with exemplary clarity in *Culture and Imperialism*.[32] Trinidadian blacks had to deal with ideas of racism that were advanced by Edward Long and other West Indian whites which, in the 1860s, were being reinvoked in the United States and Britain to support white fears of interracial mixing. Indeed, it is not for nothing that Long received the title: "father of English racism,"[33] so influential was his writings on shaping the English imagination on these issues.

Signs and Wonders

When Kingsley and his daughter, Rose, arrived in Trinidad at the end of 1869, Keenan had already presented his *Report* to Governor Gordon, and Thomas had completed his *Creole Grammar*.[34] Invited to Trinidad by Gordon, Kingsley's visit

31. *Colonial Desire*, pp. 87, 91–92. Young also notes that, in the popular realm in Britain, "it can be plausibly argued that it was the conjunction of three historical events that dramatically altered the popular perceptions of race and racial difference and formulated the basis of widespread acceptance of the new, remarkably up-front claims of permanent racial superiority: the shocked reaction in Britain to the Indian 'Mutiny' of 1857, the debates surrounding the question of slavery which developed at the time of the Civil War (1861–1865); questions which were then given a 'local' British reference with the controversy surrounding Governor Eyre's merciless suppression of the Jamaica Insurrection at Morant Bay in 1865" (*Colonial Desire*, p. 92). Of course, this suggests that the Caribbean was very much a part of the discussion—perhaps the driving force around which the question of racism and white superiority revolved. In this context, see also Stephen Jay Gould, *The Mismeasure of Man* (New York: W.W. Norton, 1996).

32. Said observes that, across the Third World in the nineteenth century, "[a]long with armed resistance in places as diverse as nineteenth century Algeria, Ireland, and Indonesia, there also went considerable efforts in cultural resistance almost everywhere, the assertions of nationalist identities, and, in the political realm, the creation of associations and parties whose common goal was self-determination and national independence. Never was it the case that the imperial encounter pitted an active Western intruder against a supine or inert non-Western native; there was *always* some form of active resistance, and in the overwhelming majority of cases, the resistance finally won out" *Culture and Imperialism*, p. xii).

33. Quoted in Young, *Colonial Desire*, p. 150.

34. Burrow points out that "[s]cience in the first half of the nineteenth century benefited enormously from the journeys of traveler-naturalists or men of scientific interest who obtained berths on survey

was a dream come true. His friendship with the governor also provided a definite advantage. Having dreamt of "the lush landscapes of the West Indies and South America" for well-nigh forty years and remembering his family ties to the islands, Kingsley wrote back to London: "Tell my mother that the old fig-tree at Harmony Hall, of which she dreamt, is standing still, and that we are going to visit a planter in Trinidad, who began in Barbadoes with Douglas, who managed Clapham for her father. So do things come around."[35] In Trinidad, Kingsley also reflected fondly on his West Indian memories when, on the beach on Monos Island, he collected "such shells as delighted our childhood in the West India cabinet at home" (*AL.*, p. 131). Biographer Bernard Martin writes that Kingsley felt "a sense of identity with the places where his forebears had lived, and to visit the West Indies was to return to the land where his mother had spent her youth. The mysterial kinship he felt with the West country and which he was to experience in Chester was paralleled in the New World."[36]

In coming to the West Indies, it did not take Kingsley long to detect "the savagery" of Caribbean people. Bearing all of the baggage of Trollope and Carlyle, and his participation in the racial discourse of his time, Kingsley describes Africans in negative terms and emphasizes the savagery of their nature.[37] He compares them with the Russians, who "is but a savage polished over: you have only to scratch him, and the barbarian shows underneath" (*AL,*, p. 88). Of his first encounter with a Negro in the Caribbean, Kingsley portrays him as "blacker than the night; in smart white coat and smart black trousers; a tall courtly gentleman, with the organ of self-interest, to judge from his physiognomy, very highly developed" (*AL.*, p. 17). For the naturalist, "the Negro may have had the *corpus sanum* without the *mens sana.*" Commenting on Daaga's heroic behavior, in spite of all of the odds against him, Kingsley writes that "[i]t was altogether owing to the unwisdom of military authorities at home, who seem to have fancied that they could transform, by a magical spurt of the pen, heathen savages into British soldiers" (*AL.*, p. 205). Commenting on a gang of workers singing (what must have been a mixture of the calypso and negro spiritual) on the wharf, Kingsley writes that "[a] lad, seeming the poet of the gang, stood on the sponson, and in the momentary intervals of work improvised

---

ships as naturalists or surgeons. Already there had been Alexander von Humboldt, whose *Personal Narrative of Travels to the Equinoctial Regions of the New Continent* first inspired by Darwin with the desire to travel and to make some contribution to science. Later there were to be Alfred Russell Wallace, and Darwin's younger friends T. H. Huxley and Joseph Hooker, who obtained posts similar to Darwin's on H.M.S. *Rattlesnake* and H.M.S. *Erebus*" (*The Origin of Species,* p. 25). Kingsley, a man of scientific interest, also profited from this kind of treatment, especially since he was a friend of Governor Gordon and, by 1869, had established quite a literary reputation in English society. Thomas who was invited by Gordon to meet Kingsley was described by the latter as "at once no mean philologer and no mean humorist" (*AL.*, p. 320).

35. Martin, *Dust of Combat,* p. 270.

36. Ibid., *p. 270.*

37. At times, during this chapter, I use the term "negro" in the way that writers at the time used it so as to reemphasize its racist nature.

some story, while the men below took up and finished each verse with a refrain, piercing, sad, running up and down large and easy intervals. The tunes were many and seemingly familiar, all barbaric, often ending in the minor key, and reminding us much, perhaps too much, of the old Gregorian tones" (*AL.*, p. 20). Kingsley goes on to contrast the songs of the blacks with those of the whites:

These were all the scraps of negro poetry which we could overhear; while on deck the band was playing quadrilles and waltzes, setting the Negro shoveller dancing in the black water at the barge-bottom, shovel in hand; and pleasant white folks danced under the awning, till the contrast between the refinement within, and the brutality without, became very painful. For brutality it was, not merely in the eyes of the sentimentalist, but in that of the moralist; still more in the eyes of those who try to believe that all God's human children may be somewhen, somewhere, somehow, reformed into His likeness. We were shocked to hear that at another island the evils of coaling are still worse; and that the white authorities have tried in vain to keep them down. The coaling system is, no doubt, demoralizing in itself, as it enables Negros [*sic*] of the lowest class to earn enough in one day to keep them in idleness, even in luxury, for a week or more, till the arrival of the next steamer. But what we saw proceeded rather from the mere excitability and coarseness of half-civilized creatures than from any deliberate depravity; and we were told that, in the island just mentioned, the Negros, when forced to coal on Sunday, or on Christmas-day, always abstain from noise or foul language, and if they sing, sing nothing but hymns. It is easy to sneer at such a fashion as formalism. It would be wiser to consider whether the first step in religious training must not be obedience to some such external positive law; whether the savage must not be taught that there are certain things which he ought never to do, by being taught that there is one day at least on which he shall not do them. How else is man to learn that the laws of Right and Wrong, like the laws of the physical world, are entirely independent of him, his likes or dislikes, knowledge or ignorance of them; that by Law he is environed from his cradle to his grave, and that it is at his own peril that he disobeys the Law? A higher religion may, and ought to follow, one in which the Law becomes a Law of Liberty, and a Gospel, because it is loved, and obeyed for its own sake; but even he who has attained to that must be reminded and again and again, alas! that the Law which he loves does not depend for its sanction of his love of it, on his passing frames or feelings; but is as awfully independent of him as it is of the veriest heathen. And that lesson the Sabbath does teach as few or no other institutions can. The man who says, and says rightly, that to the Christian all days ought to be sabbaths, may be answered, and answered rightly, "All the more reason for keeping one day which shall be a sabbath whether you are in a sabbatical mood or not. All the more reason for keeping one day holy, as a pattern of what all days should be." So we will be glad if the Negro has got thus far, as an earnest that he may some day get further still (*AL.*, pp. 21–22).

The notion that the savage negro needed some form of religious training to save him from his heathenist darkness appears more blatantly when Kingsley speaks of the nature of the education that the negro ought to receive at that stage of his evolutionary development. After reviewing Keenan's recommendations, the naturalist concludes that the latter needlessly stressed the secular or scientific (the teaching of reading, writing, and arithmetic) over religious training. He believes that, in an "ideal system," secular and religious education ought to be separate and should be taught by "different classes of men." He continues:

> But, like all ideals, it requires not only first-rate workmen, but first-rate material to work on; an intelligent and high-minded populace, who can and will think for themselves upon religious questions; and who have, moreover, a thirst for truth and knowledge of every kind. With such a populace, secular and religious education can be safely parted. But can they be safely parted in the case of a populace either degraded or still savage; given up to the "lusts of the flesh;" with no desire for improvement, and ignorant of that "moral ideal," without the influence of which, as my friend Professor Huxley well says, there can be no true education? It is well if such a people can be made to submit to one system of education. Is it wise to try to burden them with two at once? But if one system is to give way to the other, which is most important: to teach them the elements of reading, writing, and arithmetic; or the elements of duty and morals? And how these latter can be taught without religion is a problem as yet unsolved (*AL.*, pp. 344–45).

Calling upon Huxley to assist him in his argument is telling since, in a previous context, Huxley had observed that "[n]o rational man, cognizant of the facts, believes that the average Negro is the equal, still less the superior, of the average white man. And, if this be true, it is simply incredible that, when all his disabilities are removed, and our prognathous relative has a fair field and no favour, as well as no oppressor, he will be able to compete successfully with his bigger-brained and smaller jaw rival, in a contest which is to be carried on by thoughts and not by bites."[38] Moreover, in alluding to his proposition that the Trinidad population was still "degraded" and "still savage," Kingsley points to the Roman Catholic Church as the "the chief (I had almost said the only) civilizing and Christianizing influence at work on the lower orders of their own coloured people." He feels that Africans not only must be instructed, they must also "be reclaimed from gross and ruinous vices. It was not a question in Port of Spain, any more than it is in Martinique, of whether the Negros should be able to read and write, but of whether they should exist on the earth at all for a few generations to come" (*AL.*, p. 345).

For Kingsley, then, the problem inhered in how the slaves were liberated by his government. Bearing in mind his own antipathy toward the slaves, he believes that "the British had set the slaves free without letting them go through the immediate stage of feudalism, by which alone, the white races of Europe were educated to true freedom" (*AL.*, p. 345). Given the fact that "the utterly unimaginative Negro" is also incapable of thought—that he can only be reached through an appeal to the senses—it is, therefore, necessary to intersperse religious teaching with pomp and cere-

---

38. Quoted in Gould, *The Mismeasure of Man*, p. 105.

mony since the condition of the Negro was analogous to that of the "half-savage Europeans of the early Middle Ages" (*AL.*, p. 348). In short, in spite of whatever Keenan recommended, what the Negroes actually need is an education that consists primarily of "moral discipline" so as to bring them up from their savage state.

Betwixt Savagery and Civilization

In picturing Trinidad as in a savage state, Kingsley reveals more about himself and his civilization than he does about Africans in the Caribbean. Colin Rhodes remarks that "primitivism or savagery describes a Western event and does not imply any direct dialogue between the West and its 'Others.'" Moreover, savagery or primitivism "refers to the attraction to groups of people who were outside Western society, as seen through the distorting lens of Western constructions of 'the primitive' which were generated in the later part of the nineteenth century."[39] At its worse, some Europeans, such as Ernst Ludwig Kirchner in the *Negro Couple* (1911), did not even have to leave Europe in order to depict Africans as savages.

Coming to the Caribbean after an immense amount of reading about that exotic part of the world and in the aftermath of Darwin's *On the Origin of Species*,[40] Kingsley possessed definite notions about the society that had little to do with the reality of the place itself. Since the entire notion of primitivism and savagery lies at the heart of colonialism and was fueled by an unprecedented period of European colonial expansion, it is not difficult to see why so many colonialist notions structured Kingsley's views.[41] Committed as Kingsley was to the superiority of the white race and the subordination of the black and brown people, his revelations, therefore, can be considered an integral part of the colonial enterprise.

Although Kingsley tried to retrace the steps of his heroic English forebears ("sea heroes," such as Drake and Hawkins; Carlyle and Cavendish; Cumberland and Raleigh; Preston and Sommers; Frobisher and Duddeley; Keymis and Whiddon), his immediate model was Raleigh's early, disastrous trip to Trinidad. Just to be sure that he, and his ancestor had lost nothing of their sturdy Englishness in the three hundred years that had intervened, the naturalist declares: "Yes, there were heroes in England in those days. Are we, their descendants, degenerate from them? I, for one, believe not. But they were taught—what we take pride in refusing to be

39. Colin Rhodes, *Primitivism and Modern Art* (London: Thames and Hudson, 1994), p. 8.

40. Rhodes notes that "Charles Darwin's theory of evolution lies behind many early anthropological and sociological definitions of the primitive [and the savage]" (*Primitivism and Modern Art*, p. 14). Much of Kingsley's taxonomic information about Trinidad negroes and their relative position in the evolutionary process was taken from Darwin.

41. In *Primitivism and Modern Art*, Rhodes writes that "[c]olonialism, in fact, lies at the heart of theories about Primitivism. The colonial enterprise, in the eighteenth and nineteenth centuries provided a wealth of examples of cultures new to the West, set within a system of unequal power relations which determined that the primitive, or more often in contemporary writings, 'the savage,' was invariably the dominated partner. Geographically, European beliefs placed the savage in Central and Southern Africa, the Americas and Oceania" (p. 7).

taught—namely, to obey" (*AL.*, p. 6). Among other things, it was this obedience and reverence to the Crown that Kingsley sought to teach the savages of the island. Only by being obedient could Her Majesty's needs be fulfilled on this side of the Atlantic. Only in creating an atmosphere in which colonial boys and girls obeyed their master would Kingsley have considered his mission a success. According to the London *Spectator* in 1882, steady industry was "in English opinion, the single virtue, except reverence for white faces, to be demanded of black men."[42]

Given this frame of reference—this idealized relationship between the civilized and the savage—Kingsley's encounter with an Africa woman proved to be immensely illustrative. As Kingsley tells it:

> R[ose] drew out a large and lovely flower, pale yellow, with a tiny green apple or two, and leaves like those of an Oleander. The brown lady, who was again at her post on deck walked up to her in silence, uninvited, and with a commanding air waved the thing away. "Dat machineel. Dat poison. Throw dat overboard." R—, who knew it was not manchineel, whispered to a bystander, "Ce n'est pas vrai." But the brown lady was a linguist. "Ah! mais c'est vrai," cried she, with flashing teeth; and retired, muttering her contempt of English ignorance and impertinence.
>
> And, as it befel, she was, if not quite right, at least not quite wrong. For when we went into the cabin, we and our unlucky yellow flower were flown at by another brown lady, in another gorgeous turban, who had become, on the voyage, a friend and an intimate; for she was the nurse of the baby who had been the light of the eyes of the whole quarter-deck ever since we left Southampton—God bless it, and its mother, and beautiful Mon Nid, where she dwells beneath the rock, as exquisite as one of her own humming-birds. We were so scolded about this poor little green apple, that we set to work to find out what it was, after promising at least not to eat it. And it proved to be Thevetia neriifolia, and a very deadly poison (*AL.*, 24).

That the brown woman is correct shows that she possesses knowledge (that is, a truth) of her natural environment that the visitor does not. This raises the following question/ Who possesses the truth of the colonial reality: the black woman who lives on the island or the visitor who, because of his book-learning, is convinced he knows better than she. Time and time again, this question has been raised in the colonial world. Within the context of Trinidad's history, this question was asked about Carnival in the 1880s, about the quest for political representation in the 1890s, and about the call for self-government, sounded by C. L. R. James in *The Case for West Indian Self Government* (1933).

The African Response

Kingsley, to be sure, had no love for the Afro-Trinidadians or "the oppressed," as the editors of the *New Era* referred to themselves. He admitted to his mother: "'I am afraid I don't like the negroes, specially the women; but I delight in the coolies, who are graceful and well-mannered, and will be the saving of the poor West Indies,

42. Quoted in Brereton *Race Relations*, p. 148.

I verily believe.'"[43] Martin observes that "[t]he most vivid sections of his writing about the inhabitants are those in which he tells of native magic and the 'obeah man,' showing how they parallel demonism in the ancient world."[44]

Such intense disdain for Afro-Trinidadians was not lost upon those who championed their rights and who possessed distinct notions of themselves and their place in the world. Spearheaded by a local press that felt it necessary to defend the interests of African people, the Afro-Trinidadians fiercely rejected Kingsley's ideas.[45] In an editorial response to *At Last*, the *New Era* took strong exception to Kingsley descriptions of Afro-Trinidadians. Writing as though the editors were taking up where Maxwell Philip had left off, they point out that the major feature of "the social history of the West Indies over the past 30 years…[was] the antagonism which exists between the two races of which these beautiful islands are their home." Putting the racial conflict in its historical context, the editorial continues:

That antagonism began in an oppression on the part of the stronger two, and a passive protest on the part of the weaker, and time has best shown how hard it is for the oppressor to forgive even the patience and endurance of the oppressed under all the misery and injustice he had borne. Forgiving, if ever they are unable to forget the past, the coloured population of the West Indies have striven to work out, side by side, the social problem which, up to this day, perplexes the CARLYLES and the KINGSLEYS of the world's wise school; but their efforts far from mollifying, have but added fire to the fuel of hatred and mistrust which burn in the bosom of the once dominant race. Undismayed, however, they have striven on, and the result has been that a struggle which at first was one of the merest recognizance of human rights, has, through perseverance, become a rivalry for power and social and intellectual distinction. In this rivalry the fullness of the maxim, that "knowledge is power" is made apparent, and accepting of they set to work on a foundation cemented by intellectual culture.

The *New Era* placed its response in the same context as the people of color had earlier in the century. The latter had based their appeal on reason, noting that, since the oppressed coloreds possessed intelligence and reason, they ought to be treated with the same respect as the whites. In this context, the education of the population was very important since those who held them in "social and moral thralldom, did so through the strength and power of a superior intellect and the advantages of education" which they kept among themselves. To the editors of the *New Era*, who described themselves as "the faithful exponents of the people we represent," education was the only means of closing the social divide between the two "social rivals."[46]

The criticism of Trollope, Carlyle, and Kingsley weighed heavily on the minds

43. Martin, *The Dust of Combat*, p. 272.
44. Ibid, p. 272.
45. See Brereton, "The Liberal Press of Trinidad," in which she describes the role of the "liberal" black press of Trinidad during that period.
46. *New Era*, January 22, 1872.

of the black and coloured middle classes of Trinidad. Always proud of their education (their being self-made scholars and intellectuals), they took umbrage at the comments of their English antagonists. In an editorial in the *Trinidad Monthly*, a literary magazine founded by J. J. Thomas in 1871, Thomas writes that the non-whites, "the largest group in the community, are in advance of some others in the matter of intellectual culture and literary endeavor." He observed that "in the humbler walks of life there are men who without the advantages of European education…are able to hold their own against the best of them. These men would be Carlyle's heroes if only they belonged to a different race."[47]

These observations set the stage for the criticisms that other members of the black and coloured elite leveled at Kingsley's work. Without being aware of it, the newspaper editors understood that the "literary is inherently critical," in that it opens "the way to the mobilisation of mass challenge to the existing order."[48] In this sense, the vigilance of Thomas, Carter, William Herbert, and others not only revealed the emergence of an alternative voice, but in fact, paved the way for works such as *Froudacity*, ideologies such as Pan-Africanism, and the vigorous exposition of George Padmore. In other words, while Trollope, Carlyle, and Kingsley were reviling the society, Thomas, Carter, and Herbert were building a counter discourse from the ground up.

A Continuing Discourse (Scientific)

Kingsley's visit to the island not only signaled an attempt "to compare books with facts, and judge for myself of the reported wonders of Earthly Paradise [never mind to whom?]," but it also represented a continuation of a discourse between the colonizer and the colonized initiated in the writings of M'Cullum, Dauxion-Lavaysse, Davy, Joseph, Carlyle, Keenan, Trollope et al. This discourse was picked up on the other side of the Atlantic (either as echoes or challenges) by such thinkers as Philippe, Philip, de Verteuil, Thomas, Lewis, Samuel Carter and other indigenous scholars. Apart from a purely social and cultural discussion, a scientific conversation was also taking place between botanists who worked in the local environment (among them Dr. Crueger, David Lockhart,[49] William Purdue,[50] Henry Prestoe[51] and Dr. A. Grisebach) and such naturalists of international repute as

47. Quoted in Brereton, *Race Relations in Colonial Trinidad*, p. 95.
48. Quoted in Outram, *The Enlightenment*, p. 18.
49. Lockhart, a botanist who accompanied Tuckey up the river Congo in 1816, was brought to Trinidad by Sir Ralph Woodford in 1818 to be the director of the botanical gardens. Lockhart, who served as director from 1817–1846, visited Venezuela and many of the countries of the Orinocco and imported many plants from South America and other West Indian countries for the botanical gardens. He was noted for his contributions to successful cultivation of orchids.
50. Purdie succeeded Lockhart as director of the gardens (1846–1857). He introduced the Ivory Hart (*Phytelephas macrocarpa*) and other valuable plants to the gardens.
51. Prestoe, the director of the Trinidad Botanical Gardens from 1864 to 1887, was present when Kingsley visited in 1869. Responsible for the intrastructural development of the gardens, he was responsible for making it a modern botanical exhibit, a reputation that it retains to this day.

FIGURE 14. Herbert Crueger, director of the
Trinidad Botanical Gardens, contributed substan-
tially to Dr. A. Grisebach's *Flora of the British
West Indian Islands* (1859–1864).

Humboldt, Spix, Martius, Schomburgk, Waterton, Bates, Wallace, and Goose,
whom Kingsley admired (and called his masters).[52] Significantly, when the Kew
Herbarium in London decided to catalogue the vegetation of the British Empire
and Sir William Hooker, head of the Kew, conceived the idea of doing some books
on colonial floras, Grisebach's *Flora of the British West Indian Islands* was the first
volume selected because Trinidad's flora was represented so well in the Herbarium.
Since the governors of Trinidad and Jamaica were helpful in the past, "the botanical gardens in Jamaica and Trinidad could be relied upon to give assistance"[53] to
Grisebach's project. At a time when the Kew was exploiting tropical plants for
imperial purposes, Kingsley also used the findings of the Trinidad scientists to document his study and to understand tropical plants and fauna.[54] In 1937, Kingsley's
descriptions of island's plants were still being used as a point of reference to speak

52. Visiting the high woods of Trinidad, Kingsley looked at them in amazement: "In the primaeval
forest; looking upon that which my teachers and masters, Humboldt, Spix, Martius, Schomburgk,
Waterton, Bates, Goose, and the rest, had looked already, with far wiser eyes than mine, comprehend-
ing somewhat at least of its wonders, while I could only stare in ignorance. There was actually, then such
a sight to be seen on earth: and it was not less, but far more wonderful than they had said" (*AL.*, p. 157).
53. Ray Desmond, *Kew: The History of the Royal Botanic Gardens* (London: Harvest Hill Press, 1995),
p. 216. Dr. Crueger of the Trinidad Botanical Gardens contributed considerably to Grisebach's work.
54. Apart from products such as cocoa and sugar that were being exported to Europe during the
eighteenth and nineteenth centuries (especially by the Germans and the British), the Caribbean and
Latin America were also spreading cultural ideas via the exchange of scientific explorations in botany.
Outram observes that "[t]he increasing volume of goods made and sold included many consumer items
such as books, pamphlets, newspapers, pictures, all of which were media for the transmission of ideas
and attitudes" (*The Enlightenment*, p. 17). Since Europe was in scientific contact with the Caribbean (for
example, the botany collections made by Europeans in the Caribbean were sent back to the European
museums, herbaria, and scientists, who were busily competing to find the best species) Caribbean ideas
impacted upon Europe and shaped her ideas of the world. In other words, the colonial compact was a
two-way, rather than a one-way street.

about the island's flora.[55] Through the work of the local scientists and Kew's interest in tropical plants, increasingly Trinidad was brought into contact with Europe, even as the latter learned more about the former.

* * *

At Last can be read as a part of an extended conversation with local writers who attempted to chart and to describe the unconscious of Trinidad and Tobago. Because Kingsley framed the unknown in terms of his racist concerns, he could not help but perpetuate ideas and beliefs that were detrimental to the development of Caribbean peoples. Moreover, his ideas contributed to the continuing English justification for the (post) colonial project, that is, of presenting the colonized person as always being prepared and/or ready to be assimilated or consumed by the colonizer for whatever purposes the latter had in mind.[56] Such a position allowed the colonizers to speak for and on behalf of the colonized. This is why, after spending six weeks on the island, Kingsley had no compunction about speaking for and about the savages in the following manner:

> The good people of Trinidad have long since agreed to let bygones be bygones; and it speaks well for the common sense and good feeling of the islanders, as well as for the mildness and justice of British rule, that in two generations such a community as that of modern Trinidad should have formed itself out of materials so discordant. That British rule has been a solid blessing to Trinidad, all honest folk know well. Even in Picton's time, the population increased, in six years, from 17,700 to 28,400; in 1851 it was 69,600; and it is now [in 1869] far larger. (*AL.*, 84).

Kingsley had no problem with excusing Picton's cruelty against early Trinidad inhabitants. In the naturalist's eyes, such conduct proved the beneficence of British imperial rule. Despite Kingsley's depiction of well-fed and comfortable natives, poverty existed in the land, and many Trinidadians would have taken exception to his characterization of Picton's rule as mild and just. C. S. Salmon, a liberal Englishman who had lived in the West Indies for some time, wrote that West Indians could "look to Nature" for their food no more than modern Englishmen

55. While he was in Trinidad, Kingsley stayed at "The Cottage," a building that was adjacent to the Royal Botanical Gardens. In his work, he describes some of the species that he saw there. In his 1937 *Guide to the Royal Botanical Gardens*, R. E. Dean uses *At Last* "to find out how many on his [Kingsley's] old 'friends,' or plants of similar species still remain." In other words, by that time, *At Last* had become an important point of references in the scientific literature of the society. See R. E. Dean, *Guide to the Royal Botanical Gardens, Trinidad* (Port of Spain: J. D. Gorrie, 1937), p. 35.

56. According to Bart Moore-Gilbert, postcolonial criticism "can still be seen as a more or less distinct set of reading practices, if it is understood as preoccupied principally with analysis of cultural forms which mediate, challenge, reflect upon the relations of domination and subordination—economic, cultural, political—between (and often within) nations, races, and cultures, which characteristically have their roots in the history of modern European colonisation and imperialism and which, equally characteristically, continue to be apparent in the present era of neocolonialism" (*Postcolonial Theory* (London: Verso, 1997), p. 12).

could. The editor of *Public Opinion* felt that the people were pauperized and lived "from hand to mouth."[57] Reading Kingsley, one would have thought he went to Trinidad to rewrite the history of the island's relationship to Britain, a rewrite that began with the premise that Trinidadians, as free-born Britons, ought to be thankful for their lot and happy that Britain had condescended to be their benefactor. Only peace and happiness could have resulted from such rule.

At Last also clarifies the relationship between the metropole and the islands. Smith argues that "by probing Kingsley's relationship to the Caribbean, we can recast the usual implications of 'mother country'-usually understood as the colonial subject's ambivalent relationship to the metropole-and move the Caribbean from its typically imagined location at the margin on imperial center to the center of the metropolitan subject's dream life."[58] Although he preferred not to get into British politics, his book is inundated with the politics of his time. While he did not speak of British politics specifically, he immersed himself in the politics of the margin thereby revealing the racial biases of his class. Whether he liked it or not, the political issues that were playing themselves out in Britain found ready echoes Kingsley's analysis of the society. Metropolitan politics could not be separated from the politics of the colonies.

As an important naturalist, Kingsley enjoyed his excursion in Trinidad and was overwhelmed by the diversity of plant life he found on the island: "I soon found that, where the flora was endless, & all new, I must give up every other source of information & interest, if I intended to collect all I saw, & so only picked certain things which struck me—& too often lost them again." At the end of January, he wrote to his wife: "I have seen enough already to last me my life. I keep saying, 'I cannot *not* have been in the tropics" (*DOC.*, p. 200). Trinidad possessed everything Kingsley expected to find, and he luxuriated in the beauty of the island.

Five years after the appearance of *At Last*, the magazine *Friend of India* was full of praise for the book. It argued that Kingsley rendered a unique "insight into the conditions under which our Indian coolies are working on the other side of the globe....To people who want simple verities, the pure aims, [and] the accurate observation, the graphic pen of Canon Kingsley are [*sic*] are invaluable."[59] In 1886, Henry James found that *At Last* "retains its [Trinidad's] the freshness and its beauty as a glowing word-picture of the wild luxuriance of tropical vegetation and the richness and grandeur of tropical beauty."

As a successor to de Verteuil's and Leotaud's work, *At Last* certainly assisted in mapping the island and describing its beauty with a vigor and strength that only Kingsley's rhetorical opulence could have managed. In so doing, the naturalist

57. Quoted in Brereton, *Race Relations*, p. 146.
58. Smith, *John Jacob Thomas*, p. 121.
59. "The Late Canon Kingsley on Coolie Labour," reprinted in *Trinidad Chronicle*, February 16, 1875.

inserted Trinidad into the continuing international discourse on race, evolution and natural science. By using Trinidad flora for his scientific/theological purposes, inescapably, he drew the island into the modern world of ideas and demonstrated how much scientists in Trinidad were reshaping ideas about the world.

CHAPTER 10

Bodies *in* the West…

Bodies *in* the West but not *of* the West;
The nighttime is the right time;
Oh Lord, don't stop de carnival!
The road make to walk on carnival day!
Ah feeling to wine on something!
Hosay, I say?
Get something and wave.

—SELWYN R. CUDJOE

How do we learn the great secret wrapped in words? We see that a for-
eigner apparently generally fails to acquire a perfect, native sense of their
import. He has not lived from infancy in the quiet reception and
unconscious study of them, and felt how one word is allied to others
and how one age—with its writings, its unrecorded traditions and its
common style of conversation—flows into another.

—VLADIMIR NABAKOV, "The Butterfly, Memory," quoted in
The Guardian Weekend, April 17, 1999

From the point of view of the creative or world-constituting self, the
culture of a people may be defined as the expression of a distinct consciousness of existence articulated in a variety of discourses.

—PAGET HENRY, *Caliban's Reason: Studies
in Afro-Caribbean Philosophy*

The racist attitudes Charles Kingsley aired in *At Last* influenced Pierre Gustave
Borde's *Historie de l'ile de la Trinidad sous le gouvernement Espangnol,* that is, the
History of the Island of Trinidad Under the Spanish Government (1876, 1883, hereafter *History of Spanish Trinidad*) and later, Abbé Masse, a French missionary, who
travelled to some of the Leeward Islands and lived in Trinidad from 1876 to 1883.
However, Kingsley's endorsement of Governor Gordon's position on education
(that is, the latter's support of denominational rather than secular schooling) was
opposed strongly by Mr. Knox, a Protestant, who argued that Kingsley spoke
favourable of Gordon's scheme because he was not "intimately acquainted with the
peculiar circumstances of this island—its differences of race and creed, and many

other considerations of a more delicate nature." Unfortunately, coming at a time when the society was seeking to determine its direction and a fierce debate was taking place between the Protestants and the Roman Catholics about the character of the island's inhabitants, Kingsley's comments, as Knox observed, gave the debate "a higher stamp and character."[1]

It is no wonder then that, in Abbé Masse's diary, translated and organised into four volumes, *The Diaries of Abbé Masse, 1878–1883,* we see a continuation of the racist sentiments that Kingsley articulated. Bringing a Eurocentric bias to bear on his work, Abbé Masse, a Roman Catholic curate, made many derogatory comments about Africans. He opined that, if Africans "have a common origin with us [whites], their race is a degenerate one which carries on it the sign of the curse."[2] He once advised a white colleague how the latter should have responded to an African who dared to presume he was equal to whites: "Does he forget that he has been a slave, that his father is a Congo savage from the depths of Africa. If he has something, does he think that it is not that he has paid with money which he earned under the whips of his master. A Negro to put himself on a level with a Frenchman!"[3] To Abbé Masse, "[t]he Negroes are children and they must be treated as such, and in decreeing their liberty they should [have] be[en] given it gradually....Through forced labour and bad treatment, they have been made into brutes."[4]

Abbé Masse felt similarly about the Caribs of Dominica: "Perhaps before the introduction of Christianity these forests were peopled by Carib tribes who under their shade have cooked the living members of their enemies to eat them after" (*AM.,* 1, p. 101). With these beliefs, Abbé Masse hewed close to the line taken by European missionaries who were bent on bringing civilization to the colonials. Anne Claire Ince writes that "the African slave [and Amerindian "savage"] was himself an integral part of the missionaries' theology....The pagan ignorance of the African and his subsequent enslavement by the Europeans were thus conveniently seen as part of the original curse, and missionaries saw themselves divinely appoint-

1. "Mr. Knox's Speech on the Education Question," *Trinidad Chronicle,* January 25, 1870. See also the circular letter of Joachim Louis, archbishop of Port of Spain, on this matter (*Trinidad Chronicle,* February 11, 1870). Among other things, Gordon's proposals placed the schools under the local direction of one or more patrons, ecclesiastic or lay, and allowed religious instructions to be given in the schools.

2. *The Diaries of Abbé Masse, 1876–1883, Vol. 1,* translated by M. L. de Verteuil (Port of Spain: Script-J Printers, 1988), p. 69 (hereafter referred to as *AM.*). Although there were many important differences in the theology of various missionary societies, they all shared similar beliefs about Africans. All referred to Africans as "Sons of Ham," by which they meant the descendants of Noah's youngest son, Ham, who was cursed by Noah for exposing his father's nakedness as he lay drunk in his tent after the flood. According to E. Wilmot Blyden, "Ham then left his family and according to later interpretation, went off to Africa where he founded the black race"(*Slavery and Abolition,* 1, No 1 [May 1980].. The religious societies also called Africans savages and accused them of possessing "savage customs."

3. *AM.,* . 2, p. 273.

4. *AM.,* 1, p. 69.

ed to deliver the sons of Ham from spiritual darkness."[5] This thinking permeated the intellectual repertoire of the European traveller cum missionary who visited the Caribbean during the period. Borde in *History of Spanish Trinidad* and Jean-Ch. de St. Avit in *Les Deux Premiers Martyrs de la Trinidad* (1885) would repeat some of the same invectives against Africans.

Given his hostility, the downright hatred Europeans felt toward Africans, and his conviction of the presumed superiority of Western customs, Abbé Masse looked condescendingly upon African socio-cultural practices, such as wakes ("fetes which the Negro likes"), concubinage, their love of drumming, dancing and fêting.[6] Needless to say, what missionaries saw as diabolical activities were aspects of African religious practices that defined a way of life. Ince points out that Africans marked all their important rites of passage "by sacrifice, ritual, dance and posses-sion. At times of famine, hurricane, disease, or other calamity, slaves would hold dance ritual 'services' in order to placate the spirits or to beg them for help. For mis-sionaries, religion was not something that could be celebrated with dance or with music other than hymns and psalms. They saw all dance as evil, especially African dance which incorporated 'lascivious' bodily contortions."[7] In many cases, the mis-sionaries condemned dancing, theatre, masquerade, and balls, all of which they characterised as evil. As we will see, the respectable white people of the society broke into a frenzy when they saw these "lascivious bodily contortions" in African street dance. But, as Paul Gilroy cogently asserts, within the Atlantic context, "the black body is here celebrated as an instrument of pleasure rather than an instrument of labour. The night time is the right time and the space allotted for recovery and recuperation is assertively and provocatively occupied by the pursuit of leisure and pleasure."[8]

Although Africans were willing to co-operate with the dominant group, they openly defied attempts to disregard and disrespect their cultural practices, especial-ly the strictures against concubinage. Many preferred to go to hell rather than give up spouses with whom they had lived for many years. Abbé Masse tells the story of an African woman who "was living in concubinage. She was going to die. Abbé Chouit, parish priest in Grenada (he was then visiting that island) before giving her the last Sacrament wanted her to promise to abandon the man with whom she lived in disorder (concubinage). She refused. In the evening she was in hell. A woman living in adultery gave the same refusal and went to join her" (*AM.*, 2, p. 210).

Africans also resisted the cruelty and insults of whites by taking the law into their hands. Abbé Masse tells of the response of villagers in Oropouche:

5. Anne Claire Ince, "Protestant Missionary Activities in Five South Caribbean Islands during Slavery, 1765-1826," Ph.D. Dissertation, Faculty of Modern History, Oxford University, 1984, p. 64.
6. Ibid, pp. 62 – 63.
7. Ince notes that Protestant missionaries considered such worldly amusements as horse-racing, dancing, drinking, card playing, mirth, and self-esteem as evidence of Africans depravity. Although Catholics tended to be more tolerant about these practices, Abbé Masse would have agreed that many of them demonstrated African depravity. Ibid., p. 64.
8. Quoted in Raminder Kaur and John Hutnyk, *Travel Worlds* (London: Zed Books, 1999), p. 23.

A Parish Priest…by his insults to the Negroes, by the horse whipping which he gave them, prepared for himself some terrible reprisals. A crowd stopped him one day, burst the bridle of his horse, and showered him with so many blows that he died of them later. If the Parish Priest of the Bande de l'Este had not left lately, the Negroes had decided to throw him into the sea (*AM.*, 2, p. 225).

In spite of attempts to impose a "propertied whiteness" on Africans, the indigenous population continued to follow their own customs and to express themselves creatively at the various levels. Stuart Hall reports that "African religion which has been so profoundly formative in Caribbean spiritual life, is precisely *different* from Christian monotheism in having, not one, but a proliferation of gods. These gods live on, in an underground existence, in the pantheon of black saints [Abbé Masse destroyed a painting of one such saint] which people the hybridized religious universe of Latin American Catholicism."[9] Ince writes that Africans not only resisted "missionary evangelism," but also put something creative in its place. "Slave culture," she says, "provided the consolidation of a world-view especially suited to the rigors of plantation life [and which] functioned as a psychological weapon."[10] Africans' capacities to express themselves through their cultures and to develop systems of communication (through their languages, dances, and dramas) allowed them to construct ways of life that evaded white surveillance. At the base of their culture, African and Indian oral literary traditions (such as Anansi stories, kheesas, etc.) provided cutlural cohesion as they reflected the conditions of the folk.

Cultivating a Written Tradition

During this period, many citizens were involved in a public debate about the future of the society. At the secular level, the colonial government was putting into place the fundamentals of a public educational system designed to promulgate the values of the dominant power. (Between 1868 and 1878, the average attendance at primary schools grew just over three hundred percent, from 1,333 in 1868 to 4,393 in 1868.) It was not surprising that the texts selected reinforced colonial values and the inherent supremacy of whiteness. In this enterprise, English literature played an important part in indoctrinating the colonial subject. Gauri Viswanthan reminds us that English literature was organized "to perform the functions of those social institutions (such as the church) that, in England, served as the chief disseminators of value, tradition, and authority."[11]

9. Stuart Hall, "Cultural Identity and Cinematic Representation," in Houston A. Baker, Jr., Manthia Diawara and Ruth H. Lindborg, *Black British Cultural Studies* (Chicago: University of Chicago Press, 1996), p. 214.
10. Ince, "Protestant Missionary Activities," p. 166.
11. Gauri Viswanthan, *Masks of Conquests* (New York: Columbia University Press, 1989), p. 7. According to Viswanathan, the introduction of English literature into India, another of Britain's colonies, marks the effacement of colonialist expropriation, material exploitation, and class and race oppression. "The English literary text," he says, "functioning as a surrogate Englishman in his highest and most perfect state, becomes a mask for economic exploitation, so successfully camouflaging the

Such an emphasis was reflected in the texts that were required of the candidates who offered themselves for the Teachers Examination (there were three levels) in the 1870s. Candidates for a Third Class Certificate in 1871 were expected to be able to read a passage in prose and another in verse; to write from dictation, to display penmanship as used in setting copies of "Text hand and Small hand," and to be able to paraphrase a passage from Cowper's *Task*, Book III. In addition to a knowledge of the above, each candidate applying for a Second Class Certificate was required to be able to paraphrase a passage from Wordsworth's *Excursion*, Book II. In addition to knowledge of the above, a candidate for a First Class Certificate had to "paraphrase a passage from Shakespeare's *Merchant of Venice*, to answer questions on the language and subject-matter of the work; and to quote passages from it."[12] Such a system tended to buttress colonial rule and was designed to produce docile, amiable subjects. However, things turned out to be more complex, as a cadre of colonial-nationalist intellectuals emerged who contested the intellectual dominance of the colonial class and articulated the aspirations of an emerging indigenous conscious-ness.[13]

In the 1870s, the newspapers (in 1871, there were seven on the island) continued to play their part in the literary and cultural education of the society. Many of the colonists felt that they needed their own vehicle to express their views since the chief function of the newspaper was "to direct criticism upon government." Taking the position that "West Indian literature is, as yet, an unopened book," the proponents of the newly formed *Trinidad Monthly Magazine* wondered aloud where was their Mrs. Harriet Beecher Stowe who have would awaken our sympathies and arouse our indignation "against the brutality of despotism?" The editors made the case for a magazine in which the highly cultivated talent could express themselves:

> There are thinking minds everywhere, but their non-development may be the want of opportunity and facilities to afford scope for the exercise of their powers. Thinking—is said to be the essence of the soul; without, however, wandering among the labyrinthine mazes of its philosophy, we might here accept it as that inward perception which Carlyle calls "the grand thaumaturgic faculty," enabling us to commune with nature when she unfolds to our rapturous senses the fragrance of

---

material activities of the colonizer that one usually self-conscious British colonial official, Charles Trevelyan, was prompted to remark, '[The Indians] daily converse with the best and wisest Englishmen through the medium of their works, and form ideas, perhaps higher ideas of our nation than if their intercourse with it were a more personal kind" (Ibid., p. 20).

12. *The Star of the West*, July 20, 1872. In this context, the uses to which Cowper's poems were put are very important. Poets such as Pollock and Cowper were known to be "favorite reading of the Evangelicals" and their work "were prescribed in the missionary curriculum" (Viswanthan, *Masks of Conquest*, pp. 54–55).

13. In an interesting essay, Saurabh Dube warns that the colonial project is never a one-way affair. He asserts that the link between the colonial state and its subjects cannot be transformed into a "crude question of cause and effect." He warns: "the idioms of dominance embedded within colonial cultures of rule" cannot be seen as "the mere reflection of the exercise of authority through the formal apparatus of power" (Saurabh Dube, "Travelling Light," in Kaur and Hutnyk, *Travel Worlds*, pp. 29–50).

the flowers; robes the mountains in grandeur; invests the sun with meridian splendour; decks pale Dian with slivery beauty; lights up the fields and landscapes with glories hues; and studs the firmament with stars like shinning crystals. Not having this faculty, culture, which gives keenness to literary insights, is almost powerless,—the potency of thought is boundless, illimitable, unfathomable; and when purely and purposefully exercised, its magic impulses elevate the aspiration, enlarge the capabilities, purify the imagination, and the mind revels in the enjoyment of its own ideal inspiration.[14]

Recognising that in the West Indies, literature was not as lucrative as sugar making, the editors realised that they had to create an appetite for this "mental luxury." Encouraged by the fact that men of letters were beginning to receive some recognition, the *Trinidad Monthly Magazine* dedicated itself "to give scope to progressiveness—both morally and intellectually."[15] Welcoming the magazine, the editors of the *New Era* observed that "[w]e have long felt the need for such a publication, and therefore hail this project with pleasure."[16] Although the fiction of the *Trinidad Monthly Magazine was* not first-rate, still it focussed on local happenings and that was good for a start.[17]

In spite of the ambition of the *Trinidad Monthly Magazine*, the newspapers continued their fine work with regards to promoting literature. In an interesting series of articles, "Etchings in Trinidad," presumably in response to a "Prospectus" that had been issued, the importance of the press and public opinion—or the voicing of public opinion—were remarked upon. Reaching back to the effete example of Don Chacon's *"poco a poco"* behavior[18] when General Ralph Abercromby took the island for the British, the author claims that Trinidadians were too lazy to promote their own interests, a result of having been "under the aristocracy of pure Castillian blood." Noting that the "political aspect of Trinidad may be justly photographed through the episode of the Spanish surrender," the author argues:

14. "Introduction," *Trinidad Monthly Magazine*, 1, No. 1 (September 1, 1871), p. 6.
15. Ibid., p. 10.
16. *New Era*, March 13, 1871.
17. See J. H. "Scraps from an Enumerator's Note Book" and Thomas Weathehall, "Spokes in His Wheel." Other contributions are discussed in other parts of this text.
18. "The story runs that when tidings of the invasion reached the ears of the Spanish Commander, the chivalrous Don [Chacon] merely shrugged his shoulders, and with true Spanish gravity, ejaculated poco a poco ['little by little gentlemen, little by little']; when the armament entered the gulf, and the terrified inhabitants were fleeing to the woods for safety or imploring protection of the Governor, he only sough to quiet their fears with responses of *poco a poco;* it was not until the English General [Ralph] Abercrombie was marching up through the street which now bears his name that Don Chacon was at least roused to action. Muttering his *poco a poco,* he marched down, and surrendered without striking a blow" (*New Era*, March 13, 1871). There is every reason to believe the English-Spanish rivalry was behind this story and promulgation of this attitude. As we will see, it became a point of disagreement between Gustave Borde and Francisco Paul when the latter reviewed Borde's book some years later. See *History of Spanish Trinidad, Vol. 2*, pp. 276–77 for a historical discussion of this event. The saying, "poc a poc" remains popular in Trinidad.

Looking at the immobility which prevails with respect to matters that are necessary to an advancing civilization; thoughts, incredulous, may intrude; and we may refuse to believe that the damsel is not dead and only sleepeth—thrust them out of the inner chambers of the mind and look forward, hopefully, to her reawakening into a beauteous existence. Ancient Socrates walked about the thoroughfares of Athens, confronted and exposed the false maxims and shams of his day. Is not the life of the Athenian philosopher the type of an enlightened public opinion? And is not the Press its marvellous exponent, whose mission is never to let falsehood pass unchallenged? Come, public opinion! Go around the squares, traverse the streets, and stroll along wharves. Have a quiet talk with Tyranny—bid him desist, nor exact such hard service that even devils would be ashamed to bargain for....

As the Prospectus which has already issued assures us, there seems to be wanted here an authoritative exponent of educated opinion, it was this want which led to the disputations of the philosopher in the market place of Athens, and which now seeks to awaken the dormant energies in Trinidad. Is not this Prospectus the herald proclaiming the advance of an enlightened public opinion in Trinidad? What, ho! Let the standard be unfurled—Its inscription is excelsior!"[19]

Quite clearly the press saw itself in the role of philosopher dedicated to exposing the shortcomings of the society and playing an important role in social reconstitution.

The *Trinidad News* also got into the act. It, too, felt it necessary to talk about expanding the literary culture of the society. Lamenting the absence of a space in the society where intellectual matters could be discussed and building on the system of popular education that was coming into fruition, the editors of the *Trinidad News* offered the following sociological formulation:

Man is a social being and the establishment of associations for defined objects is found to be the best method by which those objects can be obtained. In the one broad stream of intellectual improvement there are no hidden religious or political rocks whereon our bark may wreck. At the present moment there is no society in Trinidad for the mental improvement where one may spend an evening. We have received a few verbal and written communications since the publication of our last article upon the subject; and we now propose to establish a society for mutual improvement upon the broadest basis. The world is advancing at such a rate that we cannot afford to delay even until our little colony feels the effects of the system of popular education so recently organised. We must "Act—act in the living present!"

The push to develop the "mental improvement" of the citizens continued as the decade wore on and sparked the development of a larger educated class. Although Thomas recorded the Creole language because it was thought to be dying, Abbé Masse discovered that French was spoken as frequently as English in the island.

19. "Etchings in Trinidad," *New Era*, March 27, 1871.

Spanish was also present in several parts of the island. Muir Marshall, the largest bookstore in the country, offered a wide variety of books on different subjects.[20] For those who could afford it, it was even possible to buy books directly from France. For instance, Abbé Masse found that Mlle. Winnett, "an old woman, …sells books and takes our orders for the libraries of France" (*AM.*, 2, p. 295)

On the literary front, many indigenous writers continued to explore their world in creative ways. Yet, the "real" literary action was taking place in the newspapers with innumerable letters to the editors on every conceivable subject. Even if they were not acting as the Greek philosophers of old, the newspaper encouraged serious disputations in the society. Primarily because these periodical was more accessible to more people, they became the space in which the literary and writing ambitions of most of the citizens and noncitizens were played out.

The Rise of Literary Criticism

Further interest in the literary and writing life evinced itself by what can be called the inauguration of literary criticism in the society and the reviewing of books that examined local subject matter. For example, the *Trinidad Chronicle* reprinted a review of Thomas's *The Theory and Practice of Creole Grammar* that appeared in the *Anti-Slavery Reporter* of December 31, 1869. For the reviewer, the publication of *Creole Grammar* proved that someone of "pure African descent" possessed "the natural capacity…for purely intellectual pursuits."[21] Almost as though he was responding to the review above (in fact, Thomas's article was in response to a request of an eminent philologist in London), the *Trinidad Chronicle* printed an excerpt from Thomas's "An Essay on the Philology of the Creole Dialect," which he delivered at the London Philological Society. In it, Thomas reiterated the extent to which "Creole, Negro-French or *patois*" was spoken throughout the Caribbean, although as he asserts, the "very curious question which remains as yet undetermined, [that] is, the extent and nature of the modifying influences which the idioms of Africa had on the formation and characteristics of the Creole….There seems to be wanting but little evidence more to prove the existence of a dominant African language, bearing to the dialects whose peculiarities characterise the Creole in a relation similar to that is borne by Sanskrit to the Indo-European languages, or less remotely, the relation which the Latin bears to the Romantic dialects."[22] This

20. See a description of the books offered by Muir Marshall in one of its ads in the *New Era*.

21. *Trinidad Chronicle*, February 15, 1870. The *Anti-Slavery Reporter* applauded the fact that *Creole Grammar* is "the product of a self-educated man, deprived of book-help and therefore labouring under the great disadvantage of not knowing what has already been written upon the Science of languages. It is further remarkable as a literary effort because its author, a native of Trinidad, is of pure African descent, affording another illustration of the natural capacity of the negro for purely intellectual pursuits of which the elusive capability is so arrogantly claimed for the Caucasian family by certain ethnologists."

22. "Creole Philology," *Trinidad Chronicle*, November 22, 1870. There is evidence to suggest that Thomas authored another book, *Philology vs. Physiology*, published in London and advertised for sale in the *Trinidad Chronicle* on December 26, 1873.

attempt to search for the specifics of Africanness and/or Asianness in the society characterized many of the literary and writing endeavours of the 1870s.

In their writings, Africans protested the social and racial inequality that pervaded the society. Africanus, a pen name for an outstanding African in the society, notes that "we are debarred from much of that Freedom and the rights of Equality which as British subjects we are entitled to, and which is secured to us by the Constitution of her Laws. But such is the principle of equality, that whether among the different Executives, in the several Councils, or in the many Courts, our rights and privileges are always held and acted upon as subservient to those of our fair neighbours. The tendency thus to rob us of our rights does not only exist in this Colony but could be traced to the Home Government and to the individual influences of both English and Colonial residents." Critiquing the tendency of many Africans to be obeisance to those of a fairer complexion, Africanus observes:

> The arrogance which our fairer neighbours assume towards us can more be traced to our own attitudes and deportment, than to any self confidence in themselves in the possession of any superior quality by reason of their being of a fair hue. Were we less anxious to associate with them; could we feel as much honour in being seen with friends of our own class in public as with them; were we less ambitious to select our friends and partners in life from that very class, indifferent as to their qualities, we would most assuredly have less of that arrogance, and would subject ourselves to less of that social abuse than we have now. The tendency to believe them a higher order of creation than ourselves, particularly amongst the more ignorant, is one of the many baneful influences of slavery, countenanced and encouraged by those whose interest it is to do so, and can only be eradicated by time and enlightenment. It is, therefore, the duty of those who have learned to the contrary to destroy this evil, which, without exaggeration, is the greatest stumbling block to our more rapid intellectual, moral, and social advancement. It is left to us to dispel this belief, and to let every Negro know that he has fully as much right as any other class to try to better his position; that the field would no more be his sphere of action than it would be that of his white employer, if he were socially and intellectually qualified to remove from it; and that he was never ordained by his Creator the "Subject-Race," as some has striven to stigmatise him. When these precepts shall have instilled into him the proper feeling, we shall find that this skin question shall have ceased to occupy men's minds, and that intellectual and social qualities shall be the only differences to distinguish our positions, one from the other. It would then be as ridiculous to pride oneself on the colour of one's skin, as would be to pride oneself on the colour of one's habiliments.[23]

It was not as though Europeans acted as passive vessels in their attempt to debase Africans. In this period, the dominant class worked hard to delegitimize all expressions of indigenous culture that arose, promoting the ensuing discussion as a debate between civility (the behaviour of the whites) and savagery (the practices and

---

23. Africanus, "To the Editor of the New Era," *New Era*, September 21, 1874.

behaviour of Africans and Indians). One critic, in another context, puts it this way: "legitimation discourse [was] premised on [an] investment of whiteness as uniquely valuable property in a society predicated on the power differentials inscribed in phenotype."[24]

In fact, this civilization-versus-savage debate was at the center of the education that was offered at the primary school level. Among others things, the discussion manifested itself in the arguments of those who supported Ward schools (secular) and the prelates and their adherents who supported church schools. As one editorial put it:

> We are accused of attacking and maligning the R. C. Clergy. We do protest our extreme unwillingness to do anything of the kind, and have avoided as much as possibly all references to them. The most painful stories have reached us, one after another; in some cases with the names, places, and dates; but we have not published and do not intend to publish them. When, however, we are possessed of such information we cannot altogether stifle the fact that some of the R. C. Clergy, from the pulpit and otherwise, do use threatening language against those of their flock who continue to send their children to the Ward Schools, and do fling vile epithets at those Schools themselves (such as *École du Diable*).[25]

This debate also took place at the secondary school level. The *Palladium*, a newspaper that promoted the Catholic point of view and which sought equal financial support for the College of Immaculate Conception (CIC), a Roman Catholic college, argued that "[t]he education of the present day is secular and irreligious, and it is only capable of turning out a man who may be a learned scholar if you wish, but who neither fears God, nor respects his fellow-man." For the editor, learning was the main ingredient that made a person civilised.[26] It contrasted the performance of CIC students (religious) with those of QRC (secular) who were not doing as well on the standardized tests of that day to prove the superiority of a religious education.[27]

The church and the school transmitted these ideas, so central to Europe's civilizing mission. Inadvertently, Robert John Lechmere Guppy (1836–1916), chief inspector of schools from 1868 to 1890, also found himself participating in this

24. Koushik Banejea, "Ni-ten-ichi-ryu: Enter the World of the Smart Stepper," in Kaur and Hutnyk, *Travel Worlds*, p. 19

25. "Meeting at Santa Cruz," *Trinidad Chronicle*, February 1, 1870.

26. According to the *Palladium*, "Our idea of civilization, which is derived from the very etymology of the word, represents to us a man living on terms of good will and peace with his fellow-men, a man instructed in his duties as a member of society and fulfilling them, in a word, a good citizen. A civilized man cannot allow self-interest to override the rights of his fellowman, nor permit himself to forget his duties as a citizen." (June 29, 1878).

27. As early as 1870, several Trinidadians were doing well on the Cambridge overseas examination and several had gone on to study at Cambridge University.

alienating discourse.[28] In his *Report* of 1875, he bemoans that the children of the poor in the primary schools spoke patois. Pouncing on this (mis)reading, the editors of the *Trinidad Chronicle* reminded Guppy that, if he took "the trouble to read a work written by a Creole author [Thomas] upon the subject, he will see that what is known here as 'Creole' is a perfectly distinct language, and that there is no reason why it should not be treated as such. The fault lies, not with the children or their parents who speak the language of *their* fathers, but with the Teachers who, if natives of the Island, too often affect an ignorance of the only language they can speak with any facility, or who, if strangers to Trinidad, will not condescend to learn the mother tongue of those they profess to teach." Arriving at a perfectly enlightened conclusion, the editors continued: "It is most desirable, nay most essential, that the children in our schools should be taught the English language, but this should not be done in a way to teach them at the same time to be ashamed of being Creoles or of foreign extraction. This would indeed be a serious blunder, and one which it is to be hoped the recollection of the past will always prevent our Rulers from committing....Let the Inspector of Schools then leave us in possession of our Creole *patois*—he may rest assured that it will never become the language of sedition."[29] During this early period of Trinidad's history, *Creole Grammar* was not an object of veneration as it is now sometimes made out to be. It was viewed as an active agent of social transformation that offered the colonial subjects a different way of understanding their condition of existence.

The missionary-educational discourse participated in fashioning and supporting authoritarian discursive practices that lay at the heart of the colonial enterprise. Although Christianity spoke about the ideal of human equality in the eyes of God, it used metaphors such as "satanic travesties," "savage customs," and "sons of Ham," stock metaphors and images that structured its discourses, "in inherently ambivalent ways, constituted and reinforced—but also questioned and subverted—powerful cultural idioms of colonial domination."[30] Although the missionary discourse, with its emphasis on individual self-determination and a degree of religious freedom of the converted, may have led to the development of one's individuality, its insistence that colonial people were perpetual children, unable to grasp rational thought,

28. R. J. L. Guppy was a remarkable man. For twenty-three years he was a part of the school system. After he retired in1890, he devoted himself to scientific study and produced several important scientific papers. According to his daughter, Yseult Bridges, "his collection of marine fauna and his geological discoveries in Trinidad brought him considerable esteem in his lifetime and a recognition that continued to grow, so that after his death even his slight papers were collected and published by Cornell University Press under the title of *A Reprint of the more Inaccessible Palaeontological writings of Robert John Luchmere Guppy*. At the age of eighty he died, retaining to the end a freshness which made any meeting with a delightful experience" (Yseult Bridges, *Child of the Tropics*, edited by Nicholas Guppy (Port of Spain: Aquarela Galleries, 1988), p. 19). See also *Addresses Presented on the Retirement of R. J. L. Guppy, Esq.*, (London: Hazell, Watson, & Viney, 1891), for an appreciation of the esteem in which teachers held Guppy.

29. *The Palladium*, September 21, 1878.

30. Dube ,"Travelling Light," in Kaur and Hutnyk, *Travel Worlds*, p. 36

shows that "within the interstices of these overlapping and tension-ridden movements, the missionaries [and some colonial officials] participated, wittingly or unwittingly, in the construction of colonial mythologies of racial supremacy, the establishment of paternalistic authority, and the reinforcement of the legitimacy of bureaucratic colonial rule."[31] In this phase of social development, the alliance between education and religion was an essential element in promoting authoritarian practices that were so necessary to consolidate colonial rule.

The Hosay Continuum

At the same time that this savage debate was going on about the importance of formal education and whether the Ward Schools were "devil schools," the East Indian and African masses were articulating the specificity of their social being by expressing a "world-constituting self," as Paget Henry calls it.[32] Consisting of about 20 percent of the population in 1871, the East Indians began to make its demands on the society. Like other groups who had immigrated to Trinidad, they wanted to practise their culture and religion freely in their new home. Growing tired of how their various festivals (expressions of their culture) were being treated by the colonial government, a group of Indians, signing themselves as "Combination," wrote to the governor of the island, via the *Trinidad Chronicle*, to make their concerns known. On March 28, 1871, the editors published their letter "*verbatim et litevatim* with the exception that we could not allow it to appear, as sent in,—addressed to the Governor, a needless impertinence, as His Excellency should be addressed with more respect, and direct or through the Colonial Secretary, in person or by deputation, by petition or memorial,—not through the public newspaper." The letter reads as follows:

> We Coolies have combined of preinforming you that as our FETE DAY is rapidly advancing, we shall indeed be exceedingly joyous of beholding everything clear before us for the same purpose. Example. As there are varieties of Nations as well as Sexes, there are also a great diversification in their rites and ceremonies. For instance, take the first for granted: the English takes a great delight in attending to his Church, for he believes it pleaseth God; in like manner the Pagan, by paying his homage to his God *Hosa*, he also believes it pleaseth the same God. Hence we deem it necessary to strive all efforts of avoiding all obstacles, which withstands or deters us from perpetrating that homage which is a tribute to God.
>
> Before delaying so long a time in expressing our wishes, we shall now in few words express it, and they are as follows:

---

31. Ibid., p. 37.

32. Paget Henry, *Caliban's Reason* (New York: Routledge, 2000), p. 4. In this important, insightful book, Henry notes that "the culture of a people may be defined as the expression of a distinct consciousness of existence articulated in a variety of discourses" (p. 4).

FIGURE 15. A taj of the hosay festival in the 1930s. From Paria Archives.

This year, Sir, there will be a great obstacle withstanding our paths, consequently, our *Hosaes* will be rendered impassable on account of the "Telegraphic wire."

We do not wish to have the wires removed at several places, on the opposition (i.e., on the contrary)—but there is a essential passage, in which partly all the *Hosaes* are compelled to pass, for the purpose of executing their decisions, and that spot is at San Fernando.

Whether the editors liked the grammar or not, the Indians had made their point. They placed their argument in context of civilization and demanded that their rights, like those of the whites, be respected. In effect, they affirmed that they possessed similar civilized impulses as their white brethren. The editors, however, could not help but give the writers a good tongue-lashing, for although they conceded that the Indians possessed certain rights, they advised that "[i]n a free country like this, a man is free to commit many follies, but he must neither make free with his own life, nor injure his neighbour in person or goods; nor must the public convenience suffer for the fancy or freak of individuals."[33] Since the wire was

33. I am reminded of Cheryl Harris's comments about the link between whiteness, property, and native dispossession: "In many ways so embedded [are the laws of whiteness and property rights] that it is rarely apparent, the set of assumptions, privileges and benefits that accompany the status of being white have become a valuable asset that whites sought to protect....The origins of property rights...are rooted in racial domination....Race and property were thus conflated by establishing a form of property contingent on race—only Blacks were subjugated as slaves and treated as property. Similarly... in native American land...only white possession and occupation...was validated and therefore privileged as a basis for property rights." Quoted in *Travel Worlds*, p. 19.

removed for the "planting interest," it was correct to move it for "the coolie labour-ers on the occasion of their great fete." Having made such a concession, the news-paper inquires:

> Who in the name of mystery was Hosay? And how come there to be two Hosays, a hindoo and a mussulman Hosay; as some say there are? And what is the proper Hosay fete day, in the Christian calendar? For it seems to wander from April to June, and even later. How is the anniversary computed? We speak of the Hindu Hosay. Does the Mussulman's Hosay day always correspond with the Hindoo one? Is Hosay a synonyme of Krishna, the Apollo and Antinous, the beloved of the Gangetic milkmaids. Krishna the preserver, the continuer of life, as Brahma is the creator and Siva the destroyer—the triad representing the three great stages of human existence? Why is the only hindu fete day consecrated to this "unknown god" while of the better known we hear naught? Why is the richly begilt, many-storied ark thrown, with its mystic contents, at the end of the ceremony, into the Gulf? And what do these things typify? Can anyone, in decent English, instruct us benighted Christians, as to the meaning of these curious matters?[34]

The editors were being facetious. As the last sentence of their inquiry suggests, they were also contemptuous of the Indians. Although the writers did not express themselves as elegantly as the editors would have liked (yet, they were certainly very eloquent) or were not as respectful of the governor as the editors felt proper, the Indians were contesting the privileged position of the whites (and whiteness) and their dominance in the society. Such a confrontation was not comfortable for the privileged class. That act of domination itself was seen as a great insult to the whites of the society. Truly, these natives were forgetting their place. Yet, despite such con-descension, the subalterns were beginning to speak out against, nay, to challenge, the self-righteousness of whites (and whiteness) and their appropriation of the pub-lic space. In unique Trinidad style, the Indians were saying: "[t]he road make to walk on Carnival day." It is this spiritual boldness that inhered in Thomas's polem-ical attack against James Anthony Froude years later.[35]

It took another white man, John Morton, a Canadian missionary who had arrived on the island three years previously and who acted as a defender of the Indians, to respond to the editors of the *Trinidad Chronicle*. Observing that some of their questions could be "very summarily disposed of" (No! there is no Hindu Hosay, No, Hosay is not a synonyme for Krishna), Morton made the astute point that the celebration of *hosay* was a creolism (Morton's word) and an Indian cultur-al practice adapted to its Trinidad environment. Taking pains to describe Hosay to the uninitiated, Morton advised that "[t]he Hosay is a funeral possession. The Hosays [the pagoda-like models, are here meant] are called tazzias from the Arabic

---

34. *Trinidad Chronicle*, March 28, 1871.
35. See "The Press" in Dennison Moore, *The Origins and Development of Racial Ideology in Trinidad* (Tunapuna: Chakra Publishing House, 1995), for a discussion of how the press depicted East Indians.

word taziya—mourning or condolence. They are representations or models of the tombs of Hussan and Hossein. In each of the large tazzias there are two small coffins fitted up in every respect as the Coolies do the coffins of their most honored dead. The women singing songs of sadness; the men smiting their breasts and crying, 'hae hae! (woe or alas!) Hussan! Hossein!'—the throwing of rice, &c, are all in perfect accordance with their ordinary mode of conducting funerals."[36] The editors may not have been satisfied with this explanation, but it opened up a discourse that escalated as the society developed.

"Playing hosay"— that is, the East Indian street procession—became widespread in the 1870s and assumed its place in the evolving Creole society. Although it represented a funeral possession initially, the hosay celebrations, central to the Shiite's religious tradition, demonstrated how a community interiorized a tradition and made it a basis for its hopes and aspirations. Significantly, in Muslim philosophy/theology, Jesus was seen as "a brother of Husayn," the slain martyr of the Muslim religion, a saint whom the Muslims commemorated in their Hosay festival. In other words, the Muslim community was using its religion to construct a new life in a strange land. Maymoud Ayoub has observed that "The tragic death of Husayn, the third Imam of the Shii community, has become for Shii Muslims a cosmic event touching all of human history, nature, the entire universe. Husayn's martyrdom, moreover, was integrated very early into the history of revelation, more specifically into the traditions of the ancient biblical prophets and the Christ of the Gospel."[37] Therefore, when "Combination" asked that their religious preference be placed on the same standing as that of their Christian counterparts, they were asking that their humanity be given the same respect as that of the Europeans. Whereas the English took "great delight in attending to his Church, for he believes it pleaseth God," the mussulman took great delight in worshipping Allah by commemorating the martyrdom of Husayn, "regarded by the Shi-i community as a cosmic event around which the entire history of the world, prior as well as subsequent to it, revolves."[38]

The literary-theatrical aspect of this festival was also important to the Muslim community. As practised by its adherents, hosay, a passion play, was analogous in

36. John Morton, "The 'Hosay' Fete," *Trinidad Chronicle*, April 11, 1871. In May, 1868, in a letter to his home mission in Canada, Morton described the playing of Hosay and the participation of Hindus and Africans in the festival: "The Mohurrum is called in Trinidad the Hossee. This has probably arisen from the Creoles, seeing the Coolies beating their breast and calling out Hussan! Hussein! This name is applied alike to the whole observance and to the Tazzias carried in the procession, and it has been universally adopted by the Coolies....The festival, for it is that rather than a fast, lasts ten days. Wherever a hossee is built an altar of mud is set by the house, and here flowers and offerings are set, and during the first nine days companies gather during the evening to play at sword exercises. This is their great sport but it is dreaded by the better thinking among the Hindus....These gatherings are always enlivened by the sound of the tom tom often played by Creoles. The Hossee day fell on Sunday, but it was postponed till Monday....[On that day] over sixty Hossees accompanied by at least four, and probably as much as six thousand men filled the street and swept slowly onward towards the wharf" (*The Home and Foreign Record* (Canada), July 1868, p. 180).

37. Mamoud Ayoub, *Redemptive Suffering in Islam* (The Hague: Mouton Publishers, 1978), p. 136.

38. Ibid., p. 141.

many ways to the ramleelas and Carnival. Fred Halliday writes that the hosay (he spells it "hoosai") represented "the theme of the martyrdom and sacrifice, celebrated every year in the passion plays of commemorating the death of the Shi'ite leader Hussein in the seventh century."[39] Aboub reveals that, by the tenth Islamic century (fifteenth century A.D.), the hosay procession "began to evolve in the familiar passion play, or what may be more accurately termed the representation (shabih) of the entire battle of Karbala, with people playing the various roles of its major characters."[40] Like Carnival and the ramleelas, hosay was nothing less than theatre in the street, a display of bodily expression as a people enacted their histories in their place and time. According to Dennison Moore, it "was the only occasion on which Indians from different plantations came together once a year."[41] By the end of 1870, there were "different bands of Hose' celebrators,"[42] and many Africans began to take part in what the authorities called "heathen" celebrations.

In February 1875, *Fair Play* reported that the Hosay, held annually, was celebrated with "greater eclat than ever, judged from the number of showily decorated temples, which they paraded about our streets yesterday. At one time we counted a procession of thirteen of them, preceded by music of a tambourine-drum kind, and attended by crowds of Coolies. Collisions between the various bands was guarded against and prevented by the police, and the occasion passed off without disorder. A curious proof of the importance of our Coolie population, now, is that, whilst estates were comparatively at a standstill, our stores closed early, there being nothing to do, as the Coolies were holiday-making."[43] Although Muslims constituted about 15 percent of the East Indian population, a large portion of the East Indian population participated in these celebrations.

The Hosay celebration of 1878, described by one newspaper as "the great annual religious Coolie fete," drew large crowds to Port of Spain. In a much more charitable report, *Fair Play* reported that "[i]n Marine Square and various other parts, members were to be seen gathered round their singers and sword-stick players. But the largest crowds attended the various temples which they construct with so much taste and elegance. There must have been at least 45 of these parading about the town."[44]

By 1880, the festival had grown in intensity. This placed many Christian whites in a defensive position. Described as revealing "grotesqueness, fanatic barbarism and repulsive ignorance," the festival could be construed as having descended to the level of the African Carnival. And, the festival continued to draw more Africans into its ranks. *Fair Play* write that "[t]here were about twenty two temples of widely differing pretensions to grandeur and importance....Another curious sight was

39. Fred Halliday, *Islam and the Myth of Confrontation* (London: I. B. Tauris, 1995), p. 60.
40. Ayoub, *Redemptive Suffering in Islam*, p. 155.
41. Dennison., *Origins and Development of Racial Ideology in Trinidad*, p. 177.
42. "The Coolie Hosea," *Fair Play*, November 23, 1882.
43. *Fair Play*, February 18, 1875.
44. *Fair Play*, January 15, 1878.

the women and children sitting placidly on the carts under the shadow of the frail temples overhead, their earnest faces and chants denoting the sense of security which filled their breasts! The procession, which was very long, passed on its *route* down (Abercrombie) street towards King Street. It was preceded by a *posse* of the most abandoned women of the City and attended by a large contingent of its *canaille*, and it required all the patience of the policemen who were of the company to keep the seething mass of barbarism, lewdness, and rascaldom in anything like tolerable order." The newspaper ended its account poetically: "After throwing their temples into the sea, the Coolies dispersed and quietly wended home their weary way."[45]

Such abandon (and dedication in this case) was too much for the "respectable people" of the city. To members of the official establishment, "the danger of Hose' day is that it brings together in different parts of the Island, large masses of men who are showing strong and menacing marks of isolated discontent for which they can give no proper reason." Like the Carnival, the annual celebration of the hosay said more about the social and political status of the Indians than any political orator could have. The editor of *Fair Play* noted that "[f]orty years ago he [the Indian] came here as a poor despised heathen immigrant; now his race has become formidable on account of its homogeneity, religion and numbers, the action of law is stayed to conciliate him, and his leading men are taken into the counsels of the Governor as of importance in the maintenance of peace and security. A portion of the scum and offscourings of heathen India has thus been concentrated into a power by its agglomeration in this Christian Island."[46]

In terms of expression of self and the construction of a community, Hosay was playing a role similar to that of Carnival and the ramleelas. To draw on Gilroy, black bodies were celebrating and being celebrated as instruments of pleasure and devotion rather than instruments of labor in a public space they carved out for recovery and recuperation. Why should they stop the hosay, a Creole bacchanal? As "Combination" understood so well: each nation has its rites and ceremonies. These Muslim-Trinidadians, with some help from Africans and Hindu-Indians, simply expressed their dark-skinned selves in a strange land. To the dominant culture, this display was a manifestation of their savagery, while to the Indians, it was a celebration of their civilization writ large on the canvas of the New World.

Carnival Continum

Like the Hosay, the annual Carnival celebration faced similar ridicule and abuse. Only, it was thought to be more savage and to present a bolder challenge to the civilized ways of the Europeans who lived on the island. Unlike Hosay, however, plans "to put down the Carnival" had been afoot since 1857 when Governor Keate

45. *Fair Play*, December 16, 1880.
46. "The Coolie Hosay," *Fair Play*, November 23, 1882.

attempted to end the event. Those plans failed because "the inhabitants interpreted the movement as an infringement of the privileges of the people, as established by long custom."[47]

In the 1870s, however, renewed attempts were made to repress Carnival since members of the dominant order interpreted it as the manifestation of a diabolical presence in the society. In 1871, the Inspector Commandant sought to confine masking and other disguises to Carnival Monday and Tuesday and to limit "the blowing of horns or other noisy instruments (and the) carrying of torches."[48] In 1877, the *Trinidad Palladium,* described Carnival as an "abomination" and noted that "the masquerade, as it is practised on the two days and several nights immediately preceding Lent, is a revel more fit for the hall of devils, than the public thoroughfares of a Christian community. We might afford a laugh even for the absurdities which pain us; but for the obscene and brutal practices which are yearly enacted in our midst, the severest reprobation and denunciation fail to convey our sentiments." Condemning Carnival and wishing that it was "among the things that were," the editorial reiterated its determination to see the festival brought to an end:

> For years we have heard it said by some wiseacres that if left to itself the "masquerade" would "die out," and that any attempt to suppress it would only result in confirming it, and provoking its continuance. In one respect they were right,—the "masquerade" *praper* is almost, if not altogether, extinct; but the evil of which we write, and which has grown out of it, has been yearly assuming greater, and, to some extent, alarming proportions, which it could never have acquired had the whole thing been abolished ere this....To remove this abomination an old institution which has struck its roots deep in the superstitions and ignorance of some weak-minded people would have to be rooted out, and to them it may be like the severance of another link with the past, the removal of another ancient landmark. But if these would only perceive that their sympathies are really with a thing of the past, and that the thing which has usurped its place is but an abnormal growth, the offspring of ignorance and depravity, nourished by superstition, they would join in the effort to exterminate it root and branch."

The editor also recommended "a diversion" that would turn "the ruffians" away from their diabolical ways. Since "[m]usic hath charm to soothe the savage breast," he reasoned than if the Police Band marched and played a few "lively airs" at several corners on Carnival day, in little time the "savage breast" of the lower orders would be soothed. What was his rationale? "The lower orders are fond of music, and we do not doubt that a crowd assembled to fight in one street would quickly disperse and scamper off to enjoy the music, if the Band struck up in the next street. And what is more, they would not return but follow the Band for the next tune. In this way the musicians would not be fatigued, and they would be doing their duty

---

47. Several Inhabitants, *The Trinidad Palladium,* February 10, 1877.
48. "The Carnival," *Trinidad Chronicle,* February 14, 1871.

FIGURE 16. A Gelede mask dancing in the Gelede festival in Imeko. The carnival masqueraders, in part, have their origins in the Gelede festival.

as men of the Force, and doing it effectually and in a way agreeable to all parties."[49] Lest one wonder, how serious the editor took this suggestion, this gentleman was the embodiment of sobriety when he made this statement. Were we writing today, we would say that these two cultures (the European and the African) were engaged in a serious cultural war.

A week later, "Several Inhabitants" added their voices to the above remarks and endorsed the notion that Carnival brought out a savage dimension in Africans. They contended that "these annual orgies are the source of much of the vagabondage and lawlessness that characterise a great portion of the low orders, cannot be denied. But apart from the effects on these people, they are a blot on civilization, and a burning shame to the country, which tolerates them....How long shall we continue to countenance and uphold such disgusting scenes as are enacted yearly in our public streets? Trinidad stands unique amongst civilised countries for these barbarous proceedings; and the sooner this ugly blot is wiped out the better."[50] These correspondents also called for the suppression of Carnival, a goal, they assured the reader, with which "every honest person concurs." In fact, the dominant class felt so superior to the lower classes that it had no problem in making this smug pronouncement: "Were these individuals likely to read this unpretending article we

49. *The Trinidad Palladium*, February 3, 1877.
50. *The Trinidad Palladium*, February 10, 1877.

should admonish them how to pursue their pleasures, but as they seldom or ever read a newspaper, we conclude by offering our readers our congratulations that so little injury has been done, and expressing our hope that, in years to come, the abstinence system, in regard to drinks, may so largely pervade the lower classes that less mischief and harm may be done to others, while indulgence may be realized by masquerades without humiliation and degradation themselves."[51] Needless to say, the writer of these words clearly sees himself as superior to the lowly people who celebrated Carnival.

Poets also got into the act of demonising the masquerades. Poeticising about the worthlessness of Carnival, R. Hill wrote:

> Masquerade again is over,
> > Fools and folly once more seen;
> Human things like apeing Monkeys,
> > Or like Demons, so I ween.
>
> Insults many and abuses,
> > Tricks of knaves or something worse,
> Gestures vile and looks indecent,
> > Odious pest and deadly curse.
>
> Why this relic of dark ages
> > Where the fruit of Gospel light?
> Are the people now no better
> > Than in heathenism's night?
>
> Shame on you, ye masquerades,
> > Heaven's gift ye prostitute—
> Stigmatise your human nature,
> > Sink it low beneath the Brute.
>
> Have you no respect for virtue,
> > No regard for what is right?
> Do you covet black dishonour—?
> > Emulate the Sons of night?
>
> Surely you are aiming higher?
> > Where then is your sense of shame?
> Why like heathens flaunt and fluster?
> > Why disgrace your place and name?
>
> Rise above such mean device;
> > Wipe the stain of shame away;
> Act no more like fools and Demons;
> > Show you're people of the day...

---

51. *The Trinidad Palladium*, March 1, 1879.

Show advance in civilisation
>   And contempt of all that's base;
Aim at purity and honour,
>   And as Christians take your place.

Then we'll see no masquerading;
>   All its follies then are o'er.
Fools no more like apeing Monkeys
>   Nor like Demons as before.

No more insults and abuses,
>   No more tricks and nonsense base.
Men and women in their senses
>   Then will walk with open face.[52]

Like much of the other discourses on Carnival, one again hears civilized contrasted with savagery and barbarism; morality with immorality; and "animal spirits" with "civilized modes" of behaviour interwoven in every argument offered in favor of suppressing Carnival. In 1877, the *Port of Spain Gazette* called for "suppression by force, if necessary" to control what they thought were the undesirable aspects of Carnival. Such suppression, they argued, "would contribute much more towards the refinement of vulgar tastes than all the learning and labour of our primary schools put together for a year."[53] Two years later, *Fair Play and Trinidad News* disagreed with the full-scale banning of Carnival and argued that this ancient institution, which had "struck its roots... deeply in the hearts and customs of a people, [is] not to be, and should not, be torn up in the rough-and-ready way suggested by purists and extremists. This often result in a destruction of what is good along with what is evil, and experience has proved that the mere attempt to adopt such crude measures has often been productive of the most disastrous consequences, social, political and moral." Calling for the repression of all aspects of the Carnival celebrations that were opposed to "public decency, morality and order," the newspaper concluded: "It would be impolitic and even tyrannical for the Government to attempt to interfere in the matter beyond these limits."[54]

Apart from the violence and licentiousness that attended the Carnival of the 1870s, the "respectable people" feared the changes that had taken place in the celebrations, claiming that these alterations had ruined Carnival for them. That the lower classes had begun to monopolise the fête was not a desirable condition for those who wished to maintain their control over the society. *Fair Play and Trinidad News* reminisced about the Carnival of forty years before when "maqueraders personated in rich and characteristic costumes all the conceits and peculiarities of

52. R. Hill, "The Masquerade," *Trinidad Chronicle*, February 14, 1880
53. Quoted in the *Trinidad Chronicle*, March 16, 1881.
54. *Fair Play and Trinidad News*, March 6, 1879.

human, even sometimes animal, life. Living caricatures went abroad who wittingly hit off in the happiest and most laughable manner the peculiarities of individuals whom they wished to compliment or satirize. Cavalcades of gentlemen, finely dressed up in character, swept through the streets. There were magnificent chateaux in which kings and queens sat, drawn by numerous horses, and preceded and sur- rounded by bands of musicians. Indians with bows and arrows, jesters, tumblers, and a thousand and one personated characters. If the sexes were imitated, it was done in good and not in vile satire and form." In those golden days, on the cusps of slavery's demise, "People of all classes," they say, "enjoyed themselves, and commerce was extensive [and] benefited by the lavish expenditure of those easy monetary times. All this, however, has been gradually changed and little now remains but features of a dangerous and disgraceful character."[55]

By 1880, forty-six years after slavery had ended; the content and character of Carnival had changed. It had become a medium through which those in the "lower order" could express and be themselves. Despite all efforts to denigrate "the Creole Bacchanal," the editors of the *Trinidad Palladium* inadvertently revealed Carnival's wide appeal to "the lower class." Describing the Carnival celebrations of 1880, the newspaper observed that "hosts of idle boys and girls, and men and women, follow these bands with the greatest glee, and recognise in their leaders persons of real con- sequence, who occupy a central commanding position. [They] are the people of the hour, if not of the day. Domestics leave their duties at home, to the great inconven- ience of their employers, in order to behold the heroes and heroines of the season."[56] Although these people did not read the papers, they had established their own ways of life, had selected their leaders, and had revealed what was important in them. The editors may have had the pen, but these people possessed and controlled their bod- ies. On those two days, as the newspaper insisted, "there is a temporary madness,"[57] a throwing off of all social restraints so as to realize, in all of its sensuous beauty, the only thing they possessed: bodies *in* the West that were not *of* the West. An old African observed:

Camboulay was played [in the streets?] during slavery by many members of the middle and in some cases [by] the upper classes: it was intended to "take off" slave life on a plantation, and hence a driver with the whip pretending drive the people before him to extinguish a night-fire in the cane-piece, the slaves tramping in time and singing a rude refrain to a small negro drum and carrying torches to light their way along the road. The town players danced to the music of drums 'tis true, but their dances—so says my informant [the old African]—were wholly unlike those generally danced at modern Camboulays, done mostly by females, accompanied by ribald songs full of double entendres and vile allusions, the dance or properly speak- ing the serpentine wrigglings the offspring (both of them) of corrupt imaginations

55. Ibid.
56. *The Trinidad Palladium,* February 4, 1880.
57. Ibid.

principally of frail daughters of Eve not overtroubled with puritanical restraints such as morality and decency, and whose drapery incommodes them as little as their consciences, to judge from the scanty amount they bother themselves to wear.[58]

Carnival took Africans to a place that represented an important marker of their social being and resonated in spaces where the European could not inhabit. When, in 1881, the latter tried to stop Carnival and to prevent Africans from carrying lighted flambeaux, all hell literally broke loose. Never again would Carnival be, if it ever were, "a season of lively, elegant and witty recreation, a source of universal enjoyment whilst conferring a benefit on trade."[59]

Gustave Borde

The publication of Pierre Gustave Borde's *The History of the Island of Trinidad under the Spanish Government* (hereafter *History of Spanish Trinidad*) was the most important literary event to take place in Trinidad up to that time. Reviewed by English, Trinidadian and Venezuelan scholars, in English, French, and Spanish, it turned out to be the work that the literary establishment awaited; J. J. Thomas translated it from the French to the English to make it available to English readers. A beautifully written work, Borde's study explores many of the themes, albeit historical, that de Verteuil, Leotaud, and Thomas raised (that of interrogating the geographic, natural, and linguistic spaces around them) and anticipated many of the concerns (particularly those of the Amerindians) that writers, thinkers, and citizens explored in the following decade. Borde employed the works of Humboldt, de Verteuil, Leotaud, and Crueger to document and to support his findings, defended Dauxion-Lavaysse passionately, and was extremely critical of E. L. Joseph's *History of Trinidad*.[60] In fact, Borde's *History of Spanish Trinidad* can be read as a celebration of the French way of life in Trinidad and as a testimony to the energy and foresight of our forebears: "We, who are the children of this country, have a sacred duty to render homage and thanks and eternal gratitude to those people who have created such a glorious history. It is due to these energetic pioneers that the colony, now confident of her destiny, was to walk with firm steps under the guidance of the English government" (*HST*, 2, pp. 341–42). [61] Yet, like the first group of writers, primarily French, Borde had to search for sources to authenticate his work in a society in which there was not a tradition in this kind of scholarship. Determined not to write a traditional history, Borde used as little documentation as possible. His

58. "The Origin Of Canboulay," quoted in *Trinidad Chronicle*, March 16, 1881.

59. *Fair Play and Trinidad News*, March 6, 1879.

60. It is not coincidental that Joseph who lived in Trinidad from 1820 to 1840 was Scottish. In his preface, Borde writes that "[i]n so short a work in which E. L. Joseph records a few historical landmarks buried under a mass of error and omissions, he deliberately finds ways and means to declare himself a rival of Washington Irving, and to make himself the adversary of Humboldt" (*History of Spanish Trinidad*, 1, p. xxxiii; hereafter referred to as *HST*.). During this period, the work of Dauxion-Lavaysse was used to clarify the Venezuelan boarder dispute. See *Trinidad Chronicle*, July 21, 1870.

61. See especially Part 2, chapter 14, a virtual panegyric of the French way of life after 1783.

"historical essay," as he calls it, reads more as a dramatic narrative than a formal history; an attempt, as he says in volume one, to promote "the heroism which we shall admire in the history of conquest of the New World and [which] inspired the great actions which we shall here relate" (*HST.*, 1, pp. 63–64). In its treatment of materials, this work predates C. L. R. James's *The Black Jacobins* as a dramatic and literary reading of history.[62] Francisco A. Paul, a reviewer of *History of Spanish Trinidad,* observed that Borde's history "will always be read with pleasure by persons capable of appreciating the beauties of French literature."[63] Even Borde's editorialising gives the text an immediacy and a poignancy that is not usually present in traditional histories.

History of Spanish Trinidad ought to be perceived as one node in a larger discursive space in which the inhabitants sought to map their space and to locate themselves in time. Borde used the historical mode to explore the particularity of his Frenchness (he was concerned to show the uniqueness of "the colonization of a Spanish island with a French population"), as he sought to bring to the surface historical materials that were either forgotten or had the possibility of being lost if they were not gathered quickly, hence his urgency "to gather and to co-ordinate…all the historical material still in existence before the action of time and the negligence of men destroy them" (*HST.*, 1, xxiv–xxv). He also saw his book as serving a practical function: it was intended "to instruct our youth in the history of their country, so that on reaching maturity, they should be able, in the interest of the general public, to impart true facts and not futile experience. Without this teaching, there is no patriotism. Little by little we become strangers to our country, and following our weaknesses or our inclinations, we make ourselves British, French or Spanish, when, in spite of everything, we are Trinidadians, though today subject to England" *(HST.*, 1, p. xxvi).

Borde reflected the racist (on occasions, patrician) sentiments of his time and presented Christianity as the saving grace of mankind ("It is Christianity and Christianity alone which can establish itself on the generous instincts of humanity" [*HST.*, 1, p. 134]), and the Christianization of the Indians as the highest human vocation. He argued that "Christianity alone" raised the Amerindians to the dignity of the missionaries" (*HST.*. 1, p. 57). He defended Las Casas's justification of slavery—that since one Negro had the strength of four Amerindians, the former ought to be enslaved in place of the latter—when he argued (or supported Washington Irving's position) that Las Casas "thought that the Indians were a superior race and that their preservation and welfare were of greater interest to humanity" (*HST.*, 1, p. 87). Drawing on aspects of missionary discourse, he argued that Africans were the sons and daughters of a "degraded and perverted civilization" and

---

62. For a discussion of *The Black Jacobins* as a literary text, see Kara M. Rabbitt in Selwyn R. Cudjoe and William Cain, ed., *C. L. R. James: His Intellectual Legacies* (Amherst: University of Massachusetts Press, 1995).

63. Francisco Paul, "A Review," *Trinidad Chronicle,* April 14, 1883; hereafter, "A Review."

saw them as "grown children who had been handed over to their masters for instructions, and this comparison is far from being imaginary, as they formed a part of the families of their masters" (*HST.*, 2, pp. 312–13). He also believed that Africans who came to the Caribbean were civilized by the Christians and French [European] culture. He spoke of the Amerindian revolt against the cruelty of the Spanish in a more insidious manner:

> We have seen them rise up and demand that they return to their barbarity rather than carry out an order which had been given to them, perhaps in a brusque manner, or lift a load which was a little heavy. Exclusively governed by a patriarchal discipline, with no thought for tomorrow and without any communication with the outside world, how could it be expected that one day, they would be able to accustom themselves to the exigencies of civilisation? Thus deprived of seeing the example set by other races which formed the population of the island, they were forced to vegetate in complete ignorance of the responsibilities of life. Without habitual contact with Christians, how could it be imagined that even religious sentiments itself could continue being developed in them only by the instruction of the missionaries? How could it be admitted that in these conditions they would be able to assimilate their higher ideas of an entirely mysterious religion which they had not imbibed with their mother's milk, and for this reason, it was with great difficulty they did assimilate it. And finally, how could they arrive at a loving God who disapproved of their natural desires especially for polygamy, which was the one to which they were particularly attached (*HST.*, 2, pp. 76–77).

Although one of the earliest historical expression of our nationness is in Borde, the concept was couched in terms of Europe's superiority (in this case, Christianity), especially at a time when the subaltern was seeking social equality and the recognition of the integrity of their culture. Yet, until 1883, when his second volume appeared, *History of Spanish Trinidad* remained the most detailed reading of Trinidad's history of the Spanish period. Borde's self-consciousness in speaking about the need for a sense of nationness earns him a special place in our literary and historical studies. Although one cannot defend Borde's missionary impulses, as Bridget Brereton asserts, he "was the first Trinidadian to express 'nationalist' sentiments as opposed to British or empire loyalty."[64]

If Borde's history represented the first indigenous history that spoke to the question of nationness, it was also one of the first local works that was subjected to a sustained critical examination internationally as well as on the island. The first substantive review, written by an English person, appeared in the *Trinidad Chronicle* on September 22, 1876. The writer complimented Borde's scholarship and observed that "[s]uch a book, full of historical details, and embodying the ripe erudition of one who has been long and patiently labouring at his task, will satisfy a want, for the materials for a study of the history of the colony are few and rare, and not gen-

---

64. Bridget Brereton, *Race Relations in Colonial Trinidad,* p. 59.

erally available, and they deserve to be treated in such a manner as will secure the permanent record of a large number of facts" The reviewer admonished Borde gently for dwelling "upon the usefulness of making known *qui nous sommes* to the high functionaries who are sent from Europe to govern the island, and to the clergy whose duty it is to teach its population." In his attempt to defend the colonial power, he notes defensively that " [i]t is quite true that a governor does very little during his first year of office, simply because he knows nothing of the country and the people, and that when he begins to comprehend the real needs of the people, his term expires and he goes away. M. Borde, however, will probably be ready to admit that it is sometimes a great advantage to have a fixed term for the rule of a governor, which term, short as it is, is occasionally found long."[65] To the reviewer, *History of Spanish Trinidad* was a "valuable book," even though some parts of it were objectionable to English readers. Recommending the book to his readers, he observed that it "deserves special attention from his countrymen as being written by a Trinidadian."

Another evaluation of the book, part of a larger review, "French Literature," appeared in the *Saturday Review* of London. It remarked that it was "a work deserving attention....[It] will be found full of curious and important matter; it begins with a geographic sketch of the island and gives us the history of the colony down to the year 1822."[66] Like most other reviewers, this one was attentive and respectful of Borde's accomplishments.

It was Aristides Rojas's review, however, that catapulted *History of Spanish Trinidad* into the limelight of American writing. Rojas, a Venezuelan historian who abandoned the profession of medicine to write fiction and historical studies, paid Borde the ultimate compliment by saying that *History of Spanish Trinidad* was "an important acquisition in the literature of American history, already rich with works by Prescott, Washington Irving, Acosta, Plaza, Baralt, and other modern writers from the two Americas. Historical truth, sustained by an integrity, is the quality of the author. This is found in each chapter of the book. Clear and simple diction, a sustained organisation, impartial criticism in regard to original sources and a growing desire to bring to light all that is related to the history of this former Castillian colony—such are the merits Mr. Borde's book."[67]

Coming from Rojas, this was fine praise indeed, and this review confirmed Borde's standing in the American intellectual tradition. Not only was Rojas a distinguished historian, he had assumed a subversive role in Venezuelan letters and was accused of bringing "the threat of history into literature" and "mingl[ing] history and poetry in his *Leyendas* and *Estudios*." Cecilio Acosta, on the other hand,

65. "West Indian in London," *Trinidad Chronicle*, September 22, 1876.

66. "French Literature," *Saturday Review of Politics, Literature, Science and Art* 42, No 1093 (October 7, 1876), pp. 459–60.

67. First published in *De La Opinion Nacional* (Venezuela) on March 16, 1878, this review was reproduced subsequently *in Fair Play and Trinidad News*, April 30, 1878, from which this quotation is taken.

was viewed as Venezuela's "most important thinker" of the second half of the nine-teenth century. His "letters, speeches, and essays were an attempt to define the moral nature of the nation."[68] Thus, it was no surprise that Borde was welcomed into that American community of letters. He was doing for Trinidadian letters what Rojas, Acosta, and Rafael Maria Baralt were doing for Latin America.[69] Ramon Diaz, a Venezuelan historian and novelist of the twentieth century, repaid the com-pliment in *Meme: A Venezuelan Novel* (1933) that documents the plight of Trinidadians who went to Venezuela in the 1920s to work in the petroleum fields of Cabimas on the eastern coast of Lake Maracaibo.

In spite of his fine praise for Borde's work, Rojas felt the former did not exhaust all the bibliographic sources/references at his disposal. Because of this shortcoming, Rojas contended that Borde repeated some of the errors of the earlier historians (compilers), especially with regard to the martyrdom of the Franciscan and Dominican fathers (Fathers Cordova and Garces) that took place in 1513 on the west coast of Cumana rather than in Trinidad as Borde claimed. In spite of this dis-agreement, Rojas viewed Borde's history not simply as a Trinidadian work but as a significant American work that he recommended "to enthusiasts of the early histo-ry of America." As studies of James, Naipaul, and Williams demonstrated, the his-tory of Trinidad was always imbricated within the larger context of American and European studies.

Rojas's review elicited a sustained, respectful response from Franciso A. Paul, a Spanish instructor at Queen's Royal College and a Trinidadian by adoption. Although Paul called Borde "a correct writer, an impartial historian, and an enlight-ened Christian philosopher," he supported Rojas's contention (although he dis-agreed with Rojas on some minor points) about the martyrdom of Cordova and Garces.[70] Such a correction was important to Paul since, among other things, Borde wanted to rectify "a large number of historical and geographical mistakes."[71] After he praised Borde and Rojas, Paul writes that "[h]ow unpleasant it must be for me to disagree from such competent authorities, is easier to be conceived than expressed; but a love of truth and an ardent desire to contribute as much as lies in my power, towards saving from oblivion the true historical annals of this Island, have encouraged me to devote some of my leisure hours to the elucidation of the

68. Guillermo, Moran, *A History of Venezuela*. Edited and translated by John Street (London: George Allen & Unwin, 1964), p. 200.

69. According to Dillwyn F. Ratcliff, "the Venezuelan men of letters of the second half of the nine-teenth century wrote romantic novels and tales and retold the traditions and legends of colonial and rev-olutionary times." Since the Venezuelan novel did not arrive fully until the 1880s (Eduardo Blanco's *Zirate* [1882]), as in Trinidad and Tobago, the newspapers provided space for these stories, sketches, leg-ends, and *cuadros de costumbres*. Rojas became a heavy contributor to the newspapers and magazines that popularized science and historical sketches. See Dillwyn F. Ratcliff, *Venezuelan Prose Fiction* (New York: Instituto de las Espanas, 1933,p. 47, 17–18.

70. Francisco A. Paul, "Detached Pages of the history of Trinidad," *Fair Play and Trinidad News*, May 14, 1878.

71. Quoted in "Detached pages of the History of Trinidad."

important question treated by Dr. Rojas in his above-mentioned letter."[72] The polite manner in which Paul disagreed with Rojas and Borde was analogous to the "politeness" Sir Robert Walpole introduced into his society when he became the Prime Minister of Britain in 1720.[73] Such civilised self-restraint, particular in discoursing about the work of a fellow scholar was an important gesture for the critical enterprise that was developing in the society. It did not hurt that Paul acted occasionally as the Venezuelan Consul to the island.

Paul also reviewed the second volume of the *History of Spanish Trinidad*. A more extensive and scholarly review, he evinced as much pride in Borde's achievement in this second volume as he had in the first. In this examination, Paul offered a complimentary rather than oppositional reading, even though he was more sympathetic toward Spanish aspirations and achievements in Trinidad than Borde.[74] In a way, Paul's review is almost an act of collaboration since he used documents that Borde did not possess nor have access to. Recognizing this synchrony, the editors of the *Trinidad Chronicle* noted: "His production may be considered as an appendix to Mr. Borde's excellent work, and for this reason we have made up our mind to print it in a pamphlet form, provided a sufficient number of subscribers can be found to defray the expense of publication." [75]

Paul called *History of Spanish Trinidad* "the most valuable contribution to the history of the Colony, during the rule of the Spanish government" and argues that Borde "was moved...by the noblest motive. I cannot but recognise in him a true patriot" ("A Review," April 14). Paul also made some corrections to Borde's work. Yet, he reserved his strongest critique for Borde's condemnation of Don Maria Chacon, the last Spanish governor, who capitulated the island to the English:

> I cannot but protest against the unjust and very severe censure passed by Mr. Borde on Don Joseph Chacon, who, during the last four years of his government was a victim of the negligence and stupidity of a man who then sat on the throne of Spain: several documents might be produced to prove that, on different occasions, our excellent Governor and other Spanish authorities in South America had brought prominently before the King the perilous situation of the Colony, and the impossibility of resisting a well-combined attack....We are told by Mr. Borde that a larger number of men might have been enlisted [to face the English]; but there was no time to lose; the enemy was marching at rapid strides towards the capital, and Chacon was compelled to choose between the two horns of a dilemma: either make

72. Ibid.

73. Simon Schama describes the form of politeness that Sir Robert Walpole introduced as "not just in the modern sense of good manners (although that was not unimportant), but rather a civilized self-restraint. The polite man, unlike the passionate man, wanted to strengthen the social bonds between men rather than sunder them; to give society an appreciation of the interdependence of its parts rather than the inevitability of its conflicts and incompatibilities." Such behaviour was surely desirable when Borde and Paul wrote; a period of national self-recognition. See Simon Schama, *A History of Britain* (London: BBC, 2001), p. 352.

74. Paul's review appeared in three issues of the *Trinidad Chronicle*, April 14, 18, and 21, 1883.

75. "A Review," *Trinidad Chronicle*, April 14, 1883.

a desperate, ineffectual resistance; or, by surrendering to a stronger enemy, to save the town from destruction. He wisely adopted the latter course, and, for having done so, deserved well of mankind. His administration, besides, was, the golden age of Trinidad: 'his ears,' says the learned writer of *Free Mulatto* 'was open to every complaint, his arm extended to the support of every feeble petitioner.' He long since has mouldered in the dust; but if the fervent prayers of a grateful people can, naught avail the soil lies gentle on him ("A Review," April 21, 1883).

Undoubtedly, Paul's Hispanic origins shaped his evaluation of Chacon and, subsequently, Borde's work. That the unnamed English reviewers, Rojas, and Paul were careful, circumspect, and laudatory showed that Borde's work was judged an international success. That Paul compared Borde's achievement (certainly his writing) to those of Thiers, Michelet, and Addison demonstrates that the society's literary culture had begun to take shape as men of erudition conducted a public debate about the meaning of Trinidad's story in its larger international context. That Thomas took the time to translate *History of Spanish Trinidad* into English so as to make it available to English readers in Trinidad and abroad supports the idea that the work had an important impact on Trinidad's consciousness. It also spoke to the tremendous work that Thomas was rendering to the intellectual culture of the society.

It is to the *New Era* that we must turn to get a complete sense of the international implications of *History of Spanish Trinidad* and the breath of Borde's undertaking:

> Of our native Island, the people who inhabited it at first, the part which it played in the great drama of Spain's transatlantic discoveries and conquests, even the best informed of us knew heretofore but little, and that little only in a vague, unsatisfactory manner. The works of Robertson, Caulin, de Lorgues, Raleigh, Joseph and others cited by Mr. Borde, are either absolutely out of the range of ordinary Creole reading, or—from the brief and casual nature of their reference to Trinidad in their details of events we have mentioned—of but little value, taken singly, for imparting a clear and consecutive knowledge of what may be called, the ancient history of the Island. The fact, then, that Mr. Borde has been the first to collect and arrange in scientific order the items of information bearing on our earliest history, and which heretofore could be obtained only by laborious gleanings throughout the whole literature of the conquest of the New World is of itself no trivial distinction. But when to the praise of industry in collecting the materials, are added the commendations due to his other no less conspicuous merits, it is clear that the claims of Mr. Borde to a foremost place among the celebrities of his country, are both unquestionable and great."[76]

In one fell swoop, Borde had placed the history of Trinidad in an international perspective. Those who came after him would have to contend with his accomplishments.

---

76. *New Era*, October 23, 1880.

Metageographies and Travel Writing

During the same period in which Borde was producing his history, the travel narrative or *récit de voyage* was also assuming an important part in the *belle lettres* of the island. Not merely first-person accounts of travellers' journeys throughout the island, these metageographies, "sets of spatial structures, through which people order their knowledge of their world,"[77] allowed inhabitants (and those visiting the island) another means of encountering and knowing the Trinidad world. Within the spirit of this new enterprise, the editor of *Fair Play and Trinidad News* visited various parts of the island and, in several editorials, reported what he saw.

These accounts, in many instances as thrilling as fiction, were located in a tradition that went back to Europe's original encounter with the New World, particularly as established by the travels of Sir Walter Raleigh (fictionalised so brilliantly in V. S. Naipaul's *The Loss of El Dorado)* and the exploits of Humboldt. Peter Adams writes that "it was the new lands opened up by the sailing ships of old lands made more accessible that produced, and still produced, most of the world's travel literature."[78]

In the Trinidadian context, the newspaper took great pleasure in publishing accounts of the island's geography that appeared in international newspapers, and as the decade wore on, they encouraged the writing of narratives that described the island. These accounts allowed the members of the society a better understanding of themselves even as the travellers got a better understanding of the commercial possibilities of the island.[79] Thomas William Carr, author of "Notes of a Voyage Round the Island of Trinidad in October 1868," averred that he intended to present his findings to the Trinidad Scientific Society, an organization that was set up to explore and to examine the natural science of the island. As he travelled around the island, Carr collected many botanical specimens, the importance of which he discussed with the scientific society. Apart from opening up the land and giving us a better understanding of our geographic space, these *récit de voyage* allowed us to see other aspects of the European encounter with the local underclass and their attitudes towards them. It also demonstrated the knowledge that the local people had about their natural environment.

One of the first travel sketches published in 1870 was chapter ten of Grenville John Chester's *Transatlantic Sketches in the West Indies, South America, Canada and the*

77. Quoted in Kaur and Hutnyk, *Travel Worlds*, p. 32.

78. Percy G. Adams, *Travel Literature and the Evolution of the Novel* (Lexington: University of Kentucky Press, 1983), p. 50

79. The traveller is neither innocent nor curious. His activities have much to do with exploring the commercial possibilities of the island that was part of the rationale for the establishment of the Trinidad Botanical Gardens. In fact, the Trinidad Botanical Garden maintained a valuable scientific link to Kew Gardens, London. In 1886, as *Grenada People* reported, the Garden pays "for itself and has an annual surplus" (May 19, 1886). It must be remembered that this was a time, the aftermath of the age of Darwin, when an examination of the flora of the tropics, played an especially important part in an understanding of the natural history of the world. An extended examination of this phenomenon, however, is outside the scope of this study.

United States (1869) that was republished in the *Trinidad Chronicle* on July 29, 1870. A member of the Royal Archaeological Institute of Great Britain and Ireland, Chester liked the island.: "{I} could grow *fond* of Trinidad, a sensation I have never felt anywhere else in the West Indies, which, to be enjoyed, ought to be seen before, and not after the glorious classic shores of the Mediterranean."[80] However, his description was more impressionistic than detailed.

Carr's "Notes" gave a more detailed and intimate look at the island and offered a more scientific study of its flora. A Trinidadian, Carr also participated in the scientific work that was being done by Lockhard, Sieber, Purdie, Crueger (all associated with the Botanical Gardens and Trinidad Scientific Society), and Grisebach, author of *Flora of the British West Indian Islands*. Carr's sketch was published in the *Trinidad Chronicle* on April 28 and May 5, 1871. He began his journey in the Bocas Islands and took his readers on a tour around the island as he described the places he saw and the botanical species he discovered. Apart from describing the landscape, he also sought to name the island properly, a constant preoccupation of these early Trinidadians.[81] Enamoured by various place names of the island and their origins, he writes:

> Chaguramas is the aboriginal and Spanish name of our queenly Palmiste or Cabbage tree, the *Oreodoxa oleracea Mart.* It may be noted here that Carenage is only a modern misnomer as applied to the large valley now known by this name; even the large and very shallow bay in front of its mouth, popularly called the Carenage, is no Carenage at all, and could not be. The true Carenage or Carenero was one of the wedge-shaped inlets of Point Gourde peninsula on the south side of the so-called Carenage or Carenage Bay. The old and proper name of the valley is Cuesa, after the palm of that name, described as a species of *Bactris* (having long black spines and a comparatively thin stem). Nor is Point Gourde named, as popularly believed, after the sunken dollars of Apodaca's squadron, but is a corruption of Punta Gorda, the big or broad Point, which describes it very appropriately, as any one who has helped to pull a boat round the long gloomy promontory will acknowledge.[82]

80. See Grenville John Chester, *Transatlantic Sketches in the West Indies, South America, Canada and the United States* (London: Smith, Elder, 1869), p. 135–41.

81. This attempt to name the place properly became a passion of the early inhabitants. For example, in a discussion of the inspector of schools' report of 1875, the editors of the *Trinidad Chronicle* were very angry at Guppy for spelling San Juan, San Fernando, and Corbeau Town incorrectly: "By what right does the Inspector of Schools take upon himself to change names of certain places? Why does he write 'Sanfernando' and 'Sanjuan' for San Fernando and San Juan? The names give by the old Spanish Colonists have a sense and a meaning, but as he has travestied then....We notice also that he has adopted the absurd suggestion that the Western suburb of Port of Spain was originally named Coburg Town. We are sorry to have to disappoint the gushing loyalty which doubtless promoted the desire to establish this nomenclature; but the tradition of the oldest inhabitants as well as official documents dating from the earliest years of this century, proved beyond a doubt that the name 'Corbeau Town' was given to that district from the fact that in consequence of slaughterys have always existed there, it was the favourite resort of the useful but unsavoury birds who have given it their name" (September 21, 1878).

82. Thomas William Carr, "Notes of a Voyage Round the Island of Trinidad in October 1868," *Trinidad Chronicle*, April 28, 1871; hereafter "Notes."

Carr also took a certain pleasure in his naming skills. His sketch reveals how other parts of the island were named. Maraval in the old Spanish time was named after Mararaval, which in turn was named after a palm tree, the Mararave, meaning the place of the Maravaves; Morichal came from Moriche, the Mauritia palm. As Carr reflects on the expressiveness of these names, he conclude a that "[t]hese aggregative words are so economical, expressive and convenient, that they should not be allowed to fall into disuse, and might even be usefully imported into the English language, with power of extension" ("Notes," April 28). Carr also compliments the skills of the local woodsmen who lived in intimate connection with the forest: "When he [the woodsman] speaks it is with deliberation, and you may accept this fruit of his woodcraft in perfect faith; he may be very simple and ignorant in matters beyond the range of his observation, but of the forest and its organisms, animate or inanimate, he knows more, and a good deal too, than you and I, good urban reader, who knows it but by book or an infrequent ramble in the still shade of its magnificent arcades" ("Notes," May 5).

"The Great Oropouche Lagoon" was another subject of the traveller's pen. One "J," presumably a visitor to the island, describes his rapture when he encountered the lagoon, even though he was not too kind to the birds that lived there: "Here, for the fist time of my life I witnessed the beauties of the tropics: the pink flamingo and white heron perched on their tall legs, were fishing for their breakfast with that careless ease peculiar to aquatic birds; but on seeing us they stretched out their necks and suddenly flew away with cries of alarm; but we were equal to the occasion, and, all at once, six well-directed shots brought down an equal number of our red-coated friends. The white-feathered gentry escaped our fire."

One is not too sure of J's reading of Africans, his relationship to them, or how he regarded the friendship they offered him. He certainly has views on Africans, particularly with regard to their relationship to Christianity. On the other hand, his observation about the heathenism of the Indians takes us back to the articulation of the missionary discourse we encounter frequently in the writings from this period:

We were carefully scrutinised by the inhabitants of this "tight little island"—uneducated Negroes are quickly scared by white faces, particularly bearded ones (we had but one bare-faced fellow in our party) but we shewed the "true-hand of fellowship" to the good man "Jimbo" and his laughing "Sally" who, after all, greeted us cheerily. We drank to their health in bumpers of the sweet milk of the Coconut—a real nectar to the wary and worn excursionist—and parted with our sable friends with their expressions and gesticulations of much love to our party. We gave them *pin money,* for which, bless me, how thankful they were....So much for the good graces and comely manners of the poor Africans; but, we have neglected to administer to their physical and moral wants since the abolition of Slavery, and alas! They are dying rapidly. I regard the black race, in every conceivable form, to be a better description of people for the permanent colonisation of a country than the Indians from Calcutta and Madras, and strange as this may appear to a great many men in this island, I advance as a reason, and a very reliable one too—that the Africans are easily converted to the pure principles of Christianity, and are consequently very superior to the heathens we have amongst us now—imperilling the spread of Christian brotherhood, as well as fostering by their miserable habits the cursed customs of heathen worship; and this, too, permitted by a Christian government, seems rather inconsistent.[83]

On April 28, 1875, "determined to know the country, and to see with his own eyes," Governor Irving left Government House to explore the wonders of Caroni, Arima, Tumpuna, Valencia, and the Chacharo Cave in the Cabaceras of Oropouche. Although he did not write about his travels, Irving's exploration of the land and his meeting with the "ordinary" inhabitants revealed to him their evolving psyche and gave him a better feel for the geography of the island. At Caroni, the governor met with the Indians to whom he "listened patiently." Next, he went to Arima, where "the merry peals of the church bells announced his arrival, and the loyalty of the people loudly manifested itself in the discharge of guns and even of a diminutive cannon belonging we believe to the Indians."[84] The next day, His Excellency, "accompanied by their Spanish porters and guides, all furnished with long sticks, hooks and *'pabilos'* (torches made of rags dipped in molten native wax)," visited Guanapo Cave. Located in the Heights of Guanapo, a steep-sided valley on the south side of the Northern Range, the cave is easily accessible and is usually occupied by bats, the most common of which is *Carollia p. perspicillata*, a small fruit-eating bat.[85] The *Trinidad Chronicle* gives what might well be the first description of this part of the country:

Here, an exploration of these curious caverns was begun, by lantern and torch-light, and completed by the burning of blue lights and magnesium wire, which had a really grand effect and brought out in bold relief the weird and fantastic forms of the numberless stalactites pendant from the domed roof and rugged sides of the caves. In two instances stalactites and stalagmites have met, and formed a couple of columns, which have the appearance of supporting the dome.

A few "unfeathered" young *Guacharos* or "*diablotins* (the *Steatorius caripensis* of Humboldt, perfect lumps of fat) were taken from their nests, among the deafening screeching of their frightened parents, who flew madly in all directions, evidently in the wildest state of excitement. One of them was caught alive.

The party, wading through the river nearly up to their waist, went to the extreme end of the Caves, through which the spring of the Oropouche river forces itself with a gurgling sound and a pretty strong current. The water is there deliciously cool and light....

We believe His Excellency is the first Governor of Trinidad who has visited those Guacharo caverns.

83. "The Great Oropouche Lagoon," *Trinidad Chronicle*, September 12, 1871.

84. *Trinidad Chronicle*, May 11, 1875.

85. Johanna P. E. Darlington, "Guanapo Cave," *Living World: Journal of the Trinidad and Tobago Field Naturalists' Club* (July 1996), p. 15.

After three exhausting days, the governor returned to his mansion.

The newspapers' editors also visited the country and reported their findings. On occasion, a newspaper omitted its editorial while the editor was off visiting the country districts. The editor of *Fair Play* took a leading role in such explorations. In April 1878, he and his party set out on one of their "periodical trips to San Fernando." Since travelling between those Port of Spain and the other town was done by sea, they left in the steamer *Albert* which made stops at Couva and Claxton Bay. When they arrived at San Fernando, several lighter boats took them to the shore. In his report, the editor offers a magnificent view of San Fernando: "The sea that we were traversing was evidently swarming with fish, as the air and sea were alive with pelicans plunging into the sea to seize their funny food and with frigate pelicans who on their sharply finely-cut wide wings now rose, now sank, then made short graceful curves, or swiftly sped from one point of sight to the other, until at last, suddenly and skilfully skimming the surface of the sea, they bore off their unfortunate prey high up into the air. Whilst the ordinary pelican plunges into the sea to feed, it is different with the frigate pelican, for if one tip of its six feet long wings were to touch the water it would no more rise from the sea and would become the prey of those inhabitants of the ocean which are its daily food."[86]

Six weeks later, the *Fair Play* editor made another trip to the south of the island, this time to Mission Village, a villages that was populated by African Americans who had fought on the side of the British in the 1812 and who were settled in Trinidad as a reward for their services. Enjoying new prosperity because of its proximity to San Fernando and the laying down of the railway lines, Mission Village had become the third most important town in the Colony. Because of its financial prosperity, the editor took great pains to describe the physical geography of the town, concluding:

> The erectors of the various Churches and schools seem to have been alive to the growing importance of the place, as they have given them proportions which will meet its requirements for many years to come, although new houses, some of them large and handsome, are being steadily erected. The population of the Village is not very large in itself, perhaps it may not exceed a thousand people; but it is the centre of a large number of thriving sugar-estates which are the sources of its prosperity, as they give employment to some 4,000 souls. San Fernando and even Port of Spain get a good deal of their food supply from the Mission in the shape of salted *Lap*, poultry and eggs. The future extension and importance of this Village mainly rests upon the thousands of acres of fertile uncultivated lands lying away to the eastward of it. The extension of the Railway in its direction will help powerfully to stimulate its progress.
>
> The situation of the Mission Village, on a table land of varying breadth formed by the junction of several hill ridges, is most dry, cool and healthy. It commands, also, magnificent views towards the North and West, of the fine-rolling country

86. *Fair Play and Trinidad News,* April 9, 1878.

bounded in the distance by that conspicuous object, the San Fernando Hill, and by the hills of Montserrat. Towards the South another noble basin of rich, undulating, picturesque land stretches away over South Naparima and towards Oropouche.[87]

None could mistake the beauty and richness of this land. It only awaited the energies of a free population to make it revel in its prosperity.

In getting to know the island and trying to maximize its potential, it was necessary to have an accurate sense of distance from one place to another. That the country was busily undertaking surveys to open the island to trade via the insertion of a railway demanded that there be a more reliable way to measure the possibilities of the land. Mallette's map, the first map commissioned when the English arrived in 1797, turned out to be inaccurate, and the island needed to be remapped. The editors of the *Trinidad Chronicle* claimed that Mallette's map "exaggerat[ed] the area of the island, stated by him as 2,400 square miles. Mallet relied also, to some unknown extent, on Spanish maps or charts, as proved, we think, by the expression (applied to S. E. hills) 'Mountains of the South, in accessible, covered with incorruptible woods,' as well as the word 'Breakers,' frequently repeated in the Gulf and off the North coasts, a mistranslation of the Spanish word 'brasso' signifying fathoms. How much of the so-called original map is really Mallett's work, is probably not known."[88] Subsequent maps, the editors of the *Trinidad Chronicle* argued, inculcated many of "Mallet's false scales and many of his errors and guesses have been copied into subsequent maps."

At the end of the 1870s, remapping Trinidad was important as the society sought a better understanding of its geographic space. Naming the land and measuring its spaces also became important preoccupations of the 1870s and thereafter. As a result, at the end of the decade, the editors of *New Era* called for the introduction of geography at all schools. To those in control, getting to know their land and flexing their muscles in their space were important signs of possessing their land more fully. Such imperatives would have tremendous (and in some cases violent) ramifications as the society developed. For the writers, it allowed for new areas of expression and exploration. For others, it represented an important phase of the society's development and a conscious desire to make the island more habitable.

87. *Fair Play and Trinidad News,* May 21, 1878.
88. *Trinidad Chronicle,* April 2, 1879.

CHAPTER 11

Cultural Self-Assertion:
Savagery Versus Civilization

I do not believe in the divine rights of kings, but I do believe...in a divine right of a great civilising people—that is their divine mission.

—H. Rider Haggard quoted in Wendy R. Katz,
Rider Haggard and the Fiction of Empire

Can't beat me drum
In my own, own native land
Can't have we Carnival
In my own, my native land
Can't have we Bacchanal
In my own, my native land.

In my own native land,
Moen pasca dancer, comme moen viel
(I cannot dance as I wish).

—Quoted in Bridget Brereton, *Race Relations
in Colonial Trinidad, 1870–1900*

All me cheren born hyar
  All ah dem married hyar
All a dem de same place
  I plantam rice
Plantam damadole
  Plantam ochro
Orking de estate
  Minam de cow
Rentam land

Some fella gwine before de five year
  India
Some fellar working ten year
  Gwine India.

—Noor Kumar Mahabir, *The Still Cry*

The 1880s, part of the age of Empire, was a time when imperialist ideology dominated the Anglo-Saxon world of which the Caribbean was a part. It was a time when Joseph Chamberlain (1836–1914), secretary of state for the colonies, could say that "the Anglo-Saxon race is infallibly destined to be the predominant force in history and civilization of the world,"[1] and Leonard Hobhouse (1864–1929), a sociologist and philosopher who taught at the Universities of Oxford and London, could assert that "[t]he white man is the stronger, and to the strong are the earth and the fruits thereof. If the black man owns land and lives on its produce, he is an idler. His 'manifest destiny' is to assist in the development of gold mines for the benefit of humanity in general and the shareholders in particular."[2] It is no wonder then that the 1880s was also a time in which the romance of the noble savage found an honorable place in British literature and was a time when works such as H. H. Henty's *By Sheer Pluck: A Tale of the Ashanti War* (1883) and H. Rider Haggard's *King Solomon's Mines* (1885) busily promulgated an ideology of empire. These stories, "based upon an unquestioning assumption of British superiority over all foreigners, especially [Indian and African] natives," reflect Britain's dominance in the world.[3] Wendy Katz has observed that Haggard "was an ideological presence, part of his period's popular culture; and he contributed to a certain state of mind. He assisted in the propagation of imperial ideas and created for Britain an image of greatness and superiority, an image of the world with the British in control."[4]

This robust impulse by the colonial elite to colonize the world, particularly India and Africa, was shared by the dominant white group in Trinidad. In 1880, a correspondent for the *Trinidad Palladium* referred to the inhabitants in the "lowest strata" as "specimens of…human animals" who "habitually lead lives of vice allied to barbarism….They are ignorant of civilised life, but cunning enough in their way, and, of course, have never been to school, and perhaps cannot read the alphabet."[5] Such comments led Bridget Brereton to conclude that a "wide cultural gap separated Afro-Creole elements from middle- and upper-class Trinidadian society….They felt that civilisation was fighting against barbarism, and that the victory of civilisation could be achieved only by controlling or eliminating debasing and primitive influences."[6] Robert Young observed that from the 1860s onwards, the need to differentiate between the civilized and the savage (that is, the barbarian) became an absolute imperative as imperialism and the notion of the 'civilizing mission' assumed "a basic differentiation between white and non-white races, and this was

1. Quoted in Wendy R. Katz, *Rider Haggard and the Fiction of Empire* (New York: Cambridge University Press, 1987), p. 28.

2. L. T. Hobhouse, *Democracy and Reaction* (London: T. Fisher Unwin, 1904), p. 61–62.

3. Dennis Butts, "Introduction," in H. Rider Haggard, *King Solomon's Mines* (Oxford: Oxford University Press, 1989), p. xi.

4. Katz., *Rider Haggard and the Fiction of Empire*, p. 4.

5. "The Moral and Religious Condition of Trinidad," *Trinidad Palladium*, September 4, 1880.

6. Bridget Brereton, *Race Relations in Colonial Trinidad, 1870–1900* (Cambridge: Cambridge University Press, 1979), p. 153.

made in increasingly absolute and derogatory terms, signalled by the increasing use of the term 'nigger' for any non-European colonial subject."[7] V. S. Naipaul might have said of the lower stratum, they were just seeking to make their way in the world.

This attitude of superiority (that is, the possession of so-called civilized behavior) among the dominant class, already apparent in the 1870s, took on greater urgency in the 1880s, no doubt because of the growing cohesion of Indians and Africans and their desire to express their dark-skinned selves. As Africans and Indians began to assert themselves culturally, cries of their savage practices became more strident as officialdom became more determined to wipe out or to control these unwanted—at least in ruling circles—expressions. What had begun as purely cultural-religious expressions took on a political (nationalist) thrust that shaped much of the debate that took place in the 1880s and that led to the Reform Movement that agitated for greater political autonomy and to the protest by Indians against the Immigration Ordinance.[8]

Yet, the louder colonial subjects shouted for their freedom, the more determined colonial authorities became to stamp out cultural practices of the "lowest strata." To tolerate such practices was to show weakness that could lead to a crack in the colonialist resolve designed to keep the natives in their place. In 1896, W. D. Ellis, an official in the Colonial Office, reiterated the imperial mandate:

> We go too far in our toleration of the customs of the natives. The raison d'être of the empire is to raise the subject races to a higher level of civilization. I am afraid that this principle has not been carried out very well in the West Indies. There has, I think, been rather a tendency to regard that part at least of the empire as a joint-stock company where dividends might be decreased if any attempt was made to "impose" Western ideas on negroes and Indians.[9]

This is how those persons conducting the business of Empire thought about "the natives." At the end of the decade, therefore, when James Anthony Froude pronounced his ideological findings after his visit to the West Indies, he was merely repeating what those in control thought about the natives in the first place. One critic writes that he was in "a constant struggle to define himself in his own and in other's eyes as a capable historian and intellectual....When we place his letters to his family and friends during this trip the eventually-published text of *The English in the West Indies* a fuller picture emerges of someone who was anxious about his reputation and prestige."[10] On the other hand, Thomas's response to Froude repre-

---

7. Robert J. C. Young, *Postcolonialism: An Historical Introduction* [Oxford: Blackwell, 2001], p. 33).

8. See chapter 8 of Brereton's *Race Relations in Colonial Trinidad* for a detailed examination of the cultural aspect of this period.

9. Quoted in H. B. D. Johnson, "Crown Colony Government in Trinidad, 1870–1897," D. Phil, Dissertation, Oxford University, 1969, p. 304.

10. Smith, *John Jacob Thomas*, p. 108.

sented a culmination of a debate begun in the 1870s and was part of the quest of a people to define themselves.

In retrospect, it must be appreciated that Africans and Indians engaged in democratic practices and participatory governance independent of what the dominant class thought or wanted. Brereton writes that the Afro-Christian cults "were democratically organised, they offered leadership positions to working-class blacks, opportunities not usually available in the orthodox churches. They represented a democratic thrust, a desire for social equality, a protest against the Establishment and the European churches with their white priests or ministers."[11] The same was true for the Indians who brought from India the concept of the self-governing village system in which was embedded the *panchayat,* a tribunal of some five people who adjudicated in village disputes.[12] In these panchayats, one finds an articulation of a democratic consensus that allowed the group to carry forward a democratic project in a foreign land.[13] Not only were these alternative forms of social organization, they were also another way of apprehending the world. In *Nations and Nationalism since 1780,* E. J. Hobsbawn asserts that, although the concept of nations did not exist prior to the 1870s, "after 1880 it increasingly did matter how ordinary common men and women felt about nationality. It is therefore important to consider the feelings and attitudes among pre-industrial people of this kind, on which the novel appeal of political nationalism could build."[14]

Although Hobsbawn was talking about Europeans, such an observation had much pertinence to the colonial subject. The confidence of the latter in their self-autonomy led them to believe that they had a right to "dance their native dance" wherever they found themselves. As they agitated for their freedom in a new land, they were not prepared to accept the notion that theirs was an inferior culture or that Europeans could teach them much about themselves, civilization, or the process of democracy. This attitude of self-confidence was summarized best in a calypso of the period when the colonial authorities banned the dancing of the calinda:

> Can't beat me drum
> In my own, own native land
> Can't have we Carnival
> In my own, my native land
> Can't have we Bacchanal
> In my own, my native land.

11. Brereton, *Race Relations in Trinidad,* p. 159.

12. J. C. Jha, "Indian Heritage in Trinidad," *Research Papers: Indentured Indians in Trinidad and Tobago, 1845–1917,* St. Augustine, Trinidad, 1985, p. 9. Jha adds that "in the late nineteenth century some features of rural leadership which existed in North India could be seen in Trinidad Indian villages: pundits, money lenders and landholders having a say in the important matters of the community" (Ibid.).

13. J. C. Jha offers an interesting discussion on the formation of "the national panchayat" in 1899. See "East Indian Pressure Groups in Trinidad, 1897–1921," in *Research Papers, 1985.*

14. E. J. Hobsbawm, *Nations and Nationalism since 1780* (Cambridge: Cambridge University Press, 1990), p. 45.

In my own native land,
Moen pasca dancer, comme moen viel
(I cannot dance as I wish)[15]

Savagery and Civilization

A central issue that shaped the discourse of the 1880s was the ideological position that branded the colonized as savages and portrayed their religion and culture as inferior to that of the Europeans. By contrasting the civilization, and by extension the civilized behavior of the Europeans, to that of native peoples, the former hoped to prove that the Christainization was the only way to redeem the natives from their savagery. In other words, the colonizers had to practice what Paulin J. Hountondji calls "a double problematic." While they tried to "civilize" the native or the primitive (that is, to obtain "practical mastery...over the black man's psychological wellsprings"), they also had to hold out the possibility of the presence of "the fine spirituality of the primitive" to justify their dehumanizing practices. Hountondji puts it this way: "The colonizers 'civilize,' but only on condition that they rehumanize themselves and recover their soul."[16]

To achieve their end, the colonizers banned and labeled as savage and heathenistic all cultural practices that manifested any salutary aspect of native agency. Using their ideological apparatus (for example, the church, school, and civil service), they defined what they termed "civilization" and then applied the definition to negate the actions of the colonized population. For example, on April 24, 1880, the editors of the *Trinidad Palladium,* a defender of the status quo, spoke of civilization as "a large word and though its meaning is immutable, this meaning gains potency as the world advances in what the term denotes: Education, Knowledge, and Refinement. Formerly the term was used to denote a person 'reclaimed from savageness and brutality.'" Such a definition was used to brand Indians and Africans as savages and to show them as being deficient in education, knowledge, and refinement and to brand them as people who had to be reclaimed from their savageness and brutality. Interesting enough, this definition contained all of the notions of civilization and savagery that writers such as Haggard and Henty had articulated. Although Indians were said to possess knowledge, such knowledge "includes artifice, dissimulation, and often falsehood as a consequence....They have not the knowledge which brings other blessings in its train, amongst which is the refinement and yet they are refined to be a polite people in the ordinary sense of greeting

15. Quoted in Brereton, *Race Relations in Trinidad,* p. 162.
16. Paulin J. Hountondji, *African Philosophy: Myth and Reality,* 2nd edition. Trans. By Henri Evans (Bloomington: Indiana University Press, 1996), p. 49. While Hountondji's context is Placide Tempels, *Bantu Philosophy,* the concept is applicable to the relentless drive on the part of the Europeans to redeem themselves by Christianizing the primitive (in this case, the Africans and the East Indians), a position they can assume by believing "the primitive" is different and the "other." As Hountondji points out "[t]he primitive is still... the 'absolute other' of the 'civilized' man. His otherness is simply redefined." (p. 80).

which some often manifest even to obsequiousness." To be sure, Indians were not
to be blamed entirely, for their shortcomings had more to do with the land from
which they came."

> Our Oriental labourers do not come to us from Colonies where the Parent hand of
> civilization has been working for centuries, and some there are who are of [the]
> opinion that we have no authority to denominate our East Indian immigrants as,
> strictly speaking, heathen, for they betray external signs of something which looks
> like the fragments of an ancient grandeur, and exist to testify that something nec-
> essary and vital has been lost, and that the vessel which bears the fragments of an
> antiquated civilization is only shattered and requires the kind hand of an infinitely
> wise and benevolent nature to revive and restore it to what it probably once was in
> centuries past and gone, and to what it may yet attain if Christianity alone could
> but enlighten the mind, and touch and melt the feelings, purify the heart, and rec-
> tify the will, and thus implant graces which would fructify and adorn human nature
> however rugged and torn its exterior may be in many instances.

After contrasting the Indian's idyllic condition with that of the Africans ("naked
savages captured and sometimes purchased for a few beads, knives, or similar trifles,
and transported to the West Indies in sailing ships in which they were so closely
packed that many of the unfortunate wretches perished and became food for sharks
ere they reached their place of destination"), the editor asks, "How then is the
Civilization, we all commend and admire, to be promoted in regard to our Asiatic
labourers?" The answer: civilize them through schooling and Christianization. The
writer continues: "Every Estate should contribute to the necessary and important
task of christianising, and thus civilising, our Asisatic labourers and their beautiful
and interesting children." From this source, all other blessings will flow. Wife mur-
ders, the chief charge against Indians—and presumably an indicator of their heathenism—will diminish and all shall be refined, happy to join the angelic train.

If the editor of the *Trinidad Palladium* was severe on the Indians, the editor of
Fair Play and Trinidad News was even more severe on the Africans.[17] Without beating around the bush, he declared what, to him, amounted to a self-evident truth:

> It is an acknowledged fact that the animal organs of the African race are far more
> developed than their intellectual ones and that this constitutes one of the greatest
> barriers against their moral and social elevation. Of course among the teeming
> black races which people Africa you find quite as wide a range of character as is to
> be found in Europe, and we have had and have in the West Indies men and women
> of pure African blood with an intellectual and moral development comparatively
> equal to that of any European. But this does not affect the general truth of the

---

17. One has to be careful to whom one attributes these views since an editor might absolve himself
from blame by claiming that "the articles which appear in these columns are not necessarily from the pen
of the Editor." However, since these pieces came from members of the dominant class, one can be sure
that the views contained within reflected those of the class.

proposition with which we started, that the great majority of the black races are more contracted in their views and aspirations, low in their desires and animal in their propensities than Europeans and other civilized races.

Needless to say, many of the ascription of animal qualities to the African race (what they claim to be "an acknowledged fact") stemmed from the new field of anthropology, whose theories were being used to buttress Europeans' claim about African inferiority. Such a coincidence led Abiola Irele to observe that "it was no accident that it was precisely the period of greatest European colonial expansion that saw the development of anthropology as a constituted discipline devoted exclusively to the study of non-Western peoples, to whom were attached the labels 'savage', 'inferior', 'primitive' as qualifications to their full participation in a human essence."[18] Necessarily, the conclusions of the colonizers in Trinidad were in sync with those of their counterparts abroad.

Thus, if "insane jealousy" led to the "moral degradation" of the East Indians, it is the "unbridled immorality of the intercourse of the sexes amongst the West Indian negroes" that is the greatest impediment to their social and moral elevation in the society. Here, the author is careful to make the connection between the African's cultural practices and the participation of the latter in his own degradation. In this context, the drum evoked the most hostility from Europeans. The author claims that "Drum Dances was one of their social customs which most help to foster this licentious characteristic of their normal condition," even though the calinda and the Bongo were danced by men and the Belair by women. Like the drum dances, the "beastly carnival" represented "a blot on our civilization;" the masqueraders, "a disgrace to civilization."[19] It seems that everything associated with the African testified to his savagery and brutality.

Contrawise, at the beginning of the 1880s, some people were prepared to see the Carnival as having "metamorphosed into 'innocent amusement.'" Actus, a correspondent for the *Trinidad Chronicle,* placed Carnival in its larger, civilizational context:

> The carnival, a national fete ingrained into the nature of our people, regarded as one of their dearest enjoyments, for which they will spend their last halfpenny, that fete sanctioned by law and held sacred by long custom and transmission to them by their forefathers; as much so as the carnivals of continental Catholic Europe are to their peoples—as the turf, the theatre, and the ball-room are to English aristocrats &c., as the May-day festivities in England are to the English rustics, as the torchlight processions of Europeans and American citizens are to their peoples—and Her Majesty the Queen's birthday is to her loyal subjects.

After he condemns the brutality against the masqueraders, Actus argues that, if the colonial masters wished to "advance the civilization of our people" and to raise them

18. Hountondji, *African Philosophy,*" p. 12.
19. "A Lover of Justice," *Trinidad Chronicle,* March 16, 1881.

from "antiquated or obscure customs," they ought to proceed slowly and by recognizing the value of this group's cultural habits or customs. To achieve their aim, they had to trust to time, education, and example.[20] However, simply calling people savages because their customs differed from those of one's own and the using brute force to crush and obliterate such distinctions are not the most efficient ways to demonstrate the superiority of "civilization." As years went by and members of the "lowest strata" of the society began to make political demands on the system, conceptions of what constituted savagery and civilization began to change.

The Calypso

By 1880s, the calypso had assumed a permanent place in the society. Attila the Hun (1892–1962), an early Trinidadian calypsonian, notes that the calypso, "a particular form of folksong undeniably African in origin,…was brought by African slaves to the West Indies. Conditioned historically by its new environment and by French acculturation, the kaiso developed most distinctively in Trinidad into a form of mass art in song and dance uniquely or typically West Indian." In his estimation, the calypso takes two forms: the single and double tone. The lyrical style of the first "is epigrammatic and has been the ideal dress for the 'picong' kaiso in which spontaneous wit, humor, scorn and ridicule of men and matters may together or alternately be employed. The style of the double tone calypso is rhetorical and it has become the versatile vehicle for a coherent, programmatic presentation of ideas on a limitless range of subjects and themes, local, foreign and international." The calypso, he adds, is distinguished by its "basic African rhythm," a derivation from "African folk songs and their progeny in the West Indies such as the bongo, kalenda, shango, belair, and worksong, in all of which the African drum (and later the *tambour bamboo*) provided the accompaniment."[21]

Brought to Trinidad in the seventeenth century, "the earliest forms of calypso were transmitted orally from generation to generation by the descendants of the slaves." Rendered in an African language, the calypso was sung at religious ceremonies, harvest festivals, and displays of martial arts. One of the earliest calypsoes, "Ja Ja Romey Eh/ Ja Ja Romey Shango," was sung at the calinda or stickfights, an African martial art form, and was associated with the Shango. According to Atilla, this song was handed down and interpreted "wherever the ritualistic ceremonies of the Shango cult are practiced [as] 'I am coming to the dance of the Gods.'"[22] Atilla alerts us to the fact that one of the earliest calypsoes described the massacre of hundreds of Africans in Marabella in 1838.

Another interesting example of the power of the calypso in the period prior to the 1880s is revealed in a composition about the Africans' revenge on Bakeway, a racist colonial officer, who was very cruel to them. One evening Bakeway's two sons

20. "The Attack on the Canboulay Masquers," *Trinidad Chronicle*, March 2, 1881.

21. Ramond Quevedo, *Atilla's Kaiso: A Short History of Trinidad Calypso* (St. Augustine: Department of Extra Mural Studies, University of the West Indies, 1983), p. 2–3.

22. *Ibid.*, p. 6.

came home and did not find their father. As a result, they searched for him and finally found him in his office, tied to his chair and liberally daubed with tar from head to foot. Questioned by his sons, Bakeway replied, as related in song:

> Bakeway, what happen
> Who did this?
> Is two black man tar poppa
> I look like a negro
> But I am white my children
> Is two black man tar poppa
> Is two black man tar poppa.[23]

Given the fear of black people and the horror of being transformed into blackness, albeit temporarily, the Africans could not have humiliated Bakeway in a more devastating way. The joy of singing about such humiliation, perhaps behind his back, must have been their supreme triumph.

By the 1880s, the calypso was a common form of expression among the lower classes. Apart from hosay and Carnival, it provided another means of verbal-musical expression, another avenue to articulate their dark-skinned selves. The note of resistance that we hear in "Can't beat we drum/ In my own, own native land/ Can't have we Carnival/ In my own, my native land" reveals that the calypso as an art form had reached a level of verbal sophistication that allowed it to critique the foibles of society. Therefore, when the editor of *Fair Play*, in his enthusiasm, condemned the savage nature of the drum and those who performed for and with it, he demonstrated his own biases rather than the tenacity with which the Africans had retained his drum and his oral culture.[24] One literally had to read between the lines to understand where he was coming from when he wrote: "The state of civilisation of people whose members can be set in movement by the repetition of such barbarous sounds can be easily gauged, and yet, when heard from a distance, they seem to exercise an almost electric and magnetic influence upon the nervous system of the low class negro."

The drums, it seems, still maintained its hypnotic power over the Africans and remained an integral part of their lives. In spite of the author's obvious bias, he gave us an early description of the calypso tent, its link with the African drum, and the centrality of Yoruba culture in its proceedings when he writes:

> An open yard in some suburb of the town, sufficiently private for the proceedings not to be seen from the street but with no hindrance to the ingress and egress of visitors; a man in a dirty shirt and trousers, a bench and a drum; a few dirtily dressed women who serve as Chorus, mixed crowds of dirtily dressed men and women who dance to the sound of the drum independently of each other, and a

23. Ibid., p. 10.
24. *Fair Play*, March 1, 1883.

gaping crowd who are attracted to spot the noise. If it is not moonlight, a flickering flambeau to enlighten the scene—such is all that is required to constitute a drum dance! And what are the songs? Generally, a few foolish sentences composed by the leader of the Chorus to provoke some obnoxious persons or band, and the sickening repetition of a refrain which gives the greatest possible amount of exercise to the lungs compatible with the least possible disturbance of the brains. As for the dancing, it is nothing but the most disgusting obscenity pure and simple, being an imitation more or less vigorous and lustful by the male and female performers of the motions of the respective sexes whilst in the act of coition.

The connection that this author makes with the chorus, the lead singer, the drums, and the dance is significant; the African connection is also important. In *Negro Musicians and Their Music*, Maud Cuney-Hare discusses the link between dance and African social and ceremonial life.[25] She also adds that "[t]he songs of the Africans are chiefly a species of recitative or chant with a short chorus. The soloist gives the melody while a chorus sings a refrain, which at times are but ejaculations. The chief singer remains standing while the members of the chorus are seated around him; and as the melody is given out, they turn to one another, each improvising in turn. Their power of invention and improvisation may last for hours. Experts in adapting songs to current events, they indulge in mockery, ridicule and sarcasm, or in flattery or praise of men and happenings."[26]

Atilla uses Cuney-Hare's insight to connect calypso to its African origin and calls it "the forerunner of kaiso."[27] This connection is plausible since the calypso represents the literary dimension of traditional Yoruba culture from whence much of the Trinidad Carnival originated. Indeed, many of the characteristics of Carnival reflect aspects of the Gelede, one of the most important multidimensional art forms of the Yoruba-speaking peoples of Dahomey and Western Yorubaland, while the calypso itself is derived from Yoruba oral literature and culture. A.I. Asiwaju writes:

> [Gelede] production is a combination of Yoruba excellence in wood carving, painting, metal work, costume design, satire, poetry and music. The outfit of the Gelede dancer [the Moko Jumbies of Trinidad and Tobago], made up of beautifully painted woodcarving for the head, special clothes for the main body, and brass or iron jingles for the ankles, illustrate the co-operation that must exist between the carver, the painter, the tailor and the blacksmith. The actual performance takes with it not only the important auxiliaries of drumming and dancing but also the more basic talent of creativity in musical composition.[28]

25. See Maud Cuney-Hare, *Negro Musicians and their Music* (1936, New York: Da Capo, 1974), p. 13.
26. Ibid., p. 19.
27. Quevedo, *Atilla's Kaiso*, p. 5
28. A. I. Asiwaju, "Efe Poetry as a Source for Western Yoruba History," in Wande Abimbola, ed., *Yoruba Oral Tradition: Poetry in Music, Dance and Drama* (Ife-Ife, Nigeria: Department of African Languages and Literatures, University of Ife, 1975), p. 199.

In many ways, the Gelede singers resemble the calypsonian. Analogous to efe, the Gelede song-poems of the Yoruba-speaking people, the calypso falls within the verbal arts and inculcates aspects of poetry, satire, and musical composition. Usually sung and rendered by the Gelede artist, these song-poems are satirical in content, critique the actions of those in authority, and ridicule undesirable social behavior among members of the community. Although the Yorubas have other forms of musical composition, efe is "easily the best patronised and the most popular from of public entertainment among the people." Like the calypso, these efe song-poems perform a function similar to that of the press and radio in literate societies. Like the calypsonians, these song-poets "behave as spokesmen for the general public vis-à-vis policies pursued by persons in authority. Equally, they hold themselves as custodians of society's cultural values and accordingly pose as critics of factors and forces threatening existing standards."[29] Needless to say, this aspect of the art form was brought to the Caribbean by Yoruba-speaking peoples during slavery.

Another consideration that suggests a comparison between the calypsonian and the Gelede artists is the relative freedom, status, and authority the latter enjoys within the group. Asiwaju observes that the "efe poets, like most talented musical composers elsewhere, are generally of very humble origins. Their reflections are therefore often representative of the feelings of the masses of the people." The protection offered the efe singer (the original calypsonian) that allowed him to comment freely and openly on all aspects of community life, particularly political events, has much in common with a similar freedom the calypsonian enjoyed within his own community, but which he had to struggle to gain outside of the group. According to Asiwaju, this freedom was derived from two sources:

> The first is the Yoruba custom which ordinarily permits singers to say what they wish in their songs. The widespread character of this guarantee is attested to in an Egungun chant (iwi), known to most parts of Yorubaland. The second set of security is provided by the magico-religious sanctions usually ascribed to traditional musical organizations. In the case of Gelede, this second type of guarantee is obtained principally from the widespread belief that the Gelede poet is a servant of witches. For this reason, all efe concerts are, in principle, dedicated to witches. Efe artists therefore enjoy considerable protection based on the customary fear of witchcraft.[30]

The calypsonians are an extension of the efe singer-poets that they resembled in essential ways. Errol Hill's description of Attila's conception of his role as a calypsonian ("more than any other of his time, [Atilla] held fast to the ancient role of the calypso as the poor man's newspaper and the voice of the people. He was a tena-

---

29. According to Asiwaju, "efe refers to a dusk-to-dawn concert of music and humor, which constitutes the most important of the activities connected with the Gelede organisation as found among the Ketu and related groups in Western Yorubaland (ibid., p. 200); see also, pp. 237–38.

30. Ibid., pp. 203–204. The Egungun chant reads as follows: "Say it on.? Say it on./ A singer is never arrested by the Oba [King]. After all, the frog says its own in the river."

cious defender of the traditional rights enjoyed by the calypsonian to comment fear-lessly on local and world affairs, debunking the high and mighty and protecting the downtrodden"[31]) could have been a description of any of the efe singer-poets. More significantly, it is in Attila's evaluation of "Ja Ja Romey Eh/ Ja Ja Romey Shango/ Ja Ja Romey Eh Mete Beni/ Ja Ja Romey Shango" that one gets a deeper sense of the Yoruba connection with the verbal arts of the calypso. Speaking of the sango-pipe (or Shango chants) of the Yorubas, Akinwumi Isola observes that "to appease Sango and to inspire him to offer his good services to the worshippers, Sango pipe artists chant his epithets and tell of his great powers."[32] Here, the leader-chorus (or call-and-response) performance is analogous to the chanting practiced by Shango initi-ates in Trinidad and Tobago. In this performance, as Oyn Ogunba explains, the tendency is "to have a refrain—usually something complimentary—which is first sung by the leader and then taken up by the chorus. The leader then recites a seg-ment of the praise epithet of the person, god or goddess being honored, followed by the refrain which is sung."[33] In this way, the entire personality of the king or the ancestors is articulated. When Ogun or any other deity is praised, similar patterns are followed. The significant aspect of Atilla's evaluation of this Shango chant lies in the fact that it was sung in an African language and came down through slavery. Additionally, he emphasizes the "religious slant" of the chant that was always used in Shango celebrations and its relation to the calinda that "was transported almost bodily into the kaiso and kalenda melodies [that] have been used for kaiso even without modification."[34] In other words, Shango and calinda are part of the con-tinuum leading to the calypso and were adapted to the specific needs of the colonial society, a point that is supported by Funso Aiyejina and Rawle Gibbon's "Orisa Tradition in Trinidad."

In the 1880s, the calypso, like hosay, the ramleelas, and the Carnival celebration emerged as one of the earliest manifestations of a people's thrust to nationness. Although we are mindful, as Hobsbwan observes, that the "real 'nation' can only be recognized a *posteriori*,"[35] still, during this period, the underclass was groping for ways to express themselves and to give expression to their imitative faculties.[36]

31. Raymond Quevedo, *Atilla's Kaiso: A Short History of Trinidad Calypso* (St. Augustine: Department of Extra Mural Studies, University of the West Indies, 1983), p. viii–ix.

32. Akinwumi Isola, "The Rhythm of the Sango-Pipe," in Abimbola, ed., *Yoruba Oral Tradition*, p. 780.

33. Oyin Ogunba, "Performance of Yoruba Oral Poetry," in Abimbola, ed., *Yoruba Oral Tradition*, p. 814.

34. Quevedo, *Atilla's Kaiso*, p. 6.

35. Hobsbawm, *Nations and Nationalism since 1870*, p. 9.

36. I use the term "imitative" in its Aristotelian sense; that is, as a fundamental aspect of human nature. Aristotle wrote that "the instinct of imitation is implanted in man from childhood, one differ-ence between him and other animals being that he is the most imitative of living creatures, and through imitation learns his earliest lessons; and no less universal is the pleasure felt in things imitated." In this sense, the practice of drama lies not so much in the text but in the capacity for improvisation, that is, disguising, masking, mimicry, and role-playing. See *Aristotle's Poetics*, translated by S. H. Butcher (New York: Hill and Wang, 1961), p. 55.

Through a dexterous use of its artistic repertoire, Africans found ways to turn up their noses at Europeans' imperialist pretenses, create a space to express themselves, and define their uniqueness. Although seen by the authorities as "doomed victims of a bestial degradation,"[37] Africans reveled in their specific humanity and thereby rejected European depictions of them as savages.

The Ramleelas

In very much the same way that Africans adapted their literary culture to their new environment, the Indians did likewise. When they arrived in 1845, they brought with them their epics, folk tales (*kheesas*), their folk sayings or folk wisdom (*kahanis*), and music, which became part of the new island society. Religion, the core of Indian culture and the source of its attendant philosophy, continued to play an important part in their lives. According to J. C. Jha, "[t]o the Indians who emigrated to far-off lands religion was a great sustainer and at times a tranquilizer."[38] The Muslims brought the Koran, whereas the Hindus brought their three great holy texts: the *Bhagwat Puran*, the *Ramayana*, and the *Bhagwat Gita*. For example, the Hindus conducted prayer services called yags (or Bhagwats) that lasted for three to four days. Usually, these services were presided over by a pundit and involved readings from one of the texts. In "Politics and Hegemony in Guyanese Nationalism, 1945–1965," Rishee Thakur observes that these readings were often followed or sometimes "interlaced with the singing of Bhajans (religious ballads and local compositions with strong moral overtones) and 'words of advice' from local notables. The Yag or Yagna (the appropriate Hindu expression) is name after one of the three texts the family chooses for the occasion."[39]

Of the three texts, the *Ramayana* had the greatest impact in shaping the literary consciousness of the Indians. In its original form, the narrative was told over forty days and covered the period from "Rama's birth to his coronation, and would be addressed to an audience numbering anywhere from a couple of hundred thousands, each installment of the narration occupying no less than three hours."[40] Hindus throughout India performed and read from this work, and those who came to Trinidad (some 85 percent of the Indians on Trinidad were Hindus) were intimately aware of and connected to the precepts of the *Ramayana* that they practiced in their daily lives.[41] The *Ramayana* was recited as well as sung. Like the *Odyssey*, its distant cousin, the *Ramayana* was an oral narrative recited among Hindus and subsequently taken to every part of the world they settled during the Indian dias-

---

37. *Trinidad Chronicle,* March 1, 1883.

38. J. C. Jha, "Indian Heritage in Trinidad," in *Research Papers: Indentured Indians in Trinidad and Tobago, 1845–1917,* St. Augustine, Trinidad, 1985, p. 2.

39. Rishee S. Thakur, "Politics and Hegemony in Guyanese Nationalism, 1945–1965," Ph.D., Dissertation, York University, Ontario, 1994, pp. 104–105.

40. R. K. Narayan, *The Ramayana* (London: Penguin, 1972), p. 171.

41. The *Ramayana,* a work of sacred literature, is believed to have been written in Sanskrit between 400–200 BC .

pora.[42]   In 1866, Daniel Hart observed: "After work, the [Hindu] men sit for hours in circles listening to some story."[43] Presumably, that story was the *Ramayana*.   In 1888, J. H. Collens, superintendent of the Boys Model and Normal School in Port of Spain, in a condescending aside, related the East Indian's familiarity with their religious texts: "Even amongst the humble labourers who till our fields there is considerable knowledge of them, and you may often find in the evening, work being done, see and hear a group of coolies crouching down in a semicircle, chanting whole stanzas of the epic poem, *Ramayan,* etc."[44]

   The Indians in Trinidad took to performing the ramleelas, an open-air reenactment of the *Ramayana* that they brought from the United Provinces where it was "the greatest festival in the late nineteenth and early twentieth centuries."[45] Jagessar Ganesh, president of the Dow Village Ramleela Cultural Organization says that the ramleela was first celebrated in Dow Village in 1880. "Since then," he continues, "this religious play has continued in this village until today.   The first organizer or leader was Ragoonath Maharaj, assisted by Fitz Simon, the general manager of Gordon Sugar Estate, who donated a parcel of land for this religious celebration. This is the only Ram-leela ground that has performed the Ram-leelah continuously since 1880."[46] Adapted to its Trinidad environment, the ramleela was given over a period of ten to twelve days and lasted about four hours each evening.   Performed by amateur actors, the story involved the entire community and thereby provided a sense of continuity, solidarity, and solace in a strange world.   Each villager could tell what episode would be performed on which given night.   Both Hindus and Muslims took part in this drama.[47]   Thakur concludes that this devotion to their religious texts (and the worldview it depicts) may have led to a sense of political ambiguity in their new home.[48] Jha believes that "professional or occupational seg-

42. In his Nobel Lecture, Derek Walcott made a remarkably insightful comment about the connection between the *Odyssey* and the *Ramayana* and the Trinidadian's awareness of the latter: "I had recently adapted the *Odyssey* for a theatre in England, presuming that the audience knew the trials of Odysseus, hero of another, Asia Minor epic, while nobody in Trinidad knew any more than I did about Rama, Kali, Shiva, Vishnu, apart from the Indians, a phrase I use pervertedly because that is the kind of remark you can still hear in Trinidad: 'apart from the Indians'" (Derek Walcott, *The Antilles; Fragments of Epic Memory* [New York: Farrar, Straus and Giroux, 1992]).

43. Daniel Hart, *Trinidad and the Other West India Islands and Colonies* (Port of Spain: The Chronicle Publishing Office, 1866), p. 101.

44. J. H. Collens, *Guide to Trinidad* (London: Elliot Stock, 1888).   When Lalchan Balroop put together the story of the *Ramayana* in 1992 to be acted by his fellow villagers, he spelt the "Ramayan" in the same way Collens spelt it in 1888.

45. Jha, *Indian Heritage in the West Indies,* p. 10.

46. Private correspondence with Jagessar Ganesh, 1992.

47. At Felicity, another village in which the ramleela was held beginning at the turn of the century, the play is broken up into the following episodes: Introduction to the *Ramayana;* The Conception; Viswaamitra Seeks the Assistance of Rama; The Bringing of Lord Shiva's Bow and Wedding Ceremony; Proposed Coronation and Eventual Exile; The Soorpanakha Episode; The Kidnapping of Sita; The Burning of Lanka; The Burning of the Bridge to Lanka; The Defeat of Raavan; Raam, Bharat, and Milaap.

48. Thakur writes that, at the end of the 1930s, East Indians occupied "precarious if not contradic-

regation and an attitude of derision" may have created "a sense of exclusiveness" among the Indians. He notes that, in the evening, they would tell their children "tales from the epics, inspiring them through the exploits of Rama of the *Ramayana* or Krishna and the Pandavas of the *Mahabharata*."[49]

The ramleelas, however, remained important to the Indians. Performed in a village setting by players the villagers knew and trusted, this ancient epic came alive each time it was retold and reminded East Indians of their homeland. Over the years, not only was it adopted to its local setting, but also both its tone and in language changed. Thus, while it was performed originally in Hindi, by 1980, the language was English. Even its amateur actors made the drama unique, as Walcott notes: "They were not amateurs but believers. There was no theatrical term to define them. They did not have to psych themselves up to play their roles. Their acting would probably be as buoyant and as natural as those bamboo arrows criss-crossing the afternoon pastures. They believed in what they were playing, in the sacredness of the text, [and] the validity of India."[50] A contemporary rendition of the play alerts one to the richness of language and the literary power of the work:

(This introductory scene takes place on the river bank of the Tamasa River)

– He [Vaalmeeki] walks on the river bank and sees on a nearby tree two loving birds, sporting and singing in their joy of life and love. and singing in their joy of life and love.

– The male bird suddenly falls, hit by a hunter's arrow. The female bird, seeing her love rolling on the ground, laments in piteous fashion.

– Vaalmeeki burst into a curse: "Oh hunter, as you have killed one of these love-intoxicated birds, you will wander homeless all your long years."

– In a moment the Sage recovers himself and wonders why he lost himself in anger: "What right had I to curse the hunter/ Why was I deceived by my emotions?"

– Recalling the words of his curse, the Rishi marvels at the rhythm of his words. He discovers that his pity has taken shape in a beautiful sloka. He thinks that all this is part of the mysterious Leela of God and goes into meditation.

– Lord Brahma appears to him saying: "Be not afraid. These things happen to start you on the story of Rama. From sorrow (soka) sprang verse (sloka) and in this metre and rhythm the story should be told. I shall give you the vision to see all that happened, aye, even how the characters thought and looked, as clearly as one sees a thing lying on the palm of one's hand. And you shall sing it, with my blessings, for the benefit of the world."

---

tory place in British Guiana. While they had been brought, encouraged, supported, and eventually achieved success as economic immigrants their cultural location and political status as citizens were very much in doubt. Citizenship in other words, was much dependent on inclusion within the idiom of civilization and since East Indians continued to be marked with traces of 'the immigrant' his/her status remained uncertain and precarious." Such a marker, i.e., his immigrant status "became a powerful trope not only to marginalize and exclude but also a mark of the ultimate 'outsider' in the idiom of citizenship. For some, it was the essential condition of the East Indian in the Caribbean, a temporary sojourn in the great Indian diaspora" ("Politics and Hegemony in Guyanese Nationalism, 1945–1965")

49. Jha, *Indian Heritage in the West Indies*, p. 12.

50. Walcott, *The Antilles*.

– Vaalmeeki fixed the pattern of the verse firmly in his mind and then composes the Ramayana in that metre and rhythm

– Thus the Holy Ramayan was born and which was later translated into Hindi by the great sage, Sant Tulsidas

(The revelation of this great Hindu Epic will follow).[51]

Walcott captures the beauty of this dramatic story in his Nobel Lecture as he meditates "on the sacred celebration of joy, the rehearsal of collective memory, that is the very essence of human experience, beyond history."[52] For the Indians, the performance of the *Ramayana* constituted vital intellectual and cultural sustenance upon which their early existence in Trinidad depended.

These popular dramas (Carnival/calypso, hosay, and the ramleelas), unlike Western forms, emphasized song, spectacle, music and dance rather than plot, character, thought and diction,[53] and through the articulation of these latter, Africans and East Indians constructed a way of life that evaded white surveillance. These dramas are also outward looking, participatory forms rather than "the spectatorial" of cultural forms in British society.[54] Forced to look backward, these people recouped aspects of their culture that were forced underground during slavery and indentureship by reviving these dramatic forms in the 1880s, a period of self-assertion and social development.

Such cultural confrontations also represented attempts to rearticulate the relationship among forces within the society. Michel Foucault suggests that confrontation ought not to be seen as an opposition "between the legitimate and the illegitimate,…but between struggle and submission."[55] The more the colonial authorities suppressed the indigenous practices of Africans and Indians, the more the latter

51. "The Ramayan" as compiled by Lalchan Balroop, First Felicity Ramleela Group, September 7, 1992.

52. Walcott, *The Antilles*, cover copy.

53. In his *Poetics*, Aristotle argues that plot, character, thought, diction, spectacle, and song are central to the dramatic performance. For Aristotle, however, song and spectacle were mere embellishments and emotional attractions and thus were/are of secondary importance. In African and Asian drama, song, spectacle, music, and dance take precedence over plot, character, diction, and thought. See *Aristotle's Poetics*, particularly chapter 6.

54. In *Rider Haggard and the Fiction of Empire*, Katz writes that "[t]he initial stages of professional athleticism, the deification of the championship performer, and the beginning of modern spectator sports, all of which cover the same period [late nineteenth century], entertain a similar spirit of heroism. John Hobson, who singled out the spectatorial aspect of English society as a particularly characteristic of its jingoistic atmosphere, suggested that field heroes and war heroes, by providing vicarious experiences of action, fed a neurotic imagination" (p. 59).

55. In *Power/Knowledge*, Michel Foucault differentiates between what he calls "contract-oppression" and "war-repression." Of the latter, he says, "repression…. is not abuse, but is, on the contrary, the mere effect and continuation of a relation of domination. On this view, repression is none other than the realisation, within the continual warfare of the pseudo-peace, of a perpetual relationship of forces" (*Power/Knowledge* [New York: Pantheon Books, 1980],p. 92).

rebelled against attempts to name their practices illegitimate and to call them inhuman or barbaric, that is, the more the colonial authorities tried to oppress them, the more they refused to submit to European racism. As a result, this period of cultural self-assertion was matched by corresponding demands for greater political self-control and autonomy. In the final analysis, African and Indian oral literary traditions reflected their nationalist aspirations, consolidated their emerging position in the society, and kept their people alive. Needless to say, it gave a much needed impetus to the political forces of resistance that were being arising among colonial people throughout the world.

Joseph Annajee and Other Narratives

Apart from the open-air dramas, the society produced other narratives as well. For example, "The Story of Joseph Annajee," a conversion narrative, was published in 1879. Written by Sarah Morton, the wife of John Morton, this work tells of Annajee's early life. It also chronicles his persecution of Christians while he lived in India, his being brought to Trinidad from India, his being set to work on the plantation as an indentured servant, and his eventual conversion and devotion to missionary work.[56] As an educated Indian, Annajee speaks of his disappointment and humiliation at being made to do manual work:

> Three years I worked on Ben Lormond Estate, and out of that time I was three hundred days in the Hospital. The reason was this: in my own country I had never worked with my hands, nor been exposed to the weather. Now, in crop time, I had to carry bundles of canes on my head, to be ground at the mill, from early morning till evening. In the wet season I was weeding the fields, and the rain and sun together made me very much sick. My health came quite broken, and my heart was breaking too. The Manager of the Estate was kind to me, and so was the Hospital nurse; but my life was weary to me. This punishment I suffered for my sins.

While Annajee worked on the plantation, he came into contact with missionaries from the Canadian Mission Indians. Subsequently, he accepted Jesus as his personal savior and became a member of the Presbyterian Church. After his baptism, Mr. Morton compensated the Ben Lormond Estate for Annajee's last two years of indentureship and made him "a teacher of Coolie children, first on Palmyra Estate, and afterwards at Couva." While he was at Couva, Annajee lost his wife. After spending some time there, he was transferred to San Fernando with his two children, and later, he was sent to Cedar Hill and Savanna Grande. Finally, in 1878,

---

56. Morton, it seems, acted more the amanuensis than a biographer. She also assisted in the production of other conversion tales. In March 1890, the *Maritime Presbyterian* published "A Short Sketch of My Life" by Francis Victor. The editor's note reads as follows: "Mrs. Morton has kindly forwarded the following sketch, written, at their request, by a young man who recently came from India to Trinidad, and who is now employed as a teacher in one of Mr. Morton's schools" (p. 79).

he settled in Morichal, where he became "a respectable and meritorious Teacher of youth and others."

Reviewing "The Story of Joseph Annajee, in the *Trinidad Palladium*, one Theta recommended the pamphlet to his readers. He predicted that "[a]ll who give the work a perusal will be much pleased to find that a man mind and energy, and of Christian principle, has pushed himself forward very deservingly aided and encouraged of course, by the Rev. Mr. Morton and Mrs. Morton."[57]

Like "Maria," "The Story of Joseph Annajee" was the kind of story (that is, "savage saved by Christianity") missionaries liked to send back to their headquarters. Thus, the impulse behind the publication of Annajee's story was not simply to tell of his life, but to tell his story in the service of an ideal, that is, the superiority of Christianity over the pagan religions of Hinduism or Islam. In fact, Sarah Morton's greatest glee came when she tells of Annajee's conversion: "Annajee gave up his books to me, which I will keep as a trophy. It is Sanskrit with explanations in the vernacular of Bombay, and has as a frontispiece, Arjun and Krishau with chariot and horse."[58] Ten years later, Morton was overjoyed when Rev. D. Hutton, the Superintendent of Mission Press in Mizrapore, India, wrote to inform her that "he had taken the liberty of translating 'The Story of Annajee,'…into Hindi and that the Vernacular Society for the promotion of Christian knowledge had ordered five thousand copies to be printed and circulated among the people."[59] The pamphlet had achieved its objective. It became an active agent of Empire in encouraging, instructing, "christianiz[ing] and civiliz[ing] these Asiatic labourers and their children who come to Trinidad, and many of these children are Creoles, having been born in the island."

At the same time Annajee was being converted, the Presbyterians had won another significant victory for their Lord when they converted Aziz Ahmad, a Mohammedan to Christianity. Rev. Kenneth Grant, another Presbyterian minister, described Ahmad as "a gift from the Lord" and wrote to Mr. Mc Gregor at Missionary Headquarters in Canada about the new convert:

[Ahmad] traveled to Calcutta, and finding a ship about to leave for Trinidad with Coolie immigrants, he embarked too. He arrived here in April 1870 and shortly after found himself plying with his hoe in the "cane piece." The work to hire was altogether new. The allowance for a task is 25 cents, and it often took him three days to accomplish one. There he remained about eight months, and often has said to me, "Ah, I was in very real trouble." Weak, disheartened, and unable to do his task, he would fall down and cry to Allah, for he was educated in the Mohammedan faith….

His mother tongue is high Urdu, a dialect of the Hindustani, but he can make

57. All quotations on this work are taken from the *Trinidad Palladium*, July 31, 1880.

58. *The Home and Foreign Record*, August 1871, p. 281

59. *The Maritime Presbyterian*, May 1881. See also Sarah Morton's letter, April 25, 1881, in the *Scrapbooks of John and Sarah Morton, Tunapuna, Trinidad, BWI, 1863–1912*, Tunapuna, Trinidad, W.I. Knox College (Toronto), 1912.

himself quite intelligible to those who have only the Hindu dialect. He speaks also the Parsee and can read the Arabic. For two years he studied the English language in school, and has acquired not only a fair knowledge of words, but also of the grammatical construction of the language. But with all his attainments he is entirely ignorant of the Gospels.[60]

Taking a deep interest in Ahmad, Rev. Grant devoted two hours a day to his instruction. After a probationary period of a year, Ahmad was baptized in March 1871. Thereafter, he began to help Rev. Grant on his daily rounds and assisted him in translating. He also became a teacher at Presbyterian Church under Rev. Grant.

In November 1873, Ahmad wrote a stinging letter to Revs. Morton and Grant after he was removed from his position. Ahmad, it seems, had used some "insulting English before Mr. Robert Mitchell," and Morton had demanded he apologize for his indiscretion. It also appeared as though he disagreed with Morton and Grant's methods of conversion. Ahmad further complained about the paltry pay he received and the cruel way in which the Indians were treated. As he wrote:

You say I hold a very low opinion of you [Mr. Morton]. Hear me with patience then. How you know? Because I said Europe is [a] drunken nation. Think upon it yourself and know whether it is true or not. Then you blame Mahommadanism of the same crime. Of course you do not call all of them as I do not mean all European, neither I meant all Chinese but speak in general. If there is any fault of drunkards less in Arabia, Persia, India, in the Island, etc., say then what people are devil or authors of crime. You may in vain point out to deprive the poor Indian merchant of their little money.

Certainly they are blameless and if any blames them ought to be blamed themselves.

Again you say selling and drinking is the same and both [are] guilty. I agree with your masters but I differ in this that as the seller is guiltier than the drinker so the maker or one who allows it to be made is the one to whom if you can say any thing that will kill the seed and will prevent all its future....

I am told I [am] reproaching you by telling the truth that you are pork eaters. Are you not then of that you are offended. If you know it is write [sic] do hear me and rejoice. You would be grieved if I say Mr. Morton eats bread, certainly not— then you should not be offended. . .

Remember my hardship in being your cook, butler, house servant, most respectable work given me to do: groom, interpreter, school teacher, your public and some your teachers too.[61]

Years later, Ahmad declared he had suffered a great deal in Trinidad. "For 5 years," he added, "that when I was in Trinidad and British Guiana, the Christians never

60. *Home and Foreign Record,* February 1871, p. 95.
61. This letter, dated "Port of Spain, 27/11/73" is to be found in the *Scrapbooks of John and Sarah Morton,.*

took a cup of tea with me. I place my trust in the Lord who will help me as in the past."[62]

In 1880, Ahmad published *Testimonials and Criticisms,* a résumé of sorts that listed his accomplishments. Upon leaving Trinidad in 1874, he became an itinerant preacher, traveling eventually to the United States via Venezuela and Guyana and landing at Yale Divinity School. One is not too sure what he did there, but in 1876, George Day of Yale School of Theology, testifies that, "since his arrival in New Haven, in November last, he has occupied a room one of the Theological Halls, and has diligently pursed his studies in preparation for the Seminary....He delivered, a few weeks since, a very interesting Lecture in this city, and would be listened to with interest by any audience." Ahmad also lectured in New York, Connecticut and Massachusetts before going in 1878 to England, where he did the same thing. In Britain, similar testimonials followed about his geniality. Yet, at the end of the day, he seemed not so much to renounce Islam as to argue for its acceptance. The *Leuth Times* of March 1880 ends its report of his lecture by noting that "Recitals from the Koran, intoned, were also given, and were evidently pleasing to audience."[63] When Rev. Grant commended Ahmad to his superiors, he allowed that "God has endowed him with a kind, winning disposition, which renders him a favorite with his countrymen."[64] That winning personality seemed to have taken him through life in a fairly satisfactory manner.

On July 31, 1880, the *Trinidad Chronicle* reviewed *An Autobiography: or the Ups and Downs of Life (in Europe, Asia and America) by an Unfortunate Planter,* a work that described the adventures of a British planter on three continents. Excited that the booklet was "produced *here,* depicting adventures among people we know and amid scenes in which we live," the reviewer recommended it to his readers and observed that "[s]uch a mixture of folly and good-nature, with an alternating round of desperate straits and luck, jerked by his own mercurial temper or the peremptory necessity of a change of scene over three quarters of the world in the oddest contrasts of occupation bringing him in near contact with an endless variety of characters...would have delighted the heart of Defoe or Tobias Smollett, of humorous memory."[65]

The year 1881 also saw the development of more literary and cultural productions in the island, the literary and the artistic being closely intertwined.[66] On

---

62. Ibid.

63. Aziz Ahmad, *Testimonials and Criticisms,* (London: Times Gate, nd.)

64. *Home and Foreign Record,* February 1871.

65. "Review," *Trinidad Chronicle,* July 31, 1880.

66. For example, in June 1882, at a meeting of the Creole Amateurs, Michel Cazabon moved the following motion: "As Music is so essential to enliven Dramatic performances, and the Art of Painting so indispensable to carry them out, and the members being novices in both of these arts, this meeting invites the co-operation of gentlemen friends in both arts to assist in the future as they have hitherto done." In a moving tribute to Cazabon's presence at this meeting, the reporter wrote: "Mr. Michael Cazabon was requested to occupy the chair, pro-tem. At this stage of the proceedings it was imposing and serious to see in the chair the respectable and grey-haired citizen, Mr. Michael Cazabon. He looked so venerable; and surrounded by distinguished Creole gentlemen, and the Amateurs seated all in a row at his back, one felt ready to exclaim: *Vivent les Creole Amateurs!*" (*Trinidad Chronicle,* June 24, 1882)

January 8, 1881, the *Trinidad Chronicle* announced that 1880 was very "prolific in amateur entertainments, some of a very high class and displaying an amount of local talent and ability surprising everybody. We allude particularly to the wonderful rendering in January of Mendelssohn's difficult oratorio 'Elijah,' by the Port of Spain Choral Society, conducted by the Rev. W. S. Doorly; the School Concert of 400 voices by pupils of the Government Schools, conducted by Mr. Collens, Superintendent of the Normal School; the several musicals and dramatic performances in aid of the new Church of the Sacred Heart given, we believe, under the guidance of Mrs. Revell."

In April, the editors of the *Trinidad Chronicle* returned to the savage-civilization debate. In describing a Public School Concert by the students of the Normal and Model schools (about ten schools) that was attended by Sir Sanford Freeling, governor of the island, they contrasted the performance of these privileged children with those of the lowest strata:

> It is impossible to regard these children and their behaviour, after the experience of our late carnival, without contrasting the sweetness and grace of this pretty flock—in which we would hope to perceive the prefigurement of a better time, a sweeter ear for the Island—with the coarse and brutish heathenism of *that* swinish *abandon.* The one exhibits to us a great a great chorus of sweet accords, and gentility and self-respect in conduct—the other their precise opposites joined with the vulgarest disfigurement and the grossest license in ribaldry: yet to their eternal shame the latter scenes are championed by whole circles who indignantly assert their claims to gentility![67]

At the end of the year, the Port of Spain Dramatic Company had added females to their company which led the *Trinidad Chronicle* to comment that "[f]emale parts will no longer be laughed at because they were (mis) represented by strapping, waistless and hipless fellows with deep masculine voices, who, however good their acting (as *Evade's,* for instance, last year) could possible blind one to the awful sham and lible of the sweet gentle sex."[68]

In 1882, Guppy produced his annual *Almanack,* an enterprise he and his brother Francis started in 1866. Each edition included more and more local material. In the 1882 edition, Guppy updated the historical information in his introduction and carried a summary of the recent census of the island. The editors of *Trinidad Chronicle* observed that the book presented, "in concise form, a compendium of reference, indispensable to all, strangers or home-staying, who require to know who's who and what is what in the island."[69] In 1886, when Francis died on a rescue mission up the Orinoco river, Guppy continued to edit the Almanack until old age pre-

67. *Trinidad Chronicle,* April 9, 1881.
68. *Trinidad Chronicle,* July 27, 1881.
69. *Trinidad Chronicle,* February 11, 1882.

vented him from doing so, and "the Government took it over and adopted it as the official year book."[70]

Meanwhile the newspapers continued to expose its readers to literary and cultural productions. In April, in two issues, the *Trinidad Chronicle* republished "Romance of an Aristocrat," which appeared initially in the *New York Times*. In May, there was a public reading from *Uncle Tom's Cabin* at St. John's Baptist Church in Port of Spain that was "illustrated" with songs and magic lantern views. According to the reviewer, "a large and appreciative audience" attended it.[71] On August 4, 1883, the *Trinidad Chronicle* carried "Trinidad," C. S. Salmon's *Capital and Labour in the West Indies*. Salmon, it must be noted, was also a very vocal critic of Froude's attack on West Indians. Such articles kept the reading public informed of what was current in the literary world.

The Trinidad Review

Consistent with the literary and cultural concerns of the time, there was a corresponding interest by the local black elite in the political affairs of the country. In 1882, for example, E. Maresse Smith, later to become very prominent in reform politics at the end of the decade, complained about the privileges of the Creoles—the ruling elite—and the need to open the franchise to more persons. Complaining of the "cliquism" of the members of the Port of Spain Borough Council, he argued:

> The Borough Council is not a Creole Institution. It is the Institution of—one for the benefit of all the Citizens....The Borough Council ought to be composed of persons of independence, who have already given proofs to the Public of their liberal-mindedness and disinterestedness and of whom one could reasonably expect some zeal, nay, some self-sacrifice in the discharge of their duties as Councillors and Auditors. Patriotism not being inborn in all men, it would be more judicious to entrust the interests of the Borough to persons who take a lively interest in its prosperity although not having seen the light within its precincts, rather than to misconfide such an important mission to either individuals whose egoism and love of ease are patent and who can only advance in support of their pretensions the fact that Trinidad has had the honour of being the cradle and sepulchre of several of their relatives.[72]

Such newfound political activism would lead to the rise of the Reform Movement at the end of the nineteenth century. During these early years there was not a very strict demarcation between culture and politics. Rather, in many important ways, politics and culture were intertwined. Maresse Smith was a member of the Creole Amateurs, a literary, cultural, and artistic group, even though he was politically active. To speak of the cultural development of the society, demanded

70. Bridges, *Child of the Tropics*, p. 17. This memoir offers a good insight into Guppy's life.
71. *Trinidad Chronicle*, May 2, 1883.
72. *Trinidad Chronicle*, November 15, 1881

some involvement with political affairs, particularly to those who felt alienated from the system.

On August 2, 1883, the *Trinidad Review of Politics, Literature, and Science in Trinidad and Other West India Colonies* (hereafter, *Trinidad Review*) published its first number. It observed that there was an "abundance amongst us of subjects for intelligent and scientific observation" and that the "absence of any systematic provision on the part of the local Press for assisting enquiry in that useful and commendable direction, the founders of the *Trinidad Review*." It signaled its intention to "venture to supply, however inadequately, that desideratum." Moreover, the "almost universal prevalence of evil-speaking and defamation" in the society, convinced the *Trinidad Review* that it needed to elevate the intellectual level of its readership so that it could participate in what it called "higher things."

Concerned especially with politics, "the cardinal element in West Indian Journalism," the *Trinidad Review* took exception to the presence of "the despotism known as Crown Colony Government." It noted that, if s/he were educated, every Caribbean person "must recognise that under the so-called paternal system, he is deprived of many valuable rights which he surrenders to Might alone, and, therefore, cannot be otherwise than [be] hostile to that system." The editors of the *Trinidad Review* felt they had to work at modifying the governmental system that prevailed and to move toward the implementation of a more representative form of government. Sounding very much like the Americans of the eighteenth century, the paper concludes that "[w]hen, therefore, the question of governing and taxing enlightened men in the colonies, without their consent as to, or even their prior cognizance of, what is intended, shall again be raised before the British Public, we are certain of the hearty support of eminent men whom Mr. Gladstone's confession has converted. But the sheet-anchor of our hope, however, is the inherent badness of the Crown Colony system itself. No one who has studied the history of oligarchism can be ignorant of the fact that irresponsible power, while it begins by enslaving the weaker majority, invariably ends by making its wielders themselves the slaves." Certainly, the nationalist flames were burning very brightly.

In its first issue, *Trinidad Review* reviewed the second volume of Gustave Borde's *History of Spanish Trinidad*, with the reviewer arguing that "a manual of this kind had long been a desideratum not only of our local Schools and Colleges, but in the libraries no less than the professional student than the mere man..."[73] The reviewer speaks of Borde's disinterested approach to scholarship and his "erudition and carefulness" and goes on to observe:

> Truly must this work be described as a 'labour of love.' Nineteen years of a talented life spent and spending in researches to give his native land the annals of its past,

---

73. Bridget Brereton describes Borde as a historian of high rank "among nineteenth century writers on the West Indies...he identified himself as a Trinidadian rather than a French Creole. He wanted to instruct Trinidad's youth in the history of the country only from a knowledge of the past" (*Race Relations in Colonial Trinidad*, pp. 58–59).

and that without the hope, or even the desire, or reward—such has been the obla-tion which Gustave Borde has laid on the altar of patriotism. He comes not before us with 'an obtrusive air,' demanding 'the honours Nature bade him share,' but, 'like the modest violet,' he has shed the sweetness of his rare powers on the 'desert air' of his scarcely appreciative country. Nevertheless, his reward is ample. To men like him, praise from even a solitary competent voice, the 'barren laurel' placed on his brow by any hand which the world of letters recognizes as competent thus to grace a worthy denizen, brings about that climax which Aspiration signed, and Genius toiled for. The gifted of the world can afford to be poor in the world's goods; for the ineffable ecstasies that mark the pulsations of the truly intellectual life, are emo-tions which the world can neither give nor ever take away.

The reviewer believes that scholarship, a disinterested act, has its own rewards. Even though the review was not critical of Borde's work (it reads more as a paean to Borde's greatness), it managed to critique the activities of the buccaneers and the support they received from the imperial governments. It delights in the fact that this work is taken seriously by others (the Europeans) and is structured by a nation-alist paradigm.

In its second issue, the *Review* examined the legal restrictions that prevented the building of a theatre in Port of Spain,[74] while the third dealt with the "Coolie Disturbance and Immigration." In this issue, there were also complaints against the textbooks that were being used in the primary schools. Although the editors argued that the textbooks were changed too often (a complaint that has become all too familiar in Trinidad), the Creoles also complained about the content of the reading material found in their children's texts. The editor asked: "What has become of the project once mooted, of getting up elementary works on local subjects for use in our primary schools?" Arguing that the topics were much too alienating, the essay states:

> In Trinidad—as indeed in most dependent countries—the obstructive system pre-vails, of instructing children in books treating of subjects of which they are igno-rant, and of which the facts and phenomena that surround them suggest no notion whatsoever. Nothing but the extraordinary aptitude of Creoles could overcome the obstacles thus presented in the earliest stages of instruction; but this triumph of tal-ent is gained by an exorbitant waste of time and effort that might have secured much larger benefits. We, in our boyhood, have been, and they, who have taken our places on the school-forms, are, unconscious victims of a system, the fatal vice of which is, that it habituates the mind to the dissociation of words from the ideas they

---

74. During this period, the building of a theatre in Port of Spain was of great interest. Because of the inadequacy of the Prince's Building and Prince Edward's theatre, the two places where most of drama was performed, it was argued that there was "no proper accommodation for the production of a drama or opera approaching in the slightest degree to the spectacular....If it should once become known that Trinidad possessed a nice theatre, we should have no lack of visitors in the shape of travelling comedi-ans, and the reproach of there being no amusement of an evening in Port of Spain would be removed" *Trinidad Chronicle*, April 14, 1883.

represent. What, for example, can a mere child in these colonies conceive of *snow, hail,* an *oak tree, acorns, hail, giraffes,* and such like outlandish things, that form the subject-matter of our elementary manuals? No conception in any way definite and pertinent to the purpose of instructions. Yet—such is the supineness of the Government and the perversity of the Inspector-of-Schools—primary instruction goes on in the same groove as from time immemorial; and thousands on thousands of pounds are all but thrown away yearly on a system which has the recommendation only being better than none at all.[75]

Calling on Mr. Guppy, the Inspector of Schools, to create books that contained local subject matter, the article made it known that the journal's intervention was the beginning of an open discussion on the subject of primary education in Trinidad, as well as a deepening and extended debate of the nature of public education that was raised in the previous decade.

The October issue of the *Review* reviewed "The Lyre and the Harp," a poem written by Jose Antonio Parez Bondalde who lived in Trinidad before moving to New York. The poem reads in part:

> Niagara, the thundering: which now appears,
> Surrounded with resplendent glories,
> Before my dazzled sight, and fills
> My soul with awe sublime,
> And strikes my tongue with muteness,
> Oppressive with its majesty immense?...
>
> Come thou: between each tearful pause
> Recite unto a wonder-stricken world
> A Poem of the Sublime.
> Tell of the grand beauteousness expanding
> My saddened breast into noble aspiration;
> And of the unutterable feelings
> And mysterious horror that were thine,
> Whilst on the brink of the Cataract immense!

Calling the poem an "exquisite contribution to the pleasures of the intellect," the editors quoted Jose Marti's reading of the poem to supplement their analysis. To be sure, Bolivar, liberator of Venezuela and Columbia, could be expected to be expansive in his praise for Bondale since the poem supported the Latin American liberation struggle. He described the poem as "the Titanic dialogue between Man impatient and Nature in disdain; the despairing shout of a son of the Great Father, asking of his voiceless Mother the secret of his birth." For Trinbagonians, however, this work represented a continuing connection beyond its boundaries; a world from which its writers and thinkers drew much intellectual sustenance and which allowed them a way to speak about their part of the universe.

75. The *Trinidad Review,* August 16, 1883, p. 23.

CHAPTER 12

The Romanticization
of the Amerindian

Two strangers have come to our island
    They are white, they are handsome
But they belong to the vile and impious race
    Which several times made the population of our
        village scarcer?
    Faced with this peril for our country
Our chiefs are going to give a decision on their fate;
Are you going to let them live?
Or inflict death upon them?
        —*The Two First Martyrs of Trinidad*

What bring'st thou, Colon, here as gifts to these
Bright, gemmy isles, that basks in peerless seas?
Civilization, say? to elevate
The savage breast, and teach to emulate
The virtues, ay! Alas, and vices too,
Thou bringest from an old world to a new?...
Alas! thy higher culture's power is such,
That at its soft yet scathing, withering touch
(Like their own upas' soft but treacherous shade)
Their feebler life will shrink, their manhood fade;
And tribes and nations wither day by day,
Sad victims of mysterious decay;
Till swept from off the earth, to live at last
Alone in fading memories of the past.
        —Horatio Nelson Huggins, *Hiroona*

The Revival of the Amerindian

Prompted, no doubt, by the romantic inclinations of the time and Borde's examination of the Amerindians, the mid-1880s showed a renewed interest in the
Amerindians. Unable to come to terms with the cruelty the Spanish had inflicted
upon them, they became a part of the mythic history of the society. Marianella

Belliard-Acosta writes that in the nineteenth century, "[t]he figure of the [Amer]Indian became an important trope to Latin American Romantic writers expressing nationalistic, anti-Spanish sentiments. The victimized and heroic Indian represented in Latin American literature a symbolic weapon to denounce Spanish ideology and oppression."[1] Although Trinidad writers did not use the Amerindian primarily to denounce the Spanish, the former figured prominently in the nationalistic ferment that was taking place in the society at the time. More than ever, Amerindian's plight provided local writers an opportunity to continue their nationalist discourse in the colonial space.

In October 1888, *Public Opinion* published "Étymologie Caraibe de Quelquest mots Creole," a fascinating academic article on the etymology of Carib names. Writing in a rapturous manner of "the days when these lovely isles were inhabited by the unsophisticated races which the ruthless conquistadores swept from off the face of the land," the editor of *Public Opinion* hoped the article would raise in "our minds an affectionate longing for new facts connected with the language, customs and manners of those races."[2] Undoubtedly, the scholars of the time (the paper called the author of "Étymologie Caraibe" a "modest savant") were paying some attention to a subject that had been excised from the national memory. Turing to the Amerindians to emphasize the nation's origins, L. B. Tronchin's *Inez* (1885), Jean-Ch. de St Avit's *Les Deux Premiers Martyrs de la* Trinidad (*The First Two Martyrs of Trinidad*) (1885), and Horatio Nelson Huggins's *Hiroona* (published in 1930 but written in the 1880s) made the Amerindians the focus of their attention. Apart from reflecting nostalgia for a past heroic age, there was a desire to connect that dimension of Trinidad's history with the nationalist evolution of the society and an attempt to collapse the Amerindian presence into a Trinidad imaginary.

For the Amerindians and the society at large, these texts performed a function similar to that of the calypso, the ramleelas, and the hosay, which allowed all these groups to be presented with authenticity and autonomy. However, with the Amerindians, there was one notable exception: they were the original inhabitants of the island (they called it *Kairi*). One commentator observed that "[t]he principal tribal groups [whom Columbus met when he came] were the Arawaks and a people who called themselves a name variously spelt by Europeans as Carina, Callinago, and Carinepogotoes. Because they resisted the 'toys and other trinkets' displayed by Columbus and defended themselves against attacks by the newcomers, they were renamed CARIBALES or 'consumers of human flesh' by Columbus and other Spanish colonisers."[3]

Because Amerindians resisted European exploitation like the Africans and East

---

1. Marianella Belliard-Acosta, "Writing Nations, Creating Race: Identity in Cuban and Dominican Literatures in the Nineteenth and Twentieth Centuries." Ph.D., Dissertation, New York University, New York.

2. R. D M, "Étymologie Caraibe de Quelques mots Creoles," *Public Opinion,* October 19, 1888.

3. Elma Reyes, "The Santa Rosa Community of Arima, Trinidad, West Indies," Santa Rosa Carib Community: Research, Education, Publications & Public Relations Unit, nd.

Indians who came after them, they also were labeled by Europeans as "savage" peoples. Resisting early attempts to Christianize them, they successfully kept the Spanish exploiters out of their society until the King of Spain issued a degree that permitted their enslavement because they persisted in "retaining their devilish practices."[4] According to Stephen Greenblatt, European observers interpreted the resistance and ultimate extermination of the Amerindians as "a sign of God's determination to cast down the idolaters and open the New World to Christianity."[5] As we will see, *Les Deux Premiers Martyrs de la Trinidad* captures that first important moment of European self-fashioning on the island and the corresponding resistance by the Amerindian.

Les Sauteurs à la Grenade, ou Ina la Caraibe

Frank Kums's poem "Les Sauteurs à la Grenade, ou Ina la Caraibe," one of the earliest examples in the Amerindian genre, highlights the nobility and defiance of the Amerindians as depicted in the heroic act of Ina, a Carib woman, as the poem tells of a particularly infamous episode in Caribbean history. Confronted by the Spanish, Ina and the other Caribs preferred to commit suicide by leaping from the Sauteurs rather than become Spanish prisoners or slaves.

Contrasting the nobility of "the unfortunate Carib" with the cruelty and treachery of the Spanish soldiers, the poet celebrates Ina's defiance:

> Three times, in the midst of the woods
> The proud victor surrounded her;
> Three times the fearless Amazon
> Had the warriors awestruck.
> Like an eagle clearing the air
> She takes them by surprise, strikes and threatens
> And under the legs of her horse
> Crushes in the dust
> The often audacious boldness
> Of many a noble warrior!

Overwhelmed by the might of the invaders, Ina is captured and brought into "the Castillians' cruel hands." So grave is Ina's situation that even nature mourns:

> Suddenly a muffled roar
> Followed by an underground grumbling
> Frightened by the whole of nature;
> Everything shook with the shaking
> The ocean was covered with foam

4. Ibid.

5. Stephen Greenblatt, *Renaissance Self-Fashioning* (Chicago: University of Chicago Press, 1980, p. 226.

The volcano erupted in smoke!
Horrible swirls of fire
Rolling down the mountain
Ran to invade the countryside.
Everything flees in this awful moment!

Eventually, Ina escapes from the Spaniards and joins her people as they defy the Castillians. In the end, "she found/ the path to the deadly plains," where the Caribs planned their final act of defiance against their conquerors:

All the Caribs were there!
Waiting for her before they would die!
"Here is the bold, the beautiful Ina!"
They all shouted aloud.

"The Great Spirit inspired me;
Ina is safe;
But He only save me
To unite me to Him!
Let everyone get ready to jump!
What! Not to crush ourselves
In order to escape from our victors!"
Suddenly, a large noise in the abyss
Announced the sublime fall
Of the Jumping Caribs![6]

Although there is every reason to believe that Kums is using this tragedy to demonstrate the evils of the Spanish colonizers, there is also a sense that Trinbagonian society had to address this grave wrong done to the Amerindians

6. Frank Kums, "Les Sauteurs à la Grenade, ou Ina La Caraire," *New Era*, June 12, 1871. This infamous incident is also found in Nelson's *Hiroona*:

> In yon Grenada, so you name it now,
> Before the holy cross, with prayer and vow,
> The murderers knelt and took the Sacrament;
> Then rising, straight to the slaughter's work they went;
> Their vow (could sacred things be more defiled?)
> To leave alive nor man, nor maid, nor child.
> They lost scarce one, while they their thousands slew;
> For what could bow and feeble arrow do?
> Until the few they left, like helpless sheep,
> Were driven and huddled on a rocky steep
> O'er-hanging far the breaking surf below;
> And when drew near the unrelenting foe,
> With one long wail their cruel faith [*sic*] they wept,
> And then adown they yawning abyss leapt.
> That fatal rock, where perished thus a race,
> But where they left for aye the crime's sad trace,
> (Its granite cheeks are trickling down with tears,)
> The heartless conquerors, mocking, name "Sauteurs."

(Port of Spain: Franklin's Electric Printery, 1930, p. 86).

before it could move forward. This poem with its tinge of anti-Spanish feeling came at a time when the English were trying to anglicize the society and when the dispossessed groups were making a case for greater equality. *Hiroona,* however, would turn the focus upon the English, for it speaks of the brutality to which the English subjected the Caribs of St. Vincent and the Carib's heroic battle to assert their independence.

Inez

The tremendous intellectual energy that manifested itself in the second part of the nineteenth century was reflected in the work of Louis Bernard Tronchin, the preeminent man of letters of the second half of the nineteenth century. More than likely a self-made scholar, Tronchin was the superintendent of the Woodbrook Model School for Boys and an active member of the Trinidad Literary Association, at whose gatherings he read many of his works. His contemporaries considered him "one of the most brilliant and one of the most accomplished" Creoles on the island.[7] Together with Thomas and Philip, he was one of the foremost figures of the Creole intelligentsia, a personage around whom most of the colored intellectuals of the day congregated and to whom they turned for advice. He was a friend and colleague of Thomas, who acknowledged Tronchin's assistance in the preface of *Creole Grammar.*

Like Maxwell Philip, and Thomas, Tronchin displayed an unusual knowledge of and appreciation for the classics. Keenan acknowledged his brilliance in grudging manner:

> Mr. Tronchin is a respectable, intelligent, and, I am convinced, industrious teacher. In matters connected with school accounts or statistics, I have never met with a readier or more intelligent person. He is candid and unaffected; and, in the ranks of the primary teachers of the colony, he legitimately occupies a foremost position. But I have to add that this is only a *relative* estimate. Were I to compare him with model-school masters at home, I could not assign him an equally exalted place.[8]

Tronchin, a brilliant essayist, wrote illuminating essays/eulogies on Lord Henry Brougham, Charles Warner, Maxwell Philip, Dr. Davis, and others.[9] Barry Lydgate,

---

7. See "The Great West Indian Orator," *Public Opinion,* December 18, 1888. These were the sentiments of Francis Damian, J.P., mayor of Port of Spain (elected in 1886) and president of the Trinidad Literary Association, formed on September 12, 1887.

8. Keenan, *Report,* p. 26.

9. See, for example, "Dr. Davis," *New Era,* January 30, 1871; "Charles Wm. Warner and His Times," *Public Opinion,* September 28–October 2, 1888; and "The Great West Indian Orator," *Public Opinion,* December 18–21, 1888. The essay was a popular form at the time. Rev. A. Caldecott, writing in the *West Indian Quarterly* listed the essays of Addison, Carlyle, Emerson, and Ruskin as being an indispensable part of the library collection of any "Englishman, in this last quarter of the nineteenth century, and living in the English colonies" ("A Home Library: For an Englishman of Today," *West Indian Quarterly,* Vol. 2 [July 1886]).

a professor of French language and literature at Wellesley College, argues that in his essays, Tronchin adopts two complementary characteristics of French academic writing of the period. First, Tronchin employs a highly rhetorical, declamatory style reminiscent of speeches (he was always writing in praise of outstanding men) in which he trots out the arsenal of Ciceronian rhetoric transmitted down through the French university system (long, multi-segmented periodic sentences, asides, exclamations, invocations, personifications, and rhetorical questions). Expectedly, his prose became more florid as he warmed up to his subject.

Second, Tronchin believes in the rationality and perfectibility of man that comes directly out of the *philosophes* and the French revolution. In his essays, he takes a high moral tone and uses many abstract nouns to carry forward his project. His was a "high-flown literary style," a strategy that "many non-metropolitan Francophone writers used to impress scholars in the metropole who tended to turn their noses down on the works of writers and scholars from the islands."[10]

"The Burning of Rome, or The Origin of the Persecution of Christians by the Romans" (1848), one of Tronchin's earliest essays, demonstrates his intellectual prowess. Written in French and brimming over with emotions, this short essay describes Nero's behavior at the burning of Rome. It offers a dramatic and vivid picture of that city under fire and contrasts Nero's behavior with that of Caesar. He concludes that the former "tarnished the imperial dignity."[11]

"Lord Brougham," also written in French, pays tribute to this "great liberator of the African race" and concludes that Brougham looked upon humanity as "a cosmopolitan philosopher, a universal statesman, rather than a sectarian whose views were circumscribed by narrow views and whose conception are not circumscribed by their nationality. Only the great human family was worthy of his exalted vision. His goals were a general fusion of all international interest."[12] As in other essays of this bent, Tronchin paints Lord Brougham as the perfect citizen. This essay also demonstrates Tronchin's ongoing concern with the plight of Africans in the Caribbean and his awareness of the major social questions and intellectual issues that affected his people and those who spoke on his people's behalf.[13]

Although Tronchin wrote continuously for the newspapers—even his poems were published in these periodicals[14]—his most ambitious creative contribution to Trinidad and Tobago's literature is *Inez,* a romantic tale, about an Amerindian woman of the same name, who was betrayed by a stranger from the "vaunted civi-

---

10. Private communications, December 20, 1999.

11. L. B. Tronchin, "The Burning of Rome," *The Trinidadian,* August 12, 1848.

12. L. B. Tronchin, " Lord Brougham," *The Trinidad Monthly Magazine* 1, No. 1 (September, 1871), p. 42.

13. Lord Brougham was among the foremost abolitionists of his time. Chester New writes that William Wilberforce, James Stephen, Zachary Macaulay, and Lord Brougham "became the greatest leaders in the later movement for the emancipation of the slaves." See Chester W. New, *The Life of Henry Brougham to 1830* (Oxford: Clarendon Press, 1961), p. 120.

14. See "Night Thoughts on the Sea-Shore," *Public Opinion,* November 2, 1888.

lization."[15] Although the plot is slim, one is impressed by the setting, the attempt to capture a dying way of life and a sadness at its passing, and a philosophizing about the evils of civilization. As the subtitle, "Tale of the Indians of the Aroucas," suggests, this work is designed to explore the fate of "the last of the Aroucas," one of the many Indian ethnic groups (tribes) that lived on the island.[16]

Set in Arima in the 1840s, the tale describes how strangers (that is, the French, the Spanish, and the English) invaded the area and violated a peaceful, tranquil way of life. It tells the story of Inez Cabrena, "the angel of her tribe," who is betrayed by a rich Anglo-Saxon, a stranger to the peasant (read unsophisticated) way of life. Padre Lopez, a Sacristan of the quarter and a descendant of Montequma, the magnificent, makes this point as he talks with the village schoolmaster:

> "Among the Indians, as you are well aware, my dear good Sir, all disputes, litigation or differences are immediately settled by the king of the tribe. This is an institution which has descended to us from the remotest antiquity, therefore the *stipended solicitude* of the magistrate is perfectly superfluous to the Indians. If you visit the court when the Assizes are held, you will not fail to observe that they are attended only by strangers who seem to be more in need of a magistrate than the quiet and peaceful Indians.
>
> Nothing daunted him. The school master resumed the enumeration of the facts he had to advance in favour of the position he defended and continued:
>
> "You have two Alquazils whose duties are to defend our interest, protect our property when we are absent or asleep, and keep order in the village during the day as well as the night. Would have the courage to maintain that they are superfluous too?"
>
> "Perfectly so," said Padre Lopez, "and you ought to remember that previous to the advent of strangers here, the Indians never bolted or locked their doors at nights, as they had entire confidence in the honesty of their neighbors. If stealing during the night, house breaking and the like are complaints of today, and become subject of Judicial interference, we ought to be thankful to the strangers...."
>
> "Civilization and Progress," continued Padre Lopez, walking to and fro as if unconscious of the presence of his antagonist, "these are the big words, the sespedalia verba, which are constantly in the mouth of the Progressives of the age, but what do they mean after all? Nothing, absolutely nothing."[17]

15. Although this tale possesses elements of the gothic—nightmarish elements of the uncanny—it fits more neatly into Nathaniel Hawthorne's definition of the romantic, which he says "attempts to connect a bygone time with the present that is flitting away from us." In this context, the moral temperament that Hawthorne suggests ought to be present in the romance—"that the wrong-doing of one generation lives into successive ones, and, divesting itself of every temporary advantage, becomes a pure and uncontrolled mischief"—is not present in *Inez*. However, Tronchin captures the sense of a bygone era that is passing and renders it attractively. See the preface to Nathaniel Hawthorne's *The House of the Seven Gables*, (Boston: Houghton Mifflin, 1924), p. 14.

16. In *Les Deux Premiers Martyrs*, de St. Avit names all of the Indian ethnic groups that lived in Trinidad before the coming of the Spaniards.

17. L. B. Tronchin, *Inez or the Last of the Aroucas* (Trinidad: R. J. Allers, 1885), pp. 4–5. All other references to this work are referred to in the text as *I*.

In this idyllic setting, *Inez* recaptures the Arcadian delight of an uncorrupted past that Antonio, a poor peon, rejected suitor and brother of Inez (he was not aware of his relationship to her at the time he offers his suit), shares with the latter. In an effort to capture her love, Antonio appeals to a past they shared and asks:

Do you remember the days of our infancy Inez, happy and delightful days that have fleeted away like an agreeable dream? Do you remember our solitary walks in the evenings, along the borders of the river, collecting shinning pebbles for your amusement at home? Afterwards when we were more advanced in age, we rambled during the cocoa-trees, or in the world forest behind the plantation, gathering wild flowers, and picking wild fruits. Sitting on the large flat rocks, and the placid surface of the basin slightly ruffled by the aromatic wind coming from the mountain nights. During our long moon-lit night in the dry season, how delectable and pleasant it was to be sitting on the same bench, listening attentively to the interesting narrations of Don Diego; sometimes it was the wars between the Indian tribes; sometimes some episodes of hunting expedition, but more commonly domestic life, and the happiness he enjoyed for twenty-five years with your dear mother (*I*, p. 18).

In presenting this version of the past, the author wishes the reader to sympathize with Antonio, who describes himself as "a common labourer, who earns his bread with his cutlass; a despicable Indian, uncivilized and rough" (*I*, p. 19). Although her father prefers that she marry "an Indian like myself," he is committed to honor his wife's dying command that "[y]ou should never make violence to her [Inez's] affection, or inclination. I have learnt from experience, and you know it well, what a woman suffers when the aspirations of her heart are disregarded" (*I*, p. 25). To the great sorrow of her father, the unfaithfulness of Lorenzo, Inez's husband, leads to her insanity. Don Diego should not have ignored the warning contained in the nocturnal cry of the Chouette, "the ill-omened bird of death," when he approved his daughter's marriage to Lorenzo.[18]

---

18. The mythology associated with the call of the Chouette bird has its parallel in the Souffriere bird, which also acts as the harbinger of death. In his epic on the Caribs of St. Vincent, *Hiroona: An Historical Romance in Poetic Form*, (188?, Port of Spain: Franklin's Electrical Printery, 1930), Horatio Nelson Huggins writes:

> One other augury there yet remained,
> Before th' assurance sough was fully gained;
> Could they but reach the plains or ere were heard
> The plaintive notes of dread Souffrière bird—
> Mysterious Songster, which had never been,
> And could not be, 'twas said, by mortals seen,
> From inmost shades, where deepened solitudes
> Enthral with strange still awe the gloomy woods,
> Thence weirdly sweet yet mournful notes would swell,
> And send the thrilling warning through the dell,
> O'er wood, round bluffs and heights of grimSouffrière,
> Till th' echoes floated faintly o'er the mere.
> Those phantoms notes the Caribs heard with dread
> As voice of warning sent them from the dead. (p. 62.)

Tronchin's elaborate thesis about the supernatural in human affairs and the part it plays in Amerindian mythology is also woven into this story.[19] He also examines Amerindian customs and contrasts them with the European mores. Yet, the moral temperament that Hawthorne sees as the *sin qua non* of the tale is not present in *Inez* even though Tronchin appeals to aspects of moral rectitude that have been violated in the Amerindian society. For him, the Europeans introduced modes of civilization that did not always represent steps in the right direction. Inez's crazed condition is a result of the evils of certain aspects of European civilization.

Inez displays Tronchin's wide-ranging knowledge of the classical authors and French literature. His many references to historical figures in his tale reveal a colonial scholar bent on demonstrating his mastery over the colonizer's culture. In the first three pages of *Inez*, one encounters such phrases such "[t]he school-master who was a typical representation of the *genus* Dominnie Sampson, immortalized by Sir Walter Scott" (*I*, p. 1); "[t]he Dominique...was in the habit of brainwashing his vardassa just as Virgil represents Aeneas on the banks of the Styx" (*I*, p. 2); and "[a]lthough I am very much inclined to accept the views of Jacques Rousseau on the superiority of the natural state...." References to Dante, Shakespeare's Othello, and Orsiris of Ancient Egypt also appear in the text. Although these references confirm Tronchin's erudition and scholarship, they do not carry forward the meaning of the text nor, for that matter, are they tightly integrated into the tale. They remain surface signals, telling the reader *what* he ought to feel rather than arousing the reader's sympathy and interest through dialogue and narrative thrust.[20] These interventions provided the editor of *Public Opinion* with the opportunity to advise Tronchin "to avoid such incursions into the domains of natural science as the paragraph on the descent of man.... They can add nothing to the interest of his work, and placed as is the one referred to, they savour rather of the grotesque than of philosophic research."[21]

Although *Inez* is not artistically successful, it does offer Tronchin a showcase to display his erudition. Perhaps, not surprisingly, he seemed more at ease in his essays and his commentaries that display an analytical turn of mind. Within the Trinbagonian tradition, he stands out for his erudition and his capacity to capture

19. In this romance, Tronchin see the human being as "the most perfect of the created forms. He is the last link of material perfectibility. But he possesses duality. In him, there is another being which is not subjected to material laws. That being which is the real man, is called the soul. It forms the first link of spiritual perfectibility. Standing as it does on the threshold of the two worlds—the Material and the Spiritual—has he not sometimes the means of obtaining a glimpse of that unknown state in which he is shortly to enter? Yes, sleep, mesmeric trance, and death, afford him that means. They differ in degrees but not in kind. While their influence is exercised the Spiritual body is perfectly free. Second-sight, mesmeric trance are of frequent occurrence, and explain satisfactorily and scientifically those supernatural coincidences and phenomena which are unjustly denominated superstitious practices" (*I*, p. 27).

20. *Hiroona*, by contrast, is a more organized narrative than *Inez*. All of its parts (cantos) are designed to tell the story of the Carib war in St. Vincent. Although Huggins draws on external episodes (mostly mythological), they are marshaled together carefully to carry forward the meaning of the story. As such, they tend to enhance rather than detract from the central content of the work. Tronchin's references or allusions, it seems, are more ornamental than they are functional.

21. "Inez," *Public Opinion*, October 27, 1885.

and synthesize the currents of the age. Yet, the very qualities that made him an out-standing essayist paralyzed him when he wrote his tale.

Although little is known of his private life and his other novels, Tronchin's work embodies the intellectual attitudes and aspirations of his age.[22] His work signals the passing of the torch from a white French-speaking to a native intellectual class. Undoubtedly, his intellectual prowess, his command of the language and academic fearlessness make him the quintessential Trinidadian man of letters of his time. He was a prototype of the kind of scholars that Trinidad produced in the nineteenth and twentieth centuries.

Les Deux Premiers Martyrs de la Trinidad

The attempt of Kums and Tronchin to connect with the Amerindian experience and to inculcate the Amerindian story into Trinidad and Tobago's [his]tory also became the thrust of Jean-Ch. de St. Avit's, *The First Two Martyrs of Trinidad*, a drama that was serialized in *Public Opinion* from April 24 through May 15, 1885, and which was later turned into a book.[23] This beautifully wrought work, replete with historical Indian names, places, and incidents, is the first dramatic work that attempts to recreate the Spanish-Amerindian rivalry of the period.

Set in 1513, the drama represents the betrayal of the original inhabitants and the pressures placed on them to conform to the white man's way of life.[24] In his intro-duction, St. Avit notes that *The First Two Martyrs of Trinidad* is a part of Trinidad's history: "It is not merely fiction. It is based on historical fact." Although the exact location of this massacre (some say martyrdom) was the subject of debate, its real-ity created an historical base from which to explore the national memory, even if that memory was being changed in historical time.[25] The massacre's reenactment

22. Tronchin was also the author of *Phantom Nun of Mount Moriah* which, as he says, describes "the unheard ravages of the cholera [epidemic]" that ravaged Port of Spain during the second half of the nineteenth century. See "The Great West Indian Orator," December 18–21, 1888.

23. Although I do not possess the necessary evidence, there is every reason to speculate that St. Avit, like Philip and Tronchin, was a part of the native intellectual group that was prominent during the sec-ond half of the nineteenth century. They spoke and wrote in French and were versed in the classics. *Les Deux Premiers Martyrs de la Trinidad* (hereafter, *The First Two Martyrs*) was published originally in French, as were many of Tronchin's early essays. *Les Deux Premiers Martyrs de la Trinidad* was translat-ed into English by Jacqueline Morin, agregee d'anglais, lycee Saint-Louis, Paris. Professor Morin also translated "Les Sauteurs à la Grenade, ou Ina la Caraibe."

24. The spirit of this play evokes sentiments to those of Charlot, the Indian of the Flathead Indians of present-day Idaho and northeast Montana, who chastised the U.S. government when the proposal was made that his group should pay taxes: "What is he? Who sent him here? We were happy when he first came; since then we often saw him, always heard him and of him. We first thought he came from the light, but he comes like the dusk of the evening now, not like the dawn of the morning. He comes like a day that has passed, and night enters our future with him.... In his poverty we fed, we cherished him—yes, befriended him, and showed [him] the fords and defiles of our land." Quoted in Nina Bayam et al., *Norton Anthology of American Literature, Vol. 2*, Fourth Edition (New York, 1994), p. 269.

25. See, for example, Francisco Paul, "Detached Pages of the History of Trinidad," *Fair Play*, May 14, 1878.

allows us to understand who our ancestor were and why it is important that we see their fate as being inexorably linked to our own.[26]

Drawing on the historical record, St. Avit notes that Father Francois de Cordoue [from Cordova] and Juan Garces, both Spanish Dominican monks, who had first evangelized Santo Domingo Indians, faced "insurmountable difficulties when they tried to protect the unfortunate Indians against Spaniards who exploited them." They decided to leave Santo Domingo to preach the Gospel to people who had not previously been under the yoke of Spanish domination. "They chose the island of Trinidad where they landed in 1513, not quite 15 years after Christopher Columbus had discovered the island." Their fate, it turned out, was not that different from what it might have been in Santo Domingo. Only, in this case, the dramatist's tone seems to be sympathetic to the missionaries, a feeling that they, too, were victims of the Spanish treachery and brutality.

As the play opens, several caciques ("the council of caciques") from different ethnic groups are seen sitting in a "carbie," or communal house, located on the very spot of the present "catholic cathedral of Port of Spain." They meet to decide the fate of two Dominican missionaries whom they believe participated in their betrayal. As they seek council from the Great Spirit, they sum up their dilemma in words that have a contemporary ring:

> Two strangers have come to our island,
> They are white, they are handsome,
> But they belong to the vile and impious race
> which several times made the population of
> our village scarce.
> Faced with this peril for our country
> Our chiefs are going to give a decision on their fate
> Are you going to let them live
> Or inflict death upon them?
> Are you going to let them live
> Or inflict death upon them?[27]

For the Amerindians, the conflict is real and poses devastating consequences. When the missionaries first came to their island, they were greeted with great joy at the promises they and their religion offered. Caroaori, one of the chiefs, gives voice

26. The history of the Dominican missions in the Caribbean is important. Although these missions were established "among those tribes who were sunk in heathenish darkness, and given up to the grossest kinds of idolatry," Thomas Cook acknowledges that the motive to "enlighten" was soon defeated by the "insatiable avarice" of the Spanish. Abbé Raynal notes that between 1503 and 1511 the Indian population of Hispaniola decreased from 1,200,000 to 14,000. As the Indians were being exterminated, Africans were being imported into the island to fill the breach. It is this vast cruelty and betrayal—this relationship between the two groups—that St. Avit attempts to capture in his drama. See Thomas Cook, *A History of the West Indies, Vol. 1* (Liverpool: Nuttall, Fisher and Dixon, 1808), pp. 180–86.

27. Interestingly enough, in *Inez*, Tronchin also depicts the presence of Europeans as strangers who have disrupted a particular way of life.

to the joy he felt at seeing those "heavenly strangers" in their midst: "Just watching them triggered something in me, an unparalleled happiness." Carapana, son of Guarionex and chief of Tunapuna, tells of breaking his idols when he first encountered these holy men and the contents of a vision he had: "Listen to their advice, be obedient./ They will be a treasure for your wandering tribes./ Welcome them." By the end of the first act of this four-act play, the people of Cairi (the Indian name of the island)[28] say:

> The divine messengers have promised plenty blessings
> Upon our fathers and mothers,
> If we agree to love with a sincere heart
> The sacred law of Jesus Christ.

The missionaries, themselves, are pleased with the reception they receive. Father Juan Garcia, seeing the enthusiasm of the Indians and their reception of Jesus's word, says to his fellow missionary:

> What a splendid dawn!
> Dear Brother, what will daylight then be?
> Its brightness, its splendor will make of our stay here
> A foretaste of heaven.

Cardova, the more cautious and mature of the pair, responds:

> Dearest Brother, let us be able
> To contain our enthusiasm. Doubtlessly, an era
> Of sweet hope may be heralded in our hearts;
> But we will have to fight the anger of watchful enemies
> Who may be preparing our entire ruin.

In another exchange, in which he seems to anticipate his fate, Cardova offers an introspective look at his condition and his life's ambition:

> Oh! My heart is overwhelmed!
> Oh, God of my youth, Oh Lord of my soul.
> Who in my earliest years has kindled this flame
> In my bosom, the wish to suffer
> While spreading your Holy Name and to die for you.
> I feel content. I saw two ripe ears gather by my sythe.
> The celestial family of the chosen will sing their joy
>   And happiness,

28. Huggins refers to the island as Iere, "the aborigines name for Trinidad" and notes admiringly that "[n]o Island in the West Indian Tropics can compare with Iere in the richness of its animal and vegetable kingdoms." According to the author of "Étymologie Caraibe," the "aborigines" called the island Iere or Cairi. See, *Hiroona*, p. 85, and "Étymologie Caraibe," *Public Opinion*, October 28, 1888.

To welcome today, the pleasant prime
Of this unhappy people. Of God of my youth
For whom, with no sadness, I forsook
My sorrowful father, my tearful mother
All that I loved, my brothers and sisters,
My fields and my friends of my merry young years
For thee, I have ignored the sacred
Duties of gratitude. In this faraway land, I stand
Deprived of all human help for thy sake…
Should you demand our lives, let a bloody martyrdom
Make us join you. How my soul
Yearns for the sacred palm.
I once caught sight of the gall
Given to Jesus, His nails and His very cross.
Others would come here, and preach in our stead
And they would reap the fruit ripened by your grace.

As the missionaries, at the invitation of the leaders of the various ethnic groups, prepare to go to the villages to spread the word of God, a frightening cry is heard in the distance, accompanied by "Woe are we!/ We have been betrayed." While the missionaries were dealing with the Indians, the Spaniards who were marauding the island took their chiefs as prisoners. Foaming with rage, Aterima, one of the chiefs who did not trust the Spanish entirely, shouts, "I had foreseen this;/That they [the caciques] would be enslaved [made captives] by this cursed people."

Along with the chiefs, the Spanish seized women and children. A woman who escaped from the Spanish gives this account of what she saw:

Barbaric strangers! They seemed so honest!
They dazzled us with stones.
They gave us a profusion of glass,
And bright objects and a thousand trinkets.
With curiosity having deprived us of our wisdom,
We all climbed into their enormous pirogue.
Suddenly, their big chief gave a signal
Showed us the horror of the fate that awaited us;
The men and women were seized together
And tied by those beasts.
All gave shouts loud enough to move
Even rocks. A few, however, managed to flee
By diving into the sea—That's how, I, myself,
Was able to escape at the cost of great effort.

After such treachery, a sentence of death is pronounced on the two missionaries. Although they played no part in the specific betrayal, they are thought to be part of a larger plot to betray the people of Cairi. The punishment meted out to the missionaries is more horrible than that which is committed by the Spanish, and their plea for mercy is of no avail. When they contemplate the fate of those captured by the Spanish, the anguished cries of the people chill the ear:

> Cairi, my dear country,
> You were the glory and love of the Indian tribes.
> Under the Spanish sword, your glory has faded.
> Will the good old days every come back?
>
>   . . . .
>
> Weep, oh tribes of Cairi,
> Weep for your captives brave.
> Their nimble feet are in fetters!
> Weep, tribes of Cairi, weep!

The dramatist comments on the treachery of the Spaniards, who turn on the Indians despite the warm reception they received. Aterima, who is wounded in the arm when he attempts to fight the Spanish, tries to rouse his fellow Indians. However, they are bewildered when confronted with a war with which they are not familiar, either in its moral implications (that is, the white man's betrayal) or with the weapons the Spanish used. Such a combination leads to dread and foreboding on the Indians' part:

> Those strangers are entirely without souls and without pity
> Among them, I knew there was no friendship.
> Their hearts are hearts of stone, equally scorning threats and prayers.
> We had come fairly close to their ship
> Used as a jail or as a living grave
> For our wretched chiefs. Their daughters and their wives
> Were still groaning in a heart-rending way.
> In this barbaric language, my prisoner [one of the missionaries] then
> Spoke to them for long time, apparently beseeching them
> Not to endanger the lives of saintly apostles
> (Without, I think, demanding our people's freedom).
> Eventually, I proposed to exchange captives
> For their two spies. Believing we were naïve,
> They asked us to come on board their ship
> To explain better what we actually meant.
> Seeing that stratagem did not work
> They did not hesitate to attack us.
> I saw lightening flashing in the distance
> Followed by an awful noise
> Then iron and rocks falling in the pirogue and all around us.
> We started to flee; but then those fiends, firing a second time
> Smashed my oars and I saw dark blood spilling on my hands.
> I was wounded in the arms and in the back.
> What accursed art is that, which spreads awe
> Freezes you in horror, makes your soul faint

And puts in your body stones and iron?
It is an evil art coming from hell, worthy of them.

The people of Cairi have their revenge by making Francisco de Cordova and Father Juan Garces suffer slow deaths. Throughout the play, however, there lingers a tragic sense of betrayal and incomprehension about what transpired between the Indians and the Spanish. The former are bewildered by the events that took place. If the playwright is to be believed, it is a tragedy with which the Indians never came to grips. In the end, the martyrs are presented as the victorious ones, "their transfigured faces," glorifying in the sacrifices they had made for their Jesus:

> Their faces were so beautiful
> When they were speaking to each other!
> The cloudless sun shines less
> Than their transfigured faces.
> How bright were their eyes
> When raised towards heaven,
> They were looking beyond the clouds.

These are the sentiments upon which *The First Two Martyrs of Trinidad* ends.

Although it is difficult to tell how successful this play was or what reception it received, *The First Two Martyrs* elicited a poetic response three months after its publication. An unnamed writer offered a mock-heroic poem, "The Misfortune of a Rabbit destined to die in Captivity," which supposedly took place during 1858 and which the writer claims he rediscovered when he read *The First Two Martyrs*. This anonymous writer contends, "the short piece, though the work of a beginner in poetry, shows however a lot of talent on the author's part and comprises some really beautiful literary points which connoisseurs will probably appreciate."[29] Like Tronchin's work, this poem contains literary references to Corneille (a parody of act II of *Le Cid*), "troubled Aeneas," and La Marseillaise.

---

29. *Public Opinion*, August 4, 7, 11, 1885. A bit of the neo-classical style is employed by this writer:
>   Chant IV
> So that he can sing the glory and defeat the rabbit
> Please, daughter of the Night, inspire this poet,
> Come and quicken the springs of my weak voice
> And give harmony to my emotional song—
> Lefus was still running when he saw in the arena
> His proud enemy leaning back breathless.
> He flies back to the fight, quicker and more ardent
> Than lightning flashing and striking at the same time
> Leporis, in his turn, left the place;
> The victor of three enemies, the youngest of Horatius's sons
> Seemed less fierce to the eyes of the proud Romans
> Than valiant Lefus, the rabbits' hero.

Hiroona

Given the education that Trinidadians received at the time and the various parts of the world from which their ancestors came, it is clear that they were caught up in a culture that extended beyond their shores. And, the practice of reaching beyond boundaries was also in evidence in Huggins's *Hiroona,* an historical romance in the poetic form, as he subtitled his epic work. Although born in St. Vincent and cradled in the epical struggle of the Amerindians in that country, Huggins only found the time to write in Trinidad about the Amerindian struggle in St. Vincent against the Europeans. Immigrating to Trinidad early in life, Huggins became a Canon in the Anglican Church, a member of the Diocesan Synod, and pastor of St. Paul's in San Fernando and St. Matthews in Oropouche. He was also the president of the Order of the Sacred Cross, a Social and Friendly Society. Because of his closeness to the freedom struggle, he was able to depict the Amerindian in an authentic and sympathetic light. More than anything else, these qualities may have led to his authorship of what Paula Burnett calls "the Caribbean's first epic poem."[30]

Published posthumously, *Hiroona* was composed in the 1880s when the Amerindian, as subject, drew intense scrutiny. In his poem, Huggins demonstrates his love for the dignity of the Amerindian and his admiration for their exploits. Analogous to the sketches and legends that were being reproduced in Latin America during the same period, Huggins's works offers a gripping account of the Carib's insurrection on St. Vincent. For his part, Huggins brought together the legends associated with the Amerindian presence in the Leeward Islands (including Trinidad and Tobago).[31] Further, he judges the Amerindians to be of equal status with Europeans and to possess a strength and a bravery not articulated as strongly in earlier works about the Amerindian presence in the Caribbean. For example, the encounter between Chetewaye, an Amerindian hero, and Norman, his English counterpart, is portrayed in a way that respects the courage of each character:

> No craven-soul submission's token this
> In self-respect our Carib pride remiss—
> (That pride to Hiroon's Indian souls inborn,
> Rejecting claims of Kings or lords with scorn—)
> But pledge and token, meant and understood,
> That man to man in equal manhood stood;
> That Honour plighted troth upon that brand,

---

30. Paula Burnett, ed., *The Penguin Book of Caribbean Verse in English* (Harmondsworth: Penguin, 1986), p. 1. Although *Hiroona* was published in 1930, Lottie and Evelyn Huggins, heirs of Horatio, attest that he left the manuscript when he died on July 27, 1895. George F. Huggins concludes that Horatio wrote this epic in the latter part of his life. As such, it seems reasonable to treat it as a part of this period. Needless to say, *Hiroona* contains many thematic similarities with the other works of this time.

31. According to George F. Huggins, "the Indian name for St. Vincent was 'Hiroon,' which means 'The Blessed.'" In the poem the author uses Hiroon "for poetic euphony and 'for endearment sake'" (*Hiroona*, Preface).

And placed its very life in friendship's hand:
And breach of friendship's bond no Carib knows,
Though treacherous, implacable to foes.
One moment Norman held the proffered sword,
Accepting thus the troth; and then restored
The pledge. His own good word he gave with clasp
Of honest hand, the hearty English grasp.
The shades of night were deepening fast around,
Before the friends had left the sacred ground.[32]

Thus, in *Hiroona*, the Caribs are depicted as individuals who possess free will and have their own outlook on the world. Even in death, after the English has cut him down in battle, Chetwaye, the leader of the Indians, is portrayed as honorable:

But o'er Chetwaye's prostrate form,
Still through such vigorous life-blood warm,
Stood Leith in flush of victory
And pride of conscious gallantry;
And gazed upon his fallen foe
With reverence such as brave men know.
Around the chieftain's shoulders lay
(The gift of England's prince, they say,
Who thus in sort had dubbed him knight)
A silver collar, glittering bright.
With reverent hand unclasping this,
The victor claimed it now as his.
"A splendid soldier here has died
"Of honours due be none denied
"A soldier's grave refuse him not."
With glistening eyes thus spoke the Scot.
But Caribs crept, how none can say,
And bore the honoured corpse away (*H.*, p. 196).

We are also made acquainted with the complexity of the culture through the depiction of characters such as Nannette, "the dreaded Carib queen, / The Obeah-working fiend" (*H.*, p. 97) and the presence of the Socucouan, "a dark and terrible [figure of] superstition, imported by the slaves from Africa."[33] How African myths

32. *Hiroona*, p. 76. All other citations from this poem will appear in the text as *H.* Huggins intimacy with the Indians—and his tendency to humanize them more—stemmed from the fact that St. Vincent had a larger, more active Indian population in the nineteenth century than did Trinidad and, as George F. Huggins notes in his preface to the book, the author "heard and committed to memory the many stories of the Caribs as handed down by tradition" (Ibid., Preface).

33. According to Huggins, the soucouan a "hag from the lower world is supposed to come forth underground, like a vampire to suck [an individual's] blood, but is under the necessity of leaving her skin at the place of exit. Should anyone carry off the skin, the Soucouan would be helpless. Her feast of blood over, the Soucouan recovers her skin and vanishes" (*H.*, p 99).

are imbricated into the Amerindian spiritual world is also highlighted in this text. It also shows how these multicultures were beginning to melt into one society.

Huggins uses the Carib war against the British on St. Vincent and the losers' subsequent deportation to Rattan Island in the Bay of Honduras to structure his poem.[34] Like previous works, the Amerindians' rage is directed against the Europeans in general ("But then in evil day the white man came,/And brought from hell itself its brands of flame." [*H.*, p. 85]). By fixing his gaze on the British, Huggins implicates them in the drama of the Indians' dispossession: "Duvalle— Hiroona's fiercest child,/ In action vehement and wild,/ Cruel, in war infuriate,/ For England full of deadliest hate—" (*H.*, p. 142). Significantly, the maroons joined the Indians in their assault at "Exterminating England's power" (*H.*, p. 142) even though enslaved Africans felt the sting of the Indians' wrath.

In spite of his heroic and dignified portrayal of the Amerindians, Huggins fell into the trap of stereotyping them as noble savages and primitives:

> Ay! Savages they surely were!
> Yet man's own royal form they bare;
> A fine and well-formed race, high-souled,
> With love for kith and kin, and bold
> To admiration to defend
> Their hearth, to save or serve a friend (*H.*, pp. 14–15).

Africans are also depicted in a negative, childlike, trusting manner. In some descriptions, stock stereotypes such as Uncle Tom and Aunt Jemima come to mind:

> Now came two ancient grey-haired slaves,
> Old Claire the nurse, the butler Greaves;
> Most faithful honest pair. The one
> Regarded Norman as her son;
> Had nursed him thirty years ago,
> And now she nursed his babes; and so,
> A strangely privileged old dame,
> And slave in nothing but the name,
> She deemed herself, good soul, to be
> Head member of the family.
> E'en more important still, old Greaves

34. The signing of the Treaty of Paris of 1763 transferred control of St. Vincent to Britain. This led to the displacement of the French planters by English colonists. As a result, the Caribs lost most of their land. With the assistance of the French, the Caribs carried out many military operations to revenge the British. After years of fierce battles, Sir Ralph Abercromby arrived with reinforcements and subjugated them. On March 11, 1797, 5,080 Caribs were deported "as a tribal nation, to Rattan Island in the Bay of Honduras" (*Hiroona*, Preface). This conflict is also celebrated in "King Shadoway," one of the first African-American dramas presented at Mr. Brown playhouse, in New York in 1821 (See John Dewberry, "The African Grove Theatre and Company," *Black American Literature Forum*, 16, No. 4 [Winter 1982], pp. 128-131).

Looked down upon his fellow slaves;
Mere *negroes* they, worth so much pelf,
But *he,* his master's second self!
And by that master humoured much:
The country's customs then were such (*H.*, p. 106).

It might be that Huggins's religious persuasion forced him to believe that the Europeans came to the Caribbean to bring salvation, that is, Christianity, to the savages. He suggests that the greed of gold thwarted this noble ambition:

Ay! Go, Columbus, on thy fated way
Nor dream a nation's doom thou'st seal'd this day!
Go! Proud Civilization's pioneer,
And carve in new-found worlds a new career!
Yet know thy well-meant zeal, that led thee here
Doth bode th'unmeasured grief, th'unnumbered tear!
O'er those fair lands shall havoc's deluge sweep;
And while recording Angels write they'll weep!
Mysterious fingers trace, as on the wall,
Spain's misused day of grace and Spain's downfall (*H.*, p. 15).

Even Ranee, the heroine of the text, is a victim of this tendency to present Christianity in this superior light. Huggins says that "she'd happily outgrown/ Her people's sterner hates and fiercer traits,/Imbibing much of white man's thoughts and ways" (*H.*, p. 115). In the end, she accepts Crayton's love, flinging "her arms around/His feet imprinted there a kiss,/Murmuring, 'I will die content with this.'" With that act, she turns her back on her people and gives herself to the Christian God. In failing breath, she proclaims her faith:

My spirit now has found its rest:
I yield it to the Christian's God,
The same Who left high Heav'n's abode
And came to earth, I've heard, to save
The spirit of the life He gave.
So lay me in the Christian ground,
That there I may with them be found (*H.*, pp. 294–95).

The epic comes to an end when, in the final climatic scene, Warramou, Cheywaye's son, exiled to Rattan Island, pronounces his final curse on the English. Ultimately, he believes that justice will be done: "White men, I curse you to your face, /Curse you and all your hated race!/Great war has placed me in your power;/I am your captive: this your hour/ To wreck your bitterest thought of ill;/To bind or slay me as you will;/ But speech you cannot bind—'tis free!" (*H.*, p. 340). He believes that the great injustice that was done to the Caribs "will be avenged by a corresponding expulsion." His apocalyptic vision seemed to be confirmed by the explosion of the St. Vincent volcano in 1812 in which many British subjects lost their lives. His speech "of passion, fire, and righteous wroth/Of patriot and of prophet both" (*H.* p. 340) had certainly come to pass.

Hiroona was the most important and sustained poetical work written in Trinidad in the nineteenth century. Huggins's intimacy with the Caribs—he had heard many of the Amerindian stories—allowed him to humanize the Amerindian. The coming together of the Amerindians and the Africans also proved fortuitous for Huggins. Although the epic has romantic tendencies and reflects European biases against the Amerindian, it also captures an important episode in Caribbean history, and Huggins rendered that historical moment with deftness and poetic sophistication. Such was his poem's importance, it led Paula Burnett to conclude that for "all his imperfections, [Huggins] was the first to relate it [the extinction of the Caribs] to the British, and the first to question the whole role of empire" in this enterprise.[35] That he should do so when other groups were interrogating the power relations within the society makes it an important addition to Trinidad and Tobago literature.

* * *

For a brief moment in the 1880s, the Amerindians were placed at the center of the national stage. Significantly, Manuel de Jesus Galvan's *Enriquillo*, published in 1886, also assumed a central position in the consciousness of the citizens of the Dominican Republic. In a way, *Inez, The First Two Martyrs of Trinidad*, and *Hiroona* were doing for Trinidadian literature what *Enriquillo* was doing for Dominican society. As members of a vanishing minority, the Amerindians demonstrated how far the dominant society would go to achieve its inhumane objectives. This attempt to reevaluate the position of the Amerindian within the national psyche coincided with the attempt to understand what it meant to be a Caribbean person in a society that was violated by Europeans in their drive to "civilize" the native. Necessarily, this attempt to reclaim an autochthonous language (tongue/nation) reflected itself in the Warramou's desire to repossess the language of his people:

> "What ho! Chattoyer! You, my friend, what now?"
> Grow dark with gathering shade his swarthy brow
> Before he answer made, "No, e'en from you,
> "I'll hear a foreign name—I'm Warramou!
> "Chetwaye, like my father, I might claim
> "To be. But Chattoyer, the barbarous name
> "Is French. 'John Demmy,' that the English gave.
> "These tainted names I bury in the grave.
> "E'en from my youth to bear them I was loth,
> "But from to-day renounce and scorn them both.
> "I'm Warramou! My blood as pure and red
> "As ever Hiroon's warrior-sons have shed.

---

35. Burnett, *The Penguin Book of Caribbean Verse in English*, p. li.

"I tell thee England's reckoning-day has come,
"And Carib war hath quit his mountain-home" (*H.*, p. 79).

This sense of national purification seems necessary before the society could come to terms with its specific identity. The concern with the naming process and the search for authenticity (i.e., recovery of a past glory) reveal an attempt to situate the Amerindian in the evolving national consciousness. It was also part of a process that reinscribed the Amerindian within the national space, part of a continuing desire to come to terms with the many strands of the nation's population, and another attempt to make sense of the mélange of cultural tendencies that were the society's inheritance.

CHAPTER 13

The Negro's Grievance:
Literature in the Service of a Cause

There has been no saint in the West Indies since Las Casas, no hero unless philonegro enthusiasm can make one out of Toussaint. There are no people there in the true sense of the word, with a character and purpose of their own, unless to some extent in Cuba, and therefore when the wind has changed and the wealth for which the islands were alone valued is no longer to be made among them, and slavery is no longer possible and would not pay if it were, there is nothing to fall back upon.

—JAMES ANTHONY FROUDE, *The English in the West Indies*

We of the Caribbean are a people more than any other people constructed by history, and therefore any attempt not only to analyze but to carry out political or social activity, in connection with ourselves and in relation to other peoples, any such attempt has got to begin and constantly to bear in mind how we came into being, where we have reached, who we are and what we are. We were brought from Africa and thrown into a highly developed modern industry and a highly developed modern language. We had to master them or die.

—C. L. R. JAMES, "The West Indian Intellectual"

Santa really take a big man from St. James and tie he like a cow in
    Morvant;
Sun and rain wetting de man but he can't get away, poor fellar.

—KING SOLOMON (Samuel Ryan), "Santa"

The primary issue that plagued African people at the beginning of the nineteenth century came to the fore with renewed intensity as the century came to a close: that is, the right of black people to rule themselves in their new environment. In 1888, fifty years after formal emancipation, there were obstructionists who believed West Indian blacks still wallowed in savagery and barbarity and that white rule represented the *sin qua non* of progress. Thirty-three years after Maxwell Philip alluded to the height to which Egyptian civilization reached during antiquity, Edward Blyden reasserted that Africans were not a barbaric people but the founders of a great civilization: "From Ethiopia, the Blacks had penetrated the desert westward to find the great West African civilization and it was from these great civilizations of the West that slaves were taken in the sixteenth century to the New World."[1] Deeply impressed by the nonracial dimension of Islam, Blyden "came to feel that its doctrines of brotherhood and lack of racial prejudice made it a more suitable religion for Africans than missionary-Christianity."[2] A commentator in *Public Opinion* complained that fifty years after formal freedom, "the sequel to emancipation has not been historically creditable." He asked that preference be given to Africans over "aliens," whom he believed had become a danger to the common weal.[3] Blyden, himself, came to believe that "the Negro, notwithstanding his two hundred years' residence with Christian and civilized races, has nowhere received anything like a correct education. We find him everywhere—in the United States, in the West Indies, in South America—largely unable to cope with the responsibilities which devolve upon him. Not only is he not sought after for any position of influence in the political movements of those countries, but he is even denied admission to ecclesiastical appointments of importance."[4]

When James Anthony Froude visited the Caribbean in 1887, he found a society bent on ruling itself, a society that believed it was not receiving the benefits emancipation promised, and a society that felt it had to make its frustration known to the mother country. Froude believed that West Indian blacks were incapable of governing themselves and that, if the English left, everything would return to barbarity and cannibalism. C. L. R. James points out that Froude was "an intimate friend, in fact perhaps the closest friend, of Thomas Carlyle, and forty years before Carlyle had made clear that he, among all others, was foremost in his attack upon not only colored people on the whole but on the West Indian black people in particular."[5] At the end of his journey, almost as though he were responding to Charles Kingsley, Froude concluded that "[t]o the man of science the West Indies may be delightful and instructive. Rocks and trees and flowers remain as they always were, and Nature is constant to herself; but the traveler whose heart is with his kind, and cares only to see his brother mortals making their corner of this planet into an orderly and rational home, had better choose some other object for his pilgrimage." For him, these "specimens of black humanity" were not people "in the true sense of the word with a character and a purpose of their own."[6] When he saw over 15,000

1. Quoted in Leonard E. Barret, Sr., *The Rastafarians* (Boston: Beacon Press, 1997), pp. 75–76.

2. Edward W. Blyden, *Christianity, Islam and the Negro Race* (Edinburgh: Edinburgh University Press, 1967), p. xiv.

3. "The Negro Grievance, " *Public Opinion*, October 16, 1885.

4. Blyden, *Christianity, Islam and the Negro Race*, p. 74.

5. C. L. R. James, "The West Indian Intellectual, " in J. J. Thomas, *Froudacity* (1889, London: New Beacon, 1969), p. 24.

6. James Anthony Froude, *The English in the West Indies* (New York: Scribner's Sons, 1900, pp. 349, 348, 347.

citizens gathered in the Queen's Park Savannah, the largest piece of open space in Trinidad, speaking boldly about their desire for freedom, he saw only "political agi-tators."[7] His derogatory comments, captured in *The English in West Indies* (1887), brought forth a stinging response from J. J. Thomas, the quintessential Trinidad scholar of the nineteenth century.

J. J. Thomas

The reality of color prejudice, or what Thomas called "skin-dread," always received critical attention in his work. In the latter part of his life he began to write a history of emancipation.[8] A dark-skinned man who obviously was doubled-dis-criminated against because of his race and his complexion, Thomas always inveighed against those who used race to depreciate the ability of African people. In 1886, Thomas wrote two pamphlets, "Rowdy-Dowdy" and "Rowdiana," to expose what he considered a public scandal in the school system. "Rowdy Dowdy," a vigorous public invective, was directed against Josephine McKay, a Scottish woman, brought to Trinidad in 1884 to be the head mistress of the girls' depart-ment of San Fernando Borough School. Shortly after she arrived, McKay demand-ed that the school be divided, boys and girls to be kept separate. The Borough Council agreed. Such an action displeased Thomas terribly since he had been appointed to head the entire school with great fanfare a few months previously. He thought that McKay was incompetent and believed that she received her position primarily because she was white. Michael Anthony observes that "looking at the correspondence in the letter-books of the [San Fernando] Town Hall it is…clear that the Borough Council sided with the Scottish lady against John Jacob Thomas."[9]

"Rowdiana" attacked William Spencer Clerk and James Wharton, two members of the Borough Council, who employed McKay. Thomas rationalized that by their actions, they conspired to deprive "a fellow creole–talented, a good teacher, a lady–of bread in order to please Miss MacKay whom all admit had nothing save her skin to recommend her." In his pamphlet, Thomas accused Wharton of dermophobia, "the fear, on the part of a dark-complexioned person, of those who have a fairer com-plexion than he."[10] In his polemic, Thomas emphasized the need for Africans to be treated fairly in the society. A reviewer in *Grenada People* observed that "*Rowdy-*

---

7. Ibid., p. 354.

8. See Donald Wood biographical sketch of Thomas in J. J. Thomas, *Froudacity* (London: New Beacon, 1969), p. 9. Wood writes that "[o]ne of the sorrows of his comparatively early death is that this [book] was never finished for it was undertaken by a descendant of slaves, close enough to the events to have received authentic impressions of their value in human terms, and moreover by a scholar gifted with a sense of the perspectives of history and an acute awareness of the hard road traveled by his peo-ple from their African beginnings—unique attributes in that Trinidad of eighty years ago" (p. 9).

9. Michael Anthony, *Anaparima: The History of San Fernando and Naparimas, Vol. 1, 1595–1900* (Laventille: City Council of San Fernando, 2001), p. 436.

10. J. J. Thomas, "The Reviewer Reviewed," *New Era*, June 7, 1886.

Dowdy is ably written, in a lofty style reminding us somewhat of Gibbon, and here and there bringing forcibly to our recollection the incomparable letters of *Junuis*. The command of language, the nervous style, and the copiousness of his vocabulary, stamp Mr. Thomas as a first rate English scholar capable of anything in prose."[11] In June 1886, Thomas responded to *Public Opinion* criticism of his pamphlets. He insisted that Miss McKay was an unfit teacher and role model for the girls and that her practice of corporal punishment was unbecoming of her status. More importantly, Thomas indicated that he had a public duty to use his pen to vindicate his profession (teaching) and his race:

> You speak, Sir, of talents 'wasted' by me, in exposing public impostures, fraud, civic corruption, cruelty to the young, and the degradation of our educational standards. You pity me for being so misguided in the selection of my subject as not to have known that a historical romance was worthier of my skill. Permit me, Sir, to differ entirely from you. There is no talent in the world lofty or powerful enough for the vindication of Right and the rebuke of Wrong. In my letter of resignation to the Borough Council of San Fernando, I "reserved to myself the right of vindicating Local Instruction, as a cause, and my own claims as an individual and a Teacher." That pledge I have imperfectly redeemed by *Rowdy-Dowdy*, which is not, as you would have your readers believe, an attack upon a woman not worth the while, but an exposure of men in power who, for one whole year and nine months, upheld that woman [Miss McKay] at the expense of their constituents in a post for which, from the very first day, she had given the strongest possible proofs of utter unfitness.... Finally, Sir, let me ask: Does it lie with you, the Editor of *Public Opinion*, to rebuke any one for wasting their time and talents?.... If the destruction of a public educational institution in the second town of the Colony, and the unrighteous dealings of the representatives of the people, are matters unworthy of the pen of a man of talent, it would be difficult to see how those topics are surpassed in public importance by the private disagreement and personal recriminations of the Proprietor of a newspaper and its former editor.[12]

Thomas, it seems, was justified in his attacks against McKay, Wharton, and Clerk. The evidence indicates that the headmistress was disrespectful toward Thomas and was indeed incompetent. She knew little of Thomas's achievements in education and linguistics and did not care overmuch for Africans. She even had the temerity to complain that Thomas was not servile enough. She complained that "I am having trouble for water. Formerly, Mr. Thomas used to fill up the buckets. Now he gives the key to the boys and they waste the water."[13] Not only did the Borough Councilors show open favoritism toward her; they even tried to cover up her incompetence.

Thomas must have been very angry. He announced he would write an autobi-

---

11. *Grenada People,* June 1886.
12. Thomas, "The Reviewer Reviewed.
13. *Anaparima,* p. 436.

ography in which he would "speak plainly of certain personages with whom I have come into contact, some of them wise enough to allow for an African to be enlightened and to be master his own soul, and others, in the ignorance of race and office, ignoring all such a possibility."[14] In 1885, Thomas openly accused the members of the Borough Council of acting with bias in favor of McKay. Small slights took on greater significance. For instance, Anthony reveals that Thomas was not given "the splendid accommodation that had been enjoyed by the former headmaster, Samuel Proctor."[15] Failing health, problems with his eyes, and a worsening financial school situation aggravated his condition. In March, he took a month's leave of absence to go to Port of Spain to see about his eyes. It was extended to three months. By June, he was in Grenada. Fed up with the Borough School controversy, he submitted his resignation to the Council: "Situated as I am, with my sight very much impaired, and with treatment for the infirmity in a strange land, I feel it incumbent on me, especially in view of the facts affecting my relations with the Borough Council of San Fernando…to tender my resignation of the post I once held as Master of the Boys' High School."[16] Thomas was proven right in the end, for soon after his departure, McKay was fired for incompetence.

The English in the West Indies

Thomas's desire to vindicate his people via his pen found its most eloquent expression in *Froudacity*, his response to *The English in the West Indies*. Although his experience with the San Fernando Borough Council bought him much pain, other discussions in the society about the "laziness of the entire Negro race"[17] made him feel uncomfortable. Some people even argued that Africans were inferior to the Indians. A local reader of *Public Opinion* who described himself as "a negro of a very pronounced type and moreover a native" critiqued J. H. Collens's *Guide to Trinidad* when it appeared. He observed that although Collens may be a "very harmless person,…it is exactly such men who, unconsciously, sow seeds of discord that bring forth, in the course of time, fruitful harvests of evils of all kinds. It is to such men that we are indebted for the present state of things in Ireland; that the English look upon the Irish as an inferior race and treat them with thorough contempt, which is repaid with the most intense hatred…. His book…is an insult to the native population of Trinidad and I think it a crying shame that the money of the tax-payers should have been spent to print such a libel on the inhabitants of the island."[18]

14. Ibid., p. 446.
15. Ibid., p. 466.
16. Ibid., p. 467.
17. See J. H. Collens, *Guide to Trinidad* and an evaluation of the text in *Public Opinion*, March 11, 1887. Collens wrote that blacks "are proverbially lazy and naturally indolent." Similar views are found in his detective novel, *Who Did It?* Collens, an Englishman, was the superintendent of the Boys Model and Normal School in Port of Spain.
18. "A Negro," *Public Opinion*, March 25, 1887. See also, *Public Opinion*, March 11, 1887, for a review of *Guide to Trinidad*.

The *English in the West Indies* echoes Collens's sentiments, albeit in a more reactionary and racist way. Froude believes in "the natural superiority" of whites and their God-given right to rule Africans, and he advocates closer imperial ties with English men and women in British territories. He claims that West Indian blacks needed a religion to keep them from "falling back into devil worship" since, in Hayti, "child murder and cannibalism have reappeared," in spite of the presence of Christian priests. Froude does not believe that slavery per se was a bad thing: "The negroes who were sold to the dealers in the African factories were most of them either slaves already to worse masters or were *servi*, servants in the old meaning of the word, prisoners of war, or else criminals, *servanti* or reserved for death. They would otherwise have been killed; and since the slave trade has been abolished are again killed in the too celebrated 'customs.'" Froude even proposes that there must have been "something human and kindly" about slavery in that "it left upon the character [of the Negro] the marks of courtesy and good breeding".[19] Yet, he has no faith in the ability of "these children of darkness" to make any progress without white guidance: "They knew their own deficiencies, and would infinitely prefer a wise English ruler to any constitution which could be offered to them. If left entirely to themselves, they would in a generation or two relapse into savages" (*EIWI.*, p. 56) These, of course, were Kingsley's exact sentiments when he left Trinidad in 1870.

In February 1888, after the first copies of Froude's book reached the West Indies, "anger and sharp editorials" greeted it.[20] On February 17, an editorial in *New Era* observed that the journal had looked forward, with great interest to *The English in the West Indies*. However, the "numerous inaccuracies with which it abounds render it totally useless to the seeker after truth." Apart from its vivid descriptions, "not inferior to the descriptive passages in Kingsley's *At Last*," the book reveals "the most stupidly malignant calumny" on the character of the Negro. Taking offense at "the contemptuous terms in which our native population is spoken of," the newspaper averred: "Mr. Froude must certainly have remarked [*sic*] how here in Trinidad there are many gentlemen of black and coloured extraction who worthily occupy positions of trust and influence. In many cases these gentlemen are the architects of their own fortunes, and several are indebted for the completion of their education to the admirable incentives to learning offered by the Government in the shape of the scholarship annually competed for by the pupils of our two great colleges, the principals of which could have given Mr. Froude trustworthy information regarding the *real* mental calibre of Trinidadians."

A few months after the *New Era* editorial, C. S. Salmon, the president of Nevis and former colonial secretary and administrator of the Gold Coast responded to Froude. Elsa Goveia, a distinguished West Indian historian, believes that Salmon might have been a West Indian. In any case, he complained about the hurried manner in which Froude and Anthony Trollope, another occasional visitor to the West

19. James Anthony Froude, *The English in the West Indies* (New York: Scribner's, 1900), p. 246; hereafter, *EIWI.*

20. Wood, *Froudacity*, p. 20.

Indies, wrote about the Caribbean and noted that their views "have been put forth without that adequate research of the subject—not necessarily on the spot—which its importance demands." He averred that "the history of the African races has yet to be written" and wondered why distinguished writers such as Froude and Trollope "did not handle the subject more seriously, when it embodied the history and qualifications of one of the largest, and one of the growing, divisions of the human family."[21] He took umbrage at Froude's contention that the laziness of the Africans led to "the ruin of the resident English families in the West Indies" and observes that "class legislation" was used to keep the Africans poor.[22]

The editors of the *New Era*, also subjected Salmon's book to a long editorial. They pointed out the unrealistic, that is, fantastic, nature of Froude's work: "In so far as accuracy is concerned, the writer of the *Bow of Ulysses* need never have left England to collect the materials for his work; he might have his descriptions of scenery from Kingsley, and of the inhabitants from any novel of naval life at the beginning of the century, and the result would have been quite as accurate a portrayal of these islands and their inhabitants. Of course, the black inhabitants have the usual 'damned nigger' stigma cast in their teeth—and behold the picture is complete."[23] The editors insisted that Froude only wanted to convince his English compatriots that theirs was a superior form of civilization and thus that they need not worry about these "savages" as they lingered in the wilderness (Froude's term was "laziness"). The West Indian Negro was everything that the European was not, hence, Froude's savage attacks on the blackness (both metaphorically and literally) of the West Indian Negro, a condition that Salmon defined as Froude's negrophobia.[24]

N. Darnell Davis, presumably an Englishman who resided in Guyana, also took exception to Froude's sentiments and repudiated "the rampant Negrophobia displayed by that gentleman." He called *The English in the West Indies* "a mere piece of Book-making, containing no real study of past History and still less of the present life, of the English and African races in the West Indies." Davis also took exception to the class bias of most of Froude's criticism, even though Davis himself seemed to be immersed in the dominant colonial attitude about the special "guiding" role of the English in the West Indies:

> The African, like the European, cannot all at once divest himself of the degraded form of Religion in which he and his fathers were brought up: hence those who live in the West Indies cannot but be struck with the marvelous progress made by the Black Man towards a more civilising view of Religion. So far from relapsing into Obeah, the majority of West Indians Africans have emerged from that form of Religious Bondage, and the remainder will do so in due time.[25]

21. C. S. Salmon, *The Caribbean Confederation* (London: Cassell, 1888), p. iv.
22. Ibid., pp. 85–87.
23. "The Caribbean Confederation," *New Era*, June 8, 1888.
24. See also, "Froudism Refuted," *Public Opinion*, June 12, 1888.
25. N. Darnell Davis, *Mr. Froude's Negophobia or Don Quixote as Cook's Tourist* (Demerara, British Guiana: Argosy Press, 1988), pp. 1, 3, 11.

Davis then speaks of the important role that the school master played in the development of the black man in the Caribbean and points the "the good example of the resident whites whose high tone of life our Tourist can bear testimony."[26]

Thomas's rebuttal to *The English in the West Indies* was the strongest and most personal. In a letter to *New Era,* he outlined his reasons for responding to Froude: "It is, in purpose, a traversing, by means of historical and commonsense arguments, of the main allegations which, as the spokesman of certain hankerers after slavery, Mr. Froude has confidently printed and published against *my* people"[27] (my italics). From March 24 to the end of July, Thomas turned out a series consisting of fifteen articles and titled "Mr. Froude and the Negroes of the British West Indies," which appeared in the *St George's Chronicle and Grenada Gazette*. The series formed the first draft of *Froudacity*. By March of the following year, Thomas's fellow citizens were doing everything in their power to assist him financially to respond to Froude's calumny.[28] For Thomas, his was a task of "self-vindication" and "patriotic duty" against the "bastard philosophising"[29] of Froude. Thomas wished to demonstrate that the latter had little knowledge of the Caribbean and thus was only a "conjuror-up of inconceivable tales" (F., p. 54). In his critique, Thomas observes that Froude never visited "the abode of any Negro" and that the Englishman's intercourse, "was exclusively with 'Anglo-West Indians', whose aversion to the Blacks he has himself, perhaps they would think indiscreetly, placed on record" (F., p. 73). Although Froude's book is filled with "rhetorical flowers," it lacks accuracy and depth and does not possess a consistent intellectual principle that kept the work together. Thomas observes:

> So far as we feel capably of intelligently mediating on questions of this inscrutable nature, we are forced to conclude that since 'natural development' could be so reg-

26. Ibid., pp. 35–36.

27. *New Era*, July 5, 1889. In Froude's eyes, Africans in the Caribbean represented nothing more than anti-types of those that he knew. Writing about how European travel writers depicted "Wild men" or "Wildness" after the sixteenth century, Haden White argues that "reports of travelers and explorers about the nature of the savages they encountered in remote places could be read in whatever way the reader *at home* desired. In any event the Wild Man was being distanced, put off in places sufficiently obscure to allow him to appear as whatever thinkers wanted to make out of him, while locating him in some place beyond the confines of civilization." Reading Froude in such a manner places him in a specific tradition—that is, writing about the ontological "other" that pervaded the writings of Machiavelli, Hobbes, and Vico down to Jean-Paul Sartre and which underlines Montainge's conclusion that "each man calls barbarism whatever is not his own practice" (Haden White, *Tropics of Discourse* [Baltimore: The Johns Hopkins University Press, 1978], pp. 174–75).

28. Thomas says that *The English in the West Indies* came into his hands in April 1888. On March 1, 1889, the following announcement appeared in the *New Era*: "A meeting was held on Tuesday evening at St. Thomas's school room to consider what steps should be taken towards raising funds for the publication of Mr. Thomas's rejoinder to Froude. It was decided to send around subscription lists and remit the amount required (£140) when raised to Messrs. Unwin & Company, publishers…. The work is already in the publisher's hands, and will be ready in very short time, so that the money must be remitted at an early date."

29. J. J. Thomas, *Froudacity: West Indian Fables by James Anthony Froude* (1889, London: New Beacon, 1969), p. 53, 179; hereafter, *F.*

ular, so continuous, and withal so efficient, in the production of the marvelous results that we daily contemplate, there must be existent and in operation—as, for instance, in the case of the uniformity characterising for ages successive generations of mankind, as above adduced by our philosopher himself—some controlling LAW, according and subject to which no check has marred the harmonious progression, or prevented the consummations that have crowned the normal exercise of human energy, intellectual as well as physical (*F.*, p. 123).

James believes that this observation was Thomas's most brilliant insight and demonstrated his intellectual superiority over Froude. According to James, "Thomas bases himself on a sense of history which he defines as a controlling LAW. And if you have no sense of historical law, then anything is what you choose to make it, and history almost automatically becomes not only non-sense, i.e., has no sense, but is usually a defence of property and privilege, which is exactly what Froude made of it." (*F.*, p. 32). Wilson Harris, however, contends that both Thomas and Froude were locked in an intellectual prison that was shaped by the intellectual assumptions of the nineteenth century and that "neither possessed the genius to penetrate intuitively or otherwise the ironic trap of the ornament, of the prison of the wasteland."[30] While Froude contended that West Indians were not capable of self-governance, Thomas made it clear that the whole population—white, black, mulatto and other island inhabitants—were an integral part of the movement toward self-government. As far as Thomas was concerned, the Europeans who were permanent residents in the West Indies never made any complaints against the political ability of the blacks to control their lives. Thomas believed rather that the enemy was colonialism, the creed of a few residents who labored under the assumption of "race-madness." He took offense at the assumption that Anglo-Saxons "have a right to crow and dominate in whatever land they chance to find themselves, though in their own country they or their forefathers had had to be very dumb dogs indeed" (*F.*, p. 132). As to the good breeding that slavery was supposed to have imposed upon Africans, Thomas concludes:

Granting the appreciable ethical value of hat-touching, smirking and curtseyings of those Blacks to persons whom they had no reason to suspect of unfriendliness, or whose white face they may in the white man's country have greeted with a civility perhaps only prudential, we fail to discover the necessity of the dreadful agency we have averted to, for securing the results on manners which are so warmly commended. African explorers, from Mungo Park to Livingstone and Stanley, have all borne sufficient testimony to the world regarding the natural friendliness of the Negro in his ancestral home, when not under the influence of suspicion, anger, or dread (*F.*, 135).

---

30. Wilson Harris, *History, Fable and Myth in the Guianas and the West Indies* (Wellesley, Mass.: Calaloux, 1995), p. 17. Harris also argues that neither Froude nor Thomas possessed "the complex creative perspective" to transcend the historical stasis that "afflicts the West Indian sensibility ... for which the historical convention would appear to possess no criteria" (Ibid., p. 17.)

Long before James, Eric Williams, and Walter Rodney, Thomas offered a plausible account of how Europeans acquired Africans to work as slaves in the Caribbean. From his childhood, Thomas mingled and conversed with island African ethnoi (the Mandingoes, Foulahs, Houssas, Calvers, Gallahs, Karamenties, Yorubas, Aradas, Cangas, Kroos, Timnehs, Veis, Eboes, Mokoes, Bibis, and Congoes). As a result, he affirms that not "even three in ten of the whole number [of Africans in Trinidad] were slaves in their own country, in the sense of having been born under any organised system of servitude" (*F.*, p 142). Thomas was also aware of the work of Conrad Reeves and Frederick Douglass, among others. To his credit, he understood that these men were products of a particular social and economic system. James would say of Thomas, that "his sense of history was strong and headed in the right direction, the direction which has strengthened and illuminated all our finest Caribbean politicians and writers, the struggle for human emancipation and advancement" (*F.*, p. 43). At the end of the nineteenth century, his "self-vindication" of Africans certainly gave colonial people the breathing room to assert their humanity against the negative philosophies of negrophobes such as Froude, Kingsley, and Carlyle.

Writing and publishing *Froudacity* were very important, though difficult, tasks for Thomas. He saw it as part of his national duty to respond to Froude who had acquired a reputation for arousing "furious protests in every Colony about which he has written in his fitful rushes around the world."[31] Although Salmon and Davis had responded to Froude, Thomas's response became the most celebrated. It was seen as "crowning the edifice of refutation…possessing greater weight and sounder arguments than the more hasty rejoinders elicited by Mr. Froude's fabulous collections of falsehoods, when it originally appeared."[32] The editor of the *New Era* pointed out that Thomas threw himself enthusiastically into his project and produced a major work of scholarship.[33] In September 1889, *Froudacity* "was launched to an ocean of publicity and pronounced a success." Yet, at a moment when Thomas should have reaped the rewards of "his talents and industry, [he] was called away to the 'Great Unknown.'"[34] As Smith writes, "his books killed him; or that he paid a high price for producing them."[35]

When the news reached Trinidad that he had died "rather suddenly" at Kings College Hospital, London, on September 20, 1889, the whole country went into mourning. They knew that his death resulted partially from the arduous labors he had undertaken on their behalf to demonstrate his profound belief that the power of the intellect is a tool of liberation. On October 18, 1889 *New Era* wrote:

> In August last year he came to England for the express purpose of dealing with the
> baseless charges made by Mr. Froude in his *English in the West Indies* against the

31. Taken from *The Echo*, an English publication, and quoted in *New Era*, September 13, 1889.
32. "Froudacity," *New Era*, September 6, 1889.
33. Ibid.
34. *New Era*, October 25, 1889.
35. Smith, *John Jacob Thomas*, p. 138.

Negroes of the islands and, in spite of tremendous difficulties, he succeeded in publishing his *Froudacity* which is now going through a second printing. Mr. Thomas was an ardent champion of the rights of his race, and was constantly engaged in fighting the battle of his people. Indeed, he may have said to have died in the struggle for, no doubt, had he remained in his own warm climate, his valuable life would have been prolonged for a good many years, as he was only 49 years when he died.

Thomas, the quintessentially Caribbean scholar of the nineteenth century, used his pen "with skill and address." *New Era* emphasized that "his language, always forcible, becomes eloquent when the libels on his people induce him to expose the perversity and untruthfulness of their traducer."[36] Unlike Jean-Baptiste Philippe and Michel Maxwell Philip, Thomas was self-taught. Like Philippe and Maxwell, Thomas mastered several classical and modern languages "with no other assistance than a few text books and his own natural ability…and established his claim to be considered one of the first, if not the first, scholar of his race and country."[37] More than the other two, Thomas's dark skin presented him with more barriers to overcome. Yet, overcome them, he did. Perhaps, more than others, James recognized Thomas's centrality in Caribbean letters. He was correct when he asserted that "It was the Caribbean human condition which produced Jacob Thomas. To know him well is to know ourselves better" (*F.* p 48). More than anyone else, James would continue the tradition of scholarship that Thomas pioneered. Thus, it is no wonder that James referred to Thomas as the quintessential West Indian intellectual.

French Creole Verse, 1850-1900

On July 6, 1887, when Thomas announced that a second edition of *Creole Grammar* would be published, he simply confirmed that the *Grammar*, as he called it, had done well in the United States, the Caribbean, and even in Venezuela. Yet, he craved the fuller support of Trinidadians. He chided them for not supporting him financially and concluded that "as more praise than helpful patronage characterised the reception, in my native country, of the [first] issue of the *Creole Grammar*, even so would it be a pleasant experience to me to find from tangible proofs that practical support is preferred by my supporters as an evidence of their appreciation of what I have accomplished."[38] In supporting this initiative, *Public Opinion* encouraged its readers to back Thomas and concluded: "We, ourselves, have tried hard to procure a copy of the work, but without success. We have no doubt that those who appreciate Creole talent will hasten to inscribe their names in support of Mr. Thomas's happy idea of reprinting a work which has run out of print and for which there is now a great demand."[39]

36. *New Era*, September 6, 1889.
37. *New Era*, October 25, 1889.
38. J. J. Thomas, "New Edition of the Creole Grammar," *Public Opinion*, July 6, 1887.
39. Ibid.

Apart from outlining the grammar of African people in Trinidad, *Creole Grammar* also revealed how deeply the French language had penetrated the island's culture. In *this book*, Thomas made a case for the use of Creole proverbs and other idiomatic expressions of the language. "Africans," he wrote, "are not, after all, the dolts and intellectual sucklings that some would have the world believe" (*CG.*, p. 120). He noted that their proverbs, characterized by "their figurativeness" and "rhythmical arrangement" gave "an insight into the mental habits and capabilities of the people who invented them" (*CG.*, p. 120). By examining these sayings, one got a good sense of what the Creoles thought about their world.

In presenting the idiomatic expressions and proverbs, Thomas exposed a prosaic dimension of African oral literature that, together with riddles and folktales, suggested a persistence of African literary forms in the culture of which he wrote. Although the idioms and proverbs cited by Thomas are brief, some are still used in the society today. They characterized the determination, the sorrow, and the wit of a people under pressure. They were didactic in that they were used to instruct the people in their daily lives. Yet, Thomas's desire to record this language for posterity and to help those who had problems with the new *lingua franca* (English) points to the important role that Creole and French played in the island. That many newspapers published in both French and English shows the influence and importance of the French population until anglicization began to take its toll in the 1870s. Tronchin's "The Burning of Rome" (1850) and "Lord Brougham" (1871), published in French in the *Trinidadiana* and the *Trinidad Monthly Magazine*[40] respectively reveal the scope and quality of the subjects that were tackled by these home-grown intellectuals.

In the period 1850–1900, the French Creoles also produced a systematic body of work even if, in many instances, it did not achieve a distinctive and original mark. Most of this considerable output of verse and songs were published in newspapers, such as the *Echo*, the *Palladium*, and the *Star of the West*, a French-Creole newspaper. Some of this literature took the form of printed leaflets that were sold to the public, while several of these poems were circulated among families in the form of manuscripts. Anthony de Verteuil, *the* authority in this area of scholarship, has written that the poetry and song of this period reflect "the social, political and religious situation in Trinidad...[They] undoubtedly exerted a formative influence on attributes at the time, since [they were] very much more in the public ear than is verse at the present time. From the literary standpoint, there was only one poet of first rank, Sly (Sylvester) Devenish."[41] Besides Devenish, in de Verteuil's collection of Trinidad's French verse, many important French-Creole personages are represented: Pierre Gustave Borde, author of *History of Spanish Trinidad*; Marie-Bertrand Cothonay, author of *Trinidad* (1893); Leon de Gannes; Alphonse Ganteaume; and Charles Le Cadre.

40. L. B. Tronchin, "Lord Brougham," *The Trinidad Monthly Magazine*, 1, No. 1 (September 1871).
41. Anthony de Verteuil, *Trinidad's French Verse, 1850–1900* (Port of Spain: Instance Print, 1978), p. 4. I am indebted to de Verteuil for much of my information on these poets.

In analyzing the works of these poets, de Verteuil makes several observations. He notes that these poems and songs "originated from the custom in France of composing and singing songs on convivial occasions, while other types might be based on workmen's songs or the custom of publishing eulogies in newspapers." The use of "periphrasis and of cumbrous mythological allusions" by such poets as Devenish indicated a dependence on a form of poetry that had long outlived its usefulness. The same could be said of the high-flown, almost archaic prose that Tronchin used in some of his fictional and nonfictional work. As these writers became less and less attached to France, their poetry "became less classical and more romantic. From 1850 to 1900 it was written mainly to be sung and this [was done] often to the music of Beranger. It is not surprising, therefore, that the latter's poetic style, as well as his rhythms, left their mark on the poetry in Trinidad."[42]

According to de Verteuil, Creole poems can be classified as poems for special occasions, religious poems, and political poems. Charles Reneaud's "Élégie à Monseigneur Spaccapietra" (1859), a poem written when Archbishop Vincent Spaccapietra,[43] one of the most controversial archbishops, left the island, illustrates the occasional poem:

> Break your lute, O Muse who should inspire me,
> And silence the syllables of your song.
> And see leave now in the midst of frenzy,
> This holy Priest to whom all thanks belong.
>
> Observe how tears flow from the eyes at all,
> And notice how his eyes are close also,
> Notwithstanding the row his tears too fall
> Our homage though now constrained to forego.
>
> . . . . .
>
> And what are those cries, sad echoes one hears,
> Are they from the dead who bid him goodbye?
> Yes, they are those he has saved by his prayers;
> Though happy, for him they weep and they sigh.
>
> . . . . .
>
> Ha! it is done, it is finished, my Father.
> Nothing again, oh nothing can stop you.
> Our cries...our hearts...the island would rather...
> Oh, may you be happy whatever you do!
>
> Oh Holy Father, August and Venerable,
> You who must know all the secrets of man,
> Spread over him from your throne adorable,
> Happiness, peace—the gifts that You can.

42. Ibid., pp. 12–13.

43. Maxwell Philip, a staunch Roman Catholic, represented Archbishop Spaccapietra when the British government denied him his allowance/stipend.

Devenish wrote another poem for Special Events when Mr. Ribiero's "Standard Hotel" opened in 1899. Typical of the calypsoes of the time, this was written partly in French and partly in *patois* and set to music. It commented on an event that was important to some of the citizens and can even be termed a "never see, come see" calypso. Devenish's tribute went as follows:

> Everyone in Trinidad came to see,
> One thing believe it or not:
> 'Standard Ribirio' an open house
> For black, for Indian, and for white!
> For everyone you have a good word,
> English, French, Spanish, Patois.[44]

Interestingly enough, up until 1899, all calypsoes were sung and written in *patois*. Speaking of the movement of the calypso from its purely African roots to one informed by the French element, Seepersad Naipaul observes that around the latter part of the nineteenth century, "the French element intruded itself in the carousals of the liberated slaves or bongo dancers. The songs gradually lost their pure African vernacular, and were sung in patois instead. Still later, they became a blend of English and patois, until in 1895 Norman Le Blanc sang the first calypso in English alone."[45] This accumulated musical/poetic tradition of the French influenced the calypso art form and made the latter what it is today. Even Devenish's poem/calypso was printed and sold for a penny.[46]

Religious poems, fostered by the French Dominican priests, also found a place in this French-Creole literary outpourings. The most notable of the religious poets were Marie-Bertrand Cothonay, Marie-Joseph Guillet, and Armand Masse. Cothonay also wrote some pieces that were inspired by the beauty of the island. All of them wrote hymns for the Church.[47] In his letters, Cothonay insists on the superiority of Europeans provided they were Roman Catholics. As a result, he had only negative things to say about Africans and Indians. Daaga is described as sounding "so little human, so savage and so terribly," even though he could not have possibly heard Daaga.[48] Africans, Cothonay says, are not fervent in their Catholicism "because faith did not have time to throw deep roots in their natures since they were scarcely out of paganism. Because they received an inferior intelligence, one must recognize that metaphysical truths penetrate very slowly into their brains."[49] "Hindus," he continues, "are a barbaric people," with most of those who were imported to the island being

44. De Verteuil, *Trinidad's French Verse,* pp. 14–15.

45. Seepersad Naipaul, "Carnival Calypsos and the Creole Troubadours," *The Trinidadian* (February-March, 193?), p. 13.

46. De Vertueil, *Trinidad's French Verse,* p. 15.

47. Ibid., p. 15.

48. Father Marie-Bertrand Cothonay, *Trinidad: Journal of a Dominican Missionary* (Paris: Victor Retaux et Fils, Libraires-Editeurs, 1893), p, 30.

49. Ibid., p. 61.

"*pariahs* without education and if they appear cunning, they are not intelligent."[50] Like the Africans, Hindus were unable to accept Christianity because "they are still too impregnated with paganism and moral corruption in the midst of which they, as well as their ancestors, lived. Christian ideas do not make an immediate impression upon them and faith find it difficult to penetrate mind that are filled with thick darkness."[51] Cothonay also has nasty things to say about the Chinese and the Jews. However, to show that he was not racist, he insisted "on partaking a dish [perhaps callaloo] that the Black people seem to relish but it was indicated to me that is was not fit for 'well-to-do people.'"[52] So much for his piety and truth.

The political poems played to and spoke about the fears of the French Creole community. In many ways, the French Creoles used their poems/songs to attack the anglicizing tendencies and other perceived threats that were rampant in the society from 1870 through the 1890s. Many of Cothonay's letters speak of the "war" his priests led against the Protestant church. Eugene Lange "La Section Britannique" and Devenish's "La Cues de Jupiter et Anglomanie a la Trinidad" were two of the angriest political poems. These poets were angry because the society was inundated with Anglomania and a stultifying sense of Englishness. Further, the Creoles felt a sense of political ostracism and feared speaking out against the English. Devenish used the following verse to express his outrage and to assert his patriotism:

> From Jupiter's thigh, mythology states,
> Come forth the Gods of famous name.
> Now men whom no genealogy rates,
> For him, proud fools, descent they claim.
>
>> Chorus
>>
>> In our tiny country,
>> My friends, it's so,
>> Where each knows the other
>> From head to toe.
>
> On this delicate subject, I do not dare say much,
> In fear to anger all in vain,
> The great '*parvenus,* of importance such.
> To laugh at whom would be insane.
>
> Chorus
>
> But, well I can without slightest sin,
> This common crime condemn most strongly,
> For you, my friend, will keep it all within in
> And names we need not mention wrongly.
>
> Chorus

50. Ibid., p. 44.
51. Ibid., p. 89.
52. Ibid., p. 42.

. . . . .

Be true sons, O Creoles, of your country,
Forget the land of your descent.
Leave to the few fools, their effrontery,
Use for your nation your talent.

Chorus

> O be Creoles in heart,
> Honorable men;
> 'Neath your nation's proud flag
> United then.

Despite being caution about how they projected their creoleness, the French Creoles circulated their verses among themselves and put some of the poems to music. It was an effective way to get their message out. De Verteuil writes that "[a]t this period when musical evenings at the homes of the educated were common, and every young lady was expected to play the piano and/or sing, these local songs were very popular. They had an important effect in rallying public opinion before the time of radio or television. Some of the senior citizens of present day Trinidad still remember 'Zalare' [song/poem about an unpopular political figure] and its tune quite well."[53]

Finally there were what de Verteuil calls the "pure poems," which consisted of the "kind of personal expression we nowadays associate with poetry."[54] Included among this verse were poems about love, nature, and other miscellaneous topics. Leon de Gannes's poem, "Exile," is a prime example of the pure poem:

Long did darkness weigh upon my days;
For an instant light broke on gloom,
Leaving deeper shadows in this womb
Where once borne I live for always.

Burning eyes, a gentle soul reveals,
Formed of tenderness and flaming zeal.
Hair so fair, smile so pure, voice enchanting,
Happy magic for a heart's a-haunting.
Why, oh why, did you appear to me
Since so soon, from you I must depart?
You are mine, and when from you I must flee,
Sad exile, will surely break my heart.
When, far from your scintillating beauty,
Then, the hard times and unpleasant duty.
More unpleasant still and harder will seem;
As hard days succeed a happy dream.
Yet, I must flee. Take again my route

53. De Verteuil, *Trinidad's French Verse*, p. 16.
54. Ibid., p. 17.

Cross the deserts, the shadows, the doubt;
With a destiny unknown to face
Though distressed, I have at least this grace
Hidden in my heart, - your image dear,
Gentle souvenir of times less hard,
As a pledge over given or earth here
For exchange with heaven's happy Bard.

The range and relative sophistication of some of these poems suggest that these writers did a lot of literary work, even though their collective efforts never gelled into a literary movement. Still the existence of Creole verse filled an aesthetic yearning and helped to articulate a way of life. De Verteuil observes that these poems and songs reflect "a life of peaceful appreciation of the good things, and a willingness to improve on the strictly human level the insuperable hardships of life [at that time.]" These Trinidadians wrote as they did because they wished "to express the mystery and the wonder and the beauty of life."[55] In doing so, they demonstrated the range of voices that permeated the society as Trindiadian literature came into being. Merely to have access to their verse gives one a sense of how they saw their world. It also expands the literary richness of the society.

Victor Hugo and his Trinidad Connection

In a curious way, Cothonay's journal ties Trinidad in the (mis)fortunes of Victor Hugo, one of the most prominent writers of French literature, and Adèle Hugo, his youngest daughter. Three years after he was sent to evangelize in the island, Cothonay was asked to lead the Catholic mission in the area. While in Trinidad, he conceived the idea of writing a diary about his experiences in the form of letters to interest those who wanted to devote their lives to missionary work. In a letter dated September 8, 1885, Cothonay relates a fascinating story about Madame Céline Alvarez Baa, an African woman from Trinidad, who brought him a small sum of money to say a mass for Hugo who had died earlier that year. Amazed by this request, Cothonay asked her why she wanted to say a mass for someone she did not know, or so he thought. Although she could not tell him everything about her relationship with the French writer, the little she could connected the great author with this descendant of slaves.

Years earlier, while Baa lived in Barbados, she took pity on a French woman who was roaming the streets of Bridgetown and gave her refuge. This woman turned out to be Adèle Hugo, who had run away to Halifax, Canada, in 1863, to marry Albert Andrew Pinson, an English officer, with whom she was madly in love. Pinson refused Adèle's entreaties to marry her because she had turned down an 1855 proposal of marriage that he had made. In 1866, when Pinson's company sailed to Barbados, Adèle followed him there, but the officer was adamant. He was too immersed in a

55. Ibid., pp. 19–20.

life of debauchery. In 1869, he left Barbados for England where, one year later, he married Catherine Edith Roxburgh, the grand daughter of Dr. William Roxburgh, a noted botanist in India.

Deserted in Barbados, Adèle had no one to turn to. Given to bouts of melancholia, she began to walk the streets in her heavy winter clothes mumbling to herself. After Baa found out her identity, she wrote to Hugo to tell him about his daughter's condition. In 1872, taking matters in her own hands, Baa took Adèle to her father, nine years after she had deserted her family. Upon her arrival in Paris, her condition saddened her father, and he wrote in his diary that " Adèle arrived this night at four o'clock at Dr. Allix's. He told me about her state. My poor, dear child. [Francois-] Victor will see her today. She did not recognize Emile Allix. The negro woman who accompanied her, Mme. Baa, is devoted to her."[56] Quickly, thereafter, Hugo placed his daughter in a mental institution.

Although Hugo was happy to see Adèle, he was even happier to see Baa whom he described as "black, nevertheless a lady in the colony" (AH., p. 162), and attracted to Baa, he lost no time in seducing her. Even at seventy, he was still active sexually. While Baa was in Paris, she and Hugo visited each other regularly. In his diary, Hugo recorded that " [Céline was] the first negress of my life" (AH., p. 162). Eventually, he reimbursed her for the expenses she incurred in bringing Adèle back to Paris. Other than that, he was not overly generous to Baa, and on March 12, she left for Barbados. In token of her affection, she left him her portrait.

Nine years later, Baa visited Adèle and Hugo once more; this time bringing a bouquet of colored bird feathers for her lover. It was the last time they saw each other. In 1885, when Baa received news of Hugo's death, she cried out in sorrow: "What a loss! He was such a generous man, so good! God should give him peace" (AH., p. 172).

At the end of this story, she revealed to Cothonay that Hugo's final words to her were "[w]hen you hear I am dead, would you have three masses said for me?" (AH., p. 172). Thus, by asking the priest to say a mass for the dead writer, Baa was only keeping a solemn promise made to someone she had loved very dearly.

Sylvester Devenish, "Papa Bois" (1819-1903)

In examining French Creole verse of the latter half of the nineteenth century, it is important to pay close attention to the work of Sylvester Devenish, the leading French Creole man of letters of the period. Born in Nantes and educated in Paris, Devenish was fond of "philological studies." His biographer writes that he was a linguist of some distinction: he studied Modern Greek, was "a complete master of the mother tongue [French], knows modern Spanish, a smattering of Italian, Polish, and Hebrew, all of which, with the exception of Spanish, through disuse, he has allowed to get somewhat rusty. We may also add that he has very fairly mastered the African dental language known as Eboe."[57] While Devenish lived in Paris, he made the

---

56. Leslie Smith Dow, *Adèle Hugo: Le Miserable* (Fredericton, New Brunswick: Goose Lane Editions, 1993), p. 160. All other quotes from this book are noted in the text as *AH*.

57. "Mr. Sylvester Devenish, MA," *Public Opinion*, May 8, 1888.

acquaintance of Jules Janin and Honoré Balzac, of whom, it is said, "procured for him journalistic work."[58] Apart from Janin and Balzac, Devenish also met Chateaubriand at Paris and Beranger at Tours. In Paris, he also studied painting, a love of which he took to Trinidad with him.

When Devenish came to Trinidad, his "adopted land," in 1842, he made use of his mathematical training and became a land surveyor. In 1850, he entered the Civil Service at the request of Lord Harris; in 1857, he became director of the Irois Forest Convict Settlement and, in 1869, the crown surveyor. At the request of Sir Arthur Gordon, he drew up the new rules for the Survey of Crown lands. In 1876, he became the surveyor-general of the island.

In these varied capacities, he had much contact with the island's forests and thus spent much time observing the natural fauna of Trinidad.[59] In *Public Opinion*, his biographer asserts that his various assignments allowed him to "practice his hitherto theoretical knowledge of medical botany and forestry. In 1848, he began his first collection, which we believe were the first ever made in this colony, of timber trees and medical plants." When Kingsley visited Trinidad in 1869, he called Devenish an "excellent forester."[60] In 1882, he received a pamphlet of the experiments that had been made with his medicinal plants, "an autograph letter from Baroness Burdett Coutts and another from Dr. Hunter thanking him for the plants."[61] Devenish's impressive collection was displayed in Paris, Vienna, and Philadelphia, as well as in London at the Colonial and Indian Exhibition of 1886.[62]

Devenish's life embodied the exuberance of his time and place. He was active in public life. He defended his group, rhapsodized about their events, and participated in almost every aspect of his community's life. A satirical sketch of Devenish appeared in the *New Era:*

> He makes accounts—puns, plans; tells anecdotes; caricatures you; talks "chemistry, gaurdiole," metaphysics, buffoonery, natural history, gymnastics, wood-craft, serpents, cholera, theatricals, plays the trumpet; dances, improvises ten couplets, sings them to thirty-six tunes; gets impatient, laughs, kicks his dog, kisses his wife, eats and drinks as he does everything else—and all these in less time that your would take to manage a single one. This man—to be explicit—is an exceptional nature, encrusted with jokes, exuberant with energy—a body of tempered steel loaded with and quicksilver.[63]

58. Ibid.

59. See, for example, Sly Devenish, "Memorandum of a Trip from Naparima to Bande De L'Est (Mayaro) and Guayaguayare, and Back, by order of His Excellency, Rear-Admiral Elliot, in January, 1856," *Trinidad Monthly Magazine*, 1, No. 1 (September 1871), pp. 11–18, for a description of one of Devenish's trips.

60. Charles Kingsley, *At Last* (London: Macmillian, 1887), p. 162. Apart from de Verteuil and Leotaud, Devenish was one of several Trinidadians (born or adopted) who were interested in the natural geography of Trinidad.

61. *Public Opinion*, May 8, 1888.

62. See "Handbook and Catalogue," *The Colonial and Indian Exhibition of 1886* (London: William Clowes and Sons, 1886), pp. 29–33, for the 235 types of woods in Devenish's collection.

63. From "A Photograph," reprinted in *Public Opinion*, May 11, 1888.

Yet, like Maxwell Philip, after serving the Colonial government for most of his life, he was retired (or suspended from office) on "a miserable pittance of £50…another instance of the habitual neglect, by Home Authorities, of native worth. According to the rules, it should have been nearly £700." It chanced that he had fallen out with the governor of the time and this led to his poor treatment.[64] After much public agitation, his pension was increased by £50. Writing in his defense, *New Era* noted that "[i]t is very suggestive of the present status of the administration, that every Governor preceding Governor Irving during the tenure of office of Mr. Devenish (a long one), appreciated the sterling talents and untiring zeal of that officer, and testified to the value of his public services. It is only left to Governor Irving to fall foul of one our most deserving public officers."[65]

The same energy that Devenish devoted to his outdoor life, he also gave to his literary endeavors: indeed, he was an extraordinarily prolific writer. Some of his compositions included "Chants de guerre"; "Le Mexicaine," dedicated to the French Army in Mexico; and "Au Drapeau," written during the Franco-Prussian war. Additionally, he wrote sonnets, poesies legeres, chansons, melodies, satins epigrams, religious poems, hymns, and canticles.

Neither a great nor brilliant poet, Devenish's verse offered a lot of platitudes and showed little originality. Even his political satires, which were more original and personal than his other poetry, turned out to be steeped in a techniques that had been developed some two centuries previously. The more he looked to France for his inspiration, the more he became immersed in a past that had little relevance to Trinidad. The notion that poetry was supposed to be a spontaneous free creation never characterized Devenish's work. According to Michele Lemettais:

> When one reads Devenish, one thinks of the elaborate and painstaking verses of the Great Rhetoriqueurs of the 16th century. His answer to Max Hilarie on the eman-cipation of women reminds us vividly of the same type of poems, about the same subjects that were written in the late Middle Ages and at the beginning of the 16th century.[66] His appeals to his friends for help and understanding about his political troubles, reflected in "My Political Troubles," are reminiscent of the many poems Marot wrote to the King and other influential people from 1518 to 1535 in which he defended himself against the accusation of heresy, being sent into exile, or being made a prisoner.[67]

Without being too harsh on Devenish and realizing the political backwardness of Trinidad at the time, it can still be argued that his poems were dated. Although he

---

64. *Public Opinion,* May 8, 1888.

65. Quoted in *Public Opinion,* May 8, 1888.

66. The reference here is to a response that Devenish wrote "To the learned doctor Max Hilairie (from St. Pierre, Martinique) in answer to his little gallant article, "Let's not emancipate women," (*Colibri,* No. 4), written on March 18, 1897.

67. Correspondence with Michele Lemettais, September 16, 1996. I am also indebted to Lemettais for translating many of these poems from French and sharing her analysis of them with me.

was exposed to the most modern writers of France, his literary endeavors served a purely didactic function in Trinidad. In France where the Romantic poets were singing without restraint about their passions, rhapsodizing about nature in harmony with the soul; talking about the awesomeness and horror of death; and philosophizing about the certitudes and doubts of religious faith, Devenish anchored his verse in the ordinariness of experience. If a friend married, he sent him a poem; when a governor arrived on the island, he wrote a poem; if a friend suffered a loss, he sent him a verse to cheer him up. Nor was there anything really elevating or memorable about the sentiments Devenish expressed. As de Verteuil reminds us, sending a poem under those circumstances was very much like our sending a greeting card to someone under similar circumstances. Where, in the present, the verses of such cards are composed by professionals, in Devenish's day, writers penned their own.

So, unlike the romantic poets in France who broke out of the narrow constraints of classical poetry, Devenish was content to use the medieval decameter or the classical alexandrin. For him, poetry was more a means of communication—remember the greeting card analogy—than a sophisticated art in itself. His poetry never displayed the complexity, density, or sophistication of Huggins's or Derek Walcott's verse.

Devenish's poetry, however, had its message. For him, humanity had to reconcile itself with itself and human beings needed to improve while they live. His attacks against the pretentiousness of some people and Anglomania stemmed from his deep conviction that human beings should accept their lives and assume their responsibilities even as they kept in mind the goodness and the goodwill of God. He wrote in "Anglomania in Trinidad":

> O stupid fellows, do not complain
> Of your descent. Here you were begot.
> To go against your nature brings no gain,
> You can never be what you are not.
>
> Be faithful always to the name you bear,
> Be loyal subjects, models too.
> Be not ashamed of the blood you share,
> Be yourself, not English un-true.

Devenish's used his verse to come to grips with a world that was shifting around him constantly. Indeed, the second half of the nineteenth century was an uncertain time for French Creoles who felt they were political "outcasts, at least until the dramatic exit of the Francophobe Charles William Warner from his post as Attorney General in 1870, and even after that they continued in opposition."[68] In terms of reli-

68. De Verteuil, *Trinidad French Verse*, p. 11. See *Public Opinion*, March 1, 1887, for a short sketch of Charles William Warner's life. At his death, Warner was described as "one of the greatest intellects that ever adorned the annals of any of England's colonies....As a barrister, Charles Warner never had an equal in Trinidad."

gion, the French Creoles, most of whom were Roman Catholics, were put on the defensive when, as early as 1840, attempts were made to give the English Catholics a greater say in the religions affairs of the country. According to de Verteuil, "the motto of their paper, *Star of the West*—'L'Union fait la Force'—betray[ed] their attitude; and though there was some improvement in 1870, it was only with the advent of Sir Hubert Jerningham in 1897, the first Catholic Governor, that they were able to get a fair deal."[69]

A deeply religious man, Devenish sought to live according the tenets of his religion and had great compassion for all people. As a French Creole who had a certain allegiance to France, he had to keep a delicate balance between defending the group interest and remaining loyal to Trinidad. Thus, his poems revolve around his affection for the island, a country of exile that had become his home, and France, a country for which he felt an undying love. Lemettais structures the contradiction the following terms: "Although France is the Motherland from which he came, Trinidad is the land that has accepted him and therefore deserves his allegiance."[70] Devenish captures the demands of these competing interests—an unease to which many French Creoles were subjected—when, on March 10, 1881, his sixty-second birthday, he offered the following verse:

> For twenty-nine years I have worked relentlessly
> For my adoptive country.
> And I had hoped that, finally, in my old age
> For so much zeal at least to be repaid...
> But we know that very often the bee
> Sees her honey drunk by thieving hornets;
> My destiny is to theirs similar...
> Others have taken the fruit of my labour!

> Therefore, I bury my old birthday
> And softly go my own sweet way...
> For how much longer can I still tread upon it,
> Where shall I be next year on this day?
> When, without complaining, I give in to my fate,
> I think also that the end must be coming...
> It is not enough to have known how to live long,
> One must also learn how to die well!

On May 8, 1888, *Public Opinion* offered an elaborate biographical sketch of Devenish. Alarmed that he "was struck down by a severe illness and for weeks was hovering between life and death" and recognizing the importance of "this great poet," the newspaper felt it had to offer its appreciation for his accomplishments. The editor offered the following rationale for publishing the sketch: "During that time [of his

---

69. De Verteuil, *Trinidad's French Verse*, p. 1.
70. Private Correspondence.

FIGURE 17. Sylvester Devenish, a leading man of French letters in Trinidad during the second half of the nineteenth century.

illness] the kindest enquiries were made about him by the highest and the lowliest in the country and a great relief was felt by every one when it was announced that this kind, genial and hearty old favorite was out of danger and in a fair way to recovery."[71] Devenish recovery lasted thirteen years after these flattering words appeared. His life spanned the century, and he outlived most of the outstanding literary and intellectual figures that graced the Trinidad stage during that time. When he died on February 2, 1903, the country fell into mourning for this devoted servant.

De Verteuil claims that Devenish "was more of an institution than a person"[72] and that might be true. Yet, Devenish's life brings the literature full circle in that he married Marie Laure d'Abadie, a granddaughter of St. Hilarie Begorrat, whom Picton ordered to investigate the charge against Louisa Calderon. It was Begorrat who wrote that "the said Luisa [*sic*] cried 'Ay, ay,' repeating the same several times, calling on God and the Holy Virgin." Begorrat also introduced the Otaheite sugar cane plant into Trinidad from Martinique in 1782 and thereby set in motion the sugar cane industry in the island.[73] It might be that the marriage between Devenish and Begorrat's granddaughter only shows how small the society was and how life commingled with art. While Devenish's poetry brought us great joy, Begorrat's life and activities were the source of much of our suffering and our shame. The matrimonial coming-together of the families reveals to us just how far Trinbagonian society had come.

71. "Mr. Sylvester Devenish, M.A." *Public Opinion*, May 8, 1888.
72. De Verteuil, *Trinidad's French Verse*, p. 172.
73. See Henry James Clark, *Trinidad: A Field for Emigration* (Port of Spain: Government Printing Office, 1886), p. 26. The first sugar estate was established by M. Picot de Lapeyrouse in 1787.

CHAPTER 14

"Knights of the Mask"

To think of the bitter sufferings of the hundreds of those—once innocent and virtuous maidens who were cruelly victimized on that occasion
by some fiendish monsters in human shape, whose lust could not be
exercised at any other time, but who found every opportunity by means
of the Carnival to accomplish the downfall of so many who would have
proven faithful and loving wives, kind mothers and ornaments to their
country, and who today are neither one nor the other, is simply distress-
ing. And the cause to which such painful and deplorable occurrences
can be attributed is a monstrosity unsurpassed by all others on the face
of the earth.

> —EUGENE FRANCIS CHALAMELLE, *Some Reflections
> on the Carnival Of Trinidad*

As opposed to the official feast, one might say that carnival celebrated
temporary liberation from the prevailing truth and from the established
order; it marked the suspension of all hierarchical rank, privileges,
norms, and prohibitions. Carnival was the true feast of time, the feast of
becoming, change, and renewal. It was hostile to all that was immortalized and completed.

> —MIKHAIL BAKHTIN, *Rabelais and his World*

Let every man think on the sublimity of the origin and nature of
mankind and he will never despair—since he is a God himself.

> —HENRY MARIOL RODRIGUES, *The Siren Goddess
> of South America*

The 1890s ushered in narratives that examined issues different from those of the
previous decades. Rather than race-based narratives that spoke urgently to questions of ethnicity, suffrage, and placedness, these new works were more concerned
with historical, anthropological, sociological, legal, and cultural topics that were
emerging to shape Trinbagonian society. Indeed, by 1890, most of the personalities
who had shaped the intellectual tenor of the age (such as Philippe, M. Philip,

Leotaud, Cazabon, Borde, and Thomas) were dead. A new generation, with new concerns, had arisen to carry forward the literary and scholarly projects that now shaped the nationalist discourse. When Jose Bodu's *Trinidadiana: A Chronological Review of the Events which Occurred in the Island from the Conquest to the Present Day, with Brief Notices of the Careers of Some Eminent Colonists* (1890) summed up, in meticulous fashion, the significant events of the century, he sought neither to offer a history of the island—he noted that de Verteuil, Leotaud, and Borde had already done so—nor to rewrite the society's beginning. Instead, he sought to impose academic order on the discordant incidents that had taken place in the society since the arrival of the British and produced, in the words of one of his contemporaries, "the indispensable hand book of interesting local events."[1] A reviewer of the book in *New Era* argued that Bodu must be credited "for the great amount of conscientious labour and research" that he had put into his book.[2]

In *The Old Bar and the New Bar* (1899), Anthony Richard Delamere performed a similar service for the legal profession when he offered biographical sketches of the members of the profession. Since the death of George Lewis Garcia in 1897 snapped "the last link that bound the Trinidad bar to the traditions [of the past],"[3] it was necessary "to preserve so as to popularize, in print, any historical narrative of the liberal professions."[4] Interestingly enough, this book appeared a decade after William Seaton offered his seminal essay, "Vicissitudes of the Profession of Attorney and Solicitor in Trinidad" (1889). It was almost as though Bodu and Delamere were saying one had to take stock of the past even as one made room for the emergence of the future.

The centenary of the colony under British rule was also cause for celebration. Lewis O. Inniss did just that in his historical drama, *Carmelita: The Belle of San Jose* (1897), while Ivry Hart's *Centenary Reminiscences* (1897) performed a similar function. Eugene Chalamelle's *Some Reflections on the Carnival of Trinidad* continued a line of attack against "the rabble" as he called for "the total annihilation of Carnival" (*SRTC.*, p. 13). He was concerned also about the transgressive sexual aspects of Carnival. By the end of the century, Charles Assee's *Laus Reginae* (1902), an epic poem, celebrated the achievements of Queen Victoria and her imperial rule, while Stephen Nathaniel Cobham's *Rupert Gray: A Tale of Black and White* (1907), a spirited, sentimental novel, lauded the achievements of Africans in a world that sought to despise them.

Although the question of race-consciousness did not come up explicitly in the creative literature of the 1890s, African cultural practices continued at the base of the society. In this context, concerns about Africa's place in the world became more

1. Eugene Francis Chalamelle, *Some Reflections on the Carnival of Trinidad* (Port of Spain: Fair Play Type, 1897), p, 15; hereafter included in the text as *SRCT*.
2. "Trinidadiana," *New Era*, March 7, 1890. Bodu, a cocoa merchant, was a citizen of Venezuela even though he had worked several years in Trinidad.
3. Chalamelle, *Some Reflections on the Carnival of Trinidad*, p. 33.
4. Anthony Richard Delamere, *The Old Bar and the New Bar* (Port of Spain: The Daily News, 1899), p. 1; hereafter included in the text as *OB*.

incessant as the fight against European colonialism in Africa intensified. In Arouca, in 1891, a major riot occurred when the police prevented Africans from beating their big African drums, dancing the *bamboula*, performing their drum dance, or the calinda, a stickfighting dance. This banning of their music, their dance, and their religion were methods aimed at wiping out a way of life since African music, dance and religion were closely intertwined with West African ontological practices.[5]

During this period, political and literary activities became tightly interrelated. Several officers of the Trinidad Literary Association were members of the Reform Movement, an organization that was agitating for internal self-government. Clerics such as Canon Philip Douglin became active in the Pan-African movement, a more visible and vocal thrust for African empowerment and self-consciousness. Owen Mathurin observes that "Maresse-Smith and such persons as [Alexander Pulcheire] Pierre, Douglin, C. E. Petioni and Emmanuel M'Zukbo Lazare, who were either on the black side of the jubilee celebration controversy [about the public celebration of Emancipation in 1888] or in the Gray's Inn Literary Association, were to be among [Sylvester] Williams's collaborators in the Pan African Association."[6] So that while many qualified Africans turned their energies to politics, teaching and preaching, several others engaged in a sustained assault against colonialism and racism. To most of the African and colored citizens, there was little contradiction between these two forms of activity.

Also during the 1890s, having moved in large numbers from the estates to newly established villages, the East Indians emerged as a political force. By 1897, they formed the East Indian National Association of Trinidad, an organization that acted in defense of their interests. Eventually, it became "one of the major Indian political organizations during the early twentieth century."[7] Further, during this period, Indians participated in mayoral politics in San Fernando and the movement for constitutional change. Girad Tikasingh writes that Indians reconstructed the panchayat, "the one traditional Indian social institution, which had the potential capacity for channeling political activity."[8] In 1888, Juppy, an Indian immigrant who had resided in the country for thirty-four years, "thought that the panchayat should select Indian electors in the event the elective principle was granted with respect to the Legislative Council."[9] The permanent panchayat had emerged as the

5. See Charles Espinet and Harry Pitts, *Land of the Calypso* (Port of Spain: Guardian Commercial Printery, 1944), pp. 66–67, for the laws that were passed to outlaw music, dance, and religion.

6. Owen Charles Mathurin, *Henry Sylvester Williams and the Origins of the Pan-African Movement, 1869–1911* (Westport, CT.: Greenwood Press, 1976), p. 11. Pierre was the founder of the Trinidad Literary Association and a delegate to the Pan-African Conference in 1900; Petioni was a committee member of the Gray's Inn Literary Association, of which Maresse-Smith was the president (ibid., p. 14).

7. Girad Tikasingh, "The Emerging Political Consciousness Among Trinidad Indians in the Late 19th Century," History Conference, University of the West Indies, St. Augustine (Trinidad), 1973, p. 282.

8. Ibid., p. 261.

9. Ibid.. p. 261.

most politically sophisticated community apparatus, "the highest native tribunal," as the *Port of Spain Gazette* described it.[10]

The impetus toward a much more articulate political community took place when, in 1897, an Immigration Ordinance sought to deny the Indians many of the freedoms to which they were entitled after having served their period of indenture-ship. Things reached a boiling point in June 1899 when Rev. John Morton, vice president of the Agricultural Society, proposed that East Indian immigrants who were being recruited as permanent settlers were not entitled to a free passage back to India. Jugmohun Singh, one of the wealthiest shopkeepers from Tacarigua, summoned a panchayat to consider Morton's motion which, according to B. Beharrysingh "had never been submitted to the consideration of the Indian people whom it would affect."[11] In the presence of at least one thousand Indians from all parts of the island, Morton assured the gathering he was only doing what he thought was "for the good of the Indian people."[12] He argued that he only wanted to ensure "that those who came to Trinidad in the future should come under a new contract whereby they could remain here permanently."[13]

By his actions, Morton had ceased to speak for the Indians. Charles Ragmundin Singh, a participant at the deliberations, observed that Morton was concerned primarily with the prosperity of his schools, "well-known to be profitably investments" and with a desire to "enable the planters to have a continuous supply of cheap labour."[14] Since the planters had spent £12,100 in return passages in 1898, the intent of Morton's motion was to ease their economic burden. Even the *Mirror* conceded that "[t]he planters and the Colony in general are interested on economic grounds in the reduction of the cost of back passages."[15] However, the Indians were determined to speak for themselves and to articulate their ethnic/national interest. Nine years earlier, Morton took pride in how he used his influence to place Charles Soodeen, one of his catechists, on the Education Board alongside Governor Sir William Gordon and the Chief Justice Sir John Gorrie.[16] In 1899, Morton had to defend his actions in front of an Indian Council who demanded that he take responsibility for his injudicious behavior. Although initially he refused to attend,

10. "Panchyat at Tunapuna," *Port of Spain Gazette,* July 23, 1899.

11. Ibid.

12. Ibid.

13. J. C. Jha, "East Indian Pressure Groups in Trinidad, 1897–1921," *Indentured Indians in Trinidad and Tobago, 1845–1917* (1985), p. 15–18.

14. "Panchyat at Tunapuna."

15. "Coolies as Permanent Settlers," *Mirror,* June 17, 1899.

16. In a letter to his superiors, he boasted: "Our new Education Board met for the first time on the 2ⁿᵈ. On that Board, along with Sir. William Robinson, K.C.M.G., Governor, Sir John Gorrie, Chief Justice, and several Honorables, sat 'Charles Clarence Sooden, Esquire'. The proposal to appoint an East Indian to represent his countrymen came spontaneously from His Excellency the Governor, and the choice fell on Sooden. He came here as an orphan boy not able to read. More than twenty years ago he became my first Indian teacher." Most of the persons who took umbrage to his motion studied in the Presbyterian schools. (See "Later Letter from Mr. Morton," *Maritime Presbyterian,* October 1890.)

his fear of losing influence among the Indians insured that he was present to answer the charges against him.[17]

The panchayat signaled that the Indians had become a part of the national community. It was the first time they had come together so publicly, in such a fashion, for such a cause. The *Mirror* wrote that "[T]he East Indians of Trinidad form a very important part of the body politic and there is no doubt that it will not be very long before we shall find them represented in every walk in our social and political economy, and that the day is not far distant when they will claim, and we doubt not successfully claim, an unofficial seat at the Legislative Council table."[18] By their actions, the East Indians gave notice of their ethnic cohesion and nationalist aspirations. Gellner notes that, "when the confrontation is not merely one between rivals for power and benefits, but between *kinds* of men, nationalism is approaching."[19] The nationalist phase of the East Indian presence had arrived.

Amidst this new assertiveness amongst the African and the Indians, several fiction and nonfiction works were published. While the former explored the emotional aspect of people's lives, the latter spoke of the economic possibilities, the history, and the folklore of the island. Just as romanticism influenced Cuban works of the 1860s, a similar romanticism began to show its influence in Trinbagonian literature of the 1890s. Even the language had to change to accommodate this new literary thrust, as writers and citizens took a sensuous joy in language.

However, in the *Mirror,* a skeptical reader took exception to "the wretched manner in which the English language is written by many inhabitants of even a very fair social standing." He observed sarcastically that "[t]he poorer classes of the island have a great command of language! Words flow eloquently enow [*sic*] from their pens; big words, of course, but these are invariably strung together without any regard to their meaning, and the result of it all is a heterogeneous concourse of rubbish which would send any little boy from an English boarding school into fits of laughter."[20]

17. In response to Jugmohun Singh's invitation to attend the Panchayat, Morton noted: "If my attendance was considered a matter of any importance I should certainly have been consulted before hand. I am not even now informed who are the members of your Panchayat, or whether other members of the Agricultural Society which passed the Resolution are invited. In these circumstances, and as a protest against the idea that any man is to be held responsible for his opinion to any self-constituted and unnamed Panchayat, I respectfully decline to attend. Had a proposal been made for a select number to meet me at my own place to talk over the matter, I should have gladly agreed to it." Letter dated July 21, 1899, in the *Scrapbooks of John and Sarah Morton.* At the last moment, Morton changed his mind and attended the panchayat.

18. "Return Passage," *The Mirror,* July 26, 1899.

19. Ernest Gellner, *Nationalism* (New York: New York University Press, 1997), p. 42.

20. Spectator, "English as 'She is Wrote' in Trinidad." *Mirror,* February 4, 1901. This affliction with or affection for "big words" seemed to be a Caribbean phenomenon. A report in the West Indian Paper wrote that "[t]he Creoles and Negroes of the West Indies have a deep love for long words, and use them on all occasions." The correspondent them went on to repeat a rather obsequious letter that came from a Grenadian who applied to become a cook in the home of an Englishman. See "West Indian Long Words," *Mirror,* February 21, 1902. This love of big words could also be seen as a love for the use of language, something that has characterized West Indian literature and rhetoric.

Even the title of the article, "English as 'She is Wrote' in Trinidad," was meant to ridicule the Trinidadian way of speaking English, even though, at a closer phonological level, a West African pattern of language informed the Trinbagonian way of rendering English. More to the point however, was that these users of the language were studying neither in an English boarding school nor living in the English countryside. They were a heterogeneous group of citizens thrown together in a helter-shelter fashion, trying to make their way in a new world, using language to describe the particularity of their social being. That the major contributors to the language had come from Venezuela (Bodu), England (Collens and Seaton), Guyana (Inniss and Rodriques), Barbados (Douglin), China (Assee), and India (Jugmohun Singh) reveal that these writers and speakers were trying to assimilate a culture and a language and to make it their own during a critical moment of political and social unrest.

Who Did It? (1891)

James Collens, an Englishman who became very active in Trinidad society during the last two decades of the nineteenth century, came to Trinidad in the 1870s. He was the secretary of the Church of England Temperance Society, superintendent of the Government Training Institution and Model School (Boys), and inspector of schools. In 1902, he was the second in command of the contingent that represented Trinidad at the coronation of Edward V11. Collens felt so at home in Trinidad he even referred to the Trinidad Cricket Team that visited Barbados in 1891 as "our representatives."[21] R. C. Cato, the vice president of the Tranquillity Boys Model Schools Ex Pupils, described Collens as "one of the few Englishmen who thoroughly appreciate and have affection for the West Indies."[22] Owen Mathurin, on the other hand, calls him "a liberal imperialist."[23] In 1881, when Kofi Nti, son of the late King Kofi Calcali of the Ashantee arrived in Trinidad, he was placed under Collens's tutelage.[24]

Collens was also a prolific author. As the government's statistician, he was privy to much information, and in 1886, he published *Guide to Trinidad: A Handbook for the Use of Tourists and Visitors.* For several years, he compiled *The Trinidad Official & Commercial Register and Almanack.*

Collens turned to fiction in 1891 when he published *Who Did It?* Written in a very lively manner, this "West Indian novelette," its subtitle, is a detective story about the murder of an Englishman, Captain Larry Webster, that takes place in Port of Spain. Very much a portrayal of island society from an English point of view, this story invites readers to participate in the tropical beauty and mystery of

21. James H. Collens, *The Trinidad Official and Register and Almanack* (Port of Spain: Government Printing Office, 1891), p. 75.
22. "Model School Ex Pupils Association," *Mirror,* November 20, 1901.
23. Mathurin, *Henry Sylvester Williams,* p. 20.
24. Jose M. Bodu, *Trinidadiana* (Port of Spain: A. C. Blondel, 1890), p. 44.

this exotic culture. As added spice is the love story of another Englishman, Lieutenant Thomas Cartwright, who is accused initially of the murder, and Margaret Tracy, the daughter of a member of the Legislative Council of Trinidad. Stanley Stubbs, a Grenadian, who prior to the book's opening, had "made the Royal Goal his temporary head quarters on at least two occasions, once for larceny and again for ill-using his paramour"[25] is also a suspect in the case. All ends well when Luke Darbin, an English sailor, is arrested for the crime and Cartwright is freed. In this novelette, the honorably Englishman (the honored and the true) is counter-poised against the lowly West Indians (liars, cheats, and scoundrels), the scum of the earth. Apart from the young Creole lawyer who is presented as a worthy, intel-ligent person, the Indians and Africans are depicted as unworthy "specimens of humanity." The Trinidadian home or "shanty" is described as "a glorious accumula-tion of dirt, and the usual congregation of cockroaches and other insect vermin that delight therein" (*WDI.*, p. 177).

Although *Who Did It?* has much that is derogatory to Trinidadian Africans and Indians, nonetheless, given the newness of the mystery genre and this being one of the earliest crime stories of the literature, Collens did a tolerably good job. Still, the story was not received well at the time of its publication. One critic saw the charges against Cartwright, the theme around which the tale revolves, as being "very, very farfetched." In the future, he recommended, Collens should so guide himself (and his writing) "to more generally get the good will of the public."[26] Interestingly enough for the sociological evolution of Trinbagonian society, *Who Did It?* opens with a cricket match, albeit from the point of view of an English person. It might have been the first Trinidadian work of fiction to do so. Set in the Queens Park Savannah, "the envy of the whole West Indies, smooth as a billiard table," the nov-elette begins with the following observation:

Trinidad is an out-and-out cricketing country if ever there was one…. It must not be thought for a moment that in this tight little island the noble game of cricket is monopolised by the well-to-do or even middle class. Not a bit of it. Any day you may see small boys clad in a minimum of the reggedest apparel bowling and bat-ting away to their heart's content. Why, just outside my window at this moment, is a group of urchins engaged in the game, and the entire sum total of raiment of the batsman nearest to me comprises about three-fourths of a shirt! Yet these same shoeless scantily-clad rascals still mange, goodness knows how, to scrape together sufficient dollars and cents to purchase decent bats and other apparatuses. To be sure their style of scoring is primitive, not to say unique…. All the same, and in spite of these little drawbacks, the young ragamuffins play a tolerably game (*WDI.*, pp. 1–3).

25. James H. Collens, *Who Did It?: A West Indian Novelette* (Port of Spain: Muir Marshall, 1891), p, 149; hereafter cited in the text as *WDI*.

26 A Wicked Critic, "Who Did It?" *New Era*, June 17, 1891.

FIGURE 18. Photograph of cricket being played at the Queen's Park Savannah, 1897.

Such observations were significant, given the role cricket was beginning to play in national life, how it would affect national consciousness, and the way the game would shape the people's response to their world, a process that C. L. R. James described in *Beyond a Boundary*.[27] By the 1900s, the newspapers, especially the *Mirror*, were filling their pages with ball-by-ball commentaries of the international games.

By now, the game had also taken on a racial edge. While, in 1883, most of the teams fielded by the Queen's Park Cricket Club were all white, by 1895, the All-Trinidad team that played a visiting English side had five nonwhite members.[28] By August 1900, a West Indian team, touring England, defeated Surrey's County Cricket team by an inning and thirty-four runs, leading the editor of the *Mirror* to exclaim: "How are the Mighty Fallen." In case one missed the significance of this victory, the editorial proclaimed: "before the cricketing world... a team of West Indians, some of them members of the 'woolly headed' race, have overthrown the mighty Surrey team in open contest with leather and willow." That this victory

27. One of the earliest descriptions of a Trinidadian game of cricket was offered in 1841. Rev. John Blackman, a Wesleyan minister, wrote that "[y]esterday, which was Sunday, I was out to enter the dead [*sic*], and on my return home was shocked to see the awful desecration of God's Holy Day. Scores of young men and boys were playing at cricket, and not having witnessed such publick [*sic*] outrage on the sacredness of the Christian Sabbath in any other colony [I became] so excited as to go up to them for the purpose of affectionately remonstrance. But scarcely had I uttered a sentence when one more brave than the rest aimed a blow at my head, with his cricket bat but he in whose hands are the issue of life and death, averted the stroke, or I had not been able to [I would not] reach my home much less preach to the people the following hour" (John Blackwell, Port of Spain, April 24, 1841, Baptist Missionary Society Papers).

28. Bereton, *Race Relations*, p. 57.

occurred when England was trumpeting its superiority all over the world and Joseph Chamberlain was boasting about the superiority of the Anglo-Saxon race must have bruised the English psyche.

More than ever, one realized that cricket was not just cricket, a position that James elucidates with tremendous acuity when he asks rhetorically, "What do they know of cricket who only cricket know?"[29] A black person who represented the West Indies not only played for his country, he also played for and represented his race.[30] The same was true for writers as the cases of Thomas and Douglin demonstrate. For Caribbean people, the victory of a West Indian team over an English team was an event of world-shaking proportions. The editorial continued:

> It is a proud performance, and one which will do more than anything we can at this moment think of, to boom the West Indies among the English public, many of whom still associate these islands with the nude, uncultured savage, and whose feeling toward us is rather one of spasmodic curiosity than lasting interest in our welfare as an integral part of the great British Empire (vide Mr. Chamberlain last speech).[31]

There, plain to see, was the link between savagery and civility even in a game as simple as cricket. But, then, cricket was not simply a game. As James would assert some sixty three years later, "to establish his own identity, Caliban, after three centuries, [had to] pioneer into regions Caesar never knew."[32] Therefore, when these "woolly headed" savages, playing "the noble game of cricket," in the home of the invincible, could inflict such a licking on members of the superior race, then all assumptions of superiority of one race over another had to be reexamined. Moreover, when one recognized that the term nobility, in its agrarian sense, "wobbles between referring to membership of a status group, and possession and display of values summed up as honour,— a touchy sensitivity about one own status,"[33] then one begins to understand how victory in this noble game threatened all of the boundaries of honor and values that were prized by defenders of the status quo.

Since such a victory over the cultured Anglo-Saxon constituted a crisis in civilizational terms, introduction of cricket into the literature was a cultural signpost. Significantly, the literary arts were pointing to social and cultural practices that would revolutionize the relationship between the colonized and the colonizer. Needless to say, by the middle of the twentieth century, the black ragamuffins of whom Collens spoke would emerge as innovators of the game and make some of the finest statements about their colonial status through their cricket bats and the fury they released in their acts of bowling.

29. C. L. R. James, *Beyond a Boundary*, (1963, Durham: Duke University Press, 1993), p. xxi.
30. See P. T. Pollard's note sent to Learie Constantine on May 22, 1900. "Farewell Presentation to Mr. L. Constantine," *Mirror*, May 24, 1900.
31. "How Are the Mighty Fallen," *Mirror*, August 2, 1900.
32. James, *Beyond a Boundary*, p. xxi.
33. Gellner, *Nationalism*, p. 19.

L. O. Innis and Caribbean Folklore

Lewis Osborne Inniss, a deacon in the Trinidad Baptist Church, was the most interesting and certainly one of the most prolific writer of the 1890s. Born in Guyana in 1848, he was the son of a remarkable father, Augustus Inniss, who before coming to Trinidad in 1852, worked conscientiously for the Baptist Missionary Society in Trinidad and Guyana in the 1840s and the early 1850s. During the 1840s, the elder Inniss was a clergyman, schoolmaster, and assistant to Rev. George Cowen, the aneusesis of *Maria Jones* before he was fired.[34] In August 1850, he wrote an eloquent letter to the Baptist Missionary Society in London about the work he was doing in Trinidad (like his son, he reflected some of the biases of his mentors). In an early description of his career, Augustus Inniss was seen working among the "Africans or their children, who have been rescued from the grasp of slavery some thirty-three years ago in the United States of America, a few of whom may have been Christians, but left to themselves, without the advantage even of reading the scriptures, they have degenerated so as scarcely to be known as the good seed of the kingdom, and have contracted ideas and habits contrary to the gospel."[35] While he was in Guyana in 1851 he tried "to raise a Baptist interest" there.[36] In Trinidad, he worked in Savannah Grande under the supervision of Rev. John Law, Rev. Cowen having died on October 17, 1852.

However, things did not work out with Law. In 1854, Inniss was fired because he was unwilling "to act under the direction of Mr. Law."[37] He seems to have had definite opinions about how things ought to proceed within the Mission. According to Lewis, after his father left the employment of the Baptist Missions, he became a teacher in the newly created Ward Schools that Lord Harris set up in the mid 1850s.[38] Lewis bore no malice toward Law, whom he described as possessing "a kind and generous dispossession and very fond of young people, whom he sought, by kind words and faithful teaching, to lead into the right way. He was very much beloved by them. If he did wrong he was sorry for it and did his best to remedy it."[39] Lewis remained a member of the Missionary Society and rose to prominence within the Church. A pharmacist by profession, Lewis took a very strong interest in anthropology and, in the process, left us with several important books and pamphlets about the folklore of Trinidad and Guyana and an insider's view of the historical development of the Baptist church in Trinidad.

34. See Barry V. Pierre, *Verbum Sap: A Tribute to L. O. Inniss* (B. V. Pierre: Port of Spain, 2000), for a short description of Inniss's life.
35. *The Missionary Herald*, No. 85 (August 1850), p. 122.
36. *The Missionary Herald*, No. 110 (November 1852), p, 175.
37. Committee Meeting of the Baptist Mission Society, August 15, 1854. There seems to have been problems between Law and Inniss. A Baptist Missionary Society Committee Meeting of November 1, 1853, of the Baptist Missionary Society makes the following observation: "Read a letter from Mr. A. Inniss, #993 acceding to the Resolution of the Committee as to his engagement in Mission service in Trinidad, and stating that he has 'no objection to the general direction of Mr. Law.'"
38. Lewis O. Inniss, *Diamond Jubilee of Baptist Missions in Trinidad, 1843–1903* (Port of Spain: Franklin's Electric Printery, 1904), p. 17.
39. Ibid., pp. 8–9.

The *Adventures of Reginald Osborn,* a tale of adventure that is set in Guyana, is one of Lewis's earliest works, which could be subtitled, "How Gold Was Discovered in British Guiana." Protagonist Osborn leaves Georgetown, Guyana, because of an altercation with Frank Denman, both being suitors for the affection of Eliza Dickson. Osborn comes into contact with several Amerindian ethnoi (the Caribs, the Macusi, and the Warraus) before he discovers a gold field in the interior of Guyana. Returning to Georgetown, he tells his father of his discovery, and discovers that Eliza is really in love with him (eventually they marry). Together with his father and father-in-law, Osborn returns to the gold field to exploit its riches. When the secret of his discovery can no longer be kept, "there was a rush to those quarters, and the gold industry was established in British Guiana and has since grown to magnificent proportions."[40]

An interesting anthropological guide to the folklore of Guyana, the *Adventures of Reginald Osborn* informs the reader of some Indian legends, charms, and incantations, as well as their use of medicinal herbs and plants, while Osborn works with a Piai man, analogous to "the obeah man in Trinidad."[41] The former also learns much about the Amerindians' superb knowledge of their natural geography. Osborn is not above making "careful notes of the names [of the herbs and plants he used] in a little tablet book which he had."[42] In the process, he discovered a remedy for Rheumatism which he gives as a present to a relative in Trinidad "who patented it under the name of OSBORN'S RHEUMATIC COMPOUND, and it has become famous as THE CURE for Rheumatic pains of all kinds."[43]

This interest in the medicinal properties of plants and herbs would consume Lewis Inniss for the rest of his life. His broader academic and scholarly interests were revealed in articles such as "Opium," presented to the Trinidad Pharmaceutical Society, and his exposition on Shakespeare, given at the Victoria Institute.[44]

Inniss's *Centennial Tourists Companion to Trinidad* reflects his sustained interest in folklore and anthropology. After offering a brief historical and political description of the island and a discussion of places of interest (government buildings, churches, squares, and parks), much of the work is a recitation of the folklore and popular superstitions of the people of the island. This particular section of the text, "Folklore and Superstitions," proved so popular that it was republished, with slight variations, several times over the next thirty years.[45] It introduces the reader to some of the folkloric characters of the society: jumbies (the Trinidadian term for ghosts); douaines, "the spirits of little children who have died before they were christened"; Soucouyan, "a Darwinian creature belonging to the *genus homo,* but possessing the

---

40. Lewis O. Inniss, *Adventures of Reginald Osborn* (Port of Spain: Mole Brothers, 1895), p. 36.

41. Ibid., p. 16.

42. Ibid., p. 27.

43. Ibid., p. 36.

44. See "Opium," *Mirror,* June 17, 1901, and "A Paper on Shakespeare," *Mirror,* March 18, 1902.

45. See "Folklore and Popular Superstition" in T. B. Jackman, ed., *The Book of Trinidad* (Port of Spain: Muir Marshall, 1904), pp. 111–24, and *Creole Folk Lore and Popular Superstitions* (Port of Spain: Yuille's Printerie, 1923).

extraordinary faculty of divesting itself of its epidermis, and thereby acquiring the power of flying through the air"; and diabless, "another specimen of the uncanny family of hybrids and is supposed to be a human being, who, by dealing with the evil one, has acquired the power of changing itself into the form of any animal that it wishes to stimulate and, in that form, doing harm to people."[46] In recounting "these ghost stories," Inniss affirms that "the folk lore of all peoples, was derived from one stock and goes to prove the Biblical assertion that God made, of one blood, all nations to dwell upon the face of the earth."[47] Such a statement reflects Inniss's religious sentiments.

Folk tales such as "How the Crab Got that Crack in Her Back," "How the Agouti Lost Its Tail," "How Compere Crapaud (the Frog) beat Compere Chival (the Horse) in a 3 Mile Race" also play a prominent part in this section of the book. They are extremely funny stories and complement the folk literature Thomas offered in *Creole Grammar*. These stories reveal another aspect of the prose dimension of African oral literature. Inniss argues that these tales, generally told at wakes by a good raconteur or at evenings to pass the time away, lose much of their spontaneity and humor when they are committed to paper. He insists that they are "equivalent to La Fortains [*sic*] fables or Grimm's fairly tales; only the Fairies, Giants, and Genii, are generally absent and the actors are animals, after the style of the American stories about Brer Rabbit and his doings among the other animals. Whether these are importations or not, I cannot say, but the adventures of compere Lapin and compere Tigre, seem to bear a strong family likeness to those of Brer Rabbit and Brer Wolf, with which uncle Remus entertains us" (*CCT.*, p. 20). This conclusion recognizes the common African literary culture out of which these stories emanate.

In his work, Inniss also talks about popular superstitions as ways of dispensing valuable advice to devotees. There are also superstitions that connected with weddings, which explain how to ensure a successful marriage, along with means to ward of evil forces. Yet, Inniss recounts one superstitious practice that still possesses currency in my adult life. It was handed down from mother to son: "If you are setting out on an important mission and you turn back, from any cause, you will be unsuccessful in your mission" (*CCT.*, pp. 40–41.) Such an example demonstrates how deeply these beliefs burrow into one's psyche and how they construct our realities. Inniss's recounting of folkloric and superstitious practices suggest that the society may have arrived at a position where it wanted to reflect upon itself.

Diamond Jubilee of the Baptist Missions in Trinidad, 1843–1903 recounts the accomplishments of the Baptist Mission in Trinidad from Rev. Cowen's arrival in the island in 1838 when he made his first convert, Maria Jones, to the abandonment of the Mission at the end of the century. In his accounting, Inniss describes Maria

---

46. Lewis O. Inniss, *The Centennial Companion to Trinidad* (Port of Spain: Daily News, 1897), pp. 24–25; hereafter included in the text as *CCT*.

47. Ibid., p. 22.

"as a chief's daughter who was stolen away [from Africa] and sold to this island as a slave."[48] *Diamond Jubilee* also possesses autobiographical elements that recall Inniss's involvement with the Church. Perhaps, the most revealing aspect of this short history is the religious practices of the American blacks or "shouters" as he calls them:

> The all-night shouting meetings [of the American Baptists] have also been a bone of contention between the missionaries and the Churches and I regret to say that it is still giving trouble. The meetings, although perhaps they originally had good results, had gradually resolved themselves into orgies, owing principally to the presence of unsympathetic visitors, who made it a practice of attending those meetings to have a lark and laugh at the antics of the "shouters" and the presence of numerous sellers of strong drink, who attended as it were a theatrical performance, and plied a busy trade. The shouting consisted of singing in a loud voice and clapping of the hands of the whole congregation, while now and then some one worked up by the excitement would begin to jump up violently, and shout until they had worked themselves into a kind of cataleptic fit, when they fall down unconscious and remain so for some time. They are supposed to be then under conviction of sin and after coming out of the fit are expected to make a profession of faith.[49]

The religious practices of the African American were more in keeping with those of the Shango and the Orishas of Trinidad. Like their African counterparts in Trinidad, they, too, "got the spirit" or "felt happy" when the spirits possessed them. Such practices were in keeping with African ways of worship in which the spirits (ancestors) descended among devotees. Inniss, a convert to a Eurocentric religion, could not appreciate the zeal of devotees to an African-centered religion because he was indoctrinated into the somberness of a European religion in which the gods, it is said, preferred to remain in their heaven.[50] Even in Trinidad, one was hearing echoes of Jonathan Edwards and the "Great Awakening." Neither Inniss nor Chalamelle could understand how these Africans had taken the religion and culture of their forefathers and adopted them to suit their purposes in a new land.

The Siren Goddess of South America

In *The Siren Goddess of South America*, a romance, Henry Martiol Rodrigues uses the intrigue of South American politics and the avarice and ambition of so-called revolutionary leaders, "the Siren Goddess of South America," as the basis of his story set in an unnamed, but typical, South American Republic (since the republic

48. Ibid., p. 5.
49. Ibid., pp. 5–6.
50. Espinet and Pitts point out that, through a process of "doption," Africans "become 'possessed' during the service and slouch or become restless in their seats... . In effect, by the application of 'doptions,' the worshippers reduce the staid, reverent religious hymns of the Anglo-Saxon into a strongly vibrant, intoxicating rhythm in which neither words nor melody has any particular resemblance to the original.' (*Land of the Calypso*, pp. 70–71).

is not named, it could be any on that vast continent). This interesting work examines the bad faith of those who promote themselves as the "liberal defenders" of these South American republics only to fulfill their own avariciousness. [51] The author is concerned to show how ambition, gone astray, sometimes overpowers the individual and leads decent people to commit dastardly deeds.

Don Pedro Sanchez is one of the main characters in the romance and is willing to sacrifice his daughter, Manuelita, to become the president of the republic. Archibald Graham, an Englishman who is betrothed to Manuelita, becomes a willing participant in Don Pedro's scheme to overthrow the government for reasons that are not made clear in the work. Interwoven into this political romance are idealized depictions of Lucana, "half Indian, half-white and belonging to the tribe of the Maracay" (*SG.*, p. 32), and Jose, a faithful servant of Graham, who remains loyal to his master unto death. Love, too, is idealized. Manuelita remains faithful to Graham, in spite of the fact that her father betrayed her. Lucana continues to love Sebastien Nunez, the villain of the novel, even though, in the end, she kills him to assuage her honor. In the world depicted by Rodrigues, retribution is a central value. No evil deed goes unpunished.

The novel also idealizes nature and the Amerindians. When asked if she dislikes the white race, Lucana responds: "I prefer the Indian race… In the midst of this race I live a far happier and purer life. I have nature in its grandest form as my teacher and I do not crave the baubles of that civilized world which the white race claim as theirs and boast of it" (*SG.*, pp. 33–34). At times, it takes a philosophical turn and speaks about the uniqueness of love and the power of prayer.

Given its idealism, this political romance offers a cynical twist to some events and certain characters. For example, all the revolutionaries are depicted as criminals, "worthless men who ambition are corrupted. They may have been moral men, but the moment they plunge headlong into an inconceivable life; into a life of bloodshed, it is because they do not trust themselves any longer. They may have been brought up to be honorable and just. They may follow the course or they may not. But if they were to follow that course, do you think that they would require to be assassinators, thieves, vile men, as I call all revolutionaries" (*SG.*, p. 33).

After Don Pedro, a revolutionary, fails in his attempt to overthrow the government, he is arrested and taken to prison. Mortally wounded, he is visited by his daughter, who forgives him. Don Pedro then consents to her marriage to Graham, gives the latter his blessings, and says, "You have been an honorable and noble man, Graham, for you have not taken advantage of the love that Manuelita had for you and married her without my consent, and neither did you try to sully her maidenly honor" (*SG.*, p. 26). As we observe the death of Don Pedro, the narrator asks the reader "to picture to yourself what I cannot fully describe. Picture the deathbed with the dying being—his ghastly and sunken eyes, his hallow cheeks, his purple lips, his

---

51. Henry Martiol Rodrigues, *The Siren Goddess of South America* (Port of Spain: Daily News, 1897), p. 22; hereafter quoted in the text as *SG.*

dark brow and shriveled and emaciated form. Picture the mother, the father, the wife, the sister, the brother, all trembling with fear at the expected moment, at that dreadful moment, when they convulsed in tears and painful sorrow, must take the last embrace, the last kiss that was so often given, so often felt.... Death is the saddest truth to contemplate" (*SG.*, p. 68). Where words cannot do the trick, the author asks the reader to intervene and use his or her imagination.

There is nothing else like *Siren Goddess* in Trinidad's literature. It revels in highly wrought sensibilities, overblown sentiments, and overwhelming sentimentally. Set firmly in the nineteenth century, the book depicts women as being subservient to their husbands and fathers. Honor, duty, and chastity are the cherished values, and deference to conventions is prized. When Manuelita ask Graham why, if he loves her so much, they do not elope, he answers, "I respected his fatherly rights, not in a worldly light but in a moral and religious one" (*SG.*, p. 70). Graham, however, never quite explains one of the central mysteries of the text: why he signed Don Pedro's declaration against the government that Don Pedro used. It is this act that gets Graham him into so much trouble.

In the end, love triumphs. In "his pathematic, lyrical voice, as he laid his face against hers," Graham whispers, "Manuelita, dearest, most precious sublime jewel of my supreme felicity, let us never speak any more about the bitter, bitter past." To which she responds, "Yes, most dearest, most dignified idol of my heart, let us not." Nestling closely together, they "cursed the Siren Goddess to oblivion" (*SG.*, p. 70). Neither ambition nor avarice can desecrate their love, although such vices have done much damage to the lives of the ones they love. If only these lovers can think of the sublimity of the origins of nature and mankind, as Rodrigues advises, all will be well with them in their future lives.

Centenary Reminiscences

The year 1897 marked the centenary of the English occupation of the island. Ivry Hart, head teacher of the Chacachacare School, sought to extend "the triumph of the English language" through two offerings, *Centenary Reminiscences* and *Some Sketches and Songs*. Like Rodrigues and Inniss, Hart possessed links to Guyana, his having taught at an Amerindian mission there. In his *Centenary Reminiscences*, he offers his recollections of Trinidad, whereas in *Some Sketches and Songs*, he "tunes a simple lay."[52] In the first, Hart tells the story of the English occupation of the island in verse and asks his readers to be lenient in their criticism: "The English language has only passed its see-time among the majority of those that are not English by birth or descent, and desiring to see the language developed, they...should reduce their criterion when judging the literary productions of the colonists, bearing in mind that the writers are, for the most part, the Caedmons of colonial literature."[53]

---

52. "Two Pamphlets Reviewed," *Mirror*, February 3, 1898.
53. Ivry Hart, *Centenary Reminiscences* (Port of Spain: Daily News, 1897), Preface.

Indeed, Hart needs much understanding, as he is not the most sophisticated versifier, although his verse does have a soothing lilt. He was familiar with the works of the masters of English poetry and did his best to imitate them. In "The Capture of Trinidad, 1797," he tells of Abercromby's entrance to Trinidad:

> The budding morn is more like eve than morn;
>   The blooming radiance comes like one forlorn,
> And like a tender child by fear confined
>   Blushingly peeps the eastern mounts behind.
>
> Benignant is his ray and softly bright,
>   Traversing darkness with regretful might,
> Like some grand conqueror, potent but kind,
>   By duty devastates against his mind... .
>
> Paria sleeps as tranquil as a child;
>   And Sol's bright beams with breath so softly mild
> O'er the wide expanse of her water (wild
>   Yestreen, to peace, to calm now reconciled.) ....
>
> Oh war, Destroying Angel stern and strong,
>   Thy shadowy Peace, precede thee long!
> All with this balmy moon seems—oh! Divine!
>   But lo! What sails within the Bocas twine?...
>
> And on its wings in place of halcyon
>   Rode eagles Abercrombie and Picton:
> These British eagles on the island bore,
>   To meet but slight resistance from the shore... .
>
> The martial elements their voices raise,
>   That drowns the birds and convent's songs of praise,
> Awake the echoes of the silent hills
>   Whose sparkling fountains feed the gushing rills.
>
> Their lurid lightning with a ghastly smile
>   Kiss the sulphurous clouds that heav'nward pile.
> But these efforts of 'Crombie and Picton
>   Were little needed to subdue Chacon... .
>
> Self-set flames suffused their Admiral's ship!
>   Chacon signed the capitulating script—
> Oh! Hast though searched the clouds when storms do part?
>   Such was the pall-like vapour o'er his heart.

After this poetic rendition of the capitulation, Hart tries to imagine how the early days of English occupation were. He calls his imaginative projections, "Personal Reminiscences," in which he reflects on his craft and explains what he is trying to accomplish. Thus, in the preface to one of his "personal reminiscences," he writes:

I cannot undertake to give in poetry an interesting and detailed account of the events of the other days [of the occupation]; for I am fully aware that the mere rhyme is not true poetry, and I have not the power of a Byron to invest with suffi-cient poetical interest all the prosaic events (such as dinners, processions, etc.) Therefore, have I, with a necessary variation, taken Colderidge as a precedent (so far as the calling up of an ancient spirit to suit a modern purpose), and introduced an "Ancient Buccaneer" to wind up with a *multum-in-parvo* retrospect.[54]

In this work, Coleridge's "Ancient Mariner" becomes "an Ancient Buccaneer," with whom Hart ends his reminisces.

Some Sketches and Songs (1898) is a more interesting and original work. Although Hart recognizes that there were better writers than he, he wants "to be a pioneer, and encourager [since] this mission on the part of myself and others may be need-ed for a long time yet."[55] In this work, a mixture of prose and verse, the author pro-vides an original insight into the life of a Caribbean peasant woman, Alice Clive, who demonstrates the dignity of the peasant as she strives to find her way in her world. Hart describes her so: "On the East Coast of Demerara and on the east and west coasts of Berbice...one sees a girl coming from the 'backdam' with sleeveless garments much the worse for wear, a large basket on a head bare of any covering save a cloth 'pad' that rests on several large plaits of hair. The basket is filled with various kinds of agricultural produce, and across it is a cutlass, while sugar cane and a hoe are borne in the hands: it is Saturday." The next day, in the church, Alice is transformed: her "fingers traverse the keys of a well-tuned harmonium, and the voice of their owner rise in exquisite melody to lead their choir: after much peering and shifting of view, and enquiry, we recognise the (now) comely form tastily and decently clad, as our quondam heroine of the field is transformed."[56] To Hart, Clive represents the quintessential Caribbean woman. He also speaks of Georgetown and its special charms and uses it as a setting in some of his poems.

In seeking to extend the triumphs of the language, Hart out-Englished the English. A Trinidad reviewer commented that, although the pamphlets are "read-able and aptly expressed," they strain too much toward the "high falutin." While it is true that Hart showed promise in his work, the remarks of the Trinidad review-er ring with much truth: "If this new writer will only put off attempts at lofty flights until his wings are fully fledged, we have every hope that the improvement clearly perceptible in the course of the two small samples of his craft...will be maintained and increased."[57] Surely, there is no a better evaluation of Hart's efforts.

Carmelita: The Belle of San Jose

Like everything else in Trinbagonian society, theatre operated at two levels: the formal and the informal. Ken Corsbie has observed that, from as early as 1827, for-

54. Ibid., p. 12.
55. Ivry Hart, *Some Sketches and Songs, Part 1* (Port of Spain: Daily News, 1898), Preface.
56. Ibid., p. 8.
57. "Two Pamphlets Reviewed."

mal theatre "was a part of the cultural heritage of the ruling class, and plays performed in the 19th century said little or nothing about Caribbean life…. Nearly all
of the full-length plays, which were staged in the 19th century, originated in
England. They were written by English people, some of whom were living and
working in the Caribbean."[58] On the other hand, open-air, communal theatre in the
form of Carnival, ramleelas, and hosay were always an integral part of the society,
the product of the non-European people of the culture. In 1897, Inniss wrote
Carmelita: The Belle of San Jose, an historical drama, under the auspices of the
Church of England Union. Performed on the occasion of Trinidad's Centenary
Celebration of British rule, it marked the first occasion that a full-length play, written by a person from the English-speaking Caribbean, was performed on the island.
According to Barry V. Pierre, this play proved to be such a success that Inniss was
"publicly presented with a Silver Medal by the Bishop of Trinidad as a mark of
appreciation."[59]

Set in 1797, this four-act play celebrates "a day of mutual capitulation." It is a
day when Chacon surrendered to the British "to avoid useless bloodshed," and an
English heart , belonging to Frank Norton, surrendered "to the irreversible charms
of the Indian Cacique's daughter, as many other English hearts will, when they
come under the sway of the lovely Creole girls."[60] In this interesting play, Inniss sets
the Spanish against the French in whom he has no confidence and announces his
preference for British rule. Rather than accept the assistance of French volunteers
and ships from Guadeloupe, Don Jose Maria Chacon, Governor of Trinidad,
prefers that the island be turned over to the English from whom, he believes, "he
can get favourable terms for my people, protection for their religion and the observance of our laws, that will be much better than putting it under the power of those
villainous Republicans, who are a terror to the Island" (*C.,* p. 50). Although Chacon
is painted as an irresponsible leader when he encounters the British, Inniss depicts
his decision as being beneficial to Trinidad in the century that followed. One hundred years after the capitulation, the descendants of the Amerindian, Spanish, and
English (the French being left out of this glorious unfoldment) had "every cause to
rejoice, that this our island of the Humming Bird, [had] fallen under the strong but
gentle and beneficent rule of England" (*C.,* p. 58). England's "gentle and beneficent
rule" was celebrated also by Charles Assee in *Laus Reginae.*

The love story brings on stage Don Juan de Almeda, alcalde of San Jose and presumed father of Carmelita, who despises Chacon's inaction, hates the English, and
is aghast that Frank Norton, an Englishman, is courting his daughter without his
permission. Carmelita, a Spanish-Indian woman, one of "the most fascinating creatures in the world" (*C.,* p. 40), is in love with Norton and is determined to act as she
pleases, regardless of Almeda's objections. It doesn't hurt that Norton is

58. Ken Corsbie, *Theatre in the Caribbean* (London: Hodder and Stoughton, 1984). p. 16.

59. Pierre, *Verbum Sap,* p. xvii.

60. Lewis O. Inniss, *Carmelita,* in *Trinidad and Trinidadians* (Port of Spain: Mirror Printing Works,
1910), p. 58. Hereafter, all citation of this work will appear in the text as *C.*

Abercromby's relative. More perspicacious than his young friend and relative, the general warns Norton to "[b]eware how you risk the fascination of the young Senhoritas, who may have jealous lovers, who are very quick at using the knife" (*C.*, p. 53).

Additionally, Oronoko, Cacique of Toucouche, who pilots General Abercromby into the Trinidad harbour, hates Almeda who "has robbed him of his property and killed his wife" (*C.*, p. 54). The plot turns on the fact that Carmelita is actually Oronoko's daughter. On the night that the Spanish attacked the Indians, Oronoko's wife escaped to San Jose and was rescued by nuns. However, she died after giving birth to Carmelita. Almeda, being childless, adopts the baby whom he loves very much. After the signing of the capitulation, Abercromby returns Oronoko's estates to him (the estates that Almeda stole) as a reward for his services to the English. In the end, Carmelita acknowledges her real father, and all obstacles to her marrying Frank are removed. In his triumph, Oronoko is generous: "I, her real father, give her to you…. You Frank shall carry on my estates, which the generous Abercromby has restored to me and which I bestow upon Carmelita, as a marriage portion, and I will end my days, happy in seeing your happiness" (*C.*, p. 58). Even Almeda is forgiven because of the love he has shown Carmelita. Oronoko says to him: "The care you have taken of my daughter, unconscious though it was, robs me of my resentment and I forego my revenge. Depart in safety" (*C.*, p. 57). Seeing such forgiveness and such a joyous end, Anna, Carmelita's nurse, exclaims: "The saints be praised. All's well that ends well" (*C.*, p. 58).

Because Inniss wrote this play under the auspices of the Church of England, he had to place British behavior in the best light. It is no wonder that the generosity of the British is so prominent and that their rule is presented as the best thing to befall Trinbagonians. Despite this bias, *Carmelita: The Belle of San Jose* demonstrates the range of Inniss's gifts and the breath of his contributions to the literature and culture of Trinbagonian society. Indeed, no intellectual pursuit on the island seemed complete without his presence. He exemplified the best impulses of the native intelligentsia and captured an important dimension of the region's oral literature.

At the end of the century, C. D. W. Inniss, Lewis's son, won an Island Scholarship from Queen's Royal College and proceeded to study at Oxford University, from which he obtained his BA degree with honors.[61] Yet, when he attempted to serve his society, as his grandfather before him, the government refused his offer. This action elicited a strong rebuke from the editor of the *Mirror*,[62] who bemoaned that, no matter how qualified a black man was, he could never replaced a less qualified white man. But, then, such a fact was part of the entire saga of colonialism. No matter how much he achieved, the black man was never fit enough to assume positions of respect and responsibilities in the society. All of the nationalists up to and including Eric Williams when he entered Trinidad and

---

61. *Mirror,* August 16, 1900.
62. See "Preaching and Practice," *Mirror,* October 7, 1901.

Tobago's politics in 1955 struggled for the right of the colored person to be given his just rewards. It is a battle that would engage A. R. F. Webber and C. L. R. James in *Those that be in Bondage* (1917) and *The Case for West- Indian Self Government* (1933), respectively.

Reflections on the Carnival of Trinidad

In the 1890s, the annual Carnival celebrations continued to be an object of scrutiny and derision. Apart from government's prohibition against the beating of the big African drum and the dancing of the calinda, this decade also saw continuing attacks against this "lower class" fête. In his analysis of this festival, Chalamelle wished to demonstrate its devastating effects on the population. Contrasting the vulgarity of Carnival with "the manly game of cricket" [*SRCT.*, p. 9], he manages to promulgate the superiority of everything European over anything that was produced locally. In his pamphlet, Chalamelle calls for the "total abolition of carnival" since it lowered the moral climate of the island. As practiced by the "rabble," Carnival was not seen as a force for the intellectual, social, or cultural development of the people of the colony. To him, it was "a fete which is fraught with such dangers that it is like a millstone around the Colony's neck, dragging it into a slough of immorality from which it will be difficult to extricate it" (*SRCT.*, preface). As far as Chalamelle is concerned, Carnival was "a relic of medieval barbarism which should not be permitted to exist under the enlightenment of the nineteenth century." The continuation of such a practice only leads to "the moral emasculation of those who take part in it" (*SRCT.*, p. 2).

In his condemnation of Carnival, Chalamelle compares it to the "good old days" when Carnival was mainly a French upper-class activity, in which even the governor participated. In those good old days, just after the emancipation of the slaves, "people from every class and position derived the greatest amount of pleasure and gaiety from it as a holiday. Even the aristocracy of those days was known to participate and found wholesome and appreciable amusement in what, at the time, was conducted in a respectable a manner as it is observed in other civilised centres where the practice obtains" (*SRCT.*, p. 10). By century's end, the rabble had spoiled the festival and turned it into a "Creole Bacchanal," in which respectable people could not participate. Given the grip that the rabble had on Carnival , the respectable people could no longer police the event.

Chalamelle's most serious objection is that, during Carnival season, particularly on the two days of the actual celebration, hundreds of "innocent and virtuous maidens" are ruined by "some fiendish monsters in human shapes" (*SRTC.*, p. 17). As one newspaper asked rhetorically: "It is not well known that many an erstwhile innocent girl has fallen from the proud pedestal of virtuous maidenhood through the designing of some gallant Knight of the Mask?" (*SRCT.*, p. 29).[63] In spite of all of his

---

63. It is not known if the phrase, "Knight of the Mask" was taken from the chorus of the battle song of the Chicago workers of 1886 that went as follows: "Storm the fort, ye Knights of Labor/Battle for

objections about the vulgarity of Carnival, Chalamelle is most afraid of its revolutionary social potential, that is, its capacity to break down social barriers through the sexual license that occurred during the Carnival:

> It may not be generally known to the World, but to us it is an open secret, of the many families who have been brought to a state of degradation and fathomless sorrow upon the downfall of their daughters, who in deep repentance must own their ruin to the Carnival....
>
> Unknown to their parents, a good number of virtuous girls grasp the opportunities afforded by those two days, to disguise themselves and commit many an indecent and immoral act.
>
> It is the opportune time for them to indulge in all the immoral songs and gestures practised by the vulgar classes. And how many of the daughters of the respectable families, who on that occasion do not seek to meet a lover of low repute and inferior rank in disguise? For it could not be otherwise, and both of them arrange to go in disguise about the streets which they do unknown to the public and unmolested... .
>
> Not a few loving wives have proved faithless on that occasion to their husbands, and many a household tie has been broken asunder, and disgrace followed by inevitable misfortune was the sole inheritance of their children... .
>
> It is a time when virginity is lost and chastity is abased. (*SRCT.*, pp. 16–17).

One wonders if the blame should be placed on the liberating tendencies of Carnival or on the repression of sexuality from which Carnival allowed a certain release. From New Orleans to Rio, from Port of Spain to Europe, Carnival—an overturning of the social order—always allows a "freeing up" that is not possible under the guise of "normal," day-to-day existence. Therefore Carnival is, as Mikhail Bakhtin observes, a celebration of the "temporary liberation from the prevailing truth and from the established order;" a time subjected to "the laws of its own freedom."[64] Chalamelle never understood this phenomenon.

To his credit, Chalamelle recognizes that Carnival was more than the rabble coming on to the street to parade their vulgarity. What he does not grasp as firmly as he might is its psycho-sociological necessity and the sexual and social release it provides its "respectable," as well as its not-so-respectable, citizens. At least, on those two "dread" days of Carnival, all social barriers are broken down and, for a moment, people interact with one another as people rather than as embodiments of social class. It is this class-cutting aspect of Carnival that makes Chalamelle hold his head and bawl: "Oh, how monstrous! Is it not cruel that the source of all these great misfortune [of Carnival sexual liaisons] should be existing in the midst of our community and threatening every household of whatever class and position with

---

our cause;/Equal rights for every neighbor/Down with tyrant law." The Knights of the Mask played a similar function in Trinidad during that period. Members of an emergent group, they opened up new possibilities for mobility and mobilization in the society. See Oliver Cromwell Cox, *Caste, Class and Race* (New York: Monthly Review Press, 1959), p. 206.

64. Mikhail Bakhtin, *Rabelais and His World* (Cambridge: The M.I.T. Press), pp. 10, 7.

the ruin to the depths of perdition?" (*SRCT.*, p. 16). It is ironic that he should call upon the church for assistance since all carnivals had their origin in Church celebrations. It was a concession that the Church of Rome made to its recent converts as they prepared themselves for the Lenten season of fasting.[65]

Chalamelle is also disturbed by the intrusive nature of the "carnival song," or the calypso, one of the most "revolting features of the carnival" (*SRCT.*, p. 21). This song, he says, has "assumed too serious a character to be permitted to continue." It was too much a threat to the "domestic affairs of respectable families" (*SRCT.*, p. 22). During these years, the "more," as Shakespeare called them, were concerned about what the "less" made of their behavior. In tones most regretful, Chalamelle observes how the former are scandalized in song: "Whether it is a domestic squabble over the spread of dinner or the decanted wine, or whether it is some slight difference between 'boudoir' and the 'saloon' which may unfortunately find its way by the intermedium of an imprudent servant or a talkative friend—it is certain of becoming the subject of a 'carnival song,' and thus the private doings of a decent household are made a matter for scandal among the lewd community" (*SRCT.*, p. 22).

To illustrate his point, Chalamelle recalls the fate of a young woman whose behavior was subjected to these lewd and vulgar songs. The plan, according to Chalamelle, consisted of a group of revelers composing "a vulgar song in which couplets of extremely damaging exposures and other things derogatory to the young lady's character were introduced." After these maskers sang this song during the Carnival season, this young woman was scandalized: "She pined away despite the anxious care of her relatives and the careful attention of her medical attendants, and in a brief time she breathed her last into eternity" (*SRCT.*, p. 22). Such was the power of these "vulgar songs," it caused many respectable families to regard Carnival "as a life-long monument of sorrow—the cause of their grief" (*SRCT.*, p. 22).

Yet, the most pertinent aspect of Chalamelle's sociological description of Trinidad's carnival and of its history involves the case of Buckley, the leading stickfighter in San Fernando and known throughout the land as "the General." It is reported that, during the Carnival season of 1897, an attempt was made to reestablish the historic *Cannes brûlées* observances as it was in days of yore. According to Chalamelle, "a large crowd of the roughs numbering five hundred more or less—armed with sticks and carrying lighted torches—gathered together in the upper pat of town in full determination to again start the disgraceful '*Cannes brûlées*' proceedings." Seeking to prevent any return of this practice, the police intervened and Buckley was arrested and charged. The magistrate who tried the case, "severely lectured him for his imprudence and sent him to prison for a term of six months" (*SRCT.*, pp. 23–24).

To Chalamelle, such a penalty seemed justified. He could not see that the calinda (or stickfighting dance) was an African martial art, a warrior's dance, very much

---

65. See Espinet and Pitts, *Land of the Calypso*, p. 52.

like any other martial art in which artists express their virtue and their valor and thereby realize their humanity. Instead, Chalamelle reduced art to barbarity and reduced the warrior's behavior to that of a "lawless vagabond" who knew neither "decency nor prudence." It would take many years to value the achievements of these artists and their art and the part they played in keeping the spirit of their group alive.

Try as he might, Chalamelle was incapable of understanding the transgressive nature of Carnival. Although he could describe all of the outer signs of the festival (that is, its semiotic aspects), he could not unravel its essence. Given his ideological stance, he could not see that Carnival and its attendant festivities "offered a completely different, nonofficial, extraecclesiastical and extrapolitical aspect of the world, of man, and of human relations; ...a second world and a second life outside officialdom."[66] Because Chalamelle did not see Carnival as a fundamental challenge to a way of life from which these former slaves were excluded, he could not understand the profoundly humanizing content of this festival. Nor, for that matter, did he understand the laughter at or the satirizing of an order that was slowly disintegrating.

In spite of its wrong-headedness, Chalamelle's book is an important sociological document in that it records a significant moment of social transformation. According to Lord Executor, a calypsonian, 1898 was the first time that calypsoes were sung in English. It was also a time when this musical form began to break out of its lower-class provenance and to give voice to the masses. In gravitating toward this music, the younger generation were breaking "away from the apron-strings of Victorianism and, with the new spirit of the independence of youth, deliberately did 'naughty things'—daringly going into the formerly taboo calypso tents where they rubbed shoulders with the less respectable inhabitants in the back-yards. Thus it became as fashionable in Trinidad to visit the 'tents' as it was smart on Fifth Avenue to 'go slumming.'"[67]

The same was true of the growing acceptance of Carnival by the coloured population. Many of them became tired of remaining aloof from the festival and confining their Carnival activities to staying on decorated floats. Gradually, they started "to join in the parades—if the unruly mass of street-dancing masques of street dancing masques could be called parades.... They wanted something to sing and they used the 'le'gos,' at first falteringly in an unnatural disguised voice and in correct English. Later, they realised the absolute stupidity of prancing around with a stiff-shirt attitude under a wet costume and thus they accepted carnival so wholeheartedly that today [1944] the upper and middle classes not only play 'ol'mask,' but they provide the most ludicrous bands to be seen." [68]

66. Bakhtin, *Rabelais and his World,* p. 6

67. Charles Espinet and Harry Pitts, *Land of the Calypso* (Port of Spain: Guardian Commercial Printery, 1944), p. 31.

68. Ibid., p. 32. "Le'go" is a corruption of "let go," that is, a song which encourages one to "let one self go" (Ibid., p. 14). In other words, it was another dimension of "freeing up."

Chalamelle, it seemed, was not fully aware of the implications of the social situation he was describing. Not only was the young people's embrace of calypso and Carnival a sign that they were being drawn into a changing world, it was a symbol that they were also being pulled into a new society that was no longer enchained by an outmoded morality and questionable Victorian values. They were becoming Trinidadians in a way that Chalamelle could not understand, stuck as he was within the prison of Victorian sensibility.

In concluding his pamphlet, Chalamelle hoped that the Executive would "take this hint and bury into its grave this annual disgraceful fixture "so that "England's fair countenance [shall] smile upon us" once more" (*SRCT.*, p. 25). Little did he know that these younger people about whom he was so concerned had turned their eyes away from England as they sought to make their way in a new world. As one calypsonian remonstrated against Governor Jerningham in 1899:

> It is rudeness in you
> To break de laws of the Borough Council. …
> At a noble conference
> At the grand Prince's building;
> Mr. Laughlin, Mr. Agostini
> Mr. Nance fan de fire pon dem.[69]

And, as if to let the officials know how they felt about colonial impertinence, on Carnival Tuesday, two knights of the mask, dressed up as Joseph Chamberlain and his private secretary, offered "an intemperate oration upon the necessity of representation, etc."[70]

Under the guise of Carnival, the people were reassessing their relationship with the Crown and saying they were opting for their rights and their freedom. Here, the artistic was joining forces with the political to reshape the society. These people did not give a hoot whether England smiled upon them or not. Chalamelle and his generation would simply have to understand that Carnival and the carnivalesque spoke to a new order of social development and that itself was a political statement.

The Old Bar and the New Bar

In a symbolic way, the passing of George Lewis and Frederick Warner in 1897 and 1889, respectively, brought an end to the "glorious colonial" phase or the "Knoxonian period of the administration of Law in Trinidad" (*OB.*, p. 31). Their deaths also alerted the society that a literature, shaped initially by a legal text, should somehow take stock of its undertaking by an accounting of those who were responsible for interpreting the texts of slavery and colonialism. Since legal rhetoric always implies "a textual exchange or dialogue, a petition or appeal or an answer to some

69. "The Carnival," *Mirror,* February 14, 1899.
70. "The Carnival," *Mirror,* February 14, 1899.

sort of accusation,"[71] it was only fitting that a member of the bar should account to the national community about their performance over the century. Recognizing such a need, Anthony Delamere wrote a very short work, *The Old Bar and the New Bar: Reminiscences, 1820–1892,* in which he documented the achievement of the members of his profession.

The Old Bar, it seems, was a work of love and devotion. Delamere begins by acknowledging that "the history of the legal profession in Trinidad, is, in its entirety, unwritten and unpublished, and, as yet, only subject matter of tradition, as far as we know." In Trinidad, he observes, it was not customary, "as has been, and is, the case of England" to keep a record of the activities of the what he called the "liberal professions." To justify an undertaking that took approximately seven years to complete, Delamere rationalizes that there must be "some things relating to this profession, as it has been utilized here, of which the recollection has been, and is, worth preserving, but which are, regrettably, quite unknown to, at least, the stripling Practitioner" (*OB.,* p. 1). Yet, in tracing the growth of the legal profession in its native soil, Delamere manages to alert us to the intellectual minds that were responsible for shaping this noble profession. He does this by giving a vivid description of the practice of law in Trinidad and paying tribute to some of the outstanding attorneys and judges who practiced between 1820 and 1892.

According to Delemare, Charles William Warner was the first attorney in Trinidad to have studied in Great Britain and, "having done so, entered upon, or continued, in Trinidad, the practice thereof" (*OB.,* p. 1). Over the century, Charles William Gordon, William George Knox, Frederick Warner, Joseph Needham, Alexander Fitzjames, Alexander Williams Anderson, Robert Guppy (R. L. P. Guppy's father), Maxwell Philip, George Lewis Garcia, Vincent Brown, and Henry Albert Alcazar, among others, graced the profession. The most outstanding members of the Court during the early period were Messrs. Paulin Josse Delisle, Samuel Greenidge, James Driggs, and James Pendleton Ramsay. According to William Seaton, in 1889, many of the existing staff of Solicitors of the Supreme Court of Trinidad and Tobago "received his first lessons of the practice of his profession" in the chambers of Greenidge who began his professional career in 1832.[72]

Robert Guppy played an unusual role in Trinidad's development. A graduate of Oxford University, from which he received an MA in 1830, he practiced at the Bar in England and wrote *A Familiar Abridgement of the Municipal Corporation Act* (1835) before coming to Trinidad in 1839. In 1840, Sir Henry McLeod, governor of Trinidad, sent him to Sierra Leone "to enquire into the prospects of obtaining a sufficient supply of [African] labourers from that settlement."[73] Guppy also advised McLeod on the introduction of East Indians into the island. Thereafter, he engaged in a career of public service. In 1868, he was responsible for the introduction of the

---

71. Echevarria, *Myth and Archive,* p. 70.

72. William Seaton, "Vicissitudes of the Profession of Attorney and Solicitor in Trinidad," *New Era,* August 9, 1889.

73. "Mr. Robert Guppy," *Public Opinion,* October 18, 1887.

FIGURE 19. Robert Guppy, author of *A Familiar Abridgement of the Municipal Corporation Act* (1835) and mayor of San Fernando (1876–1878, 1880–1889).

electric telegraph into the island and the connecting of San Fernando and Port of Spain by telegraph. In 1876, he helped bring the railway to the island. He became mayor of San Fernando from 1876 to 1878 and 1880 to 1889 when he was ousted by the newly acquired power of the Indian voters.[74] Michael Anthony called him "one of the most brilliant but controversial figures the Borough Council had ever had to deal with."[75] Girad Tikasingh described him as a "notable liberal reformer,"[76] and Delamere described him as "a political thinker and an accomplished scholar."[77]

In 1871 Philip prepared an important piece of legislation that made it less cumbersome for Trinidadians to become attorneys and solicitors "without expensively repairing to England as a stepping stone." [78] Performing "a virtual labour of love," he guided the ordinance through the Legislative Council with enormous skill. According to Seaton, he "gave publicly some of the initial proofs of his patriotic concern for the interest of the many, by untiringly combating the objection so doggedly urged by his reactionary opponents, till after all it became the law of the land."[79] This amendment of 1871 effectively repealed an Ordinance of 1853 that prevented anyone from practicing law unless he had been admitted previously to practice as an attorney or solicitor in England, Ireland, or Scotland. As a result of

74. See Tikasingh, "The Emerging Political Consciousness Among Trinidad Indians in the Late 19th Century," for a good description of the East Indian assertion of power.

75. Anthony, *Anaparima*, p. 196.

76. Tikasingh, "The Emerging Political Consciousness Among Trinidad Indians in the Late 19th Century," p. 267.

77. Delamere, *The Old Bar and the New Bar*, pp. 15–16. See Bridges, *Child of the Tropics*, for an intimate sketch of Guppy's life.

78. The amendment embodied in Ordinance 7 of 1871 reduced the probationary period of "Creoles who may have acquired at least 10 years' experience of the practice of the law in the Chambers of a member of the legal profession." (*New Era*, August 16, 1889).

79. Seaton, "Vicissitudes of the Profession of Attorney and Solicitor," *New Era*, August 9, 1889.

this piece of legislation, many local men, such as Emmanuel Lazare, W. Seaton, and E. Maresse-Smith, were admitted to the colonial bar. Between 1886 and 1890, no less than ten legal practitioners (including Cyrus Prudhomme David, Charles Demain, and H. P. Ganteaume), educated at St. Mary's or Queen's Royal College, were admitted to the colonial bar. Thus, as with so many other aspects of the intellectual life of the society, the legal profession was being localized.

In his article, Seaton makes a case for the importance of solicitors, "the auxiliary branch of the Legal Profession," as Delamere calls them (*OB.*, p. 25), and their value to the profession. He outlines five qualities that distinguish good solicitors: a) "thorough grasp of the entire case complete with adequate perception of its legal bearings"; b) "ability to state the case with precision in writing for the instruction of Counsel"; c) "mastery of the complex rules of procedure embodied in the many Judicature Ordinances already referred to"; d) "carefulness in the management of the case"; and e) "promptitude in realizing for the client the fruits of judgment."[80]

In undertaking such a mammoth task, Delamere did for the legal profession what Thomas did for linguistics, what Leotaud did for ornithology, and what De Verteuil did for geography, even though Delamere did not do so in as exhaustive a manner as the others had done. Delamere recognized that a new generation of attorney and solicitors could gain from the experiences of those who served before him. He also recognized that societies only move forward when they look at their past critically and learn from it. He was not above identifying those whom he believed had made the most illustrious contributions to the profession. In Delamere's estimation, Charles Warner, Maxwell Philip, and Alexander Anderson were the "master minds" of the profession in the nineteenth century. At their best, the intellects of these men transcended the narrow field of law. They performed their professional duties with distinction even as they kept up "their acquaintance with English, Greek, Roman and French literatures" and lectured before appreciative audiences on topics such as "Electricity," "Truthfulness of Character," "The Fear of Death," and, "The Ethics of Work'" (*OB.*, p. 32). Warner and Philip, the authors of these lectures, were the darlings of the age. They displayed their knowledge and wisdom before "the beauty and fashion" of the colony and their compatriots reveled in their brilliance. It would take a post-1890 generation of lawyers to concern themselves more fully with the politics and social transformation of the society.[81]

---

80. *New Era*, August 30, 1889.

81. This is not to suggest that prior to 1890 there were not lawyers who worked on behalf of their people. For example, Vincent Brown defended the twenty defendants who were alleged to have taken part in the *Cannes Brûlées* riots of 1881. He did such a good job, the charges against the defendants were dismissed. (See *Public Opinion*, August 17, 1888). Maresse-Smith struggled against Governor William Robinson for the right of Africans to celebrate Emancipation Day, August 1, 1888 (*Public Opinion*, June 25, 1888). Interestingly, the disagreement between Maresse-Smith and the governor revolved around the "Governor's statement that the cause of freedom had triumphed, not by the efforts of the black race, but because white philanthropists, statesmen and warriors had fought the good fight and, at great sacrifice, had conquered." Needless to say, Marresse-Smith saw things differently (*Public Opinion*, August 3, 1888).

The proceedings of the legal institution played an important part in the intellectual development of ordinary people. Doreen Sealy who studied social sciences at the London School of Economics in the 1930s noted that, while the socially mobile gravitated toward the literary and debating societies that emerged at the end of the 1890s, grass-roots folk received much of their education from the courts. Each day, the daily newspapers devoted a substantial part of their coverage to reporting court cases. According to Sealy, "grass roots persons" would hang around the courts and then proceed to Woodford Square to discuss cases at great length and with great intelligence: "There one got a chance to expatiate, a chance to vent certain ideas, and even to test one's knowledge on legal matters. This was a very important arena."[82] The legal profession, it seems, played an important part in the education of the ordinary citizen allowing them to match their wits with one another. It taught them how to discourse about ideas and gave them a fleeting sense of what their rights were.

When Thomas died in England, penniless and alone, C. Prudhomme David, "unremitting in his attention," was one of the few Trinidadians there to be sure that he was given a proper burial.[83] This was as it should have been. Thomas, "a fast friend of Ernest David," father of Cyrus, assumed the mentorship of the latter from the time he was seven years old. Cyrus, admitted to read law at Gray's Inn, was subsequently called to the bar in July 1889.[84] Thomas spent some time with Cyrus while he was in London. Lazare also assisted in Thomas burial expenses. In a symbolic way, David and Lazare ensured (and certainly recognized) that the intellectual baton had been passed on to a new generation of legal activists who, for a certain period thereafter, became the torchbearers of the struggle for liberation and freedom.

82. Interview with Doreen Sealy, March 30, 1995.

83. "Sad Tidings," New Era, October 25, 1889.

84. Brinsley Samaroo, "Cyrus Prudhomme David—A Case Study of the Emergence of the Black Man in Trinidad Politics, Journal of Caribbean History, No. 3 (November 1971), pp. 75–76.

CHAPTER 15

The Revindication of the Races

When I visited the Sphinx I could not help thinking the figure of that
monster furnished the true solution of the enigma when I saw its features precisely those of a Negro, I recollected the remarkable passage of
Herodotus in which he says: "For my part, I believe Colchi to be a
colony of Egyptians, because, like them, they have black skins and the
frizzled hair," that is, that the ancient Egyptians were real Negroes of
the same species with all the natives of Africa.

> —E. W. Blyden quoted in *Trinidad Mirror* (1901)

The problem of the twentieth century is the problem of the color-line,
— the relation of the darker races of men in Asia, Africa, in America
and the islands of the sea.

> —W. E. B. Du Bois, *The Souls of Black Folk* (1901)

God save Old England for the higher life's humanity,
God make her great, and greater, for the higher destiny
Of Man—the lever of the world, the land that elevates
All lands that own her theirs, to higher hopes and bigger fates.
And higher heights of happiness that other lives enjoy
That educates the elder savage to discard his toy!

> —C. S. Assee, "Cecil Rhodes"

Charles Eryl Secundyne Assee's *Laus Reginae* and Stephen Nathaniel Cobham's
Rupert Gray: A Tale of Black and White brought the nineteenth century literary and
intellectual tradition to an end. In their own ways, these works embody the contradictory tendencies of the age. While the former celebrates the imperial grandeur of
the century, the latter seeks to resist the debilitating consequences of racism that the
imperial-colonialist system had engendered. Although *Rupert Gray* was not published until 1907, it has its lineage in the aspirations of the budding nationalist sentiments that showed its head at the end the nineteenth century and pointed its fin-
ger at a social and political phenomenon that emerged during the twentieth century: the problem of the color line. *Laus Reginae* harks backward to an age that had
passed, even though Assee's and his colleagues' stout defense of a nationalist poet-

ry reveals their contradictory tendencies. Taken together, *Laus Reginae* and *Rupert Gray* announce simultaneously the passing of the old imperial order and the birth of a new society. Philip Douglin's work stood some place in the center.

The Big Poetry Row

The biggest literary row in Trinidad and Tobago's history took place at the beginning of the twentieth century when an Englishman, not knowing his place and calling himself "A Cynic," attacked the literary merits of local verse. The controversy began simply enough. Cynic, a columnist of the *Mirror*, decided to pan some local poets. The result was that all hell broke loose. In his article, the critic writes that "[t]here is a very large output of alleged poetry in this colony and it appears to me that the quality of the verse is much lower than it ought to be."[1] In local parlance, "Who de hell tell him to say so?" Further, Cynic made the mistake of criticizing the work of Assee, the darling of local verse at the time. The son of a wealthy Chinese shopkeeper, Assee attended St. Mary's College before he proceeded to Gray's Inn in London to study law. When he returned to Trinidad, he had imbibed sufficient Englishness to bind him to the mother colony. It helped that he married an English woman whom he adored. Shortly after his return, bandits broke into his father's shop and murdered his father. Doreen Sealy believes that this incident may have had a traumatic effect on the younger Assee. Perhaps, it led to his becoming withdrawn and somewhat individualistic.[2] Although he practiced law, he became committed to the literary life.

When Cynic threw his words into Assee's garden, he affronted the latter's contemporaries, who felt even more put upon when Cynic affirms that "[i]n Trinidad much turgid nonsense is put forward as poetry by individuals who appear to have a very imperfect knowledge of what poetry is." Although Cynic's central target was Assee, the critic also aims a salvo at Montgomery S. Corbie's "Ode to Trinidad." Of the latter's stanza on Port of Spain, Cynic writes: "His desperate attempts to secure a rhyme in the first four lines are pathetic. His muse evidently finds the air of the town stifling, for it bolts for the seashore and finds three words that match right away." Cynic had other concerns as well: he could not understand how "our local writers of alleged poetry…cannot let a disaster alone. They must supply incoherent grotesque descriptions that arouse amused irritation in the mind of anyone who happens to read them."

Throughout this two-month row, Assee became Cynic's *bête noire*. The latter was particularly harsh on Assee's poem, "Iere," criticizing Assee's line "And when cane-arrows ripe explode and light" and the poet's use of "poui-emblazoned hills." Assee's attempt to fill his poem with local images such as the poui tree that means so much to Trinidadians, especially when its yellow flamboyant flowers decorate the forest just before the rainy season, meant little to Cynic, who would have none of it. He says that such phrases are "dragged in without good reason, for there is no sense in

1. A Cynic, "A Mysterious Phenomenon," Mirror, May 24, 1902.
2. Interview with Sealy, March 30, 1995

FIGURE 20. Charles Assee, author of
Laus Reginae. From Paria Archives.

defining a particular season of the year, marked with bush fires on the hills and the
arrow of sugar canes." Cynic's reaction might be a good case of seeing what one
wants to see and evading what is not pleasant or familiar to one. To Cynic, English
poets were the models (and the truth was, most of the local poets were imitating
English poets) of correct, acceptable verse. According to Cynic, Thomas Gray's
"Elegy Written in a Country Churchyard" was an example of a perfect poem:
"There is not an unnecessary word, not a hitch in the rhythm, not a halt in the
sense, and such a result could not have come by chance, but by the strenuous effort
of a man of genius."

In his criticism of the local poets, Cynic made one mistake. Relying on smug-
ness and a presumed superior knowledge of poetry, he asked those who disagreed
with him to offer their sentiments to the public: "Now I should very much like to
know what induces the writers of lines of the sort I have quoted to publish them. If
they have any ideas which they feel ought to be put before the public, why do they
not put them as plainly as they can in the best prose they can muster?" This was not
only a challenge. It was a rude, disdainful appraisal of the efforts of local poets and
dismissive of their intelligence as well.

Perhaps to Cynic's surprise, the responses were fast and furious. They were also
informed. One May 26, the first respondent explained to Cynic what the term
"cynic" meant and advised that he be careful less he become what he appeared to
be: "a sneering sarcastic or unruly person; a misanthrope."[3] Although Corbie offered

---

3. Joker, "A Joker to a Cynic," *Mirror,* May 26, 1902. Joker informs Cynic that "[c]ynic [is] one of a
sect of philosophers founded by Antisthenes. They were formed for the purpose of providing a remedy
for the moral disorders of luxury, ambition and avarice, the great aim of its adherents being to inculcate
a love of virtue and to produce simplicity of manners. The rigorous discipline of the first cynics degen-

a feeble response, Assee left no stone unturned in an extended response, "Apologia Pro Musa Sua." Hurt and insulted, Assee was not going to let an Englishman get away with such libel no matter how much he admired England and her culture: "Had 'A Cynic' confined himself to cynicism, I should have treated him with the contempt that is considerate, but he went outside the proverbial tub in masquerading as a mentor as well."[4] Assee goes on to inform Cynic that his poems had been published in England and Ireland, and he makes it clear that he is not averse to criticism since it allows him to correct the defects in his poetry, as was the case when "Iere" appeared in the *Jamaica Times*. However, a critic must be balanced. "Criticism," Assee writes, "is an art, and like every other art, must be acquired. 'A Cynic' has no business to play the critic unless he intends to admit evidence both of what is good as well as what is bad in the subject of his criticism." Assee adds that "the word 'critic' is from a Greek word meaning a 'judge.' One must know his part or know what it is before he tries to play it. To criticize, therefore, one must be fair. 'A Cynic' would need to cease to be a cynic for such a purpose, else how could he appreciate the worthy in aught, or perceive merit in anything."

In his defense, Assee justifies his phrases, "poui-emblazoned hills" and "cane-arrows ripe." He asks Cynic: "How could you so far forget our flora, whereas those who know their Iere know that the poui does not flower simultaneously with the sugar cane?... [H]ave I attributed in that limited sense the syzygy, or shall I say bysis, of silent explosions to cane-arrows ripe; and I say, that when scattered by the wind, cane-arrows do so silently explode, as a meteorite explodes; they also light the air like rockets and give light, in the sense that all colours impart additional light to a landscape." Thereafter, Assee explains the rationale for the stanza form he employed and, in the process, criticizes the construction and rhyming patterns of Gray's elegy. To satisfy his curiosity about Cynic's versifying, he forced the *Mirror* to publish "some specimens from his [Cynic's] museum."

Cynic's exposure as a poet in the *Mirror* left him open to the same charges of incoherence, lack of finish, etc. that he had made against the local poets. Examining the poems offered in the *Mirror*, Corbie argues that Cynic's poems display "a manifestation of the poverty of his imagination, vocabulary or coherent principle."[5] Jumping on two particularly egregious lines, "Upon the rugged mountain side and in the deep ravine,/ The undergrowth retreats before the edge of cutlass keen!", Corbie exclaims that "[t]his is simply preposterous.... Surely, one need not be a planter to know that our 'Cynic' was comparatively a stranger, and a very backward one beside, when he wrote these lines." Hitting Cynic exactly where Cynic had hit

erated afterwards into the most absurd severity. As an adjective, having the qualities or habits of a dog: currish, snarling, snappish, misanthropical. As a substantive, a sneering sarcastic or unruly person; a misanthrope. And if it was desired to call up a case in point to prove the correctness of the meaning of the word, I believe our 'Cynic' would fulfil the conditions admirably well."

4. C. S. Assee, "Apologia Pro Musa Sua," *Mirror,* May 28, 1902.

5. Montgomery Corbie, "Mr. Corbie on 'A Cynic,'" *Mirror,* May 29, 1902.

him, Corbie observes: "The muse seems to have been in disgust at having to provide not only a somewhat agreeable sound, but the facts and fiction as well."

Cynic was not intimidated by these responses. The same day Corbie attacked his poems, Cynic rejoiced that he "brought down the lot [of poets]." He confesses, however, that "I did not intend to hurt the dear creatures. In the hope of doing them good I tried to puncture their vanity and let the wind out." Still, he reserved most of his venom for Assee of whom he writes: "I think perhaps that his illusion that he can write poetry is a merciful provision of nature which, by causing him to write in short lines, checks the flow and saves the land from being submerged by a deluge of prose."[6] Admitting that he might have used "too personal a tone," he hastens to assure his "four antagonists" that he feels no animosity toward them and coos, "Let us discuss 'poetry' and not 'poets.' And not be ill-natured about it."

On June 2, E. Bernard Acham, a friend of Assee and a solicitor, jumped into the fray. Like Assee, he had studied at St. Mary's College. He was also a student of J. J. Thomas. *The Trinidad Reviewer* (1900) described him as "the first lawyer of pure Chinese extraction who has ever practised law in any British Colony other than Hong Kong."[7] Drawing on Matthew Arnold, Acham argues that all competent criticism implies "a capacity to see the object as in itself it really is…. A criticism that is not guided by a sense of appreciation is useless, if not mischievous; and probably this is the thought that prompted Wordsworth to say that if the quantity of time consumed in writing critiques on the works of others were given to original composition if would make a man find out sooner his own level, and it would do infinitely less mischief."[8] By this reasoning, Acham hoped to refute Cynic's "pedestrian prose, masquerading, as Mr. Assee would say, in the guise of verse." Using Assee's "Iere," Acham demonstrates the provincial nature of Cynic's own verse.

By this point, the row had little to do with poetry and much to do with national pride. (Interestingly enough, this unfurling of the nationalist banner was being led by two brilliant Trindadians who were of Chinese origin.) Jumping on what he considered the inadequacies of Cynic's poems, Acham sneeringly remarks, "This is the critic who would fain teach the intelligence of the colony the mysteries of poetry!"

Like the other poets, Acham felt Cynic was disdainful and unappreciative of their attempt to use local images in their poetry. He argues that one of Assee's great strength is his "merrying instinct" by which he "selects the chief feature of each locality and gives you a Morichal and Atagual, which not even a deft master like the French artist, Corot, could make more native." Contending that the chief attribute of the poet resides in the emotions he evokes, Acham elaborates on what he sees as the poet's role:

6. Cynic, "My Bag," *Mirror*, May 29, 1902.

7. T. Fitz-evan Eversley, *The Trinidad Reviewer for the year 1900* (London: Robinson Printing, 1900), p. 321.

8. E. Bernard Acham, "'A Cynic,' His Lines and Mr. Assee's Poetry," *Mirror*, June 2, 1902.

We have often heard the bursting of peas, and perhaps, now and then we may have vaguely associated it with some sort of musical sound; but it needed a poet to catch the wayward sound and see it to poetry in the word "goblin-music." And it is this selective instinct, this intuitive vision which sees the emotion throbbing in a fact, may be as simple as the opening of peas, which has given us Keat's ripened ode "To Autumn" and Shelley's matchless "Skylark" and perhaps even Gray's "Elegy Written in a Country Churchyard."

In Acham's view, Cynic is not concerned with these subtleties. Although Acham concedes that some of Cynic's criticism may have been on the mark, he cannot forgive the latter's snobbery, "the rudeness of his language…his meaningless attack on Mr. Assee, and …the patronizing manner in which he sought to teach the readers of the *Mirror* something about poetry." More importantly, and this is where national pride raises its banner, "I cannot rid myself of the impression that 'A Cynic' has been thinking to himself that Trinidadians are a pack of uncouth Philistines and it is this, perhaps more than anything else, which has set me to this protest." There was no way that Cynic could have known that Acham, who later changed his name to Eugene Chen, would become "the most distinguished Chinese American of his time," serving as Sun Yat-sen's foreign affairs adviser and personal secretary.[9]

On June 3, Thomas M. Kelshall, a friend of Assee, another solicitor, and a member of "a coterie of students of poets" (Acham's description), waded into Cynic as he lauded Assee's work. Confessing that he cannot discern "one spark of real imagination" in Cynic's poems, he makes the following flattering remarks about Assee's verse:

> I have had the pleasure of pursuing a large number of Mr. Assee's poems, and I am of the opinion that he has really got "the gift." There can be no doubt that he has faults, but they are the defects of his qualities. His wealth of allusions frequently leads him to obscurity; he writes too easily and often too long; he is by no means impeccable in technique; and he often chooses archaic words and peculiar structural forms, but when all is said and done, he exhibits a large amount of original and true poetic imagination. Let anyone who doubts this and who is capable to judge read his "Ode to a Sea-Shell" which appeared in the recent issue of the *Trinidad Magazine*. The quality of that poem is higher than that of many poems written by men with a considerable poetic reputation in England.[10]

Kelshall compares Assee's elegy on Cecil Rhodes with a similar effort by Rudyard Kipling and concludes that there can be no question that some passages in it are remarkably fine, and that the lofty tone which it strikes is fully worthy of the subject." He ends by advising Cynic "to confine his attention to observations in prose on pods and boles or to his occasional 'bag' of wild-fowl, and to abstain from

---

9. Walton Look Lai, *Indentured Labor, Caribbean Sugar* (Baltimore: Johns Hopkins University Press, 1993), p. 215.

10. T. M. Kelshall, "The Debate of the Poets," *Mirror*, June 3, 1902.

attempting to criticize poetry." It was an critique in which Assee, Acham, and Corbie took immense pleasure in reading.

One would have thought that Kelshall's balanced evaluation would have stopped Cynic in his tracks, but his response proves more emotional, more strident, and perhaps more racial than ever. As usual, Assee bore the brunt of Cynic's contempt. It might have been that "Apologia Pro Musa Sua" struck its mark. Intent on having the last word, Cynic lights into Assee: "I never had so many big words thrown at me in my life. A nigger minstrel's stump oration is unambitious compared with Mr. Assee's wonderful criticism in the *Port of Spain Gazette* of those verses of mine which you so mischievously published. I congratulate Mr. Assee heartily; he must have taken a lot of trouble over that effort in collecting such an assortment of unusual words—all without the aid of a dictionary. I understand, for Mr. Assee disdains the use of such fetters to his genius."[11] Cynic is unable to concede that Assee's work has any merit. Displaying the rage and arrogance of a white man challenged in a colonial society, he is disdainful of Assee's "injudicious friends [such] as Messrs. Acham and Kelshall [who] applauds his high-fallutin obscurities as evidence of genius."

For Cynic, Trinidadians, it seems, were not capable of producing any writer of much literary worth: "I seem to myself to be merely prospecting for gold and banging refractory lumps in order to find if they contain any of the precious metal. I don't want to be deceived by glittering mica. I think perhaps that my prospecting may be too rough and ready a method to discover the amount of gold in Trinidad poetry, and that it could only be found by assay (no pun intended)."[12]

Whatever their shortcomings, by the beginning of the century there existed a coterie of local poets who were conscious about the demands of their art and that was a good sign for the development of the literary enterprise. Cynic would have argued that such a mutual admiration society lessened the rigorous discussion of the art that was so necessary for its growth.

In the course of this two-month debate, many readers became disenchanted with the exchanges that had become vituperative. "A Constant Reader" exclaimed that he did not care if Assee was "designed for a niche alongside of Virgil and Homer, or for an apartment in the Asylum of St. Ann's."[13] He only wanted the quarrelling (as he perceived it) to stop. Drawing on Acham's admonition that they should concern themselves with "the decencies of literary criticism" rather than "the personal abuse of one's opponent," Cynic hoped that "the long-winded controversy I started has done some good.... .If the writers can be brought to see how low is the standard of excellence to which they have attained they may be persuaded to desist from their unprofitable labour."[14] He regretted their row had centered so much on Assee, "the

---

11. Cynic, "The Mysterious Phenomenon, " *Mirror,* June 7, 1902.

12. Ibid.

13. A Constant Reader, "'A Constant Reader' on Mr. Acham," *Mirror,* June 16, 1902. See also Acham's response, "Concerning a Philistine," *Mirror,* June 17, 1902.

14. Cynic, "Finally, My Brethren," *Mirror,* June 24, 1902.

most prolific and versatile of the school to which he belongs [although] his verse does not exhibit the characteristics of the poetic style which is being evolved in our midst, in such a marked degree as the writing of Mr. Corbie."

Yet, Cynic was opposed to Assee because his "verse are sold to the public as poetry, and I think that the amount of poetry they contain is not sufficient to justify the name under which they are sold."[15] Even when Kelshall informed him that Assee's poems were published in the *Weekly Sun, Sala's Journal, Pall Mall Gazette, Westminster Gazette, Echo, Evening Sun, Star,* and the *Manchester Post,* "all of them being responsible papers edited by men with, I should imagine, as much literary knowledge as 'A Cynic,'"[16] Cynic refused to concede. "Mr. Kelshall," he responded, "wanders from the point when he asserts that some of Mr. Assee's verses have appeared in certain English newspapers and periodicals. I have only been dealing with alleged poetry published here." In a paradoxical somersault, Cynic comes down on the same ground as Acham, Corbie, and Kelshall. His farewell remarks to the controversy are in line with those who demand that Trinidad allow only the finest verse to come to the fore:

> I did not say that Mr. Assee was incapable of writing better verses than those I have seen (a man sufficiently intelligent to become a barrister could surely do that). I merely stated my opinion that certain of his lines should be classed as turgid nonsense. If Mr. Kelshall's assertion be correct, Mr. Assee has attained to at least the lowest standard of verse admitted to English newspapers of standing, but I protest that his ability to write up to that standard does not justify him in dumping his rubbish on the public of Trinidad. Let us have his best or nothing.[17]

At last, it seems, there is merit in Assee's verses. However, in Cynic's eyes, Assee cannot win for losing. While Acham, Kelshall, and Corbie pointed out Assee's shortcomings, they differed with Cynic's unwillingness to acknowledge Assee's gifts. Yet, the source of their difference lay in different sensibilities and different ways of responding to the world. Where Assee writes,

> Fair ornament of Nature from the mermaid's halls of art,
> Where ocean ferns in coral-grottoes dreamland slept apart.
> 'Midst fronds of corals dancing to the rhythm of the waves
> And beds of bloom along the terraces of ocean's grave!,

Cynic can see no beauty or truth in such lines. Rather, he argues: "Why does Mr. Assee write of '*fronds*' of corals, and why does he make them supple enough to dance 'to the rhythm of the waves? All this is very unlike anything I have ever seen. With me, the coral stands stiff, or if seen through shallow water appears to waver without any rhythm. I cannot forget, too, that I have never seen the cane arrows send-

15. Ibid.
16. T. M. Kelshall, "'A Cynic,' Sir Walter Besant and Other Critics," *Mirror,* June 25, 1902.
17. Cynic, "One More Word," *Mirror,* June 30, 1902.

ing up rockets at night—I suppose since the duty of fireworks was raised they find it too expensive."[18]

And may not this be the problem? Where an Asian or African sensibility might see a coral dance or cane-arrows sending up rockets at night, someone of European sensibility might find it difficult to conceive of such a phenomenon. Where one relies upon magical realism, the other insists upon an empirical validation of truth. In their back and forth, Acham had accused Cynic of having "the trained eye of a naturalist" rather than the "wide knowledge and sympathy at once catholic and deep for those ideas and emotions which are permanent in their appeal to man's sense of beauty and reverence."[19] And it is here that their difference lay.

It was Alejo Carpentier who first spoke about the magical realism that characterized Caribbean and Latin American perception and Wilson Harris who castigated James and Thomas for being unable go beyond the stasis of their age.[20] Reading reality or history as Cynic insists that it should be read only results in the consolidation of "a fortuitous destiny or ornament of history."[21] Thus, it might not be so much that Assee is right and Cynic is wrong, as it is that each gleaned different things from the reality around them. Moreover, the inability to recognize the Caribbean writer's love of "big words" and a desire to master *Prospero's* (or Caesar's) language left Cynic at a significant disadvantage. Kelshall, Corbie, Assee, and Acham had mastered Prospero's language, were knowledgeable of Victorian poetry, and were proud to display their achievement. Even though Cynic believed these natives still "gabble[d], like/ A thing most brutish,"[22] they were intent on demonstrating they were "overs" that phase of underdevelopment and could utter their own truths.

In his defense of Assee, Acham asks Cynic if he ever surprised "a humming-bird on the wing, sipping 'nectar from the chalice of the rose,' dancing in its 'sunn'd apparel' and flashing like a gem aflame with the iridescent hues and tints…. If he has never batted his sight thereat, then I pity him and I offer him the alms of my sympathy."[23] Whatever else it was not, the image of the humming bird, sipping the nectar from the chalice of the rose as it danced in the "sunn'd apparel" was Caribbean to the bone. It was the celebration of the life of inanimate objects that Cynic could not accept. "Why do the oceans ferns sleep apart?" Cynic asks Acham, playing on a line of Assee's poems. "The best explanation I could give," Acham retorts, "is to go to some place like Fontenoy in Grenada and there look into the depths of the sea and let him surprise the ocean ferns sleeping in the coral-grottoes which may have been the haunts of some ancient hermits. If there, these things are

18. Cynic, "Mysterious Phenomenon," *Mirror,* June 7, 1902.

19. Acham, "A Cynic' and the Quality of His Criticism."

20. See Alejo Carpentier, *El reino de este mundo* (Santiago, Chile: Editorial Universitaria, 1972), and Wilson Harris, *History, Fable and Myth in the Caribbean and Guianas* (1970, Wellesley: Calaloux, 1995).

21. Harris, *History, Fable and Myth,* p. 16.

22. William Shakespeare, *The Tempest,* G. B. Harrison, ed. (London: Penguin, 1937, p. 34.

23. Acham, "'A Cynic,' and the Quality of His Criticism," *Mirror,* June 12, 1902.

blind to him, then let him forswear communion with those whom men in reverence do call 'children of the gods.'"[24] Although some of Assee's phrases and even conceptions may have arisen from Victorian forms and sensibilities, Acham points out that the poet is expressing Caribbean realities in a unique way. That was good enough for Acham.

Laus Reginae

Laus Reginae reveals a different side of Assee. A perfect royalist, Assee believed in royalty and glorified the deeds of empire. For example, he was very disappointed when he learned the government might not celebrate the coronation of Edward VII in the grandest manner. In a letter to the *Mirror*, he appealed to the editor "to further advocate the good cause for its own merits, the occasion being ready-made for us to approach Our Sire for a boon so to speak?"[25] For him, the coronation was too grand an occasion to be taken lightly. He believed that, at such occasions, "we feel the want for a Borough or other representative body to organize a public anti-Government demonstration."[26] It was blasphemous that such an occasion should pass without grand demonstrations of fealty. "How could the Coronation of our own King be celebrated without some pageant illustrative of national joy?" he asks. "In England everything is being done to make it a pageant of history. Why should Trinidad not congratulate the Mother Country and rejoice with her on the occasion? Is it possible that it is intended thereby to impeach Nature!—the pharisaism were blasphemy."[27] In sentiments that out-royaled Her Majesty's loyal government on the island, Assee rails:

> To think that a day should have dawned for us poor Crown colonialists and colonials, when we should actually have to oppose the stolid apathy of the local government upon a question of policy—nay, upon a matter of principle—to vindicate our loyalty to the Sovereign of the Empire! Yet this principle of loyalty in a Crown Colony is a principle which it would appear (however grotesque a paradox it may seem to say so) that the representatives of Crown colony government are ever frantically disposed to discountenance beforehand.... This may be the occasion of bloodshed in the land! People who in their own affairs would not fight for themselves, would fight and die, nevertheless, for a symbol of a sentiment."[28]

In April 1902, when Cecil Rhodes died, Assee got a chance to prove his loyalty to his beloved Empire. He composed a long elegy on Rhodes and adorned it with an epigram by Rudyard Kipling that calls Rhodes "the greatest living man." The subtitle of Assee's elegy describes Rhodes as "the Cromwell of the South" and "the

24. Acham, "'A Cynic' and the Quality of His Criticism."
25. C. S. Assee, "Yet Another Way of Celebrating the Coronation in Trinidad," *Mirror*, May 14, 1902.
26. C. S. Assee, "Hooliganism in Trinidad," *Mirror*, May 23, 1902.
27. Ibid.
28. Ibid.

Modern Pharaoh." Yet, it was how Assee extols Rhodes's virtues that gives the reader a deeper insight into how he thought of the Empire and his relationship to it:

> To us who foster the imperial sentiment, he boomed
> The Renaissance of Chivalry. A thousand moons he mooned
> On Earth before dead Chivalry returned—a lordlier birth—
> The chivalrous idea of reunion upon earth.

Of Rhodes, his mission, and the greatness of England, Assee offers the following paean:

> He was our England's favourite, her favourite! To her
> He was her greatest son, the Monarch-Clive of Africa.
> The Great Philanthropist, the Great Apostle of Peace here
> Endowing Earth for all time with his wealth, to make Earth fair!
> Perhaps the greatest, and the greatest that has ever been,
> The greatest of the greatest nation that the Earth has seen:
> For who is greater that who loves his land?

And, in final tribute to Rhodes, Assee ends with the following sentiments:

> The hearths of home are waiting, and shall wait e'er for them now.
> Nor weep where Cedron flows with the tears of Gethsemane,
> Rather rejoice, such sacrifice for thine redemption be!
> For him the pioneer, the statesman, the financier.
> We lose not! History will be his own monument for e'er.
> In intervenient days before the great kismetic day
> Of days, death's day, teach thou thy soul for the World's weal to pray.
> Long as shall float upon adventure—seas, or sign or rag:
> There proudly from the stelling shall the fimbriated flag
> Of England float! Long as shall last the English love of sea,
> The stirring times on Earth shall be, the reign, of Chivalry.[29]

 As seen above, Kelshall argued that this elegy was better than the one Kipling composed on Rhodes.

When Queen Victoria, head of the British Empire and the longest-reigning monarch in English history, died on January 22, 1901, Assee composed *Laus Reginae (Praise to a Queen)*, an epic poem, to her memory. Although bits of the poem appeared in local newspapers—"Cecil Rhodes" was also included in the final version— Assee did not finish composing the poem until the next year. Although the publication of Assee's poem was held up for a year and a half (an initial draft was completed in February 1901), he was determined to see it into print. When *Laus Reginae* finally appeared in print, Acham said of Assee: "For surely a child is

---

29. C. S. Assee, "Cecil Rhodes," *Mirror,* April 11, 1902.

privileged to mourn as mother in soul-shaken laments—and it is as a child of Empire that Mr. Assee sings of the death of the great Mother-Queen of England."[30] Acham should know, as the poem is dedicated to him. Still, everything we know of Assee warrants this evaluation.

As a royalist, Assee was moved by Queen Victoria's death. He felt that "we, in Creolia," should also celebrate the deeds of this legendary heroine. Fulsome in his praise, he chose an epigram from Book 6 of Virgil's *Aeneid's:* "I, decus, I, nostrum melioribus utere fatis" ("Go on, our glory go; not better fates"). This line, a throwback to Roman imperialism, testifies to his sentiments. Even the *Aeneid's* themes of death and imperialism served Assee well.[31] To Assee, Victoria had embodied of all that was good and pure, and thus he eulogized her in verse:

> To thee I'll make my song and trust
> To please. And gather throughout Earth
> A tribute, elegant and just
> To eulogize transcendent worth.
>
> O thou in heaven accept my hymn
> Of praise—accept my accents coy;
> To whom I sing through visions dim
> The panegyrics of my joy!

The predominant image of *Laus Reginae* is the contrast between the light that Victoria's reign brought her subjects and the darkness that enveloped the globe when she died. In the poem's foreword, Assee writes that "in the darkness of that obscurity [the time between composition and eventual publication] it shone the more in my thoughts. And as, that darkness did not obscure it, but enhanced its light: even so; I feel this solace—that the more remote Her day, the more appreciable this contribution as a contribution to Her Memory, becomes."[32] Although Victoria's death plunged the world into a deep darkness, "[l]ike yonder dying Orb, we'll pass/Through temporary tents of night,/ From whenceforth we shall be restored/ To other lives in other light!" (*LR.*, p. 13) To Assee, the queen's death represents a beginning even though it connotes finality to many.

Laus Reginae is divided into three parts. Part I hails Victoria's virtues and contemplates the transcendence of death, part II celebrates British imperialist expan-

---

30. E. Bernard Acham, "Queen's Praise," *Mirror,* December 24, 1902.

31. These words are those of Deiphobus (one of the Trojan heroes who died in the Trojan War) speaking to Aeneas as part of Aeneas's tour of the underworld. He is telling Aeneas to leave the underworld and to go back to the real world to his destiny as the founder of Rome. According to Virgil's tale, Aeneas is the Trojan who leaves Troy after the city's defeat at the hands of the Greeks and goes on to found the city of Rome. In many ways, this ancient epic is a celebration of Roman imperialism. Needless to say, Assee is using this poem as a model for his celebration of Queen Victoria. I am indebted to Carol Dougherty for the translation of the epigram and her comments on the poem.

32. Charles Eryl Secundyne Assee, *Laus Reginae: A Memorial Tribute* (Port of Spain: Franklin's Electric Printery, 1902), Foreword; hereafter cited in the text as *LR*.

sion undertaken during Victoria's reign, and part III mourns her demise, prepares for her burial, and speaks of her lasting contributions to mankind. In true epical style, it begins with an "Ades Musa" in which the poet calls upon the muse of poetry to inspire him to write about the majesty and grandeur of this great queen:

> Thou, muse dispassionate, be mine!
> Temper my passion while I lay
> My Cross of Tears before the shrine
> Of her glad memory—and pray
>
> For her who was our Fair Hope here.
> And I will trust that she is past
> All pain in Death's redeemed career
> Of joyance that shall ever last
>
> In the immaculate embrace
> Of the chaste mother of the world
> The ever-virgin; in the grace
> Of God, emparadised,—enfurled!

Assee is effusive in his praise for Victoria, one of the most popular British monarchs. He is correct when he speaks of how her "blood" populated the European earth: "Will fame her name the Lady of/ Immortal memory for e'er,/ Her numerous blood on earth" (LR., p. 19). Victoria's relatives and descendants sat upon many European thrones. Her grandchildren included Kaiser Wilhelm II of Germany and Alexandra, consort of Tsar Nicholas II of Russia. Assee boasts that "[h]er light obscured all lights. She'll be/ While all around be dark, still bright/ Like that fair tree—the luminous tree—In Afric's wilderness at night!" (LR., p. 26). Assee stands in awe of this achievement and the corresponding expansiveness of British imperialism. Rather than condemn the latter, he reflects on the optimism, hope, and sense of progress that typified imperialism:

> Hope was the spokesman of her Age
> And Progress was the watchword here,
> As when Hypatia held the Stage
> Of Earth—the fair Philosopher.
>
> The watchword of the World will be
> Progress. And Civilisation bring
> The fruits of fair philosophy,
> As in the song the Cycles sing (LR., p. 27).

In an age when, as some said, "the sun never sets" on the British Empire, Victoria was acclaimed for her vision and her foresight. To a Briton, it seemed as though she were sent from heaven to construct a universe for England. Her influence was so great and her reach so vast that even "we in/Creolia in our condolence/ As with the voice of culverin/ Remote—salute thy passing hence" (LR., p. 20).

Assee believes that Victoria meant as much to the colonies as she meant to England. Thus, the mourning for the Queen transcends her Englishness: she embodies universal values to which the colonized and the colonizer subscribe. The Jubilee of 1897 demonstrated how much she meant to the British Empire, how universal she had become and how much "[s]he loved her land and people here/ Her love all boundless as the ocean" (*LR.*, p. 21). Since love does not decay, she will always live on in the memories of her subjects. Thus, Assee ends this section of the epic with the ennobling thought, "[n]o, no, I do not doubt:—[t]he whole/ Of Life is Love—and Death is Love!" (*LR.*, p. 37).

In part II of *Laus Reginae*, Assee praises Victoria's dedication to her imperial domain. During her reign, the queen defended Benjamin Disraeli's imperialist polices and was made Empress of India in 1876. Assee likens Victoria's relations with colonial subjects to that of a mother and her children and demands that the latter show the necessary respect and obedience to her. In this big family, all the late monarch's subjects share similar goals, possess similar desires, and are destined to achieve the same glorious end. In Assee's version of events, imperialism (and by definition Victoria's reign) broke down all racial and geographical barriers, and her rule offered a safe haven to all who came under her imperial sway. This was the magic and glory of Victoria's rule. Therefore, Assee calls on all her subjects to celebrate the centrality of England and Victoria in their lives, regardless of what part of the globe they find themselves:

> Come in, come home, come to your mindful mother, children of the Race!
> Come in, come home, from far Australia with the gold dust in your face,
> Come in, come home, from the snow-land of Labrador with snow-wet shoes,
> From Falkland with the snow-shine on your shoes and from th' unkind Karoos.
> Come in, come home, from far West India with the sunshine in your heart,
> Come in, come home, ye backbone of the Empire, that are housed apart,
> Yet hold together! Come home, children, come to glee the mother's heart (*LR.*, p. 45).

In death, he calls for true bereavement on the part of all. His final prayer is "[t]hat He who blessed you for a Record Reign on earth, may bless again—/May bless your for a halidom in heaven—another Record Reign!" (*LR.*, p. 47).

The third section of *Laus Reginae* opens with a *threnos* (a song of lamentation for the dead) and is followed by a long *monody*, an elegy performed by one person. This section represents a gradual release of emotions and an acceptance of Victoria's passing from a terrestrial to a celestial realm. When she died, even nature recognized that she was no more: "The bird that litanied around,/ From tree to tree around did know/ That she had passed from sense of sound,/ That she had gone where all must go—/And sang no more the song of yore" (*LR.*, p. 58). Forever, she shall be enshrined in the hearts of men and women and "not another/ Would come again to take her place" (*LR.*, p. 55). Her memory, Assee assures his readers, will become the stuff of legends and posterity "shall inherit her." Her name "shall be the fief of Song and Story" and her virtues shall "permeate the whole/ Earth as her sphere of influence." Her country and ours shall be ever grateful to her name. Even in death, the poet reassures his sovereign, "our passion/ Of love for thee shall still live on!" In memory of her blest rule, we shall all pay "Our hearty duty to thy son— To thine offspring, aye, to our King." To the end, Assee remains the faithful subject to a hallowed queen.

In *Laus Reginae,* Assee celebrates Queen Victoria in a grand, ceremonious style. He captures the solemnity of the occasion of her death and unleashes a vocabulary equal to the grandeur of his poetic undertaking. Assee's learned acquaintance with the English language, his knowledge of the classics, and his awareness of the demands of the epic allowed him to weave a narrative poem that captures the meaning of Victoria's life and death. He refers to her as "the most famous queen" and "my unblemished/ pure one." Reminiscent of "Iere," Assee invents new words, such as "emparadised," "asylumned," "constitutioned," and "tantaliseth," to capture the nuances of his subject matter. In the process, he emerges as one of the most ambitious and demanding writers of the first century of Trinidad and Tobago's literature. He would have agreed with Wordsworth's assessment that "[p]oetry is the breath and finer spirit of all knowledge; it is the impassioned expression which is the countenance of all Science."[33]

Carol Dougherty, professor of Classical Studies at Wellesley College, notes that "Assee's style is rooted in the past and is in the conventions of classical literature."[34] In the *Aeneid,* Virgil sought to, and succeeded in, establishing a Roman literary tradition. In much the same way, Assee hoped to achieve a similar goal for Caribbean literature by eulogizing a figure whom he felt was larger than life. Because he was so rooted in the past and committed to a theme that was so foreign to his society (that is, anti-us), he could not hear the rhythms of a new age, the novel diction that characterized it, and the innovative themes that were thrown up by it.[35] It was left to the calypsonians to capture the rhythms of this new time and to the prose writers to explore the complexities of life in the twentieth century.

Sealy argues that "Assee was a literary individual in the old English tradition who wrote profusely in a sort of stilted English and used a lot of Latin references."[36] Yet, Assee's ambition transcended the mere writing in stilted verse. In his review of *Laus Reginae,* Acham says admiringly of his friend's poem: "I have seen nearly all the best poems on the Queen's death as well as those on the King's coronation.... A few lit the fire that burns on the Parnassus. With these Mr. Assee's poems are rightly classed."[37] Assee, however, might have been elegizing himself when he said of Cecil Rhodes, "[c]hieftain! Sleep deep, sleep Peace, after life's travails, have no care,/

33. Quoted in Richards, *English Poetry of the Victorian Period,* p. 12.

34. Personal correspondence, June 26, 2000.

35. Assee's sonnet on St. Mary's College that appeared in the *Trinidad Miscellany* in 1903 demonstrates Assee's reverence for the past.

36. Interview with Sealy, March 30, 1995.

37. Acham, "Queen's Praise."

Know that, of him that loves his country, nought's forgotten here." Although his country owes him a great deal, one cannot help but wonder if he had only used his zeal and his talent to celebrate his land and its people, what a better poet he might have been. Yet, his attention to his craft and his commitment to the "ars poetica" (Acham's description) make him one of Trinidad and Tobago's most significant poet.

African Emancipation

Whatever their faults, by the end of the 1890s, it could not be said that Afro-Trinbagonians disliked their home or the country of their forebears. While Assee, Inniss, and others were celebrating the centenary of the English occupation of the island, the Africans were taking stock of their condition at the sixtieth anniversary of their emancipation from European slavery. While Assee was busy praising the achievements and exploits of Victoria and Rhodes, Africanists were taking a new look at Africa and its contribution to civilization. When Sylvester Williams, secretary of the newly formed Pan-African Association, visited the island of his birth in 1901, Afro-Trinbagonians from all over the island welcomed him and accepted his message of African unity. They were ready to join him in working actively against a stultifying socio-economic and political order that relegated Africans to second-class citizenship. Even before W. E. B. Du Bois uttered his prophetic sentiments, Williams recognized that the problem of the twentieth century would be the problem of the color line and began actively to prepare his people to meet this challenge.

This push toward African unity led several hundred Africans, under the patronage of the Working Men's Club and the Working Men's Association, to congregate at Prince Edward's Theatre at Brunswick Square on August 1, 1898, to celebrate the sixtieth anniversary of West Indian Emancipation. According to one reporter who attended, the theme of the meeting was "the capacity of the Negro or African Race and how he was kept down by the Europeans. They spoke of the want of unity and love between the Negroes, which impeded his progress." Interestingly enough, the speakers at the meeting also explored "the uncivilization [*sic*] of the Negro and the immorality derived from the barrack yard system of dwellings."[38] Because the *Mirror* did not carry a substantive report of the meeting (the reporter arrived late), Norman Alleyne, a lecturer at the meeting, sent the *Mirror* a fuller account of his address that was published by the newspaper two days later.

In his address, Alleyne notes that a substantial portion of the African population took pride in themselves and the accomplishments of the group and were determined to rule themselves, regardless of what Froude and others said. He explains why "the Sons of Ethiopia" felt it necessary to celebrate the emancipation from slavery. Then, he argues that "the deplorable condition of the Negro Race in the West Indies has been due principally to his inactivity and, as Bishop Tucker of West

38. The *Mirror,* August 2, 1898.

Figure 21. An advertisement, "The Negro Problem," that appeared in the *Mirror* (Trinidad) on July 8, 1901.

Africa says, to his attempting in every way to imitate the Caucasian. He has been taught by his parents that the white man is his ruler, his superior, his demi-god, and that alone causes him to cringe, to be over meek, to be insignificant in the face of the Caucasian." It will only be when Africans, as a group, rid themselves of those qualities; when "we have proved ourselves to be friendly to our fellow race," can "the white man" respect us.[39] Alleyne concludes his address by speaking of his hopes for his people:

> The Negro is a race which has been destined to occupy a prominent part in the history of the world, and, despite the fact that the Carib, the Indian and later the Australian aborigines have been exterminated from the face of the globe, yet the Negro not only remains, but has multiplied tenfold. What I advocate is that the Negro should unite like his fellow race in America and Liberia. In the former country he has had no chances whatever to advance, but, by dint of self-perseverance, self-energy, self-interest, he is taking a place today among the foremost ranks of the race of civilization.

This was Alleyne's vision for his people. Although he lived in Trinidad, he was very much aware of international trends and how his people figured within them. To steal a line from Thomas, he, too, had discovered the LAW of history and used

39. Norman Alleyne, "Commemoration Meeting," *Mirror,* August 4, 1898.

it to great effect. A month and half after Alleyne's lecture was published, he received a letter from Sylvester Williams, who was residing in London. Apart from agreeing with most of what Alleyne said, Williams informed him that the Pan-African Association in London was doing great work in representing the grievances of the African race.

It was gratifying to Alleyne that what he and his brothers and sisters were preaching in Trinidad and Tobago received a ready ear in London. They were waging the same struggle in Trinidad that Williams and his organization were waging in London, albeit on a larger scale. What the Afro-Trinbagonians believed to be a national struggle was, in fact, a part of a larger international battle. Apart from the fact that a fellow national was leading that international effort, it certainly must have heartened Alleyne that they were not alone, on the fringe of the world, waging a lonely crusade. Therefore, when Williams invited Alleyne to become a member of the Association and to found a branch in Trinidad, the latter felt honored and could not reject such an offer. He must have been even more elated when Williams informed him, in that same letter, that "the Association also hopes in 1900 to be able to hold a Congress in England of all their people to demonstrate their capacities in the various branches of civilization and thus enlighten the eyes of the world as to the often ability of the 'black man.'"[40] This certainly, must have been one of the first announcement of the historic Pan-African Congress that was held in London in 1900.

For the next three years, the Pan-African debate continued in the newspaper and in discussions around the island. One reader, responding to a claim that the Negro had no history— a claim that the responder declares to be erroneous—, writes that modern historians have tried to rob "the Negro of his greatness." He goes on to prove the notable place that Africa occupied in the ancient world and, as support, he draws on Edward Blyden's *Christianity, Islam and the Negro Race,* a copy of which, he points out, "will be found in the Public Library." To give a sense of the level of exchange that was taking place in the public space, I quote this writer somewhat extensively:

> The secular poets and historians at those times also bear witness...bear witness to the excellence of Ethiopian character. Homer, the prince of poets, and Herodotus, the father of history, both speak in praise of them. In the earliest tradition of nearly all of the more civilized nations of antiquity, the name of this distant people is found. The annals of the Egyptian priests were full of them; the nations of inner Asia on the Euphrates and Tigris have interwoven the fictions of the Ethiopian with their own traditions of the conquests and wars of their heroes; and at a period equally remote they glimmer in Greek mythology. When the Greeks scarcely knew Italy and Sicily by name, the Ethiopians were celebrated in the verse of their poets; they spoke of them as the "remotest nations," the "most just of men," the "favorites

40. Norman Alleyne, "Negro Unity," *Mirror,* September 27, 1898.

of the gods." The lofty inhabitants of Olympus journey to them and take part in their feasts; their sacrifices are the most agreeable of all that mortals can offer them. And when the faint glean of tradition and fable gives way to the clear light of history, the lustre of Egyptians is not diminished. They still continue the object of curiosity and admiration, and the pen of cautious, clear-sighted historians often place them in the highest ranks of knowledge and civilization.

That was not all. Advancing arguments that Martin Bernal and others made a century later, this unknown Trinidadian brother argues that it was only with the onslaught of slavery and colonization that the African's standing as a man, a citizen, and a nobleman was questioned. "History," he concludes, "is pregnant with the most favourable references to the Negro in his primitive stage of life. The Negro, under the light of impartial civilization, shone brightly amidst the national constellation."[41] Philip had made this same point in 1854, as did Thomas in 1889. James, Padmore, and Eric Williams would modify this position when their turn came in order to refine the script. Yet, in the midst of a national debate to reclaim their heritage, these unknown Trinidadians were giving voice to arguments that would infuse the twentieth century.

When Sylvester Williams arrived on the island in May 1901, he met a population that was only too ready to receive his ideas. On June 5, at one of Williams's earliest public meetings at the Trinidad Mutual Friendly Society, he received "quite an ovation and it was a long time before he was able to open his address." One of the participants called it "one of the most important and successful meetings ever held here."[42] At that meeting, many of the leading African intellectuals and activists of the island—Emmanuel Lazare, Maresse-Smith, and Stephen Cobham, to name three—were present. At another meeting in San Fernando, two days later, "among the audience were to be seen representatives of the most intelligent and better classes (both sexes) of the coloureds and black sections of the town and the Naparimas."[43] Rev. Canon Douglin, the chairman of the San Fernando branch of the Association chaired, the meeting. Mrs. Phillip John was the secretary of the group. Interestingly enough, Williams was described as "maturing the work begun by Clarke and Wilberforce."[44]

As they traveled to the towns and villages of the island to deliver their message, the example of the "American Negro" became an important symbol of progress. A. L. Carter, who had visited the United State previously, spoke of meeting African-American men of culture who did not feel themselves "inferior to [their] Caucasian brother[s]." He bemoaned the fact that, in the United States, "there was not the want of unity which existed in the West Indies."[45] In Port of Spain, the elementary

41. "Africa Has No History," *Mirror,* January 14, 1901.
42. "The Lecture on Recorded Reflection," *Mirror,* June 6, 1901.
43. "Pan African Association," *Mirror,* June 8, 1901.
44. "Dinner to Mr. Sylvester Williams," *Mirror,* July, 8, 1901.
45. Ibid.

school teachers who dined with Williams raised similar concerns. On that occasion, Williams thanked his former teachers for their guidance and urged them to take their responsibility of "moulding the characters of the men and women of the future. He spoke of the superior political condition of the Negro in the United States and attributed it to their united action, contrasting it with the lack of unity in the West Indies. It was while in the United States that he began to feel he must do something for his people and the duty seemed plain to him while in England to represent Trinidad in a very humble way." He also urged the teachers to instruct their students in such a way that their charges would become "interested in the welfare of their country and so imbued with manly principles, that they would stand squarely together in their own cause." Although Williams knew H. A. Nurse, the head master at Tacarigua E.C, was present at that dinner, he could not have known that his son, George Padmore, would emerge as a leading Pan-Africanist activist and scholar during the first part of the twentieth century.[46] Nor could he have known how seriously Nurse and Cobham had taken his message.

In a moving a toast to Williams, C. C. Smith, the head teacher of Richmond Street E.C. School, reminisced that many of the teachers at the function observed Williams as he grew up and were pleased to welcome him home as a hero. Reminding Williams that they had followed his work in the United States and Britain, he proffered that Williams would be able "to pilot a very large deputation to the presence of the King himself and lay before him the bare, simple fact that West Indian Negroes are capable of exercising self-government in some form or another."[47] Fifty four years later when the People's National Movement began its drive for self-government under the leadership of Eric Williams, it was the teachers who provided the nucleus of the organization. Such an impetus, it seems, was the product of many years of hard work and inspiration by those teachers who had become the backbone of the new society.

Canon Philip Douglin

Philip H. Douglin (1845–1902), rector of St. Clement's Church, a former missionary in West Africa, and secretary of the San Fernando branch of the Pan-African Association, also provides a good example of how Africans moved within the diaspora and the deep knowledge they displayed about African issues. In another age, they would have been called "Race Men." However, Douglin may have been a more traveled person than Williams and certainly had better first hand experience of Africa than Thomas. Born in Barbados, Canon Douglin qualified for Holy Orders in the Anglican Church before going to Rio Pongas, West Africa, as a mis-

---

46. Malcolm Nurse, the son of H. A. Nurse, adopted the *non de guerre*, George Padmore, when he joined the Communist Party in 1927. As he wrote to his friend, Dudley Cobham, "[a]ll revolutionaries are compelled to adopt false names to hide their identity from the Government" (James R. Hooker, *Black Revolutionary* [New York: Prager Publishers, 1967], p. 6).

47. "Dinner for Sylvester Williams," *Mirror,* July 8, 1901.

FIGURE 22. Philip Douglin. Used with the kind
permission of Martin Douglin.

sionary of the West Indian Church Association for the Furtherance of Gospel in
Western Africa, in 1867. On October 6, 1882, he was appointed acting chaplain of
Sierra Leone's major Anglican Church. On July 6, 1886, after a dreadful illness,
Douglin left for England to recuperate. After spending six months there, he made
his way to the West Indies, where he ended his days.

Douglin arrived in Trinidad on January 26, 1887 and was appointed rector of St.
Clement's on February 9.[48] On December 14, 1889, Bishop Hayes conferred an
honorary Canonship on Douglin that made him "not only the only Canon in the
Trinidad Church, but the first Canon, and the only Canon in the English
Church."[49] This appointment vindicated the intelligence of the African in the
Anglican Church. Eleven years earlier, Bishop Mitchinson of Barbados, asserted at
the Pan-Anglican Council in London that experience "has taught me to be mis-
trustful of intellectual gifts in the coloured race, for they do not seem generally to
connote sterling work and fitness for the Christian ministry .... I do not think the
time has come, or is even near, when the ranks of the clergy will be largely recruited in the West Indies by the negro race."[50] William Gamble, Jr., echoed similar sentiments in 1888 when he asked the Baptist Society not to send a white missionary

48. When Douglin was appointed at St. Clement's, George Towsend Fenwick, member for Naparima
and planting attorney for the Colonial sugar company, sent a protest "to his Lordship, the Bishop
[Rawle], for having appointed the Rev. Douglin to the incumbency of St. Clement's ." He and his white
colleagues could not worship under the pastoral care of a black man (Mathurin, *Henry Sylvester
Williams*, p. 23). Bishop Rawle, a radical bishop committed to racial equality, paid little attention to this
digression. He had every reason to know Douglin better. He was Douglin's teacher at Codrington
College, Barbados.

49. Correspondence of June 4, 2000, from Bishop Rawle Douglin, former Bishop of Trinidad and
Tobago. This information is taken from "the Family Registrar of Philip Henry Douglin," which is contained in the family bible.

50. Quoted in Blyden, *Christianity, Islam and the Negro Race,* p. 74.

to replace his father.[51] "Black people," he had reported, "would only listen to a white priest." However, the support Douglin received from his African congregants proved this contention to be incorrect.

In Trinidad, Douglin discovered a yearning among Africans to know more about their ancestors. Apart from sharing his Rio Pongo experience with them, he also spoke insightfully about the psychological impact of European slavery on the colonized.[52] On August 1, 1888, the Fiftieth anniversary of the emancipation of slavery, he offered this remarkable insight: "There are secret agonies, known only to God, which are far more acute than any external torture. Oh! It is not the smiting of the back, until the earth is crimsoned with the streams of blood—it is not the pursuing of human beings with blood hounds—it is not the branding of the person, or the amputation of the limbs—it is not the killing of the body—it is not these that are the keenest sufferings that a people can undergo. These affect only the outward man and may leave the majestic mind untouched. But those inflictions which tend to contract and destroy the mind—those cruelties which benumb the sensibility of the soul—those influences which chill and arrest the currency of the heart's affection—these are the awful instruments of real sufferings and the degradation; and these have been made to operate on the Negro." [53] Until then, no other observer had articulated slavery's impact on the psychology of colonized people.

Douglin also argued that "European countries have been sustained and enriched" by the labor of "30 to 40 million Negroes" that were stolen from Africa and "reduced to slavery by European Christian nations." In return, "abuse and contempt, and insult and ill-treatment [were] their reward."[54] Yet, his involvement with the African world, allowed him to speak with remarkable eloquence of the progress African people had made:

Who could, without seeming to insult the intelligence of men, have predicted the intelligence on the day of Emancipation that the Negroes then released from the blight of the withering influence of ten generations of cruel bondage, so weakened and half-destroyed—so denationalised and demoralised—so despoiled and naked, would be in the position they are now? In spite of the proud, supercilious, and dictatorial bearing of their teachers, in spite of the hampering of unsympathetic, alien oversight, in spite of the spirit of dependence and servility engendered by slavery, not only have individual members of the race entered into all the offices of dignity in Church and State, as subalterns—as hewers of wood and drawers of water—but they have attained to the very highest places. Here in the West Indies, and on the West Coast of Africa, are to be found Surgeons of the Negro Race, Solicitors, Barristers, Mayors, Councilors, Principals and Founders of High Schools and Colleges, Editors and Proprietors of Newspapers, Archdeacons, Bishops, Judges

51. See Chapter 8 of this study.
52. See P. H. Douglin, "The Rio Pongo Mission," *San Fernando Gazette*, August 6, 1887.
53. P. H. Douglin, "Jubilee of Emancipation," *San Fernando Gazette*, August 11, 1888.
54. Ibid.

and Authors—men who not only teach those immediately around them, but also teach the world (*F.*, pp. 191–92).

This awareness of the achievements of such Africans as Frederick Douglass, Hyland Garnett, Alexander Crummel, Edward Blyden, and Tanner filled Africans in Trinidad with pride. They also took extreme pride in the achievements of African-American women writers, such as S. Harper, who were moving "shoulder to shoulder with the men in the highest spheres of literary activity." Thomas felt that Harper "had surpassed every competitor among females—white or black—save and except Elizabeth Barrett Browning with whom the gifted African stands on much the same plane of poetic excellence" (*F.*, p. 192). He referred to her as an African rather than an African-American and to other Negroid persons as Ethiopians. When Alleyne addressed the Sixtieth Anniversary of West Indian Emancipation he referred to his fellow Afro-Trinbagonians as the "Sons of Ethiopia." Such an appellation might have been part of his recognition that all "ah' we is one."

When Douglin died at the St. Clement's vicarage on June 30, 1902 after a short and mysterious illness—the one he contracted in Sierra Leone—he left an indelible record on history of Africans on the island. An obituary in the *Mirror* describes his life and contribution as follows: "Canon Douglin was a Negro, proud of his race and was at times ready to associate himself with any cause having for its object the uplifting of the people, and holding himself up as a pattern.... In his death, the Church has lost a hard-working member, and the Negro Race, a staunch and sympathising friend."[55] On July 21, Bishop Hayes reminded his audience that "Rev. Douglin loved his race, and took a lively interest in everything pertaining to the welfare of the people."[56] Douglin was also a remarkable linguist. He also published *A Reading Book in the Soso Language*, as well as translating the *New Testament* into that language.[57] The *Mirror* wrote that "he has also written another work, but for certain reasons, it is not published."[58] Although he has not received the recognition of either Thomas or Maxwell Philip, Douglin contributed enormously to the revindication of the race. His is a legacy we should cherish.

Rupert Gray (1907)

Stephen Nathaniel Cobham, an important Pan-Africanist and regular spokesman on Williams's platforms, was a "leader of the [African] race" in Trinidad at this time.[59] Like Williams, he was born in Arouca, and so they knew each other

55. "The Late Rev. Canon P. H. Douglin," *Mirror*, July 4, 1902.
56. *Mirror*, July 21, 1902.
57. See, Philip Douglin, *A Reading Book in the SoSo Language* (London: Society for Promoting Christian Knowledge, 1887) and *The New Testament of Our Lord and Savior Jesus Christ. Linjila isa.* Translated by Philip Henry Douglin (London: Society for Promoting Christian Knowledge, 1884).
58. "The Late Rev. Canon P. H. Douglin."
59. "The Pan African Association," *Mirror*, July 12, 1901.

as boys in the village. In fact, just before Williams returned to London via the United States, Aroucans raised the princely sum of twenty pounds and five shillings "in recognition of the great services [Williams] rendered on behalf of the race."[60] Cobham, an elementary school teacher at Woodbrook E. C. School, was the embodiment of those Africans who were committed to establishing a civil society on the island. On July 12, when the members of Faithful Brothers of Souls in Purgatory held their farewell ball for Williams in Port of Spain, Cobham, "in the course of an eloquent address, referred to enthusiastic manner in which Williams had undertaken the promulgation of the great and good work of the society … .He hoped one of these days he would return with a charter of liberty that would make a man of every man—a charter not from the Secretary of State, but from the foot of the throne of Edward VII—a charter calling upon Ethiopia to stretch out her hands to Heaven and advance."[61] As so many other African leaders at the time, Cobham was inspired by Williams's life and teaching and certainly wanted to emulate the latter's achievements. Apart from being an activist in his own right, Cobham had certainly taken in much of what Williams and his Association offered. When he retired from teaching in December 1901, he was determined to complete *Rupert Gray* (1907) a novel that personifies so much of the philosophy of Pan-Africanism.

In a way, *Rupert Gray*, can be seen as an intellectual bridge between Philip's historical romance and the social realism of Ralph Mendes's *Black Fauns* (1935) and James's *Minty Alley* (1936). It also amplifies and extends many of the arguments Thomas advanced in *Froudacity*. In his work on Sylvester Williams, Mathurin observes that "[t]hese Pan African and back-to-Africa thoughts of Jacob Thomas were to find full expression in the words and deeds of Henry Sylvester Williams."[62] They were also rendered fictionally in *Rupert Gray*. Even Du Bois's prophetic wisdom, at the beginning of the twentieth century, that "the problem of the Twentieth century is the problem of the color line," took its impetus from the "Address to the Nations of the World," the principal document of the first Pan-African Conference that took place in London in 1900.[63] Since the impetus for this conference originated with Williams, a student of Thomas, it might be argued that Du Bois's statement had its impetus in *Froudacity* and the early Pan-African movement that gathered so much support in Trinidad.

As one looks at available ideas on Afro-Trinbagonians at the end of the century,

---

60. *Mirror,* July 15, 1901.

61. "Farewell to Mr. H. S. Williams," *Mirror,* July 13, 1901

62. Mathurin, *Henry Sylvester Williams,* p. 12.

63. See for example, Owen Charles Mathurin, *Henry Sylvester Williams and the Origins of the Pan African Movement, 1869–1911* (Westport, CT., Greenwood Press, 1967), pp. 68–69, and Selwyn R. Cudjoe, "Eric Williams and the Pan Africanist Movement," a lecture delivered at Wellesley College, April 7, 2000. According to Thomas, "More than ten million Africans are scattered over the wide area indicated [that is in the Western Hemisphere], and possess amongst them instances of mental and other qualifications which render them remarkably among their fellow-men. But like the essential parts of a complicated albeit perfect machine, these attainments and qualifications so widely dispersed await, it is evident, some potential agency to collect and adjust them into the vast engine essential for executing the true purposes of the civilised African race" (*F.,* p. 193).

it is possible to argue that one of the major functions of *Rupert Gray* was to provide a literary vehicle to carry forward the sentiments about race pride and race development that were rampant in the society. In this novel, one experiences what can be called a Pan-African continuity of ideas that are echoed by Primrose Serle, the major representative of the colonizer class and a leading character, when he tries to deny the achievements of the race:

> I do not deny the equality of man…but I do think that the West Indian Negro barely stands within the threshold of culture. There is no greater admirer of the race of Ham than I. That a great future is in store for them I am certain. But I deem it childish to try and force the game. They must bide their virgin brain-power, we look with pleasure at the distinguished sons they have produced. The world at large now bow before the genius of Toussaint L'Ouverture, the brilliant slave of Breda-warrior and statesman—they founder of the Haytian Commonwealth. Then there are Jean Francois and Biassou. There is King Christophe, "the Henry I of the North"—the sole black royal head outside Africa—the rival of Dessalines. There is Edward Wilot Blyden, M.A., D.D., LL.D—author of "Islam"—sometimes Plenipenatiary to Liberia at the Court of St. James—a Negro scion of the Island of St. Thomas, Danish West Indies. There is Booker T. Washington, whose name will be his monument—a modern Moses leading the Black Belt to the promise land of labour—wealth—prosperity. Sir Conrad Reeves, the star of Little England—that child of opportunity—that eagle whose pinions flapped out fame all around the Caribbees. Michel Maxwell Philip, the demosthenic lawyer, who in Trinidad pantheon fill his niche: where John Jacob Thomas already is; and Vincent Brown, a titan at the forum, and Edgar Maresse-Smith, true lover of his kind, will one day be. Thomas, in spite of mistakes', is a sturdy race-vindicator. Brown, now acting, is destined to be the Attorney General some day. Who but he could have climbed to the bar-leadership under Crown Colony form? Philip could not. Reeves did not. Brown alone "arises like a giant refreshed with wine," and walks off with the gates of nominative hindrances. Maresse Smith, the idol of the average native, shall be called a philantrophist without having ever crossed the Bocas. All this is as it should be. We are ready to receive the black man with open arms into the professions, the services of the Crown and in commerce, but when it comes to mixing up in the company of our wives, and wanting to marry our daughters—I say, "No, sir." I say to them what Canute said to the waves: "Thus far and no further."[64]

For all we know, this might have been a reinventoried speech of Froude from two decades before. Serles's speech certainly reads as a catalog of the international achievements of Africans, with Toussaint and Christophe (a Grenadian) bound up with those of Blyden (St. Thomas), Booker T. Washington (United States), and Conrad Reeves (Barbados), which in turn are blended with the national achievements of Philip, Thomas, Vincent Brown, and Maresse-Smith. That the white man was not willing to allow the white woman to intermarry with the black man only seems the final barrier toward the vindication of the race. At least, this is what Cobham wants his readers to believe.

64. Stephen Cobham, *Rupert Gray* (Port of Spain: Mirror Printing Works, 1907), pp. 73–74.

At the end of the nineteenth century, however, Africans in Trinidad had begun to see their fortunes tied to the activities of Africans outside their immediate environment. This sense of fraternity gave them the impetus to break out of their narrow isolation and to comprehend issues in their larger Pan-Africanist perspective. Needless to say, the relationship between the colonial master, the emerging middle class, and the internal antagonisms within the black community would be subjected to a much more deep-going examination. Further, the question of racial uplift (or the relations between black man-white woman) was one of the remaining barriers to be overcome.

In a very succinct manner, the novel sums up the state of racial affairs in the country and tells us how far the society had traveled since the narratives of Calderon and the pamphlet of Philippe. The black man, it seems, can become a part of the professions and he can join the government services but marrying a white woman remains taboo. This conundrum, as the tale tries to argue, is a major problem between black and white. Cobham, it turns out, proved to be very perceptive as he put his hand on a wound that would become a troubling topic of discussion in the twentieth century. It is a problem that Fanon would examine in *Black Skin; White Masks*.

Conclusion

In many ways, the writers of the twentieth century would amplify the concerns of Louisa Calderon, follow the lead of Maxwell Philip and Mary Fanny Wilkins, and explore the ideas of J. J. Thomas. Perhaps they found the rhetoric of Jean-Baptiste Philippe uplifting, the concerns of E. L. Joseph overblown, the scientific explorations of Leotaud and Kingsley insightful, the Eurocentrism of de Verteuil off-putting, the linguistic concerns of Thomas fascinating, and the historical excavation of Borde intriguing. They may have fould the poetics of Huggins enticing, the high-strung verse of Assee overbearing, the mundane offerings of Devenish ingratiating, the pieties of Collens interesting, and the emotions of Tronchin overwhelming. Inniss, Rodriques, and Cobham may well have inspired a second reading. Yet, whatever their strengths or weaknesses, these writers deserve attention in that they all take us beyond native boundaries. They laid the foundation and set the stage for the writers and thinkers of the twentieth century who followed in their footsteps. C. L. R. James, George Padmore, Sylvester and Eric Williams, Oliver Cromwell Cox, V. S. Naipaul, Earl Lovelace, Merle Hodge, and Arnold Rampersad stand in a straight line of descent from these early writers and thinkers. No knowledge of these twentieth century thinkers and writers is complete until we understand the intellectual culture that underlies their development and concerns. Like their forebears, they have been shaped by a tradition that speaks to its specific needs, even as it has been inundated with international ideas. It behooves us to listen and to examine the sterling legacy the nineteenth century left us, for it is a priceless object with which we ought to become acquainted. Such a tradition is one that even Naipaul may be willing to embrace as his own.

Bibliography

This Bibliography consists of two parts: a section of resources of Trinidad and Tobago Literary and Intellectual Tradition and a section of related works that were consulted. The first part includes works written by Trinbagonians and works that played a decisive role in the development of the tradition. Trinbagonians are identified as (T), while non-Trinbagonians are Others (O). Where I am not sure of the author's origin, I use (U). The Trinbagonian works are listed chronologically. The citations for the twentieth century are slim since I intend a second volume that covers the period 1900 to 1945. The second part of the bibliography is listed alphabetically.

TRINIDAD AND TOBAGO LITERARY AND INTELLECTUAL TRADITION

Malette, F. *Descriptive Account of the Island of Trinidad.* London: W. Fadden, 1802 (O).

M'Callum, Pierre. *Travels in Trinidad.* Liverpool. W. Jones, 1805. (O)

McCallum, Pierre. *The Trial of Thomas Picton.* London: W. Lewis, 1806.

The Trial of Governor T. Picton for Inflicting the Torture on Louisa Calderon. London: Dewick & Clark, 1806. (O)

The Trial of Governor Picton. London: J. Lee and W. Mantz, 1806. (O)

"Threatened Revolt of the Slaves," *Barbados Mercury and Bridgetown Gazette,* 1806. (U)

Dauxion-Lavaysse, M. *A Statistical, Commercial, and Political Description of Venezuela, Trinidad, Margarita, and Tobago.* Edited and translated by E. B. London: G and W. B. Whittaker, 1820. (O)

[Philippe, Jean-Baptiste]. *An Address to the Right Hon. Earl Bathurst, His Majesty's Principal Secretary of State for the Colonies, relative to the claims which the Coloured population of Trinidad have to the same Civil and Political privileges with their white fellow-subjects.* London: S. Gosnell, 1824. (T)

Urich, Friedrich. *The Urich Diary: Trinidad, 1830–1832.* Edited by Anthony de Verteuil and translated by Irene Urich.. 1832, Port of Spain: Litho Press, 1995. (O)

"The Curious History of a Black Man." In Studholme Hodgson, *Truths from the West Indies, Including a Sketch of Madeira in 1833.* London: William Ball, 1833. (O)

Joseph, Edward Lanza. *Martial Law in Trinidad: A Musical Farce in Two Acts* (1833). (O)

———. *Past and Present* (183?). (O)

Bridgens, Richard. *West India Scenery with Illustrations of Negro Character the process of making Sugar, & from Sketches taken during a voyage to, and residence of Seven Years in the Island of Trinidad.* London: Robert Jennings, 1837.

Joseph, Edward Lanza. *Warner Arundell: The Adventures of a Creole, Vols. I, II, III.* London: Saunders and Otley, 1838.(O)

"Warner Arundell: The Adventures of a Creole." *Trinidad Standard,* 1838. (U)

Burnley, William. *Observations of the Present Condition of the Island of Trinidad.* London: Longman, Brown, Longmans, 1842. (O)

"Jim the Boatman." *Trinidad Spectator,* 1846. (U).

Moister, William. "A Narrative of the Dispensation of Divine Providence." *Trinidad Standard,* 1846. (O).

Ca qui pas bon pour z'oies, Pas bon pour canards. Translated by Daaga Hill. *Trinidad Spectator,* 1847. (U)

"Maria Jones." *Missionary Herald,* 1848. (O)

Tronchin, L(ouis) B(ernard). "The Burning of Rome." *Trinidadian,* 1848. (T)

Cazabon, Michel J. *Views of Trinidad.* 1851, Port of Spain: Aquarela Galleries, 1984. (T).

"Treatment of Our Indian Coolies at Trinidad." *Trinidadiana,* 1851. (U)

Adolphus: A Tale. Trinidadian, 1853. (U)

Philip, Maxwell. *Emmanuel Appadocca: Or, Blighted Life.* London: Charles J. Skeet, 1854. (T)

"The Slave Son." *Atlas Supplement.* London, 1854. (U)

Wilkins, Mary Fanny. *The Slave Son.* London: Chapman and Hall, 1854. (O)

De Verteuil, L. A. A. *Trinidad: Its Geography, Natural Resources, Administrative, Present Condition, and Prospect.* London: Ward and Lock, 1858. (T)

Captain and Mrs. Swinton. *Journey of a Voyage with Coolie Emigrants from Calcutta to Trinidad.* London: Alfred W. Bennett, 1859. (O)

Wall, G. P., and J. G. Sawkins. *Report on the Geology of Trinidad, or, Part 1 of the West Indian Survey.* London: Longman, Green and Roberts. 1860. (O)

Taylor, E. Cavendish. "Five Months in the West Indies, Part 1: Trinidad and Venezuela." *The Ibis: Magazine of General Ornithology,* 6 (1864).

Gamble, William H. *Trinidad: Historical and Descriptive Being a Narrative of Nine Years Residence in the Island, with Special Reference to Christian Missions.*London: Yates and Alexander, 1866 (T)

Hart, Daniel. *Trinidad and Other West India Colonies.* Port of Spain: The Chronicle Publishing Office, 1866. (O)

Leotaud, Antoine. *Oiseaux de l'ile de la Trinidad (Antilles).* Port d'Espagne: Chronicle Publishing Office, 1866 (T).

Sclater, P. L. "Remarks on Dr. Leotaud's *Birds of Trinidad.*" *Ibis* 3 (1867). (O).

Thomas, John Jacob. *The Theory and Practice of Creole Grammar.* 1869, London: New Beacon, 1969. (T)

Keenan, Patrick Joseph. *Report Upon the State of Education in the Island of Trinidad.* Dublin: Alexander Thom, 1869. (O)

Chester, John Grenville. *Transatlantic Sketches in the West Indies, South America, Canada and the United States.* London: Smith, Elder, 1869. (O)

Carr, Thomas William. "Notes of a Voyage Round the Island of Trinidad in October 1868." *Trinidad Chronicle,* 1871 (O).

Devenish, Sylvester. "Memorandum of a Trip from Naparima to Bande's De L'est (Mayaro) and Back, by Order of His Excellency, Rear Admiral Elliot in January, 1856." *Trinidad Monthly Magazine* 1 (September 1871). (O)

"Etchings in Trinidad." *New Era,* 1871. (T)

Kingsley, Charles. *At Last: Christmas in the West Indies.* London: Macmillian, 1871. (O)

Kums, Frank. "Les Sauteurs à la Grenade, ou Ina la Caraibe." *New Era,* 1871. (U)

Morton, John. "The 'Hosay' Fete." *Trinidad Chronicle*, 1871.(O)

"The Great Oropouche Lagoon." *Trinidad Chronicle*, 1871. (U)

"The Great Siparia Festival." *New Era*, 1871. (U)

Tronchin, L(ouis) B(ernard). "Dr. Davis." *New Era*, 1871 (T)

———, "Lord Brougham." *Trinidad Monthly Magazine*, No. 1 (1871). (T)

Africanus, "To the Editor of the *New Era*." *New Era*, 1874. (T)

Borde, Pierre-Gustave-Louis. *Historie de l'ile de la Trinidad sous le gouvernement Espangnol, Vol. I (1498–1622), II (1622–1797).*; Vol. 1 translated by James Alva Bain; Vol. II translated by A. S. Mavrogordato. 1876, 1882, Port of Spain: Paria Publishing, 1982. (T)

Paul, Francisco A. "Detached Pages of the history of Trinidad." *Fair Play and Trinidad News*, 1878. (O)

Morton, Sarah. "The Story of Joseph Annajee." 1879. (O)

Aziz, Ahmad. *Testimonials and Criticism*. London: Times Gate, nd. (1880). (O)

"The Moral and Religious Condition of Trinidad." *Trinidad Palladium*, 1880. (O)

Actus. "The Attack on the Camboulay Masquers." *Trinidad Chronicle*, 1881. (O)

"A Lover of Justice." *Trinidad Chronicle*, 1881 (U).

Paul, Francisco. "A Review," *Trinidad Chronicle*, 1883. (O)

Masse, Abbé. *The Diaries of Abbé Masse, 1876–1883, Vols. 1–4*. Translated by M. L de Verteuil. 1883, Port of Spain: Script-J Printers, 1988. (O)

De St. Avit, Jean-Ch. *Les Deux Premiers Martyrs de la Trinidad. Public Opinion*, 1885.(O)

"The Negro Grievance." *Public Opinion*, 1885. (U).

Tronchin, L (ouis) B(ernard). *Inez, Or the Last of the Aroucas*. Trinidad: R. J. Allers, 1885. (T)

Thomas, John Jacob. "The Reviewer Reviewed." *New Era*, 1886. (T).

Clark, Henry James. *Trinidad: A Field for Emigration*. Port of Spain: Government Printing Office, 1886. (O)

Huggins, Horatio Nelson. *Hiroona: An Historical Romance in Poetic Form*. 188?, Port of Spain: Franklin's Electrical Printery, 1930. (O)

"A Negro." *Public Opinion*, 1887, (T)

Thomas, John Jacob. "New Edition of the Creole Grammar." *Public Opinion*, 1887.

Douglin, Philip H. *A Reading Book in the Soso Language*. London: Society for Promoting Christian Knowledge, 1887. (O)

Douglin, Philip H. "The Rio Pongo Mission." *San Fernando Gazette*. 1887. (O)

Collens, J. H. *Guide to Trinidad: A Hand-book for the use of Tourists and Visitors*, 2nd edition. London: Elliot Stock, 1888. (O)

"Mr. Sylvester Devenish, M.A." *Public Opinion*, 1888. (O)

Tronchin, L(ouis) B(ernard). "Charles Wm. Warner and His Times." *Public Opinion*, 1888. (T)

———. "The Great West Indian Orator." *New Era*, 1888. (T)

R. D. M. "Étymologie Caraibe de Quelques mots Creoles." *Public Opinion*, 1888. (O)

"Froudism Refuted." *Public Opinion*, 1888. (U)

"Night Thoughts on the Sea-Shore." *Public Opinion*, 1888. (O)

Douglin, Philip H. "Jubilee of Emancipation." *San Fernando Gazette*. 1888. (O)

"Froudacity." *New Era*, 1889. (U).

Seaton, William. "Vicissitudes of the Profession of Attorney and Solicitor in Trinidad." *New Era*, 1889. (U)

Thomas, John Jacob. *Froudacity: West Indians Fables by James Anthony Froude Explained*. 1889, London: New Beacon, 1969. (T).

Bodu, Jose M. *Trinidadiana: Being a Chronological Review of Events which have Occurred in the Island from the Conquest to the Present Day*. Port of Spain:C. Blondel, 1890. (O)

Addresses Presented on the Retirement of R. J. L. Guppy, Esq. London: Hazell, Watson, & Viney, 1891. (O)

Collens, James H. *Who Did It? A West Indian Novelette*. Port of Spain: Muir Marshall, 1891. (O)

Cothonay, Marie Bernard. *Trinidad: Journal d'un missionarie dominicain des Antilles anglaises*, Paris: V. Retaux et fils, 1893. (O)

Inniss, Lewis O. *Adventures of Reginald Osborn*. Port of Spain: Mole Brothers, 1895.(O)

Chalamelle, Eugene Francis. *Some Reflections on the Carnival of Trinidad*. Port of Spain: Fair Play Type, 1897. (T).

Hart, Ivry. *Centenary Reminiscences*. Port of Spain: Daily News, 1897. (O)

Inniss, Lewis O. *The Centennial Companion to Trinidad*. Port of Spain: Daily News, 1897. (O)

Rodrigues, Henry Martiol. *The Siren Goddess of South America*. Port of Spain: Daily News, 1897. (O)

Alleyne, Norman. "Negro Unity." *Mirror*, 1898. (T)

Hart, Ivry. *Some Sketches and Songs, Part 1*. Port of Spain: Daily News, 1898. (O)

Delamere, Anthony Richard. *The Old Bar and the New Bar*. Port of Spain: The Daily News, 1899. (T).

Inniss, Lewis O. "Opium." *Mirror*, 1901.(O)

A Cynic. "A Mysterious Phenomenon." *Mirror*, 1902. (O)

Acham, E. Bernard. "'A Cynic,' His Lines and Mr. Assee's Poetry." *Mirror*, 1902. (T)

———. "'A Cynic' and the Quality of His Criticism." *Mirror*, 1902. (T)

———. "Concerning a Philistine." *Mirror*, 1902. (T)

———. "Queen's Praise." *Mirror*, 1902. (T).

Assee, Charles Secundyne. "Apologia Pro Musa Sua." *Mirror*, 1902. (T)

———. "Cecil Rhodes." *Mirror*, 1902. (T)

———. *Laus Reginae: A Memorial Tribute*. Port of Spain: Franklin's Electric Printery, 1902. (T)

Inniss, Lewis O. "A Paper on Shakespeare." *Mirror*, 1902. (O)

Kelshall, T. M. "The Debate of the Poets." *Mirror*, 1902. (T)

Inniss, Lewis O. *Diamond Jubilee of Baptist Missions in Trinidad, 1843–1903*. Port of Spain: Franklin's Electric Printery, 1904. (O)

———. "Folklore and Popular Superstition." In T. B. Jackman, ed. *The Book Of Trinidad*. Port of Spain: Muir Marshall, 1904. (O)

Cobham, Stephen Nathaniel. *Rupert Gray: A Tale of Black and White*. Port of Spain: Mirror Printing Works, 1907. (T)

Inniss, Lewis O. *Trinidad and Trinidadians*. Port of Spain: Mirror Printing Works, 1910.(O)

Scrapbooks of John and Sarah Morton, Tunapuna, Trinidad, W.I. Knox College (Toronto), 1912. (O)

Morton, Sarah E. *John Morton of Trinidad*. Toronto: Westminster, 1916. (O)

De Verteuil, Anthony. ed. *Trinidad's French Verse, 1850–1900*. Port of Spain: Instance Print, 1978. (T)

GENERAL

Adams, Percy G. *Travel Literature and the Evolution of the Novel*. Lexington: University of Kentucky Press, 1983.

Aiyejina, Funso and Rawle Gibbons, "Orisa Tradition in Trindidad." Research and Working Paper Series, University of the West Indies, St. Augustine, Trinidad, 2000.

Allyene, Mervyn C. *Roots of Jamaican Culture*. London: Pluto Press, 1989.

Anchor, Robert. "Bakhtin's Truths of Laughter." *CLIO*, 14, No. 3 (Spring 1985).

Anderson, Benedict. *Imagined Communities: Reflections on the Origin and Spread of Nationalism.* London: Verso, 1991.

Anthony, Michael. *Anaparima: The History of San Fernando and the Naparimas, Vol. 1, 1595–1900.* Laventille: The City of San Fernando, 2001.

Aristotle Poetics. Translated by S. H. Butcher. New York: Hill and Wang, 1961.

Asiwaju, A. I. "Efe Poetry as a Source for Western Yoruba History." In Wande Ambiola, ed. *Yoruba Oral Tradition: Poetry in Music, Dance and Drama.* Ife-Ife, Nigeria: Department of African Languages and Literatures, University of Ife, 1975.

Ayoub, Mahmoud. *Redemptive Suffering in Islam: A Study of the Devotional Aspects of "Ashura" in the Twelver Shi'sim in the Middle Ages.* The Hague: Mouton Publishers, 1978.

Bakhtin, Mikhail. *Rabelais and His World.* Translated by Helene Iswolsky. Cambridge, Mass.: M.I.T. Press, 1968.

Balderrama, Maria R. ed. *Wilfredo Lam and his Contemporaries 1938–1952.* New York: The Studio Museum in Harlem, 1992.

Banham, Martin, Errol Hill, and George Woodyard, eds. *The Cambridge Guide to African And Caribbean Theatre.* Cambridge: Cambridge University Press, 1994.

Barret, Leonard E., Sr. *The Rastafarians.* Boston: Beacon Press, 1997.

Belliard-Acosta, Marianella. "Writing Nations: Creating Race in Cuban and Dominican Literature in the Nineteenth and Twentieth Centuries," Ph.D., Dissertation, NewYork University, New York.

Benitez-Rojo, Antonio. "Nineteenth-Century Spanish American Novel." In Roberto Gonzalez Echevarria and Enrique Pupo-Walker, eds. *Cambridge History of Latin American Literature, Vol. 1.* Cambridge: Cambridge University Press, 1996.

Besson, Gerard. *A Photographic Album of Trinidad, 1783–1962.* Port of Spain: Paria, 1986.

Bhabha, Homi. "Difference, Discrimination and the Discourse of Colonialism." In Francis Barker et. al., eds. *The Politics of Theory.* Colchester, U. K.: University of Essex,1983.

Blackburn, Robin. "The Black Jacobins and New World Slavery." In Selwyn R. Cudjoe and William Cain, eds. *C. L. R. James: His Intellectual Legacies.* Amherst: University of Massachusetts Press, 1995.

Blaut, J. M. *The Colonizer's Model of the World: Geographical Diffusionism and Eurocentric History.* New York: Guilford Press, 1993.

Blyden, Edward W. *Christianity, Islam and the Negro Race.* Edinburgh: Edinburgh University Press, 1997.

Boehmer, Elleke. *Colonial and Postcolonial Literature.* New York: Oxford University Press, 1995.

Bouce, Paul-Gabriel. *The Novels of Tobais Smollett.* Translated by Antonia White in collaboration with the author. London: Longman, 1976.

Brennan, Timothy. "The National Longing for Form." In Homi Bhabha, *Nation and Narration.* London: Routledge, 1990.

Brereton, Bridget. *A History of Modern Trinidad, 1783–1962.* Kingston: Heinemann, 1981.

———. "John Jacob Thomas: An Estimate." *Journal of Caribbean History,* 9 (May 1977).

———. *Race Relations in Colonial Trinidad, 1870–1900.* Cambridge: Cambridge University Press, 1979.

Brereton, Geoffrey. *A Short History of French Literature.* Harmondsworth, U. K.: Penguin,1976.

Breslaw, Elaine. *Tituba, Reluctant Witch: Devilish Indians and Puritan Fantasies.* New York: New York University Press, 1996.

Bridges, Yseult. *Child of the Tropics: Victorian Memories.* Edited and completed by Nicholas Guppy. Port of Spain: Aquarela Gardens, 1988.

Burnett, Paula, ed. *The Penguin Book of Caribbean Verse in English*. Harmondsworth, U. K.: Penguin, 1986.

Butts, Dennis. "Introduction." In H. Rider Haggard. *King Solomon's Mines*. Oxford: Oxford University Press, 1989.

Caldecott, Rev. A. "A Home Library: For an Englishman of Today." *West Indian Quarterly*, 2 (July) 1886.

Campbell, Carl C. *Cedulants and Capitulants: The Politics of the Coloured Opposition in The Slave Society of Trinidad, 1783–1838*. Port of Spain: Paria, 1992.

——. *Colony and Nation: A Short History of Education in Trinidad and Tobago*. Kingston: Ian Randle, 1992

——. "The Rebel Priest: Francis de Ridder and the Fight for Free Coloureds' Rights in Trinidad, 1825–32. *Journal of Caribbean History*, 15 (1981).

"The Caribbean Confederation." *New Era*, 1888.

Carmichael, Gertrude. *The History of the West Indian Islands of Trinidad and Tobago, 1498–1900*. London: Alvin Redman, 1961.

Carmichael, Mrs. *Domestic Manners and Social Condition of the White and Coloured, And Negro Population of the West Indies, Vol. 2* London: Longman, Brown, Longmans, 1842.

Carter, Paul. *The Road to Botany Bay: An Essay in Spatial History*. London: Faber and Faber, 1987.

Chapman, Frank M. "On the Birds of the Island of Trinidad." *Bulletin of the Museum of Natural History* (New York), 6 (1894).

Collens, James H. *The Trinidad Official & Commercial Register and Almanack*. Port Of Spain: Government Printing Office, 1891

Conde, Maryse. *I, Tituba, Black Witch of Salem*. Translated by Richard Philcox. New York: Ballantine Books, 1992.

Corsbie, Ken. *Theatre in the Caribbean*. London: Hodder and Stoughton, 1984.

Cox, Edward L. *Free Coloreds in the Slave Societies of St. Kitts and Grenada, 1763–1833*. Knoxville: University of Tennessee Press, 1984.

Cox, Oliver Cromwell. *Caste, Class and Race: A Study in Social Dynamics*. New York: Monthly Review Press, 1959.

Crowley, John. *Carnival, Camboulay and Calypso: Tradition in the Making*. Cambridge: Cambridge University Press, 1996.

Cudjoe, Selwyn R. ed. *Michel Maxwell Philip: A Trinidad Patriot of the Nineteenth Century*. Wellesley, Mass.: Calaloux, 1999.

——. *V. S. Naipaul: A Materialist Reading*. Amherst: University of Massachusetts Press, 1988.

Cuffe, Daphne Gloria. "Problems in the Teaching of English in the Island of Trinidad and Tobago from 1797 to the Present Day." MA, Thesis, Institute of Education, University of London, 1963.

Cuney-Hare, Maud. *Negro Musicians and their Music*. 1936, New York: Da Capo, 1974.

Darah, G. G. "200 Hundred Years of Nigeria Letters." *ANA Review*, 1996.

Darlington, Johanna P. E. "Guanapo Cave." *Living World: Journal of the Trinidad and Tobago Field Naturalists' Club*, 1996.

Darwin, Charles. *The Origin of Species*. 1859, London: Penguin, 1985.

Davis, Darnell N. *Mr. Froude's Negrophobia or Don Quixote as Cook's Tourist*. Demerara, British Guiana: Argosy Press, 1888.

Dayan, Joan. *Haiti: History and the Gods*. Berkeley: University of California Press, 1995.

Dean, R. E. *Guide to the Royal Botanical Gardens, Trinidad*. Port of Spain: J. D. Gorrie, 1937.

Desmond, Ray. *Kew: The History of the Royal Botanical Gardens*. London: Harvest Hill Press, 1995

De Verteuil, Anthony. *And Then There Were None: A History of the Le Cadre Family In the West Indies*. Port of Spain: Litho Press, 1992.

———. *Seven Slaves and Slavery, Trinidad: 1777–1838*. Port of Spain: Scrip-J Printers, 1992.

———. *Sir Louis de Verteuil: His Life and Times, Trinidad, 1800–1900*. Port of Spain: Columbus Publishers, 1973.

Dow, Leslie Smith. *Adèle Hugo: La Miserable*. Fredericton, New Brunswick: Goose Lane Editions, 1993.

Driver, F. "Geography's Empire: Histories of Geographical Knowledge." *Environment And Planning D: Society and Space*. 10. (1993).

Eagleton, Terry. *The Idea of Culture*. Oxford, Blackwell, 2000.

Echevarria, Roberto Gonzalez. *Myth and Archive: A Theory of Latin American Narrative*. New York: Cambridge University Press, 1990.

Edwards, John R. *Language, Society and Identity*. London: Basil Davidson, 1985.

Ellison, Ralph. *Shadow and Act*. New York: Random House, 1964.

Emenyonu, Ernest. *The Rise of the Igbo Novel*. Ibadan: Oxford University Press, 1978.

Enekwe, Onuora Ossie. *Igbo Masks: The Oneness of Ritual and Theatre*. Lagos: The Department of Culture, Federal Ministry of Information and Culture, 1987.

Entrikin, J. Nicholas. *The Betweenness of Place: Towards a Geography of Modernity*. Baltimore: Johns Hopkins University Press, 1991.

Espinet, Charles and Harry Pitts. *Land of the Calypso*. Port of Spain: Guardian Commercial Printery, 1944.

Fanon, Frantz. *Black Skin; White Masks*. Translated by Charles Lam Markmann. New York: Grove Press, 1967.

———. *The Wretched of the Earth*. Translated by Constance Farrington. New York: Grove Press, 1963.

Finnegan Ruth. *Oral Literature in Africa*. Oxford: Oxford University Press, 1976.

Fortescue, J. W. *A History of the British Army, Vol. 4*. London: Macmillan, 1915.

Foucault, Michel. *Power/Knowledge: Selected Interviews and Other Writings, 1972–1977*. Edited by Colin Gordon, translated by Colin Gordon, Leo Marshall, Mepham, and Kate Soper. New York: Pantheon Books, 1980.

Fowler, Roger. *Linguistic Criticism*. Oxford: Oxford University Press, 1986.

Franco, Jean. *An Introduction to Spanish-American Literature*. Cambridge: Cambridge University Press, 1969.

"French Literature." *Saturday Review of Politics, Literature, Science and Art* 42, No. 1093 (October 7, 1876).

Froude, James Anthony. *The English in the West Indies, or, the Bow of Ulysses*. New York: Scribner's, 1900.

Gates, Henry Louis, Jr., and Cornel West. *The Future of the Race*. New York: Alfred A. Knopf, 1996.

Gay, Peter. *The Enlightenment: An Interpretation*. New York: Norton, 1966.

Gellner, Ernest. *Nationalism*. New York: New York University Press, 1997.

Gould, Stephen Jay. *The Mismeasure of Man*. New York: W. W. Norton, 1996.

Goveia, E. V. *The West Indian Slave Laws of the 18th Century*. Barbados: Caribbean University Press, 1970.

Greenblatt, Stephen. *Renaissance Self-Fashioning: From More to Shakespeare*. Chicago: University of Chicago Press, 1980.

Gregory, Derek. *Geographical Imaginations*. Cambridge, U. K.: Blackwell, 1994.

Hall, Stuart. "Cultural Identity and Cinematic Representation." In Houston A. Baker, Jr., Manthia Diawara, and Ruth H. Lindebor, *Black British Cultural Studies: A Reader*. Chicago Press, 1996.

Halliday, Fred. *Islam and the Myth of Confrontation: Religion and Politics in the Middle East*. London: I. B. Tauris, 1995.

"Handbook and Catalogue." In *The Colonial and Indian Exhibition of 1886*. London: William Clowes and Sons, 1886.

Hanke, Lewis. *The Spanish Quest for Justice in the Conquest of America*. Philadelphia: University of Pennsylvania Press, 1949.

Haring, J. C. *The Spanish Empire in America*. New York: Harcourt and World, 1963.

Harris, Wilson. *History Fable and Myth in the Guianas and the Caribbean*. 1970, Calaloux: Wellesley, 1995.

Henry, Paget. *Caliban's Reason: Introducing Afro-Caribbean Philosophy*. New York: Routledge, 2000

Hentscchel, Cedric. "Alexander von Humboldt's Synthesis of Literature and Science." In Alexander Homboldt and Adolf Meyer-Abich, eds. *Alexander von Humboldt, 1769–1969*. Bad Godesberg: Inter Nationes, 1969.

Hill, Donald R. *Calypso Calaloo: Early Carnival Music in Trinidad*. Gainesville: University Press of Florida, 1993.

Hill, Errol. *Trinidad Theatre: Mandate for a National Theatre*. Austin: University of Texas, 1972.

Hobhouse, L. T. *Democracy and Reaction*. London: T. Fisher Unwin, 1904.

Hodge, Merle. "Challenges of the Struggle for Sovereignty: Changing the World versus Writing Stories." In Selwyn R. Cudjoe, ed. *Caribbean Women Writers: Essays From the First International Conference*. Wellesley, Mass.: Calaloux Publications, 1990.

———. *Knots of English: A Manual for Caribbean Users*. Wellesley, Mass.: Calaloux Publications, 1997.

Holm, John A. *Pidgins and Creole, Vol 1*. Cambridge: Cambridge University Press, 1988.

Hooker, James R. *Henry Sylvester Williams: Imperial Pan Africanist*. London: Collings, 1975.

Hountondji, Paulin J. *African Philosophy: Myth and Reality*, 2nd edition. Edited and translated by Henri Evans. Bloomington: Indiana University Press, 1996.

Hulme, Peter. *Colonial Encounters: Europe and the Native Caribbean, 1492–1797*. London: Metheun, 1986.

Ince, Anne Claire. "Protestant Missionaries in Five South Caribbean Islands during Slavery, 1765–1826." Ph.D., Dissertation. Faculty of Modern History, Oxford University, 1984.

Isola, Akinwumi. "The Rhythm of the Sango-Pipe." In Wande Abimbola, ed. *Yoruba Oral Tradition: Poetry in Music, Dance and Drama*. Ile-Ife, Nigeria: Department Of African Languages and Literatures, University of Ife, 1975.

James, C. L. R. *Beyond a Boundary*. 1963, Durham: Duke University Press, 1993.

———. *Black Jacobins; Toussaint L'Ouverture and the San Domingo Revolution*. 1938, New York: Vintage, 1989.

Jha, J. C. "East Indian Pressure Groups in Trinidad, 1897–1921." In *Indentured Indians in Trinidad and Tobago, 1845–1917*. St. Augustine, Trinidad; University of the West Indies, 1985.

———. "Indian Heritage in Trinidad." In *Research Papers: Indians in Trinidad and Tobago, 1845–1917*. St. Augustine, Trinidad: University of the West Indies (nd).

Johnson, H. B. D. "Crown Colony Government in Trinidad, 1870–1897." D. Phil., Dissertation. Oxford University, 1969.

Jones, Iva G. "Trollope, Carlyle, and Mill on the Negro: An Episode in the History of Ideas." *Journal of Negro History,* 52 (1967).

Joseph, Edward Lanza. *History of Trinidad.* Trinidad: H. J. Mills, 1838.

Junge, G. C. A., and G. F. Mees. *The Avifauna of Trinidad and Tobago.* Leiden: E. J. Brill, 1958.

Katz, Wendy R. *Rider Haggard and the Fiction of Empire: A Critical Study of British Imperial Fiction.* New York: Cambridge University Press, 1987.

Kaur, Raminder, and John Hutnyk. *Travel Worlds: Journeys in Contemporary Politics.* London: Zed Books, 1999.

Kedourie, Elie. *Nationalism.* London: Hutchinson, 1961.

Konate, Yacouba. *Côte d'Ivorie Contrases.* Abidjan: Edipresse, nd.

Lalla, Barbara. *Defining Jamaican Fiction: Moroonage and the Discourse of Survival.* Tuscaloosa: University of Alabama Press, 1996.

Las Casas, Bartolme. *The Devastation of the Indies: A Brief Account.* Translated by Herman Briffaulty. Baltimore: Johns Hopkins Press, 1982.

Lee, David. "Michael J. Cazabon." *Arts Review* 39 (1987).

Lewis, Gordon. "Distant Pieces." *Times Literary Supplement,* 1986.

———. *Main Currents in Caribbean Thought.* Port of Spain: Heinemann Educational Books, 1983.

Look Lai, Walton. *Indentured Labor; Caribbean Sugar: Chinese and Indian Migrants to The British West Indies, 1838–1918.* Baltimore: Johns Hopkins University Press, 1993.

MacClean, Geoffrey. *Cazabon: An Illustrated Biography of Trinidad's Nineteenth Century Painter.* Port of Spain: Aquarela Galleries, 1986.

Manzano, Juan Francisco. *The Life and Poems of a Cuban Slave.* Hamden, CT.: Anchor Books, 1981.

Maron, Guillermo. *A History of Venezuela.* Translated by John Street. London: George Allen & Unwin, 1964.

Martin, Robert Bernard. *The Dust of Combat: A Life of Charles Kingsley.* New York: W. W. Norton, 1960.

Marx, Leo. "The American Ideology of Space.'" In Stuart Wrede and William Howard Adams, eds. *Denatured Visions: Landscape and Culture in the Twentieth Century.* New York: The Museum of Modern Art, 1991.

Matthews, Basil. *Crisis of the West Indian Family: A Sample Study.* Mona, Jamaica: Extra Mural Department, University College of the West Indies, 1953.

Maturin, Owen Charles. *Henry Sylvester Williams and the Origins of the Pan-African Movement, 1869–1911.* Westport, Conn..: Greenwood, 1976.

Mavrogordato, Olga. *Voices in the Street.* Port of Spain: Imprint, 1977.

McDonald, Lorna. "The Philips: A 'Free Mulatto' Family of Grenada." *Journal of Caribbean History,* 24. , No. 2 (1990).

McDowell, Linda. "The Transformation of Cultural Geography." In Derek Gregory, Ron Martin, and Graham Smith, eds. *Human Geography: Society, Space, and Social Science.* Minneapolis: University of Minnesota Press, 1994.

Meyer-Abich, Adolph. "Alexander Homboldt." In Alexander Humboldt and Adolph Meyer, eds. *Alexander von Humboldt, 1769–1969.* Bad Godesberg: Inter Nationes, 1969.

Millette, James. *Society and Politics in Colonial Trinidad.* Curepe & London: Omega Bookshops & Zed Books, 1964.

Mintz, Sidney. "Foreword." In Norman Whitten, Jr. and John Szwed, eds. *Afro-American Anthropology: Contemporary Perspectives*. New York: The Free Press, 1970.

"The Misfortune of a Rabbit Destined in Captivity." *Public Opinion*, 1885.

Mitchell, Loften. *Black Drama: The Story of the American Negro in the Theatre*. New York: Hawthorn Books, 1967.

Moore, Dennison. *Origins and Development of Racial Ideology in Trinidad: The Black View of the East Indian*. Tunapuna: Chakra Publishing House, 1995.

Moore-Gilbert, Bart. *Postcolonial Theory*. London: Verso, 1997.

Mudimbe, V. Y. *The Invention of Africa: Gnosis, Philosophy, and the Order of Knowledge*. Bloomington: Indiana University Press, 1988.

Naipaul, Seepersad. "Carnival Calypsoes and the Creole Troubadours." *The Trinidadian*, 193?

Naipaul, V. S. *The Loss of El Dorado: A History*. London: Andre Deutsch, 1969.

Narayan, R. K. *The Ramayana*. London: Penguin, 1972.

New, Chester W. *The Life of Henry Broughton to 1830*. Oxford: Clarendon Press, 1961.

Ogunba, Oyin. "The Performance of Yoruba Oral Poetry." In Wande Abimbola, ed. *Yoruba Oral Tradition: Poetry in Music, Dance and Drama*. Ile-Ife, Nigeria: Department of African Languages and Literatures, University of Ife, 1975.

Olaniyan, Tejumola. *Scars of Conquest/Masks of Resistance: The Invention of Cultural Identities in Africa, African-American and Caribbean Drama*. New York: Oxford University Press, 1995.

Outram, Dorinda, *The Enlightenment*. Cambridge: Cambridge University Press, 1995.

Pierre, Barry V. *Verbum Sap: A Tribute to L. O. Inniss*. Port of Spain: Barry V. Pierre, 2000.

Pope-Hennessy, James. *West Indian Summer: A Retrospective*. London: B. T. Batsford, 1943.

Pratt, Mary Louise. *Imperial Eyes: Travel Writing and Transculturation*. London: Routledge, 1992.

Prince, Mary. *The History of Mary Prince, a West Indian Slave*. London: F. Westley and A. H. Davis, 1831.

Quesnel, Victor C., and T. Francis Farrell. *Native Trees of Trinidad and Tobago*. Port of Spain: Trinidad and Tobago Field Naturalists' Club, 2000.

Quevedo, Raymond. *Attila's Kaiso: A Short History of Trinidad Calypso*. St. Augustine: Department of Extra Mural Studies, University of the West Indies, 1983.

Raby, Peter. *Bright Paradise: Victorian Scientific Travelers*. London: Chatto and Windus, 1996.

Ramdin, Ron. *The Other Middle Passage*. London: Hansib, 1994.

Ratcliff, Dillwyn F. *Venezuelan Prose Fiction*. New York: Instituto de las Esapanas, 1933.

Reinecke, John E. "William Grenfield: A Neglected Pioneer Creolist." In Lawrence D. Carrington, ed. *Studies in Caribbean Language*. St. Augustine: Society for Caribbean Linguistics, 1983.

Reyes, Elma. "The Santa Rosa Community of Arima, Trinidad, West Indies." Santa Rosa Carib Community, Research, Education, Publications & Public Relations Unit, nd.

Rhodes, Colin. *Primitivism and Modern Art*. London: Thames and Hudson, 1994.

Richards, Bernard. *English Poetry of the Victorian Period, 1830–1890*. London: Longman, 1988.

Said, Edward. *Culture and Imperialism*. New York: Vintage, 1993.

Salmon, C. S. *The Caribbean Confederation*. London: Cassell, 1888.

Samaroo, Brinsley. "Cyrus Prudhomme David—A Case Study in the Emergence of the Black Man in Trinidad Politics, *Journal of Caribbean History*, No. 3 (November 1971).

Schama, Simon. *A History of Britain: The British Wars, 1603–1776*. London: BBC, 2001.

Schomburg, Arthur. "The Negro Digs Up His Past." In Alain Locke, ed. *The New Negro: An Interpretation*. New York: A and C Boni, 1926.

Shelton, Marie-Denise. "Conde: The Politics of Gender and Identity." *World Literature Today*, Autumn, 1993.

Smith, Faith Lois. "John Jacob Thomas and Caribbean Intellectual Life in the Nineteenth Century." Ph.D., Dissertation, Duke University, 1995.

Smith, Paul. *Discerning the Subject*. Minneapolis: University of Minnesota Press, 1988.

Stoler, Ann Laura. "Carnal Knowledge and Imperial Power: Gender, Race, and Morality in Colonial Asia." In Micaela di Leonardo, ed. *Gender at the Crossroads of Knowledge: Feminist Anthropology in the Postmodern Era*. Berkeley: University Of California Press, 1991.

Sundquist, Eric J. *To Wake the Nations: Race in the Making of American Literature*. Cambridge: Harvard University Press, 1993.

Thakur, Rishee S. "Politics and Hegemony in Guyanese Nationalism, 1945–1965." Ph.D., Dissertation, York University, Ontario, 1995.

Thomas, Eudora. *A History of the Shouter Baptist in Trinidad and Tobago*. Ithaca, N.Y.: Calaloux, 1987.

Thorp, Margaret Ferrand. *Charles Kingsley, 1819–1875*. Princeton: Princeton University Press, 1937.

Tikasingh, Girad. "The Emerging Political Consciousness among Trinidad Indians in the Late 19th Century." History Conference, University of the West Indies, St. Augustine (Trinidad), 1973.

Todorov, Tzvetan. *The Conquest of America: The Question of the Other*. Translated by Richard Howard. New York: Harper and Row, 1984.

Trotman, David. *Crime in Trinidad: Conflict and Control in a Plantation Society, 1838–* Knoxville: University of Tennessee, 1986.

Turnbull, David. *Maps are Territories: Science in an Atlas*. Chicago: University of Chicago Press, 1993

Viswanahan, Gauri. *Masks of Conquests: Literary Study and British Rule in India*. New York: Columbia University Press, 1989.

Walcott, Derek. *The Antilles: Fragments of Epic Memory, The Nobel Lecture*. New York: Farrar, Straus and Giroux, 1992.

Walvin, James. *The Black Presence: A Documentary History of the Negro in England, 1555–1860*. New York: Schocken Books, 1972.

Warner, Ashton. *Negro Slavery described by a Negro, being a narrative of Ashton Warner, a Native of St. Vincent's*. London: Samuel Maunder, 1831.

Waugh, Patricia. *Metafiction: The Theory and Practice of Self-Conscious Fiction*. London: Routledge, 1988.

Webber, Thomas L. *Deep Like the Rivers: Education in the Slave Quarter Community, 1831–1865*. New York: W. W. Norton, 1978.

White, Hayden. *The Content of the Form: Narrative Discourse and Historical Representation*. Baltimore: Johns Hopkins University Press, 1987.

Williams, Eric. *A History of the People of Trinidad and Tobago*. Port of Spain: PNM Publishing, 1962.

Williams, James. *A Narrative of Events since the 1st of August, 1834, by James Williams Together with Evidence taken under a commission appointed by the Colonial Office*. London: Central Emancipation Committee, 1838.

Young, Robert J. C. *Colonial Desire: Hybridity in Theory, Culture, and Race*. London: Routledge, 1995.

———. *Postcolonialism: An Historical Introduction*. Oxford: Blackwell, 2001.

———. *White Mythologies: Writing History and the West*. London: Routledge, 1990.

Zvobgo, Rungano J. *Colonialism and Education in Zimbabwe*. Harare: SAPES, 1994.

Index